Krzysztof Panczyk & Jacek Ilczuk

S0-ARK-124

the classical
king's Indian
uncovered

EVERYMAN CHESS

Gloucester Publishers plc   www.everymanchess.com

First published in 2009 by Gloucester Publishers plc (formerly Everyman Publishers plc), Northburgh House, 10 Northburgh Street, London EC1V 0AT

Copyright © 2009 Krzysztof Panczyk and Jacek Ilczuk

The right of Krzysztof Panczyk and Jacek Ilczuk to be identified as the authors of this work has been asserted in accordance with the Copyrights, Designs and Patents Act 1988.

All rights reserved. No part of this publication may be reproduced, stored in a retrieval system or transmitted in any form or by any means, electronic, electrostatic, magnetic tape, photocopying, recording or otherwise, without prior permission of the publisher.

British Library Cataloguing-in-Publication Data
A catalogue record for this book is available from the British Library.

ISBN: 978 1 85744 517 6

Distributed in North America by The Globe Pequot Press, P.O Box 480, 246 Goose Lane, Guilford, CT 06437-0480.

All other sales enquiries should be directed to Everyman Chess, Northburgh House, 10 Northburgh Street, London EC1V 0AT
tel: 020 7253 7887 fax: 020 7490 3708
email: info@everymanchess.com; website: www.everymanchess.com

Everyman is the registered trade mark of Random House Inc. and is used in this work under licence from Random House Inc.

EVERYMAN CHESS SERIES
Chief advisor: Byron Jacobs
Commissioning editor: John Emms
Assistant editor: Richard Palliser

Typeset and edited by First Rank Publishing, Brighton.
Cover design by Horatio Monteverde.
Printed and bound in the US by Versa Press.

Contents

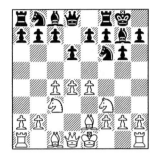

Symbols and Abbreviations

+=   White has a slight advantage
+/-   White has a clear advantage
+-   White is winning
=   The position is equal
=+   Black has a slight advantage
-/+   Black has a clear advantage
-+   Black is winning
∞   The position is unclear
!!   A brilliant move
!   A good move
!?   An interesting move
?!   A dubious move
?   A bad move
??   A blunder
Ch.   Championship
corr. Correspondence game
(D)   Diagram

Bibliography

Books

Encyclopaedia of Chess Openings vol.E (Sahovski Infomator, Belgrade 1998)
King's Indian Defence: Mar del Plata Variation, S.Gligoric (Batsford, London 2002)
Königsindisch, Awerbach-System bis Petrosjan-System, L.Polugaevsky (Sportverlag Berlin 1984)
The New Classical King's Indian, J.Nunn & G.Burgess (Batsford, London 1997)
The Offbeat King's Indian, K.Panczyk & J.Ilczuk (Everyman, London 2004)
Opening for White According to Kramnik: 1 ♘f3 (book I), A.Khalifman (Chess Stars, Sofia 2000)
Play the King's Indian, J.Gallagher (Everyman, London 2004)
Shahmatnyi uchebnik, vol II pozitionnoye idei v staroindiyskoy, V.Pozarski (Feniks, Rostov-on-Don 1998)
Staroindiskaya zashchita, E.Geller (Fizkultura i Sport, Moscow 1980)
Staroindiskaya dlinoyu v zhizn, E.Gufeld (Ripol Klassik, Moscow 2002)
Szachy od A do Z, W.Litmanowicz & J.Gizycki (Sport i Turystyka, Warsaw 1987)
Understanding the King's Indian, M.Golubev (Gambit, London 2006)

Periodicals, Magazines and Websites
Chess Informators
New in Chess Yearbooks
64 Shakhmatnoye Obozrenye
Przeglad Szachowy
MegaBase 2008
ChessBase Magazines
The Week in Chess

Introduction

This book is our second on the King's Indian. Our previous publication *The Offbeat King's Indian* taught us that writing about such a controversial opening is not an easy task. Firstly, the positions arising are often very difficult to assess. Moreover, even the best chess programs are often helpless to evaluate extremely entangled positions, and often change their assessments dramatically after a few logical moves from both sides. Secondly, the number of games available in the databases is enormous, huge enough for several books. The selection from and attitude towards the great number of comments by dozens of annotators was really hard work. An additional problem was the fact that the Classical Variation has been at the centre of theoretical discussion over several decades. It is noteworthy that even Garry Kasparov, as the world champion, refrained from playing the King's Indian after two defeats by Kramnik, exactly in the Classical Variation.

As we described in our aforementioned book, the beginnings of the King's Indian date from the 19th century. The move 1...♘f6 (after 1 d4) was mentioned by Karl Jänisch in his *A New Analysis* as far back as 1842/43. In 1848 the German chess magazine *Deutsche Schachzeitung* published a game starting with 1 d4 ♘f6. The same magazine in 1875 included a game beginning in this way which had been played by two Brahmins (Sauncheri-Moonshander). Hence the name of the defence, which was invented by Saviely Tartakower in the 1920s.

The King's Indian was used first by one of the best chess players of those times: when the German player and theoretician Louis Paulsen faced Adolf Schwarz in a match in Leipzig in 1879. At the end of the nineteenth century Mikhail Chigorin joined Paulsen in employing the defence and, as the years passed in the twentieth century, a number of the so-called hypermodern school continued the trend, with Tartakower, Nimzowitsch, Réti and Euwe among the recruits.

The Classical Variation appeared at the beginning of the 20th century. The first to use this set-up were Bogoljubow, Colle and Botvinnik. Then such prominent players as Taimanov, Gligoric, Reshevsky, Petrosian, Portisch, Korchnoi and Kasparov included it in their repertoires and considerably developed its theory. These days Karpov, Kramnik and Gelfand also play the variation.

The Classical reflects best the spirit of King's Indian – the spirit of a ruthless fight full of risk and determination; creating dynamic positions full of breakneck complications, hardly possible to evaluate or analyse, even using computers; a fight full of unpredictable, surprising moves, tactical motifs, constant tension, with play on both sides of the chessboard (sometimes including the centre), when the result of the game hovers in the balance from beginning to end. This kind of position requires extraordinary power of concentration throughout the game as any unguarded moment may result in a terrible blunder, even in a completely won position, wasting the fruits of many hours' work.

Although White usually develops his initiative on the queenside first, Black's counterplay on the opposite flank cannot be underestimated, all the more because any play against the king is always dangerous. The popularity of King's Indian has fluctuated throughout the modern history of chess, along with the opinions about this opening. Some players believe it is suspicious or even lost with perfect play by White; others think it is perfectly okay. We would not like to utter any categorical opinions on this matter; we simply studied the subject without any prejudices as thoroughly as we were able, and we hope we have managed to contribute something to the theoretical knowledge of this variation.

We would like to encourage all chess players to study this book, hoping that it will be useful for them. We believe that the Classical Variation of King's Indian is one of the most interesting openings in the whole of opening theory, and it is undoubtedly worth studying and incorporating in everybody's repertoire. The Classical Variation will surely satisfy creative players with its abundance and depth of various plans and ideas for both sides.

Krzysztof Panczyk and Jacek Ilczuk

Chapter One

Lines without 6...e5

1 d4 ♘f6 2 c4 g6 3 ♘c3 ♗g7 4 e4 d6 5 ♘f3 0-0 6 ♗e2 *(D)*

In this chapter we are going to examine sidelines in which Black refrains from ...e7-e5, or at least does not hurry with it.

6...c6 prepares active operations on the queenside with ...a7-a6 followed by...b7-b5. Black abstains from the fight for the centre (at least temporarily) and tries to obtain an advantage on the queenside, which is usually White's domain.

6...c5 is a popular idea in a great number of King's Indian variations. Black attacks the white pawn centre and, after 7 d5, usually organizes counterplay based on opening the e-file with ...e7-e6 and ...e6xd5, when c4xd5 leads to positions from the Modern Benoni. We will not discuss these transpositions in our book, except in cases where they deserve special attention as convenient for either side in a

particular position. Following 7...e6 8 0-0 ♖e8 Black can transpose to the Modern Benoni after exchanging on d5, or try for original play by maintaining the tension in the centre. For White, 8 dxe6 deserves attention, leading to positions identical or similar to those described in our previous book *Offbeat King's Indian*. White can also count on good play with 7 0-0 in the variants 7...♘a6 8 e5!, and 7...♘c6 8 d5.

With 6...♗g4 Black solves the problem of his light-squared bishop and tries to fight for the d4-square: after the exchange on f3 he will be able to advance in the centre with ...e7-e5 or ...c7-c5. On the downside, giving up the bishop pair allows White real chances of obtaining a small but long-term advantage. The exchange of light-squared bishops is usually convenient for White too; while if White hasn't castled, he can sometimes take on f3 with the pawn and gain active kingside play.

We will examine these three variations in turn.

A: 6...c6 *10*

B: 6...c5 *13*

C: 6...♗g4 *21*

Other rare continuations are:

a) 6...♘c6 7 d5! ♘b8 (7...♘e5 8 ♘xe5 dxe5 gives White a positional advantage due to Black's pawn structure; M.Galyas-G.Mester, Hungarian Team Ch. 2005, continued 9 0-0 e6 10 ♗g5 h6 11 ♗e3 exd5 12 cxd5 ♘e8 13 ♕d2 ♔h7 14 ♖ac1 +/-) 8 0-0 c6 (after 8...e5 Black would have to play normal variations two tempi down; or if 8...♗g4 9 ♗e3 ♘bd7 10 ♘d4 ♗xe2 11 ♕xe2 ♖c8 12 f4 += V.Bhat-H.Nakamura, US Chess League 2008) 9 ♗e3 ♘a6 10 h3 ♘c5 11 ♕c2 a5 12 ♖fd1 +/= V.Popov-N.Nikolaev, Peterhof 2005.

b) 6...♘bd7 is a very typical move in the King's Indian, but it is usually followed by ...e7-e5 – in particular 7 0-0 e5 transposing to Chapter Seven. A couple of independent lines are:

b1) 7 ♗e3 ♘g4 (7...e5 8 0-0 is Chapter Seven again) 8 ♗g5 h6 9 ♗h4 c5 10 d5 a6 11 a4 ♘gf6 12 ♘d2 e6 13 0-0 exd5 14 cxd5 ♖e8 when a Modern Benoni position had appeared with an extra tempo for White, M.Sorokin-A.Hoffman, Linares 2003.

b2) 7 e5!? dxe5 8 dxe5 ♘g4 9 e6 fxe6 10 0-0 ♘de5! 11 ♘xe5 (if 11 ♕xd8 ♖xd8 12 ♘b5 ♗d7! 13 ♘g5 h6 14 ♘e4 c6 15 ♘bc3 ♘f6 =+ S.Schweber-V.Liberzon, Buenos Aires 1979) 11...♘xe5 12 ♗g5

♗d7 13 ♕d2 (H.Ree-J.Nunn, Paris 1983) and if 13...♘f7!? 14 ♗e3 ♗c6 15 ♕c2 with compensation.

c) 6...♘a6 (again we will only consider atypical paths; if Black plays ...e7-e5, the game usually transposes to Chapter Six: 6...e5 7 0-0 ♘a6) 7 ♗f4 (7 ♘d2!? c6 8 0-0 e5 9 d5 c5 10 a3 ♘e8 11 ♖b1 f5 12 b4 +/= M.Illescas Cordoba-J.Arizmendi Martinez, Spanish Junior Ch. 2002) 7...♘h5 (7...♗g4!? 8 h3 ♗xf3 9 ♗xf3 e5 10 dxe5 dxe5 11 ♗xe5 ♖e8 12 ♗xf6, F.Vallejo Pons-J.Arizmendi Martinez, Spanish Junior Ch. 2002, and now 12...♕xf6 with compensation, Mikhalchishin) 8 ♗g5 h6 (8...♕e8 9 0-0 e5, I.Lutsko-A.Zhigalko, Belarus Ch. 2006, 10 ♕d2!? +/=) 9 ♗e3 e5 10 ♕d2 ♘f4 11 ♗xf4 exf4 12 ♕xf4 g5 13 ♕d2 (better was 13 ♕e3 leaving the d2-square for the f3-knight) 13...g4 14 ♘g1 (S.Arkhipov-A.Von Gleich, German League 1993) 14...c5 with compensation (Van Wely/Cifuentes).

A: 6...c6 *(D)*

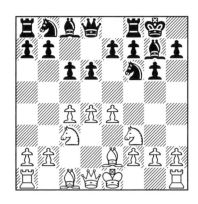

Black's prepares the ...b7-b5 advance, commencing action on the queenside. The downside of this idea is that it neglects the fight for the centre. Consequently, White usually has extra space as well as the initiative. On the other hand, Black's position is quite solid.

7 0-0

Worse is 7 ♗e3 ♘g4 8 ♗g5 f6 9 ♗h4 ♘a6 10 ♕d2 ♘h6 11 ♖d1 ♗g4 12 0-0 ♗xf3 13 ♗xf3 e5 14 d5 ♘f7 15 ♗e2 h5 16 f3 ♗h6 = V.Gavrikov-G.Kuzmin, USSR Ch., Frunze 1981.

However, 7 ♗g5 deserves serious attention; e.g. 7...a6 8 0-0 b5 (8...h6 9 ♗e3 b5 10 a3 ♔h7 11 h3 bxc4 12 ♗xc4 d5 13 exd5 ♘xd5 14 ♘xd5 cxd5 15 ♗d3 ♘c6 16 ♖c1 +/= I.Smirin-V.Tseshkovsky, USSR Team Ch. 1990; or 8...♘fd7 9 ♖c1 b5 10 c5! dxc5 11 dxc5 a5, L.Ftacnik-Kr.Georgiev, Baile Herculane 1982, 12 ♘xb5! cxb5 13 c6 ♘xc6 14 ♖xc6 b4 15 ♖c2 +/=) 9 e5 ♘e8 10 ♖e1 ♖a7 (10...f6 11 exf6 exf6 12 ♗f4 ♗g4 is unclear according to *ECO*, but in our opinion White has the upper hand) 11 h3 ♖b7 12 cxb5 axb5 13 ♖c1 ♕a5 14 d5 +/- N.Rashkovsky-T.V.Petrosian, USSR Ch., Moscow 1973.

7...a6

Other moves do not give Black chances to equalize:

a) 7...a5 8 h3 ♘a6 9 ♗f4 ♘d7 10 ♕d2 +/= S.Gligoric-R.Naranja, Manila 1974.

b) 7...♘a6 8 ♗f4!? is a rather unusual post for the dark-squared bishop in the King's Indian, but it may make sense here as Black cannot easily play ...e7-e5. V.Chuchelov-I.Glek, Bad Zwesten 2000, continued 8...♘d7 9 ♗g5! h6 10 ♗e3 e5 11 ♕d2 ♔h7 12

♖ad1 f5 13 dxe5 dxe5 14 exf5 gxf5 15 g3 ♕f6 16 ♘h4 ♘dc5 17 b4 e4 18 bxc5 ♕xc3 19 ♕xc3 ♗xc3 20 ♖d6 ♗f6 21 ♖fd1! f4 22 ♗xf4 ♘xc5 23 ♗e3 ♘e6 and now 24 ♗g4 ♘g7 25 ♗xc8 ♖axc8 26 ♖d7 +/- Chuchelov.

8 e5

White has several other reasonable continuations:

a) 8 ♗g5 transposes to 7 ♗g5 above.

b) 8 ♖e1!? is a useful move while waiting for ...b7-b5. The rook can defend the e-pawn in the future. For example, 8...♘fd7 (or 8...b5 9 e5 ♘e8 10 ♗f4 ♗g4 11 ♘g5 ♗f5, P.Benko-S.Kagan, Sao Paulo 1973, and now 12 ♕b3!? with the initiative) 9 ♗e3 b5 10 ♕d2 bxc4 11 ♗xc4 ♘b6 12 ♗b3 a5 (a typical idea: Black wants to gain space on the queenside and sometimes control the c4-square) 13 ♘a4! ♗g4 14 ♘g5 ♘xa4 15 ♗xa4 with better chances for White, L.Ftacnik-L.Karlsson, Gjovik 1983.

c) 8 h3!? is a similar idea, this time preventing ...♗g4 or ...♘g4 while preparing e4-e5. After 8...b5 9 e5 ♘e8 (or 9...dxe5 10 dxe5 ♘fd7 11 ♗f4 ♘c5 12 b4 ♘e6 13 ♗g3 +/= L.Keitlinghaus-L.Vadasz, Budapest 1997) 10 ♗f4 ♘d7 11 ♕d2 ♗b7 12 exd6 exd6 13 ♖ad1 +/= V.Hort-H.Westerinen, Nice Olympiad 1974.

d) 8 d5 ♗g4 (although White wanted to deter ...b7-b5, it was still possible; e.g. 8...b5 9 dxc6 b4 10 c7 ♕xc7 11 ♘d5 ♘xd5 12 exd5 ♘d7 13 ♘d4 +/= D.Wright-R.Persitz, Hastings 1968/69) 9 ♗e3 cxd5 10 cxd5 ♗xf3 11 ♗xf3 ♘bd7 12 ♖c1 +/= C.Ionescu-

J.Grigorov, Bucharest 1980.

e) 8 a3 (a prophylactic move, so that ...b5 Black will never have ...b4) 8...♘fd7 9 ♗g5 h6 10 ♗e3 b5 11 ♕d2 ♔h7 (V.Malakhatko-Y.Drozdovskij, Ukrainian Ch. 2004) 12 cxb5 axb5 13 d5 +/-.

8...dxe5

The passive 8...♘e8 gives Black no chances to equalize, e.g. 9 ♗f4 b5 10 b3 ♘d7 11 exd6 exd6 12 h3 h6 13 ♗d3 ♘b6 14 ♕c2 +/= J.Vilela-E.Vasiukov, Prague 1980.

9 ♘xe5 (D)

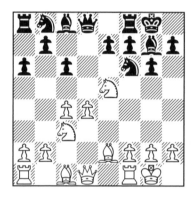

Taking with the pawn is rather weaker: 9 dxe5 (V.Mukhlisov-S.Fedoseev, St Petersburg 2005) and now 9...♕xd1 10 ♖xd1 ♘g4 11 ♗f4 ♘d7 12 e6 fxe6 with compensation.

9...♗e6

The alternative is 9...♘fd7 10 ♘f3 (White should avoid exchanging knights on e5) 10...b5 11 ♗e3 ♘b6 12 b3 ♗g4 13 ♘e5! ♗xe2 14 ♕xe2 bxc4 15 bxc4 ♘6d7 16 ♘f3 c5 17 ♖ad1 ♘c6 18 d5 ♘ce5 19 ♘xe5 ♗xe5 20 ♘e4 +/- J.Pinter-Kr.Georgiev, Baile Herculane 1982.

10 ♗e3 ♘bd7

Premature is 10...b5 11 b3 ♕a5 12 ♖c1 ♖d8? (but if 12...♘fd7 13 f4 and White's position looks imposing – Mikhalevski) 13 ♗f3 ♘fd7? (better is 13...♖c8 +/- Mikhalevski) 14 ♗xc6 ♘xc6 15 ♘xc6 1-0 G.Flear-R.Cifuentes Parada, Wijk aan Zee 1988.

11 h3

11 ♕b3 ♘xe5 12 dxe5 ♘d7 13 f4 b5 14 ♘e4 +/= Mikhalevski.

11...♖c8

11...♘xe5 12 dxe5 ♕xd1 13 ♖axd1 ♘d7 14 f4 +/= Mikhalevski.

12 ♘f3

12 a4!? Mikhalevski.

12...b5! 13 c5

13 b3!? ♘b6 14 ♘e5 ♘fd7 15 ♘e4!? Mikhalevski; 13 d5!? cxd5 14 cxb5 axb5 15 ♘xb5 ♘e4 16 ♘bd4 +/=.

13...♘d5 (D)

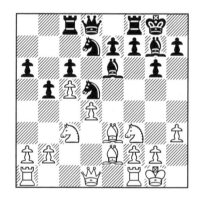

Both parties have their pluses and minuses; the position is level. The game F.Vallejo Pons-G.Kamsky, FIDE World Cup, Khanty Mansyisk 2005, continued **14 ♗g5 h6 15 ♗h4** [with these two moves White has weakened the f4-square and put his dark-squared bishop out of the game] **15...♘7f6 16 a4 ♘h5 17 ♘e5 ♘hf4 18 ♗f3 ♘xc3 19 bxc3 ♗xe5 20 dxe5 ♗d5 21 axb5 axb5 22 ♖a6 ♖e8 23 ♗g3 ♗xf3 24 ♕xf3 ♘e6 25 h4?** [25 ♖d1! =/+ Mikhalevski] **25...♕d5! 26 ♕xd5 cxd5 27 c6 ♖c7 28 ♖d1?!** [28 ♖b1 ♘c5 29 ♖b6 ♖ec8 or 29 ♖a5 ♖xc6 =/+ Mikhalevski] **28...♘c5! 29 ♖a5 e6 30 ♖xb5 ♖xc6 31 ♗f4 ♘e4 32 ♖e1 ♘xc3 33 ♖b7 ♔g7 34 ♔h2 ♖ec8 35 ♖a1 ♖6c7 36 ♖b3 d4** [better was 36...♖c4 37 ♗g3 g5 gaining space on the kingside] **37 ♗d2 ♘e4 38 ♗e1 ♖c1 39 ♖bb1 ♖xb1 40 ♖xb1 d3 41 f3?** [the only way to continue resistance was by 41 ♖d1 d2 42 ♗xd2 ♘xf2 43 ♖e1 or 41...♖d8 42 f3] **41...d2! 42 fxe4 ♖c1 43 ♗xd2 ♖xb1 44 ♔g3 ♖b3+ 45 ♔g4?! ♖b2 0-1**.

B: 6...c5 *(D)*

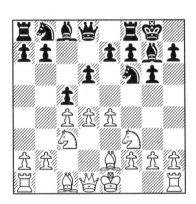

The ...c7-c5-advance is one of the typical actions in the King's Indian. It usually leads to a Modern Benoni (after d4-d5) or a Maróczy Bind (after ...c5xd4). Here we will only examine untypical lines, and will not give any transpositions unless they are espe-

cially convincing for either side.

White's two main moves are:

B1: 7 d5 *13*
B2: 7 0-0 *18*

The exchange of queens is not dangerous for Black: 7 dxc5 dxc5 8 ♕xd8 ♖xd8 9 e5 (9 ♗e3 b6 10 0-0 ♘c6 11 ♖ad1 ♗b7 = J.Sofrevski-M.Matulovic, Skopje 1970) 9...♘g4 10 ♘d5 ♘c6 11 ♘c7 ♖b8 12 e6, N.Ioseliani-Zsu.Polgar, 3rd play-off game, Monte Carlo 1993, and after either 12...♘ge5!? or 12...fxe6 Black would have had an excellent position.

B1: 7 d5 *(D)*

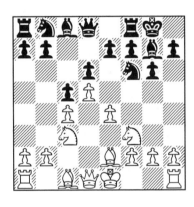

White takes the game into a variation of the Benoni.

7...e6

The most natural response. Other continuations are:

a) 7...♘a6 8 0-0 ♘c7 9 h3 e5 10 ♗g5 h6 11 ♗h4 ♕e8 12 ♘d2 ♗d7 13 ♖b1 ♖b8 14 a3 b5 15 b4 cxb4 16 axb4 bxc4 17 ♘xc4 g5 18 ♗g3 +/= J.Plachetka-B.Perenyi, Eger 1984.

b) 7...b5 8 cxb5 a6 is in the spirit of the Benko Gambit, but it's a rather worse version for Black; e.g. 9 0-0 axb5 10 ♗xb5 ♗a6 11 ♖e1 ♗xb5 12 ♘xb5 ♕b6 13 a4 ♘a6 14 ♘d2 intending ♘c4 +/- Z.Gyimesi-G.Kende, Balatonlelle 2004.

c) 7...a6 8 0-0 ♕c7 9 h3 e5 10 dxe6 ♗xe6 11 ♗f4 ♖d8 12 ♕d2 ♘e8 13 ♖ad1 +/= G.Dyballa-T.Park, Oberlinghaus 1994.

After 7...e6 White has two choices:

B11: 8 dxe6 *14*
B12: 8 0-0 *15*

B11: 8 dxe6 *(D)*

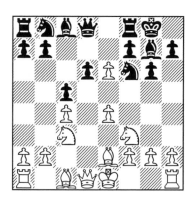

The text is a direct attempt to exploit the weakness of the d6-pawn.

8...♗xe6

Or if 8...fxe6 9 e5!? dxe5 10 ♕xd8 ♖xd8 11 ♘xe5 ♘fd7 +/= N.Karaklaic-D.Minic, Belgrade 1961.

9 ♗f4

9 0-0 ♘c6 10 ♗f4 ♕b6 11 ♖b1 ♖ad8 (or 11...♘d4!? 12 ♘xd4 cxd4 13 ♘d5 ♘xd5 14 exd5 ♗d7 15 ♗d3 +/=) 12 ♘d5

♗xd5 13 exd5 ♘b8 14 ♖e1 ♘bd7 15 ♕c2 ♖fe8, S.Flohr-M.Damjanovic, Sochi 1965, and although *ECO* assesses the position as equal, the bishop pair generally gives White the better chances in this kind of structure.

9...♕b6

Weaker is 9...♕a5 because the queen is not so well placed here; e.g. 10 0-0 ♖d8 11 ♕b3 ♘c6 12 ♖ad1 +/= M.Vukic-D.Minic, Yugoslavia 1978.

10 0-0

White also has better chances after the safe 10 ♕d2 ♘c6 11 0-0 ♖ad8 12 ♗g5 ♖fe8 13 ♖fe1 ♖d7 14 ♖ad1 M.Dyballa-A.Glyanets, Prague 1989, or 10 ♕b3 ♖d8 11 ♕xb6 axb6 12 0-0 ♘c6 13 ♖fd1 ♘e8 14 ♗d2 W.Uhlmann-U.Andersson, Vrbas 1977.

10...♕xb2 *(D)*

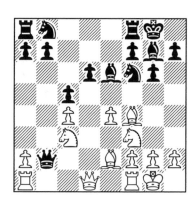

Or 10...♖d8 11 ♖b1 ♘c6 12 ♘d5 ♗xd5 13 cxd5 ♘e7 14 ♘d2 += R.Kaminski-R.Boles, corr. 1998.

After the text White can keep the upper hand with 11 ♕d3!?. Instead, V.Sherbakov-V.Arseniev, Beltsy 1979, concluded:

11 ♘a4 ♕b4?

11...♕a3! 12 ♗c1 ♕b4 13 ♗d2 ♕a3 was the correct way to draw, as the complications after 12 ♗xd6 ♖d8 are favourable for Black.

12 ♗d2?

Here White could have played 12 ♖b1!, when 12...♕a3 13 ♗xd6! ♖d8 is now good for him after 14 ♗xc5 ♖xd1 15 ♗xa3 ♖xb1 16 ♖xb1, or if 12...♕a5 13 ♗xd6 ♘xe4 14 ♗xf8 ♗xf8 15 ♖b5 ♕a6 16 ♗d3 with the advantage.

12...♕a3 13 ♗c1 ♕b4 14 ♗d2 ♕a3 ½-½.

B12: 8 0-0 ♖e8 *(D)*

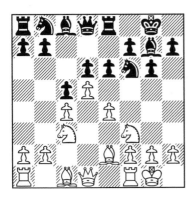

This flexible move looks most logical. Black prepares ...e6xd5, and if White does not defend his e4-pawn, he will be forced to recapture with e4xd5. Here we will only discuss lines which do not transpose to the Modern Benoni (i.e. after ...e6xd5, c4xd5).

Other options are:

a) 8...♘a6?! 9 dxe6 (a good move since the a6-knight is now out of play) 9...♗xe6 (no better is 9...fxe6 10 a3 or 10 ♕d2 intending 11 ♖d1 +/-) 10 ♗f4 (in the standard position the black knight would be on c6; whereas on a6 it is inactive and gives Black no hope of counterplay) 10...♕b6 (as usual the queen does not stand well on a5, e.g. 10...♕a5 11 ♖e1 ♖fe8 12 ♗f1 ♗g4 13 h3 ♗xf3 14 ♕xf3 ♘b4 15 ♖ac1 ♘d7 16 ♗xd6 ♘xa2, R.Ponomariov-V.Topalov, Leon rapid 2003, and now 17 ♘xa2 ♕xa2 18 e5! ♕a6 19 ♕d5 +/- Ponomariov) 11 ♕b3 ♕xb3 12 axb3 ♖fd8 13 ♖fd1 ♘e8 14 ♖d2 ♖d7 15 ♖ad1 ♖ad8 16 ♘b5 +/- V.Hort-A.Cifuentes, Havana 1967.

b) After 8...exd5 9 exd5 *(D)* White has a small space advantage, while Black has a weakness on d6, albeit an easy one to defend. On the other hand, Black position is very solid and in many lines he can exchange the f6-knight on e4, activating his dark-squared bishop.

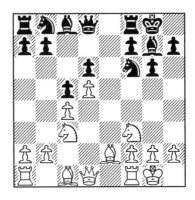

Here Black can choose from:

b1) 9...♗g4 10 ♗f4 ♘h5 (10...♖e8 11 h3 ♗xf3 12 ♗xf3 +/= Y.Averbakh-B.Vladimirov, Sverdlovsk 1957) 11 ♗d2 ♘d7 12 h3 ♗xf3 13 ♗xf3 ♘hf6 14 ♕c2 +/= G.Timoscenko-K.Hulak, Moscow 1990. As we mentioned before, this kind of structure is difficult for Black.

In our previous book, *The Offbeat King's Indian*, we explained it as follows: "Black has no serious weaknesses (the d6-pawn is quite easy to defend), his pieces are harmoniously developed. There are only two tiny factors making his position a bit worse: White has the bishop pair and a bit more space. Can they play a significant role in the practice? It is really incredible, but the answer must be positive. White has a simple plan: he wants to exchange all heavy pieces, play a4-a5 and then b4. After the exchange on b4 or c5 he places his bishops on the diagonals a3-f8 and a4-e8 (sometimes his knight may go on a4) pressing on the d6-pawn. The final stage is combining attack by advancing pawns on the kingside and other parts of the board."

b2) 9...♘a6 (again the knight is out of play here) 10 ♗f4 ♘c7 11 ♕d2 ♖e8 (11...♗f5 intending ...♘e4 is assessed as equal in *ECO*, but Black still has problems; e.g. 12 ♖fe1 ♘e4 13 ♘xe4 ♗xe4 14 ♘g5 ♗f5 15 ♗d3) 12 ♖fe1 ♗f5 13 h3 ♘e4 14 ♘xe4 ♗xe4 15 ♘g5 h6 16 ♘xe4 ♖xe4 and White has an advantage after 17 ♗d3 (or 17 ♗xh6 ♗xh6 18 ♕xh6 ♕e7 19 ♔f1) 17...♖xe1+ 18 ♖xe1 G.Sosonko-Y.Balashov, Tilburg 1977.

b3) 9...♗f5!? 10 h3 ♖e8 11 ♘h4 ♗d7 12 ♗d3 b5!? (M.Bluvshtein-O.Cvitan, Calvia Olympiad 2004) and now 13 cxb5 a6 14 ♘f3 axb5 15 ♘xb5 ♕b6 16 a4 ♘a6 (Avrukh) should be met by 17 ♘d2 +/=.

b4) 9...♖e8 10 ♗f4 (or 10 h3 ♘e4 11 ♘xe4 ♖xe4 12 ♗d3 ♖e8 13 ♗g5 ♕b6 14 ♖b1 ♘d7 15 ♘d2 ♘e5 16 ♗c2 +/=

I.Naumkin-M.Mrdja, Turin 1994) 10...a6 11 ♕d2 ♗g4 12 a4 ♕c7 13 h3 ♗xf3 14 ♗xf3 ♘bd7 15 ♖fe1 ♖xe1+ 16 ♖xe1 ♖e8 17 ♖xe8+ ♘xe8 18 ♗d1 ♘e5 19 ♕e2 ♕b6 20 ♔f1 h5 21 ♘e4 ♕c7 22 b3 ♔f8 23 ♗c2 ♕e7 24 ♗g5 f6 25 ♗d2 +/= G.Sosonko-B.Larsen, Brussels (blitz) 1987, with a similar type of position to that described above.

9 ♘d2

Alternatively:

a) 9 dxe6 ♗xe6 10 ♗f4 reaches one of the main variations of the Averbakh System with a small difference: Black's h-pawn stands on h7 instead of h6. This nuance is usually insignificant. For example, 10...♘c6 11 ♗xd6 ♘d4 12 e5 ♘d7 13 ♘xd4 cxd4 14 ♕xd4 ♘xe5 15 ♗xe5 ♕xd4 16 ♗xd4 ♗xd4 17 ♖ac1 ♖ad8 18 b3 ♗xc3 19 ♖xc3 ♖d2 20 ♗f3 ♖xa2 (20...b6!? was suggested by Hübner) 21 ♗xb7 ♖b8 (L.Barczay-P.Dely, Szolnok 1975) and now *ECO* assesses the ending after 22 ♗c6 as good for White, but Black can easily draw after 22...♖a3 23 ♗a4 ♖b4 24 ♖fc1 ♗xc4, as for example in A.Ornstein-I.Bilek, Nice Olympiad 1974. Instead, either 22 ♗e4 or Barczay's own 22 ♗f3 offer more winning chances, though Black should still draw with correct play.

b) 9 ♕c2 ♘a6 (9...exd5 is also reasonable, when 10 cxd5 reaches a harmless line of the Modern Benoni) 10 a3 ♘c7 11 ♗g5 h6 12 ♗h4 exd5 13 exd5 ♗f5 14 ♗d3 ♗xd3 15 ♕xd3 ♕d7 is about equal. Instead, 13 cxd5 again transposes to the Benoni, and now rather than the passive 13...b6? 14 ♘d2 ♗a6 15 ♗xa6 ♘xa6 16 f4 +/-

K.Sasikiran-F.El Taher, Dubai 2004, Avrukh suggests 13...g5 14 ♗g3 ♘h5 ∞.

9...♘a6 *(D)*

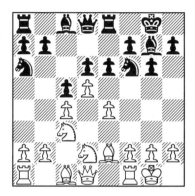

10 a3

Here 10 f3 exd5 11 cxd5 or 10 f4 exd5 11 cxd5 transpose to the Modern Benoni.

White has no chances of obtaining an advantage after either 10 dxe6 ♖xe6 11 f4 ♗d7 12 ♗f3 ♗c6 J.Plachetka-F.Gheorghiu, Bagneux 1983 (which ended abruptly 13 ♕c2 ½-½), or 10 ♖e1 ♘c7 11 ♗f1 b6 12 ♘f3 exd5 13 cxd5 ♗g4 14 h3 ♗xf3 15 ♕xf3 (S.Reshevsky-L.Christiansen, US Ch. 1981), when Black could have solved his problems with 15...b5! 16 ♘xb5 (or 16 ♗xb5 ♘xb5 17 ♘xb5 ♕a5 18 ♘c3 ♘xd5) 16...♘xb5 17 ♗xb5 ♕a5 18 ♗g5 ♖xe4! according to Christiansen, e.g. 19 ♗e2! ♖ae8 20 ♗xf6 ♗xf6 21 ♕xf6 ♖xe2 22 ♖xe2 ♖xe2 23 ♕xd6 ♖xb2.

However, 10 ♔h1 is interesting; e.g. 10...♘c7 11 a4 (or 11 f3 ♖b8 12 dxe6 ♖xe6 13 ♘b3 b6 14 ♗e3 ♘h5 15 ♕d2 ♗b7 16 ♗d3 +/= J.Ehlvest-G.Rechlis, Manila Interzonal 1990) 11...b6 12 a5 ♖b8 13 axb6 axb6 14 dxe6 ♘xe6

(A.Huss-J.Plachetka, Prague 1988) 15 ♘b3!? ♗b7 16 f3 +/=.

10...♘c7 11 ♗d3 a6 12 a4 b6 13 h3 ♖b8 14 ♘f3 exd5 15 cxd5 *(D)*

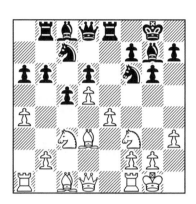

We have been following A.Cherniaev-J.Plaskett, Port Erin 2000. It seems White did not understand all the subtleties of these positions, as a variation of the Modern Benoni has now appeared with two extra tempi for Black. The game went on:

15...b5 16 ♖e1?

After this move Black's initiative develops without any obstacles. White should have opened the a-file with 16 axb5 axb5 in order to activate his rook and free the a4-square, e.g. 17 ♖e1 c4 18 ♗b1 b4 19 ♘a4, though Black's chances are still better after 19...♗d7.

16...c4 17 ♗c2 b4 18 ♘e2 b3 19 ♗b1 ♘xe4 20 ♘ed4 ♘xf2! 21 ♖xe8+ ♕xe8 22 ♔xf2

And now Black should have played 22...♗b7, followed by ...♗xd5 or ...♘xd5, when he has three pawns and a strong initiative for the piece. Instead, he chose the erroneous **22...c3?** and lost after **23 ♗d3 ♘xd5 24 ♗c4 ♘f6 25 ♖a3**

♖b4 26 ♗xb3 cxb2 27 ♗xb2 ♗b7 28
♕e1 ♘e4+ 29 ♔g1 a5 30 ♗c3 ♖b6 31
♗xa5 ♖a6 32 ♗b4 ♕d8 33 a5 ♘c5 34
♗c4 ♖a8 35 ♖e3 ♔f8 36 ♗b5 ♘d7 37
♘c6 ♕c7 38 ♘cd4 ♘e5 39 ♘xe5 ♗xe5
40 ♖xe5 1-0.

B2: 7 0-0 *(D)*

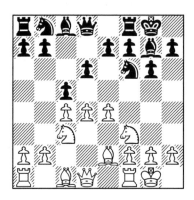

Now Black chooses between:

B21: 7...♘a6 *18*
B22: 7...♘c6 *19*

7...♖e8 does not equalize; e.g. 8 ♖e1
(or 8 dxc5!? dxc5 9 ♗e3 ♘fd7 10 ♕c2
♘c6 11 ♖fd1 +/= L.Ogaard-
U.Andersson, Copenhagen 1977)
8...cxd4 9 ♘xd4 ♘c6 10 ♗e3 ♗d7 11
♕d2 ♘xd4 (11...♘g4!?) 12 ♗xd4 +/=
G.Andruet-D.Barlov, European Team
Ch., Haifa 1989.

B21: 7...♘a6 8 e5! *(D)*
Black's set-up is suitable for a Benoni (i.e. after 8 d5), so White tries to
exploit the position of the black knight
on a6.

Alternatively, 8 ♖e1 ♗g4 9 d5 ♘d7
10 h3 ♗xf3 11 ♗xf3 ♘c7 12 ♗e2,
F.Peralta-G.Needleman, Buenos Aires
2006, or 8 ♖b1 cxd4 9 ♘xd4 ♘c5 10 f3
a5 11 ♗e3 ♘e6 12 ♕d2 ♘xd4 13 ♗xd4,
J.Bonin-R.Schmaltz, Philadelphia 2002,
are also slightly better for White.

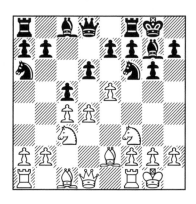

8...♘e8
Opening the centre with 8...dxe5
leads to a big advantage for White; e.g.
9 dxe5 ♘d7 10 ♗f4 ♘c7 11 ♕d2 ♘e6 12
♖ad1 B.Ivkov-V.Tseshkovsky, Sochi
1983.

9 dxc5
A good alternative is 9 ♗e3 b6 10
♘d5 (10 ♕c1!?) 10...♗b7 (10...e6!?) 11
♗g5 +/= A.Pomar Salamanca-
S.Hamann, Sant Feliu de Guixols 1974;
whereas after 9 exd6 ♘xd6 10 d5
(G.Andruet-N.Giffard, Paris 1989)
10...♗g4 Black has counterplay.

9...♘xc5 10 ♗e3
10 exd6 gives Black additional possibilities, such as 10...♘xd6 11 ♗e3
(M.Valvo-J.Benjamin, New York 1980)
and now 11...♗xc3!? is unclear. 10 ♗f4
♗g4 11 exd6 ♘xd6 12 ♖c1 ♖c8,
S.Greanias-V.Frias Pablaza, New York

Open 1991, is not dangerous for Black either.

10...♘e6 11 exd6 ♘xd6 12 ♗d3

12 ♕b3!? is slightly better for White.

12...b6 13 ♖c1 ♗b7 14 ♕e2 ♘c5 15 ♗b1

15...♗xf3!? straightaway looks better.

15...e6 16 ♖fd1 ♕e7 17 ♗f4 *(D)*

Here 17...♖fd8 would keep White's advantage to a minimum; whereas in L.Liascovich-G.Needleman, Villa Martelli 2006, Black belatedly (and incorrectly) played **17...♗xf3?! 18 ♕xf3 ♘xc4 19 ♕e2 ♘xb2 20 ♗d6** [20 ♕xb2!? ♘a4 21 ♕b3 ♘xc3 22 ♖xc3 ♗xc3 23 ♕xc3 +/=] **20...♘xd1 21 ♖xe7 ♘xc3 22 ♕f3 ♘b5 23 ♗xf8 ♖xf8 24 h4 h5 25 ♖e1 ♖d8 26 ♕c6 ♘c3 27 ♕c7 ♖d2 28 ♕b8+ ♔h7 29 ♕e8?!** [better 29 ♕xa7+/-] **29...♖b2** [here 29...♖d7!? is unclear again] **30 ♕xf7 ♘xb1 31 g4 ♖b4** [if 31...hxg4 then 32 h5 +/- intending 32...gxh5? 33 ♖e5 +-] **32 gxh5 ♖g4+ 33 ♔h2 ♖xh4+ 34 ♔g2 ♘c3 35 ♕xg6+ ♔h8 36 ♕g5 ♖d4 37 h6 ♖d7 38 ♖h1 ♗d4 39 ♖h4 ♘3e4 40 ♕g6 ♖d8 41 ♖xe4 ♘xe4 42 ♕xe4 ♖g8+ 43 ♔f1 e5 44 ♔e2 a5 45**

a4 b5 46 axb5 a4 47 ♕f3 ♔h7 48 ♕f7+ ♔h8 49 b6 a3 50 b7 a2 51 b8♕ **1-0**.

B22: 7...♘c6 *(D)*

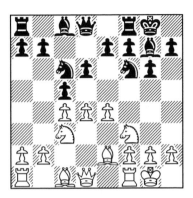

Black increases his pressure on the d4-square, forcing White to clarify the situation in the centre.

8 d5! ♘a5

The text move is reminiscent of the Yugoslav Variation of the g3-system, but the knight's position on a5 is less justified here as the c4-pawn is well defended. In fact, as Tarrasch said, the knight always stands badly on the flank. All the same, Black has little choice, as any other move entails the loss of two tempi or the weakening of his pawn structure.

a) 8...♘b4 9 a3 ♘a6 10 h3!? ♘c7 11 ♗f4 ♗d7 12 e5 dxe5 13 ♘xe5 ♘ce8 14 b4 gave Black a very bad Benoni in V.Grebionkin-M.Yuminov, Ishevsk 2005.

b) 8...♘b8 9 ♗f4 a6 10 a4 ♘h5 11 ♗e3 e5 (K.Robatsch-K.Mahdi, Austrian Team Ch. 1989) 12 dxe6!? fxe6 13 e5 +/-.

c) 8...♘e5 9 ♘xe5 dxe5 10 ♗e3 b6 11 a3 e6 12 b4 exd5 13 cxd5 cxb4 14 axb4

♘e8 15 ♗b5 ♘d6 16 ♗c6 ♗b7 17 ♗xb7 ♘xb7 18 ♖a6 +/- M.Taimanov-V.Bykov, Leningrad 1957.

9 h3

The main idea of this move is to restrict the c8-bishop. Other continuations are:

a) 9 ♗d2 b6!? 10 ♖c1 e5 11 b3 ♘e8 12 ♘e1 f5 13 a3 ♘f6 14 f3 f4 15 b4 ♘b7 16 ♘d3 ♛e7 ∞ V.Srebrnic-M.Kastelic, Slovenian Team Ch. 2003.

b) 9 ♗g5 h6 10 ♗f4 ♘h5 11 ♗e3 e5 12 dxe6 ♗xe6 13 ♘d2 ♘f6 14 ♖c1 ♘c6 15 h3 ♘d7 16 ♘f3 ♛e7 17 ♛d2 +/= Nguyen Huynh Minh-L.Szell, Budapest 2006.

c) 9 a3 b6 10 b4 ♘b7 11 ♗d2 e5 12 ♘e1 ♘e8 13 ♖b1 f5 14 exf5 gxf5 15 f4 with better chances for White, E.Postny-H.Asis Gargatagli, Andorra la Vella 2005.

d) 9 ♖b1 b6 10 a3 ♗g4 11 ♘d2 ♗xe2 12 ♛xe2 ♖e8 13 b3 e5 14 ♘d1 ♘b7 15 ♘b2 ♛e7 16 ♘d3 +/= B.Ivkov-D.Velimirovic, Yugoslavia 1987.

e) 9 ♗e3 e5 10 a3 b6 11 ♘d2 ♘d7 12 ♖c1 f5 13 f4 ♛e7 (A.Maidanik-F.Bentancor, Buenos Aires 2002) 14 exf5 gxf5 15 ♛e1 +/=.

f) 9 ♗f4 ♗g4 (or 9...♘h5 10 ♗g5 ♗g4 11 ♘d2 ♗xe2 12 ♛xe2 a6!? 13 ♖ab1 ♛c7 14 ♖fc1 and White was better when the players agreed a draw in O.Krivonosov-P.Benkovic, Biel 2003; after 9...a6 10 h3 b5 11 cxb5 axb5 12 ♗xb5 ♗a6, B.Zlotnik-J.Wetemaa, Daugawa-Lijepaja 1980, and now 13 ♗xa6 ♖xa6 14 ♛e2 ♖b6 15 e5 dxe5 16 ♗xe5 +/-, as the a5-knight is badly placed in this Benko Gambit position) 10 ♘d2

(the exchange of light-squared bishops is a typical theme in the King's Indian and Benoni, after which White can prepare action on the kingside or in the centre with e4-e5) 10...♗xe2 11 ♛xe2 a6 12 ♖ac1 e6 13 a3 exd5 14 cxd5 b5 15 b4 ♘b7 16 ♖fe1 +/= T.Doering-H.Ueter, Dortmund 1987.

9...e6 *(D)*

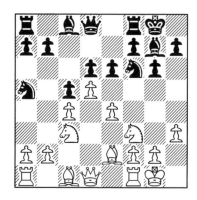

Black counters in the centre. Instead, 9...e5 fixes the pawn structure, and after 10 ♗g5 h6 11 ♗h4 b6 12 ♖b1 ♗d7 13 ♘d2 ♘b7 14 a3 ♛e8 15 b4 +/= P.Perera-K.Movsziszian, Sauzal (rapid) 2004. More flexible is 9...a6 10 a3 (10 ♗f4 is logical and transposes to 9 ♗f4 a6) 10...♛c7 11 ♗e3 ♖b8 12 ♘d2 ♗d7 13 ♖c1 +/= D.Taboas Rodriguez-P.Cabaleiro Reimondez, Marin 2002.

10 ♗g5

The most active, but other continuations also give White a small advantage; for instance, 10 ♖b1 b6 11 ♗e3 ♖e8 12 ♘d2 exd5 13 cxd5 ♛e7 14 a3 += I.Munjiza-S.Poljak, Croatian Women's Ch. 1993, or 10 ♗d3 a6 11 ♗e3 exd5 12 exd5 ♘d7 13 ♛d2 += L.Sandstrom-D.Pirrot, Baden Baden 1993.

10...h6

Otherwise White can play 11 ♕d2.

11 ♗f4

Alternatively:

a) 11 ♗h4 e5 12 ♘d2 a6 13 a3 b6 14 b4 ♘b7 15 ♖b1 ♕c7 16 ♕b3 += R.Odendahl-M.Niermann, Wuppertal 1994.

b) 11 ♗e3 also deserves attention; e.g. 11...exd5 12 cxd5 ♖e8 13 ♗d3 b6 14 ♖e1 ♗d7 15 ♗f4 c4 16 ♗c2 ♘b7 17 ♕d2 +/- D.Komljenovic-M.Veras Sanz, Saragossa 1994.

11...e5 12 ♗e3 ♘h5 13 ♕d2 ♔h7 (D)

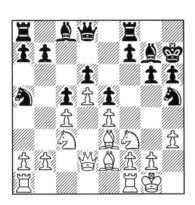

Here 14 ♖ae1!?, making ready for battle in the centre, would still leave White slightly better.

Instead, Al.David-Z.Almasi, Bastia (rapid) 2005, continued **14 ♘e1 b6 15 ♖c1 ♗d7 16 b3 ♕h4 17 ♗xh5?!** [better 17 ♘f3] **17...♕xh5 18 f4 exf4** [18...f5!? ∞] **19 ♗xf4 ♘b7 20 ♘f3 g5 21 ♗h2 ♖ae8 22 ♘e2 ♕g6 23 ♘g3 ♖e7 24 ♕d3 ♖fe8 25 ♔h1 ♔g8 26 ♘d2** [26 ♖ce1] **26...♗e5?** [Black should have played 26...g4!? when the game remains unclear] **27 ♖ce1 f6 28 ♖e2 ♘d8 29 ♖ef2 ♖f8 30 ♘f5 ♗xf5 31 ♖xf5 ♘f7 32 ♕f3**

♔g7 33 a4 h5 34 ♕d1 g4 35 ♗f4 ♗xf4 36 ♖5xf4 ♘h6 37 ♕e1 ♖e5 38 ♕g3 ♖g5 39 h4 ♖e5 40 ♕c3 ♔h7 41 a5 f5 42 axb6 axb6 43 ♔g1 ♖fe8 44 exf5 ♖xf5 45 ♕d3 ♖xf4 46 ♕xg6+ ♔xg6 47 ♖xf4 ♖e2 48 ♖f2 ♖e3 49 ♔f1 ♘f5 50 ♖f4 ♘xh4 51 ♘e4 ♘f5 52 ♔f2 ♖xb3 53 g3 ♖b2+ 54 ♔f1 ♖b4 55 ♔e2 ♖xc4 56 ♔d3 ♖d4+ 57 ♔e2 ♖xe4+ 0-1.

C: 6...♗g4 (D)

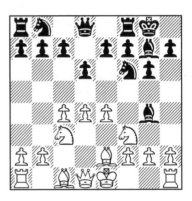

The 6...♗g4 system is the most popular sideline in the King's Indian. The main idea is to gain control of d4 by exchanging on f3 followed by ...♘fd7 and ...♘c6. Then the c6-knight can seize the central d4-square with an excellent position for Black, and sometimes he can reach a game with a well-placed knight on d4 or e5 against a weak light-squared bishop. Nevertheless, White has sufficient measures to cross Black's plan.

C1: 7 0-0 22
C2: 7 ♗e3 26

After other moves Black is okay:

a) 7 h3 is illogical as it forces Black to realize his plan with tempo: 7...♗xf3 8 ♗xf3 ♘fd7 9 0-0 ♘c6 10 ♗e3 e5 11 d5 ♘d4 = B.De Greif-M.Tal, Havana 1963.

b) 7 ♘g1 aims for the exchange of light-squared bishops, which is quite convenient for White, though it may be a little premature here. For one thing, after 7...♗d7 or 7...♗c8 White has nothing better than 8 ♘f3 repeating position. But in any case 7...♗xe2 8 ♘gxe2 c5 9 d5 ♘a6 10 0-0 ♘c7 11 a4 e6 was equal in P.Hammer-B.Züger, Biel 1981.

c) 7 ♗g5 is an interesting though rarely played idea. The bishop is more active here than on e3 and in many lines Black cannot easily play ...e7-e5. The downside is that it does not control the d4-square, and 7...♗xf3! gives Black equality; e.g. 8 ♗xf3 ♘c6 9 ♘e2 ♖e8 10 ♕d2 e5 11 d5 ♘d4 12 ♘xd4 exd4 (M.Krasenkow-V.Muratov, Blagoveshchensk 1988), when White should have preferred 13 0-0 with a level position according to Krasenkow.

C1: 7 0-0 *(D)*

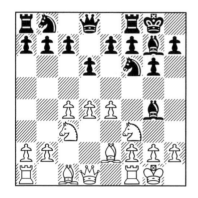

7...♘fd7

Black continues with his plan. Other continuations are less consistent:

a) 7...c5 8 d5 ♘a6 9 ♗f4 ♘c7 10 a4 a6 11 a5 ♖b8 12 ♘e1 ♗xe2 13 ♕xe2 b5 14 axb6 ♖xb6 15 ♘d3 += H.Hecht-A.Filipowicz, European Team Ch., Bath 1973.

b) 7...♘c6 8 d5 ♗xf3 9 ♗xf3 ♘a5 10 ♗e2 c5 11 ♗e3 ♘d7 12 ♕d2 ♖e8 13 ♖ab1 a6 14 b3 e6 15 dxe6 fxe6 16 ♖bc1 ♘e5 17 ♖fd1 += V.Bogdanovski-D.Ilic, Kladovo 1990.

c) 7...c6 8 ♗e3 ♘bd7 9 b4 a5 10 a3 ♕c7 11 ♕b3 ♖fc8 12 h3 ♗xf3 13 ♗xf3 += M.Quinteros-J.Diez del Corral, Montilla 1974.

8 ♗e3

Reinforcing the d4-square. Black has no problems after 8 d5 a5 9 ♗e3 ♘a6 10 ♘d4 ♗xe2 11 ♕xe2 ♘ac5 12 f3 a4 13 ♖ab1 e6 14 b4 axb3 15 axb3 ♖e8 16 dxe6 ♘xe6 17 ♕d2 ♘ec5 = V.Bogdanovski-B.Damljanovic, Pula 1990; or 8 ♘e1 ♗xe2 9 ♘xe2 e5 10 d5 a5 11 ♘d3 ♘a6 12 ♘c3 f5 with counterplay, N.Nikcevic-V.Akopian, Niksic 1991.

8...c5

Instead:

a) 8...e6 9 ♘e1 ♗xe2 10 ♕xe2 ♘c6 11 ♕d2 e5 12 d5 ♘d4 13 ♘c2 ♘xc2 14 ♕xc2 f5 15 f3 +/= J.H.Donner-M.Botvinnik, Leiden 1970.

b) 8...♘c6 9 d5 (or 9 ♕d2 e5 10 dxe5 dxe5 11 ♗g5 ♕c8 12 ♘d5 ♔h8 13 ♖ad1 ♘b6, S.Nikolic-E.Vasiukov, Moscow 1989, 14 c5 with the better chances) 9...♗xf3 (possibly Black should prefer 9...♘a5!? 10 ♘d2 ♗xe2 11 ♕xe2 c5 12 f4 a6 13 a4 ♖b8 ∞ R.Bator-J.Pribyl, Lodz

1979) 10 ♗xf3 ♘a5 11 ♗e2 ♗xc3 12 bxc3. When White plays 7 0-0 instead of 7 ♗e3 he must sometimes reckon with his pawns being doubled on the c-file. However, this is not always good for Black, as the absence of his dark-squared bishop may make itself felt; for example: 12...e5 (or 12...♖e8 13 ♖b1 c6 14 h4 ♕c7 15 h5 with an attack, V.Malakhov-A.Korotylev, Moscow 2004) 13 dxe6 (White must open the position as much as possible) 13...fxe6 14 ♗h6 ♖f7 15 f4 ♘f6 (15...♕e7, V.Chow-T.Southam, North Bay 1994, may be a little better, but White still has a dangerous initiative; e.g. 16 ♕d3 ♘c6 17 ♕e3 e5 18 c5! +/-) 16 e5 ♘e4 17 ♕d4 and White has a very strong attack; e.g. 17...d5 (or 17...♘c5 18 ♖ad1) 18 ♗g4 c5 19 ♕d3 ♖e7 (19...♕d7 20 ♖fd1 ♘xc4 21 ♕xe4) 20 ♗xe6+ ♖xe6 21 cxd5 g5 22 ♗g7 ♔xg7 23 ♕xe4 ♖h6 24 f5 +-.

9 d5 ♘a6 (*D*)

9...♗xf3 is premature as Black is not ready to play ...b7-b5, and White often plays h2-h3 to induce the exchange in any case. After 10 ♗xf3 ♘a6 11 ♗e2 ♘c7 12 ♕d2 a6 13 a4 ♖b8 14 f4 White was better in A.Ruffenach-S.Salus, Thonon les Bain 1995.

White also has an advantage after 9...♘b6 10 ♘d2 ♗xe2 11 ♕xe2 e6 12 ♖ac1 ♕e7 13 ♘f3 exd5 14 exd5 ♖e8 15 ♖fe1 += A.O'Kelly de Galway-R.Toran Albero, Torremolinos 1962; or 9...♕a5 10 ♕c2 ♘a6 11 a3 ♖fc8 12 h3 ♗xf3 13 ♗xf3 += J.Fedorowicz-J.Watson, New York 1979.

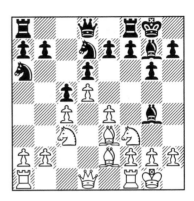

White has two main continuations:

C11: 10 ♘g5 23
C12: 10 ♕d2 24

The alternatives are not dangerous:

a) 10 ♘d2 ♗xe2 11 ♕xe2 ♘c7 12 f4 a6 13 a4 e6 14 ♕d3 exd5 15 cxd5 f5 with counterplay, E.Cobo Arteaga-L.Szabo, Salgotarjan 1967.

b) 10 h3 ♗xf3 11 ♗xf3 ♘c7 12 ♗e2 a6 13 a4 ♖e8 (or 13...e5!? 14 dxe6 ♘xe6 15 ♕xd6 ♘d4 with compensation) 14 a5 ♖b8 15 ♕d2 e6 16 ♖ab1 exd5 17 exd5 b6 ∞ H.Steingrimsson-G.Guseinov, European Ch., Plovdiv 2008.

C11: 10 ♘g5 ♗xe2 11 ♕xe2 h6 12 ♘h3 ♘c7 13 f4 (*D*)

Intending 14 e5 dxe5 15 f5 with the initiative. 13 ♖ad1 also deserves attention, since if 13...e6?! 14 dxe6 ♘xe6 15 ♖xd6 ♕e7 16 ♖d2 ♘d4 (J.Czakon-D.Gumula, Pardubice 2006) 17 ♗xd4 ♗xd4 18 ♘b5 ♗e5 19 ♖fd1 and Black does not have sufficient compensation for the pawn.

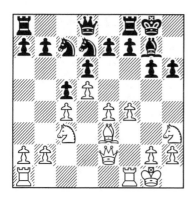

13...f5?!

But if 13...e6 14 dxe6 ♘xe6 (V.Golod-I.Kurnosov, Bad Wiessee 2004), then 15 ♘b5!? (or 15 ♕d2!? ♘d4 16 ♘f2) 15...♕e7 16 ♕d2! ♘b6 17 ♖ac1 f5 18 exf5 gxf5 19 ♖fe1 and White is better according to Golod.

14 ♔h1

14 ♘f2 a6 15 a4 b5 16 axb5 axb5 17 cxb5 ♖xa1 18 ♖xa1 ♕b8 19 exf5 gxf5 20 ♗d2 +/= I.Simeonidis-T.Hillarp Persson, European Ch., Kusadasi 2006, is not bad either. But the best move was 14 e5! dxe5 15 fxe5 ♘xe5 16 ♗xc5 with a clear advantage to White.

14...b5 15 exf5 gxf5 16 g4 (D)

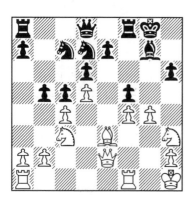

If 16 ♘xb5 ♘xb5 17 cxb5 ♘f6 (Mikhalevski) gives Black counterplay, though White's chances looks a little better after 18 ♕d3.

16...b4?!

Black should not close the queenside when his king is being attacked. Better was 16...bxc4! undermining the d5-pawn, when 17 ♖g1! ♘f6 is unclear, e.g. 18 g5!? (or 18 gxf5 ♔h8 19 ♕xc4 ♕c8 20 ♕d3 ♕b7 21 ♖ad1 ♕xb2 with counterplay) 18...♘g4 19 ♘f2 ♗xc3 20 bxc3 ♘xd5 21 ♘xg4 fxg4 22 ♕xc4 e6 23 ♖xg4 h5 (Mikhalevski).

The text was played in E.Miroshnichenko-Z.Efimenko, German League 2004, which continued **17 ♘d1 ♕e8 18 gxf5 ♖xf5 19 ♖g1 e6** [19...♕h5!?] **20 ♕g2 ♖f7?** [a blunder which allows White to open the c1-h6 diagonal; after 20...♕f8! the position would still be somewhat unclear according to Mikhalevski] **21 f5! exd5 22 ♗xh6 ♕e4** [the only defence] **23 ♕xe4 dxe4 24 ♘e3 ♔f8?!** [better 24...♘e8 +/-] **25 ♖xg7 ♖xg7 26 ♖g1 ♘e8 27 ♘d5 ♔f7 28 ♗xg7 ♘xg7 29 ♘g5+ ♔f8 30 ♘e6+** [30 f6! was simpler] **30...♘xe6 31 fxe6 ♘e5 32 e7+ ♔f7 33 ♖f1+ ♘f3 34 ♘c7 ♖h8 35 e8♕+ ♖xe8 36 ♘xe8 ♔xe8 37 ♔g2 ♘d2 38 ♖c1 b3 39 axb3 ♘xb3 40 ♖c3 ♘d2 41 ♔f2 ♔e7 42 ♔e3 ♘f1+ 43 ♔xe4 ♘xh2 44 ♔f4 d5 45 cxd5 ♔d6 46 ♖c1 1-0.**

C12: 10 ♕d2 ♘c7 (D)

White is better after 10...♗xf3 11 ♗xf3 ♘c7 12 a4 b6 13 ♗e2 += A.Ortiz-G.Needleman, Buenos Aires 2004; or 10...♕a5 11 a3 ♘c7 12 ♖fb1 ♕a6

(R.Dautov-A.Wojtkiewicz, Bad Wörishofen 1998) 13 b3 ♗xf3 14 ♗xf3 b5 15 ♗e2 bxc4 16 ♗xc4 ♕c8 17 ♗h6 += Dautov.

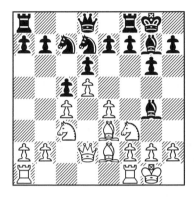

11 h3

White can also achieve an advantage after 11 ♗h6 ♗xh6 12 ♕xh6 ♗xf3 13 ♗xf3 e5 (T.Lonngren-M.Agopov, Hallsberg 1999) and now 14 ♗e2 +=, or 11 a3 a6 12 ♖ab1 ♗xf3 13 ♗xf3 b5 14 ♗e2 bxc4 15 ♗xc4 ♖b8 +=, though ½-½ G.Gajewski-A.Jakubiec, Polish Team Ch. 2005.

11...♗xf3 12 ♗xf3

White's position is better due to his extra space and greater prospects of playing in each part of the board. Moreover, Black has problems with obtaining counterplay.

12...a6

Black needs to prepare ...e7-e6, but the d6-square is weak. In V.Shishkin-D.Gumula, Barlinek 2006, Black failed in making this advance at a proper moment: 12...♖e8 13 ♖fd1 a6 14 a4 ♖b8 15 ♗e2 e6 16 dxe6 ♘xe6 17 ♕xd6 ♘e5 18 ♕xd8 ♖bxd8 19 ♖d5 ♘c6 20 ♖ad1+/-.

13 ♗e2 ♖e8

If 13...e6 14 dxe6 ♘xe6 15 ♕xd6 ♘d4 16 ♗g4 f5 17 exf5 gxf5 18 ♗d1 ♔h8 19 ♘d5 += D.Jakovenko-R.Fontaine, French Team Ch. 2008.

14 a4

14 f4 looks more active, and if 14...e6 15 dxe6 ♘xe6 16 ♕xd6!, rather than 16 ♘d5 ♘d4 17 ♗d3 ♘f6 18 ♘xf6+ ♗xf6 19 ♖ab1 b5 20 b4 cxb4 21 cxb5 ♘xb5 22 ♗xb5?! (better 22 ♕xb4) 22...axb5? (22...♗c3 -/+) 23 ♖xb4 ♕a5 24 ♖f2 ½-½ D.Tishin-V.Grinev, Alushta 2005.

14...e6! *(D)*

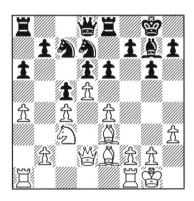

Played at a good moment.

15 ♖ab1

Now 15 dxe6 ♘xe6 16 ♕xd6 ♘d4 (Dautov) leads to excellent counterplay for Black. However, White can consider 15 ♖fe1 exd5 16 exd5 f5 +/= (½-½ V.Kosyrev-R.Mamedov, Moscow 2005) or 15 ♗g5 and Black's position remains passive.

15...exd5 16 exd5 a5!?

16...♕h4?! is met by 17 ♗g4! (A.Kharitonov-S.Mamedyarov, World Junior Ch. 2003) intending ♗g5 and wins, when objectively Black has nothing better than 17...♕d8.

17 ♖fe1 f5 18 ♗f1 ♘e5 19 f4 ♘f7

From here the knight will be quite difficult to activate. A bit better is 19...♘d7 20 ♗f2 ♘f6 21 ♖xe8+ ♕xe8 22 ♖e1 ♕d7 23 ♗d3 ♖e8 24 ♖xe8+ ♕xe8 25 ♕e1 ♘h5 26 ♕xe8+ ♘xe8 27 g3 ♗xc3 28 bxc3 ♘ef6 = R.Ibrahimov-G.Guseinov, Baku 2006.

20 ♗f2 ♕d7 *(D)*

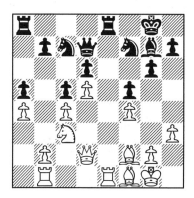

We are following R.Dautov-G.Guseinov, European Team Ch., Gothenburg 2005. In his notes Dautov now gives 21 ♕c2! ♘a6 (if 21...♖xe1 22 ♖xe1 ♖e8 23 ♕b3 ♖xe1 24 ♗xe1 ♘a6 25 ♕b6 +/-) 22 ♘b5 ♘b4 23 ♕d2 ♖xe1 24 ♖xe1 ♖e8 25 b3 when Black must still work hard to equalize. Instead the game continued:

21 ♘b5 ♘xb5 22 cxb5 b6 23 ♗c4 ♖xe1+ 24 ♖xe1 ♖e8 25 b3 ♖xe1+ 26 ♕xe1 ♗f6 27 ♕e6

White has succeeded in controlling the e6-square, but at the price of many exchanges.

27...♕d8 28 g4 fxg4 29 hxg4 ♗h4

Or 29...♗d4!? 30 ♗xd4 (or 30 g5 ♗xf2+ 31 ♔xf2 ♔f8) 30...cxd4 31 g5 ♕c7

32 ♔f1 ♕c5 and Black should draw according to Dautov.

30 ♗e3 ♕f6 31 ♕xf6! ♗xf6 32 g5 ♗d8?!

Here the best way was 32...♗c3! 33 ♗d3 ♔g7 34 ♔f2 h6 35 ♔e2 hxg5 36 fxg5 ♘e5 37 ♗e4 ♔f7 = (Dautov).

33 ♗d3 h6?!

And now 33...♔g7 =. After the text White could cause problems with 34 ♗xg6! hxg5 35 ♗xf7+ ♔xf7 36 fxg5 (Dautov) when Black must be more careful to draw. The game concluded:

34 gxh6?! ♔h7 35 ♔g2 ♘xh6 36 ♔f3 ♘f5 ½-½.

C2: 7 ♗e3 *(D)*

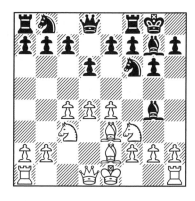

The most logical move. Black's idea consists of gaining control over the d4-square, so White prophylactically strengthens it. And as the bishop usually goes to e3 sooner or later, it seems the most flexible to play it at once.

C21: 7...e5 *27*
C22: 7...♘c6 *28*
C23: 7...♘fd7 *31*

Black has also tried:

a) 7...c5?! 8 dxc5 ♕a5 9 ♘d2 ♗xe2 10 ♕xe2 dxc5 11 ♘b3 ♕c7 12 ♘xc5 b6 13 ♘b3 ♖c8 14 ♘d5 ♘xd5 15 cxd5 +/- A.Summerscale-S.Barrett, British League 2002.

b) 7...♗xf3 8 ♗xf3 e5 9 d5 c5 10 h4 h5 11 ♗g5 ♘bd7 12 g4 hxg4 13 ♗xg4 ♕b6 14 ♗xd7 ♘xd7 15 ♕e2 with an attack, S.Djuric-Z.Ljubisavljevic, Genoa 2004.

c) 7...c6 8 h3 ♗xf3 9 ♗xf3 ♘bd7 10 0-0 a6 11 ♖c1 e5 12 d5 c5 13 a3 ♘e8 14 b4 +/= G.Kasparov-M.Dlugy, World Blitz Ch., Saint John 1988.

d) 7...♘bd7 8 h3!? ♗xf3 9 ♗xf3 e5 (9...c5 10 0-0 S.Misaka-F.Alemu, Istanbul Olympiad 2000, 10...cxd4 +/=) 10 d5 a5 11 g4 ♘c5 12 g5 ♘fd7 13 h4 f5 14 gxf6 ♕xf6 15 ♗e2 a4 16 ♕d2 +/= I.Nemet-D.Joncic, Baden 1998.

e) 7...a6 8 0-0 (an interesting plan is to attack Black's king was 8 h3 ♗xf3 9 ♗xf3 ♘fd7 10 h4 c5 11 d5 b5 12 h5 ♘e5 13 hxg6 fxg6 14 ♗g4 ♘xg4 15 ♕xg4 +/- J.Tisdall-A.Fauland, European Team Ch., Haifa 1989) 8...c6 (intending ...b5) 9 e5 ♘e8 10 ♖e1 ♘d7 11 ♗f4 dxe5 12 ♘xe5 ♘xe5 13 dxe5 ♗xe2 14 ♕xe2 ♘c7 15 ♖ad1 +/= M.Stojanovic-O.Sirotanovic, Senta 2002.

C21: 7...e5 8 d5 *(D)*

8 dxe5 dxe5 9 ♕xd8 ♖xd8 10 ♘d5 is also possible, hoping to show that ♗e3 is more useful than ...♗g4 in the Exchange Variation; e.g. 10...♘xd5 11 cxd5 c6 (C.Hughes-L.Leavell, corr. 1997), when White could have tried to fight for an edge with 12 ♗c4 ♗xf3 13

gxf3 cxd5 14 ♗xd5 ♘c6 15 ♖c1 ♖ac8 16 ♔e2. Instead Black might prefer 10...♘a6!?, when the standard ♗g5 would cost White a tempo.

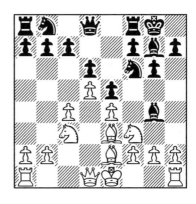

8...c5

Other continuations do not give equality, e.g. 8...♘h5 9 h3 ♗c8 10 ♕d2 f5 11 exf5 gxf5 12 g4! ♘f4 13 ♗xf4 exf4 (L.Portisch-B.Gurgenidze, Budapest 1959) 14 0-0-0! ♘a6 15 ♖dg1 with the initiative; or 8...♘a6 9 ♘d2 ♗xe2 10 ♕xe2 ♕e8 11 0-0 ♘h5 (M.Peek-T.Spaan, Amsterdam 2004) 12 ♖ab1 f5 13 f3 +/=.

9 ♖b1

With the standard plan a2-a3, b2-b4, developing an initiative on the queenside.

White can also achieve a small advantage after 9 h3 ♗d7 10 g4 ♘a6 11 ♘d2 ♘c7 12 a3 b6 13 ♘f1 ♕b8 14 b4 += S.Lputian-A.Kofidis, Panormo 1998; or 9 ♘d2 (the exchange of light-squared bishops is usually good for White unless it is connected with a loss of time) 9...♗xe2 10 ♕xe2 ♘h5 11 g3 a6 12 a3 ♘d7 13 b4 b6 14 ♘b3 += J.Ivanov-N.Sanchez, Benasque 1997.

9...♘bd7 10 a3 ♖c8 11 ♘d2

Or 11 h3!? ♗xf3 12 ♗xf3 ♘e8 13 h4 with an initiative.

11...♗xe2 12 ♕xe2 ♘h5 13 g3 *(D)*

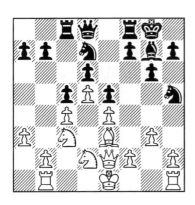

Obviously White's position is better. He has a small edge on both flanks and Black has no counterplay. On the other hand Black's position is very solid, without any weaknesses.

L.Ftacnik-W.Hug, Biel Interzonal 1993, continued:

13...a6 14 0-0 b6 15 ♔h1 ♕e8 16 ♘f3 ♔h8 17 ♖g1 ♖c7 18 ♖be1 ♕c8 19 ♘h4 ♖e8 20 ♘f5 ♗f8 21 ♕f3 ♘df6 22 g4

22 ♘h4!? would allow Black to disrupt the attack with 22...♘g4, e.g. 23 ♗c1 ♗e7 24 ♘g2 h6 when 25 h3?? loses to 25...♘xf2+ and 26...♕xh3 mate.

22...♘f4

22...gxf5 23 gxh5 f4 seems a stronger defence, though White's chances are still better.

23 ♘h4 ♘d7 24 ♘g2 ♘xg2 25 ♖xg2

Now White can arrange an attack on enemy's king.

25...♕d8 26 g5 f6 27 ♖eg1 ♗g7 28 ♕h3

28 h4! seems a better way to proceed.

28 ♕h3 ♘f8 29 f4 exf4 30 ♗xf4 fxg5 31 ♗xg5 *(D)*

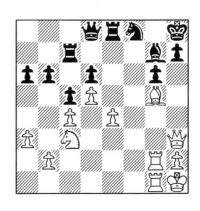

31...♕d7?

32...♕c8 was correct, and if 33 ♕h4 ♖f7 or 33 ♕g3 ♘d7! 34 ♕xd6?? ♗e5.

After the text White won without further difficulty: **32 ♕h4 ♖e5 33 ♖f1 ♕e8 34 ♖gf2 ♘d7 35 ♖f7 ♔g8 36 ♕f4 ♖c8 37 a4 ♖b8 38 ♗h6 ♗xh6 39 ♕xh6 ♕xf7 40 ♖xf7 ♔xf7 41 ♕xh7+ ♔e8 42 ♕xg6+ ♔e7 43 ♕h7+ ♔d8 44 ♘e2 ♖e7 45 ♕h4 ♘e5 46 ♘g3 ♔d7 47 ♘f5 ♖be8 48 ♕f6 ♘xc4 49 b3 ♖xe4 50 bxc4 ♔c7 51 ♕xd6+ ♔b7 52 ♕c6+ 1-0**.

C22: 7...♘c6 *(D)*

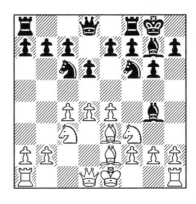

Black continues his plan of gaining control over the d4-square. However, here White can comfortably advance his d-pawn.

8 d5

The most logical move. Other continuations are:

a) 8 h3 lets Black fully realize his plan: 8...♗xf3 9 ♗xf3 e5 10 d5 ♘d4 11 0-0 ♘d7 12 ♗e2 c5 13 ♕d2 f5 14 f4 ♕e7 15 ♗d3 a6 16 fxe5 dxe5 ½-½ C.Dudek-R.Stephan, Germany 1993.

b) 8 ♖c1 ♘d7 9 0-0 (9 d5!?) 9...e5 10 d5 ♗xf3 11 ♗xf3 ♘d4 12 ♗xd4 exd4 13 ♘b5 d3 = J.Lechtynsky-K.Shirazi, Budapest 2002.

c) 8 ♕b3 ♗xf3 9 ♗xf3 e5 10 dxe5 dxe5 11 ♕xb7 ♘d4 12 ♗xd4 exd4 13 ♘d5 ♘xd5 14 ♕xd5 (14 cxd5!?) 14...♕e7 15 0-0 ♖fd8 16 ♕a5 d3 17 ♖ad1 ♗xb2 ∞ S.Kishnev-I.Rogers, German League 2001.

d) 8 0-0 e5 (8...♘d7 – *7 0-0 ♘fd7 8 ♗e3 ♘c6*) 9 d5 ♗xf3 10 ♗xf3 ♘e7 11 c5 ♘e8 12 ♗e2 f5 13 f3 +/= G.Schebler-V.Gries, Darmstadt 1996.

8...♗xf3

8...♘b8 involves the loss of two tempi. White is better after 9 0-0 c6 10 ♖c1 ♘fd7 11 h3 ♗xf3 12 ♗xf3 a5 13 ♖e1 ♘a6 (A.Delchev-O.Foisor, Mangalia 1992) 14 ♘a4!? +/=.

9 ♗xf3

9 gxf3 looks quite reasonable with the idea of attacking Black's king; e.g. 9...♘b8 (on 9...♘e5 White can try 10 ♕b3!? +/=) 10 h4!? (or 10 f4 ♘bd7 11 h4 c6 12 h5 cxd5 13 hxg6 fxg6 14 cxd5 ♕a5 15 ♗d2 ♕b4 16 ♕c2 ♘c5 17 a3 ♕b3 18 ♕xb3 ♘xb3 19 ♖d1 ♘xd2 20 ♔xd2 and

White is better in the ending, J.Granda Zuniga-T.Taylor, New York Open 1987) 10...c6 11 ♕d2 cxd5 (or 11...h5 12 f4 ♘bd7 13 0-0-0 cxd5 14 cxd5 ♕a5 15 f3 ♖fc8 16 ♔b1 a6 17 ♖hg1 with an attack, G.McKenna-J.Urbaneja, New York Open 1991) 12 cxd5 ♘bd7 13 0-0-0 ♖c8 (better 13...♕a5!? intending ...♖fc8) 14 ♔b1 ♘b6 15 ♗h6 +/- L.Van Wely-I.Rogers, Dutch Team Ch. 2000.

9...♘e5 (D)

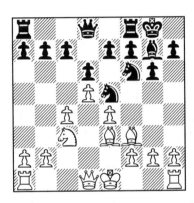

A typical position in this line. White has the bishop pair and more space. Black, on the other hand, has no weaknesses and can sometimes count on occupying the dark squares.

The alternative is 9...♘a5 10 ♗e2 c5 11 0-0 ♖e8 (or 11...♘d7 12 ♕d2 a6 13 ♖ab1 ♕c7 14 f4 +/= G.Andruet-N.Giffard, French Ch. 1989) 12 ♕c2 ♕d7 13 ♖ad1 a6 (D.Donchev-F.Portisch, Bratislava 1983), when White could have obtained a clear advantage after 14 e5! dxe5 15 ♘a4.

10 ♗e2 c6

Instead:

a) 10...♖e8 11 g4! (Black must reckon with an attack on his king) 11...e6 12 g5

♘h5 13 dxe6 ♖xe6 14 ♕d2 a6 15 f4 ♘c6 16 ♗f3 (V.Epishin-I.Rogers, Brno 1991) 16...♗xc3!? 17 ♕xc3 ♕e7 18 0-0 ♖xe4 19 ♗xe4 ♕xe4 20 ♖ae1 ♕f5 (+= Epishin) 21 ♗c1! intending b2-b4 and ♗b2 with a clear advantage.

b) After 10...c5 11 0-0 White can develop an initiative on the kingside, e.g. 11...a6 12 f3 ♘e8 13 ♕d2 ♘c7 14 ♖ad1 b5 15 b3 ♖b8 16 f4 ♘d7 17 e5 dxe5 18 f5 +/- G.Starcevic-N.Ristic, Belgrade 2005; or on the queenside, e.g. 11...♘e8 12 ♖c1 ♘c7 13 a3 ♖e8 14 b4 b6 15 bxc5 bxc5 16 ♕c2 e6 17 ♖b1 +/- T.Halasz-V.Kostic, Austrian Team Ch. 1997.

11 0-0

11 f4 ♘ed7 is often just a different move order, though sometimes it may have individual character; e.g. 12 dxc6 (more solid is 12 0-0, when 12...♕a5 transposes to the main line, or if 12...cxd5 13 exd5 ♘c5 14 ♕c2 a5 15 ♖ae1 ♘fd7 16 ♘b5 a4 17 ♗g4 f5 18 ♗f3 ♖c8 19 ♖e2 with better chances for White, B.Rytov-S.Tsetselian, Vitebsk 1970) 12...bxc6 13 0-0 a5!? 14 ♕d2 a4 15 ♗f3 ♕a5 (15...♕c7!? Ftacnik) 16 e5! dxe5 17 ♗xc6 exf4 18 ♖xf4 +/= L.Ftacnik-I.Rogers, Gold Coast 2000.

11...♕a5

Black does not equalize after 11...♕c7 12 f4 ♘ed7 13 ♖c1 e6 14 ♔h1 ♖fe8 15 ♗g1 exd5 16 cxd5! c5 17 ♗f3 ♕a5 18 g4! h6 19 h4 += M.Petursson-H.Angantysson, Reykjavik 1980; 11...cxd5 gives 12 cxd5!? ♕a5 13 f4 ♘ed7 14 a3 ♖fc8 15 ♗d4 +/- H.Salokangas-I.Svorjov, Helsinki 1990.

12 f4

Other moves give White an advantage too:

a) 12 ♖c1 ♖ac8 13 f4 ♘ed7 14 ♕d2 ♖fe8 15 ♔h1 += G.Ligterink-H.Bastian, European Team Ch., Plovdiv 1983.

b) 12 ♗d4 ♖fc8 (K.Shirazi-I.V.Ivanov, Saint John 1988) 13 f4!? ♘ed7 14 ♕d3 +=.

c) 12 ♖b1!? (this deserves attention) 12...♕c7 13 h3 a6 14 ♕b3 ♘ed7 15 ♖fc1 ♖fe8 16 ♕d1 e6 17 b4 ♖ac8 18 c5 exd5 19 exd5 ♘xd5 20 ♘xd5 cxd5 21 ♕xd5 dxc5 22 bxc5 ♖b8 23 ♕d6 ♕c8 24 ♗g4 f5 25 ♗d1 +/- A.Groszpeter-W.Hug, World Team Ch., Lucerne 1989.

12...♘ed7 *(D)*

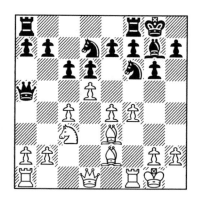

13 a3

Perhaps even better is 13 ♗d4 cxd5 14 exd5 a6 15 ♔h1 ♖ab8 16 a3 ♖fc8 17 ♗d3 ♕d8 18 ♕e2 ♘c5 19 ♗c2 b5 20 cxb5 axb5 21 b4 ♘cd7 22 ♗b3 +/- G.Agzamov-K.Lerner, USSR Ch., Moscow 1983.

13...♖fc8

13...cxd5 14 exd5 a6 15 b4 ♕c7 16 ♖c1 again leads to a small advantage for White, M.Zielinska-T.Stumberger, World Junior Ch. 1996.

14 b4

Or 14 dxc6 ♖xc6 15 ♘d5 ♕d8 16 ♘xf6+ ♘xf6 17 e5 ♘e8 18 ♗f3 with the initiative, A.Abhyankar-C.Foisor, Novi Sad Olympiad 1990.

14...♕d8 15 ♖c1 cxd5 16 exd5

Also good is 16 cxd5 ♘b6 17 ♕b3 ♘fd7 18 ♗d3 ♖c7 19 ♘b5 ♖xc1 20 ♖xc1 a6 21 ♘d4 +/- D.Belc-C.Foisor, Rumanian Team Ch. 1994.

16...a5

Or if 16...a6 17 ♕b3 ♖ab8 18 ♖fd1 ♖c7 19 g3 h5 20 ♔g2 ♘g4 21 ♗g1 ♖bc8 22 ♘e4 with the initiative, N.Rashkovsky-G.Cabrilo, Vrnjacka Banja 1988.

17 ♕b3 *(D)*

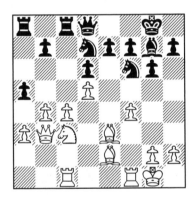

Black has a cramped position without any counterplay, and in F.Berkes-E.Cekro, European Team Ch., Plovdiv 2003, White went on to win, albeit after numerous errors from both sides:

17...♘f8 18 ♗f3 axb4 19 axb4 ♘6d7 20 ♖fd1 ♖a6 21 ♘b5 b6 22 ♗d4 ♖ca8 23 ♗xg7 ♔xg7 24 ♖e1 ♘f6 25 ♕e3 ♘g8 26 ♕c3+ f6 27 ♗d1 ♕d7 28 ♘d4 ♖a3 29 ♗b3 ♖e8 30 ♕b2 ♖aa8 31 ♖e4 e5 32 dxe6 ♘xe6 33 ♖d1 ♘c7 34 ♖xe8 ♖xe8 35 c5 bxc5 36 bxc5 d5 37 ♕f2 ♘h6 38

h3 ♘f5 39 c6 ♕c8 40 ♔h2 ♘xd4 41 ♖xd4 ♕e6 42 ♕d2 ♕d6 43 ♗a4 ♖b8 44 ♕a5 g5 45 ♕d2 gxf4 46 ♕xf4 ♕e5 47 ♕g3+ ♔f7 48 ♖h4 ♖h8 49 ♗c2 h6 50 ♗f5 ♔e7 51 ♖g4 ♔d6 52 ♖g6 ♔c5 53 ♗d7 d4 54 ♔g1 ♖a8 55 ♕xe5+ fxe5 56 ♗g4 ♔c4 57 ♖xh6 ♔d5 58 h4 e4 59 ♖h7 ♖a7 60 ♖e7 e3 61 h5 1-0.

C23: 7...♘fd7 *(D)*

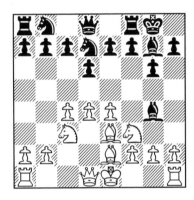

The most logical way for Black to realize his plan is by opening the a1-h8 diagonal and following up with ...♘c6. Now 8 0-0 transposes to C1 above, but White has numerous other options, the most important of which are:

C231: 8 ♖c1 *32*
C232: 8 ♘g1 *36*

Other seldom played continuations:
a) 8 h3 ♗xf3 9 ♗xf3 ♘c6 10 ♘e2 ♘a5 (the best solution here, intending ...c7-c5 to weaken the a1-h8 diagonal) 11 ♖c1 c5 12 0-0 ♘c6 13 ♕d2 cxd4 14 ♘xd4 ♘xd4 15 ♗xd4 ♗xd4 16 ♕xd4 ♕a5 = J.Tisdall-W.Wittmann, European

Team Ch., Debrecen 1992.

b) 8 h4 c5! (again the most effective counterattack) 9 d5 ♕a5 10 ♕d2 h5 11 ♗h6 a6 12 ♗xg7 ♔xg7 13 b3 (or 13 ♘g5 ♗xe2 14 ♕xe2 ♕b4 15 ♖h3 ♘e5 16 b3 ♘bd7 17 f4 ♘g4 18 ♕b2 ♔g8 19 a3 ♕a5 20 a4 ½-½ K.Spraggett-F.Izeta Txabarri, Spanish Team Ch. 1998) 13...♘f6 14 a4 ♘bd7 15 0-0 ♖ad8 16 ♕b2 ♗xf3 17 ♗xf3 e5 18 ♖ae1 ½-½ P.Schlosser-S.Martinovic, German League 1996.

c) 8 ♕d2 e5 (8...c5 9 d5 is line 'e' below) 9 d5!? (if 9 0-0-0 exd4! 10 ♗xd4 ♗xf3 11 gxf3 ♗xd4 12 ♕xd4 ♘c6 13 ♕e3 f5 14 ♘d5 ♘b6 15 c5 ♘xd5 16 ♖xd5 fxe4 17 fxe4 ♕f6 with counterplay, Y.Pelletier-B.Züger, Swiss Team Ch. 1994) 9...♗xf3 10 gxf3 ♘f6 11 f4 exf4 12 ♗xf4 ♖e8 13 f3 ♘h5 14 ♗e3 ♗e5 15 0-0-0 ♕f6 16 ♘b5 ♖e7 (M.Kanep-K.Guseinov, European Junior Ch. 2002) 17 ♖hg1!? +/=.

d) 8 ♕b3!? (now Black must decide whether to defend the b7-pawn or not) 8...♗xf3 (8...♕c8 9 ♖d1! ♗xf3 10 ♗xf3 e5 11 dxe5 ♘xe5 12 ♗e2 ♘bd7 13 0-0 a5 14 ♕c2 ♘c5 15 b3 +/= R.Janssen-S.Stojanov, Golden Sands 2000) 9 ♗xf3 ♘c6 10 ♖d1 e5 11 dxe5 ♘cxe5!? (after 11...dxe5 12 ♘e2 ♕e7, H.Genser-D.Flores, Turin Olympiad 2006, White could have taken the b7-pawn: 13 ♕xb7 ♘d4 14 ♘xd4 exd4 15 ♗xd4 +/-) 12 ♗e2 b6 13 0-0 ♘c5 14 ♕c2 ♘c6 (S.Atalik-Z.Kozul, European Ch., Istanbul 2003) and now Atalik suggests 15 f4!, e.g. 15...♗xc3 16 bxc3 ♕e7 17 ♗f3 ♖ad8 18 e5 ♘a5 19 ♕e2 dxe5 20 ♖xd8 ♖xd8 21 fxe5 ♕xe5 22 ♗d5 ♘e6 23 ♕f3 with compensation.

e) 8 d5!? c5 (other continuations lead to a small advantage for White; e.g. 8...a5 9 ♘d4 ♗xe2 10 ♕xe2 c6 11 0-0 ♘c5 12 ♖fd1 cxd5 13 cxd5 ♘bd7 14 f3 a4 15 ♖ab1 ♕a5 16 ♘db5 ♖fc8 17 ♗d4! += Z.Franco Ocampos-F.Izeta Txabarri, Elgoibar 1997; or 8...♘a6 9 ♘d4 ♗xe2 10 ♕xe2 ♘ac5 11 0-0 ♘b6 12 ♖ac1 a5 13 b3 e5 14 dxe6 fxe6 15 ♖fd1 ♕e7 16 ♘db5 += Z.Franco Ocampos-I.Morovic Fernandez, Moron 1982) 9 ♕d2!? (instead 9 0-0 – 7 0-0 ♘fd7 8 ♗e3 c5 9 d5) 9...a6 (or 9...♘a6 10 h3 ♗xf3 11 gxf3 e5 12 dxe6 fxe6 13 ♕xd6 ♘e5, K.Sasikiran-P.Harikrishna, Pune 2004, when White has a big advantage after 14 ♕xe6+!? or 14 0-0-0) 10 a4 (10 ♗h6!?) 10...♕a5 11 0-0 ♘b6 12 ♕c2 ♗xf3 13 gxf3 ♘8d7 14 f4 ♘c8 15 ♔h1 ♕d8 16 ♖g1 ♔h8 17 ♖g3 e6 (M.Gurevich-E.Sutovsky, Polanica Zdroj 1999) 18 ♖d1 +/=.

C231: 8 ♖c1 *(D)*

The main idea of this move is to protect the c3-knight, in order to forestall the possibility of (8 0-0) 8...♘c6 9 d5 ♗xf3 10 ♗xf3 ♘a5 11 ♗e2 ♗xc3 (see the notes in line C1 above); but as we think that line is good for White in any case, in our opinion the prophylactic 8 ♖c1 is unnecessary. Now Black can play:

8...a6

With this move Black usually prepares ...c7-c5, often followed by ...b7-b5. Other plans are:

a) 8...♗xf3 9 ♗xf3 e5 10 d5 allows White (as he has not yet castled) to play on both the queenside (with b2-b4) and the kingside (h4-h5). Black cannot count on equality in either case; e.g. 10...f5 11 b4 a5 12 a3 ♘a6 13 ♖b1 ♖f7 14 0-0 +/= K.Berg-P.Peev, Pernik 1984; or 10...a5 11 h4 f5 12 h5 ♘a6 13 hxg6 hxg6 14 ♔e2 f4 15 ♗d2 ♘f6 16 g3 += L.Stein-J.Rubinetti, Mar del Plata 1966.

b) 8...c5 9 d5 a6 10 0-0 transposes to the main line, but White can also play 10 a4 and if 10...b5 11 axb5 axb5 12 cxb5 ♘b6 13 ♕b3 e6 14 h3 ♗xf3 15 ♗xf3 exd5 16 ♘xd5 ♘8d7 17 ♘c3 ♗d4 18 ♗d2 ♕h4 19 0-0 ♘e5 20 ♗e2 +/- S.Atalik-M.Cebalo, Slovenian Team Ch. 2001. Otherwise Black can try 9...♘a6 10 0-0 ♘c7 11 h3 ♗xf3 12 ♗xf3 a6 13 a4 ♕b8 (this prepares ...b7-b5 and also defends the d6-pawn, thus enabling ...e7-e6) 14 ♗e2 e6 15 ♕d2 exd5 16 exd5 ♖e8 17 ♖b1 f5 18 ♖fc1 ♕d8 19 a5 ♖c8 20 ♗f1 ♖e7 21 b4 +/= A.Shariyazdanov-G.Mohr, Croatian Team Ch. 2004.

c) 8...e5 (the typical King's Indian move) 9 d5 a5 (if 9...f5 10 h3 ♗xf3 11 ♗xf3 a5 12 ♕c2 – to prevent ...♗f6-g5 – 12...♘a6 13 a3 ♔h8 14 ♖b1 ♕e7 15 b4 axb4 16 axb4 ♗f6 17 ♕c1 ♗h4 18 ♔e2!? f4 19 ♗d2 ♘b6 20 ♘d1 h5 21 ♘b2 c6 22

♕c2 ♖fe8 23 ♖he1 +/= L.Schandorff-C.Hoi, Copenhagen 2002) 10 a3!? ♘a6 (D) and now:

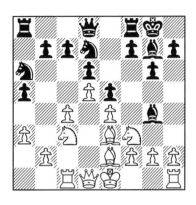

c1) 11 0-0 and then:

c11) 11...♘dc5!? 12 b3 ♗xf3?! (better 12...f5!? or 12...h6!?) 13 ♗xf3 f5 14 ♖b1 fxe4 (14...♕h4!?) 15 ♗xe4 ♕h4 16 g3 ♕h3 17 ♗f3 +/- A.Duer-C.Cuartas, Reggio Emilia 1981/82.

c12) 11...♕e7 12 ♘d2 ♗xe2 13 ♕xe2 f5 14 f3 c5 15 dxc6 bxc6 16 ♘b3 ♘c7 17 c5 dxc5 18 ♘a4 fxe4 19 fxe4 ♖xf1+ 20 ♖xf1 ♘e6 21 ♕c4 ♔h8 22 ♘bxc5 ♘exc5 23 ♗xc5 ♘xc5 24 ♘xc5 +/=, though ½-½ M.Nikolov-E.Janev, Bulgarian Team Ch. 2003.

c13) 11...f5 12 ♖b1 ♗xf3 13 ♗xf3 ♘ac5 14 b4 axb4 15 axb4 ♘xe4 and now taking with the bishop looks most logical, as after 16 ♗xe4 fxe4 (N.Rashkovsky-V.Doroshkievich, USSR Ch., Novosibirsk 1976) 17 ♘xe4 White remains with an excellently placed knight with a better game for White (Geller). Nevertheless, 16 ♘xe4 fxe4 also looks good for White, e.g. 17 ♗g4 (or if 17 ♗xe4 ♕h4 18 f3 ♗h6, Khalifman, then 19 ♗f2 +/=) 17...b6 18

♗e6+ ♔h8 19 ♕c2 ♘f6 (T.V.Petrosian-J.Bednarski, Tel Aviv Olympiad 1964) 20 ♖a1 ♕e7 21 b5 intending 22 ♖a6 with better chances for White.

c2) 11 ♖b1 is an interesting idea, aiming for b2-b4 before Black is ready with ...♘c5, ...f7-f5 and ...♘xe4. After 11...f5 12 b4 Black usually tries to exchange dark-squared bishops with 12...♗f6 13 0-0 ♗xf3 (Hübner suggests 13...♔h8! 14 ♕c1 ♕e7 ∞) 14 ♗xf3 ♗g5 15 ♗xg5 ♕xg5, though White has the initiative after 16 c5! J.Adamski-W.Hug, Stary Smokovec 1974. White can also avoid the bishop exchange, but this leaves his pieces very passive; e.g. 13 ♕c1 f4 14 ♗d2 ♕e7 15 ♕c2 ♔h8 16 h3 ♗h5 17 ♘h2 ♗xe2 18 ♔xe2 h5 = V.Korchnoi-W.Hug, 2nd matchgame, Zürich 1977.

9 0-0

White has a variety of other options:

a) 9 ♘g1 ♗xe2 10 ♘gxe2 can be compared with 8 ♘g1 in C232, and 10...c5 11 dxc5!? ♘xc5 12 b4 ♘cd7 13 0-0 in fact transposes to the note with 9...a6.

b) 9 b4!? c5 (or 9...♘b6 10 ♘d2 ♗xe2 11 ♘xe2 c6, A.Schenk-L.Vogt, Austrian Team Ch. 2003, 12 c5 +/=) 10 bxc5 dxc5 11 d5 b5 12 0-0 ♕a5 13 ♕b3 ♗xf3 14 gxf3 bxc4 (V.Chuchelov-K.Guseinov, European Ch., Istanbul 2003) 15 ♕xc4!? +/-.

c) 9 d5 ♗xf3 10 ♗xf3 (10 gxf3!? is also dangerous, e.g. 10...e5 11 h4 ♘f6, T.Hillarp Persson-M.Nouro, Stockholm 2006, 12 c5 with the initiative) 10...b5 (passive is 10...a5 11 h4 ♘a6 12 h5 ♘ac5, S.Savchenko-R.Forster, World

Team Ch., Lucerne 1997, when White can follow Khalifman's suggestion 13 hxg6 hxg6 14 ♔d2!? c6 15 ♕g1 with an attack on the black king) 11 ♗e2!? b4 12 ♘a4 c5 13 h4 ♘b6 14 ♘xb6 ♕xb6 15 ♕d2 ♘d7 16 h5 +/- V.Topalov-J.Piket, Wijk aan Zee (blitz) 1999.

9...c5

The alternative is 9...♗xf3, to divert the e2-bishop from the f1-a6 diagonal before playing ...c7-c5 and ...b7-b5; e.g. 10 ♗xf3 c5 11 d5 b5 12 ♗e2 bxc4 13 ♗xc4 ♘b6 14 ♗e2 ♘8d7 15 b3 ♕b8 16 ♕d2 ♖c8 17 ♖b1 ♕c7 18 ♖fc1 +/= J.Nikolac-M.Cebalo, Croatian Team Ch. 1997.

10 d5 b5 *(D)*

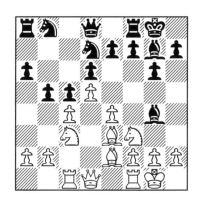

10...♗xf3 has the same idea as on the 9th move, though here White has successfully tried 11 gxf3!? ♘f6 12 f4 ♘bd7 13 a4 ♕c7 14 f5! ♖ae8 15 ♔h1 e6 16 dxe6 fxe6 17 fxg6 hxg6 18 ♖g1 +/= V.Zheliandinov-M.Cebalo, Bled 1999.

11 cxb5

Other moves are good for White too; e.g. 11 b3 b4 12 ♘a4 ♘b6 13 ♘xb6 ♕xb6 14 ♘d2 ♗xe2 15 ♕xe2 a5 16 f4 a4 17 e5 +/= P.Van der Sterren-F.Nijboer,

Gouda (rapid) 1997, or 11 ♘d2 ♗xe2 12 ♕xe2 ♘b6 13 b3 (13 cxb5!?) 13...♘8d7 14 f4 b4 15 ♘d1 a5 16 ♘f2 a4 17 ♘f3 axb3 18 axb3 ♖a3 += V.Chekhov-B.Züger, Prague 1989, though Black has some counterplay here.

11...axb5 12 ♗xb5 *(D)*

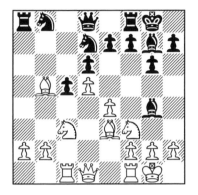

12...♘e5

Or 12...♕b6 13 a4 ♘e5 14 b4 ♘a6 15 bxc5 ♘xc5 16 ♗e2 ♘xf3+ 17 ♗xf3 ♗xf3 18 ♕xf3 ♖fc8 = S.Grunberg-B.Züger, West Berlin 1988.

13 ♗e2 *(D)*

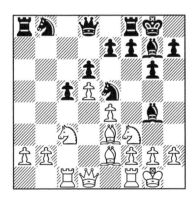

13 a4 ♘a6 (or 13...♘xf3+!? 14 gxf3 ♗h5 Mikhalevski) 14 ♗e2 ♕b6 15 ♘xe5 ♗xe2 16 ♘d7!? ♕d8 17 ♕xe2 ♕xd7 18

♘b5 ♖fb8 with compensation, V.Grebionkin-G.Guseinov, Internet blitz 2004.

13...♘xf3+ 14 ♗xf3 ♗xf3 15 ♕xf3 ♘d7 16 ♕e2 ♕a5 17 ♗g5

Mikhalevski suggests 17 ♖c2!? so that the a2-pawn is defended after a possible ...♗xc3, b2xc3.

17...♖fe8 18 f4 ♕a6

18...♗d4+ 19 ♔h1 ♗xc3 is unclear.

19 ♕g4 ♗d4+ 20 ♔h1 ♘f6 21 ♕f3 ♗xc3 22 bxc3 ♕c4! *(D)*

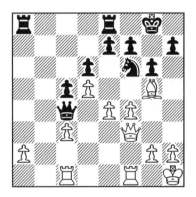

Now after 23 ♖ce1!? ♖a3! (better than 23...♖xa2 24 f5!) 24 f5 ♖xc3 25 ♕f4 ♕d4 Black should be able to hold the position, according to Mikhalevski.

So in L.Van Wely-S.Mamedyarov, Wijk aan Zee 2006, White tried **23 ♗xf6 exf6 24 e5!**, but Black was able to defend here too: **24...♖xa2! 25 exf6 ♖ae2! 26 ♖a1 h6! 27 f5! ♖2e3 28 ♕f4! ♕xf4 29 ♖xf4 ♖e1+** [or just 29...gxf5 = Mikhalevski] **30 ♖f1 ♖xf1+ 31 ♖xf1 gxf5 32 ♔g1 ♖e5 33 c4 ♔h7 34 ♖a1 ♖e4 35 ♖a6 ♖xc4 36 ♖xd6 ♖c1+ 37 ♔f2 ♔g6 38 ♖c6 c4 39 ♔e3 c3 40 ♔d3 ♖d1+ 41 ♔e3! ♖e1+ 42 ♔d4 ♖e2 43 ♔xc3 ♖xg2 44 d6 ♔xf6 45 d7+ ♔e7 46 ♖xh6 ♖g6 47 ♖h5 ♖d6 48 ♖xf5 ♖xd7 49 ♖f2 ½-½.**

C231: 8 ♘g1 *(D)*

The exchange of light-squared bishops is usually helpful to White, as after the typical ...e7-e5, d4-d5, Black's counterattack with ...f5-f4, ...g5-g4 loses its strength. However, the loss of time connected with this exchange allows Black to achieve counterplay. Moreover, White must often reckon with ...c7-c5 followed by ...b7-b5, as White's lack of castling and unprotected c4-pawn offer Black various tactical motifs.

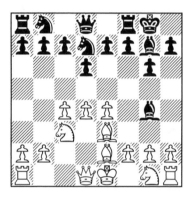

8...♗xe2 9 ♘gxe2 e5

Black has also tried:

a) 9...♘b6 10 b3 e6 11 ♕d2 d5 12 cxd5 exd5 13 e5 ♘c6 14 h4 f6 15 f4 ♕e7 16 h5 with an initiative, N.De Firmian-B.Züger, Biel 1986.

b) 9...a6 10 0-0 c5 11 dxc5 ♘xc5 12 b4 ♘cd7 13 ♖c1 ♘c6 14 ♕b3 e6 15 ♖fd1 +/= M.Cebalo-W.Hug, Biel 1986.

c) 9...e6 10 0-0 ♘c6 11 ♕d2 ♘e7 12 ♖ad1 c6 13 ♗g5 f6 14 ♗f4 d5 15 b3 e5 16 ♗g3 dxc4 17 bxc4 +/= H.Grünberg-H.Vonthron, German League 1993.

d) 9...♘c6 10 0-0 a6 11 ♕d2 ♖b8 12 ♖ac1 e6 13 b3 ♘e7 14 f4 +/= S.Pruefer-

B.Meissner, German League 2004.

e) 9...c5 *(D)* is the main alternative, when White can continue:

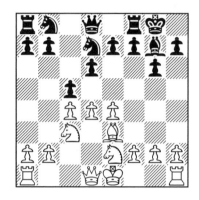

e1) 10 ♖c1 ♘c6 11 0-0 cxd4 12 ♘xd4 ♖c8 (or 12...♘xd4 13 ♗xd4 ♗xd4 14 ♕xd4 ♕b6 15 ♕d2 +/= M.Hoensch-T.Reich, German League 1989) 13 b3 a6 14 ♕d2 ♕a5 15 ♘xc6 bxc6 16 ♘a4 (16 ♘d5!?) 16...♕xd2 17 ♗xd2 c5 18 ♗c3 f5 19 ♖fe1 f4 20 f3 ½-½ H.Fioramonti-B.Züger, Swiss Team Ch. 1999.

e2) 10 0-0 cxd4 (10...a6 is 9...a6 above; or if 10...♘a6 11 ♕d2 ♖e8 12 ♖ad1 ♖c8 13 b3 ♕a5 14 f3 +/= R.Altshul-A.Kaminik, World Seniors Ch. 2006) 11 ♘xd4 ♘c6 12 b3 ♖e8 13 ♖c1 ♕a5 14 f3 ♘xd4 (14...♖ac8!?) 15 ♗xd4 ♗xd4+ 16 ♕xd4 +/= D.Yevseev-A.Gubajdullin, Russian Team Ch. 2006.

e3) 10 d5 a6 (10...♘e5 11 b3 ♕a5 12 ♕d2 a6 13 ♗g5 ♖e8 14 f4 ♘ed7 15 ♖b1 b5 was unclear in T.Nalbandian-T.L.Petrosian, European Ch., Warsaw 2005; 13 0-0!? might be more testing) 11 a4 ♕a5 (or 11...♘e5!? 12 b3 ♕a5 13 ♖c1 b5 14 axb5 axb5 15 cxb5 ♘bd7 with compensation, V.Popov-K.Guseinov, St Petersburg 2000) 12 0-0 (if 12 ♗d2 ♘e5

13 b3 ♘d3+ 14 ♔f1 ♘d7 15 h4!? h5 16 ♖h3 ♘b4 17 ♘f4 ♘f6 18 f3! ♕c7 19 g4 hxg4 20 fxg4 ♕d7 21 ♖g3, A.Beliavsky-M.Cebalo, Nova Gorica 1999, 21...b5!? 22 g5 ♘h7 23 axb5 axb5 24 cxb5!? ∞ Beliavsky) 12...♘e5 13 b3 ♘xc4 14 bxc4 ♗xc3 15 ♘xc3 ♕xc3 16 ♗h6 ♖e8 17 ♖c1 ♕d4 18 ♕g4 with compensation, J.Hultin-J.Wallace, Stockholm 1997.

10 d5

Keeping the tension in the centre with 10 0-0 deserves serious attention; e.g. 10...♘c6 (or 10...a5 11 ♕d2 ♘c6 12 f3 exd4 13 ♘xd4 ♘c5 14 ♖ad1, G.Kasparov-M.Vukic, Banja Luka 1979, and now 14...♘xd4 15 ♗xd4 ♗xd4+ 16 ♕xd4 f6 +/= Kasparov, but Black is very passive) 11 ♕d2 exd4 (11...f5 12 exf5 gxf5 13 dxe5 dxe5 14 ♖ad1 +/= Kasparov) 12 ♘xd4 ♘de5 13 b3 ♘g4 (if 13...♘xd4 14 ♗xd4 f5 15 exf5 ♖xf5, R.Vera-R.Martin del Campo, Cienfuegos 1997, 16 f3!? ♕h4 17 ♖ad1 +/= Tsesarsky; or 13...♕f6 14 ♘db5! ♖ac8 15 ♘d5 ♕d8 16 ♖ad1 ♘g4 17 ♗g5 f6 18 ♗h4 a6 19 ♘bc3 again with better chances for White, R.Vera-F.Gomez, Cuban Ch. 2001) 14 ♗g5 ♕e8 15 ♘de2 f5 16 f3 +/= V.Ilinsky-A.Krechetov, Moscow 1995.

10...f5 *(D)*

The most logical move. Black immediately starts counterplay in the centre, trying to take advantage of his good development. The passive option is to stabilize the queenside with 10...a5 11 ♕d2 ♘a6 12 0-0-0 (12 0-0!?) 12...♘dc5 13 ♔b1 f5 14 f3 f4 15 ♗f2 ♕d7 16 ♘c1 ♖f6 17 ♘d3 +/= S.Schafranietz-C.Walther, German League 1996.

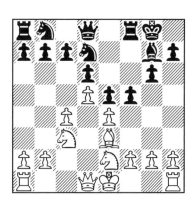

11 f3

White can also play 11 exf5 gxf5 12 f4, e.g. 12...♘f6 (12...♕h4+ 13 ♗f2 ♕e7 14 0-0 +/= F.Vallejo Pons-R.Martin del Campo, Yucatan 1999) 13 h3 ♘h5 14 0-0 ♘d7 15 ♕d2 a6 16 fxe5 ♘xe5 (16...dxe5!?) 17 b3 +/= B.Nickoloff-T.Southam, Toronto 1995.

11...♗h6

Or 11...♘f6 12 0-0 f4 13 ♗f2 ♘bd7 14 b4 ♖f7 15 c5 +/= P.Oliveira-C.Braga, Brazilian Ch. 1983.

12 ♗f2

Other moves lead to unclear positions; e.g. 12 ♕d2 ♗xe3 13 ♕xe3 (A.Piasini-S.Meo, Rome 1990) 13...f4!? 14 ♕f2 ♘b6 15 b3 a5 ∞, or 12 ♗xh6 ♕h4+ 13 ♘g3 ♕xh6 14 exf5 gxf5 15 ♕d2 ♕h4 16 0-0-0 ♘b6 ∞ M.Petursson-M.Wilder, Lone Pine 1979.

12...♘f6

Again Black should not delay with counterplay: 12...a5?! 13 h4! ♘f6 (M.Franic-G.Mohr, Zadar 1995) 14 h5! ♘xh5 15 exf5 +/-.

13 ♕d3

13 0-0!? intending c4-c5 also deserves attention, as does 13 exf5 gxf5 14

♘g3 ♘e8 15 0-0 ♘d7 16 ♕c2 +/=
B.Ostenstad-A.Poulsen, Copenhagen
1986.

13...fxe4 14 ♘xe4 ♘xe4 15 fxe4

White can count on a small advantage after 15 ♕xe4 ♘d7 16 ♘c3 ♕g5 17
0-0 ♘f6 18 ♕c2 ♖ae8 19 ♖ae1 a6 20 ♘e4
♘xe4 21 ♖xe4 ½-½ V.Kosyrev-
F.Amonatov, Moscow 2006.

15...♕g5 16 0-0 ♘d7 17 ♘c3 ♘f6 *(D)*

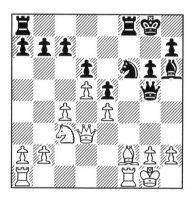

If Black wanted to draw then
17...♕d2 18 ♕xd2 ♗xd2 was good
enough, e.g. 19 ♘b5 ♖fc8 20 ♖ad1 ♗a5
21 ♖b1 a6 22 ♘a3 ♗b6 = (Avrukh). The
text is more ambitious and gives Black
an active position. In S.Lputian-
S.Mamedyarov, FIDE World Ch., Tripoli 2004, White now went wrong with:

18 ♔h1?

Better was 18 h3! ♘h5 19 ♘e2 ♘f4
(or 19...♖f7 20 c5 intending 20...♖af8?
21 cxd6 cxd6 22 ♗xa7!) 20 ♘xf4 exf4 21
♗d4 ♗g7 =.

**18...♕d2! 19 ♕h3 ♘h5 20 ♗g1 ♘f4 21
♕g3 ♕xb2**

Stronger was 21...♘e2! 22 ♕h3 ♕xb2
23 ♘xe2 ♕xe2 -/+ (Avrukh).

22 ♖ab1 ♕a3?

Here Avrukh suggests 22...♕d2!,
and if 23 ♖fd1 ♘e2! 24 ♘xe2 ♕xe2 with
the advantage.

23 ♖xb7 ♖f7 24 ♖fb1 ♔g7 25 ♖7b4

Now 25 ♘b5 was strong for White,
since if 25...♖xa2 26 ♘xc7 ♖c8 27 ♘e6+
♔g8 (Avrukh) then 28 ♘xf4 ♗xf4 29
♕g4 wins.

25...♕a6 26 ♕g4! ♕a5 27 ♕g3

White would still have been clearly
better after 27 ♕d1! ♖af8 28 ♖1b3! ♕a6
29 ♖a4 ♕c8 30 ♖xa7 ♘h5 31 ♖bb7
(Avrukh).

**27...♕a6 28 ♖a4 ♕c8 29 c5 ♖b8 30 ♖b3
♖xb3 31 axb3 ♘h5 32 ♕e1 a6 33 c6
♕g4 34 ♖a1 ♗f4 35 ♘e2 ♗g5 36 ♘c3
♗f4 37 ♘e2 ♗g5 38 ♘c3 ♗f4 ½-½.**

Conclusion

The move 6...c6 (line A) with the plan
of ...a7-a6 and ...b7-b5 is quite interesting, but Black faces serious problems to
equalize in this variation. 6...c5 (line B)
offers greater possibilities: Black often
obtains good chances in Benoni-type
positions after 7 d5, though he must
then be theoretically prepared to play
this opening. If White prefers independent variations, he can achieve
these either by holding back d4-d5 or
else exchanging on e6.

6...♗g4 (line C) is the most popular
and best-analysed sideline, perhaps
because of the clear plan of fighting for
the d4-square. However, 7 ♗e3 doesn't
grant Black equality after any of 7...e5,
7...♘c6, or the most thoroughly studied
and tested 7...♘fd7. Moreover, it seems
that with this line Black diverges from
the spirit of King's Indian somewhat.

Chapter Two

Exchange Variation: 7 dxe5

Exchanging pawns on e5 and then queens as well is too simplistic to put Black in a difficult position, but this method does have some psychological justification. By opting for the King's Indian Defence, Black has declared his preference for an aggressive and complicated fight. By taking the game into an ending – or rather a queenless middlegame – White seeks to quieten things down.

All the same, while Black can no longer expect to obtain an attack on the opponent's king, the positions arising are complex enough in a strategic sense, and White's chances of obtaining an advantage are not that great. He may be a little better developed, but the chronic weakness of the d4-square is his Achilles' heel. Indeed, White needs to be careful as he can sometimes end up in a worse ending himself due to the weak dark squares in the central zone.

1 d4 ♘f6 2 c4 g6 3 ♘c3 ♗g7 4 e4 d6 5 ♘f3 0-0 6 ♗e2 e5 *(D)*

The key position of the Classical King's Indian. Having first sorted out his kingside development, Black finally makes his challenge in the centre of the board. After the advance d4-d5, which is usually played sooner or later, Black can counterattack further with ...c7-c6 or, more usually, ...f7-f5, or sometimes both.

7 dxe5

The e5-pawn is not protected, but if matters were this simple the whole opening would be unsound. Of course Black is able to regain the pawn with a few tactics (see 9 ♘xe5 below).

Another rarely played move is 7 ♗g5 h6 (7...♘bd7 or 8...♘bd7 transposes to other chapters) 8 ♗h4 g5 (or 8...♕e8 9 dxe5 dxe5 10 ♘d5 ♘xd5 11 cxd5 c6 12 d6 f6 13 ♕b3+ ♔h7 14 ♖d1 ♘d7 15 ♕c2 ♘b6 16 ♘d2 ♗e6 17 ♘b3 ♘d7 18 f3 ∞ M.Tal-S.Bouaziz, Riga Interzonal 1979) 9 ♗g3 g4!? 10 ♘h4 exd4 11 ♕xd4 ♖e8 12 ♕d3 ♘bd7 (12...♘c6!?) 13 f3 ♘c5 ∞ J.Marcus-G.Sosonko, Dutch Ch. 1973.

7...dxe5 8 ♕xd8

The most consistent move, hoping for a better ending. Other plans are not dangerous for Black:

a) 8 ♕c2 (this and the next variation cannot be recommended, as the queen will be attacked by the black knight from d4) 8...♘c6!? 9 ♗g5 h6 10 ♖d1 ♘d4 11 ♘xd4 exd4 (S.Kamuhangire-B.Chiravorasuk, Novi Sad Olympiad 1990) 12 ♗f4 =.

b) 8 ♕b3 ♘c6 9 ♗g5 ♘d4 10 ♘xd4 exd4 11 ♘d5 c6 12 ♘xf6+ ♗xf6 13 ♗xf6 ♕xf6 14 0-0 ♕f4 15 ♕d3 c5 ½-½ E.Bende-J.Szabo, Aggtelek 1994.

c) 8 ♗g5 c6 (or 8...♘bd7 9 ♕d2 c6 10 0-0 ♕c7 11 h3 ♘c5 12 ♕c2 ♘h5 13 ♗e3 ♘e6 ∞ H.Seegers-M.Krakops, Münster 1994) 9 0-0 ♕e7 10 h3 ♖d8 11 ♕c1 ♘a6 12 ♖b1 ♘c5 = L.Havaskori-B.Martini, Budapest 2005.

8...♖xd8 *(D)*

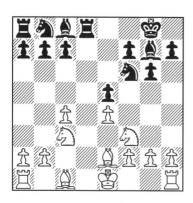

A: 9 ♘d5 *40*
B: 9 ♗g5 *42*

Other rare continuations are:

a) 9 ♗e3 ♘c6 10 ♗g5 (H.Rossetto-J.Ferre, Trelew 1972) 10...♖d7! 11 ♖d1 ♖xd1+ 12 ♔xd1 ♗g4 =.

b) 9 ♘xe5 is answered by 9...♘xe4! 10 ♘xe4 ♗xe5 11 ♗g5 ♗xb2 (or 11...♖e8 12 ♘f6+ ♗xf6 13 ♗xf6 ♗f5 14 ♖d1 ♘d7 15 ♗g5 ♘e5 16 0-0 f6 17 ♗e3 ♘g4 18 ♗xg4 ♗xg4 19 ♖d2 b6 = D.Novitzkij-S.Gavritenkov, Tula 2000) 12 ♖b1 (better 12 ♗xd8!? ♗xa1 13 ♗xc7 ♘a6 14 ♗f4 =) 12...♖e8 13 ♖xb2 ♖xe4 14 0-0 ♘c6 =/+ S.Saljova-J.Suran, Horni Becva 1993.

A: 9 ♘d5 *(D)*

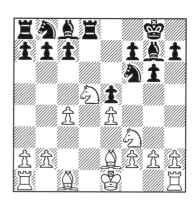

9 ♗g5 is the main line here. The text move is a little premature.

9...♘xd5

The simplest route to equality. Other moves give White better chances:

a) 9...♘a6 10 ♗g5 ♘xd5 (or 10...♖d6

11 ♗xf6 ♗xf6 12 ♘xf6+ ♖xf6 13 ♘xe5 ♖e6 14 f4 ♘c5 15 0-0-0 += L.Vogt-J.Pinter, Budapest 1976) 11 cxd5 (if 11 ♗xd8 ♘f4 12 ♗f1 f5 13 ♗e7 fxe4 14 ♘d2 ♗f5 with compensation, J.Gardner-V.Tsemekhman, Detroit 1994) 11...f6 12 ♗xa6 bxa6 13 ♗h4 g5 14 ♗g3 ♖b8 15 0-0-0 +/= J.Laruelle-M.Tissir, Metz 1998.

b) 9...♖d7 10 ♘xe5 ♘xd5 11 ♘xd7 ♘b4 12 ♘xb8 ♘c2+ 13 ♔d1 ♘xa1 14 ♗f4 ♗xb2 15 ♗xc7 a5 16 f4! a4 17 ♔d2 (we would suggest 17 ♖f1!? intending ♖f3-d3-d8 and White's chances look better) 17...a3!? 18 ♗e5! ♔f8! 19 ♗xb2 axb2 20 ♔c3 ♖xa2 21 ♖b1 ♔e8! with an extremely unclear position, S.Peric-O.Renet, St Martin 1993.

10 cxd5 c6 11 ♗c4

White gets nothing from 11 dxc6 ♘xc6 12 0-0 ♗g4 13 ♗g5 ♖d7 14 ♖fd1 ½-½ L.Perez-K.Movsziszian, Santa Cruz de Tenerife 2004; or 11 ♗g5 f6 12 dxc6 ♘xc6 13 ♗c4+ ♔h8 14 ♗e3 ♗g4 15 0-0 ♖ac8 = V.Doncea-V.Jianu, Bucharest 2004.

11...cxd5

Also good are 11...h6 12 ♗e3 b5 13 ♗b3 ♗b7 14 ♖c1 a5 = M.Roeder-B.Craps, Belgian Team Ch. 1997; and 11...b5 12 ♗b3 ♗b7 13 ♗g5 ♖c8 14 dxc6 ♗xc6 15 ♗e3 h6 16 ♖c1 ♘d7 17 ♘d2 a5 with counterplay, O.Touzane-M.Kazhgaleyev, French Team Ch. 2003.

12 ♗xd5 ♘d7

Black has to neutralize the strong d5-bishop. Another way is 12...♘a6 13 ♗g5 ♖e8 14 0-0 ♘c7 15 ♗b3 ♗e6 = S.Skembris-Kr.Georgiev, Xanthi 1990. Or even 12...♘c6!? 13 ♗xc6 bxc6 14 ♗e3

♗a6 (14...♗e6 =) 15 ♖c1 ♗d3 16 ♘d2 f5 17 f3 ♗f8, when the bishop pair compensates for the weakness on c6, M.Larrea-U.Belistri, Salto 2004.

13 ♗g5 ♖e8 *(D)*

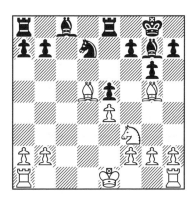

14 ♘d2

Black equalizes after 14 ♔e2 h6 15 ♗h4 ♘f6 16 ♗xf6 ♗xf6 17 ♖hc1 ♖e7 ½-½ E.Dizdarevic-M.Vukic, Zenica 1989; or 14 0-0-0 h6 15 ♗h4 ♘b6 16 ♗b3 ♗e6 17 ♗xe6 ♖xe6 J.Jimenez-S.Minero Pineda, Costa Rican Ch. 2004.

14...♘c5

14...h6 is good here too, e.g. 15 ♗e3 ♘f6 16 ♗b3 ♖d8 17 ♖c1 ♘g4 18 ♗c5 b6 19 ♗e7 ♖d7 20 ♗d5 ♖b8 21 ♗b4 ♗a6 with an excellent position for Black, O.Touzane-M.Al Modiahki, Cannes 1997.

15 0-0-0

Or 15 ♗e3 ♘d3+ 16 ♔e2 ♘f4+ 17 ♗xf4 exf4 ∞ J.Nikolac-L.Kavalek, Wijk aan Zee 1977.

15...♗e6

Or, similarly to the previous note, 15...♘e6 16 ♗e3 ♘f4 17 ♗xf4 exf4 ∞ U.Andersson-Zsu.Polgar, Bilbao 1987.

16 ♗xe6 ♘xe6 17 ♗e3 ♗f8 18 ♘b3 a5

19 ♔b1 a4 20 ♘c1 ♗c5 21 ♗xc5 ♘xc5
(D)

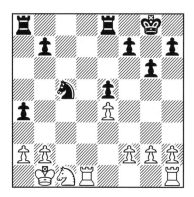

The position is equal. For example:

a) 22 f3 ♖ad8 23 ♘e2 ♔g7 = R.Jedynak-P.Czarnota, Polish Junior Ch. 2002.

b) 22 ♘d3 ♘xe4 ½-½ M.Roeder-A.Strikovic, Odivelas 2001, as 23 ♖he1 ♘f6 (or 23...f5 24 f3) 24 ♘xe5 regains the pawn.

B: 9 ♗g5 *(D)*

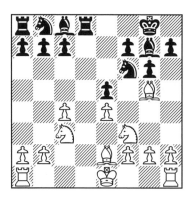

The key position for the 7 dxe5 line. Having pinned the f6-knight, White now threatens 10 ♘d5, while Black must still be ready to deal with ♘xe5.

B1: 9...♖f8 *43*
B2: 9...c6 *45*
B3: 9...♖e8 *48*

More seldom played continuations are:

a) 9...♘a6, disregarding the threat of ♘d5, and now:

a1) Black has no problems equalizing after 10 ♘xe5, e.g. 10...♖e8 11 0-0-0 ♘c5 12 ♗xf6 ♗xf6 13 f4 c6 14 b4 ♗xe5 15 fxe5 ♘d7 16 e6 ♖xe6 17 ♗g4 ♖e7 18 b5 ♔g7 19 bxc6 bxc6 20 ♗xd7 ♗xd7 21 ♖d6 ♖c8 22 ♔d2 ♗e6 = A.Haik-B.Spassky, French Ch. 1991.

a2) 10 ♘d5 is more testing; e.g. 10...♘xd5 (10...♖d6 11 ♘xf6+ ♗xf6 12 ♗xf6 ♖xf6 13 ♘xe5 ♖e6 14 f4 ♘c5 15 0-0-0! +/= P.Cramling-K.Spraggett, Biel 1990) 11 ♗xd8 ♘f4 12 g3!? ♘xe2 13 ♔xe2 ♗e6 14 ♖hd1 ♗xc4+ 15 ♔e3 +/= H.Waller-K.Neumeier, Austrian Team Ch. 2002.

b) 9...♘bd7 and then:

b1) 10 ♘d5 (although White gains the bishop pair, he may weaken dark squares, in particular c5, b4 and d4) 10...c6 11 ♘e7+ ♔f8 12 ♘xc8 ♖dxc8 13 0-0-0 ♘c5 14 ♗xf6 ♗xf6 15 ♗d3 a5 16 ♖he1 ♖e8 =/+ S.Danailov-G.Kasparov, World Junior Ch. 1980.

b2) 10 ♖d1!? ♖f8 11 ♘d5 c6 12 ♘e7+ ♔h8 13 ♗e3 (White achieved the same goal – the bishop pair – in a much better version) 13...♖e8 14 ♘xc8 ♖axc8 15 g4 ♘b6 16 ♘d2 ♖cd8 17 g5 ♘fd7 18 h4 with the initiative, S.Wolff-L.Hucks, corr. 2001.

b3) 10 0-0-0 ♖f8 11 ♘d2 (if 11 ♘d5 ♘xd5! 12 cxd5 f5 13 ♘d2 h6 14 ♗e7 ♖e8 15 ♗a3 ♘f6 16 ♗b5 ♗d7 17 ♗xd7 ♘xd7 = F.Balabaev-R.Sakic, corr. 2003; while 11 ♘e1 seeks to control the d4-square, but this move is too passive to achieve anything, e.g. 11...♘c5 12 f3 ♘e6 13 ♗e3 c5 14 ♘d3 b6 15 ♖he1 ♘d7 16 ♘d5 ♗b7 17 ♔b1 ♘d4 18 ♖c1 f5 19 ♗d1 ½-½ U.Andersson-M.Kaminski, Polanica Zdroj 1997) 11...c6 *(D)* and then:

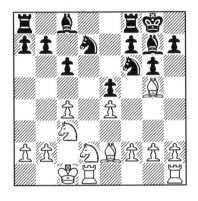

b31) 12 b4 a5 (or else 12...♖e8!? 13 c5 a5 14 a3 axb4 15 axb4 b6 16 cxb6 ♘xb6 17 ♔c2 ♗e6 18 ♖a1 ♘fd7 = N.Tolstikh-V.Shtyrenkov, Pardubice 1995) 13 a3 ♖e8 14 ♔b2, and now Black should take the bull by the horns by 14...axb4!? 15 axb4 (M.Bozovic-L.Grujic, Yugoslav Team Ch. 2000) 15...h6 16 ♗e3 ♗f8 with counterplay.

b32) 12 ♗e3 ♖e8 13 h4!? (13 c5?! is typical for this kind of structure, but here the pawn can be attacked at once by 13...♗f8! 14 b4 a5 15 a3 axb4 16 axb4 b6 =+ D.Solak-Z.Kozul, Slovenian Team Ch. 2008, or 14 ♘a4 b5 15 cxb6 axb6 16 ♘xb6 ♘xb6 17 ♗xb6 ♖xa2 =+

D.Mirschinka-R.Schoene, Karl Marx Stadt 1990) 13...♗f8 14 h5 ♘c5 15 hxg6 fxg6 16 b4 +/= O.Rubingh-M.Hebden, Hoogeveen 2003.

B1: 9...♖f8 *(D)*

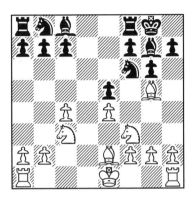

A rare move. The rook seems worse placed here than on e8 as it does not defend the e5-pawn.

10 0-0-0 *(D)*

Instead:

a) 10 0-0 ♘c6 reaches a harmless line in Chapter Eight – *7 0-0 ♘c6 8 dxe5 dxe5 9 ♕xd8 ♖xd8 10 ♗g5 ♖f8*.

b) 10 ♗xf6?! ♗xf6 11 ♘d5 ♗d8 12 ♘xe5 (12 0-0-0 and 12 0-0 are inconsistent with the exchange on f6) 12...♖e8 13 ♘f3 ♖xe4 14 ♘c3 ♖e8 and the bishop pair gives Black a good ending, J.Toikka-V.Vehkalahti, Finnish Team Ch. 1997.

c) 10 ♘d5 ♘xd5 11 cxd5 c6 12 ♗c4 cxd5 (or 12...b5 13 ♗b3 ♗b7 14 ♖c1 a5 15 a3 a4 16 dxc6 ♘xc6 = V.Gagarin-Z.Lanka, USSR 1989) 13 ♗xd5 ♘c6 14 0-0-0 ♗d7 15 ♔b1 ♖ac8 16 ♖d2 b6 17 ♗c4 ♘b8 18 ♖c1 ♗c6 19 ♗d5 ½-½ E.Kengis-E.Vasiukov, Moscow 1986.

d) 10 ♘xe5!? deserves serious attention; e.g. 10...♘xe4 11 ♘xe4 ♗xe5 12 0-0-0 ♘c6 (White maintains a small advantage after 12...♘d7 13 ♖he1 ♖e8 14 ♗f3 ♔g7 15 c5! ♖b8 16 ♗e3 Y.Korsunsky-M.Golubev, Novi Sad 1990) 13 ♖he1 (or 13 f4 ♗d4 14 ♘f6+ ♔g7 15 ♘d5 f6 16 ♗h4 ♗f5 17 ♗d3 ♗g4 18 ♖de1 +/= R.Ravisekhar-V.Bologan, Calcutta 1992) 13...f6 (if 13...♗e6 14 ♘c5 ♖fe8 15 ♘xe6 ♖xe6 16 ♗g4 ♖d6, J.Kraai-I.Zenyuk, US Ch. 2006, then 17 ♗f3!? with better chances for White due to the bishop pair) 14 ♗h6 ♖d8 15 f4 ♗d4 16 ♗f3 ♗d7 (S.Yuferov-M.Muhutdinov, Moscow 1990) and now after 17 g4!, intending g5, Black has serious problems.

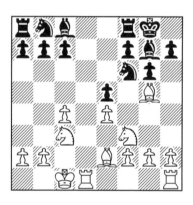

10...♘c6

The position of this knight is rather uncomfortable, as it prevents Black from playing ...c7-c6 to cover the d5-square. Instead, 10...♘bd7 transposes to 9...♘bd7 10 0-0-0 ♖f8. The immediate 10...c6 is doubtful due to 11 ♘xe5! ♘xe4 12 ♘xe4 ♗xe5 13 f4 ♗g7 14 ♘d6 f6 15 ♗h4 +/- L.Tejedor Barber-E.Grau Dominguez, Valencia 1995. Or if

10...♗e6 11 ♘xe5! ♘xe4 12 ♘xe4 ♗xe5 13 f4 ♗g7 (I.Bjelobrk-K.Hursky, Canberra (rapid) 2001) and now 14 ♘f6+!? +/-.

11 h3

Otherwise Black can control the d4-square with equality; e.g. 11 ♔b1 ♗g4 12 ♖d3 ♗xf3 13 ♗xf3 ♘d4 14 ♘b5 ♘e6 (J.Bellon Lopez-L.Oll, Oviedo rapid 1993) 15 ♗e3 ♖fd8 16 ♖hd1 ♖xd3 17 ♖xd3 ♗f8 =; or 11 ♗xf6 ♗xf6 12 ♖d2 = C.Rodrigues-M.De Pirro, corr. 2000.

11...♗e6 *(D)*

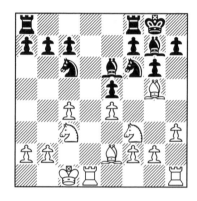

12 ♗e3

12 ♖d2 (as in D.Vaughan-R.Hardy, Newport 1997) allows 12...♘d4!? 13 ♘xe5 ♘xe4 14 ♘xe4 ♘xe2+ 15 ♖xe2 ♗xe5 and Black should gradually equalize.

12...♖ad8 13 a3

13 ♗d3!? defending the e4-pawn was better, enabling White to play ♘d5.

13...h6

Or 13...♘a5!? 14 ♘d2 ♘c6 15 ♘b3 (if 15 ♘d5 ♘d4! 16 ♗xd4 exd4 17 ♘xc7 ♗h6 with compensation) 15...b6 with equalizing chances.

14 b4 a5 15 b5 ♘d4 16 ♘xd4 exd4 17 ♗xd4 ♖xd4! 18 ♖xd4 ♘g4 19 ♗xg4 ♗xd4 20 ♗xe6 fxe6 21 ♘d1 *(D)*

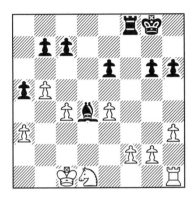

This interesting endgame was reached in Wang Yue-V.Bologan, Moscow 2006. Black has sufficient counterplay for the pawn, which indeed he soon regains.

21...♗c5

Not yet 21...♗xf2?! (or on the next move) 22 ♘xf2 ♖xf2 23 ♖d1 ♖xg2 24 ♖d7 ♖h2 25 ♖xc7 when the white pawns are more dangerous.

22 a4 ♖d8 23 ♘b2 ♗a3 24 ♔c2 ♖d4 25 f3 ♗xb2 26 ♔xb2 ♖xc4

Material is level once more, but Black must display some accuracy to draw with his slightly inferior structure.

27 ♔b3 ♖b4+ 28 ♔a3 ♖d4 29 ♖c1 ♖d7 30 ♔b3 ♔f7 31 ♖c5 ♔e7 32 f4 ♔d8 33 ♖e5 ♖d6 34 ♔c4

34 h4!? came into consideration.

34...♔d7 35 f5 exf5 36 exf5 h5 37 h4 gxf5 38 ♖xf5 ♖g6 39 ♖xh5 ♖xg2 40 ♔d5 ♖d2+

Instead of bringing the white king closer to the h-pawn, Black should

have played 40...♖g4, captured the a4-pawn, and advanced his own a-pawn as quickly as possible.

41 ♔e5 ♖e2+?

41...♖a2 was still okay, whereas after this second time-wasting check White is now winning.

42 ♔f6 ♔d6 43 ♖f5 ♖e4 44 h5 ♖xa4 45 h6 ♖h4 46 ♔g6 a4 47 h7 ♖xh7 48 ♔xh7 a3 49 ♔g6 a2 50 ♖f1 ♔c5 51 ♖a1 ♔xb5 52 ♖xa2 ♔c4 53 ♖c2+ ♔d4 54 ♖xc7 b5 55 ♖b7 1-0.

B2: 9...c6 *(D)*

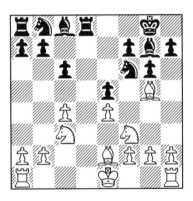

Black prevents the white knight from ever coming to d5, but in doing so he has left the e5-pawn unprotected.

10 ♘xe5

Only with this principled move can White fight for an advantage. Other continuations lead to complicated play; e.g. 10 0-0 ♖e8 11 ♖ad1 ♘bd7 12 ♖d6 ♗f8 13 ♖dd1 a5 ∞ H.Waller-G.Beckhuis, Austrian Team Ch. 2002; or 10 h3 ♘a6 11 ♘d2 ♘c5 12 0-0-0 ♘e6 13 ♗e3 ♘d4 ∞ M.Schiraldi-D.Vocaturo, Verona 2005.

10...♖e8 *(D)*

Other moves do not offer equality; e.g. 10...♞a6?! 11 ♞xc6! ♖e8 12 e5 ♞d7 13 ♞e7+ ♔f8 (S.Ekstroem-Z.Kozul, Schellenberg 1989) and now 14 ♞ed5! +/- (Karpov); or 10...h6 11 ♗h4 g5 12 ♗g3 (W.Schulz-E.Haapamaki, Winnipeg 1999) 12...♞a6 13 h4 +/=.

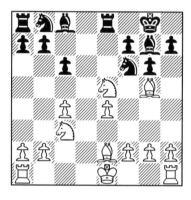

11 0-0-0

11 f4 allows Black good counterplay; e.g. 11...♞h5 12 ♗xh5 gxh5 13 ♗h4 ♞d7! 14 ♗g3 ♞xe5 15 fxe5 ♗xe5 16 ♗xe5 ♖xe5 17 0-0-0 ♗e6 18 b3 b5! 19 cxb5 cxb5 20 ♖d4 a5 = E.Maljutin-I.Glek, Moscow 1989.

11 ♗f4 may cause Black more difficulties: 11...♞a6 (after 11...♞xe4 12 ♞xe4 ♗xe5 13 ♗xe5 ♖xe5 the best move is 14 ♖d1!, C.Iglesias-A.Dumas Aviles, Santiago 1992, as after 14...♖xe4 White's king defends the e2-bishop, e.g. 15 ♖d8+ ♔g7 16 ♖xc8 and wins as Black has no way to unpin) 12 0-0-0 ♞c5 13 f3 ♞h5 14 ♗e3 ♞xe4 15 fxe4 ♗xe5 16 ♗xh5 gxh5 17 ♗d4 ♗g4 18 ♗xe5 ♖xe5 (if 18...♗xd1!? 19 ♗f6 ♗g4 20 e5 with compensation) 19 ♖d3 ♔f8 20 b3 ♔e7 21 ♖f1 +/= T.Johansen-S.Gabrielsen, Norwegian Ch. 1997.

11...♞a6

Interesting is 11...h6 12 ♗f4 ♞a6 13 h3 ♞c5 14 ♗f3 (J.Bronnum-L.Van Wely, Lyngby 1988) 14...♞h5!? 15 ♗xh5 gxh5 16 ♞d3 ♞xe4 17 ♖he1 ♗xc3 18 bxc3 ♗f5 and Black should equalize.

12 f4

After 12 ♖d6 the simplest route to equality is 12...♞xe4! 13 ♞xe4 ♗xe5 14 ♞f6+ ♗xf6 15 ♗xf6 ♞c5 16 ♗d3 ♞xd3+ 17 ♖xd3 ½-½ E.Ragozin-G.Timoscenko, Vienna 1991.

12 ♞f3 does not cause Black any problems either; e.g. 12...h6 13 ♗f4 (or 13 ♗xf6 ♗xf6 14 e5 ♗xe5 15 ♞xe5 ♖xe5 16 ♖d8+ ♔g7 = I.Nei-R.Vaganian, Tallinn 1979) 13...♞xe4 14 ♞xe4 ♖xe4 15 ♖d8+ ♔h7 16 ♗e3 ♗f6! (the white rook has no square on the eighth rank) 17 ♖d2 ♗g4 18 b3 ♗c3 19 ♖d3 ♗b4 20 h3 ♗a3+ 21 ♔d1 ♗xf3 22 ♗xf3 ♖e7 = J.Garcia Padron-V.Topalov, Las Palmas 1991.

12...h6

If 12...♞c5 13 ♗f3 ♞fxe4 14 ♞xe4 ♞xe4 15 ♗xe4 f6 16 ♗xf6 ♗xf6 17 ♖he1 ♗e6 18 b3 ♖ad8 19 ♖xd8 ♖xd8 20 ♔c2 += R.Servaty-M.Müller, Ruhrgebiet 1996, though White will have difficulty realizing his extra pawn in the ending.

13 ♗h4

Or 13 ♗xf6 ♗xf6 14 ♗f3 ♗xe5 15 fxe5 ♗e6 16 b3 ♞c5 17 ♖d6 ♞d7 18 ♞d5 cxd5 19 cxd5 ♞xe5 20 dxe6 ♖xe6 21 ♖xe6 fxe6 = Mi.Tseitlin-I.Smirin, Polanica Zdroj 1989.

13...g5 *(D)*

Or again 13...♞c5 14 ♗f3 g5 15 ♗f2 gxf4!? 16 ♗xc5 ♖xe5 17 ♗d6 ♖e8 18 ♗xf4 ♞d7 and Black has compensation for the pawn, B.Finegold-G.Barbero, Wijk aan Zee 1991.

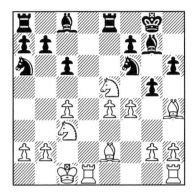

14 fxg5

Alternatively:

a) 14 ♗g3 ♘c5 15 ♗f3 g4 16 ♗e2 ♘cxe4 17 ♘xe4 ♘xe4 18 ♗xg4 ♗xe5 19 ♗xc8 ♗xb2+ 20 ♔xb2 ♖axc8 21 ♗h4 ♘c5 22 ♖he1 ♖xe1 23 ♗xe1 ♖e8 = A.Manrique-A.Villavicencio Martinez, Tenerife 2001.

b) 14 ♗f2 gxf4 15 ♘f3 ♗g4 (also good is 15...♘xe4 16 ♘xe4 ♗f5 17 ♘fd2 ♗xe4 18 ♘xe4 ♖xe4 19 ♗d3 ♖e5 =) 16 h3 (16 ♗d3!?) 16...♘xe4 17 ♘xe4 ♖xe4 (or 17...♗f5!? 18 ♘fd2 ♗xe4 19 ♘xe4 ♖xe4 20 ♗d3 ♖e5 =) 18 hxg4?! (better 18 ♗d3 ♗xf3 19 gxf3 with compensation) 18...♖xe2 19 ♗d4 ♖ae8 -/+ H.Hoeksema-J.Nunn, Groningen 1988.

14...hxg5 15 ♗g3 ♘c5

15...♘xe4 is premature, due to 16 ♘xe4 ♗xe5 17 ♗xe5 ♖xe5 18 ♖d8+ ♔g7 19 ♗d3 ♘c7 20 ♘d6 ♗e6 21 ♖xa8 ♘xa8 22 ♘xb7 ♘b6 23 b3 +/- D.Canteli Martinez-L.Prieto, Asturias 1995.

16 ♖hf1

After other moves Black can gain an advantage; e.g. 16 ♗d3 ♘h5!? 17 ♘f3

♘xg3 18 hxg3 ♗g4 =+ I.Cabezas Ayala-A.Garcia Luque, Spanish Team Ch. 1996; or 16 ♖he1 (H.Keilhack-V.Kupreichik, Berlin 1987) 16...♘fxe4 17 ♘xe4 ♘xe4 18 ♘d7 ♘xg3 19 hxg3 ♖e3 =+.

16...♗e6

Or 16...♘cxe4 17 ♘xe4 ♘xe4 18 ♗h5 ♘xg3 (18...♖xe5 19 ♖d8+ ♔h7 20 ♗xe5 ♗xe5 21 ♖xf7+ ♔h6 22 g4 ∞) 19 ♗xf7+ ♔h7 20 ♗g6+ ♔h6 21 hxg3 (R.Burlant-O.Paetzold, corr. 1997) 21...♗xe5! 22 ♗xe8 ♗g4 23 ♗f7 ♗xd1 24 ♖xd1 ♖c8 and the position is level.

17 ♘f3?!

Better was 17 ♗f3 g4 18 ♗e2 ♘fxe4 19 ♘xe4 ♘xe4 20 ♘xg4 f5 21 ♘f2 ♘xg3 22 hxg3 ♗f7 23 ♗d3 ♖e3 ∞ R.Thomas-J.Hebert, corr. 1997. Now Black can regain his pawn with impunity.

17...♘fxe4 18 ♘xe4 ♘xe4 (D)

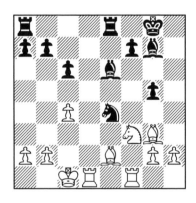

Black now stands slightly better. V.Babula-A.Jakubiec, Czech League 2003, continued **19 ♗e5** [or 19 ♘d4 ♘xg3 20 hxg3 ♗xd4 21 ♖xd4 ♖ad8 22 ♖xd8 ♖xd8 =/+ A.Sygulski-K.Wolter, German League 1995] **19...f6 20 ♗d4 g4 21 ♘h4 ♗h6+ 22 ♔c2 ♗g5 23 ♗d3?!**

[23 ♘f5] **23...♗xh4 24 ♗xe4 ♗xc4 25 ♗d3 ♗xd3+ 26 ♖xd3 ♖e2+ 27 ♖d2 ♖ae8 28 ♔d3 ♖xd2+ 29 ♔xd2 ♗g5+ 30 ♔d3 ♔f7 31 ♗xa7 ♖d8+** [31...♖a8 -/+] **32 ♔c3 ♖d5 33 ♗g1 ♖d2 34 ♗f2 ♖e2 35 h3?** [correct was 35 h4 gxh3 36 gxh3 =/+] **35...g3! 36 ♗e1 ♖xg2 37 ♖f3 ♗h4 38 ♖f4 ♖e2 39 ♖xh4 ♖xe1 40 ♖g4 ♖g1 41 ♔d3 f5 42 ♖g5 ♔f6 43 h4 g2 44 ♔e3 ♖e1+ 45 ♔f2 ♖b1 0-1**.

B3: 9...♖e8 (D)

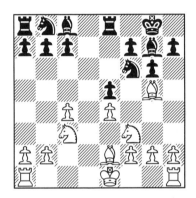

The most frequent choice. Black defends the e5-pawn and will therefore never need to be afraid of losing it. On the other hand, this move loses a tempo and allows White to control the d-file.

10 ♘d5

White jumps on the central square before Black plays ...c7-c6. Other continuations do not offer White any prospects of an advantage:

a) 10 ♗xf6 ♗xf6 11 ♘d5 ♗d8 12 0-0 c6 13 ♘c3 ♗a5 14 ♖ac1 ♘d7 15 a3 ♗c7 = A.Lehmann-G.Hub, Bad Neustadt 1991.

b) 10 ♖d1 h6 11 ♗xf6 ♗xf6 12 ♘d5

♗d8 13 ♘xe5 ♖xe5 14 ♘b6 axb6! 15 ♖xd8+ ♔g7 16 ♖xc8 ♖xa2! 17 ♖xb8 ♖xe4 18 ♖d8 ♖xb2 19 ♖d2 ♖b1+ 20 ♖d1 ♖b2 ½-½ A.Kochyev-M.Dvoretzky, USSR 1976.

c) 10 0-0-0 ♘a6 11 ♘e1 ♘c5!? 12 f3 c6 13 ♗e3 ♗f8 14 ♘d3 ♘fd7 15 ♘xc5 ♗xc5 16 ♗xc5 ♘xc5 = T.Wyrwich-M.Senff, German Junior Team Ch. 1995.

10...♘xd5 11 cxd5 c6

The right reaction. Black immediately strikes at the white pawn centre. The side attack by 11...f5 is premature and leads to an initiative for White after 12 ♖c1! h6 (if now 12...c6 13 ♗c4 ♔h8 14 ♗e3 h6, I.Kharlamov-D.Zacurdajev, St Petersburg 2005, 15 dxc6 ♘xc6 16 ♗f7 +/-) 13 ♗e3 c6 14 ♗c4 ♔h7 15 h4 ♗f8 16 h5 with the initiative, Z.Szczep-L.Gorzkiewicz, Polish Team Ch. 1999.

12 ♗c4 (D)

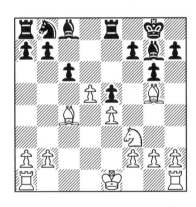

Other moves are weaker:

a) 12 dxc6 ♘xc6 13 0-0 ♗g4 14 h3 ♗xf3 15 ♗xf3 ♘d4 16 ♖fc1 ♖ac8 ½-½ R.Kholmov-R.Nezhmetdinov, Bucharest 1954.

b) 12 0-0-0 cxd5 13 ♗b5 ♗d7 14 ♗xd7 ♘xd7 15 ♖xd5 ♘b6 = M.Van Tricht-S.Korosec, corr. 2003.

After the text White has the more active bishops, which Black needs to neutralize if he is to equalize, in particular the one on c4. There are two ways of doing this: trying to exchange the light-squared bishop after ...cxd5 and a later ...♗e6; or by a queenside pawn action with ...b7-b5, ...♗b7 and often ...a7-a5.

12...cxd5

As mentioned above, the alternative plan is 12...b5 13 ♗b3 ♗b7 (the immediate 13...a5 is quite playable, e.g. 14 a4 bxa4 15 ♗xa4 ♗d7 16 dxc6 ♗xc6 17 0-0 ♗xa4 18 ♖xa4 ♘d7 = I.Khenkin-E.Sutovsky, Israeli Team Ch. 2008) 14 ♖c1 ♖c8 15 ♗e3 a5 16 a3 a4 17 ♗a2, when Black has three promising continuations:

a) 17...h6 18 ♔e2 ♘a6 19 dxc6 ♗xc6 20 ♖hd1 ♗e4 21 ♖xc8+ ♖xc8 22 ♖d7 ♖c7 23 ♗xf7+ ♔f8 24 ♗e6 ♔e8 25 ♖d6 ♘c5 26 ♗h3 ∞ G.Hertneck-S.Dolmatov, Tilburg 1992.

b) 17...♘a6 18 dxc6 ♖xc6 19 ♖xc6 ♗xc6 20 ♘g5 ♗e8 21 ♗d5 ♖b8 = B.Schmidt-W.Uhlmann, Decin 1979.

c) 17...b4 18 axb4 a3! 19 bxa3 ♖xa3 and Black's initiative is enough to regain the sacrificed pawn; e.g. 20 dxc6 (20 ♗b1 cxd5 21 ♖xc8+ ♗xc8 22 exd5, P.Staniszewski-B.Socko, Warsaw 2001, 22...♖b3 = Konikowski) 20...♘xc6 21 ♗d5 ♘xb4 22 ♗xb7 ♖xe3+ 23 ♔d2 ♖d3+ 24 ♔e2 ♖cd8 25 ♗d5 ♖a3 26 ♖hd1 ♘xd5 27 ♖xd5 ♖a2+ (G.Schebler-A.Shirov, German League 1996) 28 ♘d2 =.

13 ♗xd5 ♘d7

Black has two other ways to target White's light-squared bishop:

a) 13...♘a6 intending ...♘c7, and:

a1) 14 0-0-0 ♘c7 15 ♗b3 ♗e6 16 ♗xe6 (or 16 ♗e3 ♗xb3 17 axb3 ♖ed8 18 ♖xd8+ ♖xd8 = N.Murshed-A.Guseinov, Doha 1992) 16...♘xe6 17 ♗e3 f5 18 ♔b1 b6 19 ♖he1 ♖ad8 = J.Mellado Trivino-K.Movsziszian, Can Picafort 2008.

a2) 14 ♔e2 ♘c7 15 ♗b3 and now 15...♗d7!? is a good idea, leaving e6 free for the knight, while supporting a possible ...a5-a4; e.g. 16 ♘d2 ♘e6 17 ♗e3 (N.Tolstikh-S.Temirbaev, Cheliabinsk 1993) 17...a5!? 18 a4 ♘f4+ 19 ♔f3 h5 20 h3 ♘d3 ∞.

b) 13...♘c6!? 14 ♗xc6 bxc6 15 0-0 h6 16 ♗e3 ♗e6 17 ♖fc1 ♖eb8 was fine for Black in O.Panno-W.Browne, Madrid 1973. Instead, 14 0-0-0!? gives White more chances of obtaining an edge, but Black equalizes all the same; e.g. 14...♘b4 15 ♗b3 a5 16 a3 a4 17 ♗c4 (F.Arnold-B.Spycher, Switzerland 1988) 17...♗g4!? 18 ♔b1! ♘c6 19 ♖d3 (Kovacevic) 19...h6 20 ♗e3 ♘d4 =.

14 ♘d2 (D)

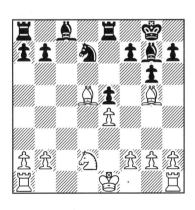

Other moves don't offer White anything either; e.g. 14 0-0-0 h6 15 ♗h4 ♘b6 16 ♗b3 ♗g4 17 ♖d3 = Kir.Georgiev-W.Uhlmann, Szirak 1985; or 14 0-0 h6 15 ♗h4 ♘b6 16 ♗b3 ♗d7 17 ♘d2 ♖ac8 18 ♖fd1 ½-½ I.Bitansky-G.Mittelman, Rishon LeZion 1998.

14...♘c5 15 0-0-0

Or if 15 ♗e3 ♘d3+ 16 ♔e2 ♘f4+ 17 ♗xf4 exf4 18 ♘c4 ♗g4+! (depriving the white king of the f3-square) 19 f3 ♗e6 20 ♗xe6 ½-½ Y.Teplitsky-E.Sutovsky, Tel Aviv 1993.

15...♗e6

Another option is 15...♘e6 16 ♗e3 ♘f4 17 ♗xf4 exf4 18 f3 ♗e6 19 ♘b3 ♖ac8+ 20 ♔b1 ♗xd5 21 ♖xd5 f5 22 exf5 ♖e2 23 ♖d2 ♖xd2 24 ♘xd2 gxf5 = J.Nogueiras-D.Anagnostopoulos, Linares 1996.

16 ♗xe6 ♘xe6

Or 16...♖xe6 17 ♗e3 ♖c6 18 ♔b1 ♖ac8 19 ♗xc5 ♖xc5 20 ♘b3 ♖c4 21 ♖c1 ♗h6 22 ♖xc4 ♖xc4 23 f3 b6 = J.Bartos-I.Baeumler, Pardubice 2005.

17 ♗e3 ♘f4

Alternatively:

a) 17...♗f8 18 ♘b3!? (or 18 ♔b1 ♗c5 19 ♘c4 ♗xe3 20 ♘xe3 ♗f8 21 ♘g4 ♘c5 22 f3 h5 23 ♘f6 ♖e6 ½-½ B.Ivkov-Z.Polgar, Wijk aan Zee 1986) 18...a5 19 ♖d5 a4 20 ♘d2 ♘f4 21 ♗xf4 exf4 22 f3 ♖ac8+ 23 ♔b1 (C.Cobb-D.Gormally, Newport 2004) 23...♖ed8 =.

b) 17...a5!? 18 ♔b1 b5 19 ♘b3 a4 20 ♘c5 ♘d4 with a good game for Black, J.Bartos-M.Bures, Ostrava 2005.

18 g3

After 18 ♗xf4 exf4 19 ♖he1 ♖ac8+ 20 ♔b1 ♖cd8 21 f3 f5 Black had an excel-lent ending in D.Berg-M.Stoeber, German League 1988.

18...♘g2! 19 ♘f1 ♖e6

Or 19...♘xe3 20 ♘xe3 ♗h6 = Mik-halevski.

20 ♖g1

20 ♖d7 is answered by 20...♖f6! 21 ♖xb7 ♘xe3 22 ♘xe3 ♖xf2, though White has sufficient counterplay after 23 ♘d1 ♖g2 24 ♖f1.

20...♘xe3 21 ♘xe3 ♖f6! 22 ♖gf1 ♗h6 23 ♔b1

23 f4 exf4 24 ♘g4 ♖c6+ 25 ♔b1 ♗g7 26 gxf4 also leaves White with a loose pawn structure.

23...♗xe3 24 fxe3 ♖xf1 25 ♖xf1 *(D)*

We have been following Kir.Geor-giev-E.Sutovsky, Gibraltar 2006. Here Black's best chance to make something of his minimal advantage was probably in the rook endgame following 25...♖d8, as White easily held the king and pawn endgame after **25...♖c8 26 ♖c1 ♖xc1+ 27 ♔xc1 f5 28 ♔d2 ♔f7 29 ♔e2 fxe4 30 h3 a5 31 ♔d2 ♔e6 32 ♔c3 ♔d5 33 ♔b3 ♔c5 34 ♔c3 a4 35 ♔c2 ♔c4 36 ♔d2 ♔b4 37 ♔c2 ♔c4 38 ♔d2 g5 39 g4 ♔b4 40 ♔c2 ♔c4 41 ♔d2 b6 42 ♔c2 b5 43 ♔d2 b4 44 ♔c2 b3+ 45 axb3+ axb3+ 46 ♔d2 ♔b4 47 ♔e2 ½-½.**

Conclusion

Black does not have serious problems in this variation. If both sides play carefully, the game usually ends in a draw. 9 ♘d5 (line A) gives White nothing, but after 9 ♗g5 Black should give most attention to 9...♖e8 (line B3), as other continuations offer White some chances of obtaining an advantage.

Chapter Three

Gligoric System: 7 ♗e3

1 d4 ♘f6 2 c4 g6 3 ♘c3 ♗g7 4 e4 d6 5 ♘f3 0-0 6 ♗e2 e5 7 ♗e3 *(D)*

7 ♗e3, known as the Gligoric System, is an alternative to the usual 7 0-0. In some lines the early ♗e3 may be convenient for White as he is ready for the manoeuvre ♘d2, but it has also its bad sides. Above all, on e3 the bishop can always be attacked by ...♘g4. All advantages and disadvantages will be discussed after particular moves.

Black has numerous possibilities here, the main ones being:

A: 7...♘c6 *52*
B: 7...c6 *54*
C: 7...♕e7 *56*
D: 7...exd4 *59*
E: 7...h6 *63*
F: 7...♘g4 *66*

7...♘a6 and 7...♘bd7 are also possible, but these moves usually transpose

elsewhere: 8 0-0 in either case enters Chapter Six or Seven respectively (variations with 8 ♗e3), while 8 d5 reaches 8 ♗e3 lines of Chapter Four (7 d5). Black cannot count on equality after:

a) 7...♖e8 8 dxe5! (this gives White an extra tempo on 7 dxe5 lines in the previous chapter) 8...dxe5 9 ♕xd8 ♖xd8 10 ♘d5 (10 ♗g5 would just return the tempo) 10...♘xd5 (10...♖d7 11 0-0-0 ♘xe4? runs into 12 ♘xc7! ♖xc7 13 ♖d8+ ♗f8 14 ♗h6 ♘d7 15 ♘xe5! ♘ec5 16 ♘xd7 ♘xd7 17 ♖d1 and wins) 11 cxd5 c6 12 ♗c4 (this position usually arises via 6 ♗e3 e5?! 7 dxe5 dxe5 8 ♕xd8 ♖xd8 9 ♘d5 etc) 12...b6?! (weak, but White is also better after 12...b5 13 ♗b3 ♗b7 14 ♖c1 += B.Larsen-R.Toran Albero, Palma 1967; or 12...cxd5 13 ♗xd5 ♘c6 14 ♗xc6 bxc6 15 0-0 += B.Larsen-R.Hübner, Leningrad Interzonal 1973) 13 0-0-0 ♗b7 14 dxc6 ♘xc6 15 ♘g5 ♖xd1+ 16 ♖xd1 ♘d8 17 ♘xf7! and wins,

Mi.Tseitlin-L.Fantin, Bagneux 1994.

b) 7...a5 can also be answered by 8 dxe5!? (8 0-0 – *7 0-0 a5!? 8 ♗e3* in Chapter Five) 8...dxe5 9 ♕xd8 ♖xd8 10 ♘d5 ♘a6 11 0-0-0 ♖e8! (S.Shipov-D.Mozetic, Belgrade 1994), when Shipov gives 12 c5! ♘xd5 13 exd5 e4 14 ♘d2 ♘b4 15 ♘c4 ♘xa2+ 16 ♔b1 ♘b4 17 d6 and White's initiative compensates for the sacrificed pawn.

A: 7...♘c6 (D)

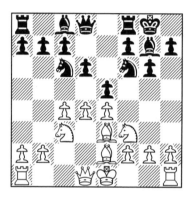

This allows White to realize his main plan – regrouping his forces with ♘d2 – and obtain all the advantages of 9 ♘d2 in the main line (see Chapter Ten), without its main drawback of blocking in the c1-bishop.

8 d5

8 0-0?! misses the point entirely and transposes to the harmless 7 0-0 ♘c6 8 ♗e3 variation in Chapter Eight.

8...♘e7 9 ♘d2

White is now ready to start action on the queenside immediately.

9...c5 (D)

Black blocks the c5-square. After other moves White achieves the c4-c5

advance and obtains at least a slight edge; for example:

a) 9...♘d7 10 b4 (or just 10 0-0 f5 11 f3 f4 12 ♗f2 g5 13 b4 ♘f6 14 c5 ♘g6 15 ♘c4 ♖f7 16 cxd6 cxd6 17 ♘b5 ♗f8 18 ♘xa7 with a very complicated position in which White's chances are more real, S.Gligoric-H.Schaufelberger, Groningen 1966) 10...f5 11 f3 ♘f6 (if now 11...f4?! 12 ♗f2 g5 13 c5 ♘f6 14 ♘c4 ♘e8 15 cxd6 cxd6 16 ♘b5 b6 17 a4 ♗a6 18 ♘ba3 ♖f6 19 b5 ♗c8 20 ♘c2 ♗d7 21. ♘b4 +/- S.Gligoric-R.Nagendra, Lucerne Olympiad 1982) 12 c5 fxe4 13 fxe4 ♘h5!? (offering a pawn; if instead 13...a5 14 cxd6 cxd6 15 bxa5 ♖xa5 16. ♘c4 ♖a6 17 a4 ♘d7 18 a5 +/- D.Sahovic-M.Nikolic, Belgrade 2003) 14 ♗xh5 (it is probably simpler to ignore the sacrifice with 14 ♘c4 ♘f4 15 0-0, when White has the better chances without any complications) 14...gxh5 15 ♕xh5 ♘g6 16 ♗g5 ♕d7 17 ♘f3 a5 18 b5 dxc5 19 0-0 +/= Y.Shulman-R.Irzhanov, Karaganda 1994.

b) 9...♘e8 10 f3 (alternatively: 10 b4 ♔h8 11 0-0 f5 12 f3 b6 13 c5 f4 14 ♗f2 g5 15 ♖c1 ♖f6 16 ♕c2 ♖h6, K.Muendle-S.Chakurira, Manila Olympiad 1992, 17 ♘c4 and White's action on the queenside is much faster than Black's on the kingside; or again 10 0-0 f5 11 f3 f4 12 ♗f2 g5 13 c5 +=, e.g. 13...♘g6 14 a4 h5 15 a5 ♖f7 16 c6 ♘f6?! 17 ♕b3 b6? 18 axb6 cxb6 19 ♗xb6 +- Di.Werner-E.Cooke, Budapest 2007) 10...f5 11 c5 (this looks the most consistent, though 11 b4 and 11 0-0 are also possible) 11...fxe4 (or 11...♘f6 12 ♘c4 ♔h8 13 a4 ♘eg8 14 cxd6 cxd6 15 0-0, B.Lalic-

R.Gunawan, Sarajevo 1988, 15...♗h6 +=
Karpov) 12 fxe4 ♔h8 (or 12...dxc5 13
♗xc5 ♘d6, Y.Shulman-A.Kovalev,
Minsk 1995, 14 ♘c4! += Kovalev) 13
♘c4 ♘g8 14 cxd6 cxd6 15 ♕d2 ♗d7 16
a4 b6 17 b4 ♖c8 18 b5 +/= A.Musat-
R.Milu, Odorheiu Secuiesc 1993.

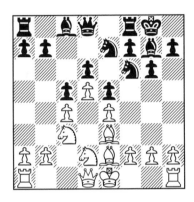

10 ♖b1

Another good plan is 10 g4 intending to play on the kingside; e.g.
10...♘e8 11 h4 f5 12 f3 ♘f6 (12...fxg4 13
fxg4 +/= A.Gutov-L.Yurtaev, Russian
Team Ch. 2006) 13 h5 f4 14 ♗f2 gxh5 15
g5 ♘d7 16 ♘b5 ♘b8 (J.Speelman-
R.Vaganian, European Team Ch.,
Plovdiv 1983) 17 ♕a4 and White can
develop an initiative by 0-0-0, ♖xh5,
♖dh1, ♕d1.

10...♘e8

Black has also tried 10...b6 11 0-0
♘e8 12 b4 f5 13 f3 f4 14 ♗f2 g5 and
now, rather than 15 a4 ♘c7 16 a5 ♘a6
(M.Garkov-H.Grünberg, Varna 1982),
better was 15 bxc5 bxc5 transposing to
the main line of the game; or if 10...♗d7
11 b4 b6 12 bxc5 bxc5, L.Baas-
O.Pleynet, Toulouse 1999, 13 0-0!? +/=.

11 b4 f5

11...b6 12 bxc5 bxc5 13 0-0 f5 14 f3
again transposes to the main line,
unless White prefers 13 ♕a4 f5 14 f3 f4
(14...♘f6!?) 15 ♗f2 g5 16 ♘b3 +/=
J.Przewoznik-K.Urban, Polish Ch. 1992.
**12 f3 b6 13 bxc5 bxc5 14 0-0 f4 15 ♗f2
g5** (D)

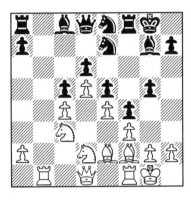

There is no room to swing a cat on
the queenside and the key c6 and b7-
squares are controlled by Black's
pieces. Therefore, although White controls the open b-file and has more
pieces in this area of the chessboard, he
cannot easily develop his initiative.
Nevertheless, a brilliant idea to sacrifice a piece on c5 gives White excellent
chances in the middlegame.

16 ♘b3

Sometimes White inserts 16 ♕a4 before continuing in similar fashion; e.g.
16...h5 17 ♘b3 g4 (after 17...a5,
A.Mirzoev-R.Gadjily, Azeri Ch. 1997,
White should continue consistently
with 18 ♘xc5 dxc5 19 ♗xc5) 18 ♕a5
♕d7 (H.Rau-P.Balcerak, German Junior
Ch. 1998) and now 19 ♘a4, with the
threats of 20 ♘b6 and 20 ♘xc5, again
would have given excellent chances.

16...♖f7 17 ♘xc5 dxc5 18 ♗xc5

White has realized his main idea and the passed c- and d-pawns give him tremendous compensation for the knight, especially as Black has no easy way to stop them.

R.Ibrahimov-E.Moradiabadi, Iranian Team Ch. 2005, concluded **18...♗f8 19 ♗f2 ♕a5 20 ♕c2 ♗a6 21 ♕a4** [21 ♘b5!?] **21...♕xa4 22 ♘xa4 ♘g6 23 ♖fc1 g4 24 ♔f1 gxf3 25 gxf3 ♖c8 26 c5 ♗xe2+ 27 ♔xe2 ♖fc7 28 ♖c3 ♔f7 29 ♖b5 ♗e7 30 ♖cb3 ♗h4 31 ♗g1 ♗d8 32 ♖b7 ♗e7 33 ♗f2** [33 c6! was also good] **33...♘f8 34 ♖3b5** [or 34 c6 again] **34...♘g6 35 ♘b2 ♔g8 36 ♖xc7 ♖xc7 37 ♘c4 ♔f7 38 ♔d3 ♗f8 39 ♖a5 ♔f6 40 h4 ♗xc5?** [but White was winning anyway] **41 ♗xc5 ♘xh4 42 ♖a6+ ♔g5 43 ♘xe5 ♘f6 44 ♗f2 ♘g2 45 ♖xa7 1-0**

B: 7...c6 (D)

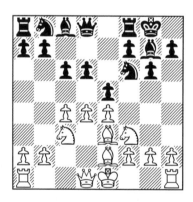

A typical move in the King's Indian. Now after any passive response Black can equalize by ...e5xd4, ...♖e8 and, at an appropriate moment, ...d6-d5.

8 d5

This looks the most consistent.

a) 8 ♕d2 ♘bd7 9 ♖d1 is not dangerous after 9...♖e8, e.g. 10 d5 cxd5 11 cxd5 ♘g4! 12 ♗g5 f6 13 ♗h4 h5 (=+ Kasparov) 14 ♗g3 a6 15 a4 ♘f8 16 0-0 ♗d7 ∞ G.Giorgadze-S.Dolmatov, Krasnodar 1997.

b) 8 dxe5 dxe5 9 ♕xd8 (avoiding the exchange gives White absolutely nothing, e.g. 9 ♘d2 ♕e7 10 c5 ♘bd7 11 ♕a4!? ♖d8 = L.Portisch-V.Ivanchuk, Reykjavik 1991) 9...♖xd8 10 ♘xe5 hopes to prove that the extra move ...c7-c6 is less than useful after 10...♘xe4 (the standard response) 11 ♘xe4 ♗xe5 12 ♗g5, e.g. 12...♗xb2? 13 ♖b1 ♖e8 fails to 14 ♘d6, or 12...♖d4 13 ♘d2 ♗g7 14 0-0-0 ♗e6 15 ♘b3 ♖xd1+ 16 ♖xd1 ♘a6 17 ♗e3 b6 18 ♘d4 += V.Chekhov-W.Uhlmann, Polanica Zdroj 1981. However, Black can play more strongly with 10...♖e8! 11 f4 ♘bd7! 12 ♗d4 ♘h5! 13 ♗xh5 ♘xe5 14 ♗e2 ♘f3+ 15 ♗xf3 (after 15 gxf3 ♗xd4 16 ♔d2 ♗e6 17 ♗d3 ♖ad8 Black has excellent compensation for the pawn) 15...♗xd4 16 ♖d1 ♗xc3+ 17 bxc3 ♗f5 18 ♔f2 ♗xe4 and Black equalized in M.Stojanovic-B.Damljanovic, Yugoslav Ch. 1996.

8...♘g4

Black has also tried:

a) 8...cxd5 9 cxd5 ♘g4 (9...♘e8 10 ♘d2 f5 11 f3 +/= V.Gefenas-V.Kirillovs, corr. 1981) 10 ♗g5 f6 11 ♗h4 ♘h6 12 0-0 ♘f7 13 ♘e1 ♗h6 14 ♘d3 ♘d7 15 a4 a5 16 ♔h1 b6 17 b4 +/= G.Rey-V.Frias Pablaza, San Francisco 1997.

b) 8...♘a6 and now:

b1) 9 a3 ♘h5 10 g3 cxd5 11 ♘xd5 ♘f6 12 ♘xf6+ ♕xf6 13 b4 ♕e7 14 0-0 b6 (now ...♗b7 will attack the vulnerable e4-pawn and the d5-square, while the c5-advance will practically be impossible) 15 ♕a4?! (15 ♕d2!? was better) 15...♘c7 16 ♕c6 ♗a6 17 ♖fd1 ♖fd8 18 ♖ac1 ♘e6 19 ♕a4 ♗b7 20 ♕c2 ♖f8 21 ♘h4 ♘d4 22 ♗xd4 exd4 23 ♗d3 ♖ae8 -/+ J.Ehlvest-V.Topalov, Vienna 1996.

b2) 9 ♘d2 ♘e8 10 0-0 (or 10 a3 f5 11 f3 c5 12 ♗d3 f4 13 ♗f2 h5 14 ♕e2 ♗d7 15 ♖b1 ♗f6 16 ♔d1 ♖f7 ∞ G.Tunik-V.Zaitsev, Vladimir 2004) 10...f5 11 f3 f4 12 ♗f2 c5 13 a3 b6 14 b4 ♗f6 15 bxc5 ♘xc5 ∞ S.Volkov-I.Zakharevich, Ekaterinburg 1999.

9 ♗g5

Instead:

a) 9 ♗d2 f5 10 exf5 (or 10 0-0 ♘f6 11 b4 ♘a6 12 ♕b3 ♔h8 13 ♖fe1 ♘c7 ∞ O.Dannevig-H.Stefansson, Gausdal 1991) 10...♗xf5 (10...gxf5 =) 11 0-0 ♘a6 12 ♘g5 ♘f6 transposes to D.Komarov-I.Smirin, Vienna 1996, which continued 13 ♗f3 ♘c5! 14 b4 e4 15 ♗e2 ♘d3 ∞.

b) 9 ♗c1 f5 10 0-0 ♘a6 11 ♘g5 ♘f6 12 ♗f3 (12 exf5) 12...cxd5 13 ♘xd5?! (13 exd5) 13...h6 =/+ G.Schebler-J.Maiwald, German League 2005.

9...f6

9...♕b6?! 10 0-0 ♕xb2 is too greedy after 11 ♘a4 ♕b4 (11...♕a3 12 ♗c1 ♕b4 13 ♗d2 comes to the same thing) 12 ♗d2 ♕a3 13 ♖b1 (M.Mchedlishvili-F.Doettling, European Junior Ch. 1997), when 13...♘a6 14 h3 ♘f6 is met by 15 ♗c1 ♕xa2 16 ♗e3 intending 17 ♖a1 +-.

10 ♗h4 (D)

10 ♗d2 f5 is the same as 9 ♗d2 above. Similarly 10 ♗c1 f5, or else 10...c5 11 h3 ♘h6 12 g4 ♘f7 ∞ G.Tunik-

V.Isupov, Russian Ch. 1990.

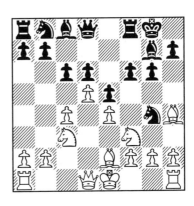

10...h5

Other moves do not give equality:

a) 10...♘h6 11 ♘d2 ♘f7 12 b4 ♘a6 13 dxc6 bxc6 14 b5 +/= H.Wirthensohn-G.Terreaux, Zürich 1993.

b) 10...♘a6 11 c5! ♘xc5 (or if 11...dxc5, S.Volkov-V.Kotronias, Corinth 2000, 12 dxc6 bxc6 13 ♘d2 h5 14 ♘c4 with excellent compensation for the pawn) 12 b4 ♘d7 13 dxc6 bxc6 14 ♕xd6 +/- A.Shchekachev-V.Isupov, Smolensk 1997.

c) 10...c5 11 ♘d2 ♘h6 12 f3 ♘f7 13 ♖b1 (or 13 a3 ♗h6 14 ♗f2 f5 15 b4 b6, S.Kiselev-V.Dydyshko, Berlin 1995, 16 ♗d3 +/= Dydyshko) 13...♗h6 14 ♗f2 a5 15 a3 f5 16 ♕c2 ♘a6 17 ♗d3 ♕g5 18 h4! ♕xd2+ 19 ♕xd2 ♗xd2+ 20 ♔xd2 += V.Saravanan-H.Banikas, Athens 2008.

11 ♘d2

Or 11 h3!? ♘h6 when, as well as 12 ♘d2 transposing below, White can consider 12 dxc6!? bxc6 13 c5 with the initiative.

11...♘h6

Other moves do not give Black equality either:

a) 11...c5 12 h3!? ♘h6 13 g4!? hxg4 14 ♗xg4 ♘xg4 15 hxg4 ♗h6 16 ♕f3 ♔g7 17 0-0-0 += J.Przewoznik-M.Ankerst, German League 1993.

b) 11...♘a6 12 0-0 ♘h6 13 f3 ♘f7 14 dxc6 bxc6 15 ♘b3 += M.Notkin-A.Galkin, Moscow 1996.

c) 11...a5 12 h3 ♘h6 13 g4 g5 14 ♗g3 h4 15 ♗h2 ♖f7 16 ♘f1 ♘a6 17 ♘e3 += S.Kiselev-S.Radzhabov, Moscow 1996.

12 h3

12 f3 is also good; e.g. 12...c5 (or 12...♘f7 13 ♗d3! ♗h6 14 ♕e2 c5 15 a3! += S.Shipov-E.Vorobiov, Moscow 1996) 13 0-0 ♘f7 14 ♗d3 ♗h6 15 ♕e2 ♘a6 16 a3 ♗d7 17 ♖ab1 b6 18 b4 ♔h8 19 ♔h1 ♖g8 20 ♗c2 ♗g5 21 ♗xg5 fxg5 22 ♗a4 ♗xa4 23 ♘xa4 +/= K.Sakaev-S.Mohandesi, Cappelle la Grande 1994.

12...♘f7

If 12...♘d7 (J.Speelman-K.Pytel, Leningrad 1984) then 13 f3 +/= Karpov, or 13 dxc6 bxc6 14 ♘b3 ♘f7 15 0-0 a5 16 ♕c2 += Zontakh.

13 g4 hxg4 14 ♗xg4 ♘a6 15 ♘b3 ♗h6 16 ♗xc8 ♖xc8 17 ♕g4 *(D)*

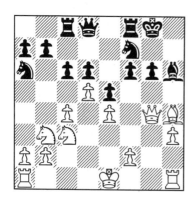

White's position is better. He has an initiative on the kingside and more active pieces. The only downside is the weak dark squares in his camp.

R.Markus-Z.Kozul, Nova Gorica 2006, continued **17...♔g7 18 ♖g1 ♗g5** [18...♘h8!?] **19 ♗xg5 fxg5 20 h4?!** [rather impatient; White could have castled before proceeding with his attack] **20...cxd5 21 exd5 ♕c7 22 ♘d2 ♘b4?!** [22...♘c5 was more logical, and if 23 ♕e2 e4 24 0-0-0 ♘e5] **23 ♕e4 ♘h8?!** [23...♖h8!?] **24 ♖g4** [24 a3 was better, as 24...♖f4 can be answered by 25 ♕b1!] **24...♕d7 25 f3 ♕f5 26 ♕xf5 ♖xf5 27 ♔e2 ♘f7 28 ♖c1 ♖h8 29 a3 ♘a6 30 ♖cg1** [30 hxg5!?] **30...♖xh4 31 ♘ce4** [31 ♘b5!?] **31...♖xg4 32 ♖xg4 b6 33 b4 ♘c7 34 ♘f1 ♘e8** [34...b5!?] **35 ♘e3 ♖f4 36 ♘g2 ♖f5 37 ♘e3 ½-½.**

C: 7...♕e7 *(D)*

A favourite move of Gufeld, who used it as early as 1966. The main idea is put pressure on the e4-pawn to force White to clarify the situation in the centre.

8 dxe5

A logical move. White wants to exploit the position of the black queen by playing 9 ♘d5.

a) 8 0-0 does not offer any advantage after 8...♘xe4! 9 ♘xe4 exd4 10 ♘xd4 ♕xe4 11 ♘b5 ♘a6 12 ♗f3 ♕xc4 13 ♘xa7 ♘c5 14 ♘xc8 ♖axc8 15 ♖c1 (L.Stein-E.Gufeld, USSR Ch., Tbilisi 1966) 15...♕xa2 16 b4 ♘e6 17 ♗xb7 ♖b8 18 ♗d5 ♕a3 =+ Gufeld, though he can try 11 ♖e1!? ♖e8 12 ♕d2 ♕e7 13 ♗f3 with compensation (Gufeld).

b) After 8 d5, closing the centre, Black doesn't usually have any problems either; e.g. 8...♘g4 (worth testing is 8...♘h5!? 9 ♘d2 ♘f4 10 ♗f1, J.H.Donner-J.Penrose, Lugano Olympiad 1968, and now 10...♘a6 with counterplay) 9 ♗g5 f6 10 ♗h4 a5 (or 10...h5 11 ♘d2!? ♘h6 12 f3 ♘d7 13 b4 ♘f7 14 ♘b3 ♗h6 with good play for Black, V.Tukmakov-L.Stein, USSR Ch., Leningrad 1971) 11 ♘d2 ♘h6 12 a3 ♗d7! ∞ V.Ivanchuk-J.Ehlvest, USSR Ch., Moscow 1988.

8...dxe5 *(D)*

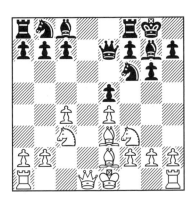

9 ♘d5 ♘xd5

The alternative is to move the queen:

a) 9...♕d6 10 ♘g4 11 ♗g5 f6 12 ♗d2

c6 13 c5 ♕d8 14 ♘e3 ♕e7 15 0-0 ♔h8 16 b4 with better chances for White, S.Ernst-Y.Visser, Hoogeveen 2000.

b) 9...♕d8 10 ♗c5 ♘xe4 (this exchange sacrifice is forced, as 10...♖e8? loses immediately to 11 ♗e7 1-0 M.Peek-G.Canfell, Dieren 1988) 11 ♗e7! (a very important zwischenzug, setting the black queen up for a potential fork on f6) 11...♕d7 (obviously not 11...♕e8? 12 ♗d3 and wins) 12 ♗xf8 ♔xf8 (12...♗xf8? would run into 13 ♘d2 and the threat of the fork works!) 13 ♕d3!? (threatening ♕a3+ in many lines; although 13 ♕c2 looks more natural, gaining time for ♖d1, Black is able to build a fortress: 13...♘c5 14 ♖d1 ♘c6! 15 0-0 ♘e6! 16 ♘b6 axb6 17 ♖xd7 ♗xd7 18 ♕d2?! ♗e8 was A.Karpov-G.Kasparov, 3rd matchgame, New York 1990, in which White came close to losing; Azmaiparashvili suggests 18 a3!? ♘cd4 19 ♘xd4 ♘xd4 20 ♕d2 += as a better try) 13...♘d6 (or 13...f5 14 ♖d1 ♘c6 15 ♕a3+ ♔g8 16 0-0 +/- K.Sakaev-P.Etchegaray, Groningen 1992) 14 ♕a3 (intending 15 ♖d1 and 16 c5 or 16 ♘xc7) 14...♘c6 (14...e4?, S.Shipov-M.Ahn, Le Touquet 1996, loses to 15 ♘g5! ♔g8 16 ♖d1 ♘c6 17 c5! +- Shipov) 15 ♖d1 ♘d4. Gufeld assessed this position as "with mutual chances", but we disagree: after 16 ♘xd4 exd4 17 0-0 White has a clear advantage; e.g. 17...♕d8 (17...c6? 18 ♘b6 axb6 19 ♕xa8 +- P.Scheeren-C.Baljon, Dutch Team Ch. 1987) 18 ♖fe1 ♔g8 19 c5 ♘f5 20 ♗f3 +/-.

10 cxd5 c6?!

This allows White to play 11 d6. The

best try here, relatively speaking, is
10...♖d8 11 ♕b3!? (or 11 0-0 c6 12 ♗c4
cxd5 13 ♗xd5 ♘c6 14 ♕b3 h6 15 h3
♔h7 16 ♖ac1 +/= J.Nielsen-H.Larsen,
corr. 1984) 11...c6 12 0-0 cxd5 (if 12...b6
13 ♖fd1 ♗g4 14 h3 ♗xf3 15 ♗xf3 c5 16
a4 +/- K.Hulak-D.Gavric, Banja Luka
1983) 13 exd5 b6 14 ♖fd1 (Ma.Tseitlin-
Y.Gruenfeld, Tel Aviv 1992) and now
14...h6 15 ♖ac1 +/= *ECO*.

11 d6 (D)

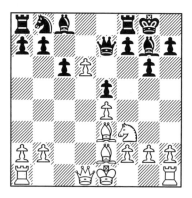

Only in this way can White maintain the initiative. The simple 11 0-0 is
less testing after 11...cxd5 12 exd5 e4 13
♘d4 a6 14 ♕b3 ♘d7 15 ♖fd1 ♗e5 16
♖d2 ♗d6 17 g3 ♘e5 ½-½ S.Reshevsky-
L.Kavalek, Netanya 1973.

11...♕d7

White has a strong initiative after
other moves too: 11...♕d8 12 0-0 ♖e8 13
♕d2 f6 14 ♖fd1 ♗e6 15 ♕c3 ♕d7 16 b4
♗f8 17 ♖d2 +/- A.Miles-E.Torre, Bad
Lauterberg 1977; or if 11...♕e6 12 h4!
(I.Sokolov-S.Djuric, San Bernardino
1988) 12...f6 13 h5 with an attack, e.g.
13...♖d8 14 ♕c2 b5 15 hxg6 hxg6 16
♘h4.

12 h4!

A strong move; White attacks on
the kingside while the d6-pawn restricts Black in the centre. After 12 ♕c2
Black finds counterplay more easily;
e.g. 12...b6 13 ♖d1 c5 14 0-0 ♗b7
(N.Kalesis-D.Vandoros, Athens 1994)
15 ♗c4 ♘c6 ∞.

12...b6?!

Black should not have ignored the
threat of h4-h5. Necessary was 12...h5!
(Tsesarsky) avoiding the direct attack,
though Black's position remains difficult.

13 h5

Now White has a standard attack
against the fianchetto: opening the h-
file, exchanging dark-squared bishops
and getting the queen on the c1-h6 diagonal.

13...♗a6

Worse is 13...c5 14 hxg6 hxg6 15
♗h6 +- Tsesarsky.

14 hxg6 hxg6 15 ♗h6 ♗xh6

Or if 15...♗xe2 (B.Avrukh-E.Grivas,
Athens 2003) then 16 ♔xe2 ♗xh6 17
♖xh6 ♕g4 18 ♖h4 ♕e6 19 ♕d2 wins
easily (Tsesarsky).

16 ♖xh6 ♖d8 (D)

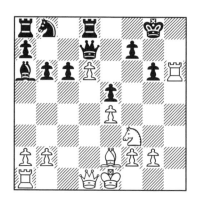

This position was reached in J.Gustafsson-H.Banikas, Fuerth 2002. White's attack is decisive and it is just a matter of accurate calculation. One nice win was 17 ♘g5! &xe2 (17...♕xd6 18 ♖h8+!) 18 ♕b3! ♖f8 (18...&h5 19 g4) 19 ♖xg6+ ♔h8 20 ♖h6+ ♔g7 21 ♘e6+ fxe6 22 ♕g3+ ♔xh6 23 ♔xe2.

The game took another course: **17 ♘xe5 ♕e6** [if 17...♕xd6 18 ♖xg6+ fxg6 19 ♕b3+ +-] **18 ♕d4 ♖xd6 19 ♕c3 ♕f6 20 ♖d1 ♖e6** [or 20...♖xd1+ 21 &xd1 ♔g7 22 ♖h3 and 23 ♖f3 wins, Tsesarsky] **21 f4** [or 21 ♖d8+! ♕xd8 22 ♘d7 f6 23 ♕h3 +-] **21...c5 22 &g4** [22 ♖d8+! ♕xd8 23 ♘d7! still works] **22...♖e8 23 ♖d6 ♕xd6** [if 23...♕g7 24 &e6!] **24 ♖h8+! ♔g7 25 ♖xe8 ♕d4 26 ♕xd4 cxd4 27 ♖e7 ♔g8 28 ♖xf7 ♘c6 29 &e6 1-0** J.Gustafsson-H.Banikas, Fuerth 2002.

D: 7...exd4 (D)

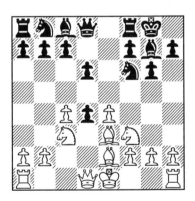

Black releases the tension in the centre, after which he usually looks for counterplay by attacking the e-pawn with ...♖e8, and breaking with ...c7-c6 and ...d6-d5.

8 ♘xd4

8 &xd4 gives White nothing after 8...♘c6 9 &e3 ♖e8 10 ♕c2 (R.Hübner-D.Suttles, Sombor 1970) and now 10...♕e7 = Karpov.

8...♖e8

Instead:

a) 8...c6 9 f3 (or 9 ♘c2!? ♖e8 10 f3) 9...♖e8 just transposes, as Black has no chances to equalize otherwise. After passive play, such as 9...♘bd7 10 ♕d2 ♖e8, White can either start an attack on the kingside with 11 g4!? ♘c5 12 0-0-0 ♕a5 13 ♔b1 &d7 14 ♖hg1 ♖ad8 15 &g5 ♕b6 16 h4 &c8 17 h5 +/- B.Larsen-L.Ljubojevic, Manila 1973; or stabilize the situation in the centre depriving Black counterplay by 11 ♖d1 ♘e5 12 0-0 ♕c7 13 ♔h1 &d7 14 &g5 ♕b6 (T.Lirindzakis-H.Skiadas, Hania 1995) 15 ♘b3 +/-.

b) 8...♘c6!? is interesting; e.g. 9 ♘c2 ♘d7 10 ♕d2 ♘c5 11 &h6 f5 with counterplay, Y.Shulman-M.Dougherty, Philadelphia 2000. White's best may be the Sämisch sideline reached after 9 f3!? (– 5 f3 0-0 6 &e3 e5 7 ♘ge2 exd4 8 ♘xd4 ♘c6 9 &e2), when 9...♖e8 transposes to the next note (or else 9 0-0 ♖e8 10 f3), while if 9...♘h5 10 ♘xc6 bxc6 11 0-0 ♘f6 12 ♕d2 c5 13 ♖ad1 ♕e7 14 ♖fe1 &b7 15 &f1 += B.Alterman-A.Kofidis, Katerini 1992.

9 f3 c6 (D)

9...♘c6 is again possible, though White is better after 10 ♕d2 (10 ♘c2 is also good, or else 10 0-0 transposing to line C3 in Chapter Five) 10...♘h5 11 ♘xc6 bxc6 12 g4 ♘f6 13 g5 ♘d7 14 0-0-0 +/= R.Döhn-H.Schaffer, German Junior Ch. 2003; or 10...♘xd4 11 &xd4

♗e6 12 0-0 c6 13 ♖fd1 ♕a5 14 a3 ♖ad8 15 b4 ♕c7 16 ♖ac1 += F.Hölzl-F.Stoppel, Austrian Team Ch. 1994.

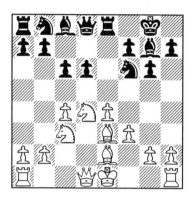

10 ♗f2

10 0-0 allows 10...d5! as in the notes to line B in Chapter Five, so White should secure his dark-squared bishop. Instead:

a) 10 ♘c2!? gives Black fewer problems after 10...d5 (if Black refrains from this advance he has a position without counterplay; e.g. 10...♕e7 11 ♕d2 ♘a6 12 0-0 ♘c7 13 ♖ad1 ♖d8 14 ♖fe1 ♗e6 15 ♗g5! ♘ce8 16 ♗f1 ♕c7 17 ♘d4 ♗d7 18 ♖c1! +/- F.Gheorghiu-Zsu.Polgar, Budapest 1989) 11 cxd5 cxd5 12 exd5 ♗f5 13 ♗f2 (or 13 ♔f2 ♗xc2 14 ♕xc2 ♘xd5 15 ♘xd5 ♕xd5 = M.Euwe-V.Pirc, Hastings 1938/39) 13...♘xd5 14 ♘xd5 ♗xc2 15 ♕xc2 ♕xd5 16 0-0 ♘c6 17 ♗c4 ♘d4!? (or 17...♕h5 18 ♖ad1, E.Karavade-L.Guliev, Balaguer 2006, 18...♖e7 and White only has a slight edge) 18 ♗xd5 ♘xc2 19 ♖ac1 ♘e3 20 ♗xe3 ♖xe3 21 ♖c7 ♗d4 22 ♔h1 ♖d8 23 ♗xf7+ ♔f8 24 ♖xb7 ♖e7 25 ♖xe7 ♔xe7 26 ♗b3 ♗xb2 and Black drew this opposite-coloured bishops ending, J.Goormachtigh-B.Van der Linden, Belgian Team Ch. 1997.

b) 10 ♕d2 is another option: 10...d5 11 exd5 cxd5 12 0-0 ♘c6 (after 12...dxc4 13 ♘db5!? ♕e7 14 ♗f4 ♖d8 15 ♕e3 ♕xe3+ 16 ♗xe3 ♘c6 17 ♖ad1 White has a small advantage in the ending, G.Tunik-A.Kovalev, Kecskemet 1989) 13 c5 (this move is positionally very logical as it leaves Black with an isolated d-pawn, and some dark squares in his camp may also be weak; on the other hand, the c5-pawn may itself prove vulnerable) 13...♖xe3!? (this exchange sacrifice is the best practical chance; other moves do not give equality, e.g. 13...♗d7 14 ♖ad1 ♕e7 15 ♗f2 ♕xc5 16 ♘e6, S.Gligoric-G.Tringov, The Hague 1966, 16...♕a5!? 17 ♘xg7 ♔xg7 +/=) 14 ♕xe3 ♕f8 15 ♘xc6!? bxc6, and now White best is probably 16 ♖ad1 (after 16 ♔h1?! ♖b8 17 ♘a4 ♖b4 18 b3 ♗e6 19 ♘b2 ♘h5 20 ♘d3 ♖h4 21 ♕f2 ♕e7 22 g4 ♗d4! 23 ♕xd4 ♖xh2+ 24 ♔xh2 ♕h4+ forced a draw in A.Karpov-G.Kasparov, 11th match-game, New York 1990) 16...♗f5 17 ♗d3 ♖e8 18 ♕f2 and Black does not have full compensation for the exchange, D.Skliarov-I.Kurnosov, Russian Junior Ch. 2000.

10...d5

Again the most consistent move. After other continuations White has a small advantage; e.g. 10...♘h5 11 ♕d2 ♘a6 12 0-0 ♗e5 13 g3 ♗h3 14 ♖fd1 += D.Kosic-M.Tosic, Serbian Team Ch. 2005; or 10...♘bd7 11 0-0 ♘e5 12 ♕d2 a5 13 b3 ♕c7 14 ♖ad1 ♘ed7 15 ♘c2 ♖e6 16 ♖fe1 ♗f8 17 ♗f1 += J.Speelman-M.Adams, Dublin 1993.

11 exd5 cxd5 12 0-0 ♘c6

Black has problems after 12...dxc4 13 ♗xc4 a6 14 ♕b3 ♖f8 15 ♖fd1 ♕a5 16 ♘d5! ♘bd7 (if 16...♘xd5 17 ♗xd5 ♘d7, M.Lepan-J.Demarre, French Team Ch. 2003, then 18 ♘e6! +/-) 17 ♘e7+ ♔h8 18 ♗xf7 +/- Z.Azmaiparashvili-Al.David, Elista Olympiad 1998.

13 c5 *(D)*

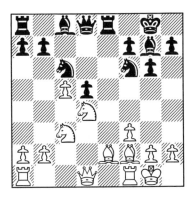

This idea appears once more. White obtains a queenside pawn majority and in the future may play against the isolated d5-pawn, while Black has to watch out for the ♘b5-d6 as well. After other moves Black equalizes easily; e.g. 13 ♕d2 ♘xd4 14 ♗xd4 dxc4 15 ♗xc4 ♗e6 16 ♗xe6 ♖xe6 17 ♖ad1 ♖d6 18 ♘b5 ♖d7 = R.Oortwijn-G.Bacino, corr. 1999; or 13 ♖c1 ♗h6 14 ♘xc6 bxc6 15 ♖c2 ♗f5 16 ♗d3 ♘e4 (or 16...dxc4 =) 17 fxe4 dxe4 18 ♗xe4 ♗xe4 19 ♖e2 ♗f5 20 ♖xe8+ ♕xe8 21 ♖e1 ♕b8 with compensation, M.Rohde-R.Francisco, Virginia Beach 2001.

13...♘h5

The threat of ...♘f4 is easy to parry; however, Black also plans the manoeuvre ...♗e5, ...♘g7 and sometimes ...♘e6

fighting for the d4-square. Otherwise White has a small advantage; e.g. 13...♗f8 14 ♔h1 ♗e6 15 ♗b5 ♖c8 16 ♕d2 ♘d7 (T.Enhbat-T.Braunlich, Ledyards 2006) 17 ♘xe6 fxe6 18 ♘a4 +=; or 13...♗e6 14 ♕d2 ♘d7 (Z.Azmaiparashvili-M.Ubach Miralda, Terrassa 1992) 15 ♘xe6 fxe6 16 ♘b5 +=; or 13...a6 14 ♕d2 ♘e5 15 ♘a4 (A.Bellaiche-P.Emmenecker, Paris 2006) 15...♘fd7 +=.

14 ♕d2

14 g3?! covers f4 but not g5. This allows Black to obtain a strong counterattack after 14...♗h3 15 ♖e1 (B.Gelfand-V.Topalov, Linares 1997) and now 15...♘xd4 16 ♗xd4 ♕g5, e.g. 17 ♔f2 (or 17 ♗f2 ♘f4 18 ♗f1 ♗xc3 19 bxc3 ♗xf1 =/+) 17...♖e6 18 ♗b5 ♖xe1 19 ♔xe1 ♘xg3 20 hxg3 ♕xg3+ 21 ♗f2 ♕h2.

More interesting is 14 ♗b5 ♗d7 15 ♕d2 ♗e5 16 ♘de2 a6 17 ♗a4 ♗e6 18 f4 ♗g7 (S.Mohandesi-L.De Briey, Tihan 1998) 19 ♘d4!? with the initiative.

14...♗e5

Black realizes his plan. Worse are 14...♗e6?! 15 ♖fd1 ♕f6!? 16 ♘db5 ♖e7 17 ♗e3 d4 18 ♘e4 ♕e5 19 ♘xd4 +/- G.Bagaturov-K.Tsarouhas, Chania 1997; or 14...♘xd4 15 ♗xd4 ♗xd4+ 16 ♕xd4 ♕f6 17 ♖ad1 ♗e6 18 b4 a5 19 a3 axb4 20 axb4 ♖a3 21 ♘b5 ♖a2 22 ♕xf6 ♘xf6 23 ♗d3 +/= J.Ehlvest-L.Bergez, Geneva 1999.

15 g3 ♘g7

If instead 15...♗h3 16 ♖fe1 ♕d7 (or 16...♘g7 17 ♖ad1 ♖c8 18 ♘db5 a6 19 ♘d6 ♗xd6 20 cxd6 d4 21 ♘e4 ♗f5 22 d7! +- G.Kasparov-M.Carlsen, Reykjavik rapid 2004) 17 f4 ♗g7 (L.Schandorff-J.Kristiansen, Danish Ch. 1992) 18

♗f3 ♗g4 19 ♗g2 with better chances for White.

16 ♖fd1 *(D)*

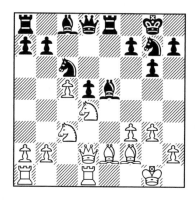

This looks most consistent, though White has also tried:

a) 16 ♖fe1 ♘f5! 17 ♘cb5!? a6 18 ♘xc6 bxc6 19 ♘d4 ♕f6 20 ♖ad1 ♖a7 = K.Islam-E.Hossain, Dhaka 2005.

b) 16 ♖ad1 ♗xd4 17 ♗xd4 ♘xd4 18 ♕xd4 ♘f5 = M.Scalcione-M.Paragua, Genoa 2001, intending 19 ♕xd5 ♕xd5 20 ♖xd5 ♘e3.

c) 16 ♗b5 ♗d7 17 ♗xc6 (if 17 ♘de2, N.Ioseliani-Peng Zhaoquin, Belgrade 1996, 17...d4! 18 ♘xd4 ♘xd4 19 ♗xd4 ♗xb5 20 ♘xb5 ♘e6 21 ♖ad1 ♗xd4+ 22 ♘xd4 ♘xc5 = Shipov) 17...bxc6 18 b4 (S.Shipov-S.Atalik, Greek Team Ch. 1996) 18...h5! intending ...h4 ∞ Shipov.

16...♗e6

Other moves allow White a small advantage, e.g. 16...♘e6 17 ♘xe6 ♗xe6 18 f4 ♗g7 19 ♘b5!? += A.Fishbein-B.Lopez, US Ch. 2004; or 16...a6 17 ♗f1 ♗e6 18 ♘xe6 fxe6 += B.Gelfand-V.Topalov, Dos Hermanas 1997.

17 ♗b5

White can also count on an advan-

tage after:

a) 17 ♘cb5 ♘f5 (17...♕d7 18 ♘xe6! fxe6 19 f4 ♗f6 20 ♗g4! +/= S.Halkias-A.El Arousy, Tanta 2002) 18 ♘xf5 ♗xf5 (Y.Kruppa-O.Goncharov, Kiev 2006) 19 f4 intending ♗f3 +/=.

b) 17 ♘xe6 (one of the most principled lines) 17...♘xe6 (or 17...fxe6 18 f4 ♗f6 19 ♘b5! +/= A.Khalifman-V.Akopian, FIDE World Ch., Las Vegas 1999) 18 ♕xd5 ♗xc3 19 bxc3 ♘f4! 20 gxf4 ♖xe2 21 ♕xd8+ ♖xd8 22 ♖xd8+ ♘xd8 23 ♖d1 with a better ending for White, R.Akesson-D.Pedzich, Cappelle la Grande 1999.

17...♕d7

17...♖c8!? is a good alternative; e.g. 18 ♗xc6 bxc6 19 ♖ac1 ♗d7 20 b4 ♘e6 21 b5 ♘g5 22 h4 ♘h3+ 23 ♔g2 ♘xf2 24 ♔xf2 ♕f6 25 bxc6 ♗g4 26 ♘ce2 (A.Gutov-S.Ershova, Omsk/Perm 1998) 26...♗e6 ∞; or if 18 ♘ce2 ♖e7 19 ♘xe6 (19 ♘xc6 bxc6 20 ♗a6 ♖b8 21 ♗d4 ♗d7 ∞) then 19...♘xe6!? ∞, rather than 19...fxe6 20 f4 ♗f6 21 ♖ac1 +/= A.Simutowe-W.Aramil, Philadelphia 2006.

18 ♖ac1

18 ♘xe6 still gives White better chances; e.g. 18...fxe6 19 f4 ♗f6 20 ♘e4 ♗e7 21 ♕c3 (or 21 ♖ac1!?) 21...♖f8 22 ♖ac1 +/= R.Markus-I.Nataf, Serbian Team Ch. 2005.

18...a6 19 ♗a4 ♖ad8

And here again 20 ♘xe6 would leave White slightly better.

Whereas in V.Ivanchuk-T.Radjabov, Morelia/Linares 2006, White played rather aimlessly and ended up losing:

20 b4 ♗h3 21 ♕h6 ♗e6 22 a3 ♕c8 23

♕g5 ♕c7 24 ♕d2 ♖f8 25 ♗c2 ♗c8 26 ♗b3 ♘e6 27 ♘de2 d4! 28 ♘d5 ♕b8 29 f4 ♗g7 30 ♕d3 [30 f5 gxf5 31 ♘ef4 ♘g5 ∞] 30...♘c7 31 ♘b6? [31 ♕f3 ♗e6 32 ♘b6 ♗xb3 33 ♕xb3 ♖fe8 =] 31...♗f5 32 ♕d2 d3 33 ♘c3 ♘d4 34 ♗xd4 ♗xd4+ 35 ♔g2 ♖fe8 36 ♖e1 ♗xc3 37 ♕xc3 ♗e4+ [or 37...♖xe1 38 ♖xe1 d2 39 ♖d1 ♖d3 -+] 38 ♔f2 d2 39 ♖xe4 ♖xe4 40 ♖d1 ♖ed4 41 ♗c4 ♘e8 42 ♕e3 ♔f8 43 ♕e5 ♕xe5 44 fxe5 ♘c7 0-1.

E: 7...h6 *(D)*

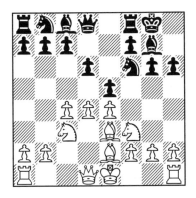

This move, popularized by John Nunn, prepares ...♘g4 which cannot now be answered by ♗g5.

8 0-0

The most common reply. Other continuations give White fewer chances of obtaining an advantage:

a) 8 dxe5 ♘g4! 9 ♗f4 ♘xe5 10 ♕d2 ♔h7 11 ♘d4 ♘bc6 12 ♗e3 ♘xd4 13 ♗xd4 c5 14 ♗e3 ♗e6 15 b3 ♘c6 16 0-0 ♘d4 17 ♗d3 a6 ∞ J.Speelman-S.Kindermann, World Team Ch., Lucerne 1985.

b) 8 h3 in turn prevents ...♘g4, but after 8...exd4 Black's pawn move is

much more useful than White's; e.g. 9 ♘xd4 ♖e8 10 ♕c2 (or if 10 ♗f3 ♘bd7 11 0-0 ♘h7 12 ♕d2 ♘g5 13 ♗d1, Wl.Schmidt-J.Tarjan, Indonesia 1983, 13...♘xe4 14 ♘xe4 ♖xe4 15 ♗c2 ♖e5 16 ♗xh6 ♗xh6 17 ♕xh6 ♖h5 18 ♕e3 ♘e5 = Karpov) 10...♕e7 11 ♗f3 (11 ♗d3 ♘a6 12 ♕d2 ♘c5 13 f3 ♘xd3+ 14 ♕xd3 c6 intending ...d6-d5 =+ L.Portisch-J.Nunn, London 1986) 11...c5 12 ♘b3 ♘c6 13 0-0 ♗e6 14 ♘d5 ♗xd5 15 exd5 ♘e5 16 ♗e2 b5 with counterplay, A.Sokolov-A.Shchekachev, Jurmala 1991.

8...♘g4 9 ♗c1 ♘c6

The most popular and principled move, though Black has other continuations at his disposal:

a) 9...♘d7 10 dxe5 ♘gxe5 11 ♘xe5 dxe5 12 ♗e3 ♔h7 13 ♕d2 ♘f6 14 ♕xd8 ♖xd8 15 ♖ad1 ♗e6 16 f3 a5 17 ♘d5 ♖d7 18 ♖d2 ♖ad8 19 ♖fd1 ♘e8 20 g4 += L.B.Hansen-I.Smirin, European Team Ch., Debrecen 1992.

b) 9...♘a6 10 dxe5!? looks good as there is no clear way for Black to equalize; e.g. 10...dxe5 (or 10...♘xe5 11 ♘d4 ♘c5 12 ♗e3 +/= B.Kelly-J.Gallagher, Saint Vincent 2005) 11 h3 ♘f6 12 ♗e3 ♘d7 13 a3 ♘ac5 14 b4 ♘e6 15 ♖a2 a5 16 ♖d2 axb4 17 axb4 c6 18 c5 += K.Sasikiran-M.Golubev, Internet blitz 2004.

10 d5

A logical move. Less effective now is 10 dxe5 ♘gxe5 11 ♗e3 ♗e6 12 ♘d2 f5 13 exf5 ♗xf5 = Z.Arsovic-J.Todorovic, Senta 2006.

10...♘e7

Obviously not 10...♘d4? 11 ♘xd4

exd4 12 ♘b5 +/- I.Sokolov-O.Cvitan, Yugoslav Ch. 1988.

11 ♘e1

The most frequently played move. The main alternative is 11 ♘d2; e.g. 11...f5 12 ♗xg4 fxg4 13 b4 ♗d7 (or 13...a5 14 bxa5 ♖xa5 15 a4 g5 16 ♗a3 += R.Yandarbiev, S.Saric-M.Cebalo, Borovo 2005, intending c4-c5, ♘c4) 14 c5 a5 15 ♗a3 ♘c8 16 ♘c4 (16 b5!?) 16...axb4 17 ♗xb4 ♖f6 18 a4 (intending 19 ♘a5 ♖b8 20 c6) 18...dxc5 19 ♗xc5 ♖fa6 20 ♕b3 b6 21 ♗e3 (R.Szymczak-M.Laskarzewski, corr. 1992) 21...♔h7 22 f4 gxf3 23 ♖xf3 +/=.

11...f5

Worse is 11...h5?! 12 h3 ♘h6 13 f4! exf4 14 ♗xf4 f5 15 ♕d2 ♘f7 16 ♘f3 fxe4 (or 16...c6!? 17 dxc6 bxc6 18 ♖ad1 ♕b6+ 19 ♗e3 ♕c7, F.Figueiredo-M.Krauland, corr. 1999, 20 c5 with the initiative) 17 ♘xe4 ♘f5 18 g4 with better chances for White, I.Smirin-B.Avrukh, Tel Aviv 1999.

12 ♗xg4 fxg4 *(D)*

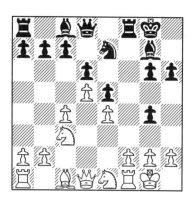

A key position, with a rather unusual pawn structure for the King's Indian. Although the doubled g-pawns cannot be regarded as weaknesses they don't coordinate very well with Black's pieces. On the other hand, he can easily get his knight to the f4- or h4-square.

13 ♗e3

Also interesting is 13 ♘c2 followed by ♘e3 to attack the key squares g4 and f5, although blocking the c1-h6 diagonal allows Black to try 13...g5 14 ♘e3 ♖f4!? and then:

a) 15 ♗d2 ♗d7 16 b4 ♘g6! (intending ...♘h4, ...♕e8-h5) 17 ♖c1 (if 17 ♘e2 ♖xe4 18 ♕c2 ♘f4 19 ♕xe4 ♘xe2+ 20 ♔h1 ♘d4 or 17 ♘f5 ♖xf5 18 exf5 ♗xf5 19 ♖e1 ♘f4 20 ♘e4 ♕e8 ∞ Nunn) 17...♘h4 18 ♔h1?! (better 18 f3 gxf3 19 g3 ♕f6! ∞ Nunn) 18...♕e8 19 f3 gxf3 20 g3 ♕h5 21 gxh4? ♖xh4 22 ♖f2 g4 23 ♘f1 ♖h3 24 ♔g1 ♕g6 with a winning attack, L.Portisch-J.Nunn, Skelleftea 1989.

b) 15 f3 gxf3 16 ♖xf3 ♕f8! 17 ♘b5 ♕d8 18 ♘c3 = O.Gschnitzer-J.Nunn, German League 1994.

c) 15 ♕d3 looks best, when the kingside attack can be met by ♘e2-g3; e.g. 15...♘g6 16 a4 ♘h4 17 ♘e2 ♕f6 18 ♗d2 ♕g6 19 ♘g3 ♗d7 20 b4 ♖af8 21 b5 ♕f7 22 ♕e2 +/- J.Tisdall-T.Sammalvuo, Gausdal 1994.

13...g5

Other moves are less energetic: 13...♖f7 14 ♘d3 g5 15 c5 ♘g6 16 a4 ♗f8 17 a5 += S.Williams-A.Hunt, Oslo 2004; or 13...c5 14 dxc6 (or 14 ♘d3!? intending b4 += Korchnoi) 14...bxc6 (S.Shipov-A.Pankratov, Moscow 1995) 15 ♕d2 d5 and White is better after any of 16 ♗c5 d4 17 ♘a4 (Korchnoi), or 16 cxd5 cxd5 17 ♗xh6, or just 16 ♗xh6!?.

14 c5

Another option is 14 f3 gxf3 15 ♖xf3 ♖xf3 16 ♕xf3 b6 17 a4 (or 17 ♕h5!? intending ♘f3, ♗xg5, ♘xg5, h4 with an attack) 17...♘g6 18 g3 ♗d7 19 ♘g2 ♕c8 20 ♗d2 ♗g4 21 ♕d3 ♗h3 22 ♘d1 a5 23 ♘ge3 +/= M.Stojanovic-B.Szuk, European Junior Ch. 1995.

14...♘g6

Planning ...♘h4, ...♕e8-h5, ...♖f3 with an attack. 14...dxc5 would be inconsistent; e.g. 15 ♗xc5 b6 16 ♗a3 ♗a6 17 ♕xg4!? (or 17 ♘d3 +=) 17...♗xf1 18 ♔xf1 ♖f7 19 ♘c2 c5 20 ♖d1 ♘g6 21 g3 ♕f6 22 ♖d2 ♗f8 23 ♘e3 +/= S.Gross-L.Salai, Czech Ch. 1990.

15 ♖c1 *(D)*

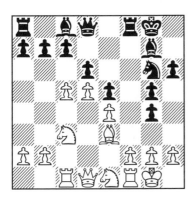

White can develop his initiative on the queenside in various ways, though it often comes to the same thing (e.g. 15 cxd6 cxd6 16 ♖c1 etc). White also has the advantage after 15 b4 ♖f7 16 a4 ♗f8 17 a5 a6 18 ♘c2 ♗d7 19 ♘a3 ♘f4 20 ♘c4 += A.Shchekachev-Gil.Hernandez, Linares 1996; or 15 a4 a6 16 b4 ♕e7 17 ♘d3 ♘f4 18 ♘b2 h5 19 ♘c4 ♗d7 20 ♖c1 ♖f7 21 cxd6 cxd6 22 ♘b6 +/= J.Ehlvest-R.Dzindzichashvili, New York 1994.

15...♖f7 *(D)*

Or 15...♕e8 16 a4 a6 17 ♘c2 ♘f4 (17...♕e7!?) 18 cxd6 cxd6 19 ♘a3 ♕g6 20 ♘c4 +/- R.Akesson-R.Meessen, Leuven 1998.

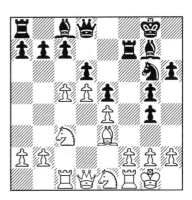

16 cxd6

Also good are 16 ♘b5 ♘f4 17 cxd6 cxd6 18 ♕c2 ♗f8 (L.Santos-I.Kopylov, corr. 1989) 19 ♘c7 ♘e2+ 20 ♕xe2 ♖xc7 21 f3 ♖xc1 22 ♗xc1 gxf3 23 ♕xf3 ♗g7 24 ♘c2 +/-; or 16 b4 ♗f8 17 a4 a5 18 cxd6 cxd6 19 b5 b6 20 ♘e2 ♖b8 21 ♘g3 ♘f4 22 ♘d3 h5 23 ♘b2 h4 24 ♘f5 ♖xf5 25 exf5 ♗xf5 26 ♖c6 +/- G.Giorgadze-D.Martinez Martin, Mondariz 1999.

16...cxd6 17 a4 ♗f8

Other moves do not give Black equality either; e.g. 17...♘f4 18 ♘c2 ♗f8 19 ♘a3 h5 20 ♘c4 b6 21 b4 += F.Peralta-E.Fernandez Romero, Andorra 2004; or 17...a6 18 ♘c2 ♗d7 19 ♘a3 ♖c8 20 b3 intending ♘c4 +=, D.Antic-M.Markovic, Serbian Team Ch. 2003.

18 ♘b5 ♗d7 19 b3

Freeing White's pieces from having to guard the a-pawn, though Kasimdzhanov later preferred 19 ♕b3!? ♘f4 20 ♔h1 ♕a5 21 ♘c3 ♖b8 22 ♘c2 intending ♘a3-c4 +/= .

19...♘f4 (D)

Or if 19...a6 20 ♘c7 ♖c8 21 ♘e6 ♖xc1 22 ♕xc1 ♕c8 23 ♕xc8 ♗xc8 24 ♘xf8 ♔xf8 25 ♘d3 +/= Ftacnik.

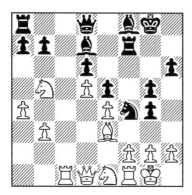

Two games have reached this interesting position. K.Sasikiran-R.Kasimdzhanov, FIDE World Cup, Hyderabad 2002, continued:

20 ♘d3

20 ♘xa7!? was tested in P.San Segundo Carrillo-B.Roselli Mailhe, Calvia Olympiad 2004: 20...♕a5 21 ♘b5 ♗xb5 22 axb5 ♕xb5 23 ♗xf4 (if 23 ♖c4, Kasimdzhanov, then 23...♖a3 with the initiative) 23...♖xf4 24 ♖c4 ♖a3 25 ♘d3 ♖xb3 26 ♘xf4 ♕xc4 27 ♘h5 ♖c3 (27...♕d3 28 ♕xg4 ♖b1 is similar) 28 ♕xg4 ♖c1 29 ♕e6+ (the immediate 29 ♘g3 was a better try for the win) 29...♔h8 30 ♕f6+ ♔g8 31 ♕g6+ ♔h8 32 ♕f6+ ♔g8 33 ♕g6+ ♔h8 34 ♘g3 b5 35 h3 b4 36 ♕f7 ♖xf1+ 37 ♘xf1 ♕c8 38 ♔h2 b3 39 ♘g3 b2 40 ♘h5 b1♕ 41 ♕f6+ ½-½.

20...♗xb5 21 axb5 ♕d7 22 ♘b2?!

An unnecessary sacrifice; better was 22 b6 (Kasimdzhanov) or possibly 22 ♖c3!? h5 (22...♕xb5 23 ♕xg4) 23 b6 +/=.

22...♕xb5 23 ♘c4 h5 24 ♖a1 a6 25 f3?!

This merely opens the f-file for the black pieces. Instead 25 ♖a5 ♕d7 26 ♘b6 ♕c7 27 ♖a2 ♖e8 28 ♖c2 ♕e7 29 ♕d2 ♕f6 ∞ Kasimdzhanov.

25...gxf3 26 ♖xf3 g4 27 ♖f1?!

Better was 27 ♖f2 avoiding ...♘e2+ tricks, as after White's next move.

27...♗e7 28 ♖a5? ♕d7

Here 28...♕xb3! wins immediately, since if 29 ♕xb3 ♘e2+.

29 ♘b6 ♕c7 30 ♖a1 ♖af8 31 ♖c1 ♗g5!
32 ♕d2

If 32 ♖xc7 ♘e2+ wins again.

32...♕e7 33 ♖fe1 ♕f6 34 ♖c8?

A final blunder, but Black was winning anyway; e.g. 34 ♔h1 ♕g6 35 ♖c4 h4 -+ Kasimdzhanov.

34...♘e2+ 0-1

If 35 ♕xe2 ♗xe3+ is decisive.

F: 7...♘g4 (D)

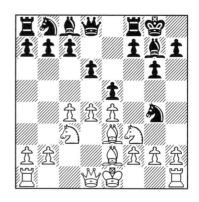

This natural continuation is the main line. Clearly White cannot allow his bishop to be exchanged, so he must play:

8 ♗g5 f6

and then choose between:

F1: 9 ♗c1 67
F2: 9 ♗h4 69

Not only is 9 ♗d2 passive, it also blocks the d-file, leaving the d4-square unprotected, which Black can exploit by 9...exd4 10 ♘xd4 f5 11 ♗xg4 ♗xd4! 12 exf5 ♘c6 13 0-0 ♗xf5 = J.Przewoznik-M.Kislov, Miedzybrodzie 1991.

F1: 9 ♗c1 (D)

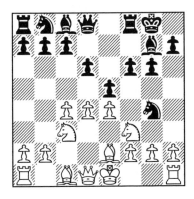

With his manoeuvre ♗c1-e3-g5-c1 White has lost two tempi. It is true that Black will return one in playing ...f7-f6-f5, but this is only possible because the ♘f6 has moved 'for free' and will only return to f6 after being prompted by a further h2-h3 which is not especially useful. In effect White will have played 7 h3 while allowing the illegal response 7...f5!?, hopping over the knight. All in all, the withdrawal to c1 cannot give White an advantage.

9...f5

In our opinion this is the most logi-cal move: with his pieces well developed, Black commences his action in the centre. Many other continuations are seen in tournament practice, but it seems Black cannot equalize so easily with any of them:

a) 9...c5? (a failed experiment) 10 dxc5 dxc5 11 ♕xd8 ♖xd8 12 ♘d5 ♘d7 13 h3 ♘h6 14 ♗e3 ♔f7?! 15 0-0-0 b6 16 g4 ♘g8 17 g5 f5 18 exf5 gxf5 19 g6+ 1-0 P.Van der Sterren-A.Romero Holmes, Wijk aan Zee 1995.

b) 9...♕e8 10 0-0 ♘a6 11 h3 ♘h6 12 ♖b1 c6 13 ♖e1 f5 (E.Gausel-M.Sagafos, Bergen 2000) 14 c5!? +/-.

c) 9...♘h6 10 dxe5! fxe5 (or 10...dxe5 11 ♕xd8 ♖xd8 12 ♘d5 +/- H.Kubikova-K.Eretova, Prague 1992) 11 c5 ♘f7 12 cxd6 ♘xd6 13 0-0 +/- A.Fishbein-S.Kagan, Tel Aviv 1992.

d) 9...c6 10 h3 (10 d5 transposes to line B) 10...♘h6 11 ♗e3 ♘f7 12 g4 ♘a6 13 ♕d2 f5 14 gxf5 gxf5 15 exf5 ♗xf5 16 0-0-0 +/= B.Ivkov-V.Ciocaltea, Havana 1962.

e) 9...exd4!? 10 ♘xd4 f5 is better, but still worse than the immediate pawn push; e.g. 11 0-0 (not 11 exf5? ♘xf2! 12 ♔xf2 ♕h4+ 13 g3 ♕xd4 -/+ S.Iskusnyh-I.Sudakova, St Petersburg 2002; or if 11 h3 ♘e5 12 exf5 gxf5 13 ♘d5 ♘a6 14 ♗e3 ♘c5 15 ♕c2 ♘g6 ∞ L.Coelho-G.Milos, Santos 2006) 11...fxe4 (11...♘c6 transposes to Chapter Eight, line A22, note with 10...exd4 11 ♘xd4 f5) 12 ♗xg4 ♗xg4 13 ♕xg4 ♗xd4 14 ♗h6 ♖f5 (or 14...♗g7 15 ♗xg7 ♔xg7 16 ♕xe4 ♘c6 17 ♘d5 ♕d7 18 ♕e3 ♔g8 19 ♕c3 ♕f7 20 ♖ae1 +/- C.Sandipan-Huang Qian, Dubai 2005) 15 ♕xe4 ♘c6 16 ♘d5

♕d7 17 ♖ae1 += D.Yevseev-Al.David, Moscow 2006.

f) 9...♘c6 is Black's choice in about 60% of games, but it does not guarantee him full equality after 10 d5 *(D)* (instead 10 0-0 again transposes to line A22 in Chapter Eight; or if 10 h3 exd4 11 ♘xd4 ♘ge5 12 ♘xc6 bxc6 13 f4 ♘d7 14 f5 with the initiative, R.Vaganian-I.Umanskaya, Moscow 1991, but here 13...♘f7!? intending ...f6-f5 deserves attention) and now:

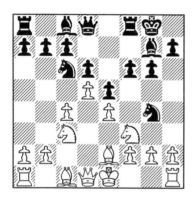

f1) 10...♘e7 11 h3! (the best move, starting an action on the kingside) 11...♘h6 12 h4 (also good is 12 g4!?, e.g. 12...f5 13 ♘g5 ♔h8 14 ♕d3 ♘hg8 15 ♗d2 ♗h6, L.Portisch-J.Polgar, Prague 1995, 16 gxf5 gxf5 17 ♖g1 with better chances for White) 12...♘f7 (if 12...c6 13 h5 g5 14 ♘h2 c5 15 ♘g4, M.Kozak-M.Ondrejat, Ostrava 2005, 15...f5 16 exf5 ♘exf5 17 ♘e4 ♘xg4 18 ♗xg4 h6 +/=; or 12...♗g4 13 h5 g5 14 ♘h2 ♗d7 15 ♗e3 +/= R.Pert-G.Buckley, British League 2004) 13 h5 g5 (if 13...f5 14 hxg6 ♘xg6 15 ♕c2 f4 16 ♗d2 ♘g5 17 ♘xg5 ♕xg5 18 g3 ♕f6 19 0-0-0 +/- V.Popov-S.Solovjov, St Petersburg 2001; or

13...c5 14 hxg6 hxg6 15 ♘h4! ♗d7 16 g3 a6 17 ♗d2 ♖b8 18 a4 g5 19 ♘g2 f5 20 exf5 ♘xf5 21 ♘e4! +/- S.Volkov-B.Kantsler, Rethymnon 2003) 14 ♕c2 (or 14 ♗e3!? h6!? 15 ♘d2 f5 16 exf5 +/= D.Solak-V.Srebrnic, Portoroz 2003) 14...h6 15 g4 c6 16 ♗e3 ♕c7 17 ♘d2 += A.Khudaverdieva-D.Harika, World Junior Ch. 2003.

f2) 10...♘d4!? (a recent try) 11 ♘xd4 exd4 12 ♘b5 (not 12 ♕xd4?! f5! 13 ♕d1 fxe4 14 ♗xg4?! ♕h4! 15 ♗e2? ♗xc3+! 16 bxc3 ♕xf2+ 17 ♔d2 ♗g4 -+ E.L'Ami-L.D.Nisipeanu, European Ch, Budva 2009} 12...f5 13 0-0! d3!? (not 13...♘xh2? 14 ♔xh2 fxe4 15 ♘xd4 ♕h4+ 16 ♔g1 ♗e5 17 f4! exf3 18 ♘xf3 ♖xf3 19 ♖xf3 +/- J.Ulko-D.Sokolov, Moscow 2005; or if 13...♘e5 14 exf5 d3 15 ♗xd3 ♘xd3 16 ♕xd3 ♗xf5 17 ♕g3 ♗e5 18 ♗g5 ♕d7 19 ♕b3 a6 20 ♘a3 ♕g7 21 ♖ae1 += D.Yevseev-A.Khruschiov, Peterhof 2009) 14 ♗xg4 fxg4 15 ♕xd3 ♗e5! 16 f4 gxf3 17 ♖xf3 ♖xf3 18 ♕xf3? (better 18 gxf3 a6 19 f4 +=) 18...a6 19 ♘c3 ♕h4 20 g3 ♕h3 21 ♗f4 ♗d4+ 22 ♔h1? (22 ♗e3 ∞) 22...g5 23 ♗xg5 ♗g4 24 ♕f1 ♕h5 25 h4 ♖f8 -+ V.Tarasova-A.Balaian, European Women's Ch., St Petersburg 2009.

10 exf5

The careless 10 h3? walks into 10...♘xf2! 11 ♔xf2 fxe4 12 ♘xe4 ♕h4+ 13 ♔g1 (not 13 ♔e3? ♗h6+ 14 ♔d3 ♕xe4+! 15 ♔xe4 ♗f5+ leads to mate) 13...♕xe4 14 d5 ♗f5 -/+ V.Ivanchuk-V.Bologan, Edmonton 2005.

Black is also fine after 10 dxe5 ♘xe5 11 exf5 ♖xf5 12 ♘xe5 ♗xe5 13 ♗e3 ♘c6 = Z.Arsovic-M.Cebalo, Bar 2006; and 10 ♗g5 ♕d7!? 11 dxe5 ♘xe5 12 ♘xe5

♗xe5, e.g. 13 exf5 ♕xf5 14 ♗e3 ♗xc3+ 15 bxc3 ♘c6 16 0-0 ♗e6 17 ♖b1 ♖ab8 18 ♕a4 ♗d7 19 ♕d1 ½-½ J.Adamski-K.Andersen, Copenhagen 1995.

10...♗xf5!?

Also playable is 10...exd4 11 ♗g5 (or 11 ♘d5 ♗xf5 12 h3 ♘h6 =, but not 11 ♘xd4? ♘xf2! again) 11...♕e8 (if 11...♕d7 12 ♘d5 gxf5 13 ♘xd4 ♘e5 14 0-0 +/= S.Valentine-A.Cabrera Pino, corr. 2003) 12 ♘d5 d3! 13 ♕xd3 (if 13 ♘xc7 ♕xe2+ 14 ♕xe2 dxe2 15 fxg6 hxg6 16 ♘xa8 ♘a6 ∞) 13...♗xf5 14 ♕d2 ♕d7 15 0-0 ♘c6 = A.Gavrilov,-F.Amonatov, Moscow 2007.

11 h3 ♘f6 *(D)*

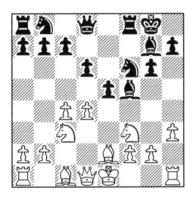

Black temporarily sacrifices the e5-pawn, but he will have good compensation for it in all variations.

12 dxe5 dxe5 13 ♕xd8 ♖xd8 14 ♘xe5 ♘e4

Or 14...♖e8 15 f4 ♘e4 16 ♘xe4 (not 16 ♘d5? ♘g3! 17 ♘xc7 ♘c6 -+) 16...♗xe4 17 0-0 ♗xe5 (17...♘c6!? looks more consistent) 18 fxe5 ♘c6 19 ♗f4 ♖ad8 (if 19...♘xe5 20 ♖ad1 +=) 20 e6?! (20 ♖fd1 +/=) 20...♘d4! 21 ♗g4 ♘xe6 22 ♗h6 ♘g7 23 ♖ad1 ♖xd1 24 ♖xd1 ♘f5

25 ♗f4 h5 26 ♗xf5 ½-½ J.Kanko-H.Laakso, Vantaa 1994.

15 ♘xe4 ♗xe4 16 ♗f3 ♗xf3 17 ♘xf3 ♘c6

Black's activity gives him sufficient play for the pawn. A.Onischuk-I.Smirin, Turin Olympiad 2006, concluded **18 0-0 ♘d4! 19 ♘xd4 ♖xd4 20 b3** [or 20 c5 ♖c4 21 ♗e3 ♗xb2 22 ♖ab1 ♖c2 =] **20...♖xc4 21 bxc4 ♗xa1 22 ♗e3 ♗f6 23 ♖d1 b6 24 g4 ♖d8 25 ♖xd8+ ♗xd8 26 ♔g2 ♔f7 27 f4 c6 28 ♔f3 ♔e6 29 ♔e4 a6 30 ♗f2 b5 31 cxb5 axb5 32 f5+ ½-½.**

F2: 9 ♗h4 *(D)*

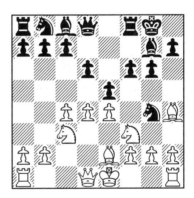

By keeping his bishop on the h4-d8 diagonal, White tries to make kingside counterplay more difficult. Black has two main responses:

F21: 9...g5 *70*
F22: 9...♘c6 *72*

Other moves allow White an easy advantage:

a) 9...♕d7 10 0-0 f5 11 dxe5 ♘xe5 12

♘xe5 dxe5 13 ♕xd7 ♗xd7 14 ♘d5 ♘a6 15 c5 += W.Uhlmann-E.Bukic, Skopje 1968.

b) 9...♕e8 10 0-0 ♘h6 11 c5 dxc5 12 dxe5 fxe5 13 ♕d5+ ♔h8 14 ♕xc5 c6 15 ♖ad1 +/- A.Zontakh-S.Martinovic, Belgrade 2000.

c) 9...h5 10 h3 exd4 (not 10...♘h6? 11 dxe5 dxe5 12 ♕xd8 ♖xd8 13 ♘d5 +- E.Jimenez Zerquera-T.Ujtumen, Palma Interzonal 1970) 11 ♘xd4 ♘h6 12 0-0 ♘c6 13 c5 +/- M.Riediger-A.Schelle, Fuerth 1999.

d) 9...♘d7 10 0-0 h5 11 dxe5 dxe5 12 b4 +/= E.Magerramov-V.Bologan, USSR Ch., Moscow 1991.

F21: 9...g5 (D)

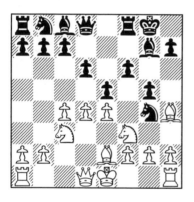

The simplest way to break the pin.
10 ♗g3 ♘h6

The knight jumps to a safe place, preparing the kingside pawn advance. Weak is 10...♘c6 11 d5 ♘e7 12 ♘xg5! ♘xf2 13 ♗xf2 fxg5 14 ♗g4 ♘g6 15 g3 h6 16 0-0 +/- V.Malaniuk-M.Szczepinski, Barlinek 2006.
11 d5

White had to reckon with 11...g4 fol-lowed by 12...f5. Other continuations are:

a) 11 c5 g4 (or if 11...♘c6 12 cxd6 cxd6 13 d5 ♘e7, S.Halkias-B.Socko, World Junior Ch. 1998, 14 0-0 += *ECO*) 12 ♘h4 f5 13 ♘xf5 ♗xf5 14 exf5 exd4 15 ♘b5 ♘xf5 16 cxd6 cxd6 17 0-0 +/= S.Shipov-K.Arakhamia, Greek Team Ch. 1996.

b) 11 dxe5 fxe5 (more aggressive than 11...dxe5 12 c5!? ♗e6 13 0-0 c6 14 b4 ♘f7 15 ♕c2 ♘d7 16 ♘d2 a5 17 a3 +/= S.Matveeva-J.Riipinen, Helsinki 1992) 12 h4 (an ambitious move after which White often wins a pawn) 12...g4 13 ♘h2 ♗e6 14 ♘d5 (also interesting is 14 ♘xg4 ♘xg4 15 ♗xg4 ♗xc4 16 ♘d5 ♔h8 P.Wells-C.Sandipan, Gibraltar 2004, and now 17 h5 with some initiative) 14...♕d7 15 ♘e3 wins the g4-pawn, but Black's active pieces give him excellent compensation after 15...♘c6 16 ♘hxg4 ♘d4 17 ♘h2 ♕c6 18 ♗d3 ♕b6 (J.Pigott-T.Gavriel, Hampstead 1998) or 15...♘a6 16 ♘exg4 ♘c5 17 ♘xh6+ ♗xh6 18 ♕c2 a5 (B.Ivkov-E.Bukic, Stip 1977).

c) 11 h3 exd4 (if 11...♘c6 12 d5 ♘e7 13 ♕d2! ♘f7 14 ♘h2 f5 15 exf5 ♘xf5 16 0-0 ♘d4 17 ♗g4 ♘h8 18 ♘e2 +/= S.Shipov-V.Golod, Minsk 1993; but 11...♘d7 12 d5 f5 13 exf5 ♘c5! 14 ♘d2 ♗xf5 15 0-0, K.Sashikiran-V.Topalov, Sofia 2007, and now 15...♗g6 followed by ...♘f5 looks good) 12 ♘xd4 ♘c6 (or 12...f5 13 exf5 ♗xf5 14 0-0 ♘c6 15 ♘xf5 ♘xf5 16 ♗h2 ♔h8 17 ♕d2 ♘fd4 ∞ K.Frey Beckman-R.G.Alvarez, corr. 2000) 13 0-0 (if 13 h4, S.Volkov-B.Socko, Neum 2000, simply 13...g4!? followed by ...f6-f5 seems playable) 13...f5 (or

13...♘xd4 14 ♕xd4 f5 15 ♕d5+ ♔h8 16 f4 fxe4 17 fxg5 ♘f5 18 ♘xe4, S.Halkias-I.Smirin, European Ch., Istanbul 2003, and now 18...♗d7 with counterplay) 14 ♘xf5 ♘xf5 15 exf5 ♘d4 16 ♗g4 ♗xf5 17 ♘b5 ♗xg4 18 hxg4 ♘xb5 19 ♕d5+ ♖f7 20 cxb5 ♗xb2 21 ♖ab1 ♗a3 22 ♖fe1 ♗c5 23 ♖b3 with compensation, S.Halkias-K.Mah, World Junior Ch. 1996.

11...♘d7

After 11...f5 the weakness of the light squares in Black's camp is more often felt; e.g. 12 exf5 ♘xf5 13 ♘d2! ♘d4 14 0-0 ♘xe2+ 15 ♕xe2 ♕e8 16 ♘de4 intending c4-c5 +/= Kir.Georgiev-V.Bologan, Gibraltar 2006.

12 ♘d2 *(D)*

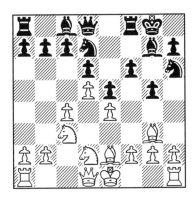

A good positional move with several purposes. Now on ...f6-f5 White either can reinforce his pawn-chain with f2-f3, or capture on f5 and follow up with ♘de4. Black must also reckon with 13 h4 as the response ...g5-g4 and ...f6-f5 is no longer possible.

Instead, 12 h3 transposes to 11 h3 ♘d7 12 d5, while after 12 0-0 Black is able to fight for the e4-square and even launch his h-pawn in some variations;

e.g. 12...f5 13 exf5 ♘xf5 14 ♘e4 g4 15 ♘fg5 ♘f6 16 ♘xf6+ ♕xf6 17 ♘e4 ♕g6 18 ♗d3 h5 with a strong initiative, O.Borik-O.Bühler, German League 1987. If instead 12 h4!? g4 13 ♘d2 (or 13 ♘h2 f5 14 exf5 ♘xf5 15 ♘xg4 ♘xg3 16 fxg3 ♘c5 with compensation, K.Ollek-N.Bensiek, corr. 1991) 13...f5 14 exf5 (D.Gurevich-I.Zenyuk, US Ch. 2007) then 14...♘f6 15 ♘de4 ♗xf5 ∞.

12...f5

Black cannot delay his counterplay for too long, or he may be deprived of it altogether; e.g. 12...♖f7 13 0-0 ♘f8 14 b4 ♘g6 15 c5 ♘f4 16 ♗xf4 exf4 (J.Wallace-S.Lewinsky, Australian Ch. 1991) 17 ♖c1 +/=; or if 12...c5 (R.Pogorelov-A.Cabrera, Albacete 2003) 13 h4 with the initiative.

13 f3

White has more chances of obtaining an edge by fighting for the e4-square: 13 exf5 ♘f6!? 14 ♘de4 ♘xe4 15 ♘xe4 ♗xf5 16 ♗d3 g4 17 0-0 ♔h8 (or 17...♕e8 18 c5 ♕g6 19 ♖e1 ♘f7 20 ♗h4 ♖ae8 21 ♖c1 +/= L.Aronian-T.Radjabov, Morelia/Linares 2006) 18 ♕e2 ♕e8 (or 18...♗d7, B.Gelfand-T.Radjabov, Russian Team Ch. 2006, 19 ♖fe1 +=) 19 c5 ♕g6 20 ♖ac1 += S.Volkov-I.Nataf, Cappelle la Grande 1999.

13...♘f6 14 h3

Preventing ...g5-g4, e.g. 14 ♗f2 g4! 15 0-0 gxf3 16 ♗xf3 ♘hg4 17 exf5 ♗xf5 18 ♘de4 ♘xe4 19 ♗xe4 ♕g5 ½-½ U.Markmann-S.Haskamp, German League 1990.

White has also tried castling long: 14 ♕c2 c6 (not now 14...g4?! 15 0-0-0, or if 14...fxe4!?, H.Leyva-R.Leyva, 5th matchgame, Holguin 1994, 15 ♘cxe4 ♘h5 16 ♗d3 ♘f4 17 0-0 ♘f5 18 ♗f2 ♘xd3 19 ♕xd3 intending b2-b4, c4-c5 and ♘c4 +/= H.Leyva) 15 dxc6 bxc6 16 0-0-0 f4 17 ♗f2 ♗e6 18 ♘b3 ♕e7 19 ♔b1 a5 20 ♘a4 ♖fb8 21 ♖d2 (H.Leyva-R.Leyva, 3rd matchgame, Holguin 1994) 21...♘f7 ∞.

14...c5!

A strong move. By blocking both flanks, Black obtains a very solid position. Less effective are:

a) 14...fxe4 15 fxe4 g4 16 ♗h4 ♕e8 17 ♕b3 ♘h5 18 0-0-0 ♘f4 19 ♖dg1 b6 20 ♕d1 +/= Zhao Xue-Ju Wenjun, Chinese Ch. 2006.

b) 14...♘h5 15 ♗f2 ♘f4 16 g3 ♘xe2 17 ♕xe2 c5!? 18 g4! f4 (B.Gelfand-I.Nataf, Cap d'Agde 2002) and now 19 h4! ♘f7 20 hxg5 ♘xg5 21 ♖h5 ♗f6 22 0-0-0 (Tsesarsky) when White has all the play.

15 ♗f2 f4 *(D)*

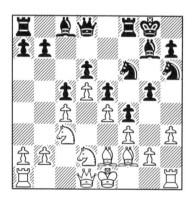

With the position closed neither side has much chance of achieving anything. B.Gelfand-T.Radjabov, Turin Olympiad 2006, continued:

16 ♖b1

White has also tried a2-a3 and b2-b4 without success: 16 a3 ♘f7 17 b4 b6 18 ♕b3 h5 ∞ E.Bacrot-T.Radjabov, Morelia/Linares 2006; or 16...♖f7 17 b4 b6 18 ♘f1 ♗f8 19 ♖b1 ♖g7 20 ♕d2 ♗d7 21 ♖b3 ♘f7 ∞ H.Grooten-F.Nijboer, Vlissingen 2006.

16...b6 17 b4 cxb4 18 ♖xb4 ♘d7 19 a4 ♘c5 20 a5 ♗d7 21 axb6 axb6 22 ♘b3 ♘f7 23 ♕b1 ♖a6 24 ♔d2 ♕c7 25 ♕b2 ♖b8 26 ♖a1 ♖ba8 27 ♖b1 ♗f6 28 ♘xc5 bxc5 29 ♖b7 ♕c8 30 ♖b8 ♖xb8 31 ♕xb8 ♗d8 32 ♕xc8 ½-½.

F22: 9...♘c6 *(D)*

Trying to force White to clarify the situation in the centre.

10 d5

The most consistent move. Other continuations are not dangerous:

a) 10 0-0 transposes to line A21 in Chapter Eight (*7 0-0 ♘c6 8 ♗e3 ♘g4 9 ♗g5 f6 10 ♗h4*). The text can go the same way if White follows with a quick 0-0 (see below).

b) 10 h3 ♘h6 11 dxe5 dxe5 12 ♕b3 g5 13 ♖d1 (G.Ajrapetian-I.Chukhno, Voronezh 2005) 13...♘d4 14 ♘xd4 exd4 15 ♗g3 f5 ∞.

c) 10 dxe5 dxe5 (or 10...♘gxe5 11 0-0 ♗e6 12 b3 ♕d7 13 ♕d2 ♖ae8 14 ♖ad1 ♘xf3+ 15 ♗xf3 ½-½ J.Adamski-Wl.Schmidt, Polanica Zdroj 1974) 11 0-0 h5 12 ♗g3 ♘h6 13 h3 (13 ♕b3!?) 13...♘f7 14 ♕b3 ♘g5 15 ♘xg5 ♘d4 16 ♕d1 fxg5 17 ♘b5 ♘e6 18 ♕xd8 ♖xd8 19 ♖fd1 ♗d7 20 f3 ♔f7 21 ♗f1 b6 22 ♖d3 c6 23 ♖ad1 ♔e7 24 ♘c3 ♗e8 = L.Janjgava-L.Van Wely, European Team Ch., Debrecen 1992.

10...&e7 11 &d2 &h6

Black can also play 11...h5!? 12 h3 (12 0-0 is Chapter Eight, line A21, note with 10...h5) 12...&h6 13 g4 (13 0-0 is Chapter Eight again) 13...g5! 14 &g3 h4 (preventing White from opening files on the kingside; now Black's position is safe) 15 &h2 c5 16 f3 (if 16 dxc6 bxc6 17 0-0 S.Iskusnyh-I.Bogachkov, Russia 2001, then 17...a5! = Bogachkov; or 16 &f1 &g6 17 &e3 &f4 18 &f1 &f7 19 f3 a6 20 &g1 &d7 ∞ M.Prusikhin-W.Uhlmann, German League 2004) 16...&f7 17 &g1 &g6 18 &f1 &e8 19 &h2 &f8 ∞ E.Moldobaev-K.Sobay, Kocaeli 2002.

12 f3 *(D)*

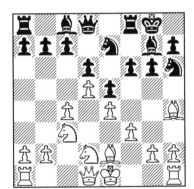

Supporting the centre, while making way for the bishop to retreat to f2. White has tried various other continuations, which also lead to complex play:

a) 12 g4 c6 13 f3 &f7 14 &c2 a6 15 a4 (V.Ivanchuk-A.Yermolinsky, Frunze 1988) 15...a5! 16 0-0-0 &h6 17 &f2 &f4 ∞ Yermolinsky/Livshits.

b) 12 b4 g5 13 &g3 &g6 14 0-0 &f4 15 c5 &xe2+ 16 &xe2 f5 17 exf5 &xf5 18 &de4 g4 with strong counterplay, L.Konings-F.Nijboer, Haarlem 1996.

c) 12 0-0 is also played and transposes again to Chapter Eight (line A21, note with 10...&h6 11 d5), although the text is more logical by the current move order.

12...c5

As mentioned above, blockading is a good strategy for Black in these types of positions. Other moves give White better play:

a) 12...f5 13 0-0 &f6 14 &f2 c5 15 dxc6 bxc6 16 b4 &e6 17 &b3 +/= L.Van Wely-F.Nijboer, Eindhoven 1988.

b) 12...&f7 13 b4 f5 14 c5 &h8 15 &c4 g5 16 &f2 &g6 17 h3 &f4 18 g3! &xe2 19 &xe2 (A.Huzman-A.Lugovoi, St Petersburg 1999) 19...&d7 +/=.

c) 12...&h8 13 0-0 f5 14 b4 &f6 15 &f2 &eg8 16 c5 &h4 17 g3 +/= S.Volkov-M.Cleven, Bad Wörishofen 1999.

d) 12...g5 13 &f2 f5 (if 13...&g6 14 g4!? &f4 15 &f1 c5 16 &e3 &f7 17 &f1 a6 18 a3 &e8 19 b4 +/= H.Grooten-J.Ocana Roca, Gibraltar 2006) 14 c5 &g6 (or 14...g4!? 15 fxg4 &xg4 16 &xg4 fxg4 17 0-0 &g6 18 cxd6! cxd6 19 &c4 &c7 20 b3 &d7 21 a4 with better chances for White, E.Magerramov-R.Maliangkay, corr. 1991) 15 g3 fxe4 16 fxe4 &h3 17 &e3 g4 18 &f1 &d7 19 &e2 &xf1 20 &xf1 &xf1+ 21 &xf1 &f7 (V.Shishkin-M.Szczepinski, Mielo 2005) 22 0-0-0 with better chances for White.

e) 12...c6!? is playable; e.g. 13 0-0 (or 13 &f2 &f7 14 b4 f5, E.Magerramov-W.Watson, Luxembourg 1990, 15 &c1 ∞ Watson) 13...c5 14 &b1 g5 15 &f2 f5 with counterplay, G.Giorgadze-J.Howell, Amantea 1995, but in this case Black might as well play ...c7-c5 straightaway and save a tempo.

13 ♖b1

Opening the b-file is thematic. White can undertake this plan in different ways, but Black has sufficient counterplay in all variations:

a) 13 ♗f2 f5 14 a3 b6 15 ♖g1 ♘f7 16 g4 fxg4 17 fxg4 ♗h6 ∞ D.Sahovic-D.Goodman, Reykjavik 1982.

b) 13 a3 ♔h8 14 b4 b6 15 ♘b3 g5 16 ♗f2 f5 17 h3 ♘g6 18 g4 fxg4 19 hxg4 ♘h4 20 ♗g3 ♘g8 21 ♘d2 ♕f6 22 ♕c2 (A.Gershon-M.Zulfugaryi, Moscow 2002) 22...♘g2+ 23 ♔f2 ♘f4 with counterplay (Wells).

13...a5

Also acceptable are:

a) 13...b6 14 b4 f5 15 bxc5 bxc5 16 ♕a4 fxe4 17 ♘dxe4 ♘hf5 18 ♗f2 ♘d4 19 ♗d3 ♘ef5 20 0-0 ♗h6 ∞ L.Koster-J.Van der Wiel, Dutch Team Ch. 1994.

b) 13...f5 14 0-0 ♘f7 15 b4 b6 16 a4 ♗h6 17 ♗f2 ♔h8 18 a5 ♘g8 19 ♕c2 ♘f6 ∞ B.Gelfand-I.Nataf, Cannes 2002.

14 a3 g5 *(D)*

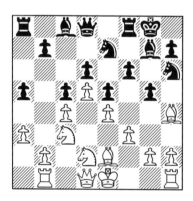

Both sides are realizing their plans. White plans b2-b4 with the initiative on the queenside, whereas Black has counterplay on the kingside. On the other hand, there is not much room on the queenside, and the white king feels quite safe.

15 ♗f2 f5 16 b4

We are following B.Gelfand-V.Bologan, Calvia Olympiad 2004:

16...axb4 17 axb4 b6 18 0-0 ♘g6 19 g3 g4?!

Allowing White to take over the central light squares is somewhat risky; and 19...fxe4?! 20 ♘dxe4 ♗h3 21 ♖e1 ♘f5 22 ♘b5 ♖a2 23 ♕b3 is similarly good for White. 19...f4 20 g4 ♘f7 (∞ Bologan) would have been more consistent, when Black can continue with ...♗f6, ...♔g7, ...♖h8 and ...h7-h5.

20 exf5 ♗xf5

If 20...gxf3 21 fxg6 fxe2 22 gxh7+ ♔xh7 23 ♕xe2 ♗h3 24 bxc5 bxc5 25 ♘de4 ♗xf1 26 ♖xf1 and White is clearly better according to Bologan.

21 ♘de4 gxf3 22 ♗xf3 ♘h8 23 ♗e3 ♘8f7 24 g4 ♗g6 25 ♕e1 ♔h8 ½-½

White's position is still better, but the opponents agreed a draw.

Conclusion

The Gligoric System with 7 ♗e3 is not so inoffensive that Black can just ignore it: 7...♘c6 (line A), 7...c6 (line B) and 7...♕e7 (line C) all allow White the better game. 7...exd4 (line D) with the plan of ...♖e8, ...c7-c6 and ...d6-d5 is playable, but White has the advantage here too, while 7...h6 (line E) is a little slow. Therefore Black should prefer the logical 7...♘g4, when after 8 ♗g5 f6 9 ♗h4, either 9...g5 or 9...♘c6 promises him sufficient counterplay.

Chapter Four

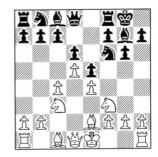

Petrosian System: 7 d5

1 d4 ♘f6 2 c4 g6 3 ♘c3 ♗g7 4 e4 d6 5 ♘f3 0-0 6 ♗e2 e5 7 d5 *(D)*

This set-up is called the Petrosian System after the Armenian former world champion. White immediately closes the centre, rules out any ...e5xd4 ideas, and intends future action on the queenside where he now has more space. Also, by forestalling the ...♘c6-e7 manoeuvre White avoids the heavy theoretical discussions of the main lines.

The drawback to this plan is that d4-d5 is both committal and inflexible. By surrendering control of the c5-square White gifts a nice outpost to a black knight. Moreover, the early release of tension in the centre allows Black to seek immediate counterplay on the kingside. Therefore White's primary concern is prophylaxis, a typical feature of Petrosian's chess. The usual follow-up is 8 ♗g5, which inter-feres with Black's plan of ...f7-f5 by preventing his knight from moving out of the way.

Nevertheless, Black has sufficient measures at his disposal. After 8 ♗g5 he can achieve the desired ...f7-f5 by breaking the pin with 8...h6 9 ♗h4 g5 10 ♗g3 ♘h5 or else 9...♕e8 and 10...♘h7. Meanwhile the other knight can go to c5 via 7...♘a6 or 7...♘bd7, or after the preliminary 7...a5, which safeguards the c5-outpost by ruling out b2-b4, at least for the time being. In any case Black's plans are very similar and the same positions often appear with a different move order.

On the whole, the Petrosian System may be a good weapon for those who like to kill the opponent's threats in the bud before trying to win, rather than allowing his full counterplay in the pursuit of a more significant advantage.

A: 7...♘a6 76
B: 7...♘bd7 78
C: 7...a5 87

Black has tried various other continuations, but these give White better chances:

a) 7...h6 (an unnecessary precaution) 8 ♘d2 ♘bd7 9 0-0 ♔h7 10 ♖e1 ♘g8 11 ♘f1 f5 12 exf5 gxf5 13 f4 += M.Ivanov-R.Radjabov, Moscow 1995.

b) 7...c5 transposes to the Old Benoni; but the blockade has little justification here – it is better to leave c5-square for a knight; e.g. 8 ♗g5 h6 9 ♗h4 ♕c7 10 ♘d2 ♘h7 11 ♘b5 ♕d7 12 a3 ♘a6 13 ♖b1 h5 14 f3 ♗h6 15 ♗f2 ♘f6 16 b4 b6 17 ♕c2 += G.Sosonko-F.Gheorghiu, Thessaloniki Olympiad 1984.

c) 7...♘h5 8 g3 ♘a6 (not 8...f5?! 9 exf5 ♕f6 10 ♘g5 ♕xf5 11 0-0 ♘f6, T.V.Petrosian-I.Zaitsev, USSR Team Ch. 1966, 12 f3 +/-) 9 ♘d2 ♘f6 10 h4 c6 11 ♘b3 ♘c7 (T.V.Petrosian-E.Gufeld, USSR Ch., Leningrad 1960) 12 h5 += Euwe.

d) 7...♘e8 8 0-0 (or 8 h4!? f5 9 ♗g5 ♗f6 10 exf5 gxf5 11 ♕d2 ♘d7 12 0-0-0 c5 13 ♖dg1 += T.V.Petrosian-L.Aronson, USSR Ch., Moscow 1957) 8...f5 9 exf5 gxf5 10 ♘g5 ♕e7 11 f4 h6 12 ♘f3 ♘d7 13 ♗e3 += G.Kuzmin-A.Malashenko, Decin 1998.

A: 7...♘a6 *(D)*
The black knight heads for c5 to attack the e4-pawn. In comparison with

7...♘bd7 (line B), the c8-bishop is not obstructed. On the other hand, the knight can sometimes find itself out of the game after b2-b4.

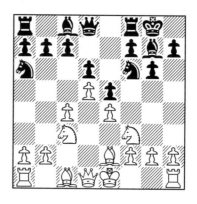

8 ♘d2

This looks best, after which the a6-knight remains isolated in many lines. White has also tried:

a) 8 ♗e3 ♘g4 9 ♗g5 f6 is obviously similar to line B1 (7...♘bd7 8 ♗e3) and will transpose if and when Black plays ...♘c5. One difference is that after 10 ♗h4 Black can consider ...♕e8, as the response ♘b5 would be pointless with the knight on a6; e.g. 10...♕e8 11 ♘d2 f5 12 a3 ♘f6 13 ♕c2 ♘c5 ∞ G.Orlov-L.Christiansen, New York Open 1990, or 10...♘h6 11 ♘d2 ♕e8 12 g4 c5 13 a3 ♕d7 14 h3 ♘f7 15 ♗d3 ♕d8 16 ♗g3 ♗h6 17 h4 ♗f4 18 ♘f1 ♗d7 19 ♕e2 ♕a5 20 ♖d1 ♖ab8 ∞ I.Radziewicz-I.Umanskaya, Koszalin 1998.

b) 8 ♗g5 is very logical, but Black has at least one forcing way to equalize: 8...h6 9 ♗h4 g5 10 ♗g3 ♘xe4 (the other plan is 10...♘h5 11 ♘d2 ♘f4 12 0-0 f5 13 exf5 ♘xe2+ 14 ♕xe2 ♗xf5 15 ♘de4 ♕e8 16 f3 ♕g6 with only a minimal edge for White, A.Ivanov-V.Savon, Ivano Frankovsk 1971) 11 ②xe4 f5 12 ②fd2 (Black has no problems after 12 ②c3 f4 13 ②d2 ②c5 14 ②de4 ②xe4 15 ②xe4 ♗f5 16 ♗d3 c6 17 0-0 cxd5 18 cxd5, A.Lugovoi-D.Jacimovic, Neum 2000, 18...♕b6 ∞) 12...fxe4 13 ②xe4 ♗f5 14 ♗d3 (or 14 ②c3 ②c5 15 0-0 a5 16 f3 e4 17 fxe4 ♗xe4 18 ♗f2 ♕e7 19 ♗d4 ½-½ Z.Rahman-J.Gallagher, British Ch. 2003) 14...g4! (now the subsequent ...h6-h5 will force f2-f3) 15 0-0 (or 15 a3 h5 16 f3 ♗xe4 17 ♗xe4 ②c5 ∞ H.Grooten-D.Brandenburg, Hoogeveen 2005) 15...h5 16 f3 ♗xe4 17 ♗xe4 ②c5 = I.Rogers-E.Mortensen, Vejstrup 1989.

8...h5

Preparing ...②h7. Black has tried numerous other moves, but White can hope for an advantage against all of them:

a) 8...♗h6 9 ②b3 (or 9 h4!? ②c5 – 7...②bd7 8 h4!? in the notes to line B) 9...♗xc1 10 ♕xc1 c6 11 0-0 cxd5 12 cxd5 ♗d7 13 ♕e3 ②e8 14 f4 +/- Y.Averbakh-Y.Sakharov, USSR Ch., Kiev 1964.

b) 8...♗d7 9 a3 c5 10 h4 h5 11 ②f3 ②c7 12 b4 b6 13 ②g5 ♕c8 14 ♗d2 += V.Malada-I.Saric, Velika Gorica 2006.

c) 8...c6 9 0-0 ♗d7 10 ②b3 cxd5 11 cxd5 ②e8 12 ♗e3 f5 13 exf5 gxf5 14 f4 += J.Alvarez del Monte-F.De la Paz, Santa Clara 1998.

d) 8...②e8 9 a3 (or 9 h4 f5 10 h5 ②f6 11 hxg6 hxg6 12 exf5 gxf5 13 g3 ②c5 14 ②b3 ②ce4 15 ②xe4 ②xe4 16 ♕c2 += S.Djuric-A.Correa, Novi Sad Olympiad 1990) 9...f5 10 0-0 ②f6 11 b4 c5 12 dxc6 bxc6 13 ♕a4 += A.Volzhin-M.Boehm, Graz 1999.

9 ②b3 *(D)*

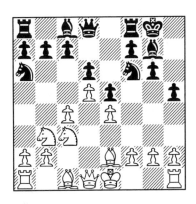

An interesting idea to control the c5-square. White can also count on better play after:

a) 9 h3 ②h7 10 g4 hxg4 11 hxg4 ♗f6 12 ②f1 ♗g5 13 ♗e3 ♕f6 (M.Stojanovic-Z.Arsovic, Belgrade 2002) 14 ♕d2 with the initiative.

b) 9 a3 c5 (otherwise after b2-b4 the a6-knight will be very restricted) 10 ♖b1 h4 (or 10...②c7 11 b4 b6 12 0-0 ②h7 13 ♕c2 += R.Kozlov-D.Brandenburg, World Junior Ch. 2006) 11 b4 ♗h6 12 ②f3 ♗xc1 13 ♖xc1 ♗g4 14 ♕g5 ♗xf3 15 ♗xf3 ♕e7 16 ♕xh4 ②xd5 17 ♕xe7 ②xe7 18 0-0 b6 19 ♖fd1 +/= M.Ivanov-M.Hebden, Cappelle la Grande 1995.

9...②c5

A rather naive response which doesn't turn out very well. 9...c5!? seems a better idea; e.g. 10 ♗g5 (or 10 dxc6 bxc6 11 0-0 ♖b8 12 ♗g5 ②c7 13 ②a5 ♕d7 14 ♖b1 ②e6 15 ♗e3 ②d4 ∞ Z.Hracek-R.Voigt, German League 2005) 10...♕e8 11 ②d2 (11 ♕d2!?) 11...②h7 12 ♗e3 h4 13 ②f3 ♕e7 when, rather than 14 g3?! h3 ∞ G.Lawton-M.Hebden, British Ch. 1995, White should play on the queenside after 14 a3!? +/=.

10 ♘xc5 dxc5 11 ♗g5

White is obviously better here.

11...a6 12 h3

Preparing to attack on the kingside. The simple 12 0-0 was also good.

12...♕d6 13 g4 ♘h7 14 ♗e3 h4 15 g5 b6 16 a4 f6 17 gxf6 ♕xf6 18 ♕d2 ♕d6 19 ♔d1 *(D)*

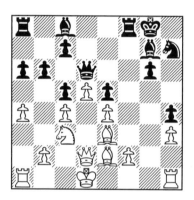

Securing the king on c2 while keeping his options open, though he could equally just attack on either side with advantage; e.g. 19 0-0-0 ♗d7 20 ♖dg1 (Tsesarsky) or 19 a5!?.

We have been following the game E.Vallejo Pons-J.Arizmendi Martinez, Spanish Junior Ch., Ayamonte 2002. Now, understandably gloomy about his long-term prospects, Black gave up the exchange, but ultimately to no avail: **19...♖f4?!** 20 ♔c2 [20 ♗xf4 exf4 21 ♔c2 is good for White in any case; e.g. 21...♘g5 22 ♗g4 ♗xc3 23 ♕xc3 ♘xe4 24 ♕e1 ♗xg4 25 hxg4 ♘g5 26 ♖a3 h3 27 f3 +/- Tsesarsky] **20...♗d7 21 ♖ag1 ♖af8 22 ♗xf4** [okay, if you insist] **22...exf4 23 ♗g4 ♗xg4 24 ♖xg4 g5 25**

♖hg1 ♕e5 26 d6 cxd6 27 ♕d5+ [simplifying to a won endgame] **27...♔h8** [27...♕xd5 28 ♘xd5 is much the same] **28 ♕xe5 ♗xe5 29 f3 ♖b8 30 b3 ♗g7?!** **31 ♖xh4 ♗d4 32 ♖g2 ♗e5 33 ♖hg4 ♔f7 34 h4 gxh4 35 ♖xh4 ♘f8 36 ♔d3 ♖b7 37 ♖h5 ♖b8 38 ♖f5+ ♔e6 39 ♘d5 1-0.**

B: 7...♘bd7 *(D)*

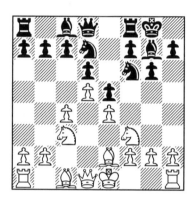

As with 7...♘a6 above, Black develops the queen's knight with an eye on c5, and at the same time plans to move the f6-knight and play ...f7-f5. The difference here is that the c8-bishop is blocked in, so lines with an early ...♗d7 are clearly impossible. On the other hand, the d7-knight can participate on either side of the board: on the queenside via c5 (as in line A), or on the kingside with a later ...♘df6.

B1: 8 ♗e3 *79*
B2: 8 ♗g5 *82*

It should be noted that 8 0-0 transposes directly into Chapter Seven (though 8 d5 is not the most testing move in that variation). Here White has also tried:

a) 8 b4?! is inaccurate due to 8...a5! (compare the Bayonet Attack where the black knight is on e7) 9 bxa5 (or 9 ♗a3 ♘h5 10 ♘d2 ♘f4 11 0-0 f5 -/+ H.Colpe-P.Gröppel, Hamburg 2001) 9...♘c5 10 ♕c2 ♖xa5 11 0-0 ♘h5 and Black is already better, A.Esparrago-J.Riveiro, Buenos Aires 1967.

b) 8 ♕c2 is a semi-useful move, defending e4 and keeping options open, including those of a kingside initiative and long castling. Black's best reply is 8...a5, securing c5 for his knight, when 9 ♗g5 h6 leads to a version of line C where the early ♕c2 is rather harmless (see also line A2 in Chapter Seven).

More interesting is 9 h3, preparing g2-g4 or ♗e3; e.g. 9...♘c5 (or 9...♘h5 10 g3 ♘c5 11 ♗e3; while if 9...c6 10 ♗e3 cxd5 11 cxd5 b6 12 0-0 ♘h5, L.Szabo-M.Najdorf, Budapest Candidates 1950, 13 a3 +=) 10 ♗e3 (10 g4 c6 11 ♗e3 a4 12 0-0-0 cxd5 13 cxd5 ♕a5 14 ♘d2 ♗d7 15 g5?! ♘fxe4! =+ L.Yurtaev-Y.Shulman, Vladivostok 1995) 10...♘h5 11 g3 f5 12 ♘d2 ♘f6 13 0-0-0 b6 14 ♖dg1 f4 15 ♗xc5 bxc5 16 g4 ♗d7 17 g5 ♘h5 18 ♗g4 += F.Vallejo Pons-T.Radjabov, Spanish Team Ch. 2005, but Black might try 12...♘a6!? and if 13 ♗xh5 f4!.

c) 8 h4!? ♘c5 9 ♘d2 ♗h6 (if 9...h5 10 b4 ♘a6 11 ♖b1 ♘g4 12 c5!? f5 13 cxd6! cxd6 14 ♘c4 fxe4 15 ♘xe4 ♗f5 16 ♗g5 ♕c7, I.Tsesarsky-I.Boim, Israeli Team Ch. 2000, 17 ♘cd2 ♖ac8 18 0-0 ♕d7 19 ♗xa6 bxa6 20 ♕e2 +/= Tsesarsky) 10 ♕c2 ♗g4 11 ♗xg4 ♘xg4 12 b4 ♘d7 13 ♘b3 ♗xc1 14 ♖xc1 f5 (or 14...♘gf6!? 15

♕d2 ♕e7 +/=) 15 h5 with the initiative, A.Aleksandrov-V.Dydyshko, 4th matchgame, Minsk 1992. Black should probably prefer 9...a5 transposing 8 h4 in line C (see note 'd1').

d) 8 ♘d2 a5 9 h4 ♘c5 leads to the same line; or if 9...h5 10 ♘f3 ♘c5 11 ♗g5 (11 ♘g5 c6 12 f3 ♕b6 13 ♖b1 cxd5 14 cxd5 ♗d7 15 ♗e3 ♖fc8 16 ♕d2 a4 17 0-0, E.Sazhin-N.Nikolaev, St Petersburg 2000, 17...♕a5 ∞) 11...c6 12 ♘d2 ♕e8 (12...♕b6!?) 13 f3 ♗d7 14 ♘b3 ♘xb3 15 ♕xb3 ♗c8 16 ♕a3 c5 17 ♘b5 ♕d7 18 0-0-0 +/= I.V.Ivanov-D.Anagnostopoulos, London Lloyds Bank 1987. White has also tried 9 ♕c2 ♘c5 10 ♘b3!?, e.g. 10...b6 11 ♘xc5 bxc5 12 a4 ♘d7 13 h4 ♘b8 14 h5 ♘a6 15 ♘a2 f5 16 hxg6 hxg6 17 ♕c3 (L.Portisch-M.Bobotsov, Moscow 1967) 17...fxe4 18 ♗e3 c6 19 0-0-0 ∞; and 9 g4!? ♘c5 (better 9...♗h6 10 h4 ♗f4 ∞ Kochiev) 10 h4 h5 11 gxh5 ♘xh5 (if 11...gxh5 12 ♖g1 with the initiative Tyomkin) 12 ♘b3 ♘f4 13 ♘xc5 dxc5 14 ♗f3 += D.Hergott-B.Kiviaho, North Bay 1997.

B1: 8 ♗e3 *(D)*

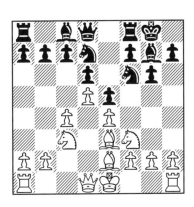

8...♘g4 *(D)*

The standard move, attacking the bishop of freeing the f-pawn to advance. Other continuations allow White to play ♘d2 with advantage:

a) 8...h6 9 ♘d2 ♘e8 10 g4!? ♘c5 (10...c5!? +=) 11 f3 a5 12 h4 ♗f6 13 ♗f2 ♘g7 14 ♕c2 ♗e7 15 0-0-0 f5 16 gxf5 gxf5 17 ♗xc5 dxc5 18 f4! +/- H.Grooten-S.Salov, Liechtenstein 1995.

b) 8...♘h5 9 g3! ♘df6 10 h3 ♘e8 (L.Konings-R.Verdonk, Dutch Team Ch. 1995) 11 ♘d2 +=.

c) 8...a5 9 ♘d2 ♘c5 10 a3 ♗d7 11 b4 axb4 12 axb4 ♖xa1 13 ♕xa1 ♘a6 14 c5! ♘g4 15 ♗xg4 ♗xg4 16 c6 +/= H.Banikas-K.Amendola, Aegina 1996.

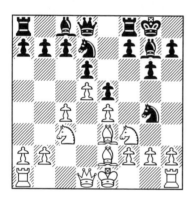

9 ♗g5

9 ♗d2 f5!? comes to the same thing. Otherwise Black can play 9...a5 10 h3 ♘gf6, when 11 ♗g5!? (Zvjaginsev) 11...♘c5 or 11...h6 12 ♗e3 ♘c5 transposes to 7...a5 8 h3 ♘a6 9 ♗g5 in the notes to C1.

9...f6 10 ♗d2

The most frequent continuation here is 10 ♗h4 ♘h6 (if 10...h5 11 ♘d2! ♘h6 12 f3 ♘f7 13 ♕c2 ♗h6 14 ♗f2! a5

15 0-0-0 ♘c5 16 ♔b1 ♗d7 17 ♘b3! +/= F.Gheorghiu-R.Kraut, Berlin 1988; instead 10...g5! 11 ♗g3 ♘h6 transposes to the line 7 ♗e3 ♘g4 8 ♗g5 f6 9 ♗h4 g5 – see line F21 in Chapter Three) 11 ♘d2 *(D)* (if 11 h3 a5 12 ♘d2 ♘c5 13 f3 ♗d7 14 b3 ♔h8 15 a3 ♕e8 = R.Markus-L.Vajda, Hungarian Team Ch. 2006) and then:

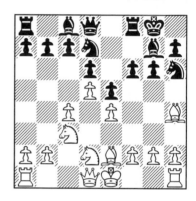

a) 11...g5! (the most energetic move) 12 ♗g3 again transposes to F21 in Chapter Three.

b) 11...♘f7 12 0-0 ♗h6 13 b4 ♗g5 (13...a5!?) 14 ♗xg5 fxg5 15 ♗g4 h5 16 ♗e6 ♔g7 17 c5 dxc5 18 ♗xd7 ♗xd7 19 bxc5 ♕e7 20 ♘b3 +/= R.Pogorelov-E.Ragozin, Linares 1994.

c) 11...a5 12 a3 ♘c5!? 13 b4 axb4 14 axb4 ♖xa1 15 ♕xa1 (R.Pogorelov-M.Todorcevic, Saragossa 1994) 15...♘xe4!? 16 ♘dxe4 ♘f5 17 ♗g3 ♘d4 18 ♕c1 f5 19 ♘g5 f4 20 ♗h4 h6 21 ♘h7 ♕xh4 22 ♘xf8 ♔xf8 with compensation.

10...f5 *(D)*

Now 10...♘h6 is met by the strong 11 h4!, e.g. 11...f5 12 ♗g5 (12 h5!?) 12...♘f6 13 h5 ♘f7 14 hxg6 hxg6 15

♕d2 ♘xg5 16 ♘xg5 ♘xe4 17 ♘cxe4 fxe4 18 ♘xe4 ♖f4 19 ♗d3 ♖h4 (J.Piket-B.Socko, European Ch., Ohrid 2001) 20 0-0-0! ♗f5 (not 20...♗h6?? 21 ♕xh6 ♖xh6 22 ♖xh6 +-) 21 ♕e2 +=.

But as usual 10...a5 is a valid alternative; e.g. 11 0-0 (or if 11 a3 ♘c5 12 b4 axb4 13 axb4 ♖xa1 14 ♕xa1 ♘b3 15 ♕a3 ♘xd2 16 ♘xd2 ♘h6 17 c5 f5 with a good game for Black, A.Gutov-A.Petrushin, Russian Club Cup 1998) 11...♘c5 12 ♘e1 f5 13 f3 ♘f6 14 exf5 gxf5 15 ♗e3 ♗d7 ∞ D.Muse-C.Syre, German League 1999.

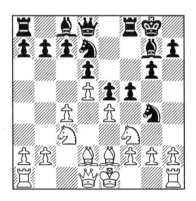

11 ♘g5
After 11 exf5 Black can choose between:

a) 11...gxf5 12 ♘g5 ♘c5 13 h3 (if 13 ♕c2 h6 14 ♗xg4 hxg5 15 ♗e2 =, or 13 b4 e4! 14 bxc5 e3 ∞) 13...♘f6 14 b4 ♘a6 15 g4 ♕e8 16 ♖g1 ♔h8 17 gxf5 ♗xf5 18 a3 c6 19 ♗e3 ½-½ V.Zvjaginsev-A.Shchekachev, St Petersburg 1994.

b) 11...♘c5!? 12 ♗g5 (or 12 0-0 ♖xf5!, C.Gabriel-K.Kachiani Gersinska, German League 1997, and if 13 b4 e4 14 bxc5 exf3 15 ♗xf3 ♘e5 16 ♗e4 ♖h5 ∞) 12...♕d7 13 h3 ♘xf2 14 ♔xf2

(V.Zvjaginsev-S.Dyachkov, Russian Ch. 1995) and now 14...♕xf5! 15 ♗e3 (or 15 ♔e1 e4 16 g4 ♕f7 17 ♘h2 ♘d3+ 18 ♔d2 ♘f2 19 ♕f1 b5 with an attack) 15...e4 16 ♔g1 exf3 17 ♗xf3 ♗d7 with an initiative.

11...♘c5 *(D)*

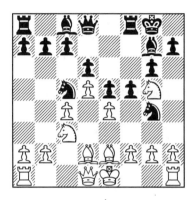

Here the knight attacks e4 and protects the e6-square as well.

11...♘df6 is less good, as after 12 exf5 (or 12 f3 ♘h6 13 0-0 +=) 12...gxf5 13 h3 ♘h6 the black knights are uncoordinated, which White can exploit with g2-g4; e.g.

a) 14 ♕c2 f4 (if 14...♕e7 15 g4! ♘f7 16 0-0-0 +/- A.Poluljahov-S.Nadyrhanov, Krasnodar 1995, or 14...e4 15 0-0-0 ♘f7 16 ♘e6! ♗xe6 17 dxe6 ♘e5 18 g4 +/- Belov) 15 ♗d3! ♘xd5 16 ♘xd5 ♕xg5 17 ♘xc7 ♖b8 18 g4 +/- R.Markus-M.Paragua, Calvia Olympiad 2004.

b) 14 g4!? may be even stronger: 14...fxg4 (not 14...♔h8? 15 ♘e5 ♗xe6 16 g5 +- P.Motwani-W.Hendriks, Vlissingen 1996) 15 hxg4 (P.Motwani-K.Van der Weide, Sas van Gent 1996) and if 15...♘hxg4 16 f3 ♘h6 17 ♗d3 ♘f5

(Zvjaginsev) then 18 ♘e2 with a clear advantage, e.g. 18...h6 19 ♘e6 ♗xe6 20 dxe6 ♘h7 21 ♕c2 ♕f6 22 0-0-0, or 18...♘d4 19 ♘xd4 exd4 20 ♕e2 ♖e8 21 ♘e6 ♗xe6 22 dxe6 ♕e7 23 ♗f5 +/-.

12 b4

If 12 f3 ♗h6!? is unclear; while 12 exf5? now runs into 12...♘xf2! 13 ♔xf2 ♖xf5+ 14 ♔g1 e4! with a strong attack.

12...fxe4 13 ♘cxe4

If 13 0-0 e3! 14 ♗xg4 exd2 15 ♗xc8 ♕xg5 16 bxc5 ♖axc8 17 ♘e4 (J.Goormachtigh-D.Taboas Rodriguez, Benidorm 2006) 17...♕h4! 18 ♕e2 dxc5 19 ♘xc5 ♗h6 20 ♘xb7 ♕d4 =+, or 15 ♘xh7 ♗xg4 16 ♕xg4 (T.Wiley-V.Rojicek, Frydek Mistek 2007) 16...♖f4! 17 ♕xg6 ♕e8 and if 18 ♕c2 ♖xc4 19 bxc5 e4 =+.

13...♘xe4 14 ♘xe4 ♗f5!?

After 14...♘f6 15 ♘xf6+ ♗xf6 16 0-0 ♗g5 17 ♗c3 ♖f7 18 a4 ♗f5 19 a5 White ground out a win in A.Miles-B.Valensi, Kusadasi 1990.

15 ♗xg4 ♗xe4 16 0-0 *(D)*

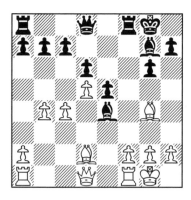

Black can be content with the outcome of the opening and in A.Belozerov-D.Abashev, Novosibirsk

2001, the players agreed a draw here. Nevertheless, there is plenty of play left in the position; in particular White can still hope to make progress on the queenside.

M.Zivanic-I.Martic, Belgrade 2007, continued **16...♕h4 17 ♖c1 ♖ae8** [17...♗f5 =] **18 ♗e3 ♔h8 19 ♗d7 ♖e7 20 ♗e6 ♗f5 21 ♕d2 h6 22 c5 a6 23 g3 ♕h3 24 ♖c4 e4?** [24...g5 ∞] **25 ♖xe4! ♖xe6 26 ♖xe6** [26 ♖h4!?] **26...♗g4 27 f3 ♗xe6 28 dxe6 ♕xe6 29 ♗xh6 ♗xh6 30 ♕xh6+ ♔g8 31 cxd6 cxd6 32 ♕d2** and with a clear extra pawn in the endgame White went on to win: **32...♖e8 33 ♖d1 ♖d8 34 ♖e1 ♕f7 35 ♕d4 d5 36 ♔g2 ♖c8 37 ♖e2 ♖c4 38 ♕e5 ♖c8 39 ♕d6 ♖f8 40 f4 ♖c8 41 ♖d2 ♖c6 42 ♕xd5 ♕xd5+ 43 ♖xd5 ♖c2+ 44 ♔h3 ♔f7 45 ♖d7+ ♔e6 46 ♖xb7 ♖xa2 47 ♖b6+ ♔f5 48 ♖c6 ♖a4 49 ♖c5+ ♔e4 50 b5 ♖a5 51 ♖e5+ ♔f3 52 b6 ♖a2 53 ♖g5 ♖b2 54 ♖xg6 a5 55 ♖c6 a4 56 ♖c3+ 1-0.**

B2: 8 ♗g5 *(D)*

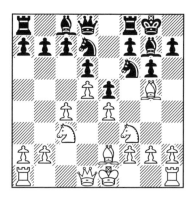

The typical move in White's strategy, developing the bishop before reorganizing with ♘d2, while interfering

with Black's counterplay on the king-side by preventing the withdrawal of the f6-knight, albeit temporarily.

8...h6

As in line B1, if White is allowed to play ♘d2 with impunity he has good chances of an advantage; e.g. 8...a5 9 ♘d2 h6 10 ♗e3 ♘e8 11 ♕c2 f5 12 f3 ♘c5 13 ♘b3 b6 14 ♘xc5 bxc5 15 0-0-0 ♕e7 16 ♗d3 f4 17 ♗d2 += F.Visier Se-govia-A.Olsson, Lugano Olympiad 1968, or 8...a6 9 ♘d2 c6 10 0-0 ♕c7 11 ♖c1 c5 12 a3 b6 13 b4 h6 14 ♗e3 ♘h7 15 ♔h1 f5 16 exf5 gxf5 17 f4 +/= A.Gokhale-P.Lakshmi, Commonwealth Ch., Mumbai 2004.

9 ♗h4

The most consistent retreat, main-taining the pin on the f6-knight. Other moves are inferior:

a) 9 ♗e3?! ♘g4 10 ♗d2 f5 11 h3 ♘gf6 12 exf5 gxf5 13 0-0 ♘c5 14 ♘e1 f4 with an excellent game for Black, P.Baixes-J.Jordan, corr. 1984.

b) 9 ♗d2 ♘c5 10 ♕c2 ♘fxe4! (this motif is worth remembering; Black eas-ily regains the piece and obtains a bet-ter position) 11 ♘xe4 ♗f5 12 ♗d3 ♗xe4 13 ♗xe4 f5 14 ♗xf5 ♖xf5 =/+ J.Zamudio-L.Olivieri, corr. 2000.

c) 9 ♗xf6 ♕xf6 10 0-0 a5 intending ...♘c5 also with excellent play for Black, D.Gunter-M.Oratovsky, Lisbon 2001.

9...g5

Black must undertake some meas-ures to unpin. The text is the simplest and most radical method, though it is also weakens the light squares on the kingside. Other plans are:

a) 9...a5!? 10 0-0 generally trans-poses elsewhere: 10...g5 11 ♗g3 ♘h5 12 ♘d2 ♘f4 is the note with 12...a5 below; while 10...♘c5 reaches line C2 (note 'c' to Black's 10th move).

b) 9...♖e8!? 10 ♘d2 (also possible is 10 0-0 ♘f8 11 ♘e1!? g5 12 ♗g3 ♘g6 13 ♘c2 intending 14 ♘e3 += Graf) 10...♘f8 11 f3!? (if 11 0-0 g5 12 ♗g3 ♘g6 13 b4 a5, A.Inants-A.Topuridze, Batumi 2003, 14 a3 h5 15 f3 ♘f4 with mutual chances) 11...c5 (11...c6!?) 12 a3 b6 13 b4 (A.Graf-L.Yurtaev, Bishkek 1993) and now 13...♕d7!? intending ...♘h5, ...f5 with counterplay.

c) 9...a6 prevents ♘b5 in advance of ...♕e8, but it's a bit slow: 10 ♘d2 ♕e8 11 0-0 ♘h7 12 b4 ♘g5 (or 12...♗f6 13 ♗xf6 ♘hxf6 14 ♘b3 ♕e7 15 ♕d2 ♔h7 16 ♕e3 ♘g8 17 c5 +/- M.Tal-R.Fischer, Candidates Tournament, Bled 1959) 13 f3 f5 14 ♖c1 ♕e7 15 ♔h1 ♘f6 16 c5 ♘h5 17 c6! b6 18 exf5 gxf5 19 g3 +/- intend-ing f3-f4, T.V.Petrosian-S.Gligoric, Candidates Tournament, Belgrade 1959.

10 ♗g3 ♘h5 *(D)*

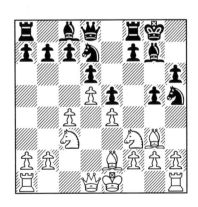

Black takes the opportunity (i.e. before White plays ♘d2) to post his knight most actively, targeting the f4-square or the g3-bishop, while making way for ...f7-f5. Other moves allow White a small advantage; in particular the exchanging operation with ...♘xe4 does not give Black full equality here:

a) 10...♘xe4 11 ♘xe4 f5 12 ♘fd2 fxe4 13 ♘xe4 ♘f6 14 ♗d3 ♘xe4 15 ♗xe4 g4 16 ♕d3 += A.Mikhalchishin-Z.Kovacs, Debrecen 1967.

b) 10...♘c5 11 ♘d2 ♘fxe4 12 ♘dxe4 ♘xe4 13 ♘xe4 f5 14 f3 fxe4 15 fxe4 c6 16 ♕d2 c5 17 0-0-0 ♗d7 18 ♖df1 += T.Tomasevic-D.Rancic, Nis 1995.

c) 10...a5 11 ♘d2 ♘c5 (or if 11...c6 12 0-0 cxd5 13 cxd5 ♘c5, M.Tal-W.Pietzsch, Riga 1959, 14 f3 intending ♗f2 += Karpov) 12 0-0 ♘fxe4 13 ♘dxe4 ♘xe4 14 ♘xe4 f5 15 f3 fxe4 16 fxe4 ♖xf1+ 17 ♗xf1 g4 18 ♕d2 h5 19 ♗f2 b6 20 ♗e2 ♗d7, P.Heitland-A.Altunbas, Dortmund 1987, 21 ♗e3 +=.

Here White has a decision to make: to attack the kingside pawn structure immediately with h2-h4; or to castle short and try to take over the light squares after the inevitable ...f7-f5.

11 ♘d2

11 0-0 ♘f4! 12 ♘d2 transposes to the text. If instead 12 ♘e1 ♘xe2+! 13 ♕xe2 f5 14 exf5 ♘f6 15 f3 (or 15 ♘c2 ♗xf5 16 ♘e3 ♗g6 17 c5 ♘h5 ∞ I.Vistaneckis-D.Lapienis, Palanga 1961) 15...♗xf5 16 ♘d3 ♕e8 17 ♘f2 ♕g6 (B.Wexler-R.Fischer, Mar del Plata 1960) 18 ♘ce4 ♘xe4 19 fxe4 ♗d7 20 ♘d3 = Boleslavsky.

The main alternative is 11 h4 *(D)* and then:

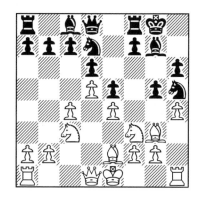

a) 11...♘f4?! (allowing the opening of the h-file, when the white rook is on it, looks suspicious) 12 hxg5 hxg5 13 ♕c2! ♘xg2+ 14 ♔d2 g4 15 ♖ag1! gxf3 16 ♗xf3 ♘f4 17 ♗xf4 exf4 18 e5 f5 19 exf6 ♘xf6 20 ♕g6 ♖f7 (20...♕e7 21 ♘e4 ♗d7 22 ♖h6 ♗g4 23 ♖gh1 ♗h5 24 ♖1xh5 1-0 I.Kanko-N.Littlewood, Havana Olympiad 1966) 21 ♘e4 c5 22 ♖h8+ ♔xh8 23 ♕xf7 ♕g8 24 ♖h1+ ♘h7 25 ♕h5 ♗d7 26 ♘g5 ♗e8 27 ♕h2 ♗g6 28 ♘xh7 ♕xh7 29 ♕f4 +/-.

b) 11...♘xg3 12 fxg3 g4 13 ♘h2 h5 14 0-0 transposes to line 'c', but this move order allows White to keep his knight in the centre with 13 ♘d2, e.g. 13...h5 14 0-0 f5 (or 14...♗h6 15 ♗d3 ♘f6 16 ♕e2 ♘e8 17 ♖f2 ♘g7 18 ♖af1 += V.Hort,V-J.Bednarski, Kecskemet 1964) 15 exf5 ♘c5 16 ♘de4 ♗xf5 17 ♘xc5 dxc5 18 ♗d3 += J.Garcia Padron-A.Rodriguez Aguilera, Ponferrada 1992.

c) 11...g4 12 ♘h2! (if now 12 ♘d2 ♘df6! 13 ♘f1 ♘f4 ∞ V.Babula-R.Kempinski, Pardubice 1994) 12...♘xg3 (12...f5 13 exf5 ♘xg3 14 fxg3 h5 15 0-0 ♘c5 transposes to 'c2'; less good is 14...♘c5 15 ♘xg4! ♗xf5 16 0-0 ♕e7 17

♕d2 ♗xg4 18 ♗xg4 e4 19 ♖xf8+! ♖xf8 20 ♖e1 ♕e5 21 ♔h2, E.Bukic-S.Gligoric, Budva 1967, 21...♖e8 22 ♕e3 +/= Karpov) 13 fxg3 h5 14 0-0 *(D)* is the critical line:

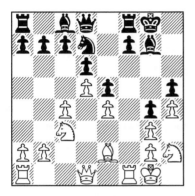

c1) 14...a5 15 ♖f5!? (if 15 ♗d3 ♘c5 16 ♖f2!? f5 17 exf5 e4, D.Monell Camarasa-R.Gonzalez Davila, Calvia Olympiad 2004, 18 ♘xe4 ♗d4 19 ♘xg4 ♘xd3 20 ♕xd3 ♗xf2+ 21 ♘gxf2 ♗xf5 ∞) 15...♘f6 (Black is not obliged to play this, having 15...♗h6!? and if 16 ♖xh5 ♗e3+ 17 ♔h1 ♘f6 18 ♕d3 ♗f4 19 ♖f5 ♗xf5 20 gxf4 ♘xe4 21 ♘xe4 ♗xe4 22 ♕xe4 f5 23 ♕e3 ♕xh4 24 g3 ∞) 16 ♖f2 ♗h6 17 ♘f1 ♘d7 18 ♗d3 ♘c5 19 ♕e2 (if 19 ♗c2 c6 20 ♕e2 ♕b6 21 ♖b1 ♗d7 ∞ A.Capoccia-M.Baviera, corr. 2000) 19...♘xd3 20 ♕xd3 (A.Yusupov-A.Correa, World Student Team Ch. 1985) and now 20...f5 21 exf5 e4! 22 ♕d4 ♗xf5 23 ♘e3 = Yusupov.

c2) 14...f5 15 exf5 ♘c5 16 b4 e4 (or if 16...♘a6!?, F.Handke-B.Socko, Groningen 1998, then 17 ♕b1 e4 18 f6 ♖xf6 19 ♕xe4 ♘xb4 ∞) 17 ♖c1 (another option is 17 f6!?, S.Estremera Panos-A.Mista, European Ch., Dresden 2007, and if

17...♗xf6 18 ♕c2 ♘d7 19 ♖ad1 +=, e.g. 19...♗xc3 20 ♕xc3 ♘e5 21 ♖xf8+ ♕xf8 22 ♕e3) 17...♘a6 (the brave 17...♘d3 does not look good after 18 ♗xd3 exd3 19 f6! ♖xf6 20 ♕xd3 ♕f8 21 ♘b5 ♗f5 22 ♖xf5 ♖xf5 23 ♘xc7 ♖c8 24 ♘e6 with more than enough compensation for the exchange, V.Kramnik-G.Kasparov, Linares 1994) 18 f6 ♖xf6 19 ♘xe4 ♖xf1+ 20 ♘xf1 ♘xb4 21 ♕d2 ♕e7 22 ♘g5 (G.Vescovi-T.Manhardt, World Junior Ch. 1995) and now 22...♗f5 ∞.

c3) 14...♗h6 15 ♗xg4!? (this intuitive sacrifice is difficult to assess, but we think it is rather doubtful; but if 15 ♗d3 c6 16 ♔h1 ♕b6 17 ♕e2 ♕e3! 18 ♕xe3 ♗xe3 19 ♖ae1 ♗d4 20 ♖f5 f6 -/+ F.Balabaev-R.Sakic, corr. 2003; White cannot play 21 ♖xh5? due to 21...♘c5 22 ♗c2 ♔g7 and ...♔g6 catches the rook) 15...hxg4 16 ♘xg4 ♗g7 and now B.Ivkov-E.Gufeld, Belgrade 1988, saw 17 ♘e3 (also possible are 17 ♕f3, A.Heyns-S.Bouaziz, Lugano Olympiad 1968, 17...♘c5 18 ♘e3 a5 19 ♖ad1!? ∞ Milic, and 17 ♖f5 ♘f6!? 18 ♘xf6+ ♗xf6 19 ♖h5!? ∞ Milic) 17...c6 18 ♘f5 ♘f6 19 g4 cxd5? 20 g5 ♘xe4 21 ♘xd5 ♗xf5 22 ♖xf5 ♖c8 23 ♕e2 ♘g3 24 ♕g4 ♖xc4 25 ♕xg3 +=. Gufeld suggests 19...♗d7 20 g5 ♘h7, but after 21 ♕h5 White has a very strong, if not decisive attack. Therefore Black should play actively with 19...♕b6+, e.g. 20 ♔h1 ♗xf5 (not 20...cxd5? 21 g5! +-) 21 ♖xf5 ♕xb2 with good chances to parry White's attack and win.

11...♘f4 12 0-0 *(D)*

12 ♗f1 f5 13 f3 is too passive: 13...♘c5 14 ♕c2 c6!? 15 ♗f2 fxe4 16

♘dxe4 =, while 16 fxe4?? (M.Najdorf-R.Byrne, Buenos Aires 1964) loses to 16...♘cd3+! 17 ♗xd3 ♘xg2+ 18 ♔d1 (if 18 ♔f1 ♘e3+ or 18 ♔e2 ♗g4+) 18...♖xf2 -+ Ftacnik.

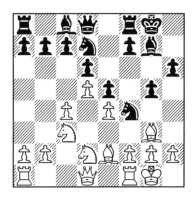

12...f5

Black has also tried:

a) 12...♘xe2+ 13 ♕xe2 f5 14 f3! f4 15 ♗f2 ♘f6 (E.Toniutti-S.Mareco, Argentine Junior Ch. 2002) 16 c5!? ♖f7 17 ♘c4 ♗f8 18 cxd6 cxd6 19 ♘b5 +=.

b) 12...♘c5 13 ♗g4 ♘xe4 (13...a5 is line 'c') 14 ♘dxe4 f5 15 f3 fxg4 16 fxg4 ♕e8 (K.Wesseln-R.Byrne, Reykjavik 1984) 17 h3 ♕g6 18 ♕d2 += Timoshchenko.

c) 12...a5 13 ♗g4 ♘c5 14 ♗xc8 (if 14 f3 ♘cd3 15 ♕c2 c6 with counterplay, T.V.Petrosian-J.Yukhtman, USSR Ch., Tbilisi 1959) 14...♕xc8 15 ♕c2 (H.Hornung-K.Schleupner, Krumbach 1981) 15...♕d7 ∞.

13 exf5 ♘xe2+

This makes sense once White has opened up the light squares with e4xf5. Black gains the bishop pair and will never have to worry about ♗g4, and plans ...♘f6, ...♗xf5 and ...♕e8-g6 with equality.

The careless 13...♘f6 allows 14 ♗xf4! exf4 15 g4 and Black does not have full compensation for the pawn, e.g. 15...fxg3 16 fxg3 c6 (or 16...♕e7 17 ♕c2 ♗d7 18 ♖ae1 +/- O.Bazan-J.Behrensen, Argentine Ch. 1960) 17 ♘b3 ♕b6+ 18 ♔g2 ♗d7 19 g4 +/- V.Hort-I.Nemet, Vinkovci 1976.

14 ♕xe2 ♘f6

Obviously the f5-pawn should be recaptured by the bishop. If 14...♖xf5?! 15 ♖ac1 ♘f8 16 ♘de4 ♘g6 17 c5 +/= M.Socko-A.Safranska, Frydek-Mistek 1997.

15 ♘de4

The other plan is 15 c5 ♗xf5 16 ♖ac1, and now 16...♕d7!? looks like a good move (rather than 16...dxc5 17 ♕c4 += V.Smyslov-P.Benko, Candidates Tournament, Zagreb 1959), e.g. 17 ♖fd1 ♗g6 18 ♘de4 ♘h5 19 f3 ♘xg3 20 hxg3 ½-½ B.Potratz-N.Bensiek, corr. 1991.

15...♗xf5 16 f3 *(D)*

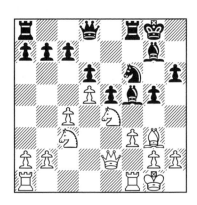

Black equalizes after 16 ♖ae1 ♕e8 17 ♘xf6+ ♗xf6 18 ♘e4 ♕g6 19 f3 b6 20 h3 ♗e7 21 ♗f2 ♕e8 22 ♗e3 ½-½

P.Clarke-A.Matanovic, Budapest 1960, or similarly 16 ♖ad1 ♕e7 17 ♘xf6+ ♕xf6 18 ♘e4 ♕g6 = Lim Kok Ann-R.Belkadi, Lugano Olympiad 1968.

16...♕e8

Black continues with his plan outlined above, though he has also tried:

a) 16...♘h5 17 ♗f2 ♘f4 18 ♕d2 (A.Garcia-J.Nunez, Uruguayan Ch. 1985) when 18...♕e8 and ...♕g6 again offers good counterplay.

b) 16...b6 17 b4 a5 18 a3 ♘h5 19 ♗f2 ♘f4 20 ♕d2 ♕e8 21 ♗e3 ♕g6 (intending ...g5-g4) 22 g4!? (a radical solution) 22...♗d7 23 c5 axb4 24 axb4 ♖xa1 25 ♖xa1 bxc5 26 bxc5 h5 27 ♗xf4! exf4 28 c6 ♗xg4!? 29 fxg4 hxg4 30 ♖a7!? (30 ♖a4 was objectively better), and now rather than 30...f3?? 31 ♖xc7 +- J.Speelman-V.Topalov, Moscow rapid 1995, Black should have played 30...♖e8! when 31 ♖xc7?! (31 ♖a4) 31...♖xe4 32 ♘xe4 ♕xe4 33 ♖xg7+ ♔xg7 34 ♕c3+ ♔f7! 35 c7 ♕b1+ lead to a draw, e.g. 36 ♔f2 ♕a2+ 37 ♔e1 f3! 38 ♕d3! (not 38 ♔d1? ♕e2+ 39 ♔c1 f2 -+) 38...♕a5+ 39 ♔d1 ♕a1+ = Speelman (but not 39...♕xc7?? 40 ♕h7+).

17 c5

If 17 ♗f2 b6 (or just 17...♕g6 =) 18 b4 a5 19 a3 ♕g6 20 c5 axb4 21 axb4 ♖xa1 22 ♖xa1 bxc5 23 bxc5 g4 with counterplay, M.Kozlov-A.Klobukov, St Petersburg 2007.

17...♕g6 18 cxd6 cxd6 19 ♖fc1

Not 19 ♘xd6?! ♗d3 20 ♕xe5 ♘e8 21 ♕e6+ ♕xe6 22 dxe6 ♗xf1 23 ♔xf1 ♗xc3 24 bxc3 ♘xd6 25 ♗xd6 ♖f6 -/+.

19...♖ad8 20 ♘xf6+ ♗xf6 21 ♘e4 ♖d7 *(D)*

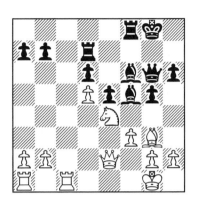

Black is fine here. A.Kharitonov-A.Khruschiov, Moscow 2002, concluded **22 ♘xf6+ ♕xf6 23 ♕e3 a6 24 ♖c4 ♕d8 25 ♕d2 ♖df7 26 ♖ac1 h5 27 h4?** [27 ♗f2] **27...♖g7?** [27...b5! takes over the initiative, e.g. 28 ♖b4 a5 29 ♖xb5 gxh4 30 ♗f2 h3] **28 hxg5 ♕xg5 29 ♕xg5 ♖xg5 30 ♔h2 ♖f7 31 ♗h4 ♖g6 32 a3 ♖fg7 33 g3 ♗f7 34 ♔g2 ♗d3 35 ♖c8+ ♔h7 36 ♖e8 ♗e2 37 ♖c3 ♖g8 38 ♖e7 ♖gf8 39 ♔f2 ♗d1 40 ♔e1 ♖xe7 41 ♗xe7 ♖f7 42 ♗xd6 ½-½.**

C: 7...a5 *(D)*

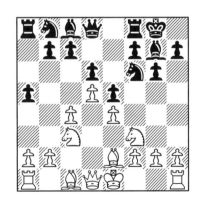

This the most popular move, by which Black prevents b2-b4 and stabilizes the future position of his knight on c5. White has two main replies:

C1: 8 h3 *89*
C2: 8 ♗g5 *90*

Most other continuations lead to unclear positions; e.g.

a) 8 ♕c2 ♘a6 9 0-0 ♘h5 (9...♘c5 transposes to line A2 in Chapter Seven) 10 g3 f5 11 exf5 ♗xf5 12 ♕d1 ♘f6 13 ♗e3 ♕d7 14 ♘h4 ♗h3 15 ♘g2 ♖ae8 ∞ I.Miladinovic-M.Markovic, Yugoslav Team Ch. 1992.

b) 8 0-0 ♘a6 9 ♘e1 (9 ♗g5 h6 10 ♗h4 transposes to line C2) 9...♘c5 10 f3 ♘h5 11 ♗e3 ♘f4 12 ♘d3 ♕g5 13 ♘xf4 exf4 14 ♗d4 ♗d7 15 ♗xg7 ♔xg7 16 ♕d4+ f6 ∞ A.Stubljar-V.Srebrnic, Ljubljana 2005.

c) 8 ♗e3 ♘g4 (also good is 8...♘a6 9 0-0 ♘h5!? 10 g3 f5 11 exf5 ♗xf5 12 ♘g5 ♘f6 13 g4 ♗d7 14 ♘ge4 ∞ J.Speelman-M.Hebden, Leeds 1990) 9 ♗g5 f6 10 ♗h4 (or 10 ♗d2 f5 11 exf5 gxf5 12 ♘g5 ♘f6 13 f4 h6 14 ♘h3 ♘e4! with counterplay, D.Solak-S.Bogner, European Ch., Dresden 2007) 10...♘a6 (or 10...h5 11 ♘d2 ♘h6 12 h3 ♘a6 13 0-0 ♗d7 14 f3 ♘f7 15 a3 ♗h6 ∞ M.Perasin-M.Chovanec, Tatranske Zruby 2006) 11 ♘d2 h5! 12 a3 ♗d7 13 0-0 ♕e7 (or 13...♕e8 14 h3 ♘h6 15 b3 f5 16 f3 ♔h8 17 ♖b1 ♖g8 18 g4 ♘f7 ½-½ T.V.Petrosian-E.Geller, Sochi 1977) 14 ♖b1 ♘c5! 15 b4 axb4 16 axb4 ♘a4 17 ♘xa4 ♖xa4 18 h3 ♘h6 19 f3 (J.Speelman-J.Piket, Tilburg 1992) 19...♖fa8 = Speelman.

d) 8 h4!? ♘a6 9 ♘d2 *(D)* is more interesting:

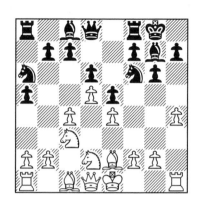

d1) 9...♘c5 10 h5 c6!? 11 g4 a4!? (or 11...♕b6 12 f3 ♗d7 13 ♘f1 cxd5 14 cxd5 ♖fc8 ∞ A.Aleksandrov-R.Leitao, Yerevan Olympiad 1996) 12 ♖b1 (if 12 g5 ♘xh5 13 ♗xh5 ♘d3+ 14 ♔f1 ♕b6 15 ♖h2, A.Aleksandrov-V.Kotronias, European Team Ch., Pula 1997, then 15...a3! intending 16 b3 ♕d4 17 ♘db1 ♘xc1 18 ♕xc1 gxh5 -/+ Huzman) 12...♕a5 13 f3 ♘e8 14 ♕c2 (D.Herder-E.McNaughton, American Open 1996) 14...♘f6!? 15 b4 axb3 16 ♘xb3 ♘xb3 17 axb3 ♕d8 ∞.

d2) 9...c6 10 h5 cxd5 (or 10...♗d7!? 11 g4 cxd5 12 cxd5 b5 13 ♘xb5 ♘xg4 14 ♘c3 ♘f6 15 ♘c4 ♕c7 16 ♗e3 ♖fc8 17 hxg6 fxg6 18 ♖c1 ♘c5 19 ♖h4 h5 20 f3 ♔f7 21 ♕d2 ♗e8 22 ♔f2 a4 ∞ ½-½ V.Savon-G.Timoshenko, St Petersburg 1996) 11 cxd5 ♘c5 12 g4 b5 13 a3!? ♕b6! 14 f3!? ♗d7! 15 ♘b3 b4 16 ♘xc5 (I.Tsesarsky-Ma.Tseitlin, Givataim 2000) and now if 16...♕xc5 17 ♘a4 ♕a7 18 b3 with counterplay (Tsesarsky).

d3) 9...h5 10 ♘f1 (or 10 ♘f3 c6 11 ♘g5 cxd5 12 cxd5 ♗d7 13 ♗e3 ♘g4 14

♗xg4 ♗xg4 15 f3 ♗d7 16 ♕e2, R.Wukits-O.Lehner, Austrian Team Ch. 2007, 16...a4 ∞) 10...♘c5 11 ♗g5 ♕e8 12 ♘d2 ♗d7 13 f3 ♘h7 14 ♗e3 f5 15 ♘b3 ♘a4! 16 ♘xa4 ♗xa4 17 g4! hxg4 18 fxg4 ∞ Y.Teplitsky-A.Istratescu, Yerevan Olympiad 1996.

C1: 8 h3 *(D)*

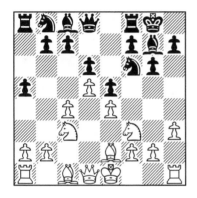

8...♘fd7 *(D)*

Alternatively:

a) 8...♘a6 9 ♗g5 h6 (if instead 9...♕e8 10 g4 ♘d7 11 ♖g1 ♘dc5 12 h4! c6 13 h5, J.Piket-J.Polgar, 1st match-game, Aruba 1995, then 13...h6 14 ♗e3 g5 15 ♘d2 intending ♘f1-g3 +/= Piket; but Black can try 9...♘c5!? 10 ♘d2 ♗d7 11 g4 a4 12 ♕c2 c6 13 b4 axb3 14 ♘xb3 ♘xb3 15 ♕xb3 cxd5 ½-½ R.De la Ro-cha-G.Agnello, Cattolica 1994) 10 ♗e3 ♘c5 11 ♘d2 ♗d7!? (or if 11...♘h7!? 12 h4 h5 13 ♘b3 b6, V.Zvjaginsev-V.Nevednichy, Yugoslav Team Ch. 1995, then 14 ♘xc5!? bxc5 15 g4 with the initiative) 12 g4 c6 13 h4 a4 14 ♗xc5! dxc5 15 ♘xa4 ♘xe4! (better than 15...♘xg4 16 ♘xc5 +=) 16 ♘xe4 ♖xa4 17 ♕xa4 cxd5 18 ♕c2 dxe4 with compen-

sation; e.g. 19 0-0-0 ♕c7 20 ♔b1 ♖a8 21 h5 g5 22 f3 exf3 23 ♗xf3 ♗a4 24 b3 e4 25 ♗xe4 ½-½ V.Sladek-R.Ottenburg, corr. 2003.

b) 8...♘h5!? 9 g3 (or 9 ♘d2 ♘f4 10 ♗f1 ♘a6 11 g3 ♘h5 12 ♘b3 c6 13 ♗e3 ♗d7 14 a4 ♘b4 15 ♖c1 ♕e7 16 c5 cxd5 17 cxd6 ♕d8 18 ♘xd5 ♘xd5 19 ♕xd5 ♘f6 20 ♕d3 ♗xa4 ∞ V.Zvjaginsev-A.Beliavsky, Yugoslav Team Ch. 1995) 9...♘a6 10 ♘h2 (or 10 ♗g5 f6 11 ♗d2 f5 12 exf5 gxf5 ∞ R.Kempinski-V.Baklan, European Junior Ch. 1995) 10...♘c5 11 ♗xh5 gxh5 12 g4 (if 12 ♕xh5 ♘d3+ 13 ♔d2 ♘xc1 14 ♔xc1 f5 with compensation) 12...hxg4 13 hxg4 c6 14 ♕f3 ♕h4 15 ♗d2 b5 16 cxb5 cxb5 17 ♘xb5 f5! ∞ W.Gschnitzer-W.Uhlmann, German League 1992.

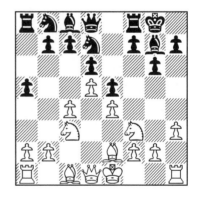

9 g4

White may do better with 9 h4!?, e.g. 9...♘f6! (less risky than 9...f5?! 10 h5 ♘f6 11 hxg6 hxg6 12 ♗g5 ♘a6 13 ♘d2 ♘c5 14 ♘b3 b6 15 ♘xc5 bxc5 16 exf5 ♗xf5 17 g4 ♗d7 18 ♕d3 ♕e8 V.Zvjaginsev-A.Beliavsky, Yugoslavia 1995, 19 ♘e4 +/-) 10 ♘g5 (10 ♗e3!?) 10...♘a6 11 g4 ♘c5 12 f3 h5 ∞

R.Markus-N.Djukic, Serbian Team Ch. 2004.

9...♘c5

Again 9...f5?! seems a bit hasty: 10 gxf5 gxf5 11 exf5 (or 11 ♖g1!?) 11...♘c5 12 ♗g5 ♕e8 (S.Giddins-H.Nordahl, Skei 1995) 13 ♖g1!? with the initiative.

10 ♗e3 ♘ba6 (D)

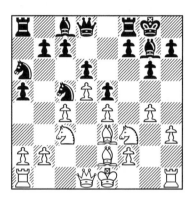

Chances are roughly balanced, although the games in our database see White scoring a meagre 2/8 from this position. For example:

a) 11 ♕d2 ♗d7 12 ♗h6 c6 13 ♗xg7 ♔xg7 14 0-0-0 ♘b4 15 ♕e3 cxd5 16 cxd5 ♖c8 with counterplay, J.Studnieka-J.Benak, Plzen 2001.

b) 11 g5 f5 12 gxf6 ♗xf6 13 ♕d2 a4 14 h4 ♗g4 15 ♘g5 ♕d7 (A.Meldrum-M.Campbell, Brisbane 1995) 16 0-0-0 +=.

c) 11 ♖g1 ♔h8 12 ♕d2 f5 13 ♗g5 ♗f6 and now 14 gxf5!? gxf5 15 ♗h6 is correct; e.g. 15...fxe4 16 ♘g5 ♘b4 ∞. Instead, N.V.Pedersen-E.Sutovsky, Reykjavik 2004, continued 14 ♗h6?! ♘xe4 15 ♘xe4 fxe4 16 ♘g5 ♘c5 17 ♕e3 ♗g7 18 ♗xg7+ ♔xg7 19 ♘xe4 ♘xe4 20 ♕xe4 ♖f4, when Black had taken over

the dark squares with the advantage, though he failed to make anything of it: 21 ♕e3 b6 (21...c6!?) 22 ♖g3 ♗a6 23 ♖f3 ♕f6 24 ♖c1 ♖xf3 25 ♕xf3 ♕g5 26 ♕e3 ♕xe3 27 fxe3 ♖f8 28 b3 ♗c8 29 a3 ♔f6 30 h4 ♔e7 31 b4 axb4 32 axb4 ♗b7 33 ♖a1 ♔d7 ½-½.

C2: 8 ♗g5 (D)

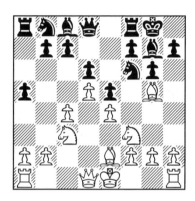

Once again the characteristic move of the Petrosian System. White develops the c1-bishop in advance of ♘d2, and gains time for his plan by stalling Black's attack on the centre with ...f7-f5.

8...h6

Black can delay this move or even do without it; e.g. 8...♘a6 9 ♘d2 (9 0-0 usually transposes after a subsequent ♘d2) 9...♕e8 (9...♗d7!? leads to similar positions) 10 a3 (White has also tried a kingside action with 10 h4 h6 11 ♗e3 h5 12 f3 ♗d7 13 g4 ♕c8 14 ♖g1 ♘c5 15 ♘b3, T.Polak-J.Bernasek, Czech Ch. 2006, 15...♘xb3!? ∞) 10...♗d7 (or 10...♔h8 11 h4 h6 12 ♗xf6 ♗xf6 13 h5 ♗g7, G.Danner-L.Vajda, Gyula 2000, 14 hxg6 fxg6 ∞) 11 b3 (D) and then we have:

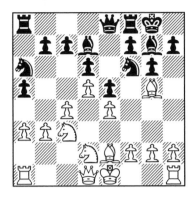

a) 11...h6 12 ♗e3 ♘h7 13 0-0 gives White a better version of 11...♗d7 12 a3 ♘h7 13 b3 in the main line, as his bishop is better placed on e3; e.g. 13...h5 14 f3 f5 15 ♗f2 f4 16 b4!? axb4 17 axb4 ♘xb4 18 ♕b3 c5 19 dxc6 ♘xc6 20 c5+ ♗e6 21 ♗c4 ♗xc4 22 ♕xc4+ ♔h8 23 cxd6 ♖xa1 24 ♖xa1 +/- A.Mirzoev-P.Balogh, World Junior Ch. 1993.

b) 11...♔h8 (intending ...♘g8 and ...f7-f5) 12 h4!? (this looks very logical with the white rook on h1 facing the king on h8; otherwise 12 ♖b1!? ♘c5 13 0-0 ♘g8 14 ♕c2 f5 15 f3 ♗h6 16 ♗xh6 ♘xh6 17 b4 ♘a6 18 c5 axb4 19 axb4 +/= P.Lyrberg-V.Kupreichik, Minsk 1994) 12...♘g8 (12...h5!? or 12...h6!? seem more sensible) 13 h5 f6 (or 13...f5 14 ♘f3 +/- M.Scalcione-D.Vocaturo, Italian Ch. 2006) 14 ♗e3 ♗h6 (E.Hedman-M.Jonsson, Swedish Junior Ch. 1993) 15 hxg6 ♕xg6 16 ♗xh6 ♘xh6 17 ♕c2 +/-.

c) 11...h5!? is an interesting idea, aiming for an improved version of line 'a'; e.g. 12 0-0 (or 12 ♖b1 ♘h7 13 ♗e3 f5 14 f3 ♕e7 15 b4 axb4 16 axb4 ♗f6 17 c5 ♗h4+ 18 g3 ♗g5 19 ♗f2 ♘f6 20 c6 bxc6 21 dxc6 ♗e6 ∞ A.Volzhin-S.Khmel-

nitsky, Minsk 1998) 12...♘h7 13 ♗e3 h4 14 ♖c1 f5 15 exf5 gxf5 16 f4 h3 17 g3 ♘f6 ∞ P.Pisk-J.Michalek, Czech Ch. 1994.

9 ♗h4 (D)

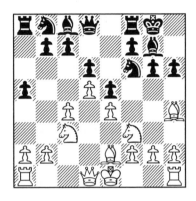

The most consistent and strongest continuation. Instead:

a) 9 ♗e3 ♘g4 10 ♗c1 has the idea 10...f5 11 exf5 gxf5 12 g3 followed by 13 ♘h4, 14 0-0 and 15 f4, though this is nothing much for Black to worry about; e.g. 12...♘a6 13 ♘h4 ♘c5 14 0-0 e4! 15 f4 exf3 16 ♖xf3 a4 17 ♘b5 c6!? (or 17...♘e4!? 18 ♘d4 f4! with the initiative) 18 dxc6 ♕b6 19 ♔g1 ♘e5 20 ♕xd6?! ♕xc6 =+ ½-½ A.Volzhin-I.Nataf, Koszalin 1999. Black can also play more solidly 10...♘a6 when 11 h3 ♘f6 transposes to 8 h3 positions with the extra move ...h7-h6; it can hardly be claimed that this is in any way detrimental here. Similarly if 10 ♗d2 ♘a6 11 h3 ♘f6 12 ♕c1 ♔h7 13 ♗e3 ♘g8 14 0-0 f5 15 exf5 gxf5 16 a3 ♗d7 17 ♕c2 ♔h8 18 ♘h2 ♕e8 19 f4 e4 ∞ U.Enkrodt-H.Kloss, Bellheim 1994.

b) 9 ♗xf6?! ♕xf6 is not good, as White will find it difficult to take effective action on the kingside without the dark-squared bishop. Therefore Black ignore things like 10 h4 and continue simply 10...♘a6 11 h5 ♘c5 etc. Instead 10...h5?! creates unnecessary weaknesses; e.g. 11 ♘d2 ♘a6 12 g4 hxg4 13 ♗xg4 ♗xg4 14 ♕xg4 ♘b4 15 ♔e2 ♘c2 16 ♖af1 ♘d4+ 17 ♔d3 ♗h6 ∞ B.Ciglic-E.Bukic, Ljubljana 1997.

9...♘a6

9...♕e8 usually leads to the main line after 10 ♘d2 ♘h7 11 0-0 ♘a6. Instead, 11...♗f6 does not equalize: 12 ♗xf6 ♘xf6 13 b3 c5 14 dxc6 ♘xc6 15 ♘f3 ♕e7 16 ♕d2 ♔g7 17 ♖fd1 +/= P.Lukacs-W.Uhlmann, Budapest 1985.

9...g5!? 10 ♗g3 ♘h5 may also transpose after 11 ♘d2 ♘f4 12 0-0 ♘a6, though White can try 11 h4 g4 12 ♘d2 (or 12 ♘h2 ♘xg3 13 fxg3 h5 14 0-0 f5 15 exf5 ♗xf5 16 ♗d3 ♗xd3 17 ♕xd3 ♘d7 = U.Gebhardt-A.Oettel, Ulm 1995) 12...♘xg3 13 fxg3 h5 14 ♗d3 (or 14 0-0 ♘a6 15 ♗d3 ♘c5 16 ♗c2 ♗d7 17 ♕e2 c6 18 ♘b3 ♘xb3 19 axb3, S.Yuferov-O.Amidzic, Krasnodar 1991, 19...♗h6 ∞) 14...c6 15 ♕e2 a4 16 ♕e3 ♘a6 17 ♘xa4 cxd5 18 cxd5 ♘b4 19 ♘c3 f5 with compensation, R.Vaganian-M.Vachier Lagrave, Kallithea 2008.

10 0-0

White can play also 10 ♘d2, though it will generally transpose to the main line after a subsequent 0-0. Deferring castling in an attempt to accelerate matters on the queenside can have its own problems; e.g. 10...♘c5 (or 10...♕e8 11 b3 ♘h7 12 a3 f5 13 f3 h5 14 ♖b1 g5 15 ♗f2 g4 16 exf5 ♗xf5 17 ♘de4 ♕g6 18 h3 gxh3 19 gxh3 ♔h8 20 ♖g1

♕h6 21 h4 ♕f4 ∞ J.Speelman-G.Kasparov, Paris rapid 1991) 11 b3 (11 0-0 is note 'c' to Black's 10th move below) 11...♗d7 12 a3 ♕e8 13 ♖b1 (13 0-0 is still possible) 13...♘h5! 14 ♕c2 (the point is that after 14 ♗xh5 ♘d3+ 15 ♔f1 gxh5 16 ♕xh5 ♘f4 17 ♕d1 f5 Black has a strong attack for the pawn) 14...♘f4 15 ♗f1 (or if 15 0-0 f5! -/+) 15...f5 16 f3 fxe4 17 ♘dxe4 ♘xe4 18 ♘xe4 g5 19 ♗f2 g4 20 g3 ♘h3 21 ♗xh3 gxh3 -/+ B.Annakov-V.Golod, Ufa 1993.

10...♕e8 *(D)*

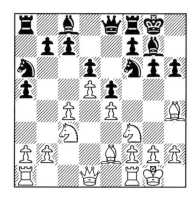

One of the key positions in the Petrosian System. Black unpins and intends ...♘h7 followed by ...f7-f5, or else ...h6-h5 and ....♗h6 activating his dark-squared bishop. White, meanwhile, will prepare the b4-advance. Other moves are:

a) 10...g5 11 ♗g3 ♘h5 12 ♘d2 (after 12 ♘e1 intending ♘c2-e3, Y.Averbakh-L.Stein, Kislovodsk 1964, simplest is 12...♘xg3 and Black stands well after both 13 fxg3 c6 and 13 hxg3 f5) 12...♘f4 13 ♗g4 ♘c5 (S.Gligoric-L.Stein, Moscow 1967) 14 ♗xc8 ♕xc8 15 ♕c2 ♕d7 =.

b) 10...♗d7 mostly transposes elsewhere; for instance 11 ♘d2 ♕e8 returns to the main line, while 11...♘c5 is line 'c' below. Two independent variations:

b1) 11 ♘e1 g5! (the most forcing and energetic) 12 ♗g3 ♘xe4 13 ♘xe4 f5 14 ♘c3!? f4 15 ♘d3 fxg3 16 hxg3 e4! 17 ♘xe4 ♗f5 18 ♘c3 ♕f6 with compensation, A.Lugovoi-V.Golod, Beersheba 1998.

b2) 11 ♘d2 ♕b8!? (a rarely played alternative, planning to activate the queen via a7) 12 ♔h1!? ♘h7 13 f3 h5 14 a3 ♗h6 15 b3 ♗e3 (or 15...♕a7 16 ♕c2 ♕e3 17 ♖ad1 ♕c5 18 ♘db1 += H.Leyva-H.Pecorelli Garcia, Cienfuegos 1996) 16 ♖b1 g5 17 ♗e1 h4?! (but if 17...♕a7 18 b4 axb4 19 axb4 ♕d4 then 20 ♘b5 ♗xb5 21 cxb5 ♘b8 22 ♕c2 and Black is strategically lost; or 17...♗c5!? 18 ♕c1 ♕a7 19 ♘a2 intending b3-b4 +=) 18 b4 axb4 19 axb4 ♘f6 20 c5 +/- M.Nedobora-V.Onoprienko, Noyabrsk 1995.

c) 10...♘c5 11 ♘d2 (11 ♘e1? drops the e-pawn after 11...g5) 11...♗d7 (if 11...c6 12 ♕c2 ♗d7, R.Schroeder-H.Pilnik, Chilean Ch. 1961, 13 ♘b3 +=; or 11...♕e8 12 b3 ♘h7 13 a3 h5!? 14 h3 ♗h6, I.Rogers-P.Thipsay, London Lloyds Bank 1991, 15 ♘b5 +/=) 12 b3 *(D)* and:

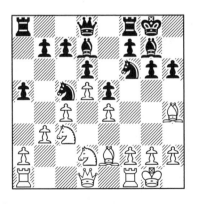

c1) 12...♘fxe4!? 13 ♗xd8 ♘xc3 14 ♕e1 ♖fxd8 is a showy idea from a Kramnik-Kasparov blitz game. Black gets two bishops and a pawn for the queen and his pieces are very active. Nevertheless, we think White's chances are better after 15 ♘b1! ♘xe2+ 16 ♕xe2 e4 17 ♘d2, e.g. 17...♗xa1 18 ♖xa1 ♖e8 19 ♕e3 ♔h7 20 ♕d4 f5 21 a3 +/- G.Lawton-D.Cummings, Maidenhead 1995; or 17...♖e8 18 ♕e3 ♖e7 (G.Laketic-G.Arsovic, Yugoslav Team Ch. 1998) 19 ♖ab1 ♖ae8 20 a3 +/-; or 17...f5 18 ♖ad1 g5 19 f4 (B.Gulko-L.Van Wely, Groningen 1994) and if 19...g4 (Gulko) then 20 ♕e3 ♖e8 21 ♘b1 ♘d3 22 ♘a3 again looks good for White.

Black probably does better to play the position normally; e.g.

c2) 12...c6 13 a3 ♕b6 14 ♖b1 cxd5 15 cxd5 ♖fc8 16 ♘c4 ♕c7 ∞ A.Huss-V.Epishin, San Bernardino 1992.

c3) 12...♕e8 13 a3 (or 13 ♕c2 ♘h7) 13...♘cxe4 14 ♘dxe4 ♘xe4 15 ♘xe4 f5 16 ♘d2 g5 17 ♗g3 f4 18 ♘e4 ♗f5 19 ♗d3 fxg3 20 hxg3 ♕g6 21 ♕e2 g4 ∞ I.Naumkin-F.Agrifoglio, Pontremoli 1998.

11 ♘d2

The alternative is 11 ♘e1 ♘c5 (or 11...♗d7 12 ♘d3 ♘h7 13 f3 h5 14 ♗f2 b6 15 a3 ♘c5 16 ♘xc5 bxc5 17 a4 ♗h6 18 ♘b5 ♕d8 = L.Polugaevsky-O.Cvitan, Sarajevo 1987) 12 f3 ♘h5 13 ♘b5 (or if 13 ♘d3, J.Kristiansen-S.B.Hansen, Danish Ch. 1993, 13...♘f4!? 14 ♘xf4 exf4 ∞) 13...♘a6 14 ♘d3 ♘f4!? 15 ♘xf4 exf4 16 ♕d2 ♕e5!? = L.B.Hansen-A.Wojtkiewicz, Wijk aan Zee 1994.

11...♘h7

11...♗d7 *(D)* is a serious alternative to the main line:

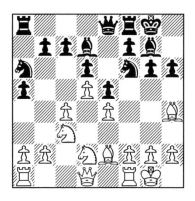

a) 12 ♘b5 ♘h7 13 a3 f5!? 14 exf5 gxf5 15 ♗h5 ∞ I.Gorin-M.Ozolin, Moscow 1998.

b) 12 ♔h1 ♘h7 (or 12...h5 13 b3 ♘g4!? 14 a3 f6 15 ♖b1 g5 16 ♗g3 f5 17 exf5 ♗xf5 18 ♘de4 ♕g6 19 h3 ♗xe4 20 ♘xe4 ♕xe4 21 hxg4, V.Kramnik-J.Polgar, Monte Carlo rapid 1994, 21...hxg4 22 ♗d3 ♕d4 23 ♕c2 ♖f6 =) 13 a3 h5 14 f3 and then:

b1) 14...♗h6 15 b3 (if 15 ♖b1 a4 16 ♘b5 b6 17 b4 axb3 18 ♘xb3 ♗g5 19 ♗xg5 ♘xg5 20 ♕d2 ♕e7 21 a4 f6 22 a5 ♖fb8 23 ♖a1 ♔f7 24 ♖a3 ∞ I.Khenkin-O.Cvitan, Geneva 1994) 15...♗e3 (15...♕b8?! 16 ♗f2 +=) 16 ♖b1 (or 16 ♕c2 f5 17 exf5 gxf5 18 ♖ae1 ♕g6 19 ♗d3, D.Komarov-Al.David, French Team Ch. 1999, 19...♕h6! =+ Komarov) 16...f5 17 exf5 (or 17 b4 f4 18 ♕c2 axb4 19 axb4 g5 20 ♗e1 ♕e7 21 ♘d1 ♗xd2 22 ♕xd2 g4 ∞ M.Nedobora-V.Bronznik, Ukraine 1994) 17...gxf5 18 b4 axb4 19 axb4 ♔h8 20 ♗d3 ♕g6 21 ♕e2 ♕h6 22 ♖fd1 ♖ae8 23 ♕e1 ♖g8 ∞

V.Topalov-S.Mamedyarov, Wijk aan Zee 2008.

b2) 14...♗f6!? is also possible; e.g. 15 ♗f2 (or 15 ♗xf6 ♘xf6 16 b3 ♕e7 17 ♕e1 ♔g7 18 ♕f2 h4 19 f4 exf4 20 ♕xf4 h3 =+ B.Gulko-G.Kasparov, Novgorod 1995) 15...♗g5 16 b3 c5 17 dxc6 bxc6 18 ♖b1 ♕e7 19 b4 axb4 20 axb4 ♖fb8 21 b5 ♘c5 22 ♘b3 ♘e6 ∞ S.Iskusnyh-S.Dolmatov, Kemerovo 1995.

c) 12 a3 ♘h7 (or 12...a4!? 13 ♘b5 c6!? 14 ♘c3 ♘c5 15 ♕c2 cxd5 16 cxd5 b5 17 ♖fc1 ♖c8 18 ♖ab1 J.Carrasco Martinez-J.Baron Rodriguez, Spanish Junior Ch. 1997, 18...♘h5 ∞) 13 b3 (13 ♔h1 returns to line 'b') 13...f5 (or 13...♗f6 14 ♗xf6 ♘xf6 15 ♕c2 b6 16 ♖ab1 ♘h7 17 b4 f5 18 exf5 gxf5 19 ♔h1 ♕g6 ∞ V.Ivanchuk-J.Piket, European Junior Ch. 1986) 14 exf5 gxf5!? (if 14...♗xf5 15 g4 e4 16 ♖c1 e3 17 gxf5 exd2 18 ♕xd2 ♘c5, I.Naumkin-L.Belov, Moscow 1984, 19 ♖ce1 +=) 15 ♗h5 ♕c8 16 ♗e7 ♖e8! 17 ♗xe8 ♕xe8 18 ♗h4 e4 and Black has good compensation for the exchange; e.g. 19 ♕c2 (or if 19 ♖c1 ♘c5 20 ♖c2!, I.Naumkin-A.Kuzmin, Moscow 1989, then 20...♘f6 21 ♘e2 ♘h5 with compensation, Karpov) 19...♕h5 20 ♗g3 ♖f8 (A.Yusupov-G.Kasparov, Barcelona 1989) 21 f4 ♘c5 (or 21...♗d4+!? 22 ♔h1 ♘f6 with an attack, Knaak) 22 ♖fd1! ♘d3 23 ♘f1 ♗d4+ 24 ♔h1 ♘f6 25 ♖xd3 exd3 26 ♕xd3 ♗c5 with compensation (Kasparov).

12 a3 *(D)*

There is no need for b2-b3 before Black has played ...♗d7, since ...a5-a4 is not an option. White also achieves nothing after 12 ♘b5 f5 13 exf5 (B.Zlotnik-

D.Rogic, Kassel 1988) 13...gxf5 14 ♗h5 ♕d7 15 a3 e4 ∞ Zlotnik.

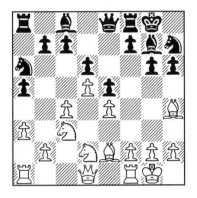

12...f5

Instead, 12...♗d7 returns to 11...♗d7 lines above (specifically 12 a3 ♘h7), while attempting to play the same way without this move allows White to achieve b2-b4 in one go; e.g. 12...h5 13 f3 ♗h6 14 b4 ♗d7 15 ♖b1 ♗e3+ 16 ♔h1 f5 17 exf5 gxf5 18 ♕e1 (18 ♕c2) 18...♕g6 19 ♗f2 ♕h6 20 ♗xe3 ♕xe3 21 ♘b5 axb4 22 ♖b3 ♕h6 23 axb4 +/- T.V.Petrosian-C.Kottnauer, Lugano Olympiad 1968.

Other moves also allow White a slight advantage; e.g. 12...♗f6 13 ♗xf6 ♘xf6 14 b4 ♗d7 15 ♕b3 ♕e7 16 ♖fc1 += H.Grünberg-Kr.Georgiev, Zinnowitz 1982; or 12...♕d7 13 ♔h1 h5 14 f3 ♗h6 15 b3 ♗e3 16 ♕c2 f5 17 exf5 gxf5 18 ♗f2 ♗xf2 19 ♖xf2 += Z.Franco Ocampos-D.Del Rey, Saragossa 1999.

13 f3

The alternative is 13 exf5 gxf5 (or if 13...♗xf5 14 g4 ♗d7 15 ♘de4 a4 16 f3 b6 17 ♗d3 ♗f6 18 ♘xf6+ ♘xf6 19 ♕d2 ♘c5 20 ♗c2, A.Veingold-G.Kasparov, USSR Spartakiad 1979, 20...g5 21 ♗xg5

hxg5 22 ♕xg5+ ♔h8 23 ♕h6+ ♔g8 24 ♕g5+ with a draw, but 14 f3!? deserves attention) 14 ♗h5 ♕d7 15 b4 (or 15 f4 e4 16 ♘b3, P.Eroes-L.Gaponenko, World Blind Ch. 1998, 16...a4 17 ♘d4 ♘c5 ∞) 15...e4 16 ♕c1 c5 (16...♗e5!?) 17 bxa5 ♗e5 18 f4 ♗d4+ 19 ♔h1 ♕g7 20 ♘b5 ½-½ L.Hetey-T.Steinkohl, German Ch. 1996.

13...♗d7

13...f4 allows 14 b4 ♗d7 15 c5 (or 15 ♕b3!? +/=) 15...axb4 16 axb4 (J.Garcia Garcia-J.Salvador Duch, Tarragona 1994) 16...dxc5 17 ♗xa6 cxb4 18 ♗xb7 ♖b8 19 ♖a7 bxc3 20 ♘c4 with the initiative.

After 13...♗d7, 14 b3 followed by ♖b1 and b3-b4 would be the expected continuation; e.g. 14...♘f6 15 exf5 (15 ♗f2 ♘h5 ∞) 15...gxf5 16 ♕c2 c6 17 ♖ad1 ♘h5 18 g3 ♘c7 19 ♘db1 c5 20 a4 ♔h8 21 ♔h1 ♗f6 ½-½ B.Damljanovic-Kir.Georgiev, Cacak 1996; or 14...♗f6!? 15 ♗f2 ♕e7 16 b4 ♗h4 17 ♕b3 ♗xf2+ 18 ♖xf2 axb4 19 axb4 ♕g5 ∞ V.Priehoda-V.Babula, Czechoslovakian Ch. 1992.

Instead, in V.Babula-A.Morozevich, Turin Olympiad 2006, White just played:

14 b4!? h5?!

This allows White to obtain his desired position without penalty. Black should take up the challenge with 14...axb4 15 axb4 ♘xb4, when V.Kramnik-G.Kasparov, Paris (rapid) 1995, continued 16 ♕b3 c5 17 dxc6 (if 17 ♖xa8 ♕xa8 18 ♗e7 ♖e8 19 ♗xd6 ♕a5 ∞, e.g. 20 exf5 gxf5 21 ♗e5 ♖xe5! 22 fxe5 ♗xe5 with compensation) 17...♘xc6 18 c5+ ♔h8 19 cxd6 ♘d4 20

♕xb7 ♖b8 21 ♕a6 ♖c8 22 ♗c4 ♖c6 23 ♕a2 ♖xd6 with a complicated game.

15 ♖b1 axb4 16 axb4 b6

16...♗h6 is reminiscent of Petrosian-Kottnauer (see the note with 12...h5 above). After 17 ♗d3 f4?! 18 c5 White was clearly better in J.Gobert-E.De Beck, corr. 1993.

17 ♗f2

17 exf5 gxf5 18 f4 is also good.

17...♘f6 18 ♕c2 ♗h6 19 ♗d3 ♔h8 20 ♖fe1 ♕e7 21 ♖e2 ♘h7 22 ♘b5 h4 23 h3

23 ♔h1!? came into consideration.

23...♗f4 24 ♔h1 ♕g5 25 ♕c3 ♘f6 26 ♘f1 (D)

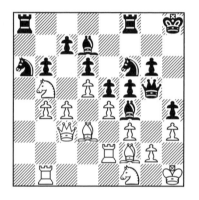

Black has managed to generate enough counterplay to equalize after

26...fxe4 27 fxe4 ♗g3 =. Instead he went for **26...♘h5?! 27 ♖a2 ♘g3+ 28 ♗xg3 hxg3 29 exf5 ♔g8 30 ♖ba1 e4 31 fxe4 ♗e5 32 ♕e1 ♘xb4?** [32...♗xa1 33 ♕xa1 gxf5 was correct, as 34 ♖xa6?? loses to 34...♖xa6 35 ♕xa6 fxe4] **33 ♖xa8 ♘xd3 34 ♖xf8+ ♔xf8 35 ♖a8+ ♔g7 36 ♕e3 ♘f2+ 37 ♔g1 ♕h4 38 ♘xc7 ♘xe4 39 ♘e6+ ♗xe6 40 fxe6 ♘f6 41 ♖a7+ ♔g8 42 ♖a8+ ♔g7 43 ♖a7+ ♔g8 44 ♕f3 ♕xc4 45 ♖a8+ ♔g7 46 e7 ♗d4+ 47 ♔h1 ♗f2 48 ♕d1** [48 ♖a1!] **48...♔f7 49 ♖a7 ♕xd5 50 ♕e2** and in this still winning position White lost on time.

Conclusion

The best method for Black against Petrosian's 7 d5 is the reinforcement of the c5-outpost by ...a7-a5 – either immediately with 7...a5, or after the preliminary ...♘a6-c5 or ...♘bd7-c5, though these often transpose to 7...a5 lines anyway. The restriction of White's queenside initiative enables Black to generate good counterplay on the other wing. After other set-ups Black risks ending up in a cramped position and White has better chances of achieving an advantage.

Chapter Five

7 0-0: Introduction

1 d4 ♘f6 2 c4 g6 3 ♘c3 ♗g7 4 e4 d6 5 ♘f3 0-0 6 ♗e2 e5 7 0-0 *(D)*

7 0-0 is the most frequently played, the best analysed and most flexible move. Now Black's primary responses involve his queen's knight emerging at a6, d7 or, in particular, c6 with the immediate central attack. The variations arising from these knight moves are the subject of the remaining seven chapters. In this chapter we are going to examine Black's less popular continuations, the most significant of which is the immediate capture 7...exd4 (line C) reducing the tension in the centre.

Of the rest, 7...c6 (line B) often just transposes elsewhere, usually to 7...♘a6, 7...♘bd7 or 7...exd4 variations. Other 7th moves may lead to original play, which is often desirable, but in these cases Black cannot count on achieving full equality theoretically speaking.

A: 7...♕e8 *99*
B: 7...c6 *102*
C: 7...exd4 *105*

Other moves:

a) 7...♖e8 cannot be recommended: the x-ray attack on the e4-pawn is easily parried by 8 d5, after which Black's rook is misplaced on e8, unable to support the counterattack with ...f7-f5; e.g. 8...♘h5 9 g3 ♘d7 10 ♗e3 ♘df6 11 ♘d2 ♗h3 12 ♖e1 ♕d7 13 f3 h6 14 c5 with the initiative, L.Ogaard-L.SAntos, Arosa 1972.

b) 7...♕e7 8 ♗g5 (the most energetic move) 8...exd4 (or if 8...c6 9 c5 ♗g4 10 cxd6 ♕xd6, G.Forintos-T.Filep, Hungarian Ch. 1969, very strong and simple is 11 dxe5 ♕xd1 12 ♖fxd1 ♘fd7 13 ♖d2 ♗xf3 14 gxf3 ♗xe5 15 ♖ad1 +/- Khalifman) 9 ♘d5! ♕d8 10 ♘xd4 c6 11 ♘xf6+ ♗xf6 12 ♗xf6 ♕xf6 13 ♕d2 ♕e5 (better 13...♖e8 +/=) 14 f4! ♕xe4 15 ♖ae1 ♕e7 16 f5 with a strong attack, A.Mitenkov-V.Zhelnin, Cherepovets 1993.

c) 7...♗g4 is reminiscent of the 6...♗g4 line in Chapter One. However, the main idea there is to exert pressure on the d4-pawn, and ...e7-e5 is not the best way of implementing this plan (see line C21 in that chapter). Here White is better after 8 ♗e3 (or 8 d5 ♘h5 9 g3 ♘d7 10 ♗e3 h6 11 ♕d2 ♗h3 12 ♖fe1 += L.Ftacnik-K.Schmidt, Aarhus 1983) 8...♘fd7 (or 8...♗xf3 9 ♗xf3 exd4 10 ♗xd4 ♘c6 11 ♗e3 ♘d7 12 ♕d2 ♘c5 13 ♖ad1 ♘e6 14 g3 ♘cd4 15 ♗g2 += Nguyen Anh Dung-D.Karatorossian, Budapest 1998) 9 d5 a5 10 a3 ♘a6 11 ♖b1 ♗xf3 12 ♗xf3 f5 13 b4 axb4 14 axb4 ♖f7 15 ♗e2 f4 16 ♗c1 h5 17 ♕c2 ♗f8 18 ♘d1 ♘f6 19 f3 g5 20 ♘f2 ♖g7 21 h3 +/= N.Spiridonov-P.Peev, Bulgaria 1981.

d) 7...a5!? is an original move found in the 1990s. Since ...a7-a5 is useful in many systems, Black plays it first and waits to see White's reaction before deciding how to develop his b8-knight.

d1) 8 ♗e3 ♘a6 is rather unclear; e.g. 9 h3 exd4 10 ♗xd4 (or 10 ♘xd4 ♖e8 11 ♗f3 ♘c5 12 ♕c2 h6 13 ♖ad1 ♘h7 14 ♘db5 ♘g5 ∞ I.Farago-I.Glek, Plzen 1992) 10...♖e8 11 ♘d2 c6 12 ♖e1 ♘c5 13 ♗f1 ♗d7 14 g3 ♘e6 15 ♗e3 c5! (A.Miles-I.Glek, Biel 1996) 16 a4!? intending ♘b5 (Glek).

d2) 8 ♗g5!? h6 9 ♗h4 ♘bd7 (if 9...♕d7?! 10 dxe5 dxe5 11 ♕c1 ♘h5 12 ♖d1 ♕e6 13 ♘d5 ♘a6 14 c5 ♘f4 15 ♗c4 +/- E.Bacrot-J.M.Degraeve, French Ch. 2002; or 9...♕e8 10 ♗xf6!? ♗xf6 11 c5!

+= Tsesarsky) 10 dxe5 (better than 10 d5 with a Petrosian System; see line B2 with 9...a5!? in Chapter Four) 10...dxe5 11 ♕c2 c6 12 ♘a4 b6 13 ♖fd1 += M.Knezevic-G.Sigurjonsson, Reykjavik 1984.

d3) 8 dxe5 dxe5 9 ♕xd8 ♖xd8 10 ♗g5 is a logical response, as White's 0-0 is much more useful in the Exchange Variation than ...a7-a5, which may just weaken the pawn structure in some lines; e.g. 10...♘bd7 11 ♖fd1 ♖f8 12 ♘d5 (or 12 ♘d2 c6 13 ♘a4 b6 14 ♗e3 ♖b8, I.Farago-A.Kosten, Nuoro 1993, 15 ♖ac1 +=) c6 13 ♘e7+ ♔h8 14 ♗e3 b6!? (14...♖e8 15 ♘xc8 ♖axc8 16 c5 +=) 15 ♘xc6 ♘xe4 16 ♘e7 ♘ec5 (A.Shariyazdanov-A.Shchekachev, Russian Ch. 1996) 17 ♘d5 +=.

e) 7...♘h5!? *(D)* is an offbeat idea which aims to gain the bishop pair after ...♘f4. In response White has tried:

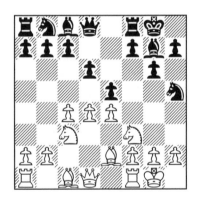

e1) 8 ♖e1 ♘f4 9 ♗f1 ♗g4 10 d5 ♕f6! and White has serious problems with unpinning, e.g. 11 ♖e3 (not 11 g3?! ♗xf3 12 ♕xf3 ♘xd5 13 ♕xf6 ♘xf6 and White has little compensation for the pawn, V.Mikhalevski-T.Remmel, Dieren 1999) 11...a5 12 h3 ♗d7 13 ♖e1 g5 ∞ A.Evdokimov-V.Shtyrenkov, Alushta 2004.

e2) 8 dxe5 dxe5 9 ♕xd8 ♖xd8 10 ♗g5 (if 10 ♘d5 ♘a6 11 g3 ♗h3 12 ♖e1 c6 =+ C.Eagle-A.Karklins, Flint 1991) 10...f6 (or 10...♖d7 11 g3, T.Taylor-A.Karklins, Chicago 1992, 11...h6!? intending 12 ♗d2 ♘f6 13 ♖fd1 ♘c6 ∞) 11 ♖fd1 ♖e8 12 ♗e3 ♘f4 13 ♗xf4 exf4 14 ♘d5 ♘a6 15 c5 (15 ♘xf4 ♖xe4 16 ♖d8+ ♔f7 17 g3 ♖e8 = Poluljahov) 15...c6 16 ♗xa6 cxd5 17 ♗b5 ♖xe4 18 ♖xd5 ♗e6 19 ♖d6 ♖b4 =+ S.Royer-M.Ippolito, Argenteuil 1997.

e3) 8 g3 ♗h3 9 ♖e1 exd4 10 ♘xd4 ♘f6 11 ♗g5 h6 (this allows White to gain a tempo after ♕d2; but if 11...♘c6 12 ♘xc6 bxc6 13 ♕d2 ♖e8 14 ♕f4 ♕e7, Z.Kozul-G.Mohr, Portoroz 1997, and here Khalifman recommends 15 g4 ♕e5 16 ♕e3, when the sacrifice 16...♘xg4 17 ♕xh3 ♘xf2 18 ♔xf2 ♕xg5 does not look fully correct, or if 15...h5 16 gxh5 gxh5 17 ♕h4 +/=) 12 ♗e3 ♖e8 13 ♕d2 ♔h7 14 f3 ♘bd7 (or 14...♘c6) 15 ♘d1!? (a good manoeuvre, intending ♘f2 to drive the h3-bishop from its active post) 15...♘e5 16 ♘f2 ♗d7 17 ♖ad1 a6 18 ♕c2 ♕b8 (18...♕e7!?) 19 b4 +/= I.Sokolov-T.Seeman, Stockholm 1998.

e4) 8 ♗g5 f6 9 ♗e3 ♘f4 (if 9...♘c6 10 c5 ♘f4 11 ♗c4+ ♔h8 12 cxd6 cxd6 13 d5 ♘e7 14 ♖e1 g5 15 ♗f1 g4 16 ♘d2 f5 17 ♘c4 += S.Krivoshey-K.Movsziszian, Salou 2008; or 10 dxe5!? fxe5 11 c5 +=) 10 ♗xf4 (the alternative is 10 c5 ♘xe2+ 11 ♕xe2 exd4 12 ♗xd4 dxc5 13 ♗xc5 ♖f7 14 e5 ♘a6 15 ♗a3 ♕e8 16 ♖ae1 fxe5 17 ♘xe5 ♕xe5 18 ♕xe5 ♗xe5 19 ♖xe5

+= V.Ikonnikov-C.Werner, Vlissingen 2001; this looks better than 12 ♘xd4 dxc5 13 ♕c4+ ♖f7 14 ♕xc5 b6 15 ♕d5 ♕xd5 16 exd5 f5 17 ♖ad1 ♘a6 intending ...♗b7 with counterplay, D.Antic-Z.Ilincic, Pale 2000) 10...exf4 11 c5 (or 11 ♕b3!? ♘c6 12 c5+ ♔h8 13 cxd6 ♕xd6 14 ♘b5 ♕e7 15 ♖ac1 a6 16 ♘c3 +/= C.Fuertes-M.Hedrera, corr. 1997) 11...dxc5 12 dxc5 c6 13 ♗c4+ ♔h8 14 ♕xd8 ♖xd8 15 ♖fd1 ♖e8 16 ♘d4 +/= G.Tallaksen-E.Gullaksen, Norwegian Team Ch. 2004.

A: 7...♕e8 *(D)*

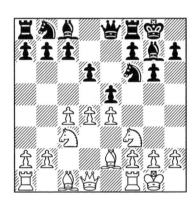

As with 7...♖e8 above, Black makes a veiled threat against the e4-pawn, but here 8 d5 is clearly less effective with the f8-rook still behind the f-pawn, while ...♕e8 is not without use in the Petrosian System. L.Psakhis-I.Smirin, Tel Aviv 1992, Black continued 8...a5 9 ♘e1 ♘a6 10 ♘d3 ♗d7 11 ♗e3 f5 12 f3 ♘dc5 13 b3 and now Black should have started an immediate action on the kingside by 13...f4!? 14 ♗f2 ♕e7 with good counterplay.

8 dxe5

A logical move; Black will now have to lose a tempo as the appropriate square for the queen in the Exchange Variation is e7, not e8.

Also interesting is 8 ♖e1 exd4 (8...♘a6 transposes to line C1 in Chapter Six) 9 ♕xd4! ♘c6 10 ♕d3 ♗g4 11 ♗g5 h6 12 ♗e3 a5 13 ♖ac1 ♘b4 14 ♕b1 ♘a6 15 h3 ♗d7 16 ♖cd1 +/= V.Babula-S.Firt, Czech Ch. 2000. The gambit attempt 9 ♘xd4?! ♘xe4 10 ♘d5 (if 10 ♗f3 ♘xc3) 10...♕d8 11 ♗f3 fails to 11...♘xf2! 12 ♔xf2 (not 12 ♕d2? ♘g4 13 ♗xg4 ♗xg4 -/+ J.Stocek-R.Kempinski, European Ch., Antalya 2004) 12...♕h4+, when White has nothing better than 13 g3 (if 13 ♔g1?! ♗xd4+ 14 ♔h1 ♗e5 15 ♖xe5 dxe5 16 ♘xc7 ♖d8 =+ J.Moreno Carnero-G.German, Buenos Aires rapid 1996, or 13 ♔f1?! ♗xd4 14 g3 ♕h3+ 15 ♗g2 ♕f5+ 16 ♗f4 ♘c6 17 ♘xc7 ♗e6 =+ L.Van Wely-R.Kempinski, German League 2004) 13...♕xd4+ 14 ♕xd4 ♗xd4+ 15 ♗e3 ♘c6 16 ♘xc7 ♖b8 17 ♗xd4 ♘xd4 18 ♖ad1 = Avrukh.

8...dxe5 9 b4 *(D)*

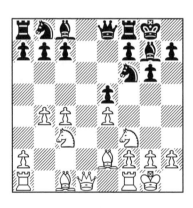

The most energetic move. White can also hope for an advantage after:

a) 9 ♗e3 b6 10 h3 (or 10 b4 ♗b7 11 ♕c2 ♘bd7 12 ♘d2 ♕e7 13 ♘d5 ♕d8 14 a4 c6 15 ♘c3 ♕e7 16 ♖fb1 ♖fb8 17 a5 += L.Van Wely-D.Khismatullin, European Ch., Warsaw 2005) 10...♗b7 (or 10...♘a6!? 11 ♕b1!? ♗b7 12 b4 ♕e7 13 a3 c6 14 c5 ♘d7 15 cxb6 axb6 16 ♖d1 += A.Lastin-P.Rozanov, Moscow 1998) 11 ♕c2 ♘a6 (the alternative 11...♘c6 hinders the natural ...c7-c6, e.g. 12 ♘d5 ♖c8 13 ♖fd1 ♘d4 14 ♘xd4 exd4 15 ♗xd4 ♘xe4 16 ♗xg7 ♔xg7 17 ♗f3 ♗xd5 18 ♖xd5 c6 19 ♖d3 ♘c5 20 ♗e3 += I.V.Ivanov-R.Menkinovski, Struga 2002) 12 a3 ♘h5 13 b4 c5 14 ♘d5 ♖c8 (M.Gurevich-V.Milov, Brussels 1995) and now 15 ♖ab1!? ♘f4 16 ♗xf4 exf4 17 ♖fe1 +/=.

b) 9 b3!? ♕e7 10 ♘d5 ♘xd5 11 cxd5 ♖d8 12 ♕c2 c6 13 ♗g5 ♗f6 14 ♗xf6 ♕xf6 15 ♖fd1 ♗g4 16 ♖ac1, L.Ftacnik-R.Kempinski, Hamburg 1999, 16...♗xf3 17 ♗xf3 ♘a6! 18 a3 cxd5 19 exd5 ♕d6 20 b4 ♖d7 +/= Ftacnik. Or if 11...c6 (R.Lev-N.Davies, Tel Aviv 1989), in our opinion White should fight for the advantage by 12 d6!?, e.g. 12...♕d7 13 ♗b2 f6 14 ♕d2 or 12...♕e6 13 ♗e3 ♖d8 14 ♗c4 ♕xd6 15 ♘g5 ♕e7 16 ♕c1 ♗e6 17 ♘xe6.

c) 9 ♘d5 ♘a6 10 ♕c2!? c6 (or 10...b6 11 ♖d1 c6 12 ♘xf6+ ♗xf6 13 a3 ♗b7 14 ♗h6 ♗g7 15 ♗xg7 ♔xg7 16 ♖d6 += R.Hrdy-J.Hostinsky, corr. 2000) 11 ♘xf6+ ♗xf6 12 ♗e3 ♕e7 13 c5 ♘c7 14 h3 ♘e6 15 ♗c4 ♘d4 16 ♘xd4 exd4 17 ♗f4 ♗e5 18 ♗xe5 ♕xe5 19 f4 ♕e7 20 ♖ad1 +/= M.Richter-M.Jolowicz, German League 1998.

9...♕e7 *(D)*

White has the advantage after other continuations too; e.g.

a) 9...♘bd7 10 b5 ♕e7 11 a4 ♘c5 12 ♗a3 ♘fd7 13 ♘d2 ♖e8 14 ♘b3 ♗f8 15 ♗g4 ♕g5 16 ♗xd7 ♘xd7 17 ♘d5 ♕d8 18 ♗xf8 ♖xf8 19 ♕c2 c6 20 ♘e3 ♕h4 21 ♖fd1 += Se.Ivanov-R.Kempinski, Stockholm 2000.

b) 9...♗g4 10 b5 c5 (or 10...♗xf3 11 ♗xf3 ♕e6 12 ♘d5 ♖c8 13 ♘xf6+ ♕xf6 14 ♗e3 += L.Van Wely-Kr.Georgiev, Kallithea 2008) 11 ♘d2 ♗xe2 12 ♕xe2 ♘bd7 13 a4 ♘h5 14 g3 ♕e6 15 ♘d5 += V.Epishin-R.Issermann, Nice 2004.

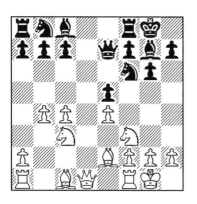

10 ♕b3

The immediate 10 b5 is also good:

a) 10...c6 11 ♕b3 (or 11 a4!? ♖d8 12 ♗a3 ♕e8 13 ♕b3 ♗g4 14 a5 += V.Ivanchuk-J.Polgar, Novgorod 1996) 11...♖d8 12 ♗a3 ♕c7 13 ♖ad1 ♖xd1 14 ♖xd1 ♘e8 15 c5 ♗e6 16 ♘d5! cxd5 17 exd5 ♗f5 18 ♗c4 +/- M.Kobalia-I.Zakharevich, Russian Ch. 2000.

b) 10...♖d8 11 ♕b3 (or just 11 ♗a3!) 11...♗g4 12 ♗a3 ♕e8 13 ♖fd1 ♘bd7 (B.Arkhangelsky-H.Karl, European Seniors Ch. 2004) 14 ♘d5 ♘xd5 15 cxd5 with better chances for White.

10...c6 11 ♗a3

Or 11 ♗e3 ♘bd7 (H.Titz-H.Herndl, Austrian League 1989) 12 ♖fd1 +/=.

11...♖e8

11...♖d8 12 b5 transposes to 10 b5 above.

12 b5 ♕c7 13 ♖fd1 *(D)*

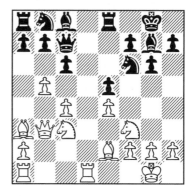

White has the advantage as Black's position is cramped, though he is not without resources:

13...♗f8 14 bxc6

Alternatively, 14 ♗xf8 ♔xf8 15 ♕b4+ (or 15 ♖ac1 ♗g4 16 ♘d2 ♗xe2 17 ♘xe2 ♘bd7, D.Aupov-I.Zakharevich, Togliatti 2001, 18 a4 +/=) 15...♔g7 (T.Gareev-I.Zakharevich, Samara 2003) 16 a4 intending a4-a5 with a better position for White.

The text was played in B.Kelly-B.Socko, European Team Ch., Gothenburg 2005, which continued **14...bxc6 15 ♗xf8 ♔xf8 16 ♕a3+ ♔g7 17 c5** [17 h3!? +/=] **17...♗g4 18 ♖d6 ♗xf3 19 ♗xf3 ♘bd7 20 ♗d1 ♖ed8 21 ♗b3** [not 21 ♗a4? ♕a5! -/+] **21...♘e8 22 ♖d3 ♘df6 23 ♖ad1 ♖xd3 24 ♖xd3 ♖d8 25 ♕a6** [not 25 ♖xd8?! ♕xd8 26 ♕xa7 ♕d2 27 ♕xf7+ ♔h6] **25...♖d4** [or 25...♖xd3 26 ♕xd3

♕d7 =] **26 ♖f3 ♗b4?** [26...h6] **27 h3?** [27 g4! +/-] **27...♕b7 28 ♕xb7 ♖xb7 29 ♗a4 ♖c7 30 ♗b3 ♖d7 31 ♗a4 ♖c7 32 ♗b3 ♖d7 33 ♗a4 ♖c7 34 ♗b3 ½-½.**

B: 7...c6 *(D)*

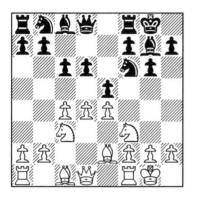

This move very often transposes to other variations; in particular 7...♘a6 or 7...♘bd7 examined in Chapters Six and Seven respectively. Black is also ready to follow up with ...e5xd4 and ...♖e8 should White respond in tame fashion.

8 ♗e3

White has a wide range of other continuations:

a) 8 ♖b1 is shown to be a waste of time after 8...exd4! 9 ♘xd4 ♖e8 10 f3 d5 11 exd5 ♘xd5! 12 cxd5 ♕b6 13 ♔h1 ♕xd4 14 ♕xd4 ♗xd4 15 ♗c4 ♗f5 16 dxc6 ♘xc6 17 ♘e4 ♘e5 =/+ K.Langeweg-R.Nezhmetdinov, Kislovodsk 1972.

b) 8 ♕c2, defending the e4-pawn and preparing ♖d1, is useful in many systems; for instance 8...♘bd7 is line B2 in Chapter Seven. But Black again seems fine after 8...exd4! 9 ♘xd4, e.g.

9...♖e8 (or 9...♘g4 10 ♗xg4 ♗xg4 11 ♗e3 c5 12 ♘de2 ♘c6 13 f3 ♗e6 14 ♘d5, D.Paunovic-S.Djuric, Yugoslav Ch. 1989; 14...f5 15 ♘ef4 ♘d4 16 ♕d2 ♗f7 ∞ Lukacs/Hazai) 10 ♖d1 ♕e7 11 f3 ♘bd7 12 ♗f1 a5 13 ♖b1 ♘c5 14 ♗g5 ♕f8 15 ♕d2 ♘fd7 ∞ L.Cyborowski-E.Miroshnichenko, European Ch., Ohrid 2001.

c) 8 dxe5 pre-empts ...e5xd4, but 8...dxe5 9 ♕xd8 ♖xd8 is a perfectly good Exchange Variation for Black, while 9 ♕c2 gives White nothing either; e.g. 9...♕c7 10 h3 ♘bd7 11 ♗e3 ♘h5 12 ♖fd1 ♘f4 13 ♗f1 ♘e6 14 b4 (J.Klingelhoefer-M.Schlicht, German Junior League 1993) 14...a5 ∞.

The next two variations, on the other hand, may cause more problems for Black:

d) 8 ♖e1 exd4 (instead 8...♘a6 is line C2 in Chapter Six, while 8...♘bd7 is line D3 in Chapter Seven; or if 8...♘g4 9 h3 exd4 10 ♘xd4 ♕b6 11 ♗xg4 ♗xg4 12 hxg4 ♕xd4 13 ♕xd4 ♗xd4 14 ♗e3 ♗xc3 15 bxc3 +/= J.Toikka-I.Kanko, Vantaa 2000) 9 ♘xd4 ♖e8 (9...♘a6 10 ♗f1 is line C22 in Chapter Six again) 10 ♗f1 and now the critical variation is 10...♘g4 11 h3 ♕f6 12 hxg4 ♕xd4 13 g5 (White should not exchange queens himself, but wait so as to gain a tempo) 13...♕xd1 (if 13...♘d7 14 ♗e3 ♕e5 15 ♕d2 ♕e7 16 ♖ad1 ♘c5 17 f3!? +/= A.Yermolinsky-K.Spraggett, FIDE World Ch., Las Vegas 1999) 14 ♖xd1 ♗e5 15 ♗e3 ♘d7 *(D)*, when White has a strong initiative in this position and can choose between the following possibilities:

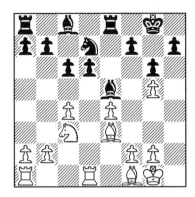

d1) 16 ♖ac1 f6 (or 16...♘c5 17 b4 ♘e6, V.Tukmakov-Z.Kozul, Croatian Team Ch. 1999, 18 g3!? +/=) 17 f4! ♗xc3 18 ♖xc3 fxg5 19 ♖xd6 gxf4 20 ♗xf4 ♘c5 21 ♖e3 ♘xe4 (or if 21...♗g4 22 e5 a5, I.Ivanisevic-B.Damljanovic, Yugoslav Ch. 1997, then 23 g3 +=) 22 ♖d4 ♗f5 23 g4 c5 24 ♖d5 ♗xg4 25 ♗g2 ♘f6 26 ♖xc5 is given as unclear by Damljanovic, but in our opinion the activity of White's pieces and the bishop pair are more important factors than the two black pawns on the kingside.

d2) 16 ♘a4 a6 (or if 16...f5!? 17 exf5 gxf5 18 f4 ♗xb2 19 ♘xb2 ♖xe3 20 ♖xd6) 17 f4 ♗g7 18 ♖xd6 ♖xe4 (Z.Kozul-V.Tukmakov, Slovenian Team Ch. 2000) and now 19 ♗f2 looks very good for White, e.g. 19...♖xf4 20 ♖e1! or 19...f6 20 ♖ad1 +/-.

e) 8 d5 is the most principled move if White does not want to risk unfavourable transpositions to other variations. Black can respond:

e1) 8...cxd5 9 cxd5 ♘bd7 10 ♘d2 a5 11 ♘c4 ♘c5 12 f3 ♘e8 13 ♗e3 b6 14 ♖b1 ♗a6 15 b4 axb4 16 ♖xb4 with the initiative, A.Huss-U.Flögel, Zürich 1988.

e2) 8...a5 9 ♘e1 ♘a6 10 ♘d3 cxd5 11 cxd5 b5 12 a3 ♗d7 13 b4 ♖c8 14 ♗d2 +/= M.Pein-W.Watson, British Ch. 1989.

e3) 8...c5 is the Old Benoni from Chapter Four (7 d5 c5) a tempo down for Black. As White is already better in that position, unsurprisingly he is better here too; e.g. 9 ♗g5 h6 10 ♗h4 ♕b6 11 ♘d2 ♗d7 12 ♖b1 a5 13 a3 ♘a6 14 ♕c2 ♖fb8 15 b3 += S.Gligoric-J.H.Donner, Madrid 1960.

e4) 8...♘a6, when White can choose between 9 ♘d2 with a good Petrosian System (7 d5 ♘a6 8 ♘d2 c6 9 0-0 – see Chapter Four) and 9 ♗e3 transposing to Chapter Six (7...♘a6 8 ♗e3 c6 9 d5 in the notes to line B1); while 9 ♘e1 also looks good, e.g. 9...♘c5 10 f3 cxd5 11 cxd5 ♘h5 12 ♗e3 a5 13 ♘d3 += G.Grigore-S.Atalik, Satu Mare 1994.

8...exd4

Again 8...♘a6 and 8 ...♘bd7 transpose to Chapter Six (line B1) and Chapter Seven (line C4) respectively. Black has also tried:

a) 8...♕e7 9 d5 ♘g4 10 ♗g5 f6 11 ♗d2 c5 12 ♘e1 ♘h6 13 ♕c1 ♘f7 14 ♘d3 f5 15 f3 f4 16 b4 += R.Cifuentes Parada-M.Gurevich, Gent 1991.

b) 8...♘g4 9 ♗g5 f6 10 ♗h4 (or 10 ♗c1 f5 11 dxe5 dxe5, P.Lyrberg-Mi.Tseitlin, Budapest 1993, 12 ♕xd8 ♖xd8 13 c5 +=) 10...♘h6 11 h3 (11 d5 would be similar to line B in Chapter Three) 11...♘f7 12 ♕c2 ♘g5 13 ♖ad1 ♘d7 14 dxe5 ♘xf3+ 15 ♗xf3 dxe5 16 b4 ♕e7 17 c5 ♖e8 (better 17...a5!? +=) 18 ♖d6 ♘f8 19 ♗e2 ♗e6 20 ♖fd1 +/- W.Addison-K.Burger, US Ch. 1969.

9 ♗xd4

A rather unusual, but good move. White more often takes with the knight, 9 ♘xd4 ♖e8 (D), but this compares unfavourably with 7...exd4 8 ♘xd4 ♖e8 9 f3 c6 (see line C2) as Black's counterplay on the e-file is stronger here:

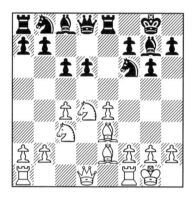

a) 10 f3 d5! 11 cxd5 ♘xd5 12 ♘xd5 cxd5 13 ♕b3 ♘c6 14 ♖ad1 ♗xd4 (or 14...♘xd4 15 ♗xd4 ♗xd4 16 ♖xd4) 15 ♗xd4 ♘xd4 (or 15...dxe4 16 ♗c3 ♕b6+ 17 ♕xb6 axb6 18 fxe4 ♖xe4 19 ♗f3 ♖e8 20 ♖d6 ½-½ C.Matamoros Franco-E.Ubilava, Linares 1994) 16 ♖xd4 ♕f6 17 ♕xd5!? (if 17 ♖f2 ♕f4 18 ♕xd5 ♕e3+ 19 ♖f2 ♗e6 20 ♕d4 ♕xd4 21 ♖xd4 ♗xa2 22 ♖d7 ♖ab8 = D.Yevseev-V.Kotronias, Reggio Emilia 2005/06) 17...♗e6 18 e5 (if 18 ♕c5 ♖ec8 19 ♕b4 a5 20 ♕d2 ♖c2! 21 ♕xc2 ♕xd4+ 22 ♔h1 ♖c8 =+ P.Ricardi-L.Bronstein, Argentine Ch. 1985) 18...♗xd5 19 exf6 ♖xe2 20 ♖xd5 ♖xb2 (½-½ D.Lima-G.Kasparov, clock simul, Rio de Janiero 1996) 21 ♖fd1 h6 and Black drew this ending, S.Pedersen-G.Burgess, Odense 1991.

b) 10 ♕c2 ♕e7 11 f3 (11 ♗f3 ♘bd7, L.Polugaevsky-V.Ivanchuk, Roque-

brune blitz 1992, 12 ♖ad1 a5 13 ♖fe1 ♘c5 14 ♗g5 h6 15 ♗f4 ♘fd7 ∞) 11...d5 12 cxd5 cxd5 (if here 12...♘xd5 13 ♘xd5 cxd5, D.Zilberstein-L.Portisch, USSR-Hungary match 1968, then 14 ♖ae1!? +=) 13 ♗b5 (or 13 ♗d3 ♘a6 14 a3 ♗d7 = A.Shirov-V.Topalov, Dortmund 1996) 13...♗d7 14 ♗f2 dxe4 15 ♖fe1 ♗xb5 16 ♘dxb5 ♘c6 17 ♘xe4 ♘xe4 18 ♖xe4 ♕f6 19 ♖xe8+ ♖xe8 20 ♘xa7 =, and ½-½ P.Van der Sterren-I.Smirin, Tilburg 1992.

9...♖e8

Other moves are also complicated:

a) 9...♕e7 10 ♖e1 (or 10 ♘d2 ♖e8 11 ♖e1 ♘a6, J.Granda Zuniga-A.Shirov, FIDE World Ch., Groningen 1997, 12 ♗f1 ♘c7 ∞) 10...♘bd7 11 ♕c2 ♘c5!? 12 ♘d2 ♖e8 13 ♖ad1 h5 14 h3 ♗h6 15 ♗f1 ♗f4 ∞ J.Pinter-M.Tal, Taxco Interzonal 1985.

b) 9...♘a6 10 ♖e1 ♖e8 11 ♘d2 (if 11 ♕c2 ♘c5 12 ♗f1 ♘e6 13 ♗e3 ♘g4 =+ S.Krivoshey-I.Glek, German League 1998) 11...♘c5 12 ♗f1 ♘e6 13 ♗e3 ♘c7 intending ...d6-d5 ∞ S.Atalik-A.Naiditsch, Budapest 1998.

10 ♕c2 (D)

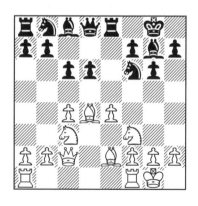

If 10 ♘d2 ♘a6 11 ♔h1 ♘c5 12 f3 a5 13 ♘b3 ♘e6 14 ♗e3 a4 = A.Beliavsky-Z.Kozul, Slovenian Team Ch. 2004.

10...♗g4

Black has also tried:

a) 10...♘a6 11 ♖ad1 ♕e7 12 ♖fe1 ♘c5 13 h3 ♘e6 14 ♗e3 += S.Matveeva-M.Chiburdanidze, Manila Olympiad 1992.

b) 10...♕e7 11 ♖fe1 ♘bd7 12 h3 (not 12 ♖ad1 ♘c5 13 ♗f1? ♗g4 14 b4 ♗xf3 15 gxf3 ♘e6 16 ♗e3 ♘h5 -/+ Y.Gozzoli-E.Miroshnichenko, Cappelle la Grande 2009) 12...c5 13 ♘d5! ♕d8 (if 13...♘xd5 14 ♗xg7 ♔xg7 15 cxd5 += Gofshtein) 14 ♗c3 ♘xe4 15 ♗xg7 ♔xg7 16 ♗d3 ♘ef6 17 ♕c3 ♔g8 18 ♖xe8+ ♘xe8 19 ♖e1 ♘df6? (but if 19...♘ef6 20 ♘e7+ ♔g7 21 g4 and White's initiative is difficult to parry) 20 ♘e7+ ♔g7 21 ♘g5! h6 22 ♘xf7 ♔xf7 23 ♗xg6+ ♔g7 24 ♕g3 ♘c7 25 ♗f5+ 1-0 L.Ogaard-Y.Rantanen, Gausdal 1981.

11 ♖ad1 ♕e7 12 h3 ♗xf3 13 ♗xf3 ♘bd7 14 ♖fe1 *(D)*

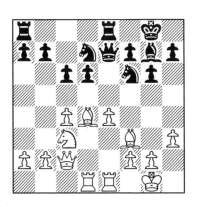

White is a little better due to his space advantage and bishop pair, though Black's position is very solid.

Three examples:

a) 14...♘b6 15 b3 ♕c7 16 a4 ♖ad8 17 a5 ♘c8 18 b4 +/- P.Salani-D.Vella, Istanbul Olympiad 2000.

b) 14...♘e5 15 ♗e2 c5 16 ♗e3 ♘c6 17 ♕c1 a6 18 b3 ♕f8 19 ♗d3 h6 20 ♖d2 ♖ad8 21 ♖ed1 +/= M.Prusikin-P.Piscopo, Steinbrunn 2005.

c) 14...h6 15 ♕d2 ♕f8 16 b3 a6 17 g3 ♖e6 18 ♗g2 ♖ae8 19 f4 += A.Beliavsky-Z.Kozul, Slovenian Team Ch. 2004. This game continued 19...♘h5 20 ♔h2 (having more space White might have avoided the exchange of pieces with 20 ♗f2!? +=) 20...♗xd4 21 ♕xd4 f5 22 ♖f1 ♘hf6 23 exf5 gxf5 24 b4 ♕g7 25 ♗f3 h5 26 ♖f2 ♖e3 27 ♖d3 ♖3e6 28 ♖e2 ♔h8 (28...c5!? ∞) 29 ♖xe6 ♖xe6 30 ♔g2 ♘f8 31 ♖e3 h4 32 ♘e2 ♖xe3 33 ♕xe3 hxg3 34 ♘xg3 ♘g6 35 ♔f2 and White maintained his pull in the endgame, though he ultimately failed to win.

C: 7...exd4 *(D)*

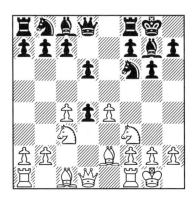

This system is not the most popular for Black, probably because it is rather contrary to the spirit of the King's Indian. By immediately easing the central tension, Black cedes to his opponent more space and freedom of action, while reducing his own attacking potential. Nevertheless, as we will see, Black is not without counterplay. He can put pressure on the e4-pawn with ...♖e8, backed up by ...♘c5 and possibly ...c7-c6 and ...d6-d5; or else seek play on the dark squares with ...♘h5 and ...♘c6.

8 ♘xd4 (D)

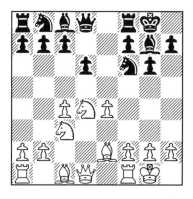

8...♖e8

Black can delay or avoid this move, but doing so does not bring him any benefits; e.g.

a) 8...♘bd7 9 ♗g5 ♘c5 10 f3 h6 11 ♗e3 (a typical manoeuvre ensuring that ♕d2 gains a tempo) 11...a5 12 ♕d2 ♔h7 13 ♘db5 (a consequence of omitting ...c7-c6 – the knight can hardly be expelled as it attacks both the c7- and d6-pawns) 13...♘a6 14 ♖ad1 ♕e7 15 ♖fe1 +/= N.Alexandria-I.Levitina, 7th matchgame, Dubna 1983.

b) 8...c6 9 ♔h1 (9 ♖e1 transposes to *7...c6 8 ♖e1 exd4 9 ♘xd4* in line B) 9...d5 (better 9...♖e8 10 f3 reaching line C2 below) 10 e5 ♘e4 11 f4 f6 12 cxd5 ♘xc3

13 bxc3 ♕xd5 (or 13...fxe5 14 ♘e6! += Ftacnik) 14 ♗a3! ♖e8 15 exf6 ♗xf6 16 f5! with a strong attack, A.Khalifman-A.Fishbein, New York Open 1998.

c) 8...♘c6!? 9 ♗e3 (9 ♘xc6?! is premature and weakens the dark squares; e.g. 9...bxc6 10 ♗g5 ♕e8 11 f3 ♘d7 12 ♕d2 ♖b8 with counterplay, B.Vukic-V.Kostic, Valjevo 1984) 9...♖e8 10 ♘xc6?! (10 f3 is better, transposing to line C3) 10...bxc6 11 ♗f3 ♘d7 12 ♕d2 ♘e5 13 ♗e2 ♗e6 14 b3 c5 15 ♖ae1 ♘c6 16 ♗d3 ♘d4 17 f4 f5 = D.Lima-A.Bachmann, Sao Paulo 2006.

9 f3 (D)

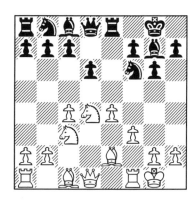

The only serious continuation. White can also defend the e-pawn with 9 ♗f3, but this is seldom a good move without f2-f4 first; e.g. 9...♘a6 10 ♗f4 (10 ♖e1 ♘c5 11 ♖b1 h6 12 b4 ♘e6 13 ♘xe6 ♗xe6 = T.Miladinovic-B.Tadic, Serbian Ch. 2007) 10...♘c5 11 ♖e1 ♘fd7 12 ♕d2 ♘e5 13 ♗e2 ♘c6 14 ♘xc6 bxc6 15 f3 ♘e6 16 ♗e3 c5 = J.Goldner-D.Hergott, Montreal 1998. Of the other moves: 9 ♕c2? walks into 9...♘xe4! 10 ♘xe4 ♗xd4 -/+ H.Rossetto-B.Larsen, Amsterdam Interzonal 1964, while 9

&g5?! h6 forces White to give up the dark-squared bishop: 10 &xf6 ♕xf6 11 ♘db5 ♕d8 =∓ J.Bello-P.Glavina Rossi, Orense 1994.

After the text Black has several tries:

C1: 9...♘h5 *107*
C2: 9...c6 *108*
C3: 9...♘c6 *113*

C1: 9...♘h5 *(D)*

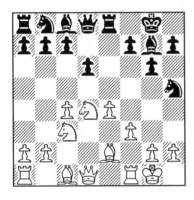

This kind of provocation is typical of various systems in the King's Indian or Benoni, and Black is sometimes willing to lose two tempi after g2-g4, ...♘hf6 in order to counterattack the exposed white pawns. Nevertheless, this move looks a little premature here.

10 g4

White is also better after:

a) 10 &e3 f5 (10...♘c6 transposes to line C3) 11 ♕d2 f4 12 &f2 &e5 13 ♖fd1 ♕f6 (13...♘a6 14 ♘b3 &e6 15 ♘a5 c5 16 ♘d5 ♖b8 17 ♘b3 ♘c7 18 ♘c1 &xd5 19 cxd5 +/= M.Panelo-G.Grigore, Barbera del Valles 2003) 14 ♘db5 (less testing is 14 ♖ac1 c6!? 15 b4 ♘g7 16 ♘b3 ♘e6 ∞

F.Krudde-M.Bosboom, Dutch Team Ch. 1994) 14...♘a6 15 ♖ab1 (or 15 ♘xa7 &e6 16 ♘ab5 ♕f7 17 b3 h6 18 ♖ac1 += F.Lipinsky-P.Issing, German League 2000) 15...♔h8 16 ♘d5 ♕g7 17 &d4 &e6 (A.Guerrero-L.Crotti, Buenos Aires 2002) and now 18 b4 +=.

b) 10 f4 c5 (if 10...♘f6 Black fails to exert any pressure after 11 &f3, e.g. 11...♘bd7 12 ♖e1 c6 13 &e3 ♕c7 14 ♕c2 ♘c5, P.Rechmann-M.Freckmann, German League 1992, 15 b4 ♘e6 16 ♘b3 +=) 11 ♘b3 ♘f6 (or if 11...&xc3!? 12 bxc3 ♘f6 13 ♘d2 ♘xe4 14 ♘xe4 ♖xe4 15 f5 with the initiative) 12 &f3 ♘c6 13 &e3 &e6 14 ♕e2 ♘a5 15 ♘xa5 ♕xa5 16 ♖fd1 ♖ad8 (G.Sosonko-T.Markowski, Polanica Zdroj 1993) 17 ♘b5! &f8 18 &d2 ♕b6 19 &c3 +/-.

10...c5

The alternative is 10...♘f6 11 &e3 (if 11 &g5 h6 12 &h4 ♘c6! 13 ♘xc6 bxc6, L.Ftacnik-A.Kovalev, Passau 1994, 14 ♕a4 ∞ Kovalev) 11...h5 (11...♘c6!? 12 ♘c2 h5 13 g5 ♘h7 14 ♕d2 transposes) 12 g5 ♘h7 13 ♕d2!? (13 f4 and 13 h4 are also promising) 13...♘c6 (if 13...♘xg5 14 &xg5 &xd4+ 15 ♔h1 &f6 16 &xf6 ♕xf6 17 ♘d5 ♕d8 18 ♕h6 intending ♖g1 with a very strong attack, V.Ruban-A.Poluljahov, Russian Ch. 1994) 14 ♘c2 (if 14 f4 &h3 15 ♖f2 f6! with counterplay, Gleizerov) 14...&h3 15 ♖f2 followed by ♔h1 and ♖g1; e.g. 15...&xc3 (or 15...a5 16 ♔h1 a4 17 ♖g1 ♘e5 18 &d4 += I.Ivanisevic-B.Miljanic, Yugoslav Team Ch. 1998) 16 bxc3 ♖e5 (E.Van den Doel-R.Polzin, Dresden 1995) 17 ♔h1 ♘xg5 18 ♖g1 with excellent play for the pawn.

11 ♘c2

White cannot count on an advantage after 11 ♘db5 a6 12 gxh5 axb5 13 ♘xb5 ∞ Gleizerov; or if 11 ♘f5 gxf5 12 gxh5 ♘c6 13 ♔h1 ♔h8 14 ♖g1 (L.Van Wely-A.Fishbein, New York Open 1993) then 14...♗d4!? 15 ♖g2 fxe4 or 15...♖g8 with a good game for Black.

11...♗e5

Not 11...♘f6 12 ♗f4 ♖e6 13 ♕d2 ♘c6 14 ♖ad1 ♘e8 15 a3 a6 16 ♔h1 ♗d7 17 b4 and Black is deprived of counterplay, M.Repplinger-A.Scheske, German League 2001.

12 gxh5

After other moves Black has an excellent position; e.g. 12 f4 ♗xc3 13 gxh5 ♗g7 14 hxg6 hxg6 R.Kleeschaetzky-J.Harm, Berlin 1995; or 12 ♕e1 ♘f4 13 ♘d5 g5 14 ♘xf4 gxf4 D.Giacomazzi-D.Chevallier, Paris 1991.

12...♗xh2+ ½-½ (D)

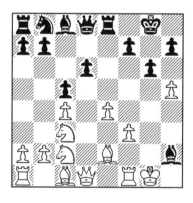

This was the abrupt end in D.Ledger-M.Twyble, British League 1996, repeated in B.Kelly-M.Twyble, British League 1999. Obviously after 13 ♔g2 ♕h4 or 13 ♔xh2 ♕h4+ Black has a perpetual check. But perhaps a future

opponent will try 13 ♔f2 ♕h4+ 14 ♔e3, after which we can see nothing concrete for Black.

C2: 9...c6 (D)

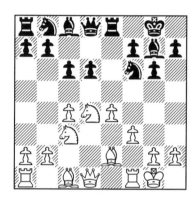

Black prepares the strike back in the centre with ...d6-d5. White can undertake some measures against it, or else allow it and make a prophylactic move.

10 ♔h1

Instead, 10 ♗e3 transposes to 7...c6 8 ♗e3 exd4 9 ♘xd4 ♖e8 10 f3 (see line B), but White clearly has better than ♗e3 here. Apart from the text, two knight moves deserve attention:

a) 10 ♘c2 is aimed against the ...d6-d5 advance and also prevents ...♘bd7.

a1) 10...d5 11 cxd5 cxd5 12 exd5 ♕b6+ 13 ♔h1 ♘a6 14 ♗e3 ♕xb2 15 ♗d4 ♘b4 16 ♘xb4 ♕xb4 17 ♖b1 ♕e7 18 ♗b5 (V.Hort-L.Barczay, Dortmund 1982) and if 18...♗d7 19 d6! +/- Hort.

a2) 10...♗e6 11 ♗e3 ♕c7 12 f4 ♗c8 13 ♗f3 ♘bd7 (M.Najdorf-H.Pilnik, Amsterdam 1950) 14 ♖c1 ♘b6 15 b3 ♘g4 16 ♗d4 +/- Ftacnik.

a3) 10...♘a6 11 ♗e3 d5 12 cxd5 cxd5 13 ♗b5 ♗d7 14 ♗xd7 ♕xd7 15 ♗d4

♘c7 (or 15...dxe4 16 fxe4 ♘xe4 17 ♗xg7 ♕xd1 18 ♖axd1 ♔xg7 19 ♘xe4 ♖xe4 20 ♖d7 +=) 16 e5 ♘h5 17 f4 ♘e6 (R.Bagirov-A.Pachmann, European Junior Ch. 1994) 18 ♗e3 d4 19 ♘xd4 ♘hxf4 20 ♖xf4 ♘xf4 21 ♗xf4 ♗xe5 22 ♗xe5 ♖xe5 23 ♘f3 ♕xd1+ 24 ♖xd1 ♖e7 and White has the better endgame.

a4) 10...♘h5 11 ♗e3 (if 11 g4 ♗e5 12 gxh5 ♗xh2+ as in line C1) 11...♗e5 12 ♕d2 ♕h4 13 f4! ♗xc3 14 ♕xc3 ♘f6 (or 14...♖xe4 15 ♗f3) 15 e5 +/- I.Akimov-A.Gubajdullin, St Petersburg 2003.

b) 10 ♘b3 *(D)* has similar aims, while hiding the b2-pawn from ...♕b6+ so that the c1-bishop can go to f4 or g5.

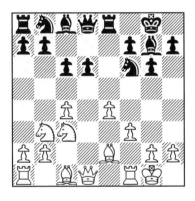

b1) 10...a6 11 ♗f4 d5 12 cxd5 cxd5 13 exd5 b5 (M.Kaabi-E.Ahmed, Cairo 1997) 14 d6! b4 15 ♘d5 +/- Khalifman.

b2) 10...♘a6 11 ♗f4 (also good is 11 ♗g5 h6 12 ♗h4 ♘c7 13 ♕c2 g5 14 ♗f2 ♘e6, R.Bagirov-D.Skorchenko, Krasnodar 2002, 15 ♖fd1 ♘f4 16 ♗f1 +/=) 11...d5 12 cxd5 cxd5 (M.Ruiz Gutierrez-J.Medina, Spanish Team Ch. 1992) 13 ♗b5 ♗d7 14 ♗xa6 bxa6 15 exd5 += Khalifman.

b3) 10...♘h5 11 ♗e3 f5 12 ♕d2 f4

(E.Gleizerov-A.Poluljahov, Krasnodar 1998) 13 ♗d4 +/= Poluljahov.

b4) 10...a5!? tries to exploit the knight's position on b3, but also weakens the light squares; e.g. 11 ♘a4 c5 12 ♖b1! ♗d7 13 ♘c3 a4 14 ♘a1 ♘h5 (or if 14...♘c6, M.Varaksin-I.Siuniakov, Prokojevsk 1998, 15 ♘b5 ♘d4 16 ♘xd4 cxd4 17 ♘c2 ♕b6 18 ♖f2 intending b2-b3, ♗b2 += Hertneck) 15 ♘c2 ♕h4 16 ♘d5 ♘c6 17 ♖f2 (G.Hertneck-G.Barbero, Austrian Team Ch. 1994) 17...♘d4 18 g3 ♘xe2+ 19 ♖xe2 ♕d8 20 g4 ♘f6 21 ♗g5 += Hertneck.

Let us return to 10 ♔h1. The purpose of this move is not to hinder the ...d6-d5 advance but be better prepared for it, by pre-empting the any check or pin with ...♕b6.

10...♘bd7

Three other moves are worth examining:

a) After 10...d5 Black has serious problems: 11 cxd5 cxd5 12 ♗g5! dxe4 *(D)* (if 12...♘c6 13 ♗b5 ♕b6 14 ♘xc6 bxc6 15 ♗xf6 ♗xf6 16 ♘xd5! cxd5 17 ♗xe8 +/- V.Eingorn-N.Rashkovsky, USSR Ch., Minsk 1987)

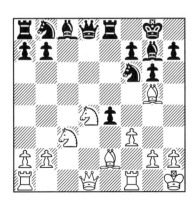

when White can choose between:

a1) 13 ♘db5 ♘bd7 14 ♘d6 (also very strong is 14 ♗f4 ♘h5, J.Bonin-R.Schutt, New York 1991, 15 ♗d6 +/-) 14...♖f8 15 fxe4 h6 (intending ...♕b6 ∞ Spraggett) 16 ♗h4 and White has a big (if not decisive) advantage; e.g. 16...a6 (if now 16...♕b6? 17 e5! +-; or 16...♘e5 17 ♘xc8 ♖xc8 18 ♕xd8 ♖fxd8 19 ♗xf6 +-) 17 ♖c1 and Black has no reasonable way to unpin.

a2) 13 fxe4 h6 (otherwise 13...♘bd7 14 ♘db5, e.g. 14...h6 15 ♗h4 g5 16 ♗g3 ♘xe4 17 ♘xe4 ♖xe4 18 ♗h5! ♖e7?! 19 ♘c7 ♖b8 20 ♘d5 1-0 V.Ikonnikov-E.Haak, Vlissingen 1998; or 14...♖e5 15 ♗f4 ♘xe4 16 ♗xe5 ♗xe5 17 ♘xe4 ♕h4 18 h3 ♕xe4 19 ♕b3 ♘f6 20 ♗c4 ♕h4, M.Tal-B.Spassky, Montreal 1979, 21 ♖ae1! +- Tal) 14 ♗h4! g5 15 ♗g3 ♘xe4 16 ♘xe4 ♖xe4 (or 16...♕xd4 17 ♘d6, Rom.Hernandez-J.Ibanez Aullana, Valencia 1999, 17...♕xd1 18 ♗xd1 ♖f8 19 ♘xc8 ♖xc8 20 ♗b3 +/-) 17 ♘b5 ♕xd1 18 ♖axd1 ♘c6 19 ♗f3 ♖e8 (or 19...♖e7 20 ♘c7 ♖xc7 21 ♗xc7 ♗e6 22 b3 +/-) 20 ♘c7 ♗e6 21 ♘xa8 ♖xa8 22 ♗d5 1-0 N.Sulava-P.Gaido, Montecatini Terme 1994.

b) 10...♘a6 (intending ...♘c7 and then ...d6-d5) 11 ♗e3 (the only way to stop the breakthrough; but 11 ♗g5!? is also good, e.g. 11...♘c5 12 b4 ♘e6 13 ♘xe6 ♗xe6 14 ♕d2 a5 15 b5 a4 16 ♖ac1 ♕a5 17 ♕xd6 ♘g4 18 fxg4 ♗xc3, N.Giertz-W.Haist, Biel 1998, 19 ♖b1 +/-) 11...♘c7 (not 11...d5? 12 cxd5 ♘xd5 13 exd5! ♖xe3 14 ♗xa6 bxa6 15 ♘xc6 +/- V.Bogdanovski-D.Jacimovic, Skopje 1991) 12 ♕d2 ♕e7 (still not 12...d5?! 13 cxd5 cxd5 14 ♘db5 ♘xb5 15 ♗xb5 ♗d7 16 ♗xd7 ♕xd7 17 exd5 +/- V.Neverov-L.Sokolin, USSR Team Ch. 1991) and now, rather than 13 ♘c2 d5! 14 cxd5 cxd5 15 exd5 ♘fxd5 16 ♘xd5 ♘xd5 17 ♕xd5 ♗f5 = A.Leniart-D.Andreikin, European Ch., Warsaw 2005, White should play 13 ♖ad1! intending 13...d5 14 cxd5 ♘fxd5 (or 14...cxd5 15 ♘db5) 15 ♘xd5 ♘xd5 16 ♗h6 +/=.

c) 10...♘h5?!, as mentioned above, seeks to weaken the white kingside, but it cannot really be recommended: 11 g4! ♘f6 (obviously 11...♗e5? just drops a piece here) 12 ♗f4 (also good is 12 ♗e3 h5 13 g5 ♘h7 14 ♕d2) 12...h5 13 g5 ♘h7 14 ♕d2 *(D)* and then:

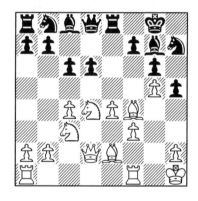

c1) 14...♘a6 15 ♖ad1 ♕e7 16 ♖g1 ♘f8 17 ♗f1 (preventing ...♗h3; this seems simpler than 17 a3 ♗h3 18 b4 ♖ad8 19 b5 += A.Shirov-L.Yurtaev, USSR Ch., Moscow 1991; or 17...♗d7!? 18 ♘db5 d5! 19 ♘d6 d4 20 ♘xe8 ♖xe8 21 ♘a2 ♘e6 ∞ M.Ulibin-A.Poluljahov, Kstovo 1997) 17...♘d7 18 ♗g3 ♘ac5 (no better is 18...♘b6 19 b3 ♘c5 20 ♗g2 ♗e5 21 f4 ♗g7 22 f5! +/- E.Bareev-A.Poluljahov, Russian Ch. 1998; or if

18...♘dc5, R.Stern-G.Lorscheid, European Ch., Dresden 2007, then 19 ♘db5! cxb5 20 cxb5 ♗xc3 21 bxc3 ♘xe4 22 fxe4 ♘c5 23 ♗xd6 ♘xe4 24 ♗xe7 ♘xd2 25 ♖xd2 ♖xe7 26 ♖d8+ ♔g7 27 ♗h3 ♖c7 28 ♖g3 +/-) 19 b4 ♘e6 20 ♘f5 (or just 20 ♘xe6 ♕xe6 21 ♗xd6 +/-) 20...gxf5 21 ♗xd6 ♕d8 22 exf5 ♘d4 23 ♕f4 ♘f8 (I.Belov-A.Poluljahov, Rostov 1993) 24 ♗c7! ♕d7 25 ♘e4 +-.

c2) 14...♗e5 15 ♗e3 doesn't help Black much: 15...♘a6 16 ♖ad1 ♗h3 (if now 16...♕e7 then 17 f4! ♗h8 18 f5 with the initiative) 17 ♖g1 ♘c5 18 ♕e1! ♕e7 19 ♕h4 ♗d7 20 ♗f1 a5 (better 20...♖ad8!? intending ....♗c8 +/= Epishin) 21 ♗g2 ♗g7 22 ♖d2 a4 23 ♖gd1 ♖a5 24 ♕g3 ♘f8 25 h3 ♗c8 26 f4 +/- V.Epishin-L.Yurtaev, USSR Ch., Moscow 1991.

11 ♗g5 *(D)*

White has also tried:

a) 11 ♘c2 ♘b6 12 ♗g5 h6 (or 12...♗e6!? 13 b3 h6 14 ♗e3 d5 15 cxd5 cxd5 16 e5 ♘fd7 17 f4, G.Grigore-M.Larios Crespo, Benasque 1999, 17...f6 with counterplay) 13 ♗h4 ♗e6 14 b3 (safer is 14 ♘e3!? g5 15 ♗g3 d5 16 cxd5 cxd5 17 ♘b5 ♖e7, P.Kindl-R.Speckner, German League 1991, 18 ♘d6 +/=) 14...♘xe4! (a brilliant idea; Black only gets two minor pieces for the queen but the bishop pair, very active pieces and lack of concrete plan for White are sufficient factors for equality) 15 ♗xd8 ♘xc3 16 ♕d2 ♖axd8 17 ♖ae1 c5 18 ♘e3 d5 19 cxd5 ♘bxd5 20 ♘xd5 ♖xd5 21 ♕c1 b5! with compensation, A.Huzman-L.Yurtaev, Tashkent 1987.

b) 11 ♗f4 ♘h5!? (sacrificing the d-pawn; passive defence with 11...♘e5 leads to a position where Black is deprived of counterplay; e.g. 12 ♕d2 a5 13 ♖ad1 a4, A.Kalka-M.Bosboom, German League 1995, 14 ♘c2 +/=) 12 ♗xd6 ♕f6 13 ♘b3! (adding useful support to the c5-square) 13...♘f4 14 c5 a5 (or 14...b6 15 ♕d2 ♘xe2 16 ♕xe2 a5 17 ♖fd1 a4 18 ♘d4 a3 19 b4 +/- D.Adla-P.Glavina Rossi, Argentine Ch. 1989) 15 a4 ♘e5 16 g3 ♘xe2 17 ♕xe2 ♗h3 18 ♖f2 ♗e6 19 ♘d2 ♘d7 20 f4 +/= P.Petran-N.Borge, Gyor 1990.

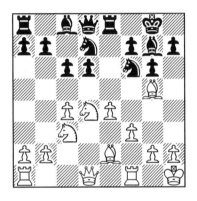

11...♕a5

Of the other options, lines 'c' and 'd' below deserve attention:

a) 11...a5 12 ♕d2 a4 13 ♖fd1 ♕a5 14 ♘c2 ♘e5 (M.Cebalo-M.Todorchevic, Yugoslavia 1989) 15 b4! +/-.

b) 11...♖e5 12 ♕d2 ♘c5 13 ♗f4 ♖e8 14 ♖ad1 ♘h5 15 ♗g5 ♗f6 16 ♗e3 +/= A.Shestoperov-B.Mirzahodjaev, Simferopol 1989.

c) 11...♕b6!? 12 ♘b3 a5 is more interesting; e.g. 13 ♖b1 (if 13 ♕d2 a4 14 ♗e3 ♕d8 15 ♘d4 ♘c5! 16 ♖fd1 ♘fd7 17 ♗f1 ♗e5 18 g3 ♕b6 19 ♖ab1 ♕a5 ∞ D.Milanovic-D.Mozetic, Belgrade 2001;

or 13 ♘a4 ♕b4 14 ♘c1 ♘c5 15 ♘xc5 ♕xc5 16 ♕d2, M.Roeder-G.Burgess, Vienna 1990, 16...♘d7 ∞) 13...a4 14 ♘a1 ♘h5!? 15 ♗d2 (or if 15 ♕xd6 h6 16 ♗d2 ♗e5 17 ♕a3 ♕c7 with compensation) 15...♘c5 16 ♗e3 ♕c7 17 ♕d2 ♗e5 18 ♘c2 ♕e7 19 ♗g5 f6 20 ♗e3 f5 21 ♗d4 ♗f4 22 ♗e3 ♗e5 ½-½ V.Hefka-O.Rusyanovsky, corr. 1999.

d) 11...h6!? 12 ♗h4 (if 12 ♗e3 ♘b6! 13 ♕d2 ♔h7 14 ♖ac1 ♕e7 15 ♖fe1, J.Norri-T.Ristoja, Finnish Ch. 1989, 15...d5! 16 cxd5 ♘fxd5 17 ♘xd5 ♘xd5 18 ♗f2 ♘b6 =) 12...♘c5 (instead, 12...♘e5 13 ♕c2 g5 14 ♗f2 c5 15 ♘b3 ♗e6 16 ♖fd1 ♕e7 17 ♘d2 ♘h5 18 ♘f1 +/= V.Chekhov-L.Yurtaev, Frunze 1988; or if 12...a6 13 ♕c2 ♕c7 14 ♖ad1 b5 15 cxb5 cxb5 16 ♕d2 ♗b7 17 ♘c2 ♖e6, E.Vladimirov-A.Yermolinsky, Tashkent 1987, 18 ♗g3 += owing to the weak d6-pawn) 13 ♕c2 (Black seems okay in other lines; e.g. 13 ♘b3 ♘xb3 14 axb3 ♕e7 15 ♕c2 ½-½ L.Kocsis-N.Stanec, Halkidiki 2002; or 13 ♖c1 a5 14 ♖c2 a4 15 b4 axb3 16 axb3 ♕b6 17 ♗f2 ♘h5 =+ L.B.Hansen-T.Radjabov, European Team Ch., Crete 2007) 13...a5 14 ♖ad1 a4 15 b4 axb3 16 ♘xb3 ♘xb3 (or 16...♘a4?! 17 ♘xa4 ♖xa4 18 ♗g3 ♕b6 19 ♗xd6 ♕a7 20 ♖d2 +/- S.Karjakin-T.Radjabov, Russian Team Ch. 2008) 17 axb3 ♕e7 18 ♖d2 ♗e6 19 ♖fd1 g5 20 ♗f2 d5 21 exd5 cxd5 22 c5 += A.Gipslis-F.Gheorghiu, Bucharest 1967.

12 ♗e3

The strongest move, though White has also played:

a) 12 ♗h4 ♘h5! 13 f4 ♘xf4! (an in-teresting motif!) 14 ♖xf4 ♕e5 (M.Makarov-T.Khasanov, USSR 1987) 15 ♘f5 ♕xf4 16 ♗g3 ♕g5 17 ♗h4 = Makarov.

b) 12 ♗f4 ♘e5 13 ♕d2 a6 14 ♖fd1 ♗e6 15 ♘xe6 ♖xe6 16 a3 b5 17 b4 ♕c7 18 cxb5 axb5 19 a4 bxa4 20 ♖xa4 ♖xa4 21 ♘xa4 d5 22 ♘c3 dxe4 23 ♘xe4 ½-½ J.Fedorowicz-A.Strikovic, New York Open 1988.

c) 12 ♗d2 ♕d8 13 ♘b3 ♘b6 14 ♖c1 ♗e6 15 ♘a5 ♕e7 16 b4 (Rom.Hernandez-M.Schlosser, Thessaloniki Olympiad 1988) 16...♘fd7 ∞.

12...♘e5

Other moves also lead to an advantage for White; e.g. 12...d5 13 cxd5 cxd5 14 ♘b3 ♕d8 15 ♘xd5 ♘xd5 16 ♕xd5 ♗xb2 17 ♖ad1 +/- B.Lalic-A.Strikovic, Yugoslav Ch. 1989; or 12...♕c7 13 ♕d2 b6 14 b4 a6 15 ♖fd1 +/= W.Kordts-H.Kunzmann, corr. 2002.

13 ♕d2 ♗e6

Alternatively:

a) 13...♗d7 14 ♖ad1 ♕c7 15 ♗g5! ♘h5 16 g4 ♘f6 17 ♕f4 ♕d8 18 ♘b3 ♕e7 19 ♖d2 +/- R.Dautov-V.Varavin, USSR 1988.

b) 13...a6 14 ♖ad1 ♕c7 15 ♗h6 b5 16 ♗xg7 ♔xg7 17 cxb5 axb5 18 f4 ♘ed7 and now, rather than 19 ♗xb5 cxb5 20 ♘dxb5 ♕c6 21 ♘xd6 ♖xe4 22 ♘cxe4 ♘xe4 23 ♘xe4 ♕xe4 24 ♖fe1 ♕f5 =+ P.Van der Sterren-J.Piket, Wijk aan Zee 1988, much stronger is 19 b4! ♗b7 (Black has no more sensible move; if 19...♘xe4 20 ♘xe4 ♖xe4 21 ♗f3 +-) 20 ♗xb5 cxb5 21 ♘dxb5 ♕b6 22 ♘xd6 +/-, when 22...♖xe4 is impossible as the ♘d7 hangs.

14 ♘xe6 ♖xe6 *(D)*

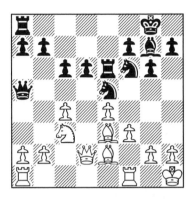

White has a clear advantage due to the bishop pair, extra space and the weak d6-pawn; for example:

a) 15 ♖fd1 a6 16 b4 ♕c7 17 ♖ac1 ♕e7 18 a4 +/- A.Kurz-O.Borik, German League 1990.

b) 15 a3 a6 16 b4 ♕c7 17 ♖ac1 ♖ae8 18 ♘d5 ♕b8 19 ♘xf6+ ♗xf6 20 ♖fd1 ♗g7 21 c5 d5 (B.Lalic-A.Strikovic, Seville 2001) 22 ♗f4! +/-.

C3: 9...♘c6 *(D)*

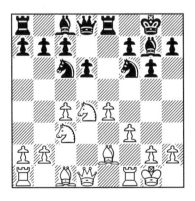

10 ♗e3

The most natural move. White has also tried:

a) 10 ♘xc6 bxc6 11 ♗g5, after which Black usually organizes play on the dark squares; e.g. 11...h6 12 ♗h4 g5 13 ♗f2 ♘d7 (or 13...♗e6 14 ♕c2 ♘d7 15 ♖ad1 c5 16 g3 ♕c8 17 f4 ♗h3 18 ♖fe1 ♘f6! with counterplay, L.Ftacnik-I.Glek, German League 1994) 14 ♖c1 a5 15 b3 ♕e7 16 ♗d3 ♘c5 17 ♗b1 ♘e6 18 ♕d2 ♗b7 19 ♔h1 c5 20 ♘e2 ♗e5 (a typical set-up with control of the dark squares) 21 ♗e3 ♔h8 22 f4 gxf4 23 ♘xf4 ♖g8! = V.Chuchelov-I.Glek, Leuven 1995.

b) 10 ♘c2 ♘h5!? *(D)* (or 10...♘d7 11 ♘d5 ♘c5 12 ♖b1 a5 13 b3 f5 with good counterplay for Black, A.Herzog-D.Vombek, Austrian Team Ch. 1996) and then:

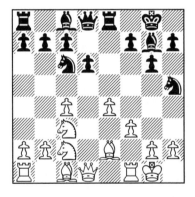

b1) 11 g4 ♗e5! leads to a familiar draw: 12 gxh5 (or 12 ♘d5 ♗xh2+! 13 ♔xh2 ♕h4+ 14 ♔g1 ½-½ D.Zagorskis-I.Glek, Böblingen 1994) 12...♗xh2+ 13 ♔xh2 ♕h4+ 14 ♔g1 ♕g3+ 15 ♔h1 ½-½ A.Yermolinsky-A.Khalifman, Hastings 1995/96.

b2) 11 ♘d5 f5 12 g4 fxg4 13 fxg4 ♘f6 14 ♗g5 ♖f8 15 ♖f2 (or 15 c5 ♗e6 16 cxd6 cxd6 17 ♘ce3 h6! 18 ♘xf6+ ♗xf6

19 ♗xh6 ♖f7 with compensation, K.Sakaev-I.Glek, Russian Ch. 1995) 15...h6 16 ♘xf6+ ♗xf6 17 ♗xh6 ♖f7 18 ♕d2 ♗e6 19 ♖af1 ♗xb2 20 ♖xf7 ♗xf7 21 ♘e3 ♕h4 (R.Pogorelov-P.Lezcano Jaen, San Sebastian 1997) and now if 22 ♘d5! ♗e5 23 ♗d1 (+= Pogorelov) then 23...♕h3 offers mutual chances in a complicated position.

b3) 11 ♗e3!? f5! (if 11...♗e5 12 ♘d5 ♘e7 13 f4 ♘xd5, V.Epishin-P.Svidler, St Petersburg 1996, then 14 cxd5 ♗xb2 15 ♖b1 ♗g7 16 ♗xh5 gxh5 17 f5, e.g. 17...♖xe4 18 f6 ♗xf6 19 ♕f3 ♖c4 20 ♘a3 ♖c3 21 ♘b5 ♗g4 22 ♕f4 ♖xe3 23 ♕xe3 +/- Epishin/Nesis) 12 ♕d2 ♗e6 13 ♖ad1 fxe4!? 14 ♘xe4 ♘f6 15 ♘c3 ♕e7 16 ♖fe1 ♖ad8 17 ♘d5 ♕f7 ∞ B.Esen-V.Jianu, European Junior Ch. 2001.

10...♘h5 (D)

Other moves are good for White:

a) 10...♘d7 11 ♕d2 ♘xd4 12 ♗xd4 ♗xd4+ 13 ♕xd4 += R.Almond-J.Munz, Gibraltar 2008.

b) 10...♗d7 11 ♕d2 ♘xd4 12 ♗xd4 ♗e6 13 ♖ad1 a6 14 ♘d5 += R.Sakic-J.Sveinsson, corr. 2004.

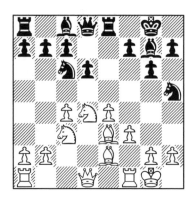

After 10...♘h5 White has a choice:

Instead:

a) 11 ♘c2 returns to 10 ♘c2 ♘h5 11 ♗e3 (note 'b3' above).

b) 11 g4?! ♘f4! (stronger here than 11...♗e5 12 gxh5 ♗xh2+ etc) 12 ♘xc6 ♘xe2+ 13 ♘xe2 bxc6 14 ♕d2 c5 15 ♖ad1 ♗b7 with excellent play for Black, M.Kijac-L.Salai, Slovakian Team Ch. 2001.

c) 11 ♘d5 is premature and leads to exchanges: 11...♘xd4 12 ♗xd4 c6 13 ♘c3 ♗e5! (S.Halkias-H.Banikas, Greece 1997) 14 ♗xe5 dxe5 15 ♕xd8 ♖xd8 16 ♖fd1 intending c4-c5 = Papaioannou.

C31: 11 f4 (D)

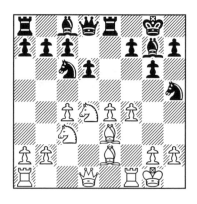

The most aggressive move, but Black can count on sufficient counterplay.

11...♘f6 12 ♗f3

Black has no problems after 12 ♘xc6 bxc6 13 ♗f3 ♘xe4 14 ♗xe4 (or 14 ♘xe4

♗f5 15 ♘xd6 cxd6 16 ♗d4 ♗e4 = A.Shirov-A.Sherzer, Clichy 1995) 14...d5! 15 ♗xd5! cxd5 16 ♕xd5 ♗e6 17 ♕xd8 ♖exd8 = Glek; e.g. 18 ♖ac1 ♗xc4 19 ♖fe1 ♖d3 20 ♔f2 ♗xc3 21 ♖xc3 ♖xc3 22 bxc3 ♗xa2 23 ♖a1 ½-½ W.Hort-K.Mallard, corr. 2003.

12...♗g4!

Other moves are weaker:

a) 12...♘g4 13 ♗xg4 ♗xg4 14 ♘xc6 ♕d7 15 ♕d3 ♗xc3 16 ♘d4! ♗xb2 17 ♖ab1 c5 18 ♖xb2 cxd4 19 ♗xd4 ♕c6 20 ♖e1 ♖ac8 (E.Lobron-I.Glek, German League 1995) 21 ♖d2 ♕xc2 22 ♕g3 ♕b4 23 ♕f2 with compensation (Lobron).

b) 12...♗d7 13 ♕d2 a6 14 h3 ♘a5 15 ♕d3 c5 16 ♘b3 ♗c6 17 ♗f2 ♕b6 18 ♘xa5 ♕xa5 19 ♖fe1 +/- A.Shirov-A.Miles, Horgen 1994.

13 ♘xc6 ♗xf3 14 ♕xf3 bxc6 *(D)*

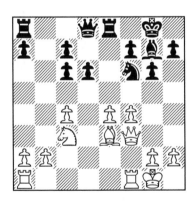

15 ♖ae1

Black was threatening 15...♘xe4 16 ♘xe4 ♕e7 -/+. Otherwise:

a) 15 ♗d2 ♕b8!? (or 15...♕c8 16 ♖ae1 ♕g4) 16 b3 ♕b6+ 17 ♔h1 ♘xe4! 18 ♘xe4 ♕d4! 19 ♘xd6 cxd6 20 ♖ad1 ♕e4 (P.Van der Sterren-I.Glek, German League 1995) 21 ♗c3! = Glek.

b) 15 ♗d4 ♕c8 (worth analysing is 15...♘xe4 16 ♗xg7 ♘d2 17 ♕d3 ♘xf1 18 ♗d4 ♘xh2 19 ♕g3 ♖b8 20 b3 c5 21 ♗f2 f5 ∞) 16 ♖ad1 ♕g4 17 e5 dxe5 18 ♗xe5 ♕e6! 19 b3 ♘g4! 20 ♗xg7 ♔xg7 21 h3 ♕e3+! 22 ♔h1 ♘f6 ½-½ A.Karpov-I.Glek, Biel 1996.

15...♕c8

The queen again makes her way to g4.

16 ♗d4

Instead:

a) 16 ♗f2 ♕g4! 17 ♕d3?! (17 ♗d4 = Glek) 17...♕xf4! 18 ♗xa7 (or 18 ♗d4 ♕g5) 18...♕h4 19 ♗f2 ♕h5 -/+ E.Solozhenkin-I.Glek, Le Touquet 1994.

b) 16 ♗d2 ♕g4 17 ♕d3 ♘d7 18 ♗e3 ♖ad8?! succeeded after 19 ♗d4? ♘e5! 20 ♕c2 ♘f3+ 21 ♖xf3 ♗xd4+ 22 ♔h1 f5 -/+ T.Haritakis-H.Banikas, Greek Ch. 1996. White should try 19 ♗xa7 with a complicated position where only he could fight for an advantage; e.g. 19...c5 20 ♘b5 ♖a8 21 ♘xc7 ♗d4+ 22 ♔h1 ♖xa7 23 ♘xe8 ♕e6 24 ♘xd6 ♕xd6 25 a3. In turn Black should probably prefer 18...♖ab8.

c) 16 e5 leads to extremely entangled positions with mutual chances, e.g. 16...dxe5 17 ♕xc6 ♘g4 18 ♗c5 exf4 19 ♘d5 ♘e5 20 ♘f6+ ♗xf6 21 ♕xf6 ♕f5! 22 ♕xf5 gxf5 ∞ L.Ftacnik-I.Glek, Wijk aan Zee 1995.

16...♕e6!?

If now 16...♕g4 17 ♕d3 ♕h5 (not 17...c5?! 18 ♗xf6 ♗xf6 19 ♘d5 +/- Bareev) 18 h3 ♘d7 19 ♗xg7 ♔xg7 (B.Bayer-K.Jürgens, Austrian Team Ch. 2004) 20 e5 and White has the upper hand. Alternatively, 16...c5 17 ♗xf6

♗xf6 18 e5 ♗g7 19 g4 (or 19 ♘d5!?, J.Lakner-B.Donaldson, Queenstown 2006, 19...c6 20 ♘f6+ ♗xf6 21 exf6 ♖b8 22 ♖xe8+ ♕xe8 23 b3 ♕e6 24 ♕xc6 ♕xf6 25 h3 +/=) 19...♖b8 20 b3 dxe5 21 f5 with the initiative; e.g. 21...e4 22 ♘xe4 (E.Bareev-S.Kindermann, Vienna 1996) and if 22...♖e5 23 fxg6 fxg6 24 ♘f6+ ♗xf6 (Bareev) 25 ♖xe5! ♗xe5 26 ♕d5+ ♔h8 27 ♕xe5+ ♔g8 28 ♕d5+ ♔g8 29 h3 +-.

17 b3 c5!? *(D)*

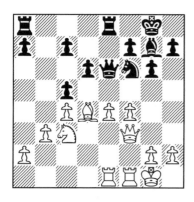

And now White has chosen between:

a) 18 f5 gxf5 19 ♗xf6 and then we have:

a1) 19...♗xf6 20 ♕g3+ (or 20 ♘d5!? ♗d4+ 21 ♔h1 fxe4 22 ♕g3+ ♕g6 23 ♕xg6+ hxg6 24 ♘xc7 ♖ac8 25 ♘xe8 ♖xe8 26 g4 +/= Svidler) 20...♔h8 21 ♘d5 ♖g8 22 exf5 ♗d4+ 23 ♔h1 ♕h6 24 ♕f4 ♕xf4 25 ♖xf4 ♖ge8 26 ♖fe4 ♖xe4 27 ♖xe4 c6 28 ♘e7 d5 29 cxd5 cxd5 30 ♘xd5 ♖d8 31 ♘f4 ½-½ A.Greenfeld-P.Svidler, Haifa 1996.

a2) 19...♕xf6! 20 ♘d5 ♕d4+ 21 ♔h1 fxe4 22 ♕xf7+ ♔h8 23 ♘xc7 (not 23 ♕xc7? e3 24 ♖e2 ♕d3! 25 ♖fe1 ♖f8 and

wins, e.g. 26 h3 ♗e5 27 ♘xe3 ♗g3 or 26 ♔g1 ♖f2! 27 ♖xe3 ♕d2 28 ♔h1 ♖af8 29 ♖g1 ♗d4 30 ♕e7 ♖2f7) 23...♖f8 24 ♕e7 ♖xf1+ 25 ♖xf1 ♖g8 26 ♘e6 ♕e5 ∞ Svidler.

b) 18 ♗xf6 ♕xf6 19 ♘d5 ♕d8 20 e5 looks a better try; e.g. 20...c6 21 ♘f6+ ♗xf6 22 exf6 ♕xf6 23 ♕xc6. Svidler gives this as equal, and P.Sinkovics-S.Videki, Zalakaros 1997, was agreed drawn on the previous move. Nevertheless, we think that White has a small advantage here.

C32: 11 ♘xc6 *(D)*

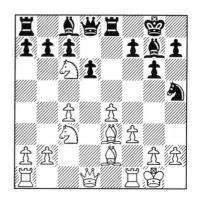

As mentioned before, this exchange often allows Black to take over the dark squares in the centre.

11...bxc6 12 ♕d2

Other moves are:

a) 12 g4 ♗e5! 13 ♖f2 (13 gxh5 ♗xh2+ is the usual draw) 13...♘f4 14 ♗f1 ♕f6 with excellent play on the weakened dark squares, M.Reta-P.Gomez, Posadas 2005.

b) 12 ♗d4 ♗h6 (or 12...♘f4!? 13 ♗xg7 ♕g5 14 g3 ♔xg7 ∞ E.Gersov-E.Meyer, Arlington 2000) 13 g3 c5 14

♞f2 ♜b8 15 b3 ♝g7 16 ♜c1 f5 with counterplay, A.Valle de Souza-E.Matsuura, Itapiruba 1997.

c) 12 ♜c1 f5?! (12...c5 seems preferable) 13 ♕d2 f4 14 ♝xf4 ♞xf4 15 ♕xf4 ♝e5 16 ♕d2 ♕f6 17 f4 ♝d4+ 18 ♚h1 +/- J.Polgar-N.Heck, Frankfurt (simul) 1999, as Black has insufficient play for the pawn.

12...f5 *(D)*

This line also arises via 11 ♕d2 f5 12 ♞xc6 bxc6, which avoids 12...c5! in note 'd' below, though it allows other possibilities (see line C33). Here Black has also tried:

a) 12...♞f6 13 ♜ad1 ♝b7 14 ♝g5 c5 (or if 14...♕b8, J.Gilbert-C.Hasman, British League 2004, then 15 c5 with the initiative) 15 ♞d5 ♝xd5 16 cxd5 ♕b8 17 ♜b1 ♕b6 18 a4 a6 19 a5 ♕b3 20 ♜fc1 += G.Giorgadze-J.Becerra Rivero, Mondariz 1996.

b) 12...♕h4 13 ♜f2! ♕e7 (E.Gleizerov-P.Lyrberg, Stockholm 1995) 14 ♜d1!? +/= intending the plan of 14...f5 15 c5.

c) 12...♝e6!? 13 ♜ad1 (13 f4!?) 13...♕e7 14 ♝g5 f6 15 ♝h4 g5 16 ♝f2 ♞f4 with counterplay, V.Grebionkin-E.Krasilnikov, Bor 2000.

d) 12...c5! looks very sensible; e.g. 13 ♜ad1 (if 13 g4 ♞f6 14 ♜ad1 ♝b7 15 ♝g5 ♕c8 16 ♞d5 ♞xd5 17 cxd5 ♝a6 18 ♝xa6 ♕xa6 = Z.Martic-Z.Jovanovic, Bizovac 2001) 13...♝e6 (or 13...♝b7 14 ♜fe1 ♜b8 15 ♝f1 ♝e5 16 ♝g5, F.Doettling-S.Brodbeck, Löwenstein 1997, and now 16...♕d7 ∞) 14 ♜fe1 ♜b8 15 ♝f1 ♝e5 16 g4 ♞g7 ½-½ V.Grabliauskas-L.Salai, European Team Ch., Pula 1997.

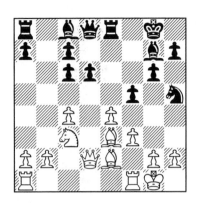

13 exf5

A logical move. White can also hope for an advantage after:

a) 13 ♝g5 ♕d7!? (or 13...♞f6 14 ♝d3 fxe4 15 ♞xe4 ♝f5 16 ♜fe1 += V.Grebionkin-A.Khruschiov, Tula 2001) 14 ♚h1!? fxe4 (N.Kalesis-G.Mastrokoukos, Karditsa 1994) and now 15 fxe4!? gives White the better chances; e.g. 15...♕e6 16 c5! a5 17 ♜ad1 or 15...♝a6 16 b3 ♕e6 17 ♝xh5 gxh5 18 ♝e3 ♕e5 19 ♜ac1 ♜f8 20 ♜f3.

b) 13 ♜ad1 ♕e7 (or 13...♞f6 14 c5 d5 15 exd5 cxd5 16 ♝b5 ♝d7 17 c6 ♝e6, R.Cornea-L.Filip, Rumanian Team Ch. 2000, 18 ♝a6 +=) 14 ♜fe1 f4 (J.Sales-A.Son, Kuala Lumpur 2005) 15 ♝d4 +/=, or if 14...♜b8 (K.Sakaev-A.Volokitin, FIDE World Ch., Moscow 2001) 15 ♝xa7 ♜a8 16 ♝f2 and Black has no compensation for the pawn.

c) 13 c5 d5 (if instead 13...♕e7 14 cxd6 cxd6 15 ♝d4 fxe4 16 fxe4 ♞f6 17 ♜ad1 += A.Nadanian-A.Matikozian, Armenian Ch. 1999; or 13...f4 14 ♝f2 ♝e6 15 ♜fd1 ♝e5 16 ♜ac1 ♞g3 17 ♝a6 ♜b8, B.Bente-U.Roemer, Seefeld 1998, 18 ♝d4 +/-) 14 ♝g5 ♕d7 15 exf5 (also good are 15 ♖ad1 ♖b8 16 ♖fe1 += or 15 exd5 cxd5 16 ♖fe1 c6 17 ♗f1 += Tsesarsky) 15...gxf5 16 ♖fe1 ♕f7?! (16...f4 17 ♗h4 +=) 17 ♗f1 ♗d7 18 ♘e2 ♕g6 19 ♗e3 +/- P.H.Nielsen-A.Volokitin, Esbjerg 2002, as 19...♗xb2? 20 ♕xb2 ♖xe3 loses to 21 ♘f4 (Volokitin).

13...♗xf5 *(D)*

The aggressive-looking 13...♕h4 (threatening ...♖xe3) turns out badly after 14 ♖ad1 ♗xf5 15 ♗g5 ♗d4+ 16 ♕xd4 ♕xg5 17 f4 ♕f6 18 ♗f3 ♕xd4+ 19 ♖xd4 ♗d7 20 c5 +/- A.Yermolinsky-A.Matikozian, Agoura Hills 2004; while if 13...♖b8 14 b3 ♗xf5 (T.Lirindzakis-I.Nikolaidis, Heraklion 1996) then 15 ♖ae1!? c5 16 ♗d3 +/=.

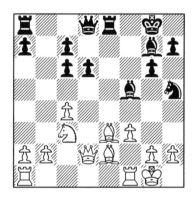

14 ♗d4

The safest and most natural move, anticipating counterplay on the e-file or a1-h8 diagonal. Instead, 14 g4 leads to a draw: 14...♗xc3 15 ♕xc3 ♕e7 16 ♔f2 ♕h4+ 17 ♔g1 ♕e7 ½-½ N.Grotnes-M.Schmidt, Panormo 2001. But 14 ♖fe1 is a valid alternative; e.g. 14...♖xe3 15 ♕xe3 ♕h4 16 g4 ♖f8 17 ♗f1 ♗d7 18 ♖ad1 (A.Chow-C.Kharroubi, Philadelphia 1998) 18...c5 19 ♘b5 +=; or 14...♖b8

15 ♗f1 ♖xe3 (not 15...♕h4? 16 g4 +- F.Doettling-U.Roemer, German League 1999) 16 ♕xe3 ♖xb2 17 ♖ad1 +/=.

14...♘f6

If 14...♗xd4+ 15 ♕xd4 ♕f6 16 ♕xf6 ♘xf6 (R.Akesson-M.Golubev, Leuven 1994) 17 ♔f2 += Dautov.

15 ♖fe1 c5 16 ♗f2 ♕d7 17 ♖ad1 ♕f7 18 b3 a6 *(D)*

ECO gives this as equal, which may be a correct assessment objectively. However, White has whatever chances are going and can make Black suffer for a long time. For example:

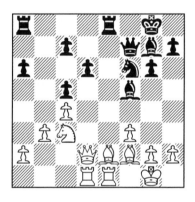

a) 19 ♗d3 ♗xd3 20 ♕xd3 ♖xe1+ 21 ♖xe1 ♖e8 22 ♖e3 ♔f8 23 g3 ♖xe3 24 ♕xe3 ♘d7 25 ♔g2 ♘e5 26 ♘e4 h6 27 f4 ♘c6? (27...♘g4! Dautov) 28 ♕f3 ♘d4 29 ♗xd4 ♗xd4 30 g4 ♔e7 31 ♘g3 += due to the stronger pawn majority, R.Dautov-I.Glek, German League 1996.

b) 19 ♗f1 ♗d7 20 ♖xe8+ ♗xe8 21 a3 ♖b8 22 ♖b1 ♗c6 23 b4 ♘d7 24 bxc5 ♖xb1 25 ♘xb1 ♘xc5 26 ♘c3 h6 27 ♘d5 g5 28 ♕b4 ♗xd5? (28...♗e5! Kramnik) 29 cxd5 ♗e5 30 ♗xc5 dxc5 31 ♕e4 ♗d4+ 32 ♔h1 a5 33 g3 +/- due to the safer king, V.Kramnik-I.Glek, Berlin 1996.

C33: 11 ♕d2 (D)

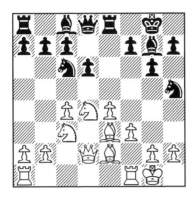

This looks best and most natural.

11...♘f4

Here Black has a few equivalent options:

a) 11...♘xd4 12 ♗xd4 and then:

a1) 12...♘f4 13 ♔h1!? (not 13 ♗xg7 ♕g5! 14 ♔f2 ♔xg7 =; while 13 ♖fd1 transposes to 11...♘f4 12 ♖fd1 ♘xd4 13 ♗xd4) 13...♕g5 (if 13...♘xe2 14 ♗xg7 ♔xg7 15 ♘xe2 +/= Belov; or 13...♗e5 14 ♖ad1 ♗e6, I.Farago-A.Czebe, Hungarian Team Ch. 1998, 15 ♗xe5 dxe5 16 ♘d5 +/=) 14 ♖f2 ♗xd4 15 ♕xd4 ♕e5 16 ♕d2 ♘xe2 17 ♖xe2 ♗e6 18 b3 +/= K.Aseev-J.Moingt, Budapest 1996.

a2) 12...♗xd4+ 13 ♕xd4 ♘f4 14 ♖f2 a5 (if 14...♗e6 15 ♗f1 +/= P.Schlosser-J.Pachow, German League 2006) 15 ♘d5 ♘xd5 16 cxd5 c5 17 dxc6 bxc6 18 ♖d1 (or 18 ♗c4 ♗e6 19 ♖d1 ♖b8, R.Vera-R.Vazquez, Cuban Ch. 2002, 20 b3!? +/= Vera) 18...♗e6 19 ♕xd6 ♕b6 ½-½ I.Sokolov-J.Piket, Groningen 1995, though White still seems better after 20 ♕a3 +=.

b) 11...f5 (D) is a serious alternative to the main line:

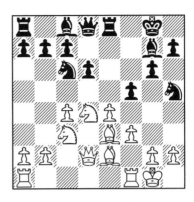

b1) 12 ♘xc6 bxc6 transposes to 11 ♘xc6 bxc6 12 ♕d2 f5 in line C32.

b2) 12 ♖ad1!? f4 (if 12...♘f4 13 ♗xf4 ♘xd4 14 ♗d3 ♘e6 15 ♗e3, A.Beliavsky-T.Nedev, European Ch., Ohrid 2001, 15...fxe4 16 ♗xe4 +/= Tsesarsky) 13 ♘xc6 bxc6 14 ♗xf4 ♘xf4 15 ♕xf4 ♖b8 16 ♕d2 g5 17 c5 +/- V.Chuchelov-A.Sherzer, Budapest 1996, or if 16...c5 (Korchnoi) 17 ♗d3 +/=.

b3) 12 ♖fd1 looks less accurate as the a1-rook has nothing to do on the queenside; the only advantage is that f1 is vacated for the bishop; e.g. 12...♘xd4 13 ♗xd4 ♗xd4+ 14 ♕xd4 ♘f4 15 ♗f1 ♕g5 16 ♔h1 ♗e6 (or 16...♘e6!? 17 ♕f2 a5 ∞ Gongora) 17 g3 ♘h5 18 exf5 ♕xf5! 19 ♗g2 ♘f6 20 f4 ♖e7! 21 b4 ♖ae8! = O.Perea-M.Gongora, Las Tunas 2003.

12 ♘xc6

Other continuations are:

a) 12 ♗xf4 (in this line Black has more chances of obtaining counterplay) 12...♘xd4 13 ♗g5 f6 (or 13...♘xe2+ 14 ♘xe2 f6 15 ♗h4 ♕e7 16 ♖fe1 ♕f7 17 ♖ac1 f5 with counterplay, J.Oms Pallise-Gil.Hernandez, Mislata 1996) 14 ♗e3 ♘xe2+ 15 ♘xe2 ♕e7 16 ♘c3 ♗e6

17 b3 ♕f7 18 ♖ad1 a6 19 ♕c1 ♖ad8 20 ♖fe1 f5 21 ♗g5 ♖b8 22 exf5 ♗xf5 23 ♘d5 ♗e6 = V.Korchnoi-Gil.Hernandez, 3rd matchgame, Merida 1996.

b) 12 ♖fd1 and then:

b1) 12...♘e6 13 ♘xe6 ♗xe6 14 ♘d5 a5 15 ♗g5 f6 16 ♗h4 b6?! (but if 16...g5 17 ♗f2 f5 18 exf5 ♗xf5 19 c5 dxc5 20 ♗xc5 +/= Pelletier) 17 f4 ♖f8 18 ♖f1 +/- Y.Pelletier-J.Becerra Rivero, World Team Ch., Lucerne 1997.

b2) 12...♘xe2+ 13 ♘cxe2 ♗d7 14 ♖ac1 a6 15 b3 ♘e5 16 ♘c3 (or 16 ♗g5 f6 17 ♗h6 ♕e7 18 ♘c3 ♗xh6 19 ♕xh6 c6 20 a4 +/= N.Doric-G.Mihalic, Velika Gorica 2006) 16...♖b8 17 ♘de2 ♗e6 18 ♘d5 c5 (if 18...b5!? 19 cxb5!? ♗xd5 20 ♕xd5 axb5 21 a3 +/=) 19 ♗g5 f6 20 ♗h6 ♗xh6 21 ♕xh6 ♗xd5 22 ♖xd5 += with an ongoing initiative, L.Psakhis-J.Manion, Chicago 1997.

b3) 12...♘xd4 13 ♗xd4 ♗xd4+ 14 ♕xd4 ♕g5 15 ♗f1 ♗e6 (15...♘e6 16 ♕f2 ♕c5 17 b4 ♕xf2+ 18 ♔xf2 a5 19 a3 b6 20 g3 ♗b7, Al.David-S.Husari, Paris 2003, 21 ♘d5! +/- Halkias; or 15...♗h3 16 ♕d2 += Y.Pelletier-G.Reichenbacher, Bad Wörishofen 2000) 16 g3 ♘h5 17 ♗g2 ♕e5 18 ♘d5 ♕xd4+ 19 ♖xd4 ♖ac8 20 f4 +/= P.Eljanov-G.Matjushin, Ukrainian Team Ch. 2000.

12...♘xe2+ 13 ♘xe2

Belov's 13 ♕xe2 bxc6 (D.Polajzer-G.Hertneck, Aschach 2001) 14 c5!? might be worth investigating.

13...bxc6 14 ♗d4 f6

Otherwise:

a) 14...♗xd4 15 ♕xd4 c5 16 ♕c3 ♗e6 17 ♘f4 a5 18 ♖ae1 ♕b8 19 ♘d3 ♕b7 20 f4 ♗d7 (D.Tishin-E.Kobylkin, Alushta

2004) 21 e5!? +/=.

b) 14...c5 15 ♗xg7 ♔xg7 16 ♘c3 ♗b7 17 ♘d1 a5 18 ♘e3 ♕f6 19 ♖ad1 h5 20 ♖f2 ♕e5 21 ♕c1 (21 ♘d5!? +=) 21...a4 22 ♖e2 ♖ab8 23 ♕c2 ♖a8 24 ♕c1 ♖ab8 = V.Golod-I.Sorkin, Dieren 1998.

15 ♖ad1

Black has no problems after 15 ♖fd1 ♕e7 16 ♖e1 (or 16 ♘c3 ♗e6 17 b3 a5 18 ♖ac1 ♕f7 19 ♘a4 ♕f8 20 ♖c2 f5 21 exf5 ♗xf5 ∞ A.Fink-R.Ullmann, Kassel 2000) 16...♕f7 (16...c5!?) 17 c5 ♗e6 18 ♘c3 ♖ad8 19 ♕f2 d5 20 exd5 ♗xd5 ½-½ S.Feller-J.M.Degraeve, Bethune 2006.

After the text Black should content himself with the peaceful 15...♕e7 or 15...♗e6 with only minimal chances for White. Instead, A.Shariyazdanov-V.Bologan, Moscow 2006, proceeded rather strangely: **15...♗a6 16 b3 d5 17 ♕a5 ♕c8 18 ♕c3 c5 19 ♗xc5 dxe4 20 fxe4** [20 ♘f4! +/-] **20...♖xe4 21 ♕d3 ♗b7 22 ♘c3 ♖e5 23 ♘d5 ♗xd5 24 cxd5 ♕d7** [24...c6!?] **25 ♕c4 ♕f7 26 ♗f2** [26 ♖fe1! +/-] **26...f5?!** [much better was 26...♖d8!?] **½-½** [27 ♗g3 +/-, but the players agreed a draw]

Conclusion

Black cannot count on equality in the lesser 7th move variations such as 7...♕e8 (line A), while 7...c6 (line B) is often just an alternate route to another variation, in particular 7...♘a6 and 7...♘bd7 in the next two chapters. After 7...exd4 (line C) White can expect a small advantage as Black's position is often cramped; however, the concluding variation C33 deserves special attention.

Chapter Six

7...♘a6

1 d4 ♘f6 2 c4 g6 3 ♘c3 ♝g7 4 e4 d6 5 ♘f3 0-0 6 ♝e2 e5 7 0-0 ♘a6 *(D)*

This line, which can also occur via 6...♘a6 7 0-0 e5, appeared in the late 1980s. Apparently Black contravenes basic chess principles by developing his knight on the flank; however, things are not so simple. The knight can be usefully placed on c5 (after d4-d5, d4xe5 or ...e5xd4), or sometimes on c7 (after ...c7-c6); and compared with 7...♘bd7 in the next chapter, on a6 the knight does not obstruct the c8-bishop. Furthermore, Black avoids the main lines of 7...♘c6, which have been studied in great depth and require equivalent theoretical knowledge.

Of course 7...♘a6 has disadvantages too. By not increasing the pressure on the centre, Black allows his opponent more latitude in his set-up. Also, the knight blocks the a-pawn from advancing and, after b2-b4, may find itself left out of the game. Therefore White can

try for an advantage with the simple 8 ♖b1 (line A). More popular is 8 ♝e3 (line B) where White has freer play and can look to play a quick c4-c5, in particular after 8...♘g4 9 ♝g5 ♕e8 10 c5!? (line B21), which deserves serious attention. White can also hope for an edge in line C with 8 ♖e1 c6 9 ♖b1 or 9 ♝f1.

In spite of the popularity of 7...♘a6 we think that White has the better game here. The advantage is not so big that the variation could be said to be in crisis. Nevertheless we think Black has more chances in the complicated main lines with 7...♘c6.

A: 8 ♖b1 *123*
B: 8 ♝e3 *125*
C: 8 ♖e1 *139*

Others:
a) 8 d5 ♘c5 transposes to 7...♘bd7 8 d5 ♘c5 discussed in the next chapter.

b) 8 a3 can be answered by 8...exd4!, when Black obtains good counterplay as a2-a3 is not very useful; e.g. 9 ♘xd4 ♖e8 10 f3 c6 11 ♔h1 ♘c7 12 ♗g5 h6 13 ♗h4 ♕e7 14 ♗d3 g5 15 ♗f2 ♘h5 16 ♗c2 ♗e5 17 g3 ♘g7 ∞ G.Geissler-M.Muresan, Dresden 1990.

c) 8 ♕c2 gets the same reaction: 8...exd4 9 ♘xd4 ♖e8 10 ♖d1 ♘c5 11 f3 (Z.Kozul-D.Kljako, Slovenian Team Ch. 1993) and now 11...♘fd7 12 b4 ♘e6 =.

d) The simple move 8 dxe5 seems to give White chances of obtaining an advantage; e.g. 8...dxe5 9 ♕c2 (if 9 ♗g5 ♕e8 10 ♗xf6 ♗xf6 11 ♘d5 ♗d8 = M.Matas-I.Armanda, Solin 2007) 9...♗g4 (or if 9...♕e8 10 a3 c6 11 b4 ♕e7 12 ♖d1 ♘h5, A.Dreev-V.Chekhov, Moscow 1989, 13 c5 with the initiative) 10 ♗e3 (10 ♘xe5 ♘b4! =) 10...♗xf3 11 ♗xf3 c6 was A.Dreev-I.Glek, Frunze 1988, when it seems to us that White's chances are better after 12 ♖fd1 ♕e7 13 ♖d2, with the two bishops and control of the d-file due to the hanging a7-pawn.

e) 8 ♗g5 (D) also deserves more attention:

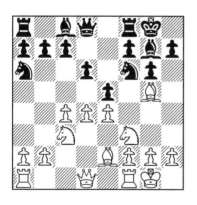

e1) 8...♕e8?! allows White to break up the black pawn structure: 9 c5 (also good is 9 ♗xf6 ♗xf6 10 c5 dxc5, A.Miles-J.Moreno Carnero, Mondariz 2000, 11 ♗xa6 bxa6 12 ♘d5! ♗d8 13 dxe5 c6 14 ♘e3 ♗c7 15 ♕c2 ♗xe5 16 ♘xe5 ♕xe5 17 ♘c4 +=, or 10...♘b4 11 cxd6 cxd6 12 ♗b5 ♕d8 13 dxe5 dxe5 14 ♕a4 ♘c6 15 ♗xc6 bxc6 16 ♕xc6 ♗e6 17 ♖fd1 ♕a5 18 ♘d5 += G.Kallai-G.Kerek, Hungarian Team Ch. 2003) 9...exd4 10 ♗xf6 dxc3 (or 10...♗xf6 11 ♘d5 ♗d8 12 ♗xa6 c6 13 ♕xd4 bxa6 14 ♘f6+ ♗xf6 15 ♕xf6 dxc5 16 ♘e5 ♕e6 17 ♕xe6 ♗xe6 +/= Y.Yakovich-M.Mrdja, Cappelle la Grande 1996) 11 ♗xg7 ♔xg7 12 ♗xa6 cxb2 13 ♕d4+ ♔g8 14 ♕xb2 bxa6 15 cxd6 cxd6 16 ♖fe1 +/= M.Roj-P.Neuman, Czech League 1995.

e2) 8...exd4 does not equalize either: 9 ♘xd4 ♖e8 (9...♘c5 10 f3 ♘e6 11 ♗e3 c6 12 ♕d2 ♕e7 13 ♖ad1 +/= N.Sadovski-I.Ljahovetsky, Alushta 2006) 10 f3 c6 11 ♕d2 ♘c5 12 ♔h1 a5 13 ♖ad1 a4 14 ♖fe1 ♕a5 15 ♗f4 ♗f8 16 ♘c2 +/= Y.Pelletier-Gil.Hernandez, Villarrobledo (rapid) 2000.

e3) 8...h6! gives Black equal play without any complications: 9 ♗h4 (other moves are no better; e.g. 9 ♗e3 ♘g4 10 ♗c1 c6 11 h3 exd4 12 ♘xd4 ♘f6 13 ♖e1 ♘c5 14 ♗f3 ♖e8 15 ♗f4! g5 16 ♗c1, V.Hort-K.Arakhamia, Copenhagen 1997, 16...a5 = Hort) 9...g5! (9...♕e8?! 10 ♗xf6 ♗xf6 11 c5!, V.Milov-J.Gallagher, Bad Ragaz 1994, is 8...♕e8 9 ♗xf6 ♗xf6 10 c5 with an extra ...h7-h6, which favours White if anything as he then has ♕d2 or ♕c1) 10 dxe5 (or if 10 ♗g3 g4 11 ♘h4 exd4 12 ♕xd4,

G.Kallai-J.Gallagher, French Team Ch. 2000, 12...♘c5 13 ♕e3 ♘h5 14 ♖ab1 ♕g5 with good counterplay for Black) 10...♘h5 (sharper was 10...gxh4!? 11 exf6 ♕xf6, H.Knuth-W.Heinig, German League 2000, 12 h3 ♖e8 13 ♖c1 ♘c5, when Black's dark square control and bishop pair compensate for the weaknesses in his pawn structure) 11 ♗g3 ♘xg3 12 hxg3 dxe5 13 ♘h2 c6 14 ♘g4 ♕xd1 15 ♖fxd1 ♗xg4 16 ♗xg4 ♖fd8 17 ♖xd8+ ♖xd8 18 ♖d1 ♖xd1+ 19 ♘xd1 ♘c5 20 f3 a5 = J.Piket-L.Comas Fabrego, Istanbul Olympiad 2000.

A: 8 ♖b1 *(D)*

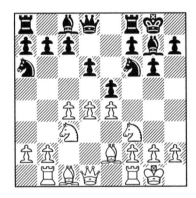

The a1-rook leaves the vulnerable a1-h8 diagonal and prepares b2-b4, gaining space on the queenside and sidelining the a6-knight.

8...exd4

A logical move; Black gives his knight the c5-square and tries to show that 8 ♖b1 is not the best idea in ...e5xd4 variations. He has also tried:

a) 8...c6 9 dxe5 dxe5 10 b4 ♕e7 11 b5 ♘c5 12 ♗a3 ♘fd7 13 ♘a4 +/- L.Renaze-J.Tihonov, Creon 2004.

b) 8...♕e8 9 dxe5!? dxe5 10 b4 c6 11 ♗a3 ♕e7 12 ♕c1 ♘c7 (D.King-Z.Quader, Calcutta 1993) 13 b5 with the initiative.

c) 8...♖e8!? is an interesting move order, threatening to follow up with 9...exd4.

c1) 9 dxe5 dxe5 10 ♕xd8 ♖xd8 11 b4 c6! (intending 12 c5 ♘c7) looks okay for Black; e.g. 12 ♗e3 ♘g4 13 ♗g5 f6 14 ♗h4 ♗e6 15 a3 ♘h6 16 ♖fd1 ♘f7 17 ♘d2 ♘c7 18 ♘b3 b6 = V.Korchnoi-B.Gelfand, Manila Interzonal 1990.

c2) 9 d5 ♘c5 is similar to 8 d5 ♘c5 (line A in the next chapter) with the black rook worse placed on e8. On the other hand, the rook on b1 prevents White from replying with 10 ♕c2 (as in line A2), because of 10...♘fxe4! 11 ♘xe4 ♘xe4 12 ♕xe4 ♗f5 with a skewer. Instead, he has to play the inferior 10 ♘d2 (as in line A1); e.g. 10...a5 11 b3 ♗h6 12 ♕c2 ♗g4 13 ♗xg4 ♘xg4 14 a3 ♕d7 15 h3 ♘f6 16 ♘f3 ♗xc1 17 ♖fxc1 ♘h5 18 b4 axb4 19 axb4 ♘a4 20 ♘e2 c6 21 dxc6 ♕xc6 with counterplay, C.Lutz-I.Rogers, Biel 1990,

9 ♘xd4 ♖e8

The most natural and flexible move, as the a6-knight can go also to c7 (i.e. following ...c7-c6).

Black has no counterplay after 9...♘c5 10 f3 a5 11 ♗e3 ♖e8 12 ♕d2 c6 13 ♘c2 ♕e7 14 ♖fd1 ♗f8 (O.Touzane-D.Poldauf, Podolsk 1991) 15 ♗f4 +/-; or if 10...♘h5!? 11 g4 ♘f6 12 ♗e3 h5 (E.Kobylkin-E.Mochalov, Yalta 1995) 13 g5 with similar ideas to Chapter Five (line C1 with 10...♘f6).

10 f3 c6 *(D)*

If 10...♘h5 11 ♗e3 f5 (or 11...♘c5 12 g4 ♘f6 13 b4 ♘e6 14 ♕d2 ♘xd4 15 ♗xd4 ♗e6 16 g5 ♘d7 17 ♗xg7 ♔xg7 18 f4 f6, T.Bosboom Lanchava-A.Areshchenko, Port Erin 2005, 19 ♕d4 +/=) 12 b4 ♘f6 13 ♕d2 fxe4 14 ♘xe4 ♘xe4 15 fxe4 c5 (not 15...♖xe4? 16 ♗f3 ♖e8 17 ♗d5+ ♔h8 18 ♖f7 c6 19 ♖xg7! +- Mikhalchishin; relatively best is 15...♕e7 +=) 16 ♘b5 ♗e5 (D.Polajzer-M.Tratar, Ptuj 1998) 17 a3 +/-.

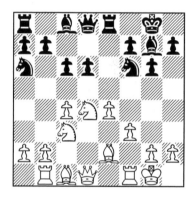

11 ♗g5

Other moves lead to unclear positions:

a) 11 ♖e1 transposes to 8 ♖e1 c6 9 ♖b1 exd4 10 ♘xd4 ♖e8 11 f3 in the notes to line C21.

b) 11 ♗e3 d5! is fine for Black (compare 9 ♘xd4 in line B, Chapter Five); e.g. 12 cxd5 ♘xd5! 13 ♘xd5 cxd5 14 ♕b3 ♘c5 15 ♕a3 (if 15 ♕b4 ♘xe4! 16 fxe4 ♖xe4 16 ♕d2 ♕e7 =+) 15...♘e6 16 ♖bd1 ♘xd4 17 ♗xd4 ♗xd4+ 18 ♖xd4 ♕b6 =.

c) 11 b4 ♘xb4!? 12 ♖xb4 c5 13 ♖b3 cxd4 14 ♘b5 a6 15 ♘xd4 ♘d7 16 ♖b1 ♘c5 ∞ P.Pinho-A.Strikovic, Portuguese Team Ch. 1998.

d) 11 ♔h1 ♘h5 12 g4 ♘f6 13 ♗f4 (or 13 ♗g5!? Karpov) 13...h5 14 g5 ♘d7 15 ♕d2 ♘e5 16 ♖bd1 ♕e7 17 ♖g1 ♗h3 18 ♖g3 ♗d7 19 ♗e3 ♖ad8 ∞ V.Epishin-V.Neverov, USSR Ch., Tbilisi 1989.

11...h6 *(D)*

11...♕a5!? is an interesting alternative; e.g. 12 ♕d2?! ♘xe4 13 fxe4 ♗xd4+ 14 ♕xd4 ♕xg5 15 ♕xd6 ♕c5+ 16 ♕xc5 ♘xc5 17 ♗f3 ♗e6 18 b3 ♖ad8 =+ V.Vales-J.Mudrak, Litomysl 2003, or 12 ♗h4 ♘h5 13 ♘b3 (D.Shapiro-M.Traldi, Philadelphia 1998) 13...♕e5!? with counterplay. Probably White should prefer 12 ♗e3!? or 12 ♗f4!?.

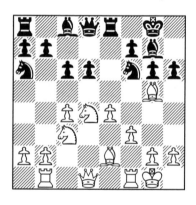

12 ♗h4

If 12 ♗e3 d5! with counterplay.

12...♘c5

Not 12...g5 13 ♗f2 d5? (I.Hogye-M.Toth, Nyiregyhaza 1994) 14 cxd5 cxd5 15 ♗xa6 bxa6 16 ♘xd5 ♘xd5 17 ♘c6 ♕c7 18 exd5 +-, or if 13...♘h5 (L.Johannessen-K.Trygstad, Copenhagen 2004) 14 g3 +=.

13 ♖e1

Not 13 ♕d2?? ♘fxe4! 0-1 R.Stone-F.Nijboer, Den Bosch 1999; or if 13 ♗f2 ♘h5 14 ♕d2 f5 15 exf5 gxf5 16 b4 ♕g5

17 ♕xg5 hxg5 18 ♖fd1 ♘e6 with counterplay, T.Likavsky-P.Czarnota, Turin Olympiad 2006.

13...a5 14 ♗f1 *(D)*

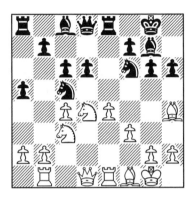

White seems a little better here. V.Ivanchuk-J.Moreno Carnero, European Team Ch., Leon 2001, continued:

14...a4 15 ♕d2 ♕b6

15...♘fxe4?! is now met by 16 ♘xe4 ♕xh4 17 ♘f6+! ♕xf6 18 ♖xe8+ ♔h7 19 ♖d1 +/-; but the immediate 15...♕c7 +/= looks more accurate.

16 ♗f2 ♘fd7 17 ♘c2 ♕c7 18 ♖ed1 h5!? 19 ♔h1

White can take the d-pawn, but perhaps Ivanchuk didn't want to allow any counterplay; e.g. 19 ♕xd6 ♕xd6 20 ♖xd6 a3! 21 b4 ♗xc3 22 bxc5 ♖a5 23 ♖d3 ♗b2 24 ♗e1 ♖a8 25 ♗b4 f5.

19...♗e5 20 b4 axb3 21 axb3 ♕d8 22 ♗d4 ♕f6 23 ♗xe5 dxe5 24 b4 ♘e6 25 c5 h4 26 ♕f2 ♕g5 27 ♘e3 ♘f6 28 ♘c4 ½-½

According to the database the players agreed a draw here – though this would be an odd decision by White, still with the better position against a lower-rated opponent.

B: 8 ♗e3 *(D)*

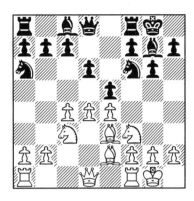

This has been White's most popular move. In reply Black has a wide range of continuations:

B1: 8...c6 *126*
B2: 8...♘g4 *129*

Also:

a) 8...exd4 must be considered, as ♗e3 is often not the best move in 7...exd4 lines. Here, however, Black is not ready with ...d6-d5, so White can play 9 ♘xd4 (rather than 9 ♗xd4 ♖e8 10 ♗d3 ♘c5 11 ♖e1 ♘e6 12 ♗e3 ♘g4 13 ♗d2 c6 ∞ Z.Adamek-A.Jedlicka, Czech League 1999) 9...♖e8 (or 9...♘c5 10 f3 a5 11 ♕d2 ♖e8 12 ♖ad1 += G.Tunik-V.Terentiev, Ekaterinburg 1997) 10 f3 when 10...c6 11 ♔h1 or 11 ♘c2 reaches variations discussed in Chapter Five (line C2), while 11 ♖e1 transposes to 8 ♖e1 c6 9 ♗e3 exd4 in the notes to line C2 in this chapter.

b) 8...♕e8 (this popular move does not give equality) 9 ♖e1 (stronger than 9 dxe5 ♘g4 10 exd6 ♘xe3 11 fxe3 cxd6

12 ♕xd6 ♗xc3 13 bxc3 ♕xe4 14 ♕d4
♖e8 ∞ C.Lutz-M.Wahls, Berlin 1989; or
9 h3 ♘d7!? ∞ A.Fishbein-Ma.Tseitlin,
Beersheba 1991) 9...♘g4 (if 9...c6 10
dxe5 dxe5 11 c5! ♘g4 12 ♗xa6 ♘xe3 13
♖xe3 bxa6 14 ♕a4 ♖b8 15 b3 +/- due to
Black's weakened pawn structure,
V.Tukmakov-T.Markowski, Geneva
1997) 10 ♗c1 f5 11 exf5 gxf5 (L.Van
Wely-B.Gelfand, European Junior Ch.
1988) 12 c5! e4 (if 12...♕d7 13 cxd6 exd4
14 ♘b5 +/-, or 12...dxc5 13 ♗xa6 bxa6
14 dxe5 ♗e6 15 h3 +/-) 13 cxd6 ♕h5
(13...cxd6 is met by 14 ♘g5, e.g.
14...♔h8 15 ♗xg4 fxg4 16 ♖xe4 +/-) 14
h3 ♘xf2 (or 14...exf3 15 ♗xf3 ♕h4 16
hxg4 fxg4 17 ♗d5+ ♔h8 18 ♗f4 cxd6 19
♗g3 ♕f6 20 ♘b5 +/-) 15 ♔xf2 exf3 16
♗xf3 ♕h4+ 17 g3 ♕xd4+ 18 ♕xd4
♗xd4+ 19 ♔g2 cxd6 20 ♗h6 ♗g7 21
♗xg7 ♔xg7 22 ♖ad1 with a clear advantage in the ending. In all variations
the important factor was the badly
placed a6-knight.

c) 8...♕e7!? 9 ♗g5 (if instead 9 dxe5
dxe5 10 ♘d5 ♕d8 11 ♕c2 ♘g4 12 ♗g5
f6 13 ♗d2!? c6 14 ♘e3 ♕e7 15 ♖ad1,
M.Gurevich-T.Markowski, Polanica
Zdroj 1999, 15...♘xe3 16 ♗xe3 f5!? with
counterplay, Huzman; or just 16...c5 =
intending ...♘b4-c6-d4 or ...♘c7-e6-d4;
or 9 ♕c2 ♘b4!? 10 ♕b1 exd4 11 ♘xd4
♘g4 12 ♗xg4 ♗xg4 13 ♘d5 ♘xd5 14
cxd5 ♖fc8 15 ♖c1 ♗d7 = Khalifman)
9...exd4 (if 9...c6?! 10 c5! +/-; or 9...♕e8?!
10 ♗xf6 ♗xf6 11 c5 +=) 10 ♘d5 (if 10
♘xd4 ♕e5!? 11 ♘f3 ♕e8 12 ♗d3 ♘c5 13
♖e1 h6 14 ♗h4 g5 15 ♗g3 ♘h5 with
counterplay, R.Kempinski-T.Markow-
ski, Pula 1998) 10...♕d8 11 ♘xd4 c6 12

♘xf6+ ♗xf6 13 ♗xf6 ♕xf6 14 ♕d2 ♘c5
15 f3 a5 16 ♖ad1 ♖d8 17 ♖fe1 ♗d7 18
♗f1 with a minimal edge, B.Gelfand-
B.Damljanovic, Istanbul Olympiad
2000.

d) 8...h6 (intending ...♘g4) 9 dxe5 (9
h3 is not dangerous either: 9...exd4 10
♗xd4 ♖e8 11 ♗d3 c6 12 ♖e1 ♘c5 13
♕d2 ♘xd3 14 ♕xd3 ½-½ B.Predojevic-
A.Areshchenko, Moscow 2007) 9...♘g4
10 ♗d2 (if 10 exd6 ♘xe3 11 fxe3 ♗xc3
12 bxc3 cxd6 with obvious compensation) 10...♘xe5 (less good is 10...dxe5 11
♕c1 ♔h7 12 ♖d1 ♕e8 13 h3 ♘f6 14 ♗e3
+/= B.Gelfand-I.Smirin, World Blitz Ch.,
Rishon LeZion 2006) 11 ♘xe5 dxe5 12
♕c1 ♔h7 13 ♖d1 ♕h4 = Zhao Xue-
Z.Efimenko, Dubai 2005.

B1: 8...c6 (D)

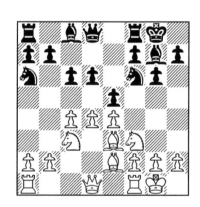

9 dxe5

White plays for a slightly favourable endgame. Instead:

a) 9 ♕d2 exd4 10 ♘xd4 ♘g4 11
♗xg4 ♗xg4 12 f3 ♗c8 13 ♖ad1 ♖e8 14
♕f2 += J.Vehre-S.Calleri, corr. 1999.

b) 9 ♕c2 ♘g4 10 ♗g5 f6 11 ♗h4 g5
(11...♕e7!?) 12 ♗g3 f5 13 exf5 += L.Van

Wely-J.Piket, FIDE World Ch., Groningen 1997.

c) 9 d5 (the most principled move, closing the centre) 9...♘g4 10 ♗g5 f6 11 ♗h4! (restricting Black's action on the kingside; after other continuations Black has no problems: 11 ♗d2 c5 12 h3 ♘h6 13 ♕c1 ♘f7 14 ♘e1 f5 15 exf5 gxf5 16 f4 ♗d7 ∞ L.Ftacnik-R.Kasimdzhanov, German League 2006; or 11 ♗c1 c5!? 12 ♘e1 ♘h6 13 ♘d3 ♗d7 14 a3 ♘f7 15 b4 b6 16 ♖b1 ♕c8 17 ♗d2 f5 18 f3 ♗f6 19 ♔h1 ♔h8 20 ♖b2 f4 21 b5 ♘c7 ½-½ E.Gleizerov-V.Isupov, Russian Team Ch. 1997) 11...c5 (otherwise White has the option of c4-c5; e.g. 11...♘h6 12 c5! ♘xc5 13 b4 ♘d7 14 dxc6 ♘b6 15 a4 +/- J.Lautier-K.Le Quang, Antwerp 1998; or 11...h5 12 h3 ♘h6 13 c5 g5!?, V.Chuchelov-R.Polzin, Hamburg 1997, 14 cxd6 ♕xd6 15 ♗g3 +=) 12 ♘e1 (D) (also good is 12 ♘d2!? ♘h6 13 a3 ♘f7 14 ♖b1 ♗h6 15 b4 ♗g5 16 ♗xg5 ♘xg5 17 ♕c2 +/= V.Ruban-C.Lingnau, Berlin 1991) and then:

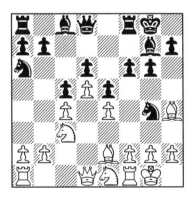

c1) 12...♘h6 13 f3!? (if 13 ♘d3 g5! 14 ♗g3 f5 15 exf5 ♗xf5 16 f3 ♗g6 17 ♗f2 ♘f5 with counterplay, Peng Zhaoqin-

A.Fishbein, Philadelphia 2002) 13...♘f7 (or 13...♗d7 14 ♘d3 g5 15 ♗f2 f5, A.Shabalov-A.Fishbein, US Ch. 2003, 16 a3 += Shabalov) 14 ♘d3 ♗h6 15 ♗f2 f5 (O.Jovanic-Z.Kozul, Croatian Ch. 2005) 16 a3 intending b4 +/=.

c2) 12...h5 13 h3 (if 13 a3 ♕e7 14 ♖b1 b6 15 b4 ♗d7 16 ♘d3 g5 17 ♗g3 f5 18 h3 ♘f6 19 bxc5 ♘xc5 20 ♘xc5 bxc5 21 ♗xh5 ♘xh5 22 ♕xh5, B.Gelfand-V.Topalov, Dortmund 1997, 22...f4 23 ♗h2 ♖f6!? 24 ♕xg5 ♕e8! 25 ♔h1 ♖h6 ∞) 13...♘h6 14 a3 ♘c7!? (if 14...♘f7 15 ♘d3 ♗h6 16 b4 ♔g7 17 ♕c2 ♕e7 18 ♕b2 ♗f4 19 ♗g3 ♗xg3 20 fxg3 ♖b8 21 bxc5 ♘xc5 22 ♘xc5 dxc5, V.Topalov-Kir.Georgiev, FIDE World Ch., New Delhi/Tehran 2000, 23 a4 b6 24 a5 += Tsesarsky; or 14...♗d7 15 ♘d3 g5 16 ♗g3 +=; e.g. 16...g4?! 17 hxg4 ♘xg4 18 ♗h4 with the initiative, D.Antic-Z.Arsovic, Jagodina 1998) 15 ♘d3 ♘e8 16 f4! g5 (not 16...exf4?! 17 ♘xf4 g5 18 ♘e6! ♗xe6 19 dxe6 gxh4? 20 ♘d5 intending 21 e7 +-) 17 fxg5 fxg5 18 ♖xf8+ ♗xf8 19 ♗e1 g4 20 h4 g3 21 ♗xg3 ♘g4 22 ♗xg4 ♗xg4 23 ♕d2 +/- Y.Kruppa-I.Lutsko, Kiev 2005.

9...dxe5 10 ♕xd8

Black has no problems after other moves; e.g. 10 h3 ♕e7 11 ♕c2 ♘h5 12 ♖fe1 ♘c7 13 ♖ad1 ♘e6 14 c5 ♘hf4 15 b4 ♘xe2+ 16 ♘xe2 ♘c7 17 ♘c3 a5 18 a3 axb4 19 axb4 f6 = E.Lobron-G.Kasparov, clock simul, Baden Baden 1992.

10...♖xd8 11 ♖fd1 (D)

The ending is a little better for White, who has more space and the more active pieces, and controls the d-file. Nothing else is particularly testing for Black:

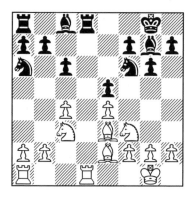

a) 11 ♘xe5 ♘xe4 12 ♘xe4 ♗xe5 = O.Lehner-J.Candela Perez, Internet blitz 2004.

b) 11 ♖ad1 ♖e8 12 a3 (12 h3!?) 12...♘g4 13 ♗c1 ♘c5 14 b4 ♘b3 15 ♗e3 a5 (or 15...♘xe3!? 16 fxe3 a5 ∞ Wells, e.g. 17 ♔f2 f6 18 ♖d3 axb4 19 axb4 ♘a1 20 ♖c1 ♗e6 with the initiative) 16 ♗b6 axb4 17 axb4 ♘f6 (A.Beliavsky-Z.Kozul, European Team Ch., Gothenburg 2005) 18 h3 ♖a3 19 ♖d3 ♘d7 20 ♘b1 ♖a4 21 ♖xb3 ♘xb6 22 ♘c3 = Wells.

c) 11 h3!? ♖e8 12 a3 ♘h5! 13 ♖fd1 ♘f4 14 ♗f1 ♘e6 15 b4 f5 16 c5 f4 17 ♗c1 ♘d4 18 ♘d2 ♗e6 with good counterplay, D.Sahovic-V.Kotronias, Novi Sad 1999.

11...♖e8!

Worse is 11...♖xd1+ (11...♗g4?! drops the a-pawn) 12 ♖xd1 ♗g4 13 a3 ♗xf3 14 gxf3 ♘c7 15 f4 exf4 16 ♗xf4 ♘e6 17 ♗e3 +/= G.Giorgadze-M.Kaminski, Yerevan Olympiad 1996.

12 h3

A good move, preventing ...♘g4 and ...♗g4 forever.

12...♗f8

Preparing to bring the a6-knight into the game via c5 and e6. Other moves do not promise Black equality:

a) 12...♘h5 13 c5 ♘f4 14 ♗f1 ♗e6 15 ♘g5 h6 16 ♘xe6 ♘xe6 17 ♗xa6 bxa6 18 ♖ac1 += R.Cifuentes Parada-N.McDonald, Andorra 1991.

b) 12...♘d7 13 a3 ♘f8 14 b4 ♘e6 15 c5 ♘ac7 16 ♖ab1 f5 17 ♗c4 ♔h8 18 ♖d6 f4 19 ♗d2 ♘d4 20 ♘xd4 exd4 21 ♘e2 ♖xe4 22 ♖d8+ ♖e8 23 ♖xe8+ ♘xe8 24 ♘xf4 += R.Libeau-S.Reschke, German League 1995.

13 ♘d2 *(D)*

13 a3!? prevents 13...♗b4 in the next note (should White think that worth doing), but otherwise is likely to transpose; e.g. 13...♘c5 14 ♘d2 (if 14 ♗xc5 ♗xc5 15 b4 ♗f8 16 c5 b6 = D.Ballesteros Gonzalez-J.Moreno Ruiz, Madrid 2002) 14...♘e6 (or 14...a5 15 b4 ♘e6 16 c5 ♘d4 17 ♗d3) 15 b4 (15 ♘f3 ♘c5 repeats) 15...♘d4 (15...b6!? is the 13...b6 line below) 16 ♗d3 a5 17 c5 is the main line.

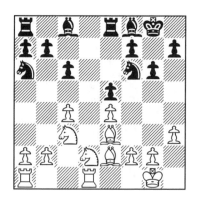

13...♘c5

Alternatively:

a) 13...♗b4 14 ♖ac1 ♘c5 15 f3 ♘e6

16 ♘b3 ♘d7!? (if 16...♘f4 17 ♗f1 ♘6h5 18 ♗f2 ♗e7 19 c5 +/= G.Giorgadze-A.Zapata, Linares 1997) 17 ♖d2 b6 18 ♖cd1 ♘dc5 19 ♘xc5 ♗xc5 20 ♗xc5 ♘xc5 21 ♖d6 ♗b7 22 b4 ♘e6 = S.Halkias-V.Kotronias, Moscow 2007.

b) 13...b6!? 14 a3 ♘c5 15 b4 ♘e6 16 ♘f3! (Black has no problems after 16 ♘b3 ♗a6 17 f3 ♘h5 18 ♗f2 ♖ed8 19 ♗f1 ♘hf4 20 g3 ♘h5 21 ♔g2 f5 22 ♖ab1 ♖ac8 23 ♖xd8 ♖xd8 24 ♖d1 ♖xd1 25 ♘xd1 fxe4 = A.Karpov-G.Kasparov, 5th matchgame, New York 1990), when Black can count on good play after 16...♘d7!? (intending ...f7-f5) 17 ♖c1 a5 or 17 b5 ∞ Wahls. Other moves give White better chances; e.g. 16...♘h5 17 ♖ac1 f6 18 ♖b1 ♔f7 19 ♗f1 ♖b8 20 a4 ♖b7 21 b5 c5 22 ♘d5 ♘hf4 23 a5 += R.Cifuentes Parada-Y.Visser, Groningen 1990: or 16...c5 17 ♘d5! ♘xd5 18 cxd5 ♘d4 19 ♗d3 ♘xf3+ 20 gxf3 ♗xh3 (S.Halkias-H.Banikas, Greek Ch. 2004) 21 ♗b5! ♖ed8 22 ♗g5 +/-.

14 b4 ♘e6 15 c5 ♘d4 16 ♗d3 a5

Not 16...b6?! 17 ♘b3! ♘xb3 18 axb3 ♗e6 19 ♗c4 ♗xc4 20 bxc4 bxc5 21 b5 cxb5 22 cxb5 ♖eb8 23 ♖a6 += R.Cifuentes Parada-M.Sion Castro, Ampuriabrava 1997.

But the immediate 16...♗e6 is possible; e.g. 17 ♘e2 ♘xe2+ 18 ♗xe2 a5 (or 18...♖ad8 19 ♖dc1 ♘h5 20 ♘c4 ♘f4 21 ♗f1, B.Gelfand-Z.Kozul, Portoroz 2001, 21...♘d3!? 22 ♗xd3 ♖xd3 23 ♘xe5 ♖a3 24 ♘c4 ♖a4 25 ♘d6 ♖b8 with counterplay, Gelfand) 19 a3 ♖ed8 20 f3 ♘h5 21 ♔h2 ♘f4 22 ♗f1 ♘d3 =+ V.Shtyrenkov-M.Annaberdiev, Alushta 2007.

17 a3 ♗e6 18 ♘e2

Cifuentes suggests 18 ♖ab1 axb4 19 axb4 ♖a3 20 ♖dc1 and if 20...♘b3?! 21 ♘xb3 ♖xb3 (not 21...♗xb3? 22 ♘b5! cxb5 23 ♖c3 +/-) 22 ♖xb3 ♗xb3 23 ♖a1 ♖d8 24 ♗e2 +/=.

18...♘b3!? *(D)*

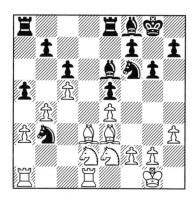

Taking advantage of the inclusion of a2-a3. Otherwise 18...♘xe2+ 19 ♗xe2 returns to 16...♗e6 above. Black seems to have good counterplay in either case.

Two examples after the text:

a) 19 ♘xb3 ♗xb3 20 ♖db1 a4 21 ♖e1 ♘h5 22 g4 ♘g7 23 ♘c1 ♗e6 24 ♗c2 h5 25 f3 ♗c4 26 ♘e2 ♘e6 27 ♖ad1 ♗e7 28 ♖d2 ♖ed8 29 ♖ed1 ∞ M.Shukurova-K.Kachiani, European Women's Ch., Kusadasi 2006.

b) 19 ♖ab1 ♘xd2 20 ♗xd2 axb4 21 axb4 ♖a2 22 ♔f1 ♘d7 23 ♖a1 ♖ea8 24 ♖xa2 ♖xa2 25 ♔e1 f6 26 ♖c1 ♔f7 27 f3 ½-½ P.Kiriakov-V.Isupov, Russian Team Ch. 1999.

B2: 8...♘g4 *(D)*

As usual this is logical and natural when White's bishop is on e3. Black frees his ...f7-pawn with tempo.

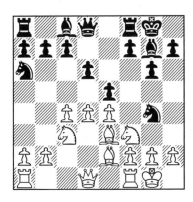

9 ♗g5 ♕e8

The alternative is 9...f6 and then:

a) 10 ♗h4!? ♕e8 (if 10...g5 11 ♗g3 ♘h6, L.Van Wely-K.Berg, Lyngby 1990, 12 c5! g4 13 ♗xa6 bxa6 14 dxe5 dxe5 15 ♘h4 f5 16 ♕b3+ ♔h8 17 ♖ad1 ♕f6 18 ♘d5 +/-; or 10...♘h6 11 d5 ♘f7 12 ♘d2 c5 13 a3 h5 14 h3 ♗d7 15 ♖b1 ♗h6 16 b4 b6 17 ♗d3! ♗f4 18 ♘e2 g5 19 ♗g3 += I.Glek-Y.Visser, Netherlands 1997) 11 c5! (this move causes Black most problems) 11...exd4 (if 11...dxc5 12 dxe5 ♘xe5 13 ♘xe5 ♕xe5 14 ♗g3, I.Sitnik-N.Fercec, Portoroz 1997, 14...♕e6!? 15 ♗xa6 bxa6 16 ♗xc7 ♗b7 +/=) 12 ♘xd4 dxc5 13 ♘b3 ♕e6 (Shipov's 13...f5 looks relatively best, e.g. 14 exf5 gxf5 15 ♕d5+ ♕e6 16 ♖fe1 ♘b4 17 ♕xe6+ ♗xe6 18 ♘xc5 ♗f7 19 ♖ac1 +/=) 14 ♕d5 ♖b8 15 ♗g3 ♘e5 16 ♗xe5 fxe5 17 ♗xa6 ♕xd5 18 ♘xd5 bxa6 19 ♖ac1 +/- W.D.Taylor-J.Hill, corr. 1996.

b) 10 ♗d2 exd4 11 ♘xd4 f5 12 ♘c2 (or 12 ♗xg4 fxg4 13 ♗e3 ♖f7 14 ♕d2 ♕f8 ∞ K.Nikuljshin-D.Khismatullin, Voronezh 2006) 12...♘f6 13 exf5 ♗xf5 14 ♘d4 ♕d7 15 ♘xf5 ♕xf5 16 ♗e3 ♘c5 17 ♖c1 a5 18 ♕c2 ♘g4! = D.Zagorskis-

G.Timoscenko, Sala 1994.

c) 10 ♗c1 ♔h8 (if instead 10...♕e8 11 c5! dxc5 12 ♗xa6 bxa6 13 d5 f5 14 ♖e1 +/= R.Pogorelov-D.Larino Nieto, Calvia 2005; or 10...♘h6 11 ♖b1! ♘f7 12 dxe5 dxe5 13 b4 c6 14 b5 += J.Benjamin-S.Kindermann, Novi Sad Olympiad 1990; or 10...c6 11 h3 ♘h6 12 c5! exd4 13 ♗xa6 dxc3 14 ♗c4+ ♔h8! 15 cxd6 +/- A.Glicenstein-M.Kozakov, Paris 2004) 11 h3 ♘h6 12 dxe5 dxe5 (if 12...fxe5 13 ♗e3 ♘f7 14 ♕d2 ♘c5 15 ♘g5 ♘xg5 16 ♗xg5 ♗f6 17 ♗e3 ♘e6 18 ♗g4 +/= A.Karpov-G.Kasparov, 7th matchgame, New York 1990) 13 ♕xd8 ♖xd8 14 ♗e3 and, as in line B1 above, White has a persistent edge in the ending; e.g. 14...♗e6 (or 14...c6 15 ♖fd1 ♖e8 16 ♘d2 ♗f8 17 a3 f5 18 f3 ♘c5 19 b4 ♘e6 20 ♘b3 += L.E.Johannessen-A.Simutowe, Istanbul Olympiad 2000) 15 a3 ♘f7 16 b4 c6 17 ♖fd1 ♖xd1+ 18 ♖xd1 ♘c7 19 ♘d2 ♗f8 20 ♖b1! b6 (if 20...♗h6!? 21 ♗xh6 ♘xh6 22 ♘b3 +/= Kramnik; or 20...f5 21 g3 +/=) 21 c5! b5 22 a4 +/= V.Kramnik-V.Topalov, Novgorod 1997.

Returning to 9...♕e8 (D):

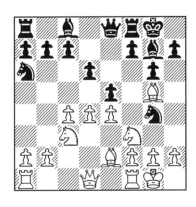

White mostly chooses between:

B21: 10 c5!? *132*
B22: 10 dxe5 *134*

But he also has a number of other continuations:

a) 10 d5 f5 (or 10...f6 11 ♗c1 f5 12 ♘e1 ♘f6 13 f3 f4 14 ♘d3 g5 15 ♖b1 ♕g6 with counterplay, F.Ercan-A.Duman, Turkish Ch. 2004) 11 ♘d2 h6 12 ♗h4 g5 13 ♗g3 ♘f6 14 f3 f4 15 ♗f2 ♕g6. Compared with 7...♘c6 8 d5 ♘e7 main lines Black's knight is out of play on a6, but he has made good progress on the kingside. V.Korchnoi-I.Smirin, Dresden 1998, continued 16 ♔h1 g4 17 fxg4 ♘xg4 18 ♗g1 ♖f7 19 ♘f3 ♗f6 20 ♖e1 ♖g7 21 ♗f1 ♘c5 22 b4 ♘d7 23 c5 ♗d8! 24 h3 ♘e3 25 ♗xe3 fxe3 26 c6 ♘f6 with an unclear position from which Black went on to win.

b) 10 ♖e1 *(D)* and now:

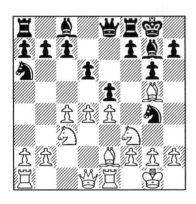

b1) 10...h6 11 ♗h4 ♘f6?! transposes to 8 ♗g5 h6 9 ♗h4 ♕e8 (which is bad for Black anyway – see the note 'e3' at the beginning of the chapter) with an extra ♖e1 for White. A.Jankovic-

H.Ziska, European Ch., Dresden 2007, continued 12 c5 (12 ♗xf6 ♗xf6 13 c5 is also good) 12...exd4 13 ♗xf6 dxc3 14 ♗xg7 ♔xg7 15 cxd6 cxb2 16 ♖b1 cxd6 17 ♕xd6 +/-. Black can improve this with 11...exd4!?, but in that case he might as well play it at once.

b2) 10...f6 11 ♗d2 is similar to 9...f6 10 ♗d2 above, the difference being that here the white rook stands on e1 (instead of f1) and the black queen is on e8 (rather than d8), but these extra moves do not have to be so important; e.g. 11...exd4 (not 11...f5?! 12 exf5 gxf5 13 c5 +/- N.Sulava-V.Milov, Geneva 1996) 12 ♘xd4 f5 or 12 ♘b5 d3!? 13 ♗xd3 ♕e7 ∞.

b3) 10...exd4 11 ♘xd4 (or if 11 ♘d5 f6 12 ♗f4, A.Huzman-L.McShane, Saint Vincent 2005, 12...♘e5!? 13 ♘xd4 c6 14 ♘c3 ♕f7 ∞) 11...♕e5! (not 11...♘xh2? 12 ♗e3 +-) 12 ♘f3 ♕c5 13 ♗h4 f5 14 exf5 ♗xf5 15 a3 (15 ♕b3 ♕b6 16 h3 ♘f6 17 ♕xb6 axb6 18 ♘d4 ♗d7 19 ♖ad1 = Dydysko) 15...♗xc3 16 bxc3 ♖ae8 ∞ E.Magerramov-V.Dydyshko, St Petersburg 1992.

c) 10 h3 *(D)* and then:

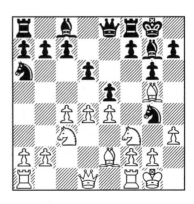

c1) 10...♘f6?! transposes to 8 ♗g5 ♕e8 (see note 'e1' at the beginning of the chapter) with the extra h2-h3 for White, who is again clearly better after either 11 c5 or 11 ♗xf6 ♗xf6 12 c5.

c2) 10...exd4 11 ♘xd4 ♘f6 12 ♗f3 ♕e5!? (if 12...h6 13 ♗e3 ♘h7 14 ♖e1 ♘g5 15 ♘db5 ♘xf3+ 16 ♕xf3 ♗e6 17 ♘d5 ♕d8 18 ♗d4 +/= H.Groffen-B.Laurent, Belgian Team Ch. 2003) 13 ♗e3 ♘c5 14 ♘db5 ♕e7 (O.Gladyszev-J.Kjetzae, Budapest 1999) 15 b4!? ♘cxe4 16 ♗xe4 ♘xe4 17 ♘d5 ♕d8 18 ♗d4 +=.

c3) 10...f6 11 ♗d2 ♘h6 12 d5 c5!? (P.Lafuente-I.Karim, World Junior Ch. 2003) 13 dxc6! (otherwise Black has a good version of 8...c6 9 d5 in the notes to line B1) 13...bxc6 14 ♗e3 ♘f7 15 a3 f5 16 b4 and White's prospects look brighter.

c4) 10...h6 11 ♗c1 (if 11 ♗h4 exd4! 12 ♘xd4 ♘f6 13 ♗f3 ♘h7 14 ♖e1 ♘g5 15 ♗xg5 hxg5 16 ♕d2 c6 17 ♖ad1 ♕e7 ∞ H.Nakamura-E.Perelshteyn, Bermuda 2003, or 13...♘d7!? 14 ♕d2 ♘e5 15 ♗e2 ♘c6 16 ♘xc6 bxc6 17 ♖ae1 ♘c5 ∞ S.Fedukovich-R.Rutkus, corr. 2000) 11...exd4!? (11...♘f6 12 dxe5 dxe5 13 ♗e3 transposes to line B22) 12 ♘xd4 ♘f6 13 ♗f3 ♘h7 (a typical manoeuvre with the white bishop on f3) 14 ♖e1 ♘g5 15 ♗g4 (or 15 ♗e3 ♕e5!?, G.Bagaturov-Z.Sturua, Protvino 1993, 16 ♖c1 c6 = Belov) 15...♘c5 (or 15...♗xg4 16 hxg4 ♘c5 17 ♗xg5 hxg5 18 ♕d2, I.Rogers-J.Gallagher, German League 1997, 18...♕d7 with excellent counterplay for Black) 16 ♘db5 ♗xg4 17 hxg4 ♕d8 18 f3 ♘ge6 19 ♗e3 c6 20 ♘d4 ♘xd4 21 ♗xd4 ♗e5! and Black's

position looks a little nicer, Hway Ik Oei-G.Mittelman, Amsterdam 1995.

B21: 10 c5!? *(D)*

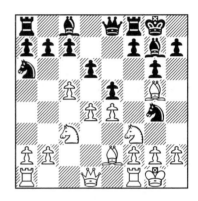

This sharp move become popular about four years ago (2005). In our opinion it is quite troublesome for Black and can be recommended.

10...exd4

Other moves are weaker:

a) 10...h6 11 ♗h4 exd4 (if 11...g5 12 ♗g3 exd4 13 ♘d5 dxc5 14 ♗xa6 bxa6 15 ♘xc7 ♕xe4 16 ♖e1 ♕c6 17 ♘xa8 ♕xa8 18 ♖c1 +/- V.Dimitrov-S.Jordanova, Plovdiv 2007; or 13...c6 14 ♗xd6! cxd5 15 exd5 with great compensation, R.Vera-J.Cuenca Jimenez, Albacete 2005) 12 ♘d5 ♕xe4!? (not 12...♘xc5? 13 ♘xc7 ♕xe4 14 ♘d2! +-; or if 12...g5 13 ♗g3 – *11...g5*) 13 ♘e7+ ♔h8 14 cxd6 (A.Zubarev-O.Gladyszev, corr. 2007) and if 14...cxd6 15 ♖e1 ♘e5! 16 ♗g3 d3 17 ♘xe5 dxe5 18 ♗xd3 ♕d4 19 ♗xg6 fxg6 20 ♘xg6+ ♔g8 21 ♘xf8 ♕xd1 22 ♖axd1 with the better ending for White.

b) 10...dxc5 11 ♗xa6 (11 ♘d5 h6 12 ♗h4 c6 13 ♘e7+ ♔h8 14 ♗xa6 bxa6 15

♘xc8 ♖xc8 16 h3 ♘f6 17 ♗xf6 ♗xf6 18 dxc5 += R.Ibrahimov-E.Moradiabadi, Moscow 2005, due to the superior pawn structure and minor piece) 11...bxa6 12 ♘d5 ♖b8 13 dxe5 ♘xe5 14 ♘f6+ ♗xf6 15 ♗xf6 ♘d7 16 ♗c3 (B.Avrukh-D.Bojkov, Greek Team Ch. 2005) and if 16...♕xe4 17 ♕d2 ♕f5 18 ♖ad1 ♘b6 19 ♖fe1 with a very strong initiative for the sacrificed material.

11 ♘d5 ♘xc5

A sharp continuation, the idea of which is seen after the next move. Other moves are again weaker:

a) 11...c6 12 ♘e7+ ♔h8 13 cxd6 +/- R.Ibrahimov-K.Lahno, Moscow 2005.

b) 11...dxc5 12 ♗xa6 bxa6 13 ♖c1 ♗b7 (or 13...♖b8 14 ♖xc5 h6 15 ♗h4 ♗b7 16 ♖e1 +/- Avrukh) 14 ♖xc5 ♗xd5 15 exd5 ♕d7 16 h3 ♕d6 17 b4 ♘e5 18 ♘xd4 +/- I.Cheparinov-C.Matamoros Franco, Dos Hermanas 2005.

c) 11...♕xe4 12 ♘e7+ ♔h8 13 cxd6 ♘c5 (or 13...cxd6 14 ♘xc8 ♖axc8 15 ♘d2 ♕e5 16 ♗xg4 ♕xg5 17 ♗xc8 ♖xc8 18 ♖c1 +/-) 14 ♗c4 d3 15 ♖c1 ♘e5 16 ♖e1 ♘xf3+ 17 gxf3 ♕d4 18 dxc7 ♕xb2 19 ♗xd3 and Black has problems, S.Knott-M.White, European Ch., Liverpool 2006.

d) 11...♗e6 12 cxd6 ♗xd5 13 exd5 cxd6 14 ♗xa6 bxa6 15 ♘xd4 ♕e5 16 ♕xg4 ♕xd4 17 ♕xd4 ♗xd4 18 ♖ad1 with a better ending for White, V.Teterev-J.Tihonov, Belarus Ch. 2007.

12 ♘xc7 ♕xe4 (D)

Black's is relying on his threat of 13...d3, while if 13 ♘d2 ♕e5 hits the bishop on g5. White has two testing responses:

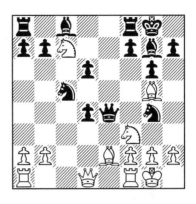

a) 13 ♖e1 ♖b8 (another option is 13...♗e6!? 14 ♘xa8 ♖xa8 15 h3 ♘e5 16 ♘xd4 ♘ed3 17 ♗xd3 ♕xd4 18 ♗f1 ♕xb2 with compensation for the exchange; but not 13...d3? 14 ♗f1 ♕c6? 15 ♘xa8 ♗e6 16 h3 ♘e5 17 ♘xe5 dxe5 18 ♖c1 +- V.Golod-M.Muse, German League 2007) 14 ♗c4 ♕f5 (14...♕c6 15 ♘d5 gives White a strong initiative for the pawns; e.g. 15...♕a4 16 b3 ♕a3 17 ♗c1 ♕a5 18 ♗d2 ♕d8 19 ♗g5 ♘f6 20 ♖e7!? ♘xd5?! 21 ♖xf7 ♕a5? 22 ♖xg7+ ♔xg7, V.Zakhartsov-D.Gochelashvili, Maikop 2008, 23 ♕xd4+! ♘f6 24 ♗h6+! ♔xh6 25 ♕e3+ ♔g7 26 ♕e7+ and wins) 15 ♗e7 ♗d7 16 h3 (16 ♗xf8 ♖xf8 17 ♘d5 ♕h5 again gives Black good play for the exchange) 16...♘xf2! (not 16...♘f6? 17 ♗xd6 ♘ce4 18 ♗xf8 ♖xf8 19 ♕xd4 when Black has no compensation, D.Navara-L.McShane, European Team Ch., Gothenburg 2005) 17 ♔xf2 b5 with a very unclear position; e.g. 18 ♗xf8 (or 18 ♗d5 ♘d3+ 19 ♔g1 ♘xe1 20 ♕xe1 ♖fc8 21 ♗xd6 ♖b6) 18...♔xf8 (or 18...bxc4!? 19 ♗xg7 ♘d3+ 20 ♔g1 ♔xg7) 19 ♗f1 d3 20 ♔g1 ♖c8.

b) 13 ♘xa8! looks like the critical

move; e.g. 13...d3 14 ♖e1 dxe2 15 ♖xe2 ♕c6 16 ♗e7 ♖e8 17 ♘c7 ♘xf2 (or 17...♕xc7 18 ♗xd6) 18 ♕d5 +/-. If Black is unable to improve this variation, he will have to choose something else at move 10 or 11.

B22: 10 dxe5 dxe5 *(D)*

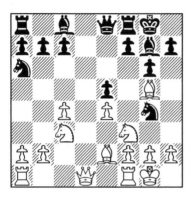

Most games have proceeded in this fashion. White releases the tension in the centre and tries to prove that the opposing pieces (♕e8, ♘g4, ♘a6) are misplaced and that Black will have to waste time improving their positions. Instead:

a) 10...♘xe5 11 ♘d4 ♘c6 12 ♘db5 f5 13 exf5 ♗xf5 14 ♕d2 ♕d7 15 ♘d5 ♔h8 16 ♖ae1 += M.Illescas Cordoba-V.Miguel Lago, Oviedo (rapid) 1991.

b) 10...h6 11 ♗h4 dxe5 (or 11...♘xe5 12 ♘d4 g5 13 ♗g3 ♘g6, Y.Shulman-B.Asanov, St Petersburg 1994, 14 ♖c1 +=) 12 ♘d5! c6?! 13 ♘e7+ ♔h7 14 ♘xc8 ♕xc8? (14...♖xc8 15 ♕d6 += A.Cherep-kov-D.Poldauf, Leningrad 1990) 15 ♗e7! ♖e8 16 ♘g5+! hxg5 17 ♗xg4 ♕c7 18 ♗xg5 +- E.Najer-R.Kempinski, Linares 2001.

11 h3

White prepares a safe place for his dark-squared bishop.

a) 11 ♕c1 does not give White chances of an advantage; e.g. 11...c6!? 12 ♖d1 f6 13 ♗d2 f5 14 h3 ♘f6 15 exf5 gxf5 16 ♗h6 ∞ P.Harikrishna-A.Volokitin, Bermuda 2005.

b) 11 a3!? worked out well for White in S.Skembris-L.Riemersma, Corfu 1996: 11...♘c5?! 12 ♘d5 f6? 13 ♘xc7 ♕f7 14 ♘xa8 fxg5 15 ♘xg5 ♕f4 16 ♗xg4 ♗xg4 17 ♕d5+ ♔h8 18 h4 ♘b3 19 ♘c7 ♘d4, at which point *Informator* breaks off with "with compensation", though White is completely winning after 20 ♖ae1. Instead, Black should prefer 11...h6 with similar play to the main line.

c) 11 ♘d2 *(D)* is the main alternative for White, and then:

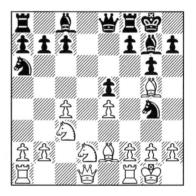

c1) 11...♘f6 12 ♘d5! ♕d8 13 f4 ♘xd5! 14 ♗xd8 ♘e3 15 ♕c1 ♘xf1 16 ♗h4 ♘xd2 17 ♕xd2 exf4 was Y.Zilberman-R.Har Zvi, Tel Aviv 1991, and ½-½ here according to the data-base, although the position is much better for White.

c2) 11...♗f6 12 h4 h6 13 ♘d5 hxg5 14 ♗xg4 ♕d8 15 h5 ♗g7 16 ♗xc8 ♖xc8 17 hxg6 c6 18 ♘e3 fxg6 19 ♘b3 ♕f6 20 ♕g4 ♖cd8 21 ♖ad1 ♖xd1 22 ♕xd1 ♕e7 23 ♕e2 ♘c7 24 ♘g4 +/=, though ½-½ again in A.Huzman-E.Miroshnichenko, Kapuskasing 2004.

c3) 11...h6 12 ♗h4 h5 13 c5 ♘xc5 14 ♘d5 ♘e6 15 h3 ♘h6 16 ♘f6+! ♗xf6 17 ♗xf6 ♘f4 (V.Mikhalevski-I.Smirin, Israel 1998) and now simplest was 18 ♘f3! ♕c6 19 ♗xe5 ♕xe4 20 ♖e1 +/-, or if 18...♗xh3!? 19 gxh3 ♘xh3+ 20 ♔h1 ♘g4 21 ♗h4 should repulse Black's attack.

c4) 11...f6 12 ♗h4 (12 ♗xg4 fxg5 is usually convenient for Black, giving him control of the dark squares and opening the f-file; e.g. 13.♘b3 c6 14.♗xc8 ♕xc8 15.♕d6 ♖f7 16.♖ad1 ♕e8 17.♕d2 g4 18.♕e2 ♕e6 19.♘a4 ♗f8 20.c5 ♗e7 =+ T.Jackelen-J.Gallagher, German League 2002) 12...♘h6 (another alternative is 12...h5 13 a3 ♘c5 14 b4 ♘e6 15 c5 ♘d4 16 ♗c4+ ♗e6 17 ♗xe6+ ♕xe6 18 ♘d5 ♖f7 ∞ V.Dydyshko-A.Zhigalko, Belarus Ch. 2005) 13 a3 ♘c5 14 b4 ♘e6 15 ♘b3 c6 16 ♖e1 f5 (Black can also consider 16...♘f4!? ∞) 17 f3 f4 18 ♖a2 g5 19 ♗f2 ♕g6 20 ♖d2 ♘f7 21 c5 h5 with counterplay, L.Van Wely-V.Milov, European Rapid Ch., Panormo 2002.

11...h6

Or 11...f6 12 ♗d2 (12 ♗c1 has no real worth here unless White wants to try 12...♘h6 13 b3!?, e.g. 13...c6 14 ♗a3 ♖f7 15 c5 ♘c7 16 ♖e1, M.Sadler-I.Glek, German League 2003, 16...♘e6!? 17 ♗c4 ♖d7 18 ♕c2 ♘f7 19 ♖ad1 b5!? 20 cxb6 axb6 21 ♗b2 b5 22 ♗xe6 ♕xe6 23 ♖xd7

♗xd7 24 a4 ∞ Glek) 12...♘h6 *(D)* and then:

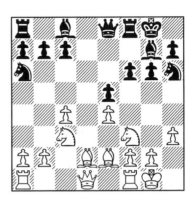

a) 13 ♕c1 ♘f7 14 c5 c6! 15 ♘a4 ♘c7 16 ♖e1 f5 with counterplay, S.Atalik-L.Comas Fabrego, New York Open 1998.

b) 13 ♗e3 c6 14 c5 ♘f7 15 ♗xa6 bxa6 16 ♕a4 ♖b8! 17 b3 f5 18 exf5 gxf5 19 ♖fe1 ♖b7! 20 ♖ac1 ♖e7 21 ♕h4 ♖e6 ∞ P.Eljanov-M.Tratar, Bled 2002.

c) 13 c5!? ♘xc5 (critical, though 13...c6 is still playable) 14 ♕c1 ♘f7 15 ♘d5 ♘e6 16 ♘xc7 ♘xc7 17 ♕xc7 ♘d8 18 ♖fc1 (or 18 ♗c4+ ♗e6 19 ♗xe6 ♕xe6 20 ♖ac1 ♖f7 21 ♕c4 ♖d7 =, e.g. 22 ♗e3 ♕xc4 23 ♖xc4 ♗f8 24 ♖fc1 ♘c6 25 ♔f1 ♖ad8 ½-½ A.Spielmann-O.Gladyszev, Nancy 2007) 18...♗e6 19 b4 (if 19 ♗e3 ♖f7 20 ♕c3 ♗f8 21 b4 ♕a4 22 a3 ♖c8 23 ♕b2, M.Gurevich-J.Lopez Martinez, Andorra 2004, 23...♖fc7!? 24 ♖xc7 ♖xc7 25 ♖c1 ♖xc1+ 26 ♕xc1 ♘f7 = Gurevich) 19...♖f7 20 ♕c3 ♗f8 21 ♕b2 (if 21 b5 b6! 22 ♕b2 ♘b7 ∞ O.Biriukov-S.Mihajlovskij, St Petersburg 2006) 21...b5!? 22 ♗e3 ♘b7 23 ♘d2 ♘d6 24 ♖c2 a5 ∞ D.Yevseev-V.Nevostrujev, Russia 2005.

d) 13 ♖b1 might be the best try for an edge; e.g. 13...♘f7 14 b4 c6 15 ♗e3 ♕e7 16 ♕a4 ♗e6 (if 16...♘c7, E.Najer-Y.Kruppa, St Petersburg 2003, 17 ♖fd1 +/=) 17 c5 +=, though ½-½ E.Najer-P.Svidler, St Petersburg 2003.

12 ♗d2

Or equivalently 12 ♗c1 ♘f6 13 ♗e3; whereas after 12 ♗h4 ♘f6 13 ♘d5 (or 13 ♘d2 c6 = V.Chekhov-L.Yurtaev, Riga 1988) 13...♘xe4 14 ♗e7 c6 15 ♗xf8 ♕xf8 Black has excellent compensation for the exchange, I.Zlatilov-I.Glek, Werfen 1990.

12...♘f6 13 ♗e3 *(D)*

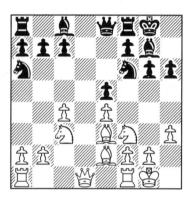

The key position. Now Black has to decide how to develop his queenside pieces.

13...b6

This avoids any structural difficulties connected with c4-c5 and ♗xa6, while ....♗b7 will exert pressure on the e4-pawn. Other moves are:

a) 13...c6 14 c5 (or 14 ♕d6!? ♕d7 15 ♕a3 ♖e8 16 c5 ♕e7, I.Nowak-D.Fillon, Kiekrz 1995, 17 ♗xa6 bxa6 18 ♖ad1 +/-) 14...♕e7 (or 14...♘h5 15 ♖e1 ♗e6 16 ♗xa6 bxa6 17 ♕a4 f5 18 ♖ad1 +/- Bu

Xiangzhi-L.McShane, Tiayuan 2005) 15 ♗xa6 bxa6 16 ♕a4 (or 16 ♕d6!? +/-) 16...♕c7 17 ♖fd1 +/- M.Gurevich-J.Hjartarson, Munich 1993.

b) 13...♘d7 14 a3 ♘ac5 (or if 14...f5 15 b4 f4 16 ♗c1 c6 17 c5 ♔h7 18 ♗b2 ♘c7 19 ♘b1 ♘e6 20 ♘bd2 ♘d4 21 ♘c4 ♘xe2+ 22 ♕xe2 b6, J.Piket-I.Smirin, Biel Interzonal 1993, then 23 cxb6 axb6 24 ♖fd1 intending ♕c2, ♖d2, ♖ad1 +/-) 15 ♘b5! (the most troublesome move, though White also keeps a positional advantage after 15 b4 ♘e6 16 c5 c6 17 ♗c4 ♕e7 18 ♕d2 ♔h7 19 ♖fd1 ♖e8 20 ♕c2! ♘df8 21 ♖d6 ♘f4 22 ♖ad1 ♘8e6, Zsu.Polgar-S.Kindermann, Munich 1991, and now 23 b5 Polgar) 15...♘e6 (or 15...♕d8 16 ♗xc5 ♘xc5 17 ♕xd8 ♖xd8 18 ♘xc7 +/- L.Van Wely-D.Reinderman, Leeuwarden 1993) 16 ♘xa7 ♖xa7!? (otherwise Black is just a pawn down) 17 ♗xa7 b6 18 a4 ♗b7 19 a5 f5?! (19...♗xe4 offered more hope) 20 axb6 (20 c5! +/- Piket) 20...cxb6 (20...c5! ∞ Piket) 21 c5 fxe4 22 ♗b5 +/- J.Piket-J.Polgar, Biel 1993.

c) 13...♕e7 14 ♘d5 (or 14 ♕c1 ♔h7 15 ♘d5!? ♕e6 16 ♕c2 b6 17 ♖fd1 ♗b7 18 b4 c6 19 ♘xf6+ ♗xf6 20 c5 +/- F.Beckmann-W.Pommerel, corr. 2002; while 14 a3 c6 15 b4 ♘h5 16 ♖e1 ♕f6 17 ♖a2 ♘f4 18 ♗f1 transposes to 13...♘h5 14 ♖e1 below) 14...♕d8 15 ♕c2 (or 15 ♘xf6+ ♕xf6 16 c5 ♘b8 17 b4 ♘c6 18 b5 ♘d4 19 ♗xd4 exd4 20 e5 += D.Korol-T.Melamed, Ukrainian Team Ch. 1998) 15...c6 16 ♘xf6+ ♕xf6 17 ♖ad1 (or 17 c5 ♘c7 18 ♖ad1 ♗e6 19 ♕c1! g5 20 ♗c4 ♕g6 21 ♗xe6 ♘xe6 22 ♕c4 ♖fd8, V.Topalov-H.Herraiz Lopez, 2nd matchgame, Albacete 2000, 23 ♖fe1! +/= Topalov) 17...♕e7 (17...c5!?) 18 c5 ♘c7 (or 18...♗e6 19 ♖d6 ♘c7 20 ♖fd1 +/= T.Jackelen-M.Borriss, German League 2003) 19 ♗c4 ♗e6 20 ♗xe6 ♕xe6 (G.Morrison-L.Trent, Blackpool 2005) 21 ♕d2 +/=.

d) 13...♘h5 (D) and then:

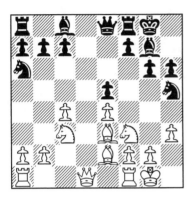

d1) 14 ♖e1 ♘f4 15 ♗f1 c6 (or 15...♘e6 16.a3 b6 17.b4 ♗b7 18.♖a2 ♔h7 19.♗c1 c6 20.♖d2 ♘ac7 21.♗b2, S.Gligoric-Z.Ilincic, Yugoslav Ch. 1995, 21...♖d8 =) 16 a3 ♕e7 17 b4 ♕f6 18 ♖a2 ♖d8 19 ♖d2 ♖xd2 20 ♕xd2 g5 21 ♖d1 ♗e6 22 ♘h2 ♘c7 23 ♘a4 ♕g6 24 ♕d6 ♖c8 25 ♗xa7 ♕xe4 with counterplay, D.Sharavdorj-C.Matamoros Franco, Calvia Olympiad 2004.

d2) 14 c5 ♘f4 15 ♗xa6 (or 15 ♗b5 ♕e6 16 ♖e1 ♔h8 17 ♖c1 g5 18 ♗f1 c6 19 ♕d6 += D.Mozetic-Z.Ilincic, Yugoslav Team Ch. 1996) 15...bxa6 16 ♕d2! (or 16 ♗xf4!? exf4 17 ♘d5 ♖b8 18 ♖e1 c6 19 ♘xf4 ♖xb2 20 e5 with the initiative, V.Topalov-V.Milov, Prague rapid 2002; or just 17 ♖e1!? ♖b8 18 ♕d2 +=) 16...♖b8 17 ♖ad1 g5 18 ♖fe1! ♕e6 19 ♗xf4! exf4?! (19...gxf4 20 b3 += Dautov) 20

♘d4 +/- V.Tukmakov-C.Landenbergue, Geneva 1997.

14 a3

Preparing the standard b2-b4 to gain space and restrict the a6-knight. Otherwise:

a) 14 ♕c2 ♘h5 15 c5 and now, rather than 15...♘f4 16 ♗xf4 exf4 17 cxb6 cxb6 18 ♖fe1 ♘c5 19 ♗b5 ♗d7 20 ♗xd7 ♕xd7 21 ♖ad1 ♕b7 22 e5! += S.Atalik-I.Smirin, Las Vegas 1998, instead 15...♘xc5!? looks better, when White has nothing special after either 16 ♗xc5 bxc5 17 ♘d5 ♖b8 or 16 ♘d5 ♘e6 17 ♘xc7 ♘xc7 18 ♕xc7 ♗e6.

b) 14 ♕c1!? ♔h7 15 a3 ♘h5 (or 15...♗b7 16 ♕c2 with similar play to the main line) 16 ♖e1 c6 17 b4 ♘c7 (S.Savchenko-S.Iuldachev, Jakarta 1997) 18 c5 +/=.

14...♗b7 15 ♕c2

There is no point in delaying this move; e.g. 15 ♘d2 ♖d8 16 ♕c2 ♘h7 (or 16...♘d7!? intending ...f7-f5) 17 b4 (V.Malaniuk-V.Chekhov, Kecskemet 1989) 17...f5!? with counterplay.

15...♘h5 (D)

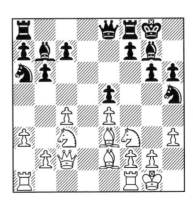

Black directs his knight to the active

position on f4. Instead, the passive 15...c6 16 b4 ♘c7 17 c5 b5 18 a4 gives White the better chances, E.Bareev-M.Manninen, Yerevan Olympiad 1996. But 15...♘c5!? is possible, not fearing the doubled pawns after 16 ♗xc5 (if 16 ♘d5 ♕a4!?) 16...bxc5 17 ♘d5 ♕b8! 18 ♖fd1 (or 18 ♘d2, A.Lastin-E.Ragozin, St Petersburg 2000, 18...a5!? and if 19 ♘b3 ♘xe4! 20 ♕xe4 ♗xd5 21 ♕xd5 ♕xb3 22 ♕xc5 e4 -/+ Huzman) 18...♖d8 19 ♘d2 (19 ♘c3!?) 19...a5 20 ♕a4 ♖a6 21 ♗f3 ♔h7 22 ♖ab1 ♗c6 23 ♕c2 a4 with counterplay, F.Peralta-C.Barrero Garcia, Ayamonte 2006.

16 b4

Here 16 ♖fe1 can be recommended as it leads to an advantage for White without any complications: 16...c6 (if 16...♘f4 17 ♗xf4! exf4 18 e5 ♘c5 19 ♖ad1 ♘e6 20 ♘d5 c6 21 ♘f6+ ♗xf6 22 exf6 c5 23 ♕c1 ♕c6 24 ♗f1 +/- M.Gurevich-R.Kempinski, German League 1999; or 16...♔h8 17 b4 ♘f4 18 ♗xf4 exf4 19 e5 c5 20 ♘d5 ♖c8 21 b5 ♘c7 22 ♘xf4 +/- A.Shirov-R.Kempinski, German League 2002) 17 b4 ♘c7 18 c5 ♘e6 19 ♖ad1 ♕e7 20 ♖d6 ♘hf4 21 ♗c4 ♖ad8 22 ♖ed1 ♖xd6 23 ♖xd6 +/= M.Ionescu-L.Vajda, Bucharest 2003, while 19 cxb6!? may be even stronger; e.g. 19...♘d4 20 ♗xd4 exd4 21 ♘a4 d3 22 ♗xd3 ♗xa1 23 ♖xa1 axb6 24 ♘xb6 ♖d8 25 ♘a4 ♘f4 26 ♗c4 ♗c8 27 ♘c5 +/- Mikhalevski.

16...♘f4

If 16...c5 17 ♘d5 ♖c8 18 ♖ab1 ♘f4 19 ♗xf4 exf4 20 ♖fe1 cxb4 21 axb4 +/= C.Marzolo-P.Toulzac, French Team Ch. 2004.

17 c5!?

It is probably better to keep the light-squared bishop; i.e. 17 ♗xf4! exf4 18 ♖fe1 ♕e6 19 ♖ad1 ♖fe8 20 ♗f1 intending ♘d5 with a slight advantage. **17...♘xe2+ 18 ♕xe2** (D)

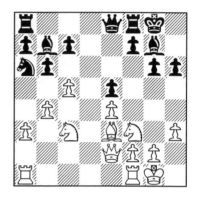

Matters are nicely unbalanced: White has space and the initiative on the queenside, while Black has the two bishops and counterplay on the other wing. However, in the three games to reach this position, Black has won every time:

a) 18...bxc5? 19 b5! ♘b8 20 ♗xc5 wins the exchange.

b) 18...♕e6 19 ♖ac1 +=; obviously better than 19 ♘d5?! c6 20 ♘c3 bxc5 21 bxc5 ∞ A.Dragomirescu-A.Zozulia, European Women's Ch., Kusadasi 2006.

c) 18...♘b8 19 b5! (not 19 ♖fd1 f5 20 ♘d5?! ♕f7 21 ♕a2 fxe4 22 ♘h2 ♔h7 =+ A.Beliavsky-Ba.Jobava, FIDE World Cup, Khanty Mansyisk 2005) 19...c6 20 cxb6 axb6 21 ♗xb6 cxb5 22 ♗c5 +/- Mikhalevski.

d) 18...f5! immediately looks like the best plan; e.g. 19 ♖fd1 bxc5 20 b5 ♘b8 21 ♕c4+ ♕f7 22 ♕xc5 ♖e8 23 ♘d5?! (it seems White just can't resist this move) 23...fxe4 24 ♘xc7 ♖c8 25 ♘xa8?? (25 ♘g5! hxg5 26 ♖ac1 remains unclear as Black has no easy way to develop his queenside) 26...♖xc5 26 ♖d8+ ♔h7 27 ♗xc5 ♘d7 28 ♗b4 ♗f6 0-1 P.Wells-R.Kempinski, German League 1998.

C: 8 ♖e1 *(D)*

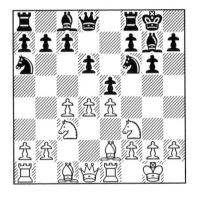

White makes a good prophylactic move, deferring the decision on where to develop the dark-squared bishop.

C1: 8...♕e8 *139*
C2: 8...c6 *142*

White should not have problems obtaining an advantage after other moves:

a) 8...♘g4 9 dxe5 ♘xe5 10 ♘d4 += N.Legky-C.Foisor, Ticino 1994.

b) 8...♗g4 9 ♗e3 (or 9 d5 ♘c5 10 ♕c2 a5 11 ♗e3 += R.Kempinski-T.Markowski, Polanica Zdroj 1996) 9...exd4 10 ♘xd4 ♗xe2 11 ♕xe2 ♘c5 12 f3 ♘h5 13 ♖ad1 += V.Popov-I.Saric, Saint Vincent 2005.

c) 8...exd4 is less valid here as Black has no appropriate moment to play ...d6-d5; e.g. 9 ♘xd4 ♖e8 (for 9...♘c5 see 7...♘bd7 8 ♖e1 exd4 in Chapter Seven, notes to line D) 10 ♗f1 ♘g4 (if 10...c6 11 ♘b3 d5? 12 cxd5 cxd5 13 ♗g5 +/- V.Malaniuk-A.Kovalev, Simferopol 1988) 11 f3 ♘e5 (not 11...♘xh2? 12 ♔xh2 ♕h4+ 13 ♔g1 ♗e5 14 f4 ♗xd4+ 15 ♕xd4 ♕xe1 16 ♘d5 ♖e6 17 b4 ♕h4 18 ♗b2 f6 19 ♕c3 +- Cu.Hansen-S.Tjomsland, Copenhagen 2005) 12 ♗e3 ♗d7 13 ♕d2 ♘c5 14 ♖ad1 ♘a4 15 ♘xa4 ♗xa4 16 b3 ♗d7 17 ♘e2 ♗c6 18 ♘c3 += U.Rueetschi-C.Maier, Swiss Team Ch. 2001.

C1: 8...♕e8 *(D)*

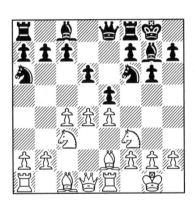

An alternative to the main line of C2, increasing the pressure on the e4-pawn. It may look a bit odd to post the queen opposite the white rook on e1, but Black has an idea to close the file.
9 ♗f1
Others:
a) 9 d5 ♘c5 transposes to 8 d5 ♘c5 (line A in Chapter Seven) with the extra moves ♖e1 and ...♕e8, which at

worst do not harm Black's position at
all; e.g. 10 ♘d2 a5 11 b3 ♗h6 12 ♗f1
♕e7 13 a3 ♗d7 14 ♖b1 ♘h5 15 ♕c2 f5
and Black had good counterplay in
A.Shirov-A.Motylev, Bastia (rapid)
2004.

b) 9 dxe5!? dxe5 10 b3 is an interesting attempt to exploit the weakness of
the a3-f8 diagonal. As Black has not
done very well trying to meet the
threat of ♗a3 (e.g. 10...♕e7 11 ♘d5 ♕d6
12 ♗g5 ♘xd5 13 cxd5 h6 14 ♗e3 f5 15
♕c1 +/- T.Bakre-J.Gallagher, British Ch.
2003), he may prefer simply to allow it:
10...♘c5 11 ♗a3 ♘fxe4 12 ♘xe4 ♘xe4
13 ♗xf8 ♕xf8 14 ♕c2 ♘c5 15 ♖ad1 a5
16 h3 ♗f5 17 ♕c1 ♖e8 with good compensation, A.Yermolinsky-V.Milov,
FIDE World Ch., Moscow 2001.

c) 9 ♗g5 became quite popular at
the end of the 1990s. White hopes for
the casual 9...h6?! 10 ♗xf6 ♗xf6 11 c5!
+= (compare 8 ♗g5 ♕e8 at the beginning of the chapter), and is also doing
quite well after 9...♗g4, e.g. 10 h3 ♗xf3
11 ♗xf3 ♘d7 12 ♗e3 c6 13 ♖b1 ♘c7 14
d5 c5 15 b4 += (though 15...♘a6 ½-½
V.Epishin-S.Movsesian, Groningen
1998). Much simpler is 9...exd4!? 10
♕xd4 ♘g4 11 ♕d2 ♘c5 and Black has
no problems, e.g. 12 ♗f1 ♗xc3 13 ♕xc3
♘xe4 14 ♕a5 ♕c6 15 ♘d4 ♕c5 16 ♕xc5
♘xc5 17 h3 f6 18 ♗d2 ♘e5 =+ V.Milov-
J.Arizmendi Martinez, Biel 2002.

9...♗g4 *(D)*

This is Black's idea; now that the e2-
bishop has withdrawn to meet the
veiled threat to e4, Black switches his
pressure to d4 by pinning the knight
on f3.

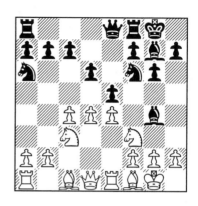

10 d5

The most usual response, though
White can also hope for a slight edge
after 10 dxe5!? dxe5 11 ♗e3 ♘d7 12 h3
♗xf3 13 ♕xf3 += L.Istvandi-
V.Dydyshko, Frydek Mistek 1995; or 10
♗e3 ♗xf3 11 ♕xf3 ♘g4 12 d5 ♘xe3 13
♕xe3, e.g. 13...c5 14 a3 f5 15 ♖ab1 ♕d7
16 ♕h3 ♖f7 17 b4 +/= G.Timoshenko-
G.Grigore, Berlin 1998.

10...♘b4

Threatening 11...♗xf3 when the
threat of 12...♘c2 would force White to
recapture with the g-pawn. Instead,
10...♘h5 plans the immediate counterattack with ...f7-f5, but Black isn't very
well set up for it here: 11 h3 ♗d7 (this
loses time, but 11...♗xf3 leads to a
permanent weakness on the light
squares, e.g. 12 ♕xf3 f5 13 exf5 gxf5 14
♗e2 ♘f6 15 ♗d3 f4 16 ♗f5 ♕h5 17
♕xh5 ♘xh5, I.Sokolov-D.Gadasi, Antwerp 1995, and now 18 ♗e6+ with a
long-term advantage for White) 12 ♖b1
♘c5 13 ♘b5! ♘a6 14 b4 f5 15 ♘c3 ♘f6
(N.Ostojic-G.Arsovic, Yugoslav Ch.
2002) 16 exf5!? ♗xf5 17 ♗d3 with a better position for White.

11 ♗e2

Nearly all games are played in this way, but White has another two interesting alternatives:

a) 11 ♕b3 a5 12 a3 ♘a6 13 ♕xb7 ♘d7 14 ♗e3 ♕e7 15 ♕b3 ♗xf3 16 gxf3 ♘ac5 17 ♕c2 a4 (S.Citak-C.Arduman, Turkish Ch. 2004) and after 18 ♘b5 Black still has to prove that he has enough compensation for the pawn, e.g. 18...♘b3 19 ♖ad1 ♘dc5 20 f4.

b) 11 a3!? basically ignores Black's threat in order to accelerate play on the queenside: 11...♗xf3 12 gxf3 ♘a6 13 b4! ♘h5 (or 13...♕e7 14 ♗e3 ♘d7 15 ♖c1 f5 16 exf5 gxf5 17 f4 += B.Larsen-K.Berg, Danish Ch. 1993) 14 c5 dxc5 15 ♗xa6 bxa6 16 bxc5 ♕e7 17 ♗e3 += G.Pankov-R.Altshul, St Petersburg 2002.

11...a5 *(D)*

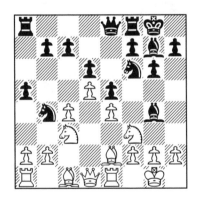

Having achieved this queenside breakwater, Black plans to return his knight to a6 so that it can reappear at c5. He is afforded the time to do so by White's own time wasting with ♗e2-f1-e2. However, the bishop doesn't really belong on g4 in these positions, so White can still hope for an advantage.

12 ♗e3 ♘a6

12...b6 is bit too passive; e.g. 13 a3 ♘a6 14 b3 ♘c5 15 ♘d2 ♗d7 16 b4 ♘a4 17 ♕c2 ♘xc3 18 ♕xc3 ♕e7 19 c5 += M.Petrekanovic-Z.Grujic, Sremska Mitrovica 2006.

13 ♘d2

As usual in these positions the exchange of bishops is favourable to White, though he can prepare his queenside expansion in other ways too; e.g. 13 b3 ♔h8 14 a3 ♘g8 15 ♖b1 ♗h6 16 ♗xh6 ♘xh6 17 b4 axb4 18 axb4 ♕e7 19 ♕d2 ♘g8 20 ♖ec1 += V.Golod-A.Weindl, Zürich 2004; or 13 a3 ♗d7 14 ♘d2 h5 15 h3 a4 16 b4 axb3 17 ♘xb3 += C.Navrotescu-G.Grigore, Rumanian Team Ch. 1998.

13...♗xe2

Or 13...♗d7 14 ♖b1 ♘c5 (14...b6?! is again too passive; e.g. 15 ♘b5 ♔h8 16 f3 ♘g8 17 a3 ♗h6 18 ♗xh6 ♘xh6 19 b4 +/- T.Gareev-A.Zhigalko, Calvia Olympiad 2004) 15 b3 ♔h8 16 a3 ♘g8 17 b4 axb4 18 axb4 ♘a4 19 ♘xa4 ♗xa4 20 ♕c1 f5 21 f3 += D.Bunzmann-G.Souleidis, German League 2007.

14 ♕xe2 ♘h5 *(D)*

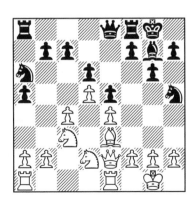

"It would be interesting to check 13...♗xe2 14 ♕xe2 ♘h5," wrote Avrukh in 2004. Two games since then have seen:

a) 15 b3 ♘f4 16 ♕d1 ♘d3 17 ♖f1 f5 18 f3 ♕e7 19 ♔h1 ♕h4 20 ♕e2 ♘f4 21 ♕e1 ♕xe1 22 ♖axe1 was fine for Black in E.Moser-C.Karner, Austrian Team Ch. 2006.

b) 15 a3 ♘f4 16 ♕f1 a4 (another benefit of ...♕e8) 17 b4!? axb3 18 ♘xb3 b6 19 ♘b5 ♕d7 20 g3 ♘h5 21 ♕e2 f5 22 exf5 ♖xf5 (S.Lputian-O.Sepp, European Team Ch., Gothenburg 2005) and now 23 a4 intending a4-a5 would offer White a slight advantage.

C2: 8...c6 *(D)*

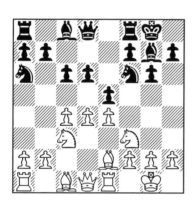

The main line.

C21: 9 ♖b1 *143*
C22: 9 ♗f1 *145*

After 9 d5 Black should play 9...♘c5!, transposing to 7...♘bd7 8 ♖e1 c6 9 d5 ♘c5 in the notes to line D3 in Chapter Seven.

White does not have much chance of achieving anything after moves such as:

a) 9 h3 exd4 (a good moment to capture, as h2-h3 is not very useful in ...e5xd4 variations) 10 ♘xd4 ♖e8 11 ♗f3 ♘d7 12 ♗e3 ♘b6 13 ♕e2 ♘c5 14 ♖ad1 ♕h4 15 b3 a5 16 ♕d2 ♕e7 ∞ S.Ibanez-M.Sorin, Rochefort 1998.

b) 9 dxe5 dxe5 10 ♕xd8 ♖xd8 11 ♘xe5 ♘c5 (not yet 11...♘xe4? 12 ♘xc6!) 12 ♗f1 ♖e8 13 f4 ♘fxe4 14 ♘xe4 ♘xe4 15 ♖xe4 f6 = V.Baikov-I.Smirin, USSR Team Ch. 1988.

c) 9 ♗e3 *(D)* deserves serious attention though:

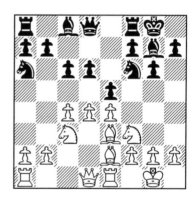

c1) 9...exd4 is less appropriate now, as the white rook eliminates any tactics on the e-file; e.g. 10 ♘xd4 ♖e8 11 f3 ♘c7 (not 11...d5?! 12 cxd5 ♘xd5 13 ♘xd5 cxd5 14 ♗xa6 bxa6 15 ♘c6 ♕f6 16 exd5 ♕xb2 17 ♖b1 ♕xa2 18 d6 ♗f6 19 ♘e7+! +/- P.San Segundo Carrillo-L.Perpinya Rofes, Spanish Ch. 2000; or if 11...♘c5 12 ♕d2 a5 13 ♖ad1 ♘fd7 14 ♘b3 ♘xb3 15 axb3 += V.Neverov-G.Timoscenko, USSR Team Ch. 1988) 12 ♕d2 +/=, and if 12...d5?! 13 cxd5

cxd5 14 ♘db5 ♗e6 15 e5 ♘d7 16 f4 +/-
H.Wirthensohn-J.Gallagher, Swiss Ch.
2006.

b) 9...♘g4 10 ♗g5 f6 (if 10...♗f6 11
♗xf6 ♕xf6 12 h3 exd4 13 ♕xd4 ♘e5 14
♖ad1 ♗xh3 15 ♕xd6 ♘xf3+ 16 ♗xf3 +/-
Y.Pelletier-A.Volokitin, Biel 2005; or
10...♕c7 11 ♗h4!? f5?!, E.Lobron-
A.Kovalev, German Cup 1991, 12 c5!
+/-) 11 ♗h4 ♘h6 12 h3 (12 c5!? looks
good here too) 12...♘f7 13 ♖b1 ♘c7 14
b4 ♘e6 15 d5 (V.Anand-V.Topalov,
Monte Carlo rapid 1999) 15...♘f4 16
dxc6 bxc6 17 b5 +/=.

C21: 9 ♖b1 (D)

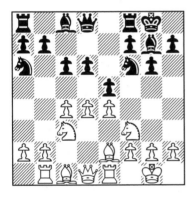

As with 8 ♖b1 (see line A) White
plans b2-b4, gaining space and restricting the a6-knight.

9...exd4

Again this is the correct decision for
Black, as the b1-rook is now rather
misplaced. Other moves lead to an advantage for White:

a) 9...♕e7 10 c5! (Black must always
watch out for this move, particularly
after he has played ...c7-c6) 10...dxc5 11
dxe5 ♘g4 12 ♗xa6 bxa6 13 ♕d6 ♖e8 14

♗g5!? ♕e6 15 ♕xc5 ♘xe5 16 ♘xe5
♗xe5 17 ♖bd1 ♖b8 18 b3 +/- D.Hergott-
R.Martin del Campo, Linares 1992.

b) 9...♘g4 10 h3 exd4 11 ♘xd4 ♕f6
12 hxg4 ♕xd4 13 ♗f4 ♕xd1 14 ♖exd1
♗e5 15 ♗h6 ♖e8 16 ♘a4 c5 17 ♗e3 ♘b4
18 f4 ♗g7 19 ♖xd6 ♗f8 20 ♖d2 ♖xe4 21
♔f2 +/- S.Guseinov-Y.Nikitin, USSR
Team Ch. 1991.

10 ♘xd4 ♖e8

The alternative is 10...♘c5 11 f3 (or
if 11 ♗f1 ♘g4! 12 h3 ♕f6 13 hxg4 ♕xd4
= L.Bass-D.Cramling, Gausdal 1983)
11...♘h5!? (more promising than 11...a5
12 ♗e3 a4 13 ♘c2 ♕e7 14 ♕d2 ♗e6 15
♖bd1 ♘e8 16 ♗d4 +/= V.Kramnik-
J.Gallagher, clock simul, Zürich 1999)
12 g3 (if 12 ♗e3 ♕h4! 13 ♗f2 ♕g5 14
♗f1 ♘f4 15 g3 ♘cd3 16 ♗xd3 ♘h3+ 17
♔g2 ♘xf2 18 ♔xf2 ♗xd4+ 19 ♔g2 =+
V.Popov-G.Kuzmin, Krasnodar 1998)
12...♖e8 13 b4 ♘e6 14 ♗e3 f5 15 f4 ♘f6
16 exf5 ♘xd4 17 ♗xd4 ∞ M.Narciso
Dublan-Y.Lederer, Andorra 2002.

11 ♗f1

White has also tried:

a) 11 f3 ♘h5 (preparing kingside action. although the plan of ...d6-d5 is
also good, e.g. 11...♘c7 12 ♗f1 d5 13
cxd5 ♘fxd5 14 ♘ce2, J.Pinter-
P.Szekely, Hungarian Team Ch. 1991,
14...♘b4!? 15 a3 c5 with counterplay)
12 ♗e3 (not 12 f4?! ♕f6!, but 12 ♗f1!?
intending 12...♕h4 13 ♘de2 and 14 g3
comes into consideration) 12...f5 (or
12...♕h4!? as in the previous note) 13
♕d2 f4 14 ♗f2 ♗e5 15 ♘c2 g5 16 ♖ed1
♗e6 17 ♘d4 ♗d7 18 a3 ♘f6 19 g4 h5 20
h3 ♔g7 21 ♔g2 ∞ J.Nilssen-D.Bekker
Jensen, Taastrup 1997.

b) 11 ♗f3 h6 (preparing the typical manoeuvre ...♘h7-g5; otherwise 11...♘c5 12 b4 ♘e6 13 ♗e3 ♘xd4 14 ♗xd4 ♗e6 15 ♗e2 ♕e7 16 ♕c2 d5! 17 cxd5 cxd5 18 ♗b5 ♖ec8! 19 exd5 ½-½ V.Neverov-I.Glek, corr. 1989, due to 19...♘xd5 20 ♗xg7 ♔xg7 21 ♘xd5 ♗xd5 22 ♕b2+ ♕f6 = Glek) 12 b4 (or 12 ♗f4 g5 13 ♗g3 g4 14 ♗e2 ♘c5 15 f3 ∞ Khalifman) 12...♘xb4 13 ♖xb4 c5 14 ♖b3 cxd4 15 ♘b5 (L.Andersen-K.Trygstad, Gausdal 2000) 15...a6 16 ♘xd4 ♘d7 =.

11...♘g4!

Other continuations allow White a small advantage:

a) 11...♘c5 12 f3 ♘h5 (White is now ready to meet this effectively) 13 ♗e3 ♘e6 14 ♘xe6 ♗xe6 15 ♕d2 += B.Raedeker-H.Bode, Ellwangen 2003.

b) 11...♕b6 12 ♘a4 ♕c7 13 f3 ♗d7 14 ♘c3 d5 15 cxd5 ♘xd5 16 exd5 ♖xe1 17 ♕xe1 ♗xd4+ 18 ♗e3 ♕b6 19 ♗xd4 ♕xd4+ 20 ♔h1 ♖e8 21 ♕g3 ♘b4 22 ♖d1 ♕e5 23 d6 ♕xg3 24 hxg3 f5 25 ♖d2 += V.Kramnik-J.Piket, Monte Carlo (rapid) 2001.

12 h3 ♕b6 13 hxg4 ♕xd4

After 13...♗xd4 14 ♗e3 ♗xe3 15 ♖xe3 Black is left with the weak d6-pawn and less space; e.g. 15...♕c5 16 a3 (E.Kublashvili-D.Daulyte, European Junior Ch. 2005) 16...♕e5 17 b4 ♘c7 18 ♖b2 ♗e6 19 ♖d2 +=.

14 ♕f3

White can also accede to the ending with 14 ♕xd4!? (if 14 g5 ♘c5 15 ♗f4 ♕xd1 16 ♖bxd1 ♗e5 = V.Babula-T.Likavsky, Slovakian Ch. 1999) 14...♗xd4 15 ♖d1 ♗e5 16 g5 ♘c5 17 f3

a6 (or 17...a5 18 ♘e2 h6 19 gxh6 f5 20 ♗e3 += A.Yermolinsky-J.Fedorowicz, Philadelphia 2002) 18 ♘e2! b5 19 ♘d4 ♗d7 20 ♗e3 ♘a4 21 ♖d2 (A.Yermolinsky-V.Ivanchuk, Wijk aan Zee 1999) 21...♖ab8 22 b3 ♘c3 23 ♖c1 b4 24 ♘e2 +/=, or if 19...♗b7 (I.Stohl-Z.Kozul, Croatian Team Ch. 2004) 20 ♘b3! +/=.

14...♕f6

Other moves allow White to play ♗f4 with advantage:

a) 14...♘c5?! 15 ♗f4 ♘e6 16 ♖bd1 ♕b6 17 ♗xd6 +/- J.Pinter-P.Sinkovics, Hungary 1990.

b) 14...♕e5 15 ♗f4 ♕e7 16 g5 ♘c5 17 ♕g3 ♗e5 18 ♖bd1 f6 19 gxf6 ♕xf6 20 ♗xe5 dxe5 21 b4 ♘e6 22 ♖d6 ♕f4 23 ♕xf4 ♘xf4 24 ♖ed1 ♘e6 (P.Lafuente-J.Lopez Martinez, Havana 2004) 25 c5 intending ♗c4 +=.

15 ♕g3 g5! *(D)*

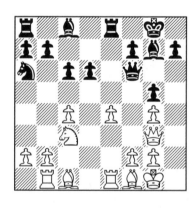

Preventing both ♗f4 and g4-g5 and taking control of the kingside dark squares. The game Z.Krnic-R.Bakic, Belgrade 2005, continued 16 ♖d1 ♗e6 (16...♕e5!?) 17 ♗e3 ♕e7 18 f3 ♘c5 19 ♘e2 and now, rather than the mistaken and unnecessary sacrifice 19...♘xe4? 20 fxe4 ♖xe4 21 ♗d4 ♗xg4 22 ♗xg7 ♔xg7 23 ♘c3 ♖f4 24 ♖e1 ♕f6 25 ♖e4 +/-, Black should have played 19...♖h6 followed by 20...♗e5 with a very satisfactory position.

C22: 9 ♗f1 *(D)*

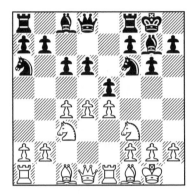

The most natural and flexible continuation.

9...exd4

This move usually leads to an ending where White has a slight edge, although winning the game can be very difficult. On the other hand, Black cannot expect much counterplay.

Other continuations lead to a small advantage for White:

a) 9...♘g4 is inaccurate due to 10 ♗g5! (10 h3 exd4 11 ♘xd4 would transpose to the main line) 10...f6 11 ♗h4 (V.Sergeev-W.Nikitin, Simferopol 1989) 11...exd4 12 ♘xd4 ♕b6 13 ♘a4 ♕d8 14 ♗g3 +=.

b) 9...♘h5 10 d5 c5 11 ♗g5 ♗f6 12 ♗d2 ♗g4 13 ♘b5 += V.Epishin-J.Polgar, Madrid 1992.

c) 9...♗g4 (as in line C1) is the main

alternative, when White usually responds 10 d5 (or 10 dxe5!? ♗xf3 11 ♕xf3 dxe5 12 ♗e3 ♕e7 13 ♖ad1 ♘d7, S.Ovsejevitsch-A.Morozevich, Jurmala 1992, 14 ♖d2 +/=) 10...c5 *(D)* (the immediate 10...♘e8 11 h3 ♗d7 allows 12 c5! ♘ac7 13 ♗g5 f6 14 ♗e3 ♕e7 15 ♕b3 +/- I.Farago-E.Toth, Budapest 2007; while if 10...♘b4, as in line C1, then 11 ♗e2 a5 12 ♗g5 h6 13 ♗e3 ♕c7 14 h3 ♗xf3 15 ♗xf3, A.Karpov-Z.Ilincic, Belgrade 1996, 15...♖fe8 16 a3 ♘a6 17 ♕d2 ♔h7 18 b3 +/= Ftacnik) and now:

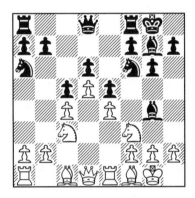

c1) 11 ♗e2 ♘e8 12 a3 ♗d7 13 g3 (13 ♕b3!? should be tested) 13...f5 14 ♘g5 ♘ac7 15 exf5 gxf5 16 f4 (+/= Pogorelov) 16...e4 17 ♗e3 ♗xc3!? (not as antipositional as it looks, since White is unable to take advantage of the weakened a1-h8 diagonal and, meanwhile, loses any dynamic pawn-play on the queenside) 18 bxc3 ♘f6 19 ♘h3 ♔h8 20 ♘f2 ♖g8 21 ♔h1 ♖g6 22 ♖g1 ♕g8 23 ♕d2 ♕g7 24 ♖g2 ♖g8 25 ♖ag1 ½-½ D.Komarov-L.Comas Fabrego, Benasque 1995.

c2) 11 h3 ♗d7 12 ♗g5 (or 12 a3 ♔h8 13 ♖b1 ♘g8 14 b4 ♗h6 15 ♗xh6 ♔xh6

16 ♕d2 ♔g7, J.Piket-V.Topalov, Tilburg 1998, 17 ♗d3 intending ♗c2-a4, Huzman) 12...♔h8 (if 12...h6 13 ♗e3 ♘h5 14 ♕d2 g5 15 ♘h2 ♘f4 16 a3 h5 17 ♗e2 ♘xe2+ 18 ♕xe2 g4 19 hxg4 hxg4 20 ♘xg4 ♕h4 21 f3 f5 22 exf5 ♗xf5 23 ♘e4 +/- A.Mitenkov-S.Ziger, Katowice 1993) 13 a3 (if 13 ♕d2 ♖g8! 14 ♗d3 ♕f8 15 ♖f1 h6 16 ♗e3 ♘h7 17 ♘h2 f5 with counterplay, Z.Gyimesi-L.McShane, German League 2006) 13...♕b8 14 ♕c2 ♘g8 15 ♗d3 f6!? (A.Miles-P.Cramling, Malmö 1996) 16 ♗d2!? intending ♖ab1, b2-b4 with better chances for White (Hazai).

10 ♘xd4 ♘g4 (D)

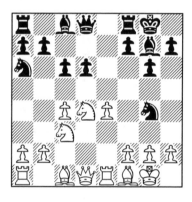

Black begins play on the dark squares, threatening 11...♕b6 and obviously 11...♕h4. White must play energetically in order to avoid some tactical motifs.

a) 10...♕b6 has similar intentions, but then White can play 11 ♘a4! (if 11 h3 ♘g4! transposes to the main line) 11...♕c7 (or 11...♕a5 12 ♗d2 ♕h5?! 13 ♗f4 ♖e8 14 ♘c3 ♕xd1 15 ♖axd1 ♗f8 16 ♘b3 +/- A.Beliavsky-Z.Kozul, Slovenian Team Ch. 2000) 12 ♗f4 ♘h5 13

♗e3 ♘c5 14 ♘c3 ♘f6 15 f3 a5 16 ♕d2 +/= L.Ftacnik-M.Muse, German League 2007.

b) 10...♖e8 is too passive here, as Black is essentially a tempo down on line C1; e.g. 11 ♘b3 ♗e6 12 ♗f4 d5 (A.Shariyazdanov-M.Tosic, Nizhnij Tagil 1998) 13 cxd5 cxd5 14 e5 ♘h5 15 ♗c1 and Black has serious problems with his h5-knight.

11 h3

Attempts to anticipate Black's counterplay are ineffective; e.g. 11 ♘f3 ♕b6 12 ♕e2 ♗e6 13 h3 ♘e5 14 ♘xe5 dxe5 = E.Bukic-D.Simic, Slovenian Ch. 1991; or similarly 11 ♖e2 ♕b6 12 ♘f3 ♗e6 13 h3 ♘e5 14 ♘xe5 dxe5! 15 ♗e3 ♕b4 16 c5 ♖fd8 17 ♖d2 ♕a5 18 ♗xa6 ♖xd2 19 ♕xd2 ♕xa6 20 ♖d1 ♗f8 = V.Topalov-V.Dimitrov, Bulgarian Ch. 1989.

11...♕b6

After 11...♘xf2 12 ♔xf2 Black does not have full compensation for the piece, although the position is very complicated: 12...♕b6 13 ♗e3 (13 ♘ce2 may be better, keeping the queenside pawns, e.g. 13...♘c5 14 ♔g1 ♘xe4 15 ♖b1 ♖e8 16 ♗f4 +=) 13...♕xb2+ 14 ♘ce2 ♘c5 15 ♔g1 ♘xe4 (or if 15...♖e8, Z.Gyimesi-R.Polzin, Austrian Team Ch. 2005, 16 ♘c2 +/=) 16 ♘b3 += B.Ivkov-M.Hebden, Las Palmas 1989.

12 hxg4 ♕xd4 (D)

After 12...♗xd4 13 ♗e3! ♗xe3 14 ♖xe3 Black is again left with his weak d6-pawn; e.g. 14...♕c5 (not 14...♕xb2?? 15 ♖b1 ♕a3 16 ♘a4 +-) 15 ♗e2 ♗e6 16 b3 ♖ad8 17 ♕d2 (L.Van Wely-S.Ernst, Dutch Ch. 2001) 17...♕e5 18 ♖h3 ♖d7 +/= Tsesarsky; or 14...♘c5 15 ♖b1 ♕c7

16 b4 ♘d7 17 ♗e2 a5 18 a3 axb4 19 axb4 ♘f6 20 ♕d4 ♕e7 21 g5 ♘e8 22 e5! +/- L.Ftacnik-G.Milos, Istanbul Olympiad 2000.

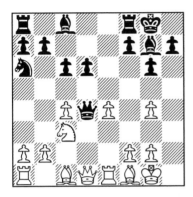

The position after the text is the same as in line C21, minus the two rook moves ♖b1 and ...♖e8. This should be in White's favour as his rook does not belong on b1 here; on the other hand the black rook may find work on f8 after a later ...f7-f5 or ...f7-f6.

13 g5

White tried a few other continuations:

a) 13 ♕f3 (avoiding the exchange of queens, but White cannot expect more of an advantage than in the ending) 13...♕b6 (if 13...♕e5 14 g5 ♕e7 15 ♕g3 ♘c5 16 ♗f4 ♗e5 17 ♖ad1 f6 18 gxf6 ♖xf6 19 ♗xe5 ♕xe5, B.Gelfand-T.Markowski, Polanica Zdroj 1998, 20 ♖e3 +=) 14 ♖d1 (or if 14 ♕g3 ♗e5 15 ♗f4, S.Savchenko-F.Amonatov, Elista Olympiad 1998, 15...f6!? 16 ♖ab1 ♘c5 17 b4 ♘e6 18 ♗xe5 fxe5 ∞ Savchenko) 14...♗e5 15 ♖b1 ♕d8 16 g3 ♕e7 ∞ P.Eljanov-L.Comas Fabrego, Spanish Team Ch. 2006.

b) 13 ♕e2 ♕e5 14 ♗e3 ♘c5 15 f3 ♕e7 (not 15...f5?! 16 gxf5 gxf5 17 f4 ♕e7 18 ♗xc5 dxc5 19 e5 += A.Rychagov-A.Motylev, Kolontaevo 1997) 16 ♕d2 ♗e5 17 ♗g5 ♕c7 18 b4 ♘e6 19 ♗e3 (Wl.Schmidt-P.Cramling, Novi Sad Olympiad 1990) 19...a5! 20 a3 f5!? with good counterplay for Black (Cramling).

c) 13 ♗f4 ♕xd1 14 ♖axd1 ♗e5 15 ♗h6 ♖e8 16 f3 ♘c5 17 ♔f2 a6 18 ♖c1 ♗e6 19 ♗e3 b5 = P.Van der Sterren-B.Gelfand, Wijk aan Zee 1998.

d) 13 ♗e3!? ♕xd1 (13...♕e5 14 g3 ♕e7 15 f3 ♘c5 16 ♕d2 a5 17 ♖ad1 ♗e5 18 ♗f2 ♖e8 19 ♗g2 +=, threatening f2-f4 to win the d6-pawn at an appropriate moment, O.Salmensuu-K.Trygstad, Gausdal 1997) 14 ♖axd1 ♗xg4 15 ♖xd6 ♖fe8 16 f3 ♗e6 17 ♖ed1 ♘b4?! (Tsesarsky's 17...f5!? is better, but after 18 c5, threatening 19 ♖xe6 or 19 ♗xa6, White still has a slight initiative; e.g. 18...♘c7 19 ♖6d3 fxe4 20 ♘xe4 ♘d5 21 ♗d4) 18 ♖6d2 b6 19 ♔f2 with a small but long-term advantage for White due his central control, N.Sanjay-T.Markowski, Calcutta 2001.

13...♕xd1

Other moves do not promise Black equality:

a) 13...f5 14 ♗f4 fxe4 15 ♕xd4 ♗xd4 16 ♖xe4 ♗xc3 17 bxc3 ♘c5 18 ♖d4 ♘e6 19 ♗xd6 ♘xd4 20 ♗xf8 ♘c2 21 ♖c1 ♘e3 22 fxe3 ♔xf8 +/= V.Kramnik-B.Gelfand, Monte Carlo (blindfold rapid) 2001.

b) 13...♕e5 14 ♗e3 ♘c5 15 f4! ♕e7 16 ♗xc5 dxc5 17 e5 h6 18 gxh6 ♗xh6 19 g3 f6 20 ♕c2 ♗f5 21 ♗d3 ♗xd3 22 ♕xd3 +/= V.Eingorn-V.Dydyshko,

USSR Team Ch. 1991.

c) 13...♞c5 and then:

c1) 14 ♕c2 ♕e5 (if 14...f5!? 15 ♗e3 ♕e5 16 exf5 ♗xf5 17 ♕d2 ♞e4! 18 ♞xe4 ♗xe4, E.Alekseev-E.Vorobiov, Krasnoyarsk 2003, 19 ♖e2!? +/=) 15 ♗e3 ♕e7 (or if 15...a5 16 ♖ad1 ♕e7 17 ♕d2, D.Berczes-W.Wittmann, Budapest 2005, 17...♗e5 18 f4 ♗xc3 19 ♕xc3 ♞xe4 20 ♕d4 with compensation) 16 ♖ad1 ♖d8 (or 16...b6 17 b4 ♞e6 18 b5 ♗b7 19 bxc6 ♗xc6 20 ♞d5 ♕d8, E.Bacrot-I.Nataf, Istanbul 2003, 21 ♕d2 +/=) 17 ♖d2 ♞e6 18 f4 b6 (H.Stefansson-M.Apicella, Reykjavik 1993) 19 g3 ♗b7 20 ♗g2 +/=.

c2) 14 ♗f4! ♕xd1 15 ♖axd1 ♗e5 16 g3! (not possible in the 13 ♗f4 line as the g4-pawn was en prise) 16...♖e8 (or even 16...b6 17 ♖xd6!? ♗xd6 18 ♗xd6 ♖d8 19 e5 ♗f5 20 ♗g2 ♖ac8 21 b4 ♞b7 22 c5 bxc5 23 bxc5 with very strong compensation for the pawn, S.Grimm-K.Wolter, Budapest 1999) 17 ♖xd6! ♗xd6 18 ♗xd6 ♞e6 (or 18...b6 19 f4 ♖d8 20 e5 ♗f5 21 ♗g2 ♖ac8 22 b4 ♞e6 23 ♔f2 +/= J.Pinter-M.Apicella, European Team Ch., Debrecen 1992) 19 f4 ♖d8 20 e5 ♞d4 21 ♔f2 ♞f5 22 c5 ♗e6 (N.Nikcevic-V.Dimitrov, Ulcinj 1997) and now 23 ♖e4! ♖d7 24 ♖a4 ♔g7 25 ♞e4 (Roiz) with a pawn and very strong play for the exchange.

14 ♖xd1 (D)

White is slightly better due to the weakness on d6, but winning that pawn is by no means easy. Black's main line of defence is a counterattack against e4, making it difficult for White to achieve the necessary f2(-f3)-f4.

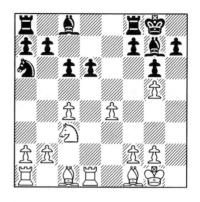

14...♞c5

Black can also play 14...♗e5 at once, when 15 ♗e3 ♞c5 16 f3 and 15 ♞e2!? ♞c5 16 f3 transpose to the text. Otherwise White has tried:

a) 15 f4 ♗xc3 16 bxc3 ♞c5 17 ♗a3 (if 17 ♖xd6 ♞xe4 or 17 e5 dxe5 18 ♗a3 b6 19 ♗xc5 bxc5 20 fxe5 =) 17...♞xe4 18 ♖e1 ♖e8 19 ♗d3 d5 20 cxd5 cxd5 21 c4 ♗e6 22 ♗xe4 dxe4 23 ♖xe4 = Se.Ivanov-I.Glek, Russian Ch. 1998.

b) 15 ♞a4!? (preparing f2-f4) 15...♞b4 (or 15...♞c5 16 ♞xc5 dxc5 17 ♗e3 ♗xb2 18 ♖ab1 ♗g7 19 ♗xc5 ♖e8 20 ♗e3 b6 21 a4 += G.Van der Stricht-P.Vandevoort, Belgian Ch. 2006) 16 a3 (also good is 16 ♗d2 ♞c2 17 ♖ac1 ♞d4 18 f4 ♗g7 19 ♗e3 c5 20 ♞c3 += Glek) 16...♞c2 17 ♖a2 ♞d4 18 b4 b6 19 ♗e3 +=, though ½-½ here in A.Huzman-L.Comas Fabrego, European Ch., Istanbul 2003.

15 f3

White can try to exploit the bishop pair after 15 ♖xd6 ♗xc3 16 bxc3 ♞xe4 17 ♖d3, but the weakness of his queenside pawns gives Black counterplay; e.g. 17...b6 18 ♗f4 ♗a6 19 ♖e1 ♞c5 20

♖d6 ♘e6 21 ♗e3 c5 22 a4 ½-½ S.Savchenko-W.Muhren, Dieren 2004.

15...♗e5 16 ♗e3

16 ♘e2!? is a good alternative, e.g. 16...a5 17 ♖b1 a4 18 ♗e3 ♖e8 19 ♘d4 (or 19 ♘f4 intending ♘d3 +/= M.M.Ivanov-P.Toulzac, Mulhouse 2002) 19...f6 20 gxf6 ♗xf6 21 g3 ♗e5 22 ♔f2 +/= P.Eljanov-L.Comas Fabrego, Ubeda 2001.

16...a5

Black remains slightly worse after other moves too; e.g. 16...♗e6 17 ♖ac1 a5 18 b3 f5 19 gxf6 ♖xf6 20 ♘e2 ♗f7 21 ♗g5 ♖e6 22 g3 ♖ee8 23 ♖c2 b6 24 ♗g2 += L.Ftacnik-E.Gullaksen, Amsterdam 2006; or 16...f6 17 gxf6 ♖xf6 18 ♖d2 a5 19 ♘e2 ♘e6 20 ♘d4 a4 21 ♖ad1 += A.Saric-J.Skoberne, Nova Gorica 2007.

17 ♖d2 *(D)*

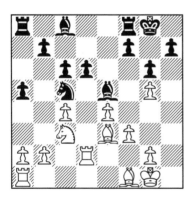

Also good are 17 ♖ab1!? ♖e8 18 ♘e2 b6 (18...a4 – *16 ♘e2*) 19 b3 ♗b7 20 ♖d2 d5 21 cxd5 cxd5 22 exd5 ♖ad8 23 ♖bd1 +/- Z.Kozul-I.Smirin, Croatian Team Ch. 2006; and 17 f4!? ♗xc3 18 ♗xc5

dxc5 19 bxc3 f6 (19...♗g4 20 ♖db1 ♖fe8 21 e5) 20 gxf6 ♖xf6 21 g3 +=.

The text was played in V.Topalov-P.Svidler, Monte Carlo (blindfold rapid) 2006, which continued **17...a4 18 ♖c1 a3?!** [18...f5!? would have provided more counter-chances] **19 b4 ♘a4 20 ♘d1** [better 20 ♘e2 c5 21 bxc5 dxc5 22 ♘f4 b6 23 ♘d5 +/- S.Zablotsky-D.Kokarev, Vladimir 2008; or 20 ♘xa4 ♖xa4 21 f4 ♗b2 22 ♖cc2 +/-] **20...♗e6 21 ♗d4** [White could have maintained a small advantage after 21 f4! ♗b2 22 ♖b1] **21...♗f4 22 ♗e3 ♗e5 23 ♗d4 ♖fd8 24 ♔f2?!** [24 ♖cc2 =] **24...c5 25 ♗xe5 dxe5 26 ♖xd8+?! ♖xd8 27 ♔e1 cxb4 28 ♖b1 ♘c3 29 ♘xc3 bxc3 30 ♖d1 ♖d4 31 ♗e2 ♔f8 32 ♖c1 ♖d2 33 ♖xc3 ♖xa2 34 ♖b3?? ♖xe2+ 0-1**.

Conclusion

White has a few interesting continuations after 7...♘a6, and even the simple 8 ♖b1 (line A) gives him chances of obtaining a small advantage. The straightforward 8 ♗e3 (line B) gives Black comparatively fewer difficulties, in particular after the logical 8...♘g4 9 ♗g5 ♕e8 (line B2), though the recent development 10 c5!? warrants more investigation. Also promising is 8 ♖e1 (line C), planning simply to reorganize with ♗f1 and decide on a specific development afterwards. In the endgame-seeking variation 8...c6 9 ♗f1 exd4 (line C22), White should probably give most attention to 13 ♗e3 or 17 ♖ab1.

Chapter Seven

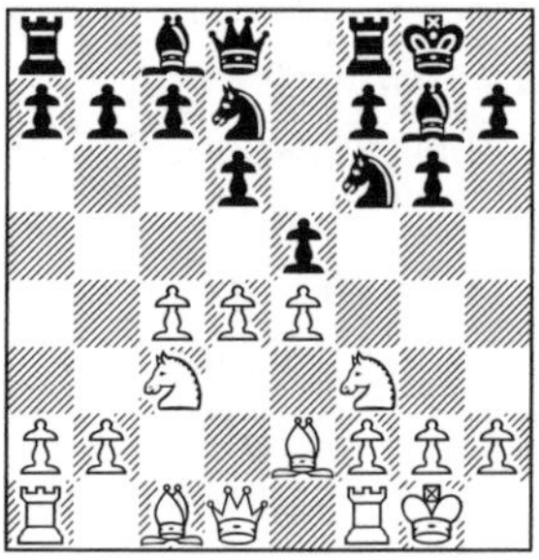

7...♘bd7

1 d4 ♘f6 2 c4 g6 3 ♘c3 ♗g7 4 e4 d6 5 ♘f3 0-0 6 ♗e2 e5 7 0-0 ♘bd7 *(D)*

The move ...♘bd7 is a typical one for the King's Indian: the knight reinforces e5 and is ready to jump to the active post on c5 should either party decide to release the tension in the centre. The position in the diagram can be reached via various move orders, not least 6...♘bd7 7 0-0 e5, which Black occasionally employs to avoid the queen exchange of Chapter Two. Nevertheless, this set-up is far less popular than with ...♘c6, because ...♘bd7 applies less pressure to the centre and leaves White with more options.

The simple 8 d5 allows Black to realize his plan: ...♘c5 followed by ...a7-a5 and further counterplay on the kingside. Therefore White should prefer other ideas. (Note that this position can also arise after 7...♘a6 8 d5 ♘c5.)

8 ♕c2 seeks to improve by waiting for 8...c6 before playing 9 d5, in order

then to utilize the half-open d-file (after d5xc6) or the open c-file (after ...c6xd5). 8 ♗e3 also gives White interesting possibilities of active play, especially as 8...♘g4 is not as strong here as is usually the case in these structures.

The anticipatory 8 ♖e1 is the most popular move. After 8...c6 9 ♗f1 White improves the position of his pieces while maintaining the tension. Black's best response is either to strengthen his game on the queenside by 9...a5 (line D32) or else clarify the situation in the centre with 9...exd4 (line D33); other ideas are less promising for Black.

A: 8 d5 *151*
B: 8 ♕c2 *157*
C: 8 ♗e3 *164*
D: 8 ♖e1 *176*

Other moves do not give White chances of obtaining an advantage:

a) 8 b3 exd4! (this is justified since White has just weakened the a1-h8 diagonal) 9 ♘xd4 c6 10 ♗f4 ♖e8! (rather than 10...♕c7, transposing to V.Korchnoi-L.Ljubojevic, Palma 1972) 11 f3 ♘h5! 12 ♗e3 f5 13 ♕d2 f4 with counterplay on the kingside.

b) 8 h3 exd4! (as mentioned before, h2-h3 is fairly useless in these positions; if White wants to play this way he should start with 7 d5 as in Chapter Four) 9 ♘xd4 ♖e8 10 f3 (the point – this natural move creates holes on dark squares) 10...♘h5 11 ♗e3 ♘c5 12 ♕d2 ♗e5 with counterplay, J.Szabolcsi-A.Czebe, Hungarian Team Ch. 1994.

c) 8 ♖b1 c6 9 d5 cxd5 10 cxd5 ♘c5 11 ♗g5 h6 12 ♗xf6 ♗xf6 13 ♘d2 ♗e7 14 ♘c4 f5 with counterplay, G.Stahlberg-G.Barcza, Saltsjöbaden Interzonal 1952.

d) 8 dxe5 dxe5 (8...♘xe5 is also playable – see Chapter Eight) 9 ♕c2 c6 10 b3 ♖e8 11 ♖d1 ♕c7 12 ♗a3 ♗f8 13 ♗xf8 ♘xf8 14 ♖d2 ♗g4 15 ♖ad1 ♘e6 with control over the d4-square and equality, N.Mantzouneas-R.Litterst, World Seniors Ch. 1993.

e) 8 ♗g5 h6 (or 8...exd4!? 9 ♘xd4 c6 10 ♕d2 ♘c5 11 ♕f4 ♕e7 12 ♖ad1 ♕e5! 13 f3 ♘e6 14 ♘xe6 ♗xe6 15 ♕e3 ♕a5 16 ♖xd6 ♘d7 17 ♖fd1 ♘b6 18 c5 ♘a4 19 e5 ♘xc3 20 bxc3 ♖fe8 21 f4 ♕xa2 = S.Palatnik-J.Gallagher, Baku 1988) 9 ♗h4 g5 (9...a5 transposes to *7...a5 8 ♗g5 h6 9 ♗h4 ♘bd7* at the beginning of Chapter Five) 10 dxe5 (not 10 ♗g3?! g4! 11 ♘h4 exd4 12 ♕xd4 ♘h5 =+ M.Palacios Perez-D.Pribeanu, World Blind Ch. 2006) 10...♘h5 11 ♘d4 (or 11 ♗g3 ♘xg3 12 hxg3 dxe5 13 ♕c2 c6 14 ♖fd1 ♕e7 ∞ C.Krishna-E.Pileckis, World Junior Ch. 2002) 11...♘f4 (even better looks 11...gxh4! 12 ♗xh5 ♘xe5 13 ♗e2 h3 14 g3 ♘c6) 12 ♗g3 dxe5 13 ♘f5 ♘c5 14 ♗g4 ♗xf5 15 ♗xf5 ♕xd1 16 ♖fxd1 ♖fd8 ½-½ W.Uhlmann-S.Gligoric, Lugano Olympiad 1968.

A: 8 d5 (D)

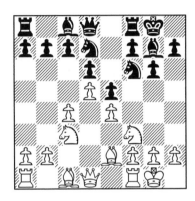

8...♘c5

The most logical move: Black immediately attacks the e4-pawn, any defence of which has its bad side for White. Instead:

a) 8...a5 allows White to play 9 ♗g5 as in the Petrosian System, when 9...h6 10 ♗h4 ♘c5 11 ♘d2 transposes to Chapter Four (10...♘c5 in line C2). If instead 9 ♘e1 ♘c5 10 ♕c2 a4!? 11 ♗e3 a3 with counterplay, F.Demelli-M.Loiza, Argentine Junior Ch. 1992.

b) 8...h6 prevents ♗g5, but basically gives White a tempo; e.g. 9 ♘e1 ♘c5 10 f3 a5 11 ♘d3 b6 12 ♘xc5 bxc5 13 ♗d2 ♘e8 14 ♗d3 ♗d7 15 ♗c2 f5 16 ♗a4 fxe4 17 ♘xe4 += S.Gligoric-O.Jakobsen, European Team Ch., Kapfenberg 1970.

c) 8...♘h5 is possible, intending

...♘f4 to gain the two bishops, while also freeing the f7-pawn. As 9 ♖e1 a5! is a clear improvement (for Black) on line D2, and other moves allow ...♘f4, White should probably resort to 9 g3, e.g. 9...♘df6 (or 9...♗f6!? 10 ♘e1 ♘g7 11 ♘d3 ♗e7 12 ♗e3 f5 13 f3 += J.Pichler-C.Troyke, German League 1999; not 9...f5? 10 exf5 gxf5 11 ♘g5 +-) 10 ♘e1! (better than 10 ♖e1 ♗h3 11 ♕c2 h6 12 ♔h1 ♕e7 13 ♘d1 ♖ac8 14 ♘g1 ♗d7 15 ♗f3 c6 ∞ S.Flohr-E.Bogoljubow, Bern 1932) 10...♗h3 11 ♘g2 += F.Ruzicka-P.Belohlavek, Moravian Team Ch. 2003.

A1: 9 ♘d2 *152*
A2: 9 ♕c2 *153*

White cannot play 9 ♗g5 h6 10 ♗h4? here as 10...g5 wins the e4-pawn; while 10 ♗xf6 ♕xf6 11 b4 ♘d7 is not dangerous for Black, e.g. 12 ♖c1 ♕e7 13 ♘b5 ♘f6 14 ♘d2 h5 15 c5 ♗h6 16 ♗f3 a6 17 ♘a3 ♗g4 18 ♘ac4 ♔g7 19 ♘e3 a5 = G.Kuzmin-S.Matveeva, Rostov 1993.

A1: 9 ♘d2 *(D)*

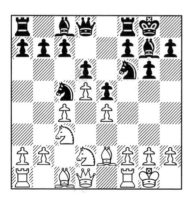

This move obstructs the c1-bishop.

9...a5

Obviously 9...♘e8? 10 b4 just costs Black two tempi; but 9...♗h6!? is possible, when 10 ♕c2 a5 transposes to the text, or if 10 f3 ♘h5! with counterplay, U.Aewerdieck-K.Arriens, Schleswig Holstein 1989.

10 ♕c2

Other moves do not cause Black any problems:

a) 10 b3 ♘e8 11 a3 f5 12 ♖b1 ♘f6 13 f3 ♘h5 14 b4 axb4 15 axb4 ♘d7 16 ♘b3 ♘f4 17 c5 ♕g5 with the initiative, M.Pardo-A.Nunez, World Junior Ch. 1990.

b) 10 ♖b1 c6 11 b3 ♗h6 12 ♕c2 ♗d7 13 a3 cxd5 14 cxd5 ♕c7 15 b4 (S.Dobranov-N.Rogers, Philadelphia 1995) 15...♗xd2!? 16 bxc5 ♗xc3 17 ♕xc3 ♘xe4 18 ♕f3 f5 =/+.

c) 10 f3 ♘h5 11 ♘b3 ♘xb3 12 axb3 ♗d7 13 g3 ♗h3 14 ♖f2 f5 with counterplay, K.Fufuengmongkolkij-S.Bouaziz, Manila Olympiad 1992.

10...♗h6 *(D)*

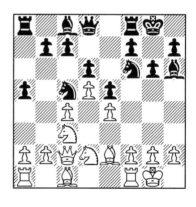

Geller's idea, which practically forces the dark-squared bishop exchange.

Also interesting is 10...a4 11 ♖b1 ♘e8 12 b4 axb3 13 axb3 f5 14 b4 ♘a6 15 exf5 gxf5 16 f4 e4 ∞ S.Flohr-A.Tolush, Leningrad 1939.

Other moves allow White a small advantage; e.g. 10...♗g4 11 ♘b3 ♗xe2 12 ♕xe2 ♘xb3 13 axb3 ♕d7 14 ♖d1 b6 15 ♗d2 ♔h8 16 ♘b5 ♘g8 17 b4 += S.Flohr-A.Vajda, Budapest 1949; or 10...♘fd7 11 ♘b3 f5 12 exf5 ♖xf5 (12...gxf5!? looks better) 13 ♗g4 ♖f8 14 ♗e3 (E.Bogoljubow-M.Euwe, 5th matchgame, Amsterdam 1928) 14...♘xb3 15 axb3 ♘f6 16 ♗xc8 ♕xc8 17 f3 += Yudovich.

11 ♘b3 ♗xc1

Less accurate is 11...♘xb3 12 axb3 ♗xc1 13 ♕xc1 ♗d7 14 ♕e3 +/= T.Zoltek-R.Grabczewski, Polish Ch. 1966.

12 ♖axc1

Obviously White should take the bishop. After 12 ♘xc5 ♗h6 13 ♘d3 ♘d7 14 ♗g4 (14 ♖ae1!?) 14...f5 15 ♗h3 ♕h4 16 ♖ae1 ♘f6 Black had excellent play on the kingside, N.Spiridonov-M.Tal, Tbilisi 1969.

12...♘fd7

White can again count on a small advantage after 12...♘xb3 13 ♕xb3 (or 13 axb3 b6 14 ♖a1 ♗d7 15 ♕d2 += F.May-P.Krause, corr. 1993) 13...♘d7 14 ♘a4 b6 (14...♕h4!? 15 ♕e3 f5 16 exf5 ♖xf5 might be better) 15 ♕g3 += A.Kolarov-J.Marsalek, World Student Team Ch. 1960.

13 ♖cd1

Other moves do not change the nature of the position:

a) 13 ♘xc5 ♘xc5 14 f4 exf4 15 ♖xf4

♕g5 16 ♖cf1 ♗h3 17 ♖1f2 ♖ae8 ∞ S.Suvrajit-L.Yurtaev, Calcutta 1998.

b) 13 ♗g4 ♘xb3 14 axb3 f5 15 exf5 ♘c5 16 ♘a4 ♘a6 = M.Bobotsov-T.V.Petrosian, European Team Ch., Kapfenberg 1970.

c) 13 ♘d2 ♘b6!? 14 b3 ♗d7 15 f4 exf4 16 ♖xf4 ♕g5 17 ♖cf1 ♖ae8 ∞ K.Prucha-O.Malcanek, Brno 1961.

13...♘xb3 14 ♕xb3 ♘c5 15 ♕c2 f5 16 exf5 ♗xf5 (D)

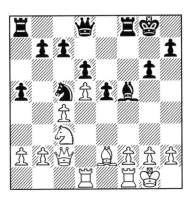

Black has a perfectly good game, e.g.

a) 17 ♕c1 g5 18 ♕e3 ♕f6 19 ♖d2 ♗d7 20 ♘e4 ♘xe4 21 ♕xe4 ♕f4 22 ♕e3 ½-½ S.Flohr-T.V.Petrosian, USSR Ch., Moscow 1950.

b) 17 ♕d2 ♗d7 (or 17...g5!?) 18 ♕e3 ♕e7 19 f3 b6 20 ♘e4 ♗f5 21 b3 ♗xe4 22 fxe4 ♖xf1+ 23 ♖xf1 ♖f8 24 g3 ♖xf1+ 25 ♔xf1 ½-½ I.Gelfer-V.Liberzon, Israeli Ch. 1974.

A2: 9 ♕c2 (D)

By defending the e-pawn with the queen White leaves the way clear for his dark-squared bishop. The drawback is that 9 ♕c2 is not very testing.

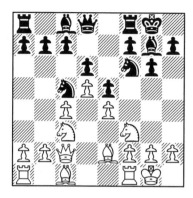

9...a5

Stabilizing the position of the c5-knight.

10 ♗g5

As in the Petrosian System (Chapter Four) the bishop's deployment to g5 is a standard idea in these positions. By hampering Black's counterplay with ...f7-f5, White hopes to gain time to reorganize his forces effectively. Otherwise:

a) 10 ♘d2 returns to line A1.

b) 10 b3 is too passive, e.g. 10...♘h5 11 ♗e3 f5 (M.Opalic-F.Stimpel, Bad Wiessee 1998) 12 ♖fe1 ♘f4 ∞.

c) 10 ♗e3 gives White nothing either: 10...♘g4 (a very principled move; otherwise Black can play 10...b6 11 ♘d2 ♘g4 12 ♗xg4 ♗xg4 13 a3 a4 14 ♗xc5 bxc5 15 ♘xa4 ♕g5 16 f3 ♗d7 17 ♘c3 ♗h6 with compensation, G.Porreca-F.Planas Garcia, Helsinki Olympiad 1952) 11 ♗xc5 dxc5 12 h3 ♘h6 13 ♘e1 f5 (Y.Pelletier-S.Ludwig, Bad Ragaz 1991) 14 exf5 gxf5 15 ♘d3 b6 ∞.

10...h6

White has a small advantage after 10...b6 11 ♘d2 (A.Yusupov-O.Romani-shin, USSR Ch., Moscow 1983) 11...h6 12 ♗h4 += Yusupov; or 10...♗g4 11 ♘d2 ♗xe2 12 ♘xe2 c6 13 ♗e3 ♘fd7 14 ♘b3 += E.Thingstad-A.Muratet Casadevall, Copenhagen 2006.

However, 10...♗d7!? deserves attention, e.g. 11 ♘d2 h6 12 ♗e3 (12 ♗h4!? – *10...h6 11 ♗h4 ♗d7 12 ♘d2* in the next note) 12...♘g4 13 ♗xg4 ♗xg4 14 a3 (V.Kostyuchenko-R.Gugnin, St Petersburg 2005) 14...a4 =.

11 ♗e3 (D)

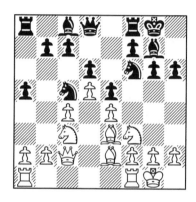

As usual exchanging on f6 is weak: 11 ♗xf6?! ♗xf6 12 a3 a4 13 ♘d2 ♗g5 14 b4 axb3 15 ♘xb3 ♘xb3 16 ♕xb3 b6 17 ♘b5 f5 and Black has the initiative, M.Ruzicka-P.Jelen, Tatranske Zruby 2003.

White achieves nothing after the passive 11 ♗d2 either, e.g. 11...♘h5 12 g3 ♗h3 13 ♖fe1 ♕d7 14 ♘h4 ♘f6 ∞ V.Borisov-N.Ogryzkov, corr. 1993.

11 ♗h4 is a natural continuation, but in this case Black has a good version of the Petrosian System, where White has played a harmless early ♕c2; e.g. 11...g5 (or 11...♗d7!? 12 ♘d2 ♕e8 13 ♘b3, B.Spassky-M.Ginsburg,

Lugano 1984, 13...♘cxe4! 14 ♘xe4 ♘xe4 15 ♕xe4 g5 with excellent play for Black) 12 ♗g3 ♘h5 (or again 12...♘fxe4 13 ♘xe4 ♘xe4 14 ♕xe4 f5 15 ♕c2 f4 = F.Berresheim-G.Eisele, Koblenz 1993) 13 ♘d2 ♘f4 14 ♖fe1 f5 15 ♗f1 (P.Dankert-N.McDonald, Hastings 1988/89) 15...♘h5 with counterplay.

11...b6

This move is very flexible and useful in different structures. However, Black has a great variety of other continuations:

a) 11...♘e8 (a bit passive as the knight has nowhere much to go from e8) 12 ♘d2 f5 13 exf5 gxf5 14 f4 e4 15 ♘b3 ♘xb3 16 axb3 ♗d7 (D.Guthrie-S.Low, Australian Junior Ch. 1995) 17 ♖a2 intending ♖fa1 +/=.

b) 11...♘h7 12 ♘d2 f5 (or 12...♕e8 13 ♖ae1 b6 14 b3 ♗d7 15 a3 f5 16 exf5 ♗xf5 17 ♘de4 g5 18 ♗xc5 bxc5 19 ♗d3 ♕d7 20 ♘g3 += L.Brunner-D.Summermatter, Switzerland 1989) 13 exf5 ♗xf5 14 ♘de4 b6 15 ♗xc5 bxc5 16 ♗d3 h5 17 ♖ae1 ♗h6 18 ♘g3 += I.V.Ivanov-J.Hjartarson, Philadelphia 1986.

c) 11...♘fd7 (at least here the knight covers c5 and e5) 12 ♘d2 f5 13 exf5 gxf5 14 f4 exf4 15 ♗xf4 ♘e5 16 ♖ae1 ♗d7 17 ♘f3 ♕f6 18 ♘xe5 dxe5 19 ♗e3 ♕d6 20 ♘b5 ♕b6 (A.Czebe-E.Sutovsky, Budapest 1993) 21 ♗f3 +/=.

d) 11...♘h5 12 g3 ♗h3 (12...b6 13 ♘e1!? looks a little better for White, e.g. 13...♗h3 14 ♘g2 ♘f6 15 f3 ♘h7 16 ♘d1 +=) 13 ♖fe1 b6 (worse is 13...f5?! 14 ♘h4! f4 15 ♗xc5 dxc5, I.Glek-L.Yurtaev, Frunze 1987, 16 ♘xg6! ♕g5 17 ♘xf8 fxg3 18 fxg3 ♘xg3 19 ♗f3! ♖xf8

20 ♗g2 ♘h5 21 ♔h1 and Black does not have sufficient compensation) 14 a3 (if 14 ♘d2 ♘f6 15 f3 ♘h7 16 ♘d1 ♗d7 17 ♘f2 f5 18 exf5 gxf5 19 f4 ♕f6 ∞ J.Piket-G.Hernandez, FIDE World Ch., New Delhi 2000) 14...f5 (14...a4!?) 15 ♘h4 (if 15 exf5 ♗xf5 16 ♕d1 ♔h7 = Karpov) 15...f4 16 ♗xc5 bxc5 17 ♘xg6 ♕g5 (N.Zilberman-T.Khasanov, USSR 1983) 18 ♘xf8 fxg3 19 fxg3 ♘xg3 20 ♗f3 ♖xf8 21 ♗g2 ♘h5 22 ♔h1 and White is again better.

e) 11...♘g4 (the most principled, forcing move) 12 ♗xc5 dxc5 13 h3 (now in contrast to the 10 ♗e3 variation, the knight cannot jump back to h6) 13...♘f6 14 ♘xe5 ♘xd5 15 cxd5 ♗xe5 16 f4 (otherwise Black would play ...♕h4 or ...♕g5 with the control over the dark squares) 16...♗d4+ 17 ♔h2 g5 18 e5 gxf4 19 ♕e4 ♕e7 20 e6 fxe6 21 ♗c4 ∞ V.Ruban-L.Oll, USSR 1984.

f) 11...♕e7 (a useful non-committal move defending e5 and c5) 12 ♘d2 (or 12 a3 ♘g4 13 ♗xc5 dxc5 14 ♖ab1 ♗d7 15 ♘e1 ♘f6 16 ♘d3 a4 ∞ R.Kempinski-T.Casper, German League 2002) 12...♘g4 13 ♗xg4 ♗xg4 14 a3 ♗d7 15 b4 axb4 16 axb4 ♘a6 17 ♕b3 f5 with counterplay, J.Rodriguez Cordoba-J.Ostos, Cienfuegos 1976.

g) 11...♘a6 (strange-looking but quite logical: Black rules out ♗xc5 in response to his intended ...♘g4) 12 ♘d2 ♘g4 13 ♗xg4 ♗xg4 14 a3 ♗d7 15 ♖ab1 f5 16 f3 f4 17 ♗f2 ♗f6 18 ♔h1 ♗h4 19 ♗g1 h5 20 b4 axb4 21 axb4 ♕e7 ∞ I.Rogers-M.Chiburdanidze, Geneva 1990.

12 ♘d2 (D)

Nothing else gives Black any problems; e.g. 12 ♘e1 ♘g4 13 ♗d2 f5 14 ♗xg4 fxg4 15 ♘d3 h5 16 ♘xc5 bxc5 17 ♘b5 h4 18 a4 ♕e7 19 ♖a3 ♖f7 ∞ M.Richter-A.Naumann, German Junior League 1995; or 12 h3 ♘h5 (12...♗d7!?) 13 ♕d2 ♔h7 14 ♗d1 ♘f4 15 ♗c2 (S.Solovjov-S.Milton, St Petersburg 1998) 15...♕f6 ∞.

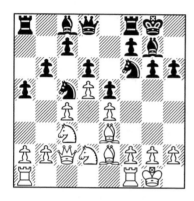

12...♗g4

Most moves lead to a small advantage for White here:

a) 12...h5 13 ♗g5 ♕e8 14 ♘b5 ♘a6 15 f3 ♘h7 16 ♗h4 f5 17 exf5 ♗xf5 18 ♘e4 g5 19 ♗e1 ♘f6 20 ♗d3 += R.Simic-V.Tseshkovsky, Yugoslav Team Ch. 1995.

b) 12...♘h5 13 ♗xh5 gxh5 14 a3 f5 15 f3 f4 16 ♗f2 ♕g5 17 ♔h1 ♖f6 18 ♖g1 ♖g6 19 ♘b5! += A.Yusupov-N.Rashkovsky, Moscow 1983.

c) 12...♘h7 13 a3 f5 (S.Palatnik-V.Anand, New Delhi 1986) 14 b4 ♘xe4 15 ♘dxe4 fxe4 16 ♘xe4 += Karpov.

d) 12...♘fd7 13 f3 f5 14 b3 f4 15 ♗f2 ♘f6 16 a3 g5 17 b4 ♘b7 18 ♘a4 g4 19 c5 g3 20 hxg3 fxg3 21 ♗xg3 ♘h5 22 ♗h2 +/= E.Iliushkin-I.Kniazev, Kazan 2006.

e) 12...♘g4 deserves attention though: 13 ♗xg4 ♗xg4 14 a3 (or if 14 f3 ♗d7 15 b3 f5 16 a3 f4!? 17 ♗f2, M.Dyballa-K.Movsziszian, Berlin 1993, 17...♘a6 ∞ Karpov) 14...♘a6 (Black can also consider Geller's pawn sacrifice 14...a4!? 15 ♗xc5 bxc5 16 ♘xa4 ♕g5 17 f3 ♗h3 18 ♖f2 ♗d7 with a strong initiative, A.Bergmann-J.Härtig, German League 1993; or 14...♗c8 15 b4 ♘d7 16 c5, I.V.Ivanov-M.Hennigan, London Lloyds Bank 1992, 16...bxc5!? 17 bxc5 ♘xc5 18 ♗xc5 dxc5 19 ♘a4 c6 with excellent counterplay) 15 ♖ab1 ♗d7 16 b4 f5 17 exf5! gxf5 18 f4 (V.Smyslov-A.Suetin, Sochi 1974) 18...axb4 19 axb4 ♕e7 ∞ Yudovich.

13 ♖ae1

Other moves allow Black good counterplay:

a) 13 ♗xg4 ♘xg4 14 ♗xc5 (V.Lukov-R.Casafus, Rio Gallegos 1986) 14...dxc5!? 15 ♘f3 ♘f6 and if 16 ♘xe5 ♘xd5 17 cxd5 ♗xe5 18 f4 ♗d4+ 19 ♔h1 f5 with counterplay.

b) 13 h3 ♗d7 14 b3 ♘h7 15 ♖ae1 (R.Vaganian-I.Smirin, Rostov 1993) 15...f5!?.

c) 13 f3 ♗d7 14 b3 ♘h5 15 ♖fe1 ♗f6!? 16 g3 (if 16 ♗xh6?! then 16...♗g5! 17 ♗xf8? ♗e3+ 18 ♔h1 ♘g3+! 19 hxg3 ♕xf8 leads to mate) 16...♗g5 17 ♗f2 ♘g7 18 ♖ad1 ∞ A.Korobov-E.Miroshnichenko, Ukrainian Ch. 2008.

13...♗xe2 14 ♖xe2 ♘g4 15 ♗xc5 bxc5

15...dxc5 is weaker here as the white rook is more active; e.g. 16 ♕a4 (or 16 ♘f3 +=) 16...♖e8 17 ♕c6 ♗f8 18 h3 ♘f6 (A.Korobov-L.Kozak, Illichevsk 2006) 19 ♘f3 +/=.

16 g3

In a later game, perhaps fearing an improvement, White deviated with 16 ♘b5 h5 17 a4 ♗h6 18 ♕c3 f5 19 f3 ♘f6 20 ♘b3? (this attempt to win the a5-pawn ended fatally; necessary first was 20 exf5 gxf5 21 ♘b3, though Black has strong counterplay after 21...h4 22 ♘xa5 ♘h5, e.g. 23 ♘c6 ♕d7 24 b3 h3 25 g3 f4 26 g4 ♘g3!) 20...fxe4 21 fxe4 ♘g4 22 ♘d2 (now if 22 ♘xa5? ♖xf1+ 23 ♔xf1 ♕h4 wins) 22...♕h4 23 ♘f3 ♖xf3! 24 gxf3 ♗e3+ 25 ♔h1 ♕h3 26 ♕e1 ♖f8 27 f4 0-1 A.Korobov-N.Kurenkov, Moscow 2007.

16...h5 17 f3 ♘h6

White is also slightly better after 17...♘f6 18 f4 h4 19 ♕d3 ♘h5 20 f5 hxg3 21 hxg3 ♕g5 22 ♖g2 +/= S.Vukanovic-Z.Arsovic, Bar 2005.

18 f4 f5

18...h4!? looks preferable.

19 ♘f3 (D)

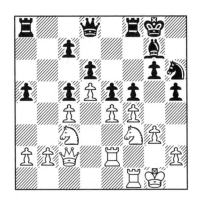

White has a clear advantage. A.Korobov-P.Czarnota, Cappelle la Grande 2004, concluded **19...exf4 20 gxf4 fxe4 21 ♖xe4 ♖f5 22 ♘e2 ♕f6** [or 22...♖b8 23 b3 +/-] **23 ♖e6 ♕xb2 24**

♕xb2 ♗xb2 25 ♖xg6+ ♔h7 26 ♖g2 ♗f6? 27 ♘g3 ♖b8 [if 27...♖xf4 28 ♘xh5 ♗d4+ 29 ♘xd4 ♖xf1+ 30 ♔xf1 cxd4 31 ♖g7+ ♔h8 32 ♖xc7 +-] **28 ♘g5+ ♔g6 29 ♘e6?!** [simpler 29 ♘xf5!? ♔xf5 30 h3 ♗d4+ 31 ♔h2 +-] **29...♖b4?** [29...♘g4 was stronger, though Black should still lose] **30 ♘xf5+ ♔xf5 31 ♖g5+! ♔e4 32 ♖g6 ♘g4 33 h3 ♔f5 34 ♖g5+! 1-0.**

B: 8 ♕c2 (D)

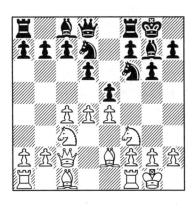

White maintains the central tension and prepares ♖d1.

B1: 8...♘h5 *159*
B2: 8...c6 *161*

Inaccurate are:

a) 8...a5?! 9 dxe5! dxe5 10 ♗e3 (10 ♖d1 looks even better) 10...c6 11 ♖ad1 (P.Cramling-A.Haik, Metz 1989) 11...♖e8 12 ♘a4 +/-.

b) 8...a6?! 9 dxe5!? dxe5 10 ♗e3 ♘g4 11 ♗g5 f6 12 ♗d2 ♘h6 13 ♖ad1 c6 14 c5 ♕e7 15 ♘a4 ♖b8 16 ♗a5! ♘f7 17 ♗c7 ♖a8 18 ♗d6 ♘xd6 19 cxd6 +/- P.Cramling-M.Todorcevic, Biel 1991.

c) 8...♘g4 (this gifts White a tempo on ♗e3 lines) 9 ♗g5 f6 10 ♗h4 h5 11 h3 ♘h6 12 dxe5 dxe5 13 ♖ad1 ♖e8 14 c5 c6 15 b4 ♕e7 16 ♘d2 ♘f8 17 ♘c4 ♘f7 18 ♘d6 ♖d8 19 ♘xc8 += J.Dorfman-A.Romero Holmes, Logrono 1991.

d) 8...♕e7 9 d5 ♘e8 10 ♗g5!? f6 11 ♗h4 h5 12 ♗g3 ♗h6 (or if 12...g5!? 13 h3 ♗h6 14 ♘e1 ♘g7 15 ♗h2! intending g2-g4 += Eingorn) 13 ♘h4! += V.Eingorn-O.Romanishin, Moscow 1986.

e) 8...h6 (preventing ♗g5) 9 dxe5! dxe5 10 ♖d1 is line D1 (8 ♖e1 h6) with the white rook better placed, e.g. 10...♖e8 11 c5 c6 12 b4 ♕e7 13 ♘a4 ♘f8 (13...♘h5!? +=) 14 ♘b2 ♘h5 15 ♘c4 ♘f4 16 ♘d6 +/- M.Krasenkow-V.Epishin, Norilsk 1987.

f) 8...♖e8 9 d5 (as usual the black rook is better on f8 with the centre closed) 9...a5 10 ♗g5 ♘c5 11 ♘d2 h6 12 ♗h4 ♗d7 13 ♖ab1 ♕c8 14 ♖be1 ♘h7 15 ♔h1 f5 16 exf5 ♗xf5 17 ♘de4 +/= A.Kryschilovskij-G.Kazakevich, St Petersburg 2007.

g) 8...exd4 9 ♘xd4 (D) deserves some attention:

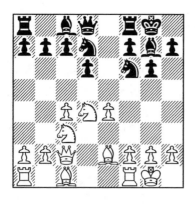

g1) 9...♘c5 10 ♘b3 ♘fd7 11 ♗e3 ♖e8

12 f3 f5 13 ♖ad1 +/= J.Martin del Campo-R.Calderin, Mexico 1996.

g2) 9...♘g4 10 ♗xg4 ♗xd4 11 ♗h6 ♖e8 12 ♖ad1 ♗h8 13 f4! ♘f6 (V.Ruban-V.Varavin, Smolensk 1991) 14 ♗xc8 ♕xc8 15 ♖fe1 with a spatial plus for White.

g3) 9...c6 10 ♗g5!? ♖e8 11 ♖ad1 a5 12 ♖fe1 a4 13 ♗f4 ♕e7 14 ♘f3 ♘e5 15 ♘xa4 ♘xe4, J.Brenninkmeijer-M.Bosboom, Dutch Ch. 1990, and now White would have had better chances after either 16 ♘b6 ♗f5 17 ♗xe5 ♗xe5 18 ♗d3 ♖xa2 19 ♗xe4 ♖xb2 20 ♗xf5 ♖xc2 21 ♗xc2 or 16 ♘xe5 dxe5 17 ♗e3 ♗f5 18 g4 ♘xf2 19 gxf5 ♘xd1 20 ♗xd1.

g4) 9...♖e8 (natural) 10 ♗e3 (10 ♖d1 c6 transposes to *8...c6 9 ♖d1 exd4 10 ♘xd4 ♖e8* in line B2; if instead 10...♘c5 11 f3 ♘h5 12 ♗e3 ♗e5, A.Shneider-A.Kochyev, St Petersburg 1993, 13 g3!? intending f3-f4 +=, or 11...a5 12 ♗e3 ♘fd7 13 ♘db5 ♘e6, G.Kern-K.Oeljeklaus, German League 1990, 14 f4 and Black has problems) and then:

g41) 10...♘b6 11 ♖ad1 ♕e7?! (11...♘g4!? 12 ♗f4 +=) 12 ♘db5 ♗e6 (Black has problems as 12...a6? runs into 13 ♘xd6) 13 b3 ♖ec8 14 h3 ♗d7 15 ♗f3 ♗c6 16 ♖fe1 ♖e8 17 ♗d4 ♕d7 18 ♕b2 ♖e7 19 a4 ♘e8 20 c5 +/- P.Lukacs-L.Vogt, Leipzig 1986.

g42) 10...♘c5 11 f3 ♘h5 (or 11...a5 12 ♖ad1 ♗d7 13 ♘db5 ♕c8 14 ♖fe1 ♗c6 15 ♗f1 +/- L.Ftacnik-R.Knaak, Trnava 1983) 12 ♖ad1 f5 13 b4 ♘a6 14 c5 f4 15 ♗f2 ♕g5 16 ♗xa6 bxa6 (M.Gurevich-R.Knaak, Balatonbereny 1987) and now 17 ♕b3+ ♔f8 18 ♕d5 would have won at once.

g43) 10...c6 11 ♖ad1 ♕e7 12 f3 a5 (not 12...d5? 13 cxd5 cxd5 14 ♘db5! dxe4 15 fxe4 ♘f8 16 ♘d6 ♖d8 17 ♗c5 ♕e5 18 ♘d5 +- A.Shirov-V.Akopian, Borzhomi 1988) 13 f3 ♘c5 14 ♗f1 ♘fd7 15 b3 ♗e5 16 a3 ♕f6 17 ♘ce2 g5 18 b4 axb4 19 axb4 ♘e6 20 ♘f5 +/- S.Lputian-A.J.Mestel, Hastings 1986/87.

B1: 8...♘h5 *(D)*

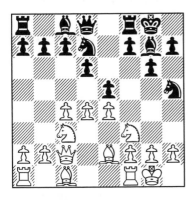

Black wants his opponent to clarify the situation in the centre.

9 ♖d1

The consistent continuation, although White can also play:

a) 9 dxe5 dxe5 10 g3 c6 11 ♗g5 ♘hf6 12 b4 ♕e7 13 c5 ♖e8 14 ♘a4 ♘f8 15 ♘b2 ♗g4 (R.Soffer-L.Vogt, Bad Lauterberg 1991) and if 16 ♘c4 ♗xf3 17 ♗xf3 ♘e6 18 ♗e3 ♘d4 19 ♗xd4 exd4 (Dautov) 20 ♖ae1 +=.

b) 9 ♗g5 f6 10 ♗e3 ♘f4 11 ♗xf4 exf4 12 ♖ad1 c6 13 b4 (or 13 ♗d3!? +=) 13...♕e7 14 c5 += B.Lalic-J.Diaz Rodriguez, Benasque 2006, e.g. 14...dxc5 15 bxc5 b6 16 ♕a4! ♗b7 17 ♗a6 ♗xa6 18 ♕xa6 with the initiative (Lalic).

9...♘f4

If now 9...c6 10 ♗e3 (or 10 ♗g5 f6 11 ♗e3 ♘f4 12 ♗f1 M.Kaabi-G.Van der Ploeg, Dubai Olympiad 1986) 10...♕e7 11 ♕d2 ♘hf6 12 ♗g5 (12 d5!?) 12...♕e8 (or 12...exd4 13 ♘xd4 ♖e8 14 f3) 13 d5 c5 14 a3 a6 15 ♖ab1 (or 15 ♘e1) 15...♘h5 16 ♗h6 f6 17 ♗xg7 ♔xg7 18 b4 (T.Tuomala-P.Salmi, Jyvaskyla 2001) with better chances for White in all variations.

10 ♗f1

10 ♗xf4 can be recommended too, e.g. 10...exf4 11 b4 g5 (E.Vovsha-C.Gregoir, World Junior Ch. 1998) 12 h3!? +/-.

10...c5 *(D)*

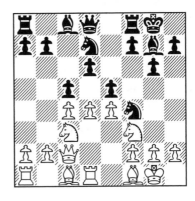

Black forces matters himself. White is better after 10...exd4 11 ♘xd4 ♘e6 12 ♗e3 ♘e5 13 h3 f5 14 f4 ♘f7 15 exf5 ♘xd4 16 ♗xd4 ♗xd4+ 17 ♖xd4 ♗xf5 18 ♕f2 += C.Kamp-H.Grünberg, German League 1994; or 10...♘e6 11 d5 ♘d4 12 ♘xd4 exd4 13 ♘b5 d3!? 14 ♗xd3 ♘c5 15 ♗e3 ♘xd3 16 ♖xd3 f5 17 f3 += S.Simonenko-M.Perelshteyn, USSR 1989.

11 d5

Closing the centre is quite a logical

decision. Nevertheless, White may do better with:

a) 11 ♘b5 cxd4 12 ♗xf4 exf4 13 ♘fxd4 ♕b6 (or 13...♘e5, O.Biriukov-A.Kochyev, St Petersburg 1998, 14 c5 +/-) 14 ♘f3 ♗e5 15 ♘xe5 dxe5 16 b4 +/- O.Biriukov-Y.Glashev, St Petersburg 1997.

b) 11 dxc5 dxc5 (or equivalently 11 dxe5 dxe5) 12 ♘d5 (12 ♗xf4!? prevents a black knight coming to d4, but also activates the g7-bishop: 12...exf4 13 ♘d5 g5 14 h3 ♖e8 15 ♖d2 h6, S.Panzalovic-S.Solonar, Lampertheim 2000, 16 ♖ad1 +=) 12...♘e6 13 ♗d2!? ♘b8 14 a3 (14 b4!?) 14...♘c6 15 b4 +/= E.Scarella-N.Robledo, Argentine Junior Ch. 1997.

11...♘f6

Otherwise, 11...h6 12 g3 ♘h5 13 ♗e2 ♘df6 14 ♘e1 ♘h7 15 ♘g2 ♘5f6 16 ♖b1 a5 17 a3 a4 18 f3 ♗d7 19 b3 axb3 20 ♖xb3 ♗c8 21 ♗e3 +/= R.Leitao-R.Martin del Campo, World Student Team Ch. 1993; or 11...♘b6!? (E.Toth-H.Leks, Budapest 2007) 12 ♘e2!? ♘xe2+ 13 ♗xe2 f5 14 ♗d2 intending b2-b4 +=.

12 ♘e1

Black equalizes after 12 ♗xf4 exf4 13 e5 dxe5 (or 13...♘e8 14 ♖e1 dxe5 15 ♘xe5 ♘d6 = A.Beliavsky-A.Shchekachev, Leon rapid 2008) 14 ♘xe5 ♕d6 15 ♘f3 ♗f5 16 ♗d3 ♗g4 17 ♗e4 ♘d7 18 ♘b5 ♕b6 19 d6! a6 20 ♘c7 ♖ad8 21 ♘d5 ♕xd6! 22 ♘e3 ♕b6 23 ♘xg4 h5 24 ♘h6+! ♗xh6 25 ♕b3 = L.Van Wely-P.Svidler, Groningen 1996; or 12 h3 ♘e8 13 ♗xf4 exf4 14 ♖e1 ♕e7 15 ♕d2 ♗e5 = F.Atakisi-M.Geenen, corr. 2001.

But 12 ♖e1 is interesting, e.g. 12...h5

13 g3 ♘h3+ 14 ♔h1 ♘h7 15 ♗g2 g5 16 ♘g1 ♘xg1 17 ♔xg1 a6 18 ♖b1 g4 19 b4 with the initiative, G.Hertneck-R.Knaak, Munich (rapid) 1991.

12...♘6h5

Other games have seen:

a) 12...♘e8 13 g3 (or 13 ♖b1 f5 14 b4 b6 15 f3 fxe4 16 ♘xe4 ♘f6 17 bxc5 ♘xe4 18 fxe4 bxc5 = G.Hertneck-L.Vogt, Bayern 1991) 13...♘h5 14 ♕e2 ♘hf6 15 ♘d3 ♘c7 16 ♗g2 ♗d7 17 b4 cxb4 18 ♘xb4 a5 19 ♘d3 b5 = D.Johansen-J.Gallagher, Dresden Olympiad 2008.

b) 12...♗g4 13 f3 ♗d7 14 g3 ♘4h5 15 ♖b1 a5!? 16 ♘g2 ♘e8 17 g4 ♘hf6 18 ♗g5 ♕b6 19 b3 ♔h8 20 ♗e3 h5 (D.Ruzele-A.Kovalev, Vilnius 1997) 21 h3 ∞ Kovalev.

13 a3 ♗g4 14 f3 ♗d7 15 b4 b6 16 bxc5 bxc5 17 ♖b1 (D)

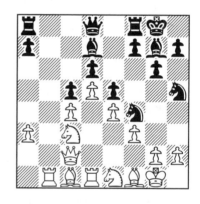

This position was reached in P.H.Nielsen-K.Sakaev, European Blitz Ch., Panormo 2002. White is slightly better as he can build up his initiative on the queenside. Meanwhile Black can't initiate kingside counterplay with ...f7-f5, as then g2-g3 would trap the knight. Black should probably sit tight with 17...h6!?, except that passive defence is not often a good strategy in blitz chess.

The game continued **17...g5?!** [giving the f4-knight a retreat so as to be able to play ...f7-f5, but weakening the light squares] **18 g3 ♘g6 19 ♘g2 g4?!** [a further loosening; again 19...h6 20 ♘e3 ♘e7 was objectively the stronger course] **20 fxg4 ♗xg4 21 ♗e2 f5 22 ♘e3 ♗xe2 23 ♕xe2 ♘hf4!? 24 gxf4 exf4 25 ♘xf5 ♗xc3 26 ♗b2** [here 26 ♕g4! would have won for White] **26...♕f6 27 ♗xc3 ♕xc3 28 ♖b7 f3 29 ♕f2 ♔h8 30 ♖db1 ♖g8 31 ♖xh7+??** [a brainstorm; instead 31 ♔h1 and White should still win] **31...♔xh7 32 ♖b7+ ♔h8 33 ♖b1 ♖ab8 34 ♖f1 ♖b2 35 ♕e3 ♕xe3+ 36 ♘xe3 ♘e5+ 37 ♔h1 ♖e2 38 ♘f5 ♖gg2 39 ♘h4 ♖xh2+ 40 ♔g1 ♖xh4 0-1**.

B2: 8...c6 (D)

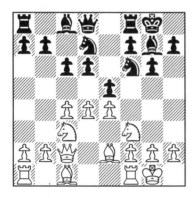

A flexible move, which can be useful in different structures.

9 d5

This was the plan noted in the introduction: White hopes to utilize the half-open d-file after a further d5xc6, or else the open c-file after ...c6xd5. Instead, 9 ♗e3 transposes to 8 ♗e3 c6 9 ♕c2 (see the notes to C4 below), while Black has no problems after 9 ♗g5 h6 10 ♗h4 ♖e8!? 11 ♖ad1 ♕c7 12 d5 cxd5 13 cxd5 a6 14 ♘d2 b5 = N.Rashkovsky-M.Hasanov, USSR 1984.

However, 9 ♖d1 with ideas of d4xe5 or b2-b4 is a serious alternative:

a) 9...♖e8 10 d5 c5 11 a3 ♖f8 leaves White a tempo up on 10 a3 in the main line, e.g. 12 b4 b6 13 ♖b1 ♘e8 14 ♗g5 += J.Van de Mortel-H.Fleger, Ruhrgebiet 1996.

b) 9...♕e7 10 d5 c5 (or if 10...cxd5!? 11 cxd5 a6 12 a4 ♘h5, Z.Kozul-S.Kagan, Portoroz 1993, 13 ♗g5 f6 14 ♗d2 +=) 11 ♗g5 h6 12 ♗d2 ♘e8 13 g3 ♘df6 14 ♖ab1 ♘h7 15 ♕c1 h5 16 b4 += P.Schlosser-D.Wachsmuth, Bad Wörishofen 1990.

c) 9...♕c7 10 ♖b1 a5 11 b3 b6 12 dxe5 dxe5 13 ♗a3 += B.Oresek-M.Nolimal, corr. 1995.

d) 9...exd4 (logical, as White's pieces are perhaps not optimally placed) 10 ♘xd4 (D) and now:

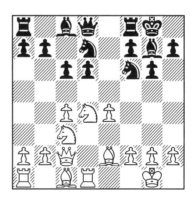

d1) 10...♕e7 11 ♖b1 (if 11 ♘b3!? ♖e8 12 f3 ♘e5 13 ♘d4 h6 14 b3 a6 15 ♕d2 b5 with counterplay, G.Muttoni-S.Kissinger, corr. 1998) 11...♘c5 (or 11...♘b6 12 ♗g5 ♖e8 13 f3 d5 14 cxd5 cxd5 15 ♗b5 ♖d8 16 ♕c1! h6 17 ♗xh6 dxe4! 18 ♗xg7 ♔xg7 19 ♘xe4 ♘xe4 20 ♕e3, E.Mochalov-V.Chernov, corr. 1991, 20...f5 ∞) 12 f3 ♘h5 with the standard plan of ...f7-f5, while g2-g4 gives Black other possibilities to construct counterplay based on the weakness (as we saw in Chapter Five); e.g. 13 b4 (or 13 g4 ♘f6 14 ♗f4 ♘fd7 15 ♗g3 ♘e5 16 ♕d2 ♖d8 ∞ Wl.Schmidt-R.Knaak, Dresden 1985) 13...♘e6 14 ♘xe6 (if 14 ♗e3 f5 15 ♕d2, K.Robatsch-H.Wirthensohn, Biel 1977, then 15...♗e5! ∞) 14...♗xe6 15 g4 ♗e5! (the familiar drawing motif; otherwise 15...♘f6 is unclear) 16 gxh5 ♗xh2+ 17 ♔xh2 ♕h4+ 18 ♔g1 ♕g3+ 19 ♔h1 ♕h3+ ½-½ M.Makarov-A.Kovalev, Leningrad 1989.

d2) 10...♖e8 11 f3 ♘h5 also looks good, e.g. 12 g4 (12 ♗e3 f5 13 ♗f2 f4 ∞ R.Pogorelov-C.Minzer, Albacete 2002) 12...♘hf6 13 ♗g5 ♕a5 (or 13...h6!? 14 ♗f4 ♘e5 ∞) 14 ♗e3 h5 15 g5 ♘h7 16 ♘b3 ♕d8 17 ♕d2 a5! ∞ J.Van de Mortel-V.Bologan, Wijk aan Zee 1996.

9...c5

Black closes the centre. He can also maintain the tension in various ways, but none of these provides him with full equality, e.g.

a) 9...a6 10 ♗g5 h6 11 ♗d2 ♕c7 12 b4 cxd5 13 cxd5 ♘b6 14 ♕b3 ♗d7 15 ♖fc1 ♖fc8 16 a4 ♘c4 17 ♗e1 b5 18 axb5 axb5 19 ♘d2! += M.Gurevich-

Y.Balashov, German League 1995.

b) 9...♕c7 10 ♗e3 a6 11 ♘d2 ♘e8 12 b4 f5 13 f3 c5 14 ♖ab1! b6 15 ♖b2 += J.Piket-B.Damljanovic, Novi Sad Olympiad 1990.

c) 9...a5 10 ♗e3 ♘g4 11 ♗d2 f5 (or 11...♘c5 12 h3 ♘f6 13 ♗e3 ♕e7 14 ♖fd1 += L.Van Wely-M.Bosboom, Dutch Team Ch. 2008) 12 exf5 gxf5 13 ♘g5 ♘df6 14 h3 ♘h6 15 ♖ad1 ♕e7 16 f4 e4 17 ♗e3 c5 18 ♕b3 ♘f7 19 ♘xf7 ♔xf7 20 ♖de1 += V.Eingorn-A.Zapata, Belgrade 1988.

10 g3 *(D)*

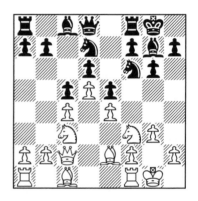

White's chances are on the queenside, to which end he should prepare b2-b4 and open the b-file. On the other hand, Black plans to initiate kingside counterplay with ...f7-f5. The text move, a favourite of GM Van Wely, has the idea of playing ♘h4, when Black has problems achieving ...f7-f5 at all.

White has two other moves deserving attention:

a) 10 ♗g5 h6 11 ♗d2 ♘h7 (or 11...♘e8 12 g3 ♘df6 13 ♘h4 ♘h7 14 ♔h1 ♗h3 15 ♖g1 ♘g5 16 a3 ♗d7 17 b4 ♘h3 18 ♖gf1 += M.Gurevich-D.Jojua,

European Ch., Plovdiv 2008) 12 ♕c1 (or 12 g3 ♘g5 13 ♘xg5 hxg5 14 ♗g4 ♘b6 15 ♗xc8 ♖xc8 16 ♘b5 a6 17 ♘a7 ♖a8 18 ♗a5 += J.Markos-L.Vogt, German League 2007) 12...g5 13 ♘e1 ♘df6 14 ♘c2 ♔h8 15 h3 ♖g8 16 ♕d1 ♘f8 17 ♘e3 +/= A.Kryschilovskij-A.Utkin, St Petersburg 2007.

b) 10 a3!? is also logical. White starts his queenside action immediately and avoids playing anything on the kingside where he does not have an advantage. After 10...♘e8 (if 10...a5 11 ♗d2 a4 12 ♗d3 ♘b6 13 b4 axb3 14 ♕xb3 ♖a6 15 a4 ♘bd7 16 a5 ♔h8 17 ♘a4 ♘g8 18 ♖fb1 ♗h6 19 ♗c3 ♗g7 20 ♕c2 ♘h6 21 ♗d2 +/= M.Krasenkow-T.Casper, German League 1993; or 10...♘h5 11 g3 ♗f6 12 ♗h6 ♘g7 13 ♕d2 ♕e7 14 ♘g5 ♗xg5 15 ♗xg5 f6 16 ♗h6 ♘b6 17 f4 with the initiative, V.Eingorn-V.Kotronias, Debrecen 1989) 11 b4 b6 White can develop his initiative on the queenside faster than Black on the kingside; e.g. 12 ♗d2 (or 12 ♖b1 h6 13 ♗d3 ♕e7 14 ♗d2 ♘df6 15 bxc5 dxc5!? 16 a4!? ♘d6, D.Habedank-H.Schoppmeyer, corr. 1991, 17 a5 bxa5 18 ♗e3 +/=) 12...♗f6 (or 12...h6 13 ♗d3 ♘b8 14 bxc5 bxc5, S.Giemsa-J.Kapischka, German League 1996, 15 ♖ab1 +/=) 13 bxc5 bxc5 14 ♖ab1 ♗e7 15 ♗h6 ♘g7 16 ♕d2 ♔h8 17 ♘e1 f5 18 exf5 gxf5 19 f4 +/= P.Van der Sterren-M.Bosboom, Dutch Ch. 1990.

10...h6

Black has also tried:

a) 10...♘e8 11 ♘h4 ♗f6 12 ♘g2 ♘g7 13 ♗d3 ♗e7 14 ♗h6 ♗g5!? (or 14...♘f6 15 f3 ♗h3 16 ♘d1 ♘d7 17 ♕d2 f5 18 ♘f2 ♗xg2 19 ♔xg2 f4 20 ♘h3 g5 21 ♖f2 ♕e8 22 ♗xg5 ♗xg5 23 ♘xg5 ♕g6 24 ♘h3 +/- J.Benjamin-A.Lesiege, Toronto 1990) 15 ♗xg5 ♕xg5 16 f4 exf4 17 gxf4 ♕e7 18 ♖ae1 += L.Van Wely-M.Riemens, Dutch Team Ch. 1998.

b) 10...♔h8 11 ♘h4 ♘g8 12 ♗d3 ♘df6 13 ♗g5 ♕d7 14 a3 ♘e8 (L.Van Wely-Z.Kozul, European Team Ch., Plovdiv 2003) 15 b4 +/=.

c) 10...♕e7 11 ♘h4 ♔h8 12 ♗g5 ♘b6 13 a3 ♗h3 14 ♖fe1 ♖ac8 15 ♖ab1 ♕c7 16 ♕d2 a6 17 b3 ♘bd7 18 f3 ♘g8 19 ♘d1 ♘df6 20 b4 +/= L.Van Wely-T.Casper, German League 1998.

11 ♘h4 *(D)*

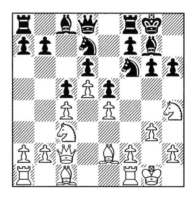

As mentioned above, Black now has problems proceeding with his kingside counterplay. Nevertheless, the position remains very complicated and White cannot easily make any progress.

The game L.Van Wely-I.Smirin, Ledyards (blitz playoff) 2006, continued **11...♘h7 12 ♗d2 ♘g5 13 ♔h1 ♘f6 14 ♖ae1 ♗h3 15 ♖g1 ♘g4 16 ♘d1 ♘f6 17 f3 ♗d7 18 ♕c1 ♘h5 19 ♘f2 ♔h7 20 ♕c2 a6 21 b3?!** [here White should have played 21 f4! exf4 22 ♗xh5 fxg3 23

♖xg3 +/-] **21...b5 22 ♘g2 bxc4 23 bxc4 f5 24 ♘h4?** [24 f4 was still correct, whereas now Black plays it himself] **24...f4 25 ♖b1 fxg3?!** [better first 25...♘f7! with the initiative] **26 hxg3 ♘h3 27 ♘xh3 ♗xh3 28 ♔h2 ♗c8 29 ♖h1 ♖a7 30 ♔g2** and having consolidated his kingside White again stood better and went on to win, albeit after numerous mistakes on both sides.

C: 8 ♗e3 (D)

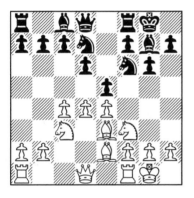

A typical move in this structure. After closing the centre White can always play ♘d2 (e.g. after ...♘c5) when all his queenside pieces are well developed.

Other seldom used moves are:

a) 8...b6 9 b4 exd4 10 ♘xd4 ♗b7 11 f3 a6 12 ♕d2 ♖e8 13 ♖fd1 c6 (L.Van Wely-M.Bosboom, Sonnevanck 1992) 14 b5! c5 15 ♘c6 ♕c8 16 ♕xd6 ♗f8 17 ♕g3 ♗xc6 18 bxc6 ♕xc6 19 ♘d5 +/- Khalifman.

b) 8...exd4 9 ♘xd4 ♖e8 10 f3 c6 is similar to the 7...exd4 and 7...c6 variations in Chapters Three and Five, except that Black has spent a move on ...♘bd7, thus delaying his ...d6-d5 break; e.g. 11 ♘c2 (also good is 11 ♗f2 returning to Chapter Three, notes to line D; or 11 ♕d2 ♘e5 12 ♖fd1 a6 13 ♗f1 ♕e7 14 ♘b3 ♗e6 15 c5 d5, J.Lautier-A.Shchekachev, Dutch Blitz Ch. 2001, 16 ♗d4 +/=) 11...♘e5 (or 11...♕e7 12 ♕d2 ♘b6, S.Vukovic-T.Gniot, Krynica 1956, 13 ♖ad1 ♗e6 14 b3 += Khalifman) 12 ♕d2 (usually the best move, as it defends the e3-bishop and c3-knight and makes way for the a1-rook) 12...♗e6 13 b3 d5 14 exd5 cxd5 15 c5 ♕e7 16 ♖fe1 ♖ac8 (or 16...a6 17 ♖ac1 ♘c6 18 ♗f1 ♖ad8 19 ♘d4 +/= I.Farago-M.Todorcevic, Montpellier 1989) 17 ♖ac1! ♖ed8?! (better 17...a6 +/= Gleizerov) 18 ♘d4 (or 18 ♘b5! +/- Gleizerov) 18...♖xc5!? 19 ♘xe6 fxe6 20 ♗xc5 ♕xc5+ 21 ♔h1 ♕f8 22 f4 ♗h6 23 ♕e3 +/- E.Gleizerov-J.Andersen, Skorping 1994.

c) 8...♕e7 9 d5 (if 9 ♕c2 exd4!? 10 ♘xd4 c6 11 ♖fe1 ♘c5 12 f3 ♘h5 13 ♕d2 a5 14 ♖ad1 a4 15 ♗f1 += R.Cifuentes Parada-V.Akopian, Spanish Team Ch. 2008; or similarly 9 ♖e1!? exd4 10 ♘xd4 c6 11 f3 ♘c5 12 ♕d2 ♖e8 13 ♗f1 a5 14 ♖ad1 a4 15 ♘c2 ♘fd7 16 ♗d4! +/= N.Farrell-C.McNab, Scottish Team Ch. 1994) 9...♘g4 (9...♘h5 10 g3 f5 11 exf5 gxf5 12 ♘g5 f4 13 ♘e6 ♘hf6, J.H.Donner-F.Olafsson, Lugano 1970, and now the simplest is 14 ♘xf8 fxe3 15

♘e6 and Black has no compensation for the exchange; 9...c5 10 ♗g5 h6 11 ♗d2 ♘e8 12 g3 ♘df6 13 ♘h4 ♗h3 14 ♖e1 ♔h7 15 ♖b1 b6 16 a3 ♗d7 17 b4 with better chances for White, V.Topalov-S.Movsesian, European Team Ch., Batumi 1999) 10 ♗g5 f6 11 ♗d2 f5 12 exf5 gxf5 13 ♘g5 ♘df6 14 h3 ♘h6 15 f4 +/= I.Belov-Y.Balashov, German League 1995.

d) 8...h6 *(D)* (planning the manoeuvre ...♘h7-g5) and then:

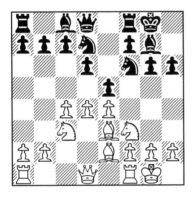

d1) 9 h3 exd4! (logical, as h2-h3 is not useful in the ...exd4 variation) 10 ♘xd4 ♘c5 11 ♕c2 ♖e8 12 ♗f3 ♘h7 13 b4 ♘e6 14 ♖ad1 ♘hg5 15 ♗e2 ♘xd4 16 ♗xd4 ♗xd4 17 ♖xd4 (J.Schultze-H.Kunas, German League 1985) 17...♘e6 ∞.

d2) 9 ♘e1 is also well met by 9...exd4! 10 ♗xd4 ♘e5! 11 f3 ♗e6 = V.Dobrov-E.Alekseev, Russian Junior Ch. 1999.

d3) 9 d5!? is a valid alternative, and if 9...♘g4 10 ♗d2 f5 11 ♘e1! ♘gf6 12 exf5 gxf5 13 f4 exf4 14 ♗xf4 ♘c5 15 ♘c2 +/= M.Muse-G.Iskov, Hamburg 1984.

d4) 9 dxe5 dxe5 10 ♘d2 (10 ♕c1 is

rightly recommended by Khalifman, as it hinders Black's intended ...♘h7-g5, e.g. 10...♔h7!? 11 ♖d1 ♖e8 12 b4 c6 13 c5 ♕e7 14 ♘d2 +/= V.Chuchelov-B.Kristensen, Eupen 1997) 10...♘h7 (or 10...c6 11 c5 ♕e7 12 b4 ♖d8 13 ♕a4 ♘f8 14 ♘c4 ♘g4 15 ♗xg4 ♗xg4 16 ♘d6 with the initiative, E.Gleizerov-K.Kalashnikov, Tomsk 1998) 11 c5 (also good is 11 b4 f5 12 f3 ♘g5 13 ♘b3, H.Wirthensohn-J.Nunn, Biel 1983, 13...c6 14 c5 +/=) 11...♘g5 12 b4 ♘e6 (or 12...f5 13 f3 f4 14 ♗f2 ♘e6 15 ♗c4 ♘f6 16 ♘b3 ♕e8 17 b5 ♔h8, J.Pinter-A.J.Mestel, European Team Ch., Plovdiv 1983, 18 ♕d3 with better chances for White) 13 ♗c4 ♖e8 (Khalifman suggests 13...♘d4 14 ♘b3 ♘b8, but after 15 ♕d2 threatening 16 ♗xh6 or 16 ♖ad1 the black knight will not get to stay on d4) 14 ♗xe6 ♖xe6 15 ♘c4 b6 16 ♕a4 bxc5 17 bxc5 ♖a6 18 ♕c2 ♘f8 19 ♘d5 ♗d7 20 ♘b4 ♖a4 21 a3 +/- Cu.Hansen-E.Mortensen, Danish Ch. 1994.

C1: 8...a5 *(D)*

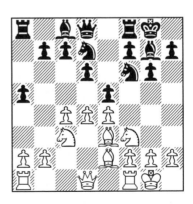

This is useful in various set-ups.

9 dxe5

Only this move can show the shortcomings of ...a7-a5; i.e. the weakening of some squares on the queenside. Instead:

a) 9 d5 is a rather anodyne version of the Petrosian System, e.g. 9...♘g4 10 ♗d2 (or 10 ♗g5 f6 11 ♗h4 h5 12 ♘d2 ♘h6 13 f3 ♘f7 14 ♗d3 ♗h6 15 ♕e2 ♔h8 16 ♗c2 ♖g8 17 ♔h1 ♘f8 = M.Najdorf-L.Stein, Moscow 1967) 10...♘c5 11 ♘e1 f5 12 ♗xg4 fxg4 13 ♗e3 b6 14 ♕d2 ♗a6!? 15 b3 ♕h4 16 f3 ♖f7 17 ♗g5?! (or 17 ♕f2 ♕xf2+ 18 ♖xf2 gxf3 19 ♘xf3 h6 =) 17...♕h5 18 ♘e2 gxf3 19 gxf3 ♖af8 =+ J.Speelman-B.Gelfand, Moscow 1990.

b) 9 ♕c2 offers more chances of an advantage; e.g. 9...♘g4 10 ♗g5 f6 11 ♗d2 exd4 12 ♘xd4 ♘c5 13 ♘b3 ♘xb3 14 ♕xb3 f5 (B.Gelfand-C.McNab, Novi Sad Olympiad 1990) and now 15 exf5 ♗xf5 is slightly better for White. Unfortunately for Black, the "drawing" combination 15...♘xh2 (intending 16 ♔xh2 ♕h4+ 17 ♔g1 ♗e5 18 g3 ♗xg3 19 fxg3 ♕xg3+ etc, McNab) fails to 16 c5+! ♔h8 17 ♖fd1 gxf5, when White can either content himself with 18 ♗f4 ♘g4 19 cxd6 cxd6 20 ♗xd6 ♖e8 21 ♕b5 +=, or try to parry Black's attack after 18 ♔xh2 ♕h4+ 19 ♔g1 ♗e5 20 ♗f3, e.g. 20...a4 21 ♘xa4 ♖xa4 22 g3 ♕c4 23 ♕xc4 ♖xc4 24 cxd6 cxd6 25 ♖ac1 or 21...♕xa4 22 ♕xa4 ♖xa4 23 cxd6 cxd6 24 ♗c3 with the better ending for White in both variations.

9...dxe5

Worse is 9...♘xe5 10 ♘xe5 dxe5 11 ♕c2 ♘g4 12 ♗c5 ♖e8 (G.Halldorsson-U.Starace, corr. 1999) 13 h3 ♘f6 14

♖ad1 with a clear advantage for White.
10 ♘d2 *(D)*

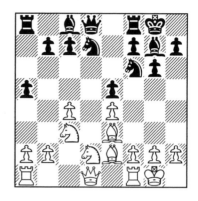

A typical move, aimed against ...♘h5 or ...♘g4. Otherwise White can play 10 ♕c2 ♘g4 11 ♗d2! c6 12 ♘a4 h6 13 h3 ♘gf6 14 ♗e3 ♘h5 15 ♖fd1 ♕e7 16 g3 ♖e8 17 ♔h2 += W.Uhlmann-R.Knaak, Leipzig 1980; or even the direct 10 c5!? as 10...♘g4 11 ♗g5 f6 12 ♕d5+ ♔h8 13 c6 leads to an advantage for White.

10...b6

The alternative, 10...c6, leaves the dark squares weak after 11 c5! ♕e7 12 ♘a4 ♘e8 13 ♘c4 and White has the upper hand, D.Pira-J.Roos, Vichy 2000.
11 ♕a4!

The most energetic move, activating the queen and vacating d1 for a rook.

11...♗b7 12 ♖fd1 ♕e7

Black needed to take control of the d5-square with 12...c6!? which is not as bad as its reputation, e.g. 13 ♕c2 ♕c7 14 ♘b3 ♖fe8 15 ♘a4 +/=. Shirov's line 13 c5!? b5 14 ♘xb5 cxb5 15 ♗xb5 ♗a6 16 c6 ♘b8 17 ♗c5 seems fine for Black after 17...♖e8 18 c7 ♕xc7 19 ♗xe8 ♕xc5 20 ♖ac1 ♕e7 21 ♗b5 ♗b7, though

White could improve with 17 ♘c4 ∞.
13 ♘d5 ♘xd5 14 cxd5 f5 15 f3! ♔h8 16 ♖ac1 ♖ac8 *(D)*

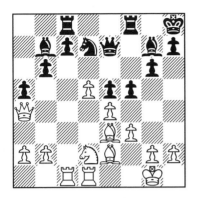

17 ♘c4

We have been following A.Shirov-R.Djurhuus, Gausdal 1991. Here 17 b4! was correct according to Shirov, when 17...axb4 allows 18 ♕a7 and wins.

Nevertheless, the text was also logical and strong, and White went on to win after **17...fxe4 18 fxe4 ♘c5 19 ♕a3 ♕h4 20 ♗xc5 bxc5 21 ♗f3 ♗h6 22 ♖c2 ♗a6 23 ♘xe5 ♗f4 24 g3 ♕g5 25 ♘g4 ♗e3+ 26 ♕xe3 ♕xe3+ 27 ♘xe3 ♖xf3 28 ♘g4 ♖cf8 29 ♖f2 ♔g7 30 ♖xf3 ♖xf3 31 ♖c1 h5 32 ♘f2 c4 33 ♖e1 ♖f8 34 ♘d1 a4 35 a3 ♖b8 36 e5 ♗c8 37 e6 ♗b7 38 ♘c3 ♔f6 39 ♖f1+ ♔e5 40 e7 ♖e8 41 ♖e1+ ♔f5 42 ♘b5 1-0.**

C2: 8...♖e8 9 d5

This is the most logical response when Black plays ...♖e8 before ...e5xd4. However, 9 ♕c2 is a valid alternative:

a) 9...♘g4 10 ♗g5 f6 (or 10...♗f6 11 ♗xf6 ♘gxf6 12 dxe5 dxe5 13 ♖fd1 +/= J.Blumenstein-P.Fink, Griesheim 2002) 11 ♗h4 c6 12 h3 ♘h6 13 ♖fd1 ♕e7 14 b4

♘f8 15 d5 g5 16 ♗g3 f5 (F.Lamprecht-D.Rogozenko, Hamburg 1999) 17 c5 dxc5 18 d6 ♕f6 19 exf5! ♗xf5 20 ♘e4+/-.

b) 9...a5 10 ♖ad1 exd4 11 ♘xd4 ♘c5 12 f3 ♘fd7 13 ♘db5 (a well-known unpleasant motif: Black has no good way to get rid of the b5-knight) 13...♘a6 14 ♕d2 ♘dc5 15 ♗g5 f6 16 ♗h4 with better play for White, F.Gheorghiu-J.Ulrich, US Ch. 1971.

c) 9...exd4 10 ♘xd4 c6 11 ♖fe1 (or 11 ♖fd1 ♕e7 12 f3 ♘c5 13 b4 ♘e6 14 ♖ab1 ♘h5 15 ♗f1 f5 16 ♕d2 fxe4 17 ♘xe4 +/= A.Mitscherling-J.Roth, Budapest 2006) 11...a6 12 ♖ad1 ♕c7 (or 12...♕e7 13 ♗g5 a5 14 ♗f1 ♘c5 15 f3 ♕c7 16 b3 ♘fd7 17 ♗e3 +/= V.Chekhov-V.Komliakov, Moscow 1996) 13 a3 b5!? 14 cxb5 cxb5 15 ♕d2 ♗b7 16 f3 d5 17 exd5 ♘b6 18 ♖c1 ∞ A.Evdokimov-V.Bologan, Moscow 2008.

9...♘g4 *(D)*

A standard reaction. Other moves are:

a) 9...♘c5 10 ♘d2 a5 11 a3 ♗d7 12 b4 axb4 13 axb4 ♖xa1 14 ♕xa1 ♘a6 15 ♕a3 ♘g4 16 ♗xg4 ♗xg4 17 c5 +/= J.Lopez Martinez-D.Svetushkin, World Junior Ch. 1999.

b) 9...♘h5!? 10 g3 ♗f8 11 ♘e1 ♘g7 (this unusual set-up features again in line D2) 12 ♘d3 f5 13 f3 ♗e7 14 ♕d2 ♘f6 15 c5 (or 15 ♔g2 fxe4 16 fxe4 ♘g4 17 ♗xg4 ♗xg4 18 h3 ♗d7 19 ♖f3 ♖f8 20 ♖af1 ♖xf3 21 ♖xf3 ♕c8 22 ♘f2 += I.Ibrahimov-F.Abbasov, Azeri Ch. 2008) 15...fxe4 16 fxe4 ♗h3 17 cxd6 cxd6 18 ♖fc1 ♘g4 19 ♗xg4 ♗xg4 20 ♘b5 ♖f8 21 ♘xa7 (not 21 ♖c3?! a6 22 ♘c7 ♖c8 23 ♖ac1 ♕d7 24 ♘f2 ♗d8 25

♕c2?! ♖f3 -/+ B.Gelfand-T.Radjabov, Wijk aan Zee 2008) 21...h5 22 ♘b5 h4 23 ♘f2 ♗d7 24 ♘c3 += M.Ulibin-B.Roktim, New Delhi 2009.

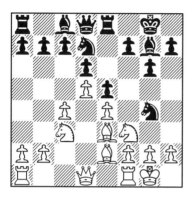

10 ♗d2

White more often inserts 10 ♗g5 f6 (if 10...♗f6 11 ♗d2 ♗g7 12 ♘e1 ♘gf6 13 b4 ♖f8 14 ♘d3 ♘e8 15 ♕c2 c5 16 dxc6 bxc6 17 b5 with the initiative, M.Ac-R.Kohlmann, Bratislava 1989) 11 ♗d2 (also possible is 11 ♗h4 ♘f8 12 ♘d2 h5 13 b4 ♕e7 14 c5 ♘h6 15 cxd6 cxd6 16 f3 ♗d7 17 ♖c1 +/= G.Buckley-C.McNab, Hampstead 1999) and then 11...♘f8 (11...f5?! transposes to *10 ♗d2 f5*, or if 11...a5 12 ♘e1 ♘h6 13 ♘d3 f5 14 a3 ♘f6 15 f3 ♗f8 16 b4 += A.Kirusha-S.Voitsekhovsky, St Petersburg 1998) 12 ♘e1 h5!? (or 12...♘h6 13 ♕c1 ♘f7 14 ♗e3 f5 15 f3 f4 16 ♗f2 g5 17 c5 a6 18 ♘a4 +/= O.Revelj-R.Barhudarian, Stockholm 2007) 13 ♘d3 f5 14 exf5 (or 14 f3!? ♘h6 15 c5 f4 16 ♖c1 a6, R.Djurhuus-Y.Shulman, Moscow Olympiad 1994, 17 a4!? g5 18 a5 intending cxd6 and ♘a4 += Chekhov) 14...e4!? (or if 14...♗xf5 15 h3 ♘f6 16 ♘e1 ♘8h7 17 ♕b3 +/= B.Montalta-J.Bouma, corr. 1999) 15

♗xg4 hxg4 16 f6! ♕xf6 17 ♘f4 ♗f5 18 ♗e3 c5 19 dxc6 bxc6 20 ♕a4 ♖ac8! (S.Shipov-Y.Shulman, Alusta 1994) and now 21 ♘fe2! ♘d7 22 ♘g3 += Shipov.

10...c5

Closing the centre and forestalling ideas of c4-c5. Other continuations are no better:

a) 10...♗h6 (N.Sulava-A.Areshchenko, Cappelle la Grande 2004) 11 ♗xh6 ♘xh6 12 ♕d2 ♘g4 13 b4 +/=.

b) 10...a5 11 ♘e1 ♘gf6 (here 11...♘h6??, S.Shipov-V.Bologan, Internet blitz 2004, just drops the knight to 12 ♕c1) 12 ♘d3 +/=.

c) 10...f5 is met by 11 ♘g5! ♘df6 (or 11...♘f8 12 exf5 gxf5 13 ♗xg4 fxg4 14 f3 ♗f5, V.Belov-L.Guliev, Baku 2006, 15 ♗e3 +/-) 12 c5 fxe4 (or if 12...♕e7, R.Sherbakov-C.McNab, London Lloyds Bank 1992, 14 cxd6 cxd6 15 ♖c1 +=) 13 ♘e6 (13 ♘gxe4 ♘xe4 14 ♘xe4 +/=) 13...♖xe6 14 dxe6 ♗xe6 15 ♗g5 ♕d7 16 cxd6 cxd6 17 ♗b5 with better chances for White, R.Sherbakov-A.Graf, Calcutta 1996.

11 ♘e1 ♘gf6 *(D)*

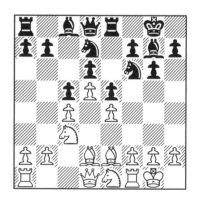

White has the advantage due to his

extra space. Furthermore, if we compare this position with 8 ♕c2 c6 9 d5 c5 in line B2 (which was already somewhat better for White), here he has swapped ♕c2 for ♘e1 and ♗d2, while Black's rook is somewhat misplaced on e8.

The game P.Wells-Zhang Zhong, Hastings 2001/02, continued **12 ♘d3 ♖e7!? 13 ♕c2 ♕f8** [making use of the absent rook] **14 a3 ♗h6 15 b4 ♗xd2 16 ♕xd2 b6 17 ♕e3 ♘e8 18 a4 f5 19 a5 ♖f7?!** [19...♖b8 would allow Black to maintain his pawn chain] **20 axb6 ♘xb6 21 bxc5 ♘xc4 22 ♕c1** [or 22 ♕g5!? +/-] **22...dxc5 23 f4** [or 23 ♘a4!? +/-] **23...♕e7 24 ♘b5?** [a serious mistake; either 24 ♘e1 (Tsesarsky) or 24 ♖e1 would keep a clear advantage] **24...fxe4 25 ♕xc4 exd3 26 ♗xd3 exf4 27 ♖ae1 ♕f8 28 d6 ♗d7 29 ♕xc5 ♗xb5 30 ♗xb5?** [better 30 ♕xb5 ♘xd6 31 ♕d5 and 32 ♖xf4] **30...♘xd6 31 ♗c6 ♖c8 32 ♖d1?! ♘f5 33 ♕a5 ♘e3 34 ♗d5 ♘xd5 35 ♖xd5 f3 0-1**.

C3: 8...♘g4 (D)

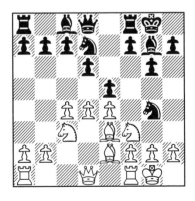

A typical response, enabling Black

to start counterplay on the kingside.

9 ♗g5 f6 10 ♗c1

White has two equivalent moves:

a) 10 ♗d2 ♘h6 (or 10...c6 11 b4!? f5 12 d5 f4, W.Uhlmann-R.Knaak, Leipzig 1977, 13 dxc6!? bxc6 14 ♗e1 ♕c7 15 ♕d3 +/=) 11 ♕c2 ♘f7 12 ♖ad1 a5 13 ♖fe1 c6 14 ♗f1 ♕c7 15 ♗e3 ♗h6 16 a3 ♗xe3 17 ♖xe3 ♖e8 18 b4 with better play for White, J.Levitt-S.Kagan, Holon 1986.

b) 10 ♗h4 ♘h6 (or if 10...h5 11 h3 ♘h6 12 ♕d2 ♘f7 13 ♖ad1 ♗h6 14 ♕c2 ♘g5, I.Farago-B.Ivanovic, Sarajevo 1983, then 15 dxe5 ♘xf3+ 16 ♗xf3 dxe5 17 c5 or 15 ♘xg5 fxg5 16 ♗g3 exd4 17 ♖xd4 with the advantage in either case) 11 dxe5 dxe5 12 b4 a5 (or 12...c6 13 c5 a5 14 a3, N.Kalesis-M.Pavlovic, Kardista 1994, and if 14...♘f7!? intending ...♕e7 Pavlovic, then 15 ♕c2 +/=) 13 a3 axb4 14 axb4 ♖xa1 15 ♕xa1 g5 (or if 15...c6 16 ♖d1 ♕e7 17 c5 b6?, S.Bromberger-Z.Ilincic, Budapest 2008, 18 ♕a7! bxc5 19 ♗a6! +-) 16 ♗g3 f5 17 exf5 e4 18 ♘d2 e3 19 fxe3 ♘xf5 20 ♗f2 ♘f6 21 ♕a2 and Black has insufficient compensation for the pawn, W.Uhlmann-D.Minic, Palma Interzonal 1970.

10...♘h6 (D)

Other continuations allow White a small advantage:

a) 10...f5 11 exf5 gxf5 12 ♗g5 ♘gf6 13 dxe5 dxe5 14 ♕c2 e4 15 ♘d4 ♘e5 16 ♖ad1 += C.Valero Fuertes-J.Quesada Vera, Malaga 1999.

b) 10...♔h8 11 b4 ♘h6 12 ♗b2 ♖e8 13 ♕c2 += P.Stempin-R.Knaak, Leipzig 1986.

c) 10...a5 11 dxe5 dxe5 12 b3 ♖e8 13 ♕c2 c6 14 ♗a3 ♗f8 15 ♗xf8 ♖xf8 16 ♘a4 += S.Semkov-A.Zapata, Saint John 1988.

d) 10...c6 11 b4 f5 (more promising is 11...exd4!? 12 ♘xd4 f5 13 exf5 gxf5 and if 14 ♘e6 ♕h4 15 h3 ♗xc3 16 ♗g5 ♘xf2 17 ♖xf2 ♕e4 18 ♘xf8 ♘xf8 19 ♗f4 ♗d4 20 ♗xd6 ♗e6 ∞) 12 d5 ♘df6 13 ♘g5 += W.Uhlmann-W.Heinig, East German Ch. 1981.

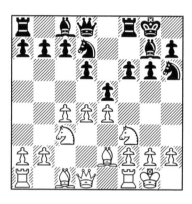

11 ♖b1

Roiz criticizes this move, so White might prefer:

a) 11 ♕c2 exd4 (if 11...c6 12 ♖d1 ♕e7 13 b4 f5 14 c5 dxc5, S.Prange-W.Heinig, Berlin 1995, 15 ♗c4+ ♔h8 16 ♗g5 ♕e8 17 dxc5 +=; or 11...♘f7 12 ♖d1 c6 13 ♗e3 ♕e7 14 c5! exd4 15 cxd6 ♘xd6 16 ♖xd4 ♘f7 17 ♖ad1 += N.Sulava-B.Badea, Nice 2001) 12 ♘xd4 ♖e8 13 ♗e3 c6 14 ♕d2 ♘f7 (B.Byjic Katanic-J.Sakotic, Yugoslav Women's Ch. 1996) when White could have obtained a small advantage after either 15 ♖ad1 or 15 f4.

b) 11 dxe5 dxe5 (if 11...♘xe5 12 ♘xe5 dxe5 13 ♕xd8 ♖xd8 14 ♘d5 c6 15

♘xf6+ ♗xf6 16 ♗xh6 +/- T.Engqvist-P.Levacic, Podgorica 1991) 12 b4 ♘f7 13 c5 ♔h8 (R.Hernandez-C.Cuartas, Bogota 1978) 14 ♗c4 c6 15 ♗e3 +=.

11...♘f7

Black has also tried:

a) 11...c6 12 b4 f5 (F.Visier Segovia-D.Minic, Praia da Rocha 1969) 13 ♗g5 ♕e8 14 d5 +=.

b) 11...a5 12 a3 (or 12 dxe5!? +=) 12...c6 13 b4 axb4 14 axb4 ♖e8 (G.Timoscenko-V.Talla, Slovakian Team Ch. 1997) 15 ♕c2 +/=.

12 dxe5

Weaker is 12 b4?! f5 (or 12...c6 13 d5 c5 14 a3 b6 15 ♘e1 f5 = Cu.Hansen-S.Bjarnason, Borgarnes 1985) 13 exf5 (if 13 dxe5 ♘dxe5!, or 13 d5 ♘f6 =+ M.Labollita-F.De la Paz, Santa Clara 2004) 13...gxf5 14 dxe5 dxe5 15 ♗b2 c6 16 ♘e1 (S.Tatai-C.Hoi, Teesside 1978) 16...♕e7 ∞.

However, 12 ♕c2 looks better, e.g. 12...f5 13 exf5 gxf5 14 dxe5 dxe5?! (but if 14...♘dxe5 15 ♘d4 += or 14...♘fxe5!? 15 ♗f4 +/=) 15 ♕xf5 ♘f6 16 ♕c2 +/- A.Zakharov-I.Lymar, Decin 1997.

12...♘dxe5

12...dxe5 is a bit worse: 13 b4 c6 14 c5 ♖e8 15 ♕b3 ♕c7 16 ♗c4 += V.Gagarin-P.Hanko, Pardubice 2000, or 13...f5 (A.Ornstein-B.Hammar, Swedish Ch. 1984) 14 ♗d3 ♘f6 15 ♕e2 c6 16 ♖d1 +/=.

13 ♘d4

Possibly White should perhaps opt for 13 ♘xe5 dxe5 14 ♗e3 (or 14 ♕c2!?) 14...♗e6 15 ♕xd8 ♖fxd8 16 ♖fd1 with an equal endgame.

13...c5 14 ♘c2 f5 *(D)*

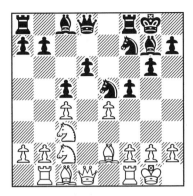

Black's active pieces give him excellent compensation for his slight structural weakness and, moreover, the easier position to play.

The game M.Roiz-P.Svidler, European Cup, Rethymnon 2003, continued (with notes by Roiz): **15 f4** [or if 15 ♘e3!? fxe4 16 ♘xe4 ♗e6 with counterplay] **15...♘c6 16 exf5** [or 16 ♗d3 ♘h6 17 ♘d5 ♘d4 with counterplay] **16...♗xf5 17 ♗d3 ♘h6 18 ♘e3 ♗xd3 19 ♕xd3 ♘b4 20 ♕d1 ♕d7?!** [better was 20...♕h4! 21 a3 ♗d4! 22 ♔h1 ♘c6 with the advantage] **21 ♘ed5 ♘xd5 22 ♕xd5+! ♕f7! 23 ♗d2 ♖ae8 24 ♕xf7+ ♖xf7 25 h3?!** [here 25 ♖fe1 is equal] **25...♘f5 26 ♖fe1 ♗d4+! 27 ♔h2 ♖fe7 28 ♖xe7 ♖xe7 29 ♖e1 ♖xe1 30 ♗xe1 ♔f7 31 b3 ♔e6 32 ♘b5 a6 33 ♘c7+! ♔d7 34 ♘d5 b5 35 g4 ♘e7 36 ♔g3!** [not 36 ♘xe7? ♔xe7 37 ♔g3 ♔e6 38 ♔f3 d5 39 cxd5+ ♔xd5 -/+] **36...♘xd5 37 cxd5 c4 38 bxc4 bxc4 39 ♗b4??** [this is a terrible blunder; instead 39 ♗f2 would hold the draw easily, e.g. 39...♗b2 40 ♔f3 c3 41 ♗d4 ♗a1 42 ♗e3 ♗b2] **39...♗b2 0-1** [as the c-pawn cannot be stopped].

C4: 8...c6 (D)

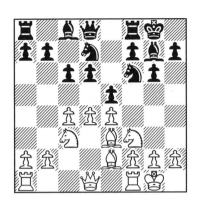

This flexible system, leaving open the possibilities of ...♘g4 or ...e5xd4, has become more popular in recent years.

9 d5

This looks the most consistent response. Instead:

a) 9 ♖e1!? transposes to 8 ♖e1 c6 9 ♗e3!? (see D3, note 'e').

b) 9 dxe5 dxe5 gives White nothing, e.g. 10 ♘d2 ♕e7 11 ♕c2 ♘c5 12 ♘b3 ♘e6 13 ♖fd1 h5! 14 f3 h4 15 c5 ♘h5 16 ♗c4 ♘ef4 17 ♘e2 (A.Luczak-J.Bielczyk, Polish Team Ch. 1986) 17...♕g5 = Bielczyk.

c) 9 ♕d2!? is more interesting: 9...♘g4 (or 9...♕e7 10 ♗g5 exd4 11 ♘xd4 ♖e8 12 f3 ♘c5 13 ♔h1 a5 14 ♖ad1 +/= K.Sakaev-A.Lukin, St Petersburg 1995) 10 ♗g5 f6 11 ♗h4 ♘h6 12 ♖ad1 ♘f7 13 b4 (or 13 ♕c2 ♖e8 14 h3 ♕c7 15 b4 +/= V.Chuchelov-B.Badea, French Team Ch. 2001) 13...g5!? (13...a5 14 a3 axb4 15 axb4 ♕b6 16 ♖b1 g5 17 dxe5 dxe5 18 c5 ♕c7 19 ♗g3 +/= E.Karavade-E.Pähtz, World Junior Ch. 2004) 14 dxe5 (14 ♗g3 g4 ½-½ O.Panno-Ye Jiangchuan, Dubai Olympiad 1986) 14...♘dxe5 15 ♘xe5 dxe5 16 ♕b2 +=.

d) 9 ♕c2 *(D)* again deserves serious attention:

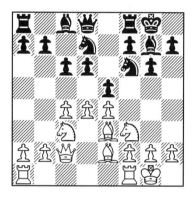

d1) 9...♖e8 10 d5 cxd5 11 cxd5 a6 12 a4 ♖f8 13 ♘d2 ♘e8 14 f3 f5 15 b4 ♘ef6 16 ♘c4 += M.Hüttinger-N.Heck, Giessen 1994.

d2) 9...♕e7 10 d5 ♘g4 11 ♗g5 f6 12 ♗d2 f5 13 exf5 gxf5 14 ♘g5 ♘df6 15 f3 ♘h6 16 ♗d3 ♗d7 17 ♖ae1 ♔h8 18 ♔h1 (V.Korchnoi-A.J.Mestel, Beersheba 1984) 18...♖ac8 += Karpov.

d3) 9...♘g4 10 ♗g5 f6 11 ♗h4 (if 11 ♗d2 f5 12 exf5 gxf5 13 dxe5 dxe5 14 ♘g5 ♘df6 15 ♖ad1 ♕e7 16 ♕c1 ♗d7 17 b4 ♔h8 18 f3 ♘h6 ∞ W.Uhlmann-R.Knaak, Szirak 1985) 11...♘h6 12 dxe5 dxe5 13 b4 ♘f7 14 c5 ♕c7 15 ♗g3 ♖e8 16 h3 += A.Groszpeter-E.Ermenkov, European Team Ch., Haifa 1989, though the opponents agreed a draw here.

d4) 9...h6!? is more promising; e.g. 10 h3 (or 10 dxe5 dxe5 11 ♘d2 ♕e7 12 a3 ♘c5 13 b4 ♘e6 with counterplay, S.Prange-M.Stoeber, Hastings 1995/96) 10...♕e7 (if 10...♘h5 11 ♖fd1 ♕e7 12 c5

dxc5 13 d5 += B.Savchenko-A.Areshchenko, Budva 2009) 11 ♖fe1 ♖e8 12 ♗f1 exd4 13 ♗xd4 ♘e5 14 ♘xe5 dxe5 15 ♗e3 ♗e6 16 ♖ad1 b6 17 c5 ♘d7 ½-½ W.Uhlmann-L.Vogt, Dresden 1988.

d5) 9...exd4!? 10 ♗xd4 (better 10 ♘xd4 ♖e8 transposing to *8...♖e8 9 ♕c2 exd4 10 ♘xd4 c6* in the notes to line C2) 10...♖e8 11 ♖ad1 ♕e7 12 ♖fe1 ♘c5 (if 12...♘e5 13 h3 ♗h6 14 b4 b6 15 c5 ♘xf3+ 16 ♗xf3 bxc5 17 bxc5 dxc5 18 ♗e3 ♗xe3 19 ♖xe3 ♕e5 20 ♘a4 ♗e6 21 ♘xc5 ♖ab8, K.Langeweg-P.Scheeren, Amsterdam 1977, 22 ♘d3 +=) 13 b4 (or 13 h3!? ♘e6 14 ♗e3, S.Matveeva-M.Chiburdanidze, Manila Olympiad 1992, 14...♘c5! ∞) 13...♘e6 14 ♗e3 ♘g4 15 ♗c1 a5 ∞ M.Sadler-J.Calvo Sanchez, Andorra 1991.

9...c5

Apart from closing the centre, Black can maintain the tension or open the c-file:

a) 9...cxd5 (this leads to better play for White) 10 cxd5 ♘g4 (otherwise White regroups with ♘d2, e.g. 10...a6 11 ♘d2 h5 12 ♘c4 ♕c7 13 a4 ♘g4 14 ♗g5 f6 15 ♗d2 f5 16 exf5 gxf5 17 h3 ♘gf6 18 f4 += V.Bhat-S.Shoker, Pula 2006) 11 ♗d2 ♗h6 12 ♖c1 a6 13 a4 f5 14 exf5 gxf5 15 h3 ♗xd2 16 ♕xd2 ♘gf6 17 ♘g5 ♘c5 18 ♗c4 ♘fe4 19 ♘gxe4 ♘xe4 20 ♘xe4 fxe4 21 ♖c3 +/- V.Chekhov-T.Casper, Leipzig 1988.

b) 9...♕e7 10 ♘d2 ♘e8 (if now 10...c5 11 a3 ♘e8, S.Chloupek-V.Vodicka, Czech League 1998, 12 ♖c1!? intending 12...f5 13 exf5 gxf5 14 f4 +/=) 11 b4 (or 11 dxc6 bxc6 12 b4 +=

Y.Kruppa-V.Kirillova, St Petersburg 2004) 11...c5 12 bxc5 ♘xc5 13 ♘b3 b6 14 ♘xc5 bxc5 15 ♕a4 f5 16 ♖ab1 += E.Bang-E.Arnlind, corr. 1984.

c) 9...♘g4 *(D)* (the typical reaction when the bishop is on e3) with two options:

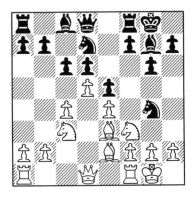

c1) 10 ♗g5 f6 and then:

c11) 11 ♗h4 ♕e7 (or if 11...c5 12 ♘e1 ♘h6 13 ♘d3 ♘f7 14 ♖b1 ♗h6 15 a3 intending b2-b4 += V.Chuchelov-K.Van der Weide, Leeuwarden 1995) 12 ♘e1 ♘h6 13 ♘d3 (R.Fyllingen-E.Mortensen, Aars 1999) 13...g5! 14 ♗g3 f5 15 dxc6 bxc6 16 f3 +/=.

c12) 11 dxc6!? (this unexpected move, based on motif of the open a2-g8 diagonal, may be a serious problem for Black as he loses a pawn without sufficient compensation) 11...♘c5 (if 11...bxc6 12 ♕xd6 fxg5 13 ♕e6+ ♔h8 14 ♕xg4 h6 15 ♕g3 ♖f4 16 ♘e1 ♘c5 17 ♕e3 ♘e6 18 ♘d3 +/- K.Robatsch-V.Kotronias, Budapest 1988) 12 cxb7 ♗xb7 13 ♗c1 with a clear advantage, as 13...♘xe4?? runs into 14 ♘xe4 ♗xe4 15 ♘d2 and White wins a piece.

c13) 11 ♗d2 ♕e7 (11...f5 transposes

to 10 ♗d2 f5, but most annotators condemn this move because it weakens the e6-square) 12 b4 ♔h8 13 dxc6 bxc6 14 b5 ♗b7 15 bxc6 ♗xc6 16 ♘d5 ♗xd5 17 cxd5 ♘c5 18 ♘e1 ♘h6 19 f3 ♘f7 20 ♘d3 ♘xd3 21 ♗xd3 ♗h6 22 ♗xh6 ♘xh6 23 ♕d2 with the better game, J.Donaldson-W.Browne, Reno 1992.

c2) 10 ♗d2!? is also possible, when V.Ivanchuk-J.Piket, Wijk aan Zee 1996, continued 10...f5 11 ♘g5 ♘df6 12 b4 cxd5 13 cxd5 fxe4? (but if 13...♕e7 then 14 f3 ♘h6 15 ♕b3 with an initiative) 14 ♘e6 ♗xe6 15 dxe6 ♘h6 16 g4 d5 17 ♗g5 ♖c8 18 e7 ♕xe7 19 ♘xd5 and White won.

It is not clear whether White should insert 10 ♗g5 f6 or not (he usually does). Although Black's f-pawn on f6 looks a little ugly, it does not harm Black at all and sometimes enables the manoeuvre ...♘h6-f7. On the other hand, after 10 ♗g5 f6 White has the additional possibilities of 11 ♗h4 and, especially, 11 dxc6!?.

10 ♘e1 *(D)*

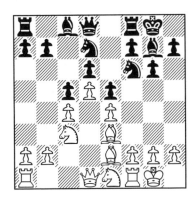

The knight heads for d3 to assist White's play on both the kingside (f2-

f4) and the queenside (b2-b4), while also preventing ...♘g4 or ...♘h5. White has several other worthwhile ideas:

a) 10 ♘d2 (with similar intentions) 10...♘e8 11 ♖b1 f5 (J.Kiedrowicz-A.Maciejewski, Gdynia 1985) 12 exf5! gxf5 13 f4 e4 14 ♕e1 +=.

b) 10 g3 (intending ♘h4 to control the f5-square) 10...♔h8 11 ♘h4 ♘g8 12 ♕d2 ♘df6 13 f3 ♘e8 14 ♗d3 += D.Gurevich-A.Soltis, Bermuda 1990.

c) 10 ♗g5 (interfering with Black's kingside counterplay) 10...h6 11 ♗h4 g5 12 ♗g3 ♘h5 13 ♘d2 ♘f4 14 ♗g4 ♘f6 15 ♗xc8 ♕xc8 16 ♖e1 ♘6h5 17 ♘f1 f5 18 ♗xf4 ♘xf4 19 ♘e3 fxe4 20 ♘xe4 += I.Farago-N.McDonald, Hastings 1989/90.

d) 10 a3 (planning direct action on the queenside) 10...♘g4 11 ♗g5 f6 12 ♗d2 ♕e7 13 b4 f5 14 ♘g5 ♘df6 15 f3 ♘h6 (L.D.Nisipeanu-L.McShane, European Team Ch., Gothenburg 2005) 16 bxc5 dxc5 17 exf5 gxf5 18 ♗d3 +=.

e) 10 ♖b1!? (with similar intentions) 10...h6 (or 10...♘e8 11 b4 cxb4 12 ♖xb4 ♘c5 13 ♘d2 f5 14 f3 ♗f6 15 ♘b3 += A.Lastin-E.Kovalevskaya, St Petersburg 1999) 11 ♘e1 ♘e8 12 ♕d2 ♔h7 13 ♘d3 ♕e7 14 ♔h1 f5 15 exf5 gxf5 16 f4 e4 17 ♘f2 ♘df6 18 b4 b6 19 a4 ♘c7 20 bxc5 bxc5 21 ♖g1 +/= V.Korchnoi-C.Landenbergue, Bern 1992.

10...♔h8

Freeing the g8-square for the knight. Black has also tried:

a) 10...a6 11 ♖b1 ♕e7 12 a3 ♘e8 (N.Stanec-E.Sutovsky, Pula 2000) 13 ♘c2 f5 14 exf5 gxf5 15 f4 +=.

b) 10...♖e8 11 a3 a5 12 b3 ♘b6 13

♘d3 ♗d7 14 ♘b2 ♕e7 15 ♗f3 ♖f8 16 ♕e2 ♘e8 17 b4 += J.Jezek-R.Blessing, corr. 1985.

c) 10...♘e8 *(D)* is the main alternative, but White can still hope for the advantage:

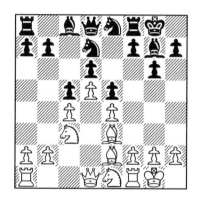

c1) 11 ♘d3 f5 12 f4 (if 12 exf5 gxf5 13 f4 e4 14 ♘f2 ♗xc3!? 15 bxc3 ♘df6 16 h3 ♔h8 17 ♔h2 ♖g8 ∞ J.Tisdall-E.Sutovsky, Gausdal 1995) 12...♘b6 13 ♕b3 exf4 14 ♘xf4 ♕e7 15 a4 ♘c7 16 a5 ♘d7 17 ♘e6 ♘xe6 18 dxe6 ♕xe6 19 ♘d5 ♖b8 20 exf5 gxf5 21 ♖ad1 ½-½ H.Olafsson-J.Lautier, Novi Sad Olympiad 1990.

c2) 11 g4!? f5 12 exf5 gxf5 13 gxf5 ♘b6 14 ♔h1 ♗xf5 15 ♖g1 ♔h8!? 16 ♘f3 e4 17 ♘g5 ♗xc3! 18 bxc3 ♕e7 19 ♖g3 ♘f6 ∞ R.Sherbakov-A.Poluljahov, Kahovka 1997.

c3) 11 a3 f5 (if 11...♕e7!? 12 ♕d2) 12 exf5 (better than 12 f3 f4 13 ♗f2 g5 14 b4 b6 15 ♘d3 h5 ∞ R.Tischbierek-L.Hazai, Halle 1981) 12...gxf5 13 f4 exf4 (if 13...♘ef6 14 ♘d3 ♘e4 15 fxe5 ♘xc3 16 bxc3 ♘xe5 17 ♘f4 += Gelfand/Kapengut; or 13...e4, M.Ronco-O.Bustamante, Buenos Aires 2002, 14

♕d2 +=) 14 ♗xf4 ♘e5 15 ♕d2 ♘f6 16 ♘f3 ♘g6 17 ♗g5 ♕b6 (I.Naumkin-B.Gelfand, Vilnius 1988) 18 ♘h4 +=.

11 ♘d3 ♘g8 (D)

11...♘b6 prevents any immediate b2-b4, but White can play in the centre instead: 12 b3 ♘g8 13 ♕d2 ♗d7 14 ♖ae1 ♕e7 15 f4 with the initiative, E.Kolesnikov-P.Czarnota, European Junior Ch. 2004.

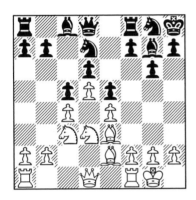

12 ♕d2

Other moves give White a small advantage too:

a) 12 b4 cxb4 13 ♘xb4 ♗h6 14 ♗xh6 ♘xh6 15 ♕d2 ♔g7 16 ♘d3 b6 17 a4 ♘c5 18 ♘xc5 bxc5 19 ♖ab1 += V.Chekhov-T.Casper, German League 1993.

b) 12 ♘b5!? ♕e7 13 b4 b6 14 a4 a6 15 ♘c3 a5 16 bxc5 bxc5 17 ♖b1 f5 (or if 17...♗h6 18 ♗xh6 ♘xh6 19 ♕d2 ♘g8 20 f4 exf4 21 ♕xf4 ♗a6 22 ♘b5 ♗xb5 23 ♖xb5 ♘gf6 24 ♖b7 ♖fb8, R.Soldo-M.Bilic, Zagreb 2007, 25 ♖c7! ♖c8 26 ♖c6! ♕xe4 27 ♕xe4 ♘xe4 28 ♖xf7 +/-) 18 f3 ♗h6 19 ♗f2 ♘gf6 20 ♕c2 += G.Van der Stricht-A.Kovalev, Belgian Team Ch. 2006.

12...f5

Otherwise Black would be deprived of counterplay, e.g. 12...♕e7 13 ♖ae1 f5 14 ♗g5 ♘df6 15 f4 h6 16 ♗h4 +/- C.Duncan-P.Thipsay, British Ch. 1999; or 12...♘e7 13 f4 f6 14 fxe5 fxe5 15 ♖xf8+ ♘xf8 16 ♗g5 ♕d7 17 h3 a6 18 a4 ♘g8 19 a5 ♕c7 20 ♘a4 ♗d7 21 ♘b6 ♖e8 22 b4 cxb4 23 ♕xb4 ♗h6 24 ♗xh6 ♘xh6 25 ♖b1 1-0 L.Janjgava-M.Chiburdanidze, Tbilisi 1991.

13 f4!?

Or again 13 exf5 gxf5 14 f4 e4 15 ♘f2 += J.Grigorov-E.Ermenkov, Bulgarian Ch. 1975.

13...g5?!

After this the c3-knight will romp throughout Black's territory. He should have decided on 13...♘gf6, though White's chances would still have been better.

14 fxg5 f4 15 ♗f2 ♕xg5 16 ♘b5 ♕g6 17 ♗f3 b6 18 ♕e2 a6 19 ♘c7 ♖a7 20 ♘e6 ♖f6 (D)

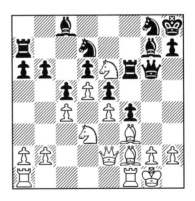

We have been following the game V.Petkov-Z.Kozul, Zadar 2005, and now 21 b4 ♘e7 22 ♖ab1 would have maintained a clear advantage for White. Instead, he somewhat greedily went for the exchange and allowed his opponent to obtain counterplay: **21 ♗h4? ♖xe6 22 dxe6 ♘f8 23 ♔h1 ♘xe6 24 ♗f2 ♘f6 25 b4 ♘g5 26 bxc5 bxc5 27 ♖ab1 ♖f7 28 ♖fe1** [if 28 ♗xc5!? ♘fxe4] **28...♗f8** [28...♖f8! ∞ was stronger] **29 ♖b6 ♖g7 30 ♗h4 ♔g8 31 ♗xg5 ♕xg5 32 ♘f2 ♕h4 33 ♖b8 ♗e6 34 ♖d1 ♘d7 35 ♖b7 ♖g6?!** [and here 35...h5!? intending ...♘f6-g4] **36 ♖db1 ♕d8?! 37 ♗h5 ♖g7 38 ♗g4 ♗xg4 39 ♘xg4 ♕g5 40 h3 ♕g6 41 ♕d3 h5?! 42 ♖xd7 ♖xd7 43 ♘xe5 dxe5 44 ♕xd7 ♕xe4 45 ♕e6+ ♔g7 46 ♖d1 ♔h8 47 ♕f7 1-0**.

D: 8 ♖e1 (*D*)

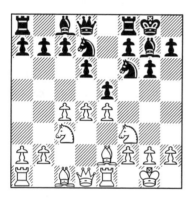

This is White's most popular continuation, reorganizing the kingside without committing to any particular plan.

D1: 8...h6 *176*
D2: 8...♖e8 *178*
D3: 8...c6 *180*

Other seldom used moves are:
a) 8...b6 9 ♗f1 (9 ♗e3 also deserves attention, e.g. 9...♗b7 10 d5 ♘c5 11 ♕c2 a5 12 ♘d2 ♗c8 13 a3 +/= B.Berndorff-A.Fiedler, German League 1994) 9...exd4 (or if 9...♗b7 10 d5 ♘e8, M.Bitelmajer-M.Jurcik, World Junior Ch. 2005, 11 ♗g5 +/=) 10 ♘xd4 ♗b7 11 f3 c6 12 ♗g5 a6 13 a4 ♕c7 14 ♕d2 ♖fe8 15 ♖ad1 ♖ac8 16 ♔h1 ♕b8 17 ♘de2 ♗f8 18 ♘g3 ♖e6 19 ♕f2 ♗a8 20 ♖d2 ♘e5 21 ♖ed1 +/= A.Mikhalevski-M.Bosboom, Leeuwarden 1994.

b) 8...exd4 is less appropriate here, as Black lacks counterplay; e.g. 9 ♘xd4 ♘c5 (or 9...♖e8 10 f3 c6 11 ♘c2 ♕e7 12 ♗e3 += J.Sloth-K.Pedersen, Randers 1970) 10 f3 a5 (or 10...♖e8 11 ♗e3 ♘e6 12 ♖c1 ♘h5 13 ♘xe6 ♗xe6 14 ♕d2 += Y.Glyzin-G.Toczek, Warsaw 2005) 11 ♘db5 (a well-known motif, preventing ...c7-c6) 11...♗d7 12 ♗e3 ♗xb5 (12...♖e8 13 ♕d2 ♕b8 14 ♖ad1 ♗c6 15 ♗f1 +=, though 15...♘fd7 ½-½ O.Lehner-N.Stanec, Ansfelden 2003) 13 ♘xb5 ♕e7 14 ♕d2 a4 15 ♖ad1 ♖fd8 16 ♗f1 +/- M.Taimanov-H.Kestler, European Team Ch., Hamburg 1965.

D1: 8...h6 (*D*)

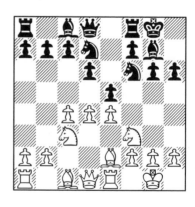

Preparing the manoeuvre ...♘h7-g5 while at the same time controlling the g5-square.

9 dxe5

Ruling out any possibility Black might throw in ...e5xd4, although in that case ...h7-h6 would not be the most useful move either. White has several other continuations:

a) 9 d5 is inconsistent, and after 9...♘h7!? 10 g3 a5 11 ♗e3 ♘c5 12 ♕d2 h5 13 ♖ab1 ♗d7 14 b3 f5 Black can count on sufficient counterplay, V.Babula-V.Sergeev, Pardubice 1998.

b) 9 ♖b1 exd4 (if 9...♘h7 10 dxe5 dxe5 11 b4 f5 12 c5 ♔h8 13 ♕c2 f4, Sr.Cvetkovic-A.Lanc, Stary Smokovec 1983, 14 ♖d1 +/-) 10 ♘xd4 ♘c5 (or 10...♖e8 11 f3 c6 12 ♗e3 +=) 11 f3 a5 12 ♗e3 ♖e8 13 ♕d2 ♔h7 14 ♗f1 ♘fd7 15 ♘db5 ♘e6 16 f4 +/= J.Martin del Campo-G.Vazquez Escalona, Mexican Ch. 2002.

c) 9 ♕c2 ♘h7 (9...exd4!? 10 ♘xd4 ♘c5 might again be considered) 10 dxe5 (or 10 ♗e3 ♘g5 11 ♖ad1 ♘xf3+ 12 ♗xf3 c6 13 ♗g4 +/= V.Epishin-K.Movsziszian, Dos Hermanas 2004) 10...dxe5 11 ♗e3 ♖e8 (if 11...f5 12 exf5 gxf5 13 ♖ad1 c6 14 c5 +/- A.Volokitin-Z.Kozul, Slovenian Team Ch. 2008; or 11...c6 12 ♖ad1 ♕e7 13 ♕c1 h5 14 c5 ♘df6 15 h3 ♘e8 16 b4 +/- A.Beliavsky-Z.Kozul, Portoroz 1999) 12 c5 ♘hf8 13 ♖ed1! c6 14 b4 ♘e6 15 ♗c4 += M.Roeder-A.Carstens, German League 1987.

d) 9 ♗f1 ♘h7 (if 9...exd4 10 ♘xd4 ♖e8 11 f3 ♘f8 12 ♗e3 ♗d7 13 ♕d2 ♔h7 14 ♖ad1 += A.Rychagov-I.Filipov, Tula 2000) 10 dxe5 (or 10 ♗e3 f5 11 exf5 gxf5

12 dxe5 dxe5 13 ♕d5+ ♔h8 14 ♖ad1 e4 15 ♘d4 c6 16 ♕d6 ♘e5 17 ♘db5 += A.Allen-M.Fuller, Australian Ch. 1991) 10...dxe5 11 ♗e3 ♘hf6 12 h3 c6 13 b4 ♕c7 14 ♕c2 ♘h5 15 ♖ad1 ♖e8 16 ♘d2 ♘f8 17 c5 ♗e6 18 ♘c4 += M.Bee-K.Scharff, German League 1988.

9...dxe5 10 ♕c2

If now 10 ♗f1 c6 11 h3 ♕e7 12 ♗e3 ♘c5 13 ♕c2 ♘e8 intending ...♘e6 with counterplay, M.Szymanski-V.Teterev, World Junior Ch. 1995; or 10 h3 c6 11 ♗e3 ♕e7 12 ♕c2 ♘h5 13 ♕d2 ♘f4 14 ♗xf4 exf4 15 ♕xf4 ♕b4 with compensation, B.Ivkov-M.Chiburdanidze, Vienna 1993.

10...c6 11 ♖b1 ♖e8 12 b4 ♘f8 13 h3 ♘h5 14 c5 ♘e6 15 ♘a4 ♘hf4 16 ♗f1 ♕f6 (D)

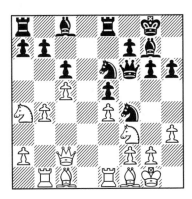

White stands slightly better with more space and plans the manoeuvre ♘b2-c4-d6. Meanwhile Black will try to further his kingside ambitions by advancing his pawns.

The game K.Panczyk-A.Lanc, Poznan 1985, continued **17 ♖b3** [reinforcing the third rank, thus preventing any tactics with ...♘xh3] **17...g5 18 a3?!**

[stronger was 18 ♖a3, threatening ♘b6, and if 18...♘c7 19 ♖d1 +/=] **18...♘c7** [the immediate 18...h5! was more accurate with good counterplay] **19 ♘b2 h5 20 ♖be3** [20 ♘c4!? g4 21 ♘d6 gxf3 22 ♘xe8 ♘xe8 23 ♖xf3 came into consideration] **20...g4 21 hxg4 hxg4 22 ♘h2 ♕g6 23 ♘c4 ♘b5 24 a4 ♘d4 25 ♕d1 ♗e6 26 ♘d6 ♖ed8 27 ♗b2 ♘h5** [if 27...♗f8 28 ♖g3 ♗xd6 29 ♘xg4 with the initiative] **28 g3 b6** [trying to undermine the d6-knight; if instead 28...a5 29 bxa5 ♖xa5 30 ♗d3 ♖d7 31 ♗xd4 exd4 32 e5 ♕g5 33 ♖3e2 ♗f8 34 ♕c2 +=] **29 ♗xd4 exd4 30 ♖d3 bxc5 31 bxc5 ♗e5?** [Black had to try 31...♕g5 32 ♗e2 ♘f6 33 e5 ♕xe5 34 ♗xg4 ♕xc5 35 ♘b7 ♕c4! 36 ♘xd8 ♖xd8 37 ♗xe6 fxe6 and if 38 ♘g4 ♘xg4! 39 ♕xg4 ♕xd3 40 ♕xe6+ ♔h8 41 ♔g2 ♕h7 42 ♖h1 (or 42 ♖e4 ♕d1+ 43 ♔g2 ♕h5) 42...♕xh1+ 43 ♔xh1 d3 ∞] **32 ♘f5! ♗xf5?** [32...♖e8 +/- was necessary; the text just loses] **33 exf5 ♕xf5 34 ♘xg4 ♗g7 35 ♖e5! ♕g6 36 ♖xh5! ♖e8 37 ♖h4 ♖ab8 38 ♘h2 ♖b4 39 ♘f3 ♖eb8 40 ♘xd4 1-0.**

D2: 8...♖e8 *(D)*

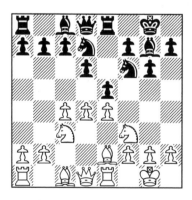

Black increases the latent pressure on the e4-pawn.

9 d5

A very logical move: as we have already mentioned, Black's rook stands badly on e8 in this type of position, and it is not out of the question that the rook will have to return to f8 at some point to support counterplay on the kingside.

The alternative is 9 ♗f1 and then:

a) 9...h6 is similar to line D1 (8...h6), though ♗f1 is slightly more useful than ...♖e8; e.g. 10 dxe5 dxe5 11 h3 c6 12 ♗e3 ♕e7 13 ♕c2 ♘h5 14 ♖ad1 ♘f8 15 c5 +/= C.Krings-M.Ivanov, Baden Baden 2001.

b) 9...c6 10 d5 (again emphasizing the misplaced e8-rook; White has less chance of an advantage after other moves) 10...c5 (compare line B2) 11 a3 (11 g3 is also good) 11...♖f8 12 b4 ♘e8 13 g3 h6 14 ♘h4 += M.Christoffel-I.Boleslavsky, Groningen 1946.

c) 9...a6!? 10 d5 a5 has the idea that White's extra ♗f1 on the main line has merely put his bishop on a worse square. Therefore in L.D.Nisipeanu-V.Chernov, Rumania 1999, White elected to return the tempo with 11 ♗d3!? ♘h5 (if 11...♘c5 12 ♗c2 followed by a2-a3, ♖b1 and b2-b4 +=) 12 ♗e3 ♗f6!? 13 a3 ♗e7 14 b4 ♘g7 15 ♕c2 b6 16 ♘b5 ♖f8 17 c5!.

d) 9...exd4 may be the best option. Black must practically give up any ideas of ...c7-c6 and ...d6-d5, but his position is quite difficult to break down: 10 ♘xd4 ♘c5 (instead 10...c6! transposes to *8...c6 9 ♗f1 exd4 10 ♘xd4*

♖e8 in the notes to line D33) 11 f3 c6 12 ♗e3 a5 13 b3! (otherwise Black plays ...a5-a4; e.g. 13 ♕d2 a4 14 ♖ab1 ♘fd7 15 b4 axb3 16 axb3 ♘e5 17 ♖ed1 ♕e7 18 ♔h1 f5 ∞ Z.Gyimesi-E.Miroshnichenko, German League 2004) 13...♘fd7 (not 13...d5?! 14 exd5 cxd5 15 ♘db5 ♘a6 16 cxd5 ♘b4 17 d6 ♗f5 18 ♖c1 ♖xe3 19 ♖xe3 ♗h6 20 ♖e1 ♖c8, I.Nei-T.V.Petrosian, USSR Junior Ch. 1946, 21 ♕d4 +-) 14 ♕d2 ♗e5 15 ♖ad1 h5 16 g3 ♕e7 17 f4 ♗g7 18 ♗g2 += J.Pelikan-J.Rubinetti, Argentine Ch. 1968.

9...♘h5 *(D)*

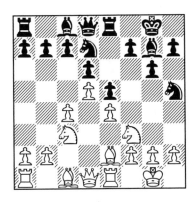

Black prepares ...f7-f5. Other play is based on building a secure outpost on c5 for the d7-knight. The variations are similar to those after 8 d5, but with the moves ♖e1 and ...♖e8 inserted which must favour White.

a) 9...h6 10 ♕c2 a5 11 ♘d2 ♘h7 12 ♘f1 ♖f8 13 ♗e3 f5 14 exf5 gxf5 15 f4 +/= R.Peiffer-L.Guillard, corr. 1956.

b) 9...a5 10 ♗g5 h6 11 ♗h4 g5 12 ♗g3 ♘h5 13 ♘d2 ♘f4 14 ♗g4 ♘c5 15 ♗xc8 ♕xc8 16 ♘f1 +/= M.Najdorf-U.Andersson, Wijk aan Zee 1971.

c) 9...♘c5 deserves attention, e.g. 10

♗f1 (10 ♗g5 h6 11 ♗xf6 ♕xf6 12 b4 ♘d7 13 ♘d2 a6 14 ♕c2 h5 with counterplay, S.Lputian-A.Bykhovsky, USSR Cup 1984) 10...a5 11 g3 ♖f8 12 ♗g5 ♗d7 13 ♕d2 ♕c8 14 ♘h4 ♘g4 15 ♕e2 f6 16 ♗d2 f5 17 f3 ♘f6 18 exf5 gxf5 19 ♗h3 ♔h8 20 ♗e3 b6 21 ♖f1 ♘g8 22 ♕c2 ♘e7 23 ♗g5 ½-½ A.Vaisser-V.Gurevich, Cappelle la Grande 1994.

10 ♗g5

In contrast to 8 d5 ♘h5 (in the notes to line A), there is no need for 10 g3 here, as ...♘f4 can be answered by ♗f1.

10...♗f6

10...f6 11 ♗e3 is just good for White as there is no ...♘g4, while 11...♗f8 12 ♕d2 (or 12 b4) 12...♗e7 13 b4 ♘g7, S.Akter-H.Koneru, Doha (rapid) 2006, was similar to the game with an extra ♕d2 for White.

11 ♗e3 ♗e7

Clearing the way for the f-pawn again.

12 b4

More logical than 12 ♕d2 ♘g7 13 ♕c2 f5 14 ♖ad1 (14 exf5!?) 14...f4 15 ♗c1 g5 with counterplay, R.Laxman-H.Koneru, Commonwealth Ch., Mumbai 2004.

12...♘g7 13 ♖c1

White might have counted on an advantage after 13 ♕b3!? intending 13...f5 14 c5, e.g. 14...♘f6 15 ♗b5 ♖f8 16 ♘xe5 dxe5 17 d6+.

13...f5 14 ♗h6 ♘f6 15 ♘d2 ♔h8 16 ♗f3 ♘g8 17 ♗xg7+ ♔xg7 *(D)*

This position was reached in C.Bauer-V.Bologan, French Team Ch. 2005. White's queenside initiative is more advanced, but Black has counterplay on the kingside and in the centre, as well as the two bishops. The game was later drawn after mutual (presumably time-induced) mistakes.

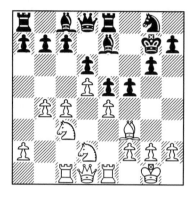

D3: 8...c6 *(D)*

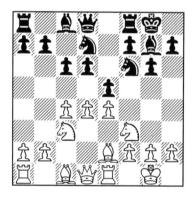

The most flexible and popular move, played over 60% of the time – and that doesn't include games reaching the same position via different routes. The main difference to the equivalent 7...♘a6 line (other than ...♗g4 being impossible) is that the advance d4-d5 will create the threat of d5xc6 as the d6-pawn is unprotected.

9 ♗f1 *(D)*

And this is the most popular reply (played in over 80% of games). White cannot expect much after such moves as:

a) 9 h3 exd4! (after any passive move the exchange on d4 is usually the best solution for Black, as he practically gains a tempo) 10 ♘xd4 ♖e8 11 ♗d3 a5 12 ♘f3 ♘c5 13 ♗f4 ♘h5 14 ♗g5 ♗f6 ∞ O.Saether-O.Reeh, Gausdal 1992.

b) 9 b3 exd4 10 ♘xd4 ♖e8 11 ♗f1 ♘g4 12 f3 ♕a5 13 ♘ce2 ♘gf6 14 ♗d2 ♕d8 15 ♗g5 d5 16 cxd5 cxd5 17 ♘c3 ♕a5 18 ♕d2 dxe4 19 ♘xe4 ♕xd2 20 ♘xd2 ♘b6 21 ♘c4 ♘xc4 ½-½ R.Har Zvi-I.Smirin, Zagreb 1993.

c) 9 ♖b1 exd4 (otherwise 9...a5 10 ♗f1 transposes to *9 ♗f1 a5 10 ♖b1*) 10 ♘xd4 ♖e8 (10...♘c5 is also possible, as in the notes to line C21 in Chapter Six) 11 f3 (or if 11 ♗f1 ♘g4! – see *9 ♗f1 exd4 10 ♘xd4 ♖e8 11 ♖b1 ♘g4*) 11...d5! 12 cxd5 cxd5 13 ♗g5 dxe4 14 fxe4 h6 15 ♗h4 (H.Corral-I.Boleslavsky, Montevideo 1954) 15...♕b6 ∞.

d) 9 d5 is a logical response to ...c7-c6, but is perhaps a little premature; e.g. 9...♘c5 10 ♕c2 (10 ♗f1 a5 transposes to *9 ♗f1 a5 10 d5 ♘c5*, while if 10 ♗g5 cxd5 11 cxd5 h6 12 ♗xf6 ♕xf6 13 b4 ♘d7 ∞ Sr.Cvetkovic-Z.Ilincic, Kladovo 1994) 10...a5 11 ♗e3 cxd5 12 cxd5 ♘h5 13 ♗xc5 dxc5 14 ♘a4 b6 15 ♕b3 ♗d7 16 ♗b5 ♖b8 17 ♘c3 ♘f4 18 g3 ♘h3+ 19 ♔g2 ♗c8 20 ♖ad1 ♔h8 21 ♖d2 ½-½ I.Porat-J.Radovanovic, Port Erin 2003.

e) 9 ♗e3!? deserves attention though; e.g. 9...♘g4 (if 9...♖e8 10 d5 c5 11.♖b1 ♘g4 12.♗g5 f6 13.♗d2 ♘h6

14.a3 ♘f7 15.♕c2 ♘f8 16.b4 +=
G.Stahlberg-O.Troianescu, Budapest
1952; or 9...exd4 10 ♘xd4 ♖e8 11 f3 d5
12 cxd5 cxd5, J.E.Martinez-J.Iliesco,
Argentine Ch. 1947, 13 ♘db5 fxe4 14
♘d6 +=) 10 ♗g5 f6 11 ♗h4 ♘h6 (or
11...h5 12 h3 ♘h6 13 dxe5 dxe5 14 b4
♕c7 15 c5 +/= M.Melnichuk-
S.Pervakov, Ukrainian Team Ch. 2006)
12 d5 ♕e7 13 b4 g5 14 ♗g3 f5 15 exf5
♘xf5 (B.Fiedler-M.Necada, Czech
League 1998) 16 ♘e4 +/=.

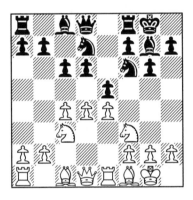

D31: 9...♕c7 *182*
D32: 9...a5 *185*
D33: 9...exd4 *189*

Black has also occasionally tried:

a) 9...♖e8 10 d5 c5 (if 10...♕c7 11 b4!
cxd5 12 ♘b5 ♕b8 13 cxd5 a6 14 ♘c3 +=
N.Rashkovsky-R.Kempinski, Biel 2001;
or 10...cxd5 11 cxd5 a5 12 ♗g5 h6 13
♗h4 g5 14 ♗g3 ♘h5 15 ♘d2 +/=
M.Taimanov-M.Aaron, Amsterdam
1964) 11 a3 ♘h5 (11...♖f8 12 b4 ♘e8 13
♖b1 h6 14 ♘d2 f5 15 ♘b3 f4 16 bxc5
♘xc5 17 ♘xc5 dxc5 18 a4 with the initiative, M.Taimanov-V.Liberzon, Moscow 1964) 12 g3 b6 13 ♖b1 h6 14 ♗d2
♘df6 15 b4 +/= W.Golz-T.Ghitescu,
Zinnowitz 1964.

b) 9...♘g4 10 d5 (otherwise 10 h3
exd4 11 ♘xd4 transposes to *9...exd4 10
♘xd4 ♘g4 11 h3* in the notes to line
C33) 10...c5 (if 10...♕b6 11 ♕c2 f5 12 h3
♘h6 13 ♘g5 ♘c5 14 ♗e3 ♕d8 15 ♖ad1
+= K.Berg-T.Utasi, Budapest 1983) 11 a3
h6 (if 11...f5 12 h3 ♘gf6 13 ♘g5 ♘b6 14
b4 ♘b6 15 ♘e6 +/- Pytel) 12 g3 ♘gf6
(not 12...f5? 13 ♘h4 +/-) 13 ♕c2 ♔h7 14
b4 b6 15 ♖b1 ♘g8 16 ♗d3 ♘e7 17 ♗d2
+/= G.Sosonko-H.Camara, Sao Paulo
1978.

c) 9...♕b6!? 10 d5 (instead 10 h3
exd4 11 ♘xd4 ♘g4 is *9...exd4 10 ♘xd4
♘g4 11 h3 ♕b6* in line C33 again; or
similarly 10 ♖b1 exd4 11 ♘xd4 ♘g4 12
♕xg4 ♗xd4 13 ♗e3 ♗xe3 14 ♖xe3 ♘e5,
A.Saric-Z.Arsovic, Zupanja 2007, 15
♕h4 +=) 10...♘c5 (or 10...♘g4 – *9...♘g4
10 d5 ♕b6*) 11 ♖b1 (if 11 dxc6?! bxc6 12
♕xd6 ♖d8 13 ♕e7 ♖e8 forces a draw)
11...cxd5 (or 11...a5 12 b3 ♗d7 13 ♗a3
cxd5 14 cxd5 ♘g4 15 ♖b2 f5 16 ♘a4! +/-
K.Commons-S.Reshevsky, US Ch.
1974) 12 cxd5 ♘g4 (if 12...a5 13 h3 ♗d7
14 ♗e3 a4 15 ♘d2 ♕c7 16 ♖c1 ♖fc8 17
b4 axb3 18 ♘xb3 +/= V.Hort-
S.Reshevsky, Petropolis Interzonal
1973) 13 ♕c2 (not 13 b4? ♘xf2! 14 ♕c2
♘cxe4 15 ♘xe4 ♘g4+ 16 ♔h1 f5 17 ♘c5
e4 18 h3 exf3 19 hxg4 dxc5 20 bxc5 ♕d8
-+ O.Korchagin-A.Kochyev, Tallinn
2000) 13...f5 14 h3 ♘f6 15 ♗e3 +=.

d) 9...♕e7 10 d5 (instead 10 ♖b1 a5
11 d5 transposes, but Black can also
play 10...exd4!? 11 ♘xd4 a5 12 ♗f4 ♖e8

13 ♕d2 ♘c5 14 f3 ♘fd7 15 ♖bd1 ♗e5 ∞ D.Adla-L.Bernal Moro, Corunna 1995) 10...a5 (or 10...c5 11 a3 h6 12 b4 b6 13 g3 ♔h7 14 ♘h4 ♘g8 15 ♖b1 += I.Nemet-V.Garabedian, Biel 1993) 11 ♖b1 ♘c5 12 b3 ♗d7 (if 12...♗g4 13 h3 ♗xf3?! 14 ♕xf3 += P.Kiss-A.Szittar, Hungarian Team Ch. 1995) 13 a3 cxd5 14 cxd5 ♖fc8 15 ♘d2 a4 16 b4 ♘d3 17 ♗xd3 ♖xc3 18 ♕e2 +/= E.Arlandi-E.Grivas, European Rapid Ch., Athens 1997.

e) 9...h6 10 ♖b1 (or again 10 d5!?, and if 10...c5 11 g3 ♘e8 12 ♘h4 += C.Niklasson-D.Uddenfeldt, Swedish Ch. 1975) 10...♘h7 (instead 10...a5 transposes to *9...a5 10 ♖b1 h6*; or Black might prefer 10...exd4 11 ♘xd4 ♖e8 12 ♘c2, V.Cengija-R.Bulajic, Sremska Mitrovica 2006, 12...♕e7 with counterplay) 11 b4 (or 11 d5 c5, H.Steingrimsson-A.Kveinys, Reykjavik 1994, 12 ♘b5!? ♘b6 13 b4 cxb4 14 ♗e3 intending 14...f5 15 ♘xd6! ♕xd6 16 c5 +=) 11...♘g5 12 d5 ♘xf3+ 13 ♕xf3 c5 (D.Dumitrache-M.Saltaev, Cappelle la Grande 1998) 14 a3 f5 15 ♕g3 ♕f6 16 exf5 gxf5 17 ♗d2 +=.

f) 9...a6!? 10 d5 (if instead 10 ♖b1 b5!? 11 b4 exd4 12 ♘xd4 ♕c7 13 ♗e3, V.Epishin-A.Romero Holmes, Logrono 1991, 13...bxc4 14 ♗xc4 ♘e5 intending ...c6-c5 with counterplay) 10...c5 (or 10...cxd5 11 cxd5 b5 12 b4 ♘b6 13 a4 ♕c7 14 ♗d2 bxa4 15 ♘xa4 ♗d7 16 ♘xb6 ♕xb6 17 h3 += J.Pinter-I.Bilek, Hungarian Team Ch. 1993) 11 a3 ♘e8 12 b4 h6 (or 12...b6 13 ♕c2 f5 14 ♘g5 ♘df6 15 ♖b1 f4 16 ♘a4 ♗h6 17 ♘e6 ♗xe6 18 dxe6 ♘g7 19 e7 ♕xe7 20 ♘xb6 ♖a7 21 bxc5 dxc5 22 ♘d5 +/- L.Bass-

A.Romero Holmes, Leon 1990) 13 bxc5 dxc5 14 ♘a4 ♘d6 15 ♖b1 f5 16 ♘d2 ♖b8 17 ♗b2 += E.Postny-G.Ginsburg, Ashdod 2003.

D31: 9...♕c7 *(D)*

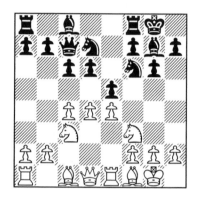

10 ♖b1

Naturally 10 d5 is still an option, but Black hasn't made any concessions as yet and so is well set up to meet it: 10...a5 (10...c5 seems less consistent, e.g. 11 a3 a6 12 b4 b6 13 ♖b1 ♘e8, E.Stauch-N.Assmann, Bayern 2000, 14 ♗e3 += intending 14...f5 15 exf5 gxf5 16 ♘g5 ♘df6 17 ♘e6 ♗xe6 18 dxe6 +/- or 14...h6 15 ♕d2 ♔h7 16 ♕c2) 11 ♖b1 ♘c5 12 b3 ♗d7 13 ♘d2 (or 13 ♗d2 cxd5 14 cxd5 b5 15 ♘xb5 ♗xb5 16 ♗xb5 ♘fxe4 17 ♗c6 ♖ab8 = O.Korneev-A.Strikovic, Ferrol 2002) 13...♖fb8 14 a3 cxd5 15 cxd5 b5 16 b4 axb4 17 ♖xb4 ♘a6 18 ♖b3 ♕a5 19 ♘db1 ♘c5 20 ♖b4 ♘a6 ½-½ N.Rashkovsky-A.Kremenietsky, Moscow 1982.

10...♖e8

Seeking to force White's hand. Otherwise Black can keep his options open with 10...a5! and then:

a) 11 d5 returns to 10 d5 a5 11 a3 above.

b) 11 a3 exd4 (alternatively 11...♖e8 12 d5 a4! transposes to *10...♖e8 11 d5 a5 12 a3* below) 12 ♞xd4 ♞c5 13 b4 axb4 14 axb4 ♞e6 15 ♞xe6 fxe6 (or 15...♗xe6 16.♗f4 ♖fd8 17.c5 ♞e8 18.♕c1 ♗e5 19.♗xe5 dxe5 = V.Harasta-S.Hazir, Bratislava 2003) 16 e5 dxe5 17 ♞e4 ♞xe4 18 ♖xe4 b6 19 c5 bxc5 20 bxc5 ♗a6 21 ♗xa6 ♖xa6 22 ♕b3 with compensation, M.Krisko-E.Meduna, Czechoslovakian Ch. 1972.

c) 11 b3 (avoiding ideas of ...a5-a4) 11...exd4!? (11...♖e8 12 d5 is *10...♖e8 11 d5 a5 12 b3* below; or if 11...♖d8 12 a3 ♞f8 13 d5 ♞g4 14 h3 ♞h6 15 b4 axb4 16 axb4 f5 17 ♞d2 ♞f7 18 ♞b3 f4 19 dxc6 bxc6 20 b5 +/= S.Gligoric-A.Bulat, Yugoslav Ch. 1953) 12 ♞xd4 ♞c5 13 a3 ♖e8 14 f3 ♞fd7 15 ♗e3 ♞e5 16 ♔h1 ♞e6 ∞ Z.Franco Ocampos-C.Ramo Frontinan, Alicante 1989.

11 d5 *(D)*

Logical and consistent now Black has played ...♖e8. Alternatively, the omission of ...a7-a5 means that White can play 11 b4!? straight away; e.g.

11...♞f8 (if 11...exd4 12 ♞xd4 a5 13 a3 axb4 14 axb4 +=, while 11...a6 12 d5! c5 13 a3 transposes to *11 d5 c5 12 a3 a6 13 b4* below) 12 d5 ♗d7 (or 12...♗g4 13 h3 ♗xf3 14 ♕xf3 ♞8d7 15 ♗e3 += N.Spiridonov-W.Dietze, Polanica Zdroj 1970) 13 ♗d2 h6 14 h3 a5 15 a3 axb4 16 axb4 ♖a3 17 ♖b3 ♖xb3 18 ♕xb3 +=.

11...c5

As we have seen, this is a typical move in such positions, but here White's prospects on the queenside look more real than Black's on the other side of the board. However, White has the better chances after other moves too:

a) 11...cxd5 12 cxd5 a6 13 ♗d2 b5 (or 13...h6 14 ♖c1 ♕d8 15 b4 ♖f8 16 g3 ♞e8 17 ♞h4 += V.Kozlov-G.Burnevsky, Jaroslavl 1975) 14 ♖c1 ♕b8 15 b4 ♞b6 16 a4 bxa4 17 ♞xa4 ♗d7 18 ♞c3 +/= J.Garriga Nualart-C.Herbrechtsmeier, corr. 1982.

b) 11...a5 12 b3! (not 12 a3?! a4! 13 ♞xa4 ♞xe4! 14 ♖xe4 ♖xa4 15 ♕xa4 ♞c5 16 ♖xe5 dxe5 17 ♕b4 ♞a6 18 ♕c3 ♗f5 19 ♖a1 cxd5 20 cxd5 ♕xc3 21 bxc3 ♖d8 =+ L.Radulov-R.Djurhuus, corr. 1988) 12...♞c5 13 a3 cxd5 (if 13...♗g4 14 b4 axb4 15 axb4 ♗xf3 16 ♕xf3 ♞a4 17 ♞d1 +/- S.Furman-M.Dvoretzky, Tbilisi 1973, or 15...♞a6 16 h3 ♗d7 17 dxc6 bxc6 18 ♗e3 +=) 14 cxd5 ♗d7 15 ♞d2 ♖f8 16 a4! (a noteworthy plan) 16...♞e8 17 ♗b5 f5 18 ♗xd7 ♕xd7 19 ♞c4 ♕f7 20 f3 fxe4 21 ♞xe4 ♞xe4 22 fxe4 ♕f2+ 23 ♔h1 ♕h4 24 ♕e2 +/- Wl.Schmidt-F.Trois, Buenos Aires Olympiad 1978.

12 a3

12 ♞h4!? is another option, e.g.

12...♘f8 13 g3 ♕e7 14 a3 ♘h5 15 ♘f5! gxf5 16 ♕xh5 fxe4 (E.Eliskases-C.Dominguez, Argentine Ch. 1950) 17 ♘xe4 ♘g6 (not 17...f5? 18 ♘xd6!) 18 b4 +/-.

12...a6

No better are:

a) 12...♘f8 13 b4 b6 14 ♘d2 ♗d7 15 ♘b3 ♕d8 16 f3 ♘h5 17 ♗e3 += M.Ziembinski-P.Martin, World Seniors Ch. 2000.

b) 12...♕d8 13 b4 h6 14 ♗d2 ♔h7 15 ♕c2 += V.Tukmakov-M.Schmid, Zürich 1997.

c) 12...♖f8 13 b4 ♘e8 14 ♗e3 b6 15 h3 h6 16 ♕d2 ♔h7 17 g3 (or 17 ♕c2 +=) 17...♕d8 18 ♘h4 +=, though 18...♘df6 ½-½ A.Botsari-E.Fahiridou, Greek Team Ch. 2004.

13 b4 ♖f8 (D)

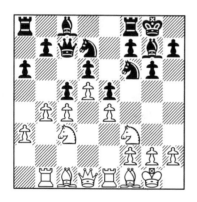

We are following P.Kotsur-L.Dominguez, FIDE World Ch., Moscow 2001. White is now two tempi up on the 10 d5 c5 variation, having already achieved ♖b1 and b2-b4 while Black moved his rook f8-e8-f8.

14 h3

Using one of his 'spare' moves to secure e3 for the bishop. Another idea is 14 ♘a4!? b6 (if 14...cxb4!? 15 axb4 a5 16 c5) 15 bxc5 bxc5 16 ♗d2 +=, e.g. 17...♗b7 17 ♗c3 ♖fb8 18 ♘d2 ♗c8 19 ♘b3 ♕d8 20 ♘a5 ♖xb1 21 ♕xb1 ♖b8 22 ♕c2 ♕f8 23 ♖b1 ♖a8 24 ♘c6 ♘e8 25 ♗a5 f5? 26 exf5 gxf5 27 ♕xf5 +- R.Cruz-J.Bolbochan, Buenos Aires 1965.

14...♘e8 15 ♗e3 h6

Not yet 15...f5? 16 exf5 gxf5 17 ♘g5 +/-.

16 ♘d2?!

Making ready for the forthcoming ...f7-f5, but in fact White can prevent it altogether with a noteworthy motif: 16 ♕d2 ♔h7 17 ♕c2 followed by 18 ♗d3, since 17...f5? runs into 18 exf5 gxf5 19 ♘h4, e.g. 19...cxb4 20 axb4 ♘b6 21 ♗xb6! ♕xb6 22 ♗d3 e4 23 ♘xe4! fxe4 24 ♗xe4+ ♔h8 (if 24...♔g8? 25 ♗h7+ ♔h8 26 ♘g6+) 25 ♘g6+ ♔g8 26 ♘xf8 ♔xf8 27 ♗f5 with a decisive attack.

16...f5 17 f3?!

17 exf5 gxf5 18 ♘b3 was better, though Black can try 18...b5!? ∞.

17...f4 18 ♗f2 g5 19 ♘b3 b6 (D)

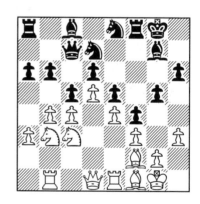

The situation from move 11 has been overturned: while White's queenside initiative has stalled, Black now has a free hand on the kingside.

The game concluded **20 ♘a2 h5 21 a4 a5 22 bxa5 bxa5 23 ♘c3 ♘df6 24 ♗e2 ♖f7 25 ♘d2 ♗f8 26 ♘f1 g4 27 fxg4 hxg4 28 hxg4 ♖h7 29 g5 ♕g7! 30 gxf6 ♕h6 31 f7+ ♔xf7 32 ♗h5+ ♕xh5** [32...♔g8 33 g3] **33 ♕xh5+ ♖xh5 34 ♘h2 ♗a6 35 ♘b5 ♗e7 36 ♖b3 ♖d8** [36...♘f6! since if 37 ♘c7 ♗xc4! 38 ♖c3 ♖ah8 wins] **37 ♖h3 ♖xh3 38 gxh3 ♗c8 39 ♔g2 ♘f6 40 ♘f3 ♖g8+ 41 ♔h2 ♖h8 42 ♗h4?!** [42 h4 was necessary] **42...♘e8 43 ♗xe7 ♔xe7** [or first 43...♖xh3+] **44 ♘g1 ♘f6 45 ♘a7 ♘g4+ 46 ♔h1 ♗d7 47 ♖b1 ♗xa4 48 ♖b7+ ♔f6 49 ♖b6 ♘f2+ 50 ♔g2 ♘xe4 51 ♘f3 ♖g8+ 52 ♔f1 ♖g3 53 ♔e2 ♗e8 54 ♘h2 ♖xh3 55 ♘g4+ ♔g5 56 ♘xe5 ♗h5+ 57 ♔f1 dxe5 0-1**.

D32: 9...a5 (D)

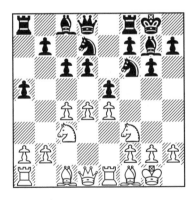

A flexible move, useful in various structures.

10 dxe5

White plans to target the queenside dark squares weakened by ...c7-c6 and ...a7-a5, while forestalling any future

...e5xd4. The numerous other options give Black fewer problems:

a) 10 h3 exd4 (the usual comfortable response to inactive moves) 11 ♘xd4 ♖e8 12 ♗f4 ♘c5 13 ♕c2 ♘h5 14 ♗e3 ♘f6 15 ♗f4 ♘h5 16 ♗e3 ♘f6 ½-½ G.Sosonko-M.Tal, Biel Interzonal 1976.

b) 10 b3 exd4 11 ♘xd4 ♘g4 12 f3 (if 12 ♕xg4 ♗xd4 13 ♕g3 f5! =+ E.Gereben-R.Wirthensohn, Bern 1974) 12...♕b6 13 ♘ce2 c5!? 14 fxg4 (White might try 14 ♘c2!? ♗xa1 15 ♘xa1 with compensation) 14...cxd4 15 ♘f4 ♘e5 ∞ S.Halkias-H.Banikas, Kavala 1995.

c) 10 ♗e3 ♘g4 11 ♗g5 f6 12 ♗h4 ♘h6 13 ♘a4 (G.Kuzmin-M.Dvoretzky, USSR 1976) 13...g5! 14 ♗g3 f5 with counterplay.

d) 10 ♗g5 h6 11 ♗h4 ♖e8 12 d5 ♘c5 13 b3 ♕c7 14 ♖c1 ♘h5 15 a3 (G.Linn-M.Dvoretzky, Saint John 1988) 15...g5!? 16 ♗g3 ♘xg3 17 hxg3 f5 with counterplay.

e) 10 d5 ♘c5 11 b3 cxd5 12 cxd5 ♗d7 13 ♘d2 (or 13 ♗g5 h6 14 ♗xf6 ♕xf6 15 ♘d2 ♕e7 16 ♗c4 f5 17 ♕e2, R.Pogorelov-J.Calvo Sanchez, Coria del Rio 1995, 17...♖ad8!? 18 ♗b5 ♗c8 ∞) 13...♘e8 14 a4 f5 15 ♘c4 ♘xe4 16 ♘xe4 fxe4 17 ♗e3 ♘f6 ∞ C.Incutto-M.Najdorf, Argentine Ch. 1960.

f) 10 ♖b1 is the main alternative (also arising via 9 ♖b1 a5 10 ♗f1) and is actually more popular than the text.

Now moves such as 10...♕b6 or 10...♕e7 return after 11 d5 to the equivalent 9th move variations. More usually Black plays one of the following:

f1) 10...h6 11 a3 (the immediate 11

d5 is met by 11...♘c5) 11...♘h7 (or 11...exd4 12 ♘xd4 ♖e8 13 f3 ♘c5 14 b4 axb4 15 axb4 ♘e6 16 ♗e3 += J.Stanke-K.Movsziszian, Hamburg 1992) 12 d5 (if 12 b4 axb4 13 axb4 f5 14 exf5 gxf5 15 dxe5 dxe5 16 ♘e2 e4 = U.Andersson-J.Mestel, London Phillips & Drew 1982) 12...c5 (not 12...♕c7 13 ♗e3 f5? 14 exf5 gxf5 15 ♘b5! cxb5 16 ♕d5+ ♔h8 17 ♘h4! +-) 13 ♘b5 ♕e7 14 g3 ♘df6 15 ♗g2 ♘e8 16 ♗d2 f5 17 ♘h4 ♕f7 18 exf5 gxf5 19 f4 +/- D.Barria-F.Barranco Cara, El Ejido 2007.

f2) 10...♖e8 11 d5! (if 11 a3 exd4 12 ♘xd4 a4! 13 f3 ♘c5 14 ♗e3 ♘fd7 ∞ T.Bosboom Lanchava-E.Kovalevskaya, Groningen 1999; or 11 b3 exd4 12 ♘xd4 ♘g4! 13 f3 ♕b6 14 ♘ce2 ♘ge5 15 ♗e3 ♘c5 ∞ L.Portisch-O.Panno, World Student Team Ch. 1958; or 11 dxe5 ♘xe5! 12 ♘xe5 dxe5 13 ♕xd8 ♖xd8 14 ♗g5 ♗e6 15 ♘a4, J.Johannes-M.Bertram, corr. 2000, 15...h6 16 ♗e3 ♘d7 =) 11...♘c5 (11...♕c7 returns to 9...♕c7 10 ♖b1 ♖e8 11 d5 a5 in line D31) 12 b3 (D) and then:

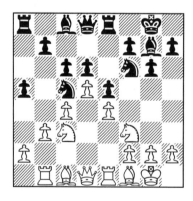

f21) 12...cxd5 13 cxd5 ♗d7 14 ♘d2 ♖f8 15 a4! ♘e8 16 ♗a3 (or 16 ♗b5 ♗xb5 17 ♘xb5 ♘d3 18 ♖e3 ♘xc1 19 ♖xc1 f5 20 ♖ec3 += J.Adamski-R.Knaak, Polanica Zdroj 1976) 16...♖c8 17 ♘c4 f5 18 b4 ♘xe4 19 ♘xe4 fxe4 20 bxa5 +/- I.Farago-Y.Rantanen, Helsinki 1981.

f22) 12...♖f8 13 a3 cxd5 14 cxd5 ♗d7 15 ♘d2 (if 15 b4 axb4 16 axb4 ♘a4 17 ♕b3 ♕c7 18 ♗d2 ♘xc3 19 ♗xc3 ♕b6 ∞ G.Cabrera-M.Tal, Las Palmas 1977) 15...♘e8 16 a4! is good even a tempo down, e.g. 16...f5 17 ♘c4 b6? 18 b4! axb4 19 ♖xb4 +/- L.Stein-L.Vadasz, Vrnjacka Banja 1971.

f23) 12...♗d7 13 dxc6 (if 13 a3 cxd5 14 cxd5 b5! ∞ Wl.Schmidt-R.Knaak, Pula 1975, or 13 ♘d2 ♘h5! 14 g3 f5 ∞ W.Kaiser-J.Pohl Kümmel, German League 1993) 13...♗xc6 14 ♕c2 ♖c8 15 ♗a3 ♕b6 16 ♖bd1 ♗f8 (this not only protects the d6-pawn but also prepares a cunning trap based on the motif of a very long x-ray f8-a3) 17 ♗c1 (17 g3? walks into 17...♘cxe4 18 ♘xe4 ♗xe4 19 ♖xe4 ♘xe4 20 ♕xe4 d5 21 ♖xd5 ♗xa3 -/+ T.Baklanova-E.Kovalevskaya, Melitopol 1992; and 17 ♕b1?, Wl.Schmidt-A.Maciejewski, Polish Ch. 1980, fails to the same combination) 17...h6 (if 17...a4 18 ♗g5! axb3 19 axb3 ♘fd7 20 ♖b1 ♘e6 21 ♗e3 ♕c7 22 b4 +/- N.Titorenko-E.Kovalevskaya, Russian Women's Ch. 1994) 18 ♗d2 ♕a7 (now if 18...a4? 19 b4! +/-) 19 ♕b1 ♕a8 20 ♖c1 b5!? 21 ♘d5 ♘xd5 22 cxd5 ♗d7 23 ♗e3 ♔h7 24 ♘d2 += S.Ionov-E.Kovalevskaya, St Petersburg 2000.

f3) 10...exd4 (a sensible response, since ...a7-a5 is more useful than ♖b1) 11 ♘xd4 ♖e8 (11...♘c5 12 f3 ♖e8 transposes, or if 12 ♗g5 h6 13 ♗h4 ♕b6 14

♕d2 ♖e8 15 ♗xf6 ♗xf6 16 ♘f3 ♗g4! 17 ♕xh6 ♗xf3 18 gxf3 ♘e6 with compensation, Comp Rebel-G.Ligterink, The Hague 1993; but not 11...♘g4?! 12 ♕xg4 ♗xd4 13 ♕g3 ♘c5, R.Markus-N.Sedlak, Budapest 2002, 14 ♗f4 ♖e8 15 ♖bd1! ♗xc3 16 ♕xc3 ♘xe4 17 ♕d4 +/-) 12 f3 (D) (if 12 ♗g5 a4 13 f3 ♘c5 14 ♕d2 ♕a5 15 ♔h1 ♘e6 16 ♗e3, A.Riazantsev-R.Weill, Cap d'Agde 2002, 16...♘d7 ∞; or 12 ♘c2!? ♕e7 13 ♗f4 ♘e5 14 ♕d2 +/= F.Baumbach-C.Syre, East Germany 1977) and now:

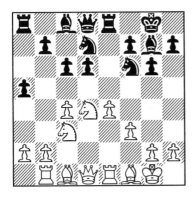

f31) 12...d5?! 13 exd5! (the simplest and best move) 13...♖xe1 14 ♕xe1 cxd5 15 ♗e3 dxc4 (Ftacnik's 15...♘e5 fails to 16 ♖d1 ♘xc4 17 ♗xc4 dxc4 18 ♘c6 +/-, or if 15...♘b6 16 ♖d1 with the same idea) 16 ♖d1 ♕f8 17 ♘db5 ♘c5 18 ♕f2 b6 19 ♗xc4 ♗a6 20 ♘d6 and Black has problems, B.Ivkov-M.Pavlovic, New York Open 1987.

f32) 12...♘c5 13 ♗e3 ♘fd7 (if 13...♘h5 14 ♕d2 f5 15 exf5 gxf5 16 ♖bd1 ♕f6, R.Servat-A.Sorin, Argentine Ch. 1995, 17 ♘c2 +=) 14 ♕d2 ♕c7 (or 14...♘e5 15 h3 f5 16 exf5 gxf5 17 f4 +/= U.Andersson-J.Nunn, Johannesburg

1981) 15 ♔h1 (if 15 ♗h6, A.Panchenko-A.Kuzmin, Kiev 1986, 15...♗xh6 16 ♕xh6 ♕b6 17 ♔h1 ♘d3 18 ♗xd3 ♕xd4 = Ftacnik; or 15 b3 ♘e5 16 ♖bc1, S.Milanovic-B.Rakic, Mataruska Banja 2007, 16...♗d7 ∞) 15...♘e5 16 ♖bd1 ♗f8 17 ♗h6 ♗xh6 18 ♕xh6 f6 19 ♕d2 ♘f7 20 b3 with persistent pressure, V.Kramnik-W.Watson, German League 1994, though Black remains very solid.

10...dxe5

Simpler is 10...♘xe5! 11 ♘xe5 dxe5 12 ♕c2 (if 12 ♕xd8 ♖xd8 13 ♗e3 ♗e6 14 ♖ad1 ♘d7 15 ♖d2 f5 16 ♖ed1 ♗f6 17 f3 ♔g7 18 exf5 gxf5 19 f4 exf4 20 ♗xf4 ♘c5 ∞ U.Ritter-H.Höcker, Recklinghausen 1995) 12...♗e6 13 ♖d1 ♕e7 14 ♗e3 ♘d7 (or 14...♖fd8!? =) 15 ♖d2 f5 16 f3 (if 16 exf5 gxf5 17 f3 ♘c5 ∞) 16...f4 17 ♗f2 g5 with counterplay, R.Sakic-F.Balabaev, corr. 2003.

11 ♘a4 (D)

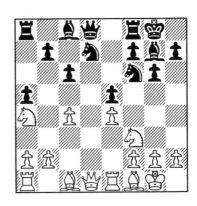

Planning to control the queenside dark squares with c4-c5.

11...♕e7

Black has also tried:

a) 11...♕c7 12 c5 ♘h5 13 ♗e3 ♖b8 14 ♘d2 ♘df6 15 f3 ♗e6 16 ♘c4 ♘e8 17

♕d2 f5 (Peng Zhaoqin-E.Kovalevskaya, Rethymnon 2003) 18 exf5 gxf5 19 ♕xa5 +/-.

b) 11...♖e8 12 c5 ♗f8 13 ♕c2 ♕e7 14 b3! (or 14 ♗e3 ♘g4 15 ♗g5 f6 16 ♗d2 ♘xc5 17 ♘b6 ♖b8 18 h3 ♘h6 19 b4! ♘a6 20 ♘xc8 ♖exc8 21 bxa5 +/- A.Shariyazdanov-S.Sale, Oberwart 2002) and if 14...♘xc5? (or 14...♖b8 15 ♗b2 ♘xc5? 16 ♗xe5 +-) 15 ♗a3 ♘fd7 16 ♖ac1 b6 17 ♘xb6 ♘xb6 18 ♗xc5 ♕xc5 19 ♕xc5 ♗xc5 20 ♖xc5 with a winning endgame (Shariyazdanov/Lisenko)

c) 11...♘e8 12 ♗e3 ♘c7 13 ♕c2 ♘e6 14 ♖ad1 followed by 15 c5 +=, since if 14...c5?? 15 ♘xc5 ♘exc5 16 ♗xc5 +- I.Jelen-O.Orel, Slovenian Ch. 1992.

d) 11...b6!? 12 ♕d6 (if 12 ♕c2 ♗a6! 13 b3 b5 14 ♘b2 ♕e7 ∞ R.Huerta-G.Garcia Gonzales, Cienfuegos 1980; but White might try 12 c5!? b5 13 ♘b6 ♘xb6 14 ♕xd8 ♖xd8 15 cxb6 +=) 12...♘c5! (if 12...♗b7 13 ♘xe5, or 12...♖a7 13 c5!) 13 ♕xd8 ♖xd8 14 ♘xb6 (or 14 ♘xc5 bxc5) 14...♖b8 15 ♘xc8 ♖dxc8 with compensation.

12 ♕c2 b6

White is better after other moves too:

a) 12...♖e8 13 c5 ♘h5 (13...♗f8 is line 'b' in the previous note) 14 ♗g5 f6 15 ♗e3 ♘f4 16 ♘d2 +/- F.Schirm-W.Rostalski, Bargteheide 1988.

b) 12...♘e8 13 c5 ♘c7 14 ♗g5 f6 15 ♗e3 ♔h8 16 ♘d2 (or 16 ♖ad1 +=) 16...f5 17 f3 f4 18 ♗f2 ♘e6 19 ♘b3 g5 20 ♗e2 += S.Brynell-R.Djurhuus, Malmö 1995.

c) 12...♖d8 13 c5 ♘f8 14 ♗e3 ♗g4 15 ♘d2 ♗e6 16 h3 ♘6d7 17 ♘c4 += T.Polak-S.Firt, Czech Ch. 2000.

d) 12...♘c5 13 ♘xc5 ♕xc5 14 ♗e3 ♕e7 15 c5 ♘g4 (if 15...a4, H.Banikas-E.Grivas, Greek Team Ch. 2004, 16 b4 axb3 17 axb3 +=; or 15...♗g4 16 ♘d2 ♗e6 17 f3 ♘d7 18 ♘c4 += G.Djurovic-M.Brigljevic, Zagreb 2009) 16 ♗g5 f6 17 ♗d2 ♘h6 18 h3 ♘f7 19 ♗c4 (or 19 b4!? axb4 20 ♗xb4 b5 21 a4 += I.Cosma) 19...♔h8 20 ♗b3 ♗e6 21 ♗xe6 ♕xe6 22 ♕a4 += V.Vostrotin-J.Krebs, corr. 2003.

13 c5 *(D)*

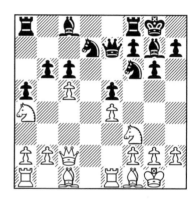

As can be seen, Black has some problems on the queenside dark squares. The text is a forcing way in order to open the play on this part of the board.

The other possibility is 13 ♗e3 ♖b8 14 ♖ad1 (or 14 h3 ♗a6 15 c5 ♗xf1 16 ♖xf1 b5 17 ♘b6 ♘xb6 18 cxb6 ♖fc8 19 a4 ♘d7 20 axb5 cxb5 21 ♕b3 ♘xb6 22 ♖xa5 ♘c4 23 ♖xb5 ♖xb5 24 ♕xb5 ♘xe3 25 fxe3 += F.Balabaev-R.Sakic, corr. 2003) 14...♗a6 15 h3 (or 15 c5 ♗xf1 16 ♔xf1 b5 17 ♘b6 ♘xb6 18 cxb6 ♖fc8 19 ♗c5 += D.Komarov-P.Svidler, St Petersburg 1997) 15...♖fc8 (if 15...b5 16 ♘c5! ♘xc5 17 cxb5 cxb5 18 ♗xc5 ♕c7 19 ♕c3 +/-) 16 b3 b5 17 c5 ♗b7 18 ♘b2

♗f8 19 ♖c1 ♘e8 20 a3 ♘g7 21 b4 a4 22 ♗h6 ♘e8 23 ♗xf8 ♘xf8 24 ♘d1 ♖d8 25 ♘e3 +/= I.Ivanisevic-N.Sedlak, Yugoslav Ch. 2000.

13...b5 14 ♘b6 ♘xb6

No better is 14...♖b8 15 ♗e3 ♘g4 16 ♗d2 ♕xc5 17 ♕xc5 ♘xc5 18 ♗xa5 f5 (V.Epishin-P.Cladouras, Bad Wiessee 1997) 19 h3 ♘h6 20 ♗b4 +/-; but 14...♖a6!? deserves attention.

15 cxb6 ♗b7 *(D)*

An improvement on 15...♗a6 16 a4 ♖fc8 17 ♗e3 ♗b7 which saw Black reach the same position a tempo down. V.Babula-A.Mista, Czech League 2004, continued 18 ♘d2 ♗f8 19 f3 ♘d7 20 ♘b3 b4 21 ♖ac1 c5 22 ♗b5 ♘xb6 23 ♘xc5 ♗c6 24 ♕e2 ♕e8?! (24...♘d7!? 25 ♘b3 ♕e6 26 ♗xc6 ♖xc6 offered more chances to resist) 25 ♘a6 ♗xb5 26 axb5 ♕d8 27 ♘c7 ♖ab8 28 ♖ed1 ♕h4 29 ♖c6 ♘a8 30 b6 a4 31 ♖d7 a3 32 bxa3 bxa3 33 ♗f2 ♕h6 34 ♕c4 ♔h8 35 g3 (not 35 ♕xf7? ♘xb6! 36 ♗xb6 a2 37 ♕xa2 ♖xb6 =) 35...♕h3 36 ♖xf7 ♘xc7 37 ♖cxc7 ♖a8 38 b7 ♖d8 39 ♖xf8+ ♖xf8 40 bxa8♕ 1-0.

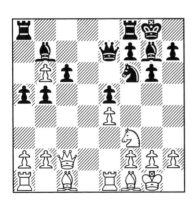

After the text Black remains somewhat worse but can put up a better de-fence. T.Polak-A.Mista, Brno 2004, saw **16 a4** [16 ♗e3 may be more accurate, and if 16...♖fc8 17 ♗c5 ♕e8 18 a4 +=] **16...♖fc8 17 ♗e3 ♗f8 18 h3 b4 19 ♗c4 h6 20 ♘d2 c5 21 f4!?** [21 ♗b3 intending 22 ♘c4 +=] **21...♘d7 22 fxe5 ♘xb6 23 e6 fxe6 24 e5 ♔g7?** [24...♔h7! 25 ♖f1 ♗g7 26 ♕xg6+!? (if 26 ♗d3 ♘d5 27 ♗xg6+ ♔h8 =+) 26...♔xg6 27 ♗d3+ ♔h5 28 ♗e2+ ♔g6 is an amusing draw] **25 ♖f1 ♘d5 26 ♗xd5 exd5?** [26...♗xd5 +=] **27 ♖f6 ♔h8 28 ♕xg6 ♕g7 29 ♕f5** [White is winning, but took a draw, presumably in time trouble] **29...♖c7 30 ♖xh6+ ♕xh6 31 ♗xh6 ♗xh6 32 ♕f6+ ♔h7 33 ♕f5+ ♔h8 34 ♕f6+ ♔h7 35 ♕f5+ ½-½**.

D33: 9...exd4 10 ♘xd4 ♘g4

Black tries to exploit White's vulnerability on the a1-h8 and a7-g1 diagonals.

The main alternative is 10...♖e8! *(D)*,

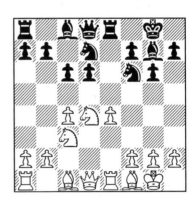

when White has a rich choice of continuations, but none of them leads to an obvious advantage for him:

a) 11 ♘b3, a good move in the 7...♘a6 line, is well met here by 11...a5!

and if 12 ♕xd6 (or 12 a4 ♘e5 = D.Gurevich-A.Fishbein, Las Vegas 1989) 12...a4 13 ♘d2 a3 with a strong initiative, e.g. 14 ♖b1 ♘g4 15 ♕g3 ♘c5 16 h3 axb2 17 ♗xb2 ♗e5 18 ♕f3 ♕xd2 19 hxg4 ♕g5 20 ♗e2 ♘e6 =+ M.Kostin-A.Gelman, Moscow 1997.

b) 11 ♗g5 h6 12 ♗h4 ♕b6 (or 12...♘c5 13 ♕c2 g5 14 ♗g3 ♘h5 15 ♖ad1 ♘xg3 16 hxg3 = W.Balcerowski-V.Ciocaltea, Bad Liebenstein 1963) 13 ♘b3 a5 14 ♘a4 ♕b4 15 ♘d2 ♘c5 16 ♘xc5 ♕xc5 = I.Novikov-I.Foygel, Kherson 1989.

c) 11 ♖b1 ♘g4! (11...a5 – *9...a5 10 ♖b1 exd4 11 ♘xd4 ♖e8* in line D32) 12 h3 (or 12 ♕xg4 ♗xd4 13 ♕d1 ♕f6 14 ♗e3 ♗xe3 15 ♖xe3 ♘e5 = R.Kleeschaetzky-A.Penzold, German League 1996) 12...♕b6 13 ♕xg4 (or 13 hxg4 ♕xd4 14 ♗e3 ♕e5 15 g5 ♕e7 16 ♕d2 ♘e5 17 ♖bd1, T.Jakat-R.Knaak, Rostock 1984, 17...♗e6 18 b3 f6 ∞) 13...♕xd4 14 ♗e3 ♕e5 15 ♖bd1 ♘c5 16 ♕f3 ♕e7 17 ♗f4 ♗e5 ∞ J.Piket-J.Nunn, Groningen 1988.

d) 11 f3 d5!? (otherwise 11...a5 12 ♗e3 ♘c5 13 ♕d2 a4 14 ♖ad1 ♘fd7 15 ♘c2 ♗e5 16 ♗d4 ♘e6 17 ♗xe5 dxe5 = M.Taimanov-S.Reshevsky, Zürich Candidates 1953) 12 exd5 (or 12 cxd5 ♘xd5! ∞ J.Rosito-C.Valiente, Santos 2006) 12...♖xe1 13 ♕xe1 cxd5 14 ♗e3 dxc4 15 ♖d1 a6 16 ♗xc4 ♕c7 17 ♗b3 (or 17 ♗d5!? ♘b6 18 ♗b3 ♗d7 ∞ A.Shneider-A.Kochyev, Pavlodar 1982) 17...♘c5 18 ♕f2 ♘xb3 19 ♘xb3 ♗e6 20 ♗b6 (A.Huzman-B.Itkis, Pavlodar 1982) 20...♕e7 =.

e) 11 ♘c2 ♘e5 (or 11...♕c7 12 ♗f4 ♘e5 13 ♕d2 ♗e6 14 b3 ♖ad8 15 f3 ♕a5 ∞ P.Trajkovic-D.Lazic, Serbian Ch. 2000) 12 h3 (or similarly 12 f3 ♗e6 13 b3 ♘h5 with counterplay, D.Ilic-Z.Arsovic, Serbian Ch. 2003; while if 12 ♘e3 ♘fg4! 13 ♕c2 ♗e6 14 ♘xg4 ♘xg4 15 ♗f4 ♗e5 16 ♗g3 ♕g5 17 ♗e2 h5 18 ♖ad1 h4 19 ♗xe5 dxe5 = H.Fioramonti-L.Vogt, Swiss Team Ch. 1995) 12...♗e6 13 b3 ♘h5 14 ♘d4 ♕h4 15 ♗e3 h6 (or 15...♘f4!? 16 ♘xe6 ♘xe6 ∞) 16 ♘xe6?! (better 16 ♖c1 ∞ Dorfman) 16...♖xe6 17 ♖c1 ♖ae8 18 ♔h1 ♘d7 19 g3 ♕e7 20 ♗g2 ♘c5 =+ N.Rashkovsky-J.Dorfman, USSR Ch., Moscow 1976.

f) 11 ♗f4 ♘c5 (not 11...d5? 12 cxd5 ♘xd5 13 exd5 ♖xe1 14 ♕xe1 ♗xd4 15 dxc6 bxc6 16 ♖d1 ♗g7 17 ♗c4 +/- S.Gligoric-H.Pilnik, Amsterdam 1950; or if 11...♘e5 12 h3 ♘h5 13 ♗e3 a6 14 a4 a5 15 ♕d2 +/= I.Maris-N.Dedes, Greek Ch. 1988) 12 ♕c2 (if 12 f3 ♕b6 13 ♕d2 ♘e6 14 ♗e3 ♘xe4! 15 ♘xe4 ♘xd4 16 ♗f2 ♗f5 17 ♘xd6 = J.Nunn-Ju.Hodgson, London Lloyds Bank 1985) 12...♘g4?! (Black should probably prefer 12...♘fd7 13 ♗e3 a5 14 b3, I.Nemet-L.Vogt, Lucerne 1994, 14...♘e5!? ∞; or even 12...♘fxe4!? 13 ♘xe4 ♗xd4 14 ♘xd6 ♖e6 15 ♖xe6 ♗xe6 16 ♖d1 ♕f6 17 ♗e3 ♗xe3 18 fxe3 ♕e5 = A.Leal-D.Bretz, corr. 1998) 13 ♖ad1 ♕e7 (or 13...♗xd4 14 ♖xd4 ♕f6 15 ♘e2 ♘xf2?! 16 ♔xf2 g5 17 ♖xd6 ♕e7 18 e5 gxf4 19 ♘xf4 ♕g5, G.Burgess-M.Schlosser, Prestwich 1990, 20 ♕d2 ♗f5 21 ♕d4 +/-) 14 ♗g3 h5!? 15 h3 h4 16 ♘xc6 bxc6 17 ♗xd6 ♕g5 (Se.Ivanov-P.Svidler, St Petersburg 1997) 18 f4! ♕h5 19 e5 +/- Huzman.

11 ♕xg4! *(D)*

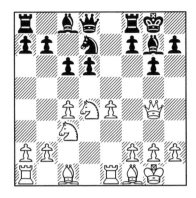

This is the difference between the equivalent variation with 7...♘a6 (line C22 in Chapter Six): here the c8-bishop is obstructed, allowing White to capture the knight with the queen.

The alternative is 11 h3 ♕b6 and then:

a) 12 hxg4 ♗xd4! (the simplest response, although 12...♕xd4 is still possible, e.g. 13 g5 ♕e5 14 ♗e3 f6 15 ♕d2 fxg5 16 ♖ad1 g4 ∞ L.Ftacnik-L.Vogt, Tallinn 1981; or 13 ♗f4 ♕xd1 14 ♖axd1 ♘e5! 15 g5 ♗e6 16 ♖xd6 ♗xc4 ∞ N.Alexandria-M.Chiburdanidze, 4th matchgame, Tbilisi 1981) 13 ♗e3 ♗xe3 14 ♖xe3 ♕c5 15 ♖g3 (or 15 ♗e2 ♘f6 16 g5 ♘e8 17 ♖g3 f6 18 gxf6 ♖xf6 19 ♖e3 ♕e5 = A.Luczak-Z.Ksieski, Lublin 1981) 15...♘f6 16 ♗e2 ♕e5 17 ♕d3 g5 18 ♖d1 ♖d8 = K.Juhnke-G.Treppner, German League 1981.

b) 12 ♕xg4! ♗xd4 13 ♕e2 ♘c5 14 ♗h6 ♖e8 15 ♕d2 ♗e5 (or 15...♘e6 16 ♖ad1 ♗d7 17 ♗e3 += V.Babula-O.Kalinin, Moravian Team Ch. 1997) 16 ♔h1 f5 17 ♖ad1! ♘xe4 18 ♘xe4 fxe4 19 ♖xe4 ♗f5 20 ♖e2 += K.Lerner-L.Vogt, Berlin East 1989.

11...♗xd4 12 ♕d1

The most straightforward and testing move. Instead:

a) 12 ♗h6? ♘e5 13 ♕f4 ♘g4 14 ♖e2? (but if 14 ♗xf8 ♘xf2 15 ♕d2 ♗c5 -/+) 14...♗e5 15 ♕g5 (P.Glavina Rossi-R.Casafus, Buenos Aires 1990) 15...♗f6 16 ♕f4 ♘xh6 17 ♕xh6 ♗g5 -+.

b) 12 ♕g3 ♘f6 13 ♗g5 (or 13 ♕d3 ♕b6 14 ♗e3 ♗xe3 15 ♖xe3 ♘g4 16 ♖e2 ♗e6 17 b3 ♖ad8 = K.Berg-H.Pöttinger, Budapest 1983) 13...♕a5! 14 ♗xf6 ♗xf6 15 ♕xd6 ♗e5 16 ♕d2 ♖d8 17 ♕c2 ♗e6 with compensation, L.Quendro-R.Knaak, Thessaloniki Olympiad 1988.

c) 12 ♗e3 ♘c5! 13 ♕d1 ♗e5 14 ♕d2 ♖e8 (or 14...♕h4!? 15 g3 ♕h5 16 ♗g2 ♗h3 17 ♗h1 ♗g4 18 f4 ♗g7 19 e5 ♖fd8 20 exd6 ♗f8 ∞ J.Pinter-R.Knaak, Szirak 1985) 15 f3 a5 16 ♖ad1 ♕f6 17 ♘e2 (if 17 ♗g5 ♕h8! =+ D.Lalev-V.Ivanchuk, Lvov 1988) 17...♕g7 18 ♗h6 ♕f6 19 ♗e3 ♕g7 20 b3 f5 21 ♗h6 ♕f7 ∞ S.Koutsin-S.Wirius, Austrian Team Ch. 1997.

12...♕f6

If 12...♗e5 13 f4 ♗xc3 14 bxc3 ♕f6 (R.Vaganian-W.Heinig, German League 1994) 15 ♗a3 c5 16 ♕d2 +/-; or 12...♕b6 13 ♗e3 ♗xe3 14 ♖xe3 ♕c5 (J.Solakian-J.Baron Rodriguez, Paris 1993) 15 ♕d2 ♘b6 16 ♖d1 +=.

13 ♗e3 ♗xe3

Black is also worse after 13...♗e5 (or 13...♗c5?! 14 ♕d2 ♖e8 15 ♖ad1 ♘f8 16 h3 h5 17 ♗d4! +/- K.Panczyk-Z.Ksieski, Polish Ch. 1982) 14 ♕d2 and then:

a) 14...♘c5 15 ♗g5 ♕e6 (if 15...♕h8!? 16 ♗e7 ♖e8 17 ♗xd6 ♗xc3 18 bxc3 ♘xe4, T.Karolyi-M.Geenen, Belgium 1990, 19 ♗f4 ♗f5 20 ♕d4 +=) 16 ♗h6

♖e8 17 f4 ♗xc3?! 18 ♕xc3 f6 19 e5 fxe5 20 fxe5 dxe5 21 ♖xe5! ♕xe5 22 ♖e1 ♕xc3 (not 22...♘d3? 23 ♖xe5 ♘xe5 24 c5! +-) 23 ♖xe8+ ♔f7 24 ♖f8+ +/- M.Sibarevic-M.Vukic, Banja Luka 1983.

b) 14 ♕d2 ♖e8 15 f4! (otherwise 15 ♖ad1 ♘c5 is similar to 12 ♗e3 above) 15...♗xc3 16 bxc3 ♖xe4 17 ♗d4! ♖xe1 18 ♖xe1 ♕d8 19 f5 with compensation (Tsesarsky), e.g. 19...♕f8 20 ♗e3! ♘e5 21 ♗h6 ♕e7 22 c5 ♗xf5 23 cxd6 ♕f6 24 ♗f4 ♘d7 25 ♗g5 ♕g7 26 ♖e7 ♗e6 27 ♗c4 ♗xc4 28 ♖xd7 +/-.

14 ♖xe3 ♘e5 15 ♕d2! ♗e6

If 15...h5 16 ♖d1 ♖d8 17 b3 h4 18 ♗e2! ♗e6 (if 18...g5 19 c5!) 19 g3! ♘g4 (or 19...hxg3 20 ♖xg3) 20 ♗xg4 ♗xg4 21 f3 ♗e6 22 g4 ♖d7 23 ♖d3 +/- K.Sakaev-P.Svidler, St Petersburg 1997.

16 b3 ♖ad8 17 ♖d1 *(D)*

Another good option is 17 ♖g3 ♕h4 18 ♖e1 (or 18 f4 ♘g4 19 ♖h3 ♕e7 20 ♖d3 f5 21 ♖e1 += T.Karolyi-M.Bosboom, Amsterdam 1988) 18...a6 19 ♘e2 ♘g4 20 h3 ♘f6 21 ♘f4 b5!? 22 ♖d3 bxc4 23 g3 ♕g5 24 ♘xe6 ♕xd2 25 ♖xd2 c3 26 ♖c2 fxe6 27 ♖xc3 += V.Epishin-P.Svidler, Budapest 1996.

After the text Black has tried three moves without achieving equality:

a) 17...a6 18 ♖g3 c5 19 f4 ♘c6 20 ♕f2 ♔h8 21 ♖gd3 += I.Nemet-J.Banas, Virovitica 1981.

b) 17...♕h4 18 g3! ♕h5 19 f4! ♘g4 20 ♖d3 f6 21 h3 ♘h6 22 g4 ♕c5+ (not 22...♕h4? 23 c5 +- E.Otero-M.Lee, Cuba 1987) 23 ♔h1 ♘f7 24 ♕b2! Camacho; e.g. 24...g5 25 ♘a4 ♕a5 26 ♕xf6 ♖de8 27 f5 ♗xc4 28 bxc4 ♕xa4 29 ♖xd6! +=.

c) 17...h5 18 ♗e2 ♗g4 (18...h4 19 g3! is similar to 15...h5 above; e.g. 19...♘g4 20 ♗xg4 ♗xg4 21 f3 ♗e6 22 g4, or 19...g5 20 f4 gxf4 21 gxf4 ♘g4 22 ♖f3 ♔h7 23 f5 ♗c8 24 ♕f4 +/-) 19 f3 ♗c8 20 g3 h4 21 f4 ♘g4 22 ♖d3 hxg3 23 hxg3 ♕h8 24 ♗f3 ♔g7 25 ♕g2 ♕h5 26 e5 f6 27 exf6+ ♖xf6 28 ♘e4 ♖f7 (or 28...♖e6 29 ♕b2+ ♔g8 30 ♗xg4 ♕xg4 31 ♘f6+) 29 ♕b2+ ♔g8 30 ♖xd6 ♖df8 31 ♘g5 ♖e7 32 ♖d8 ♖fe8 (A.Maksimenko-M.Saltaev, Tehran 1999) and now 33 ♘e4 ♕h8 34 ♕xh8+ ♔xh8 35 ♖xc8 ♖xc8 36 ♗xg4 with a winning endgame.

Conclusion

After 8 d5 ♘c5 (line A) Black obtains good play, though White can improve this by first playing 8 ♕c2 and if 8...c6 9 d5 (line B2). The natural 8 ♗e3 (line C) also gives White good chances, even after the standard 8...♘g4 (line C3). Nevertheless, the most popular option is the non-committal 8 ♖e1, to which Black should respond with equal flexibility, playing either 8...c6 9 ♗f1 a5 (line D32) or 9...exd4 10 ♘xd4 ♖e8 (see line D33), with good chances of achieving equality in either case.

Chapter Eight

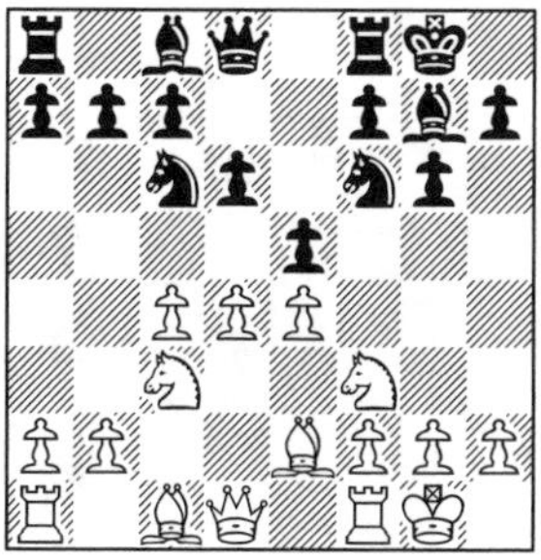

7...♘c6: Introduction

1 d4 ♘f6 2 c4 g6 3 ♘c3 ♗g7 4 e4 d6 5 ♘f3 0-0 6 ♗e2 e5 7 0-0 ♘c6 (D)

This move, discovered by the Soviet grandmaster Lev Aronin, is nowadays Black's most popular method (used in about 70% of games) of fighting against the Classical System and is one of the sharpest. It was popularized at the famous tournament in Mar del Plata in 1953, from which it took its name. The knight immediately exerts pressure on the centre and forces White to clarify the situation.

The jungle of variations arising from 8 d5 ♘e7 are perhaps the most characteristic of the present-day King's Indian. White aims for active play on the queenside, advancing his pawns towards c4-c5 and the opening of the c-file. Black, on the other hand, tries to attack the white king. These conflicting plans give rise to extremely complicated positions, difficult to analyse.

White's three primary options here are examined in the subsequent chapters: 9 ♘e1 and 9 ♘d2 both send the knight across to support White's queenside ambitions, while at the same time freeing the f3-square for the f-pawn; and the straightforward 9 b4 commences action without any preamble. In line B of the current chapter we will discuss White's rarer ninth move continuations, such as 9 ♘h4, 9 a4, 9 ♔h1, 9 ♗e3 and, in particular, 9 ♗d2 (line B1) and 9 ♗g5 (line B2).

White can also play 8 ♗e3 (line A), to which Black's most principled response is, as usual, 8...♗g4, though even the simple 8...♖e8 gives him good chances.

A: 8 ♗e3 *194*
B: 8 d5 *204*

---

8 dxe5 (D) is seen occasionally, but as with 7...♘bd7 8 dxe5 in the previous

chapter, offers White little hope of an opening advantage:

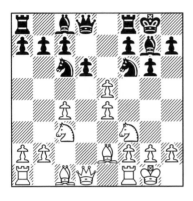

a) 8...dxe5 9 ♕xd8 (9 ♗g5 ♕xd1 10 ♖fxd1 reaches the same position; worse is 9...♗g4 10 ♘d5! ♗xf3 11 ♗xf3, G.Brajnikov-J.Reid, corr. 2001, and now 11...♔h8 is the only way to unpin so that after ...h7-h6 White cannot take on f6 with check, though 12 ♕b3 ♖b8 13 ♖ad1 h6 14 ♗h4 g5 15 ♗g3 ♘xd5 16 cxd5 ♘d4 17 ♕a3 gives him a small, but long-term advantage) 9...♖xd8 10 ♗g5 ♖f8 11 ♖fd1 ♗g4 12 ♖d3 (if 12 h3 ♗xf3 13 ♗xf3 ♘d4 14 ♘d5 ♘xd5 15 cxd5 c6! 16 dxc6 bxc6 17 ♖ac1 ♖fb8 18 b3 a5 19 ♖c4 a4 with counterplay, S.Ernst-F.Nijboer, Dieren 2006) 12...h6 13 ♗e3 ♘xe4! 14 ♘xe4 f5 15 ♘c5 (or 15 ♘c3 e4 16 ♖d2 exf3 17 gxf3 f4 18 ♗c5 ♗xc3 19 bxc3 ♖f5 ½-½ S.Perun-S.Pavlov, Kiev 2004) 15...e4 (or 15...f4!? 16 ♗d2 e4 17 ♘xe4 ♖ae8) 16 ♖b3 exf3 17 gxf3 f4 18 fxg4 fxe3 19 fxe3 ♘d4! 20 exd4 ♗xd4+ 21 ♔h1 ♗xc5 22 ♖f1 ♖xf1+ 23 ♗xf1 b6 = B.Itkis-M.Golubev, Rumanian Team Ch. 2000.

b) 8...♘xe5 is also playable, e.g. 9 ♘d4 (if 9 ♘xe5 dxe5 10 ♕xd8 ♖xd8 11

♗g5 c6 = G.Prieditis-M.Tal, Latvian Ch. 1954; or 9 ♗f4 ♘xf3+ 10 ♗xf3 ♗e6 11 b3 ♘d7 = A.Mitenkov-A.Ukolov, Moscow 1996) 9...♖e8 10 f3 c6 11 ♘c2 a6 12 a4 ♗e6 13 ♘e3 (A.Minsky-S.Iskusnyh, Moscow 1994) 13...♕b6!? with counterplay.

A: 8 ♗e3 (D)

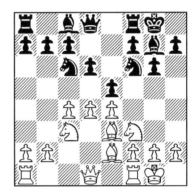

White cannot expect much maintaining tension in the centre with the black knight on its optimum square.

A1: 8...♖e8 *195*
A2: 8...♘g4 *198*

On other moves White may play d4-d5 after all and follow up with ♘d2, achieving a favourable organization of his pieces; e.g.

a) 8...♗g4 9 d5 ♘e7 10 c5 ♘e8 11 ♖c1 ♗xf3 12 ♗xf3 +/= M.Cebalo-S.Djuric, Cannes 1990.

b) 8...♘d7 9 d5 ♘e7 10 ♘d2 a6 11 b4 f5 12 f3 f4 13 ♗f2 g5 14 c5 with the initiative, N.Lakic-I.Mihevic, Pula 1990.

c) 8...h6 9 d5 ♘e7 10 ♘d2 (or 10 ♘e1 ♘e8 11 ♕d2 ♔h7 12 f4 f5 13 fxe5 dxe5

14 exf5 gxf5 15 ♗d3 +/= G.Stanciu-
G.Szmacinska, Balatonfured 1987)
10...♘d7 11 b4 f5 12 f3 f4 13 ♗f2 c5 14
dxc6 ♘xc6 15 ♘b3 ♘f6 16 a3 +=
K.Barvin-A.Al Khateeb, Decin 1997.

d) 8...♘h5 9 dxe5! (this time 9 d5
♘e7 is not so bad, e.g. 10 ♘e1 ♘f4 11
♘d3 ♘xe2+ 12 ♕xe2 f5 13 f3 f4 14 ♗f2
g5 with a probable transposition to
9...♘h5!? in line B2 as Black regains the
tempo playing ...h7-h5 in one go)
9...dxe5 10 ♕xd8 ♘xd8 (or 10...♖xd8 11
♘d5 ♖d7 12 ♖fd1 +/= Z.Lehmann-
D.Wegener, Budapest 1993) 11 ♘b5
♘e6 12 ♘xa7 ♘ef4 13 ♖fe1 ♘xe2+ 14
♖xe2 ♗e6 15 ♖c2 c6 16 b4 += J.Spesny-
A.Simunek, Czechia 2001.

e) 8...exd4 is also possible, when 9
♘xd4 ♖e8 10 f3 transposes to line C3 in
Chapter Five (7 0-0 exd4 8 ♘xd4 ♖e8 9
f3 ♘c6 10 ♗e3).

A1: 8...♖e8 (D)

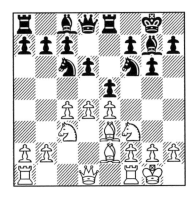

This move, increasing the pressure
on e4 is quite logical, and although it is
played less often than 8...♘g4 (at a ratio of 3:1 in the database), it scores
roughly the same for Black.

9 dxe5

The point of Black's last move is
that 9 d5 can now be answered by
9...♘d4! (otherwise the rook would
stand worse than on f8) 10 ♘xd4 (this
leads to many exchanges but other
moves give White nothing; e.g. 10 ♖e1
♘xe2+ 11 ♖xe2 ♘g4 12 ♗g5 f6 13 ♗h4
♘h6 14 ♘d2 g5 15 ♗g3 f5 with the initiative, V.Shalimov-A.Surjadnji,
Kharkov 1999) 10...exd4 11 ♗xd4 ♘xe4
12 ♘xe4 ♖xe4 13 ♗xg7 ♔xg7 14 ♗d3
♖e8 and Black is fine: 15 ♕c2 (or 15 ♕f3
♕f6 16 ♕xf6+ ♔xf6 17 ♖fe1 ♗d7 =
B.Savchenko-A.Kornev, Russian Team
Ch. 2006) 15...♕f6 16 f4 b6 17 f5 g5 18
♔h1 ♗d7 19 ♖ae1 ♖xe1 20 ♖xe1 ♖e8 21
♖xe8 ♗xe8 22 ♕e2 ½-½ V.Abramov-
V.Toporov, St Petersburg 2006.

9...dxe5

9...♘xe5 is less effective here, as after 10 ♘xe5 dxe5 (or 10...♖xe5 11 f3 ♖e8
12 ♕d2 ♗e6 13 ♖fd1 ♘d7 14 ♖ac1 f5 15
exf5 ♗xf5 16 ♗f1 ♘e5 17 ♘d5 +/=
J.Nogueiras-G.Timoscenko, Bayamo
1981) 11 ♕xd8 ♖xd8 White has an extra
move (♗e3) on the 8 dxe5 ♘xe5 variation above; e.g. 12 ♘b5 ♖d7 13 ♖fd1
♘xe4?? (but if 13...c6 14 ♘d6 ♖d8 15 c5
♗e6 16 f3 with better play for White) 14
♘xc7! 1-0 O.Gschnitzer-A.Von Gleich,
Bad Wörishofen 1991.

10 h3

Black has no problems equalizing
after:

a) 10 ♕xd8 ♘xd8! (better than
10...♖xd8 11 ♖fd1 ♗g4 12 ♘d5! ♘xe4
13 ♘xc7 ♖xd1+ 14 ♖xd1 ♖c8 15 ♘d5 +=
M.Dlugy-A.Fishbein, New York Open
1991) 11 ♘b5 (if 11 ♖fd1 ♘e6 12 h3 c5

13 ♗d3 ♘d4 ∞ J.Morgado-K.Engel, corr. 1992) 11...♘e6 12 ♘g5 ♖e7 13 ♖fd1 (if 13 ♘xa7 ♘f4 14 ♗xf4 exf4 15 ♘xc8 ♖xc8 16 f3 ♘d7 17 ♖ab1 ♖a8 18 a3 h6 19 ♘h3 ♗d4+ ½-½ B.Toth-L.Vadasz, Hungarian Ch. 1970, or 13 ♘xe6 ♗xe6 14 f3 c6 15 ♘c3 ♖d7 16 ♖fd1 ♗f8 17 ♔f2 b6 = S.Reshevsky-R.Fischer, Santa Monica 1966) 13...b6 (or again 13...c6!? 14 ♘xe6 ♗xe6 15 ♘c3 ♖d7 16 ♖xd7 ♗xd7 17 ♖b1 ♘g4 18 ♗d2 ♗e6 19 f3 ♘f6 20 ♗e3 ♗f8 = S.Reshevsky-R.Fischer, 9th matchgame, Los Angeles 1961) 14 a4 (or 14 c5 ♘xc5 15 ♖d8+ ♗f8 16 ♘xa7 ♖xa7 17 ♖xc8 ♖e8 18 ♖xe8 ♘xe8 19 ♘f3 f6 20 ♗c4+ ½-½ J.Piket-J.Nunn, Wijk aan Zee 1991) 14...c6 15 ♘xe6 ♗xe6 16 ♘c3 ♖b7 17 b4 ♗f8 18 ♖ab1 ♘d7 19 b5 ♖c8 = L.Portisch-J.Nunn, Amsterdam 1990.

b) 10 c5 ♗g4 (10...♕e7!? intending ...♖d8 is also possible, e.g. 11 ♕b3 ♖b8 12 ♗b5 ♗g4 13 ♘d5? ♘xd5! 14 exd5 ♗xf3 15 gxf3 ♖ed8 -/+ P.Martynov-A.Shchekachev, Malmö 1991) 11 ♗b5 ♕c8 (or 11...♘h5 12 ♘d5 ♖e6 13 h3 ♗xf3 14 ♕xf3 ♘d4 15 ♗xd4 exd4 ∞ I.Belov-V.Vepkhvishvili, Stare Mesto 1992) 12 h3 ♗h5 (if 12...♖d8 13 ♘d5 ♘xd5 14 exd5 ♗e6 15 dxe6 ♖xd1 16 exf7+ ♔xf7 17 ♗c4+ ♔f8 18 ♖axd1 with compensation, P.Lukacs-A.Stummer, Budapest 1992) 13 ♗xc6 bxc6 14 ♗g5 ♖b8 15 ♖b1 (if 15 b3 ♘d5! ∞) 15...♗xf3 16 ♕xf3 ♘d7 17 b4 a5 18 b5!? ♘xc5 19 bxc6 ♘e6 20 ♕e3! f6 21 ♗h6 ♖xb1 22 ♖xb1 ♕a6 23 ♘d5 ♕xc6 24 ♖c1 ♕b7?! 25 ♗xg7 ♔xg7 26 ♕f3 ♖f8 27 ♕g4 f5 28 ♕g3 ♕b2 (L.Oll-I.Smirin, Rostov 1993) and now White could have drawn with

29 ♖c6! ♕b1+ 30 ♔h2 ♕xe4 31 ♖xe6 ♕xd5 32 ♖xe5 (Smirin), e.g. 32...♕xa2 33 ♖e7+ ♖f7 34 ♕xc7 ♖xe7 35 ♕xe7+ ♕f7 36 ♕e5+ and 37 ♕xa5.

10...♗e6 (D)

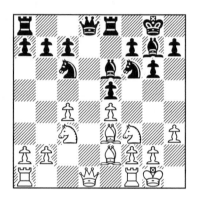

Other moves allow White a slight advantage; e.g. 10...♘d7 11 c5 ♘f8 12 ♗b5 ♗d7 13 ♗g5 f6 14 ♗e3 ♔h8 15 ♕d2 ♕c8 16 ♖fd1 ♖d8 17 ♕e2 a6 18 ♗c4 += N.Purgin-G.Piesina, Belgorod 1989; or 10...♘h5 11 ♕xd8 ♘xd8 12 ♖fd1 ♘f4 13 ♗f1 c6 14 ♖ac1 f6 15 c5 ♗e6 16 ♘d2 ♘f7 17 ♘c4 ♖ad8 18 b4 += R.Polaczek-P.Vandervaeren, corr. 1990.

11 c5

If now 11 ♕xd8 ♖exd8 12 ♖fd1 ♘e8! 13 ♘d5 f6 (or 13...h6!? intending ...f7-f5 with counterplay) 14 c5 ♔f7 15 a3 ♘b8! 16 b4 c6 17 ♘c3 ♖xd1+ 18 ♖xd1 ♗f8! 19 ♘d2 ♘d7 20 ♘c4 b6 21 cxb6 axb6 22 b5! cxb5 23 ♘xb5 ♗c5 with an even position, I.Polovodin-M.Novik, St Petersburg 1994.

11...♘h5 (D)

Black can also play:

a) 11...♕c8 12 ♕a4 ♘h5 13 ♖fd1 ♘f4 14 ♗f1 ♗d7 15 ♕c2 ♘e6 16 ♗c4 ♘ed4 17 ♗xd4 ♘xd4 18 ♘xd4 exd4 19 ♘d5 c6

20 ♘f4 b6 = V.Mikhalevski-I.Manor, Israeli Team Ch. 1996.

b) 11...♕e7 12 ♕c2 ♖ad8 13 ♖ad1 a6!? 14 ♖xd8 (14 b4!?) 14...♖xd8 15 ♖d1 ♖xd1+ 16 ♕xd1 h6 17 a3 ♕d7 18 b4 ♕xd1+ 19 ♗xd1 ♔f8 20 ♗a4 ♗d7 21 ♔f1 ♔e8 22 ♔e2 ♘g8 ½-½ V.Vaitonis-E.Rodriguez Martin, corr. 1995.

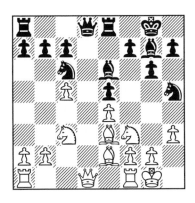

12 ♘g5

12 ♗b5 is similar to the game after 12...♖f8 13 ♗xc6 bxc6 (or 13...♕xd1!?) 14 ♕a4 ♕e8 15 ♖ad1 f5 16 exf5 gxf5 17 ♖fe1 e4 18 ♘d4 ♗d7 ∞ R.Vera-I.Teran Alvarez, Seville 1997. But not 12 ♘d5?! ♘d4 with an excellent position for Black, E.Hakulinen-R.Watanabe, Maringa 1991.

12...♘f4 13 ♘xe6 ♘xe6 14 ♗b5

Or 14 ♗c4 ♘cd4 15 ♗xe6 ♖xe6 = T.Csonkics-P.Bottyan, Salgotarjan 1998.

14...♖f8

Black can also insert 14...♕xd1!? 15 ♖axd1 ♖ed8 16 ♗xc6 bxc6 =.

15 ♗xc6 bxc6 16 ♕a4 ♕e8

Or 16...♘d4 17 ♖ad1 ♕e7 18 ♕c4 ♖ab8 19 ♖d2 a5 20 ♘e2 ♖fd8 ∞ A.Zakharov-M.Novik, Rostov 1993.

17 ♖ad1 f5 18 exf5!

After 18 f3 f4! 19 ♗f2 g5 Black would build up with ...♖f6, ...h7-h5, ...g5-g4, etc.

18...gxf5 19 f3 ♔h8 20 ♔h1 ♖g8 21 ♖d2 ♗f6 22 ♕c4 *(D)*

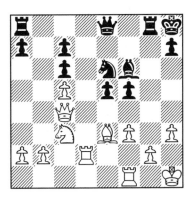

Black stands slightly better: his doubled c-pawns control important squares and can hardly be attacked while he pursues his initiative on the kingside. Two moves have been tried:

a) 22...♘g7?! allowed 23 g4! in P.Van der Sterren-B.Gelfand, Biel Interzonal 1993, and White neutralized the attack after 23...♕e7 24 ♖g1 ♗g5 25 f4! exf4 26 ♗xf4 ♗xf4 27 ♕xf4 fxg4 28 ♖xg4 ♖af8 (or 28...♕xc5 29 ♖dg2 and the extra c-pawn is of no value) 29 ♕d4 ♖d8 30 ♖e2 ♕f7 31 ♕f2 ♕xf2 ½-½.

b) Gelfand later suggested 22...♗g5 23 ♗xg5 (or 23 ♖e1 ♗xe3 24 ♖xe3 ♘f4) 23...♖xg5 (intending ...♘f4) 24 ♘e2 ♕g6 25 ♕c3 ♕g7 with the initiative. Instead, I.Jelen-M.Tratar, Slovenian Ch. 1994, concluded 24 ♕e2 ♘f4 25 ♕e3 ♖g7 26 ♖e1 ♖e7 ½-½, but Black could have played for more with 26...♕g6! 27 ♖g1 (27 ♕xe5 runs into 27...♘d3! -/+) 27...♖e8 and his initiative continues.

A2: 8...♘g4 *(D)*

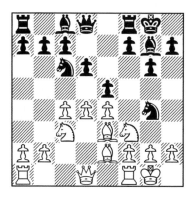

The typical reaction to ♗e3. Subsequent play is reminiscent of 7...♘g4 in the Gligoric System (see variation F in Chapter Three, in particular the lines with 9...♘c6) and can transpose directly, although White has lost a degree of flexibility having already castled short here.

9 ♗g5 f6

Other moves are less logical:

a) 9...♗f6 10 ♗xf6 ♘xf6 11 d5 ♘e7 12 ♘e1 ♘d7 13 ♘d3 f5 14 exf5 ♘xf5 (or 14...gxf5 15 f4 ♘g6 16 ♕d2 += S.Reshevsky-R.Fischer, 1st matchgame, Los Angeles 1961) 15 ♕d2 ♘f6 16 ♖ae1 += J.Horvath-W.Uhlmann, Austrian Team Ch. 1991.

b) 9...♕d7 10 d5 ♘e7 11 h3 ♘f6 12 c5 ♘e8 13 cxd6 ♘xd6 14 ♘d2 b6 15 ♘c4 += G.Garcia Gonzales-J.Kristiansen, Lucerne Olympiad 1982.

A21: 10 ♗h4 *198*
A22: 10 ♗c1 *201*

With the centre fluid 10 ♗d2 is of no value and merely blocks the d-file. After 10...f5 White has little better than to aim for A22 lines with a subsequent ♗e3 or ♗g5. Or Black can just play 10...♘xd4 11 ♘xd4 (B.Setchell-B.Milligan, corr. 1993) 11...exd4! 12 ♗xg4 (or 12 ♘b5 f5) 12...♗xg4 13 ♕xg4 f5! =.

A21: 10 ♗h4 *(D)*

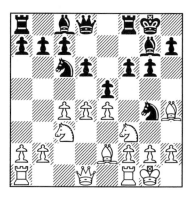

10...g5

Aiming for standard kingside counterplay. Black has also tried:

a) 10...h5 11 h3 (or 11 d5 ♘e7 12 ♘d2 ♕e8 13 b4 g5 14 ♗g3 f5 15 exf5 ♗xf5 16 ♘de4 ♕g6 17 ♖e1 a5 ½-½ G.Fahnenschmidt-J.Nunn, German League 1989) 11...♘h6 12 dxe5 (if 12 d5 ♘e7 13 ♘d2 c5! is a standard idea from the Gligoric System, e.g. 14 ♖b1 ♗d7 15 b4 cxb4!? 16 ♖xb4 b6 ∞ G.Timoscenko-S.Atalik, Nova Gorica 1999) 12...dxe5 13 ♕d5+ ♘f7 14 ♖ad1 ♕e7 15 ♕b5 (or 15 ♕d2 ♗h6, P.Rosso-C.Kinkelin, corr. 2000, 16 ♕c2 +=) 15...♘d6 16 ♕a4 ♘d8? 17 ♘d5 ♕f7 18 c5 ♘e8 19 ♘xe5! fxe5 20 ♘e7+ ♔h7 21 ♖xd8 +/- Z.Ksieski-M.Sarwinski, Polish Team Ch. 1987.

b) 10...♘h6 11 dxe5 (11 d5 ♘e7 12 ♘d2 g5 13 ♗g3 transposes to 12 d5 in the main line; or else 12...c5!? 13 f3 f5 14 ♖b1 ♗f6 15 ♗f2 f4 16 b4 b6 17 bxc5 bxc5 18 ♕a4 g5 with counterplay, L.Van Wely-H.Van der Poel, Dutch Team Ch. 1987) 11...dxe5 12 c5 (if 12 ♕b3!? ♔h8 13 ♖ad1 ♕e8 14 ♘d5 ♖f7 15 h3 f5!? 16 ♖fe1 fxe4 17 ♘g5 ♘f5 ∞ J.Speelman-J.Gallagher, British Ch. 1987) 12...♕xd1 (if 12...♗e6 13 ♕a4 ♕e8 14 ♗c4 ♔h8 15 ♗xe6 ♕xe6 16 ♘d5 ♖f7 17 ♕b3 ♖b8 18 ♖fd1, M.Suba-J.Gallagher, Biel 1987, 18...♘d4!? ∞ ECO, then 19 ♘xd4 exd4 20 ♗g3! with the initiative) 13 ♖fxd1 ♗g4 14 ♘e1 ♗xe2 15 ♘xe2 ♖fd8 16 f3 ♖xd1 17 ♖xd1 ♖d8 18 ♖xd8+ ♘xd8 = A.Maric-J.Micic, Yugoslav Team Ch. 1991.

c) 10...♔h8 11 d5 (if now 11 dxe5 dxe5 12 ♘d5 ♘e7 13 ♘d2 ♘h6 14 ♕c2 c6 15 ♘xe7 ♕xe7 16 f3 ♘f7 17 ♗f2 ♘g5! = M.Najdorf-W.Uhlmann, Moscow 1967, or 12 c5 ♘h6!? 13 h3 ♗e6 14 ♕a4 ♕e7! 15 ♗c4 ♘d4! with counterplay, T.Chekhova Kostina-N.Surshdorsh, Moscow 1991) 11...♘e7 12 ♘e1 (or 12 ♘d2 h5 13 ♖c1 c5 14 dxc6 bxc6 15 b4 += V.Mikhalevski-O.Cvitan, Ljubljana 1995) 12...h5 13 ♘d3 ♘h6 14 ♗g3 f5 15 f4! fxe4 16 ♘xe4 ♘ef5 (Burmakin also notes 16...exf4 17 ♘xf4 ♘hf5 18 ♗f2 ♗xb2?! 19 ♗xh5! or 18...♗h6 19 ♗e1 when White looks better, e.g. 19...♗g7 20 ♗c3 ♗xc3 21 ♘xc3) 17 fxe5 (or 17 ♗f2!? ♘d4 18 fxe5 dxe5 19 ♗g3 +=) 17...♘xg3 18 ♖xf8+ ♕xf8 19 ♘xg3 dxe5 20 ♗f3 ♕e7 21 ♗e4 += V.Burmakin-J.Gdanski, Cappelle la Grande 1997.

d) 10...♕e8!? 11 d5 ♘d8!? 12 ♘d2 (or

12 ♘e1 h5! 13 ♗xg4 hxg4 14 f3 gxf3 15 ♘xf3 a6 ∞ V.Blecken-V.Kupreichik, Cuxhaven 1992) 12...h5 13 h3 ♘h6 14 b4 ♘df7 15 c5 ♗d7 (or 15...g5 16 ♗g3 g4 ∞ Shipov) 16 a4 f5 17 ♘b5 ♕b8 18 f3 a6 19 ♘a3 g5 20 ♗f2 g4 21 fxg4 hxg4 22 hxg4 (S.Shipov-V.Kupreichik, Alborg 1993) 22...♘xg4 23 ♗xg4 fxg4 24 ♗h4 += (Shipov), when 24...♖h8!? followed by ...♘g6 comes into consideration.

11 ♗g3 ♘h6 (D)

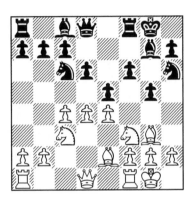

Threatening 12...g4 followed by 13...♘xd4, and thus forcing White to clarify the situation in the centre. Other moves are inferior; e.g. 11...h5?! 12 d5 ♘e7 13 ♘d2 f5 14 exf5 ♘xf5 15 ♗xg4 hxg4 16 ♘de4 +/-M.Ghorbani-H.Aryanejad, Iranian Ch. 1998; or 11...f5 12 d5 ♘b8 13 exf5 ♗xf5 14 ♗d3 ♘d7 15 ♗xf5 ♖xf5 16 ♘e4 += V.Vodicka-M.Voracek, Czech League 1999.

12 dxe5

The alternative is 12 d5 ♘e7 13 ♘d2, which can also arise via the Gligoric System (7 ♗e3 ♘g4 8 ♗g5 f6 9 ♗h4 ♘c6 10 d5 ♘e7 11 ♘d2 ♘h6 12 0-0 g5 13 ♗g3). Black generally chooses between:

a) 13...f5!? 14 exf5 (or 14 f3 ♘g6 15 b4 ♘f4 16 c5 ♘xe2+ 17 ♕xe2 f4 18 ♗f2 g4 ∞ D.Semenenko-I.Grischuk, Evpatoria 2005) 14...♘hxf5 15 ♘de4 (or 15 ♗h5 ♘d4 16 f3 b5! with counterplay, A.Onischuk-V.Bologan, Poikovsky 2004) 15...♘g6 16 c5 ♘f4 17 ♗g4 ♕e7 18 cxd6 cxd6 19 ♘b5 ♗d7 ∞ J.Speelman-M.Wilder, World Blitz Ch., Saint John 1988.

b) 13...♘g6 14 ♖c1 (or 14 ♖e1 ♘f4 15 ♘f1 f5 16 exf5 ♘xe2+ 17 ♕xe2 ♘xf5 ∞ U.Zak-F.Portisch, Budapest 1993) 14...f5 (or 14...♘f4!? 15 b4 f5 16 exf5 ♘xf5 17 ♗g4 a5 ∞ J.Ehlvest-G.Rey, San Francisco 2000) 15 exf5 ♗xf5! 16 ♘de4 ♘f4 17 c5 ♗g6 18 ♖e1 ♘xe2+ 19 ♕xe2 ♘f5 20 ♕b5?! (instead Shirov gives 20 f3 ♖f7 21 ♗f2 ♗f8 22 ♕b5 b6 23 cxd6 cxd6 24 ♕b4 ♖c7 ∞) 20...g4! 21 ♕xb7 h5 -/+ L.Van Wely-A.Shirov, World Junior Ch. 1989.

12...fxe5

Naturally 12...dxe5 is still possible, and then:

a) 13 c5 ♗e6 (or 13...g4!? 14 ♗c4+ ♔h8 15 ♕xd8 ♖xd8 16 ♘e1 f5 17 ♗h4 ♖d7 ∞) 14 ♕a4 g4 15 ♗c4 gxf3 16 ♗xe6+ ♔h8 17 ♗c4 f5 ∞ F.Zamecnik-V.Babula, Bratislava 1990.

b) 13 h3 ♗e6 (if now 13...g4!? 14 hxg4 ♗xg4, Y.Pelletier-D.Barria, World Junior Ch. 1994, 15 ♕b3!? +/=) 14 c5 ♕e8 15 ♘d5 ♕f7 16 ♕a4 ♔h8 (N.Alexandria-O.Cvitan, Tilburg 1994) 17 ♗a6!? ♘d8 18 ♗c4 +/=.

13 h3

White has fewer chances after other moves:

a) 13 h4 (G.Georgadze-J.Polgar, San Sebastian 1991) 13...g4!? 14 ♘h2 (or 14 ♘g5 ♘d4) 14...♗e6 15 ♘xg4 ♘xg4 16 ♗xg4 ♗xc4 =.

b) 13 ♘d5 ♗e6 14 ♕d2 (if 14 h4 ♖xf3! 15 ♗xf3 gxh4 16 ♗h2 ♘d4 17 ♔h1 c6 18 ♘e3 ♕g5 with compensation, A.Bangiev-C.Gil Matilla, corr. 1988) 14...♘f7 15 h4 ♗h6!? (or 15...♘d4 ∞) 16 ♕d1 ♖c8 17 h5 ♗g7 18 ♘h2 ♘h6 ∞ V.Golod-A.Prokhorov, Ukrainian Team Ch. 1991.

c) 13 c5!? g4 14 ♘d2 dxc5 15 ♘b3 ♘d4 16 ♘xc5 (if 16 ♗c4+ ♔h8 17 ♘xc5 c6 transposes, or Black can play 16...♘f7!? 17 ♘xc5 h5 18 ♘d3 ♗e6 19 ♗xe6 ♘xe6 ∞ N.Alexandria-K.Sakaev, St Petersburg 1995) 16...c6 17 ♗c4+ ♔h8 18 ♘e2 ♕e7 19 ♘b3 ♗e6 20 ♗xe6 ♘xe6 21 ♕c2 ♘f7 22 f3 gxf3 23 ♖xf3 ♘fg5 ∞ V.Chekhov-T.Pähtz, Berlin 1990.

13...♘f7

Black can also try 13...g4!? (if 13...♗e6 14 c5 ♘f7 15 cxd6 ♘xd6 16 ♕d2 h6 17 ♖fd1 ♕d7 18 ♖ac1 ♕f7 19 ♕e3 += M.Suba-A.Sznapik, Warsaw 1987) 14 hxg4 ♗xg4 (not 14...♘xg4?! 15 c5 dxc5 16 ♕d5+ ♕xd5 17 ♘xd5 ♖b8 18 ♘xc7 ♘f6 19 ♖fe1 += D.Dumitrache-A.Guseinov, Baku 1988) 15 ♗h4 (if 15 ♘e1, L.Lengyel-L.Zila, Hungarian Team Ch. 1994, 15...♗e6 =; but 15 c5!? dxc5 16 ♕d5+ ♕xd5 17 ♘xd5 may still offer White something) 15...♗f6 16 ♗xf6 ♕xf6 17 ♘h2 ♗e6 = A.Jedlicka-J.Balhar, Pardubice 2006.

14 ♘h2

14 c5 is fine for Black after 14...dxc5 15 ♗c4 h6 16 ♕xd8 (or 16 ♗xf7+ ♔xf7 17 ♕d5+ ♔g6!? ∞ R.Vera-P.Paneque, Holguin 1989) 16...♖xd8 17 ♘b5 ♖d7 18

♖fd1 ♖e7 = D.Dumitrache-D.Paunovic, Istanbul 1988; while if 14 ♘d2 ♘d4 15 ♗g4 c6!? (or 15...♗xg4 16 ♕xg4 c6 ∞) 16 ♘b3 ♕e7 17 ♗xc8 ♖axc8 18 ♕d3 ½-½ I.Kanko-T.Ristoja, Finnish Team Ch. 1989.

14...♘d4 15 ♗g4 (D)

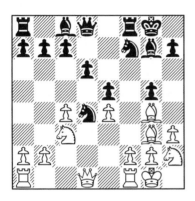

White seeks the exchange of light-squared bishops to increase his control of that colour complex and f5 in particular. On the other hand, Black is very strong on the dark squares and can aim his knights at d4 and f4. Practice has seen:

a) 15...♘h8 16 ♘b5 (or 16 ♗xc8 ♖xc8 17 ♘g4 ♘g6 18 ♘e3 ♘f4 = T.Engqvist-J.Howell, Wrexham 1995) 16...♘g6 (or 16...c6!? 17 ♘xd4 exd4 18 ♗xc8 ♖xc8 19 ♘f3 c5 ∞ Golod) 17 ♗xc8 ♕xc8 18 ♘xd4 exd4 19 ♘f3 g4! 20 ♘xd4 (20 hxg4?! ♕xg4 21 ♖e1 ♖ae8 22 ♘xd4 ♖xe4 23 ♕xg4 ♖xg4 24 ♘e6 ♖f7 is fine for Black) 20...gxh3?! (better was 20...♗xd4! 21 ♕xd4 gxh3 ∞ Golod) 21 ♘f5 ♕e6 22 ♕d5 ♖ae8 23 f3 hxg2 24 ♔xg2 += V.Golod-A.Kovalev, Israeli Team Ch. 2001.

b) 15...♘e6!? may be stronger, e.g.

16 ♖e1 ♘h6 17 ♘f1 ∞ Golod, or 16 ♕d2 c6 17 ♖ad1 ♕f6 18 ♖fe1 ♘f4 19 ♗xc8 ♖axc8 20 ♘g4 (G.Engelhardt-A.Copar, corr. 2002) 20...♕e6 21 b3 ♖cd8 with excellent play for Black.

A22: 10 ♗c1 (D)

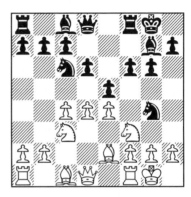

As we have seen, 10 ♗h4 leaves the bishop somewhat exposed, so White more often withdraws it to its starting square; the bishop can reappear at e3 once the knight on g4 has been driven away, or else at g5 after a subsequent ...f6-f5 or (d4xe5) ...f6xe5. Compared with the relevant line of the Gligoric System (7 ♗e3 ♘g4 8 ♗g5 f6 9 ♗c1) Black is committed to ...♘c6 here, but the dangerous attack with h2-h3-h4-h5 is ruled out.

10...f5 (D)

As usual this is the most logical move, though Black has also tried the following:

a) 10...h5 11 h3 ♘h6 12 dxe5 (also good is 12 d5 ♘e7 13 ♘e1 f5 14 exf5 ♘exf5 15 ♘f3 ♘f7 16 ♘e4 ♘d4, B.Leuchter-P.Türk, Cologne 1993, 17 ♗d3 +/=) 12...dxe5 (or 12...fxe5 13 ♗g5

♕d7 14 ♘d5 ♔h7 15 ♕d2 += A.Stromer-H.Vonthron, German League 1992) 13 ♗e3 ♗e6 14 c5 ♕e7 15 ♕a4 ♘d8 16 b4 += M.Cebalo-L.Gyorkos, Osijek 1992.

b) 10...♘h6 11 dxe5 dxe5 (if 11...fxe5 12 ♗g5 ♕d7 13 ♘d5 ♔h8 14 b4 ♘f7 15 ♗e3 ♘cd8 16 ♕d2 ♘e6 17 ♖fd1 c6 18 ♘c3 += S.Reshevsky-M.Najdorf, 1st matchgame, Buenos Aires 1953; or 11...♘xe5 12 ♘xe5 dxe5 13 ♕xd8 ♖xd8 14 ♘d5 c6 15 ♘xf6+ ♗xf6 16 ♗xh6 ♖d4 17 ♗e3 ♖xe4 18 ♗d3 ♖h4 19 g3 e4 20 ♗e2 ♖h3 21 ♖ad1 += T.Engqvist-P.Levacic, Podgorica 1991) 12 ♕d5+ ♘f7 (or 12...♔h8 13 ♗e3 ♕e8 14 ♖ad1 ♗e6 15 ♕b5 ♖b8 16 ♕a4 a6 17 ♗c5 ♖f7 18 ♘d5 += L.Portisch-K.Spraggett, Moscow 1990) 13 ♗e3 ♕e8 14 ♘b5 ♗e6 15 ♘xc7 ♗xd5 16 ♘xe8 ♗xe4 17 ♘xg7 ♔xg7 18 ♘d2 ♗f5 19 ♘b3 ♘fd8 20 ♖ad1 += J.Adamski-S.Yuferov, Naleczow 1984.

c) 10...♔h8 11 d5 (the only try for an advantage; 11 dxe5 ♘gxe5 and 11 h3 exd4 offer White nothing) 11...♘e7 12 ♘g5!? (the standard 12 ♘e1 or 12 ♘d2 are also good, e.g. 12 ♘e1 f5 13 ♗xg4 fxg4 14 f3 gxf3 15 ♘xf3 h6 16 ♗e3 ♘g8 17 ♕e1 ♗g4 18 ♕g3 ♗xf3 19 ♖xf3 ♖xf3 20 ♕xf3 ♕d7 21 c5 += S.Reshevsky-M.Najdorf, 3rd matchgame, Buenos Aires 1953) 12...♘h6 (White also has the advantage after 12...fxg5 13 ♗xg4 h6 14 ♗e3 A.Miles-M.Godena, Forli 1991, or 12...♘xh2 13 ♔xh2 fxg5 14 ♗xg5 h6 15 ♗e3 ♘g8 16 ♖h1 A.Miles-Ye Jiangchuan, Beijing 1991) 13 ♘e6 ♗xe6 14 dxe6 (or 14...♕c8, D.Byrne-L.Evans, US Ch. 1961, 15 c5!? ♕xe6 16 ♘b5 +=) 14...♘c6 15 f4 exf4 (or 15...♘d4

16 ♗e3 +/=) 16 ♗xf4 += A.Stromer-J.M.Degraeve, French Team Ch. 1992.

d) 10...exd4 11 ♘xd4 ♘xd4 (if immediately 11...f5?! 12 ♘xc6 bxc6 13 exf5 gxf5 14 h3 ♘f6 15 ♗f3 ♗d7 16 ♗g5 ♖b8 17 ♕d2 ♕e8 18 ♖ae1 ♕f7 19 b3 += P.Van der Sterren-G.Kamsky, 1st matchgame, Wijk aan Zee 1994; or 14...♘e5 15 f4 ♘g6 16 ♗e3 ♕f6 17 ♕d2 += M.Cebalo-I.Nataf, Porto San Giorgio 1997) 12 ♕xd4 f5 (or 12...♗e6 13 ♕d1 f5 14 exf5 gxf5 15 ♘d5 c6!? 16 ♘f4 ♕d7 17 h3 ♘e5 18 ♕c2 ♕f7 19 ♘xe6 ♕xe6 = M.Cebalo-B.Kutuzovic, Djakovo 1994) 13 ♕d5+ ♔h8 14 ♗xg4 (if 14 exf5 c6 15 ♕d1 gxf5 16 h3 ♘e5 ½-½ V.Inkiov-E.Ermenkov, Bulgarian Ch. 1984) 14...fxg4 (or 14...c6 15 ♕d3 fxg4 16 ♗e3 ♗e6 17 ♖ad1 ♗e5 18 ♗d4 ♕g5 19 ♘e2 ♖ad8 20 b3 b6 21 ♗e3 ♕h4 = L.Portisch-J.Piket, Wijk aan Zee 1990) 15 ♗g5 (otherwise 15 ♗e3 c6 16 ♕d3 ♗e6 returns to 14...c6 above; or if 15 ♖d1 simply 15...♗e5 and 16...c6 with excellent play) 15...♕e8 16 ♖ad1 ♗e6 17 ♕d3 ♖f7 18 ♗e3 b6 19 ♗d4 ♕f8 20 b3 ½-½ A.Khalifman-R.Byrne, London 1991.

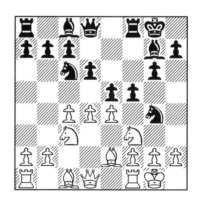

11 exf5

White has a number of other continuations, but none of them gives him the advantage:

a) 11 d5 ♘e7 12 ♘g5 ♘f6 13 exf5 ♘xf5! (better than 13...gxf5 14 f4! e4 15 ♗e3 += A.Miles-I.Rogers, Manila Interzonal 1990) 14 ♗d3 c6 15 ♘ge4 ♘xe4 16 ♘xe4 cxd5 17 cxd5 ♗h6 18 ♗xh6 ♘xh6 19 ♕d2 ♘f5 20 ♕b4 a5 21 ♕a3 b6 22 ♘c3 ♘h4 23 ♘e4 ♘f5 24 ♘c3 ♘h4 25 ♘e4 ♘f5 26 ♘c3 ½-½ J.Gustafsson-M.Van Delft, European Junior Ch. 1995.

b) 11 dxe5 ♘gxe5 12 exf5 ♗xf5 13 ♗e3 (or if 13 ♘xe5 ♗xe5! 14 ♗e3, S.Kishnev-K.Schuh, Giessen 1992, 14...♕h4 with excellent play for Black) 13...♕f6 14 ♖c1 ♖ae8 15 b3 h6 16 ♕d2 g5 ∞ J.Granda Zuniga-J.Polgar, Aruba 1992.

c) 11 ♗g5 ♕e8 (11...♕d7 12 exf5 exd4 transposes below, but 12 d5 ♘d8 13 ♘e1 ♘f6 14 f3 ♘f7 15 ♗e3 f4 16 ♗f2 h5 17 ♘d3 g5 18 c5 += C.De Saegher-F.Nijboer, Haarlem 1996) 12 ♘d5 (if 12 dxe5 fxe4 13 ♘xe4 ♘gxe5 14 ♖e1 ♗e6 ∞ J.Quintana Ortiz-V.Casas Bataller, Barcelona 2007; or 12 d5 ♘d8 13 ♘e1 ♘f7 14 ♗d2 ♘f6 15 exf5 gxf5 16 f4 ∞ K.Volke-V.Kupreichik, Berlin 1992) 12...♕f7 13 dxe5 (not 13 ♗e7?! ♘xe7 14 ♘g5 ♕e8 15 ♘xc7 ♕d8 16 ♘xa8 ♘c6 17 dxe5 ♕xg5 =+ A.Chtcherbine-L.Fusco, Vicente Lopez 2004) 13...♘gxe5!? (or 13...fxe4 14 ♘d2 ♘gxe5 15 ♘xe4 ♗f5 = Wahls) 14 exf5 ♗xf5 15 ♕d2 ♖ae8 16 ♖ae1 ♔h8 17 b3 (P.San Segundo Carrillo-V.Topalov, Madrid 1997) 17...♘xf3+ 18 ♗xf3 ♘d4 ∞.

11...exd4

Alternatively:

a) 11...gxf5 12 dxe5 ♘cxe5 13 h3 ♘xf3+ 14 ♗xf3 ♘e5 15 ♗d5+ ♔h8 16 f4 ♘g6 17 ♗e3 c6 18 ♗f3 ♖g8 ∞ C.Incutto-F.Herrera, Cordoba 1970.

b) 11...♗xf5 12 ♗g5 ♘f6 13 ♗xf6 ♘xf6 14 ♕d2 ♕e7 15 ♖fe1 ♕g7 16 ♖ad1 ♖ae8 17 dxe5 dxe5 18 b3 e4 ∞ J.Horvath-J.Reyes, Novi Sad Olympiad 1990.

12 ♘b5 (D)

Or 12 ♗g5 ♕d7 13 ♘b5 (13 ♘d5?! is pointless with Black's knight already on c6) 13...gxf5 (or 13...♖xf5!?) 14 ♕d2 ♘f6 15 ♗xf6 ♗xf6 16 ♘fxd4 ♕g7 ∞ J.Donner-L.Kavalek, San Juan 1969.

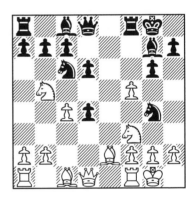

12...♖xf5

The other recaptures are also fine:

a) 12...gxf5 13 ♗g5 ♕d7 is the previous note; and not 13 ♘bxd4? ♘xd4 14 ♘xd4 (0-1 V.Zilberstein-S.Novikov, Serpukhov 2003) due to 14...♘xh2! winning a pawn.

b) 12...♗xf5 13 ♘fxd4 ♘xd4 14 ♘xd4 ♕h4 ∞; but not now 14...♘xh2? 15 ♘xf5 ♘xf1 16 ♘xg7 +/- M.Perez Lopez-J.Fernandez Gonzalez, Gijon 2000.

13 h3

13 ♘fxd4 allows 13...♘xf2! 14 ♘xc6 (not 14 ♖xf2? ♘xd4 15 ♘xd4 ♖xf2 16 ♔xf2 ♕h4+ 17 ♔e3 d5! with a winning attack) 14...bxc6 15 ♖xf2 ♖xf2 16 ♔xf2 ♕h4+ 17 ♔g1 (not 17 ♔f1? ♗e6 18 ♘a3 ♗d4 -+) and now Black can choose between: 17...♗e5 18 g3 ♗xg3 19 hxg3 ♕xg3+ 20 ♔h1 ♕h3+ 21 ♔g1 ♕g3+ with perpetual check, and 17...cxb5 18 ♕d5+ ♔h8 19 ♗e3 ♖b8 20 cxb5 ♗b7 21 ♕c4 ♕xc4 22 ♗xc4 d5 with an equal ending.
13...♘ge5 14 ♘fxd4 ♖f7 15 ♗e3

If 15 f4 ♘xd4 16 ♘xd4 ♘c6 17 ♘xc6 bxc6 18 ♗f3 ♗d7 =.

15...a6 16 ♘xc6 bxc6 17 ♘d4 c5 18 ♘c2 ♗b7 19 f4 ♘d7 (D)

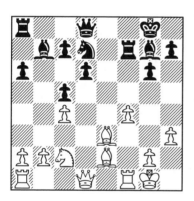

Black has a good position, his active pieces compensating for the inferior pawn structure. Bu Xiangzhi-T.L.Petrosian, Tiayuan 2005, continued **20 ♖b1 ♘f6 21 ♗f3 ♘e4 22 ♕d3 ♕e8 23 b4 ♗c6 24 ♖bd1 ♖e7 25 ♖fe1 ♘c3 26 ♗xc6?!** [better was 26 ♗xc5!? ♘xd1 27 ♖xe7 ♕xe7 28 ♗xc6 ♖f8 29 ♗d4 ♘b2 30 ♗d5+ ♔h8 31 ♕d2 with compensation] **26...♕xc6 27 ♗d2 ♖xe1+ 28 ♖xe1 ♘xa2 29 bxc5 ♕xc5+ 30 ♗e3 ♕f5 31 ♕b3?** [and here 31 ♕xf5 gxf5 32 ♗d4]

31...♘c3 32 ♗d4? [the final mistake; 32 ♗d2 was necessary, though Black should win after 32...♕d3] **32...♗xd4+ 33 ♘xd4 ♕d3 34 c5+ d5 35 ♕b7** [if the knight moves then 35...♘e2+ wins the queen] **35...♕xd4+ 36 ♔h1 ♖f8 37 ♕xc7 ♕xf4 38 ♕b7 ♕d2 39 ♕e7 ♘e4 40 ♕e6+ ♔g7 41 ♖b1 ♔h6 42 ♕e7 ♘g3+ 43 ♔g1 ♕f2+ 0-1.**

B: 8 d5 ♘e7 (D)

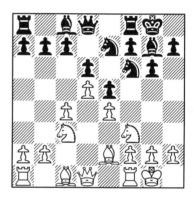

This is one of the most popular positions in the King's Indian, occurring in nearly 70% of games with the Classical Variation in recent years. It also perfectly represents the character of the opening: White achieves a space advantage in the centre and on the queenside, whereas Black, as usual, looks for his chances on the kingside, preparing counterplay with ...f7-f5.

The weak point of Black's position is often the e7-knight – it has no good squares to jump to and, in particular, is far from the c5-square. Nevertheless, after the common action ...f5-f4, ...g6-g5, the knight can go to g6 and participate in an attack on White's king.

Instead, 8...♘b8?! just gives White two extra tempi on a Petrosian System (7 d5); e.g. 9 ♗g5 a5 (or 9...h6 10 ♗h4 a5 11 c5 ♘bd7 12 cxd6 cxd6 13 ♘d2 ♘c5 14 f3 ♗d7 15 a4 ♘a6 16 ♗b5 +/= M.Gurevich-H.Karner,Tallinn 1987) 10 ♘d2 ♘a6 11 a3 ♗d7 12 ♕c2 ♕e8 13 ♘b5! h5 14 ♖ae1 ♘h7 15 ♗e3 +/= O.Panno-J.Diez del Corral, Siegen Olympiad 1970.

B1: 9 ♗d2 *206*
B2: 9 ♗g5 *209*

The main moves for White here are 9 ♘e1, 9 ♘d2 and 9 b4, which are covered in the remaining chapters of this book.

Black has no problems after such continuations as:

a) 9 ♘h4 ♘e8! 10 g3 ♗h3 11 ♖e1 f5 12 exf5 ♘xf5 13 ♘f3 h6 14 ♘e4 ♗g4 15 ♕d3 ♘f6 16 ♗d2 ♕d7 17 ♗c3 ♘xe4 18 ♕xe4 ♗h3 19 ♘d2 ♘d4 with counterplay, G.Hertneck-W.Watson, German League 1994.

b) 9 ♖e1 a5 (otherwise 9...♘h5 10 b4 transposes to the main line of Chapter Twelve) 10 ♗d3 h6 11 b3 ♘d7 12 ♕e2 f5 13 ♗b2 f4 14 a3 g5 15 ♗c2 g4 16 ♘d2 f3 17 gxf3 gxf3 18 ♘xf3 ♘g6 with a strong attack, T.Lovholt-L.Alves, corr. 2001.

c) 9 a4, hoping to gain space with a4-a5, is well met by 9...a5! 10 b3 (if 10 ♘e1 ♘d7 11 ♗e3 f5 12 f3 ♘c5 13 ♘d3 b6 14 b4 ♘xd3 15 ♕xd3 axb4 16 ♘b5 ♔h8 17 ♕b3 ♘g8 ∞ V.Korchnoi-G.Kasparov, Barcelona 1989; or 11 ♘d3

f5 12 exf5 ♘xf5 13 ♖a3 ♘b6 14 b3 c6 with counterplay, L.Ftacnik-F.Nijboer, Hamburg 2005) 10...♘d7 11 ♗a3 ♘c5 12 b4!? axb4 13 ♗xb4 and now 13...f5 14 ♗xc5 dxc5 15 a5 is a Bayonet Attack a tempo down (b2-b3-b4), but White seems better nevertheless; e.g. 15...fxe4 (15...♖a6 would return the tempo – see Chapter Eleven, line C2, note with 10...♘d7 11 bxa5 ♖xa5 12 ♗b4 ♖a6 13 a4 f5) 16 ♘xe4 c6 (B.Lalic-M.Sandu, Metz 2007) 17 ♘fg5 +=. Black should prefer 13...♘a6!? 14 ♗a3 h6 followed by ...f7-f5; or else 11...♗h6!? 12 b4 axb4 13 ♗xb4 f5 with counterplay, M.Carlsen-A.Morozevich, Biel 2006.

d) 9 ♔h1!? *(D)*

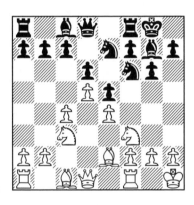

9...♘e8 (or 9...♔h8 10 ♘g1 ♘d7 11 g4 f5 12 f3 ♘g8 13 ♗e3 ♗h6 14 ♗f2 a5 = I.Kanko-L.Hazai, Helsinki 1989) 10 ♖g1 (or 10 ♘e1 f5 11 exf5 ♘xf5 12 ♘f3 ♘f6 13 ♗d3 ♘d4 14 ♘xd4 exd4 15 ♘e4 ♘xe4 16 ♗xe4 ♗d7 17 ♕d3 c5 18 dxc6 bxc6 19 ♗d2 ♖b8 20 b4, A.Miles-A.Beliavsky, Nova Gorica 1999, 20...♕f6 with counterplay) 10...f5 (if 10...♔h8 11 g4! ♘g8 12 ♗e3 ♗h6 13 g5 ♗g7 14 ♘e1 f5 15 f3 +/= Z.Arsovic-

J.Todorovic, Serbian Ch. 2007) 11 exf5 gxf5 12 ♘g5 ♘f6 13 f4!? ♘g6 14 fxe5 dxe5 15 c5 h6 16 ♘e6 ♗xe6 17 dxe6 ♕e7 or 17...♕xd1 18 ♖xd1 ♖ae8 19 ♗c4 ♖e7 with counterplay, Tsesarsky) 18 ♕b3 c6 19 ♖f1 f4 20 ♗d2 ♘h4 21 g3 ♘f5 22 gxf4 e4! 23 ♖g1 ♔h8 24. ♖g2 ♖ad8 ∞ N.Sulava-R.Ponomariov, European Ch., Ohrid 2001.

e) 9 ♗e3!? *(D)* deserves attention though.

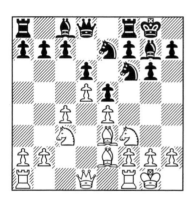

9...♘g4 (otherwise White plays 10 ♘d2 with advantage, e.g. 9...♘d7 10 ♘d2 f5 11 f3 f4 12 ♗f2 g5 13 b4 ♖f6 14 c5 ♖h6 15 ♖c1 a6 16 ♖e1 ♕e8 17 ♘a4 ♕h5 18 ♘f1 +/- V.Chekhov-C.Saksgard, Gausdal 1990) 10 ♗d2 (10 ♗g5 f6 11 ♗d2 f5 comes to the same thing, while 11 ♗h4 transposes to d4-d5 variations in line A21 above) 10...f5 11 ♘g5!? (more promising than 11 exf5 gxf5 12 ♘h4 ♘f6 13 f4 e4 14 ♗e3 c5 ∞ T.Gelashvili-A.Fedorov, Dubai 2004; and not 11 ♘e1?! ♘f6 12 f3 f4 when White is a tempo down on the 9 ♘e1 main line in the next chapter) 11...♘f6 12 exf5 gxf5!? (or 12...♘xf5 13 ♗d3 +/= L.Ljubojevic-M.Vukic, Yugoslav Ch.

1977) 13 f4 (if 13 ♕b3, E.De Castro-L.Fressinet, Internet blitz 2001, 13...f4!? ∞) 13...e4 14 ♗e3 +=, e.g. 14...h6 15 ♘h3 c5 16 ♘f2 a6 17 a4 b6 18 h3 ♕e8 19 ♖b1 ♕g6 20 ♕d2 a5 21 ♘b5 ♘e8 22 ♔h2 h5 23 g3 ♔f7 (S.Slipak-F.Peralta, Villa Ballester 1999) 24 ♖g1, with the plan of ♖g2, ♔g1-c2, and eventually g3-g4.

B1: 9 ♗d2 *(D)*

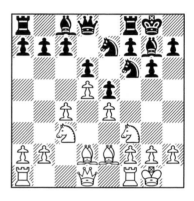

A slightly more subtle move; by leaving the knight on f3 White keeps the option of answering ...f7-f5 with ♘g5. In the meantime he can proceed on the queenside with ♖c1 and c4-c5.

9...♔h8

Black responds with a semi-useful waiting move of his own, clearing g8 for the e7-knight, and holding ...f7-f5 back until the white knight leaves f3. Naturally, Black has several other possibilities, of which lines 'd' and 'e' are the most significant:

a) 9...c5 10 ♖b1 (instead 10 dxc6 is the next note; or else 10 ♘e1 ♘e8 11 ♘d3 f5 12 f4 b6 13 ♕e1 += D.Weise-R.Oechslein, West German Ch. 1972) 10...♘e8 11 b4 b6 12 ♕c1 f5 13 bxc5 bxc5 14 ♖b3 ♘f6 15 ♘g5 ♘xe4 16 ♘cxe4 fxe4 17 g4 ♔h8 18 ♘xe4 += M.Sadler-R.McFarland, British Ch. 1995.

b) 9...c6 10 dxc6 bxc6 11 ♗g5 ♗e6?! (but if 11...♗b7 12 c5 d5, N.Ioseliani-J.Piket, Spijkenisse 1989, 13 ♘xe5!? d4 14 ♕b3 ♕c7 15 ♗f4 ♘h5 16 ♗xh5 ♗xe5 17 ♗xe5 ♕xe5 18 ♘e2 +=, or 11...♕c7 12 ♕d2 ♗e6 13 ♖ac1 +=) 12 c5 ♘e8 13 cxd6 ♘xd6 14 ♕a4 f6 15 ♗e3 ♕c7 16. ♖ac1 +/- V.Korchnoi-R.Byrne, Leningrad Interzonal 1973.

c) 9...♘d7 10 ♖c1 (better than 10 b4 f5 11 ♘g5 ♘f6 12 f3 c6 13 ♕b3 h6 14 ♘e6 ♗xe6 15 dxe6 ♕c8 16 ♖ad1 ♕xe6 17 ♗e3 ♔h7 =+ T.Tuomala-V.Maki, Finnish Ch. 1985; while 10 ♘e1 f5 11 ♘d3 is the main line C3 in Chapter Nine) 10...f5 11 ♘g5 ♘f6 12 exf5 gxf5 (or 12...♘xf5 13 ♗d3 ♘d4 14 ♘b5 c5 15 dxc6 bxc6 16 ♘xd4 exd4 17 c5 += V.Korchnoi-B.Zuckerman, New York blitz 1974) 13 f4 e4 14 ♗e3 h6 15 ♘h3 c5 16 dxc6 bxc6 17 b4 += P.Boersma-A.De Diego, Groningen 1989.

d) 9...♘e8 10 ♖c1 (D) and then:

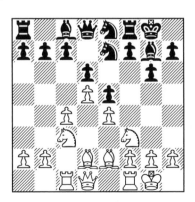

d1) 10...f5 11 ♘g5 (stronger than 11

exf5 gxf5 12 ♘g5 h6 13 ♘e6 ♗xe6 14 dxe6 ♕c8 15 ♕b3 c6 16 ♗h5 ♕xe6 17 ♕xb7 ♘f6 18 ♗e2 ♖fb8 19 ♕a6 ♖xb2 -/+ M.Taimanov-R.Fischer, 1st matchgame, Vancouver 1971; or even 11 ♕b3 b6 12 exf5 gxf5 13 ♘g5 h6 14 ♘e6 ♗xe6 15 dxe6 ♕c8 16 ♘d5 ♕xe6 ∞ M.Taimanov-Ma.Tseitlin, USSR 1973) 11...h6 (11...♘f6 – 9...♘d7) 12 ♘e6 ♗xe6 13 dxe6 ♕c8 14 ♕b3 c6 15 f4 += L.Ftacnik-Kr.Georgiev, Groningen 1976.

d2) 10...h6 11 ♘e1 f5 (or if 11...c5 12 ♘d3 f5, K.Robatsch-E.Torre, Biel 1977, 13 f4!? +=) 12 ♘d3 f4 13 c5 g5 14 ♗g4 ♗xg4 15 ♕xg4 += L.Vogt-P.Hesse, East German Ch. 1980.

d3) 10...c5!? 11 dxc6 bxc6 12 b4 h6 (not 12...f5?! 13 c5 fxe4 14 cxd6 ♘xd6 15 ♘g5 ♘ef5 16 ♘cxe4 ♘xe4 17 ♗c4+ ♔h8 18 ♘xe4 +/- E.Geller-G.Sax, Hilversum 1973; or if 12...♘c7 13 b5 d5 14 cxd5 cxd5, Z.Ribli-E.Torre, 8th matchgame, Alicante 1983, 15 ♕b3!? +=) 13 b5 (T.Gareev-O.Khamzin, Russia 2004) 13...f5!? 14 bxc6 (14 ♗e3!?) 14...♘xc6 15 ♗d3 ♘f6 16 ♘h4 ♘e7 17 exf5 gxf5 18 ♖b1 ♗e6 19 ♖e1 ∞ Gareev.

e) 9...♘h5 (D) and now:

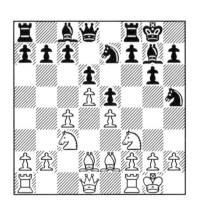

e1) 10 ♖c1 f5 (or 10...h6 11 ♖e1 ♘f4 12 ♗f1 g5 13 h4 g4 14 ♘h2 h5 15 c5 dxc5 16 ♗e3, J.Piket-B.Gelfand, Dos Hermanas 1995, 16...b6!? 17 g3 ♘fg6 18 f3 f5 with good play for Black) 11 ♘g5 (or 11 exf5 ♘xf5 12 c5 ♘f4 13 ♗xf4 exf4 14 c6 bxc6 15 dxc6 ∞ P.Boersma-P.Peelen, Amsterdam 1987) 11...♘f4 (not 11...♘f6?! – 9...♘d7) 12 ♗xf4 exf4 13 ♗f3 fxe4 14 ♗xe4 ♘f5 15 ♘e6 ♗xe6 16 dxe6 c6 17 ♖e1 ♕e7 ∞ V.Korchnoi-K.Spraggett, Montpellier Candidates 1985.

e2) 10 g3 f5 11 exf5 (11 ♘g5 ♘f6 is a clear improvement for Black on line 'c'; e.g. 12 f3 c6 13 ♕b3 h6 14 ♘e6 ♗xe6 15 dxe6 ♕c8 16 ♗e3 ♕xe6 17 ♖ad1 ♔h8 18 ♕xb7 ♖fb8 19 ♕c7 ♘e8 20 ♕a5 ♖xb2 =+ J.Plachetka-A.Rodriguez Cespedes, Tbilisi 1977). 11...♘xf5 (if 11...gxf5 12 ♘xe5 ♘xg3 13 fxg3!? +=) 12 ♘e4 ♘f6 13 ♗d3 (13 ♗g5 h6 14 ♗xf6 ♗xf6 15 ♗d3 ♗g7 16 ♔g2 c6 17 ♕b3 ♔h8 18 h4 ♕d7 V.Frias-F.Nijboer, Wijk aan Zee 1991) 13...c6 14 a4 ♔h8 15 a5 cxd5 16 ♘xf6 ♕xf6 17 cxd5, Cu.Hansen-F.Nijboer, Groningen 1990, 17...h6! with an excellent game for Black.

e3) 10 ♘e1!? ♘f4 11 ♘d3 ♘xe2+ 12 ♕xe2 f5 13 f3 f4 14 b4 ♗d7 (14...c6!?) 15 c5 c6 16 cxd6 ♘c8 17 ♘c5 cxd5 18 ♘xd7 ♕xd7 19 ♘xd5 ♘xd6 (S.Holbeck-A.Rallsjo, corr. 1990) and now 20 ♖fd1 gives White the better chances.

10 ♖c1 (D)

White has also tried:

a) 10 ♘e1 ♘e8 11 ♘d3 f5 12 exf5 gxf5 13 ♔h1 c6 14 f4 e4 15 ♘b4 ♘f6 ∞ P.Panzer-S.Farago, Budapest 1993.

b) 10 b4 ♘eg8?! (in the style of line A in Chapter Eleven, but it's a bit slow; either 10...♘h5 or 10...♘d7 looks better) 11 c5 ♘e8 12 ♖c1 f5 13 cxd6 cxd6 14 ♘g5! ♕e7 15 ♗c4 ♘c7 16 exf5 ♗xf5 17 ♗e3 ♘f6 18 f3 ♘h5 19 ♖e1 ♕d7 20 ♕d2 b6 21 a4 +/- M.Klauser-J.Gallagher, Swiss Ch. 2001.

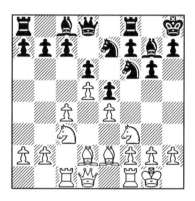

10...b6

In other games Black reverted to ...c7-c5 without success:

a) 10...c5 11 dxc6 bxc6 12 b4 ♗b7 13 ♗g5 ♘fg8 14 ♕b3 f6 15 ♗e3 f5 16 ♖fd1 +/- M.Peek-D.Coleman, Amsterdam 1996.

b) 10...♘e8 11 ♘e1 c5 12 g4!? (or 12 dxc6 bxc6 13 c5 +/=) 12...f5 13 f3 ♘g8 (13...f4!? seems preferable) 14 ♘g2 ♗d7 15 ♔h1 ♕e7 16 exf5 gxf5 17 f4! fxg4 18 ♗xg4 ♘ef6 19 ♗xd7 ♘xd7 20 ♕g4 ♖ae8 21 ♖ce1 +/- S.Atalik-Y.Visser, Wijk aan Zee 2006.

11 b4 ♘d7 12 ♘e1 f5

Now that the plan ♘f3-g5 is ruled out, Black finally makes his thematic break.

13 f3 ♘g8 14 ♘d3 ♘df6 15 c5 ♗h6 16 cxd6 cxd6 17 ♗xh6 ♘xh6 18 ♕d2 f4 19 ♘b5 ♘e8 (D)

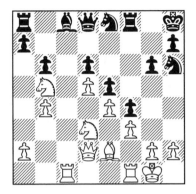

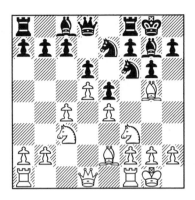

This position was reached in V.Kramnik-V.Zvjaginsev, Russian Ch., Moscow 2005. White has the better chances with his ongoing queenside initiative, whereas Black's kingside counterplay is non-existent. Nevertheless, making significant progress is not so easy, as evidenced by the remaining moves: **20 ♕c3 ♕e7 21 ♘c7 ♘xc7 22 ♕xc7 ♗d7 23 ♘f2** [23 b5!? ♖fc8 24 ♕b7 ♖cb8 25 ♕a6 ♗c8 26 ♕a3 and if 26...a6? 27 ♕b2! threatening ♘xf4 and ♘b4 +/- Mikhalevski] **23...♖fc8 24 ♕b7 ♖cb8 25 ♕a6 ♗c8 26 ♕a3 a6 27 ♖c6** [White might have tried 27 ♖c3 ♗d7 28 ♖fc1 ♘g8 29 ♗xa6!? ♕d8 30 ♖c6 ♗xc6 31 dxc6 ♕c7 32 b5 intending ♕b3, ♘d3-b4-d5 Mikhalevski] **27...♗d7 28 ♖c7 ♘g8 29 ♖fc1 ♘f6 30 ♕b2** [30 ♗xa6!? ♕d8 31 ♖7c6 ♗xc6 32 dxc6 was still possible, e.g. 32...♘e8 33 b5 ♘c7 34 ♕b3 ♘xa6 35 bxa6 ♖a7 36 ♘d3 b5 37 ♘b4 +/- Mikhalevski] **30...♔g8 31 ♗f1 ♘e8 32 ♖7c3 ♕d8 33 ♕d2 ♘f6 34 ♖c7 ♘e8 35 ♖7c3 ♘f6 36 ♖c7 ♘e8 37 ♖7c2 ♘f6 38 ♖c3 ♖a7 39 ♕c2 ½-½.**

B2: 9 ♗g5 *(D)*

The most frequent of the less frequent moves in this position. White develops the dark-squared bishop actively in advance of reorganizing with ♘f3-d2. The difference with 7 d5 ♘bd7 8 ♗g5 in the Petrosian System (line B2 in Chapter Four) is that here White has already castled short while the d7-knight has slipped across to e7, which in turn means that the f6-knight is free to move.

9...♘d7

Other plans are:

a) 9...♘e8 10 ♘d2 (also good is 10 ♕d2 f5 11 exf5 gxf5 12 ♖ac1 ♘f6 13 ♗d1 a6 14 ♖e1 b6 15 b4 +/= N.Woischke-W.Oleak, corr. 2000) 10...f5 (10...f6 or 10...h6 gives White a favourable Gligoric-type position after 11 ♗e3, e.g. 10...f6 11 ♗e3 f5 12 f3 c5!? 13 dxc6 bxc6 14 b4 ♘c7 15 ♘b3 ♘e6 16 ♕d2 +/= I.Belov-A.Petrushin, Rostov 1993) 11 f3 f4 (again if 11...♘f6 12 ♖c1 h6?! 13 ♗e3 f4 14 ♗f2 g5 15 c5 ♖f7 16 ♘c4 +/- J.Blumenstein-W.Hillgaertner, Griesheim 1998; 12...c5!? was a better try) 12 ♗h4 (safeguarding the bishop from exchange) 12...♗f6 (or 12...♔h8 13 b4 ♖g8 14 c5 ♗f8 15 cxd6 cxd6 16 ♗f2 g5 17 ♖c1 ♘g6 18 ♘c4 ♘f6 19 ♔h1 h5 20 ♘b5 +/- I.Belov-V.Zhelnin, Katowice 1991) 13 ♗f2 g5 14 c5 ♖f7 15 ♘c4 ♖g7 16 cxd6 ♘xd6 17 ♘xd6 cxd6 18 ♖c1 ♘g6 19 ♕b3 h5 20 ♘b5 a6 21 ♘a7 ♗d7 22 ♘c6! ♕f8 23 ♕xb7 won a pawn in E.Gausel-R.Djurhuus, Norwegian Team Ch. 1999, though the black attack still has to be repulsed; the game continued 23...g4 24 ♕b4 (24 ♕b6!?) 24...g3 25 ♗e1? (25 ♗b6) 25...gxh2+ 26 ♔xh2 ♗h4! 27 ♗xh4 ♘xh4 28 ♖f2 ♕f6 29 ♖h1 and now 29...♕g5! would have been decisive.

b) 9...♘h5 10 ♘e1 (to fight for the f4-square; 10 ♘d2 makes less sense here, while if 10 g3 f6 11 ♗d2 f5 12 exf5 ♗xf5 13 ♘g5 ♘f6 14 f3 c6 15 ♗e3 h6 16 ♘ge4 c5 ∞ B.Arkhangelsky-E.Brondum, European Seniors Ch. 2007; or 10 ♖e1 h6 11 ♗d2 ♘f4 12 ♗xf4 exf4 13 ♕d2 g5 14 h3 ♘g6 ∞ J.Gonzalez Zamora-V.Bologan, Turin Olympiad 2006) 10...♘f4 11 ♘d3 ♘xe2+ 12 ♕xe2 h6 (or 12...f5 13 f4 h6 14 ♗xe7 ♕xe7 15 ♖ae1, Sr.Cvetkovic-I.Simeonidis, Ano Liosia 1998, and now 15...exf4!? 16 ♘xf4 ♗d4+ 17 ♔h1 ♕g7 =) 13 ♗d2 (if 13 ♗e3 f5 14 f3 f4 15 ♗f2 g5 16 c5 ♘g6 with counterplay, e.g. 17 ♖fc1 ♖f7 18 ♖c2 h5 19 ♖ac1 ♗d7! 20 a4 a6 21 c6 bxc6 22 dxc6, Y.Pelletier-I.Nataf, French Team Ch. 2002, 22...♗xc6 23 ♘d5 ♗xa4 24 ♖xc7 ∞ Pelletier) 13...f5 (alternatively, 13...g5 14 f3 ♘g6 15 g3 f5 16 c5 ♖f7 17 cxd6 cxd6 ∞ L.Gonda-G.Papp, Balatonlelle 2007; or 13...c6!? 14 ♖ac1 f5 15 f3 f4 16 ♗e1 c5 17 ♗f2 ♗d7 18 a3 b6 19 b4 g5 20 ♖b1 h5 21 ♖b2 ♘g6 ∞ H.Draba-A.Khlystov,

corr. 2000) 14 f4!? exf4! 15 ♘xf4 g5 16 ♘h5 (not 16 ♘e6?! ♗xe6 17 dxe6 f4 18 g3 ♘g6 19 gxf4 ♗xc3 20 bxc3 gxf4 -/+ A.Blees-H.Klarenbeek, Heraklio 1993) 16...♗e5 (or 16...♗d4+ 17 ♔h1 f4 18 g3 fxg3 19 ♖xf8+ ♕xf8 20 ♖f1 ♗h3! 21 ♖xf8+ ♖xf8 ∞ G.Prakash-P.Konguvel, Indian Ch. 1999) 17 exf5 ♘xf5 18 g4 ♘g7 19 ♘xg7 ♔xg7 20 ♖xf8 ♕xf8 = D.Berczes-L.Valdes, Budapest 2006.

c) 9...h6 is the most common response, immediately asking the question of the bishop and thus preventing White's plan. After 10 ♗xf6 (other moves are inconsistent, for instance 10 ♗d2 just gives Black the useful extra ...h7-h6 on line B1, preventing any ideas of ♘g5) 10...♗xf6 11 b4 *(D)*,

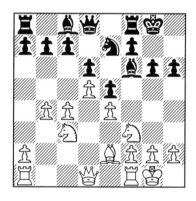

White has achieved a lead in development and started action on the queenside, but the lack of his dark-squared bishop may make itself felt in the future. Black's response depends on whether he wishes to relocate his own bishop to e7 or put it back on g7.

c1) 11...♔g7 (similar is 11...♔h7 12 c5 ♘g8 13 ♘d2 ♗e7 14 c6 b6 15 b5 ♗g5, V.Majorovas-D.Komljenovic, Augsburg 1991, 16 ♘f3 ♗f4 17 ♕c2 f5 18 exf5 ♗xf5 19 ♗d3 +/=; or 11...♔h8 12 c5 ♘g8 13 a4 ♗e7 14 c6 bxc6 15 dxc6 f5, T.Hillarp Persson-L.McShane, Copenhagen 1998, 16 ♗d3!? +/=) 12 c5 ♘g8 13 a4 (if 13 cxd6 cxd6 14 ♘d2 ♗g5 15 ♘c4 f5 ∞ P.Dussol-A.Shirov, Torcy 1990) 13...♗e7 14 c6 bxc6 15 dxc6 f5 16 ♗c4 ♘f6 (A.Vlaskov-I.Umanskaya, St Petersburg 1994) 17 exf5 gxf5 18 ♘d5 with the initiative.

c2) 11...♗g7 (or first 11...a5 12 a3, when 12...♗g7 13 c5 transposes below, or if 12...axb4 13 axb4 ♖xa1 14 ♕xa1 ♗g7 15 ♘d2 f5 16 ♕a8 c6 17 ♕b8 ♔h7 18 ♖d1 cxd5 19 exd5 e4 20 ♘b5 +/= C.Cruz-E.Sanchez Jerez, Barbera del Valles 2006) 12 c5 (12 ♘d2 f5 13 c5 again transposes, while if 13 f3 ♔h8 14 c5 ♘g8 15 ♘c4 ♖f7 16 a4 ♘f6 17 a5 ♘h5 with counterplay, Y.Pelletier-J.Hjartarson, German League 2003) 12...f5 (Black can also insert 12...a5!? 13 a3 f5, e.g. 14 ♖c1 fxe4 15 ♘d2, G.Burgess-H.Nordahl, Gausdal 1990, 15...♘f5!? 16 ♘dxe4 ♘d4 ∞) 13 ♘d2 (D) and then:

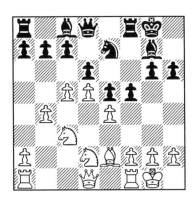

c21) 13...♔h8 (or 13...♔h7 14 ♖c1 ♘g8 15 exf5!?, I.Smirin-K.Neumeier,

Dortmund 1990, 15...♗xf5 16 ♘de4 +=) 14 ♘c4 (14 ♗d3 and 14 f3 return to 13 ♗d3 and 12 ♘d2 f5 13 f3 respectively) 14...♘g8 15 ♖c1 ♘f6 16 exf5 gxf5 17 cxd6 cxd6 (V.Todorovic-A.Srebrnic, Ptuj 2003) 18 f4 +/=.

c22) 13...fxe4 14 ♘dxe4 ♘f5 15 ♗g4 (if 15 ♖c1 ♘d4 16 ♘b5, M.Orso-C.Bognar, Budapest 2002, 16...♘xe2+ 17 ♕xe2 a6 18 ♘bc3 ♗f5 =) 15...a5 (or 15...♕e7 16 a4 h5 17 ♗h3 ♗h6 18 a5 a6 19 ♕d3 g5 ∞ ½-½ N.Nikcevic-D.Antic, Yugoslav Team Ch. 1999) 16 cxd6 cxd6 17 bxa5 ♖xa5 ∞ J.Gonzalez Zamora-S.Minero Pineda, San Salvador 2001.

10 ♘d2

The most consistent move. Instead:

a) 10 ♘e1!? transposes to *9 ♘e1 ♘d7 10 ♗g5!?* (see the notes to line C in the next chapter).

b) 10 ♕d2 leads to equality here, e.g. 10...a5 11 ♕e3 f6 12 ♗h6 f5 13 ♗xg7 f4 14 ♕d2 ♔xg7 15 ♕c2 ½-½ M.Poppe-C.Espindola, corr. 1996.

10...f5 (D)

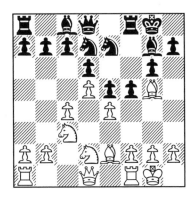

Planning to close the c1-g5 diagonal before targeting the g5-bishop. Attacking it immediately with 10...h6 or 10...f6

allows a retreat to e3 with a favourable Gligoric-type position; e.g. 10...f6 11 ♗e3 (also good is 11 ♗h4 h5 12 f3 ♗h6 13 b4 f5 14 exf5 gxf5 15 f4! ♗xf4 16 ♖xf4! exf4 17 ♗xh5 with a very strong attack, Sr.Cvetkovic-H.Banikas, Athens 1998) 11...f5 12 f3 f4 13 ♗f2 actually transposes to 7 ♗e3 ♘c6 8 d5 ♘e7 9 ♘d2 ♘d7 10 0-0 f5 11 f3 f4 12 ♗f2 (see the notes to line A in Chapter Three).

Inserting 10...a5 11 a3 doesn't help; e.g. 11...f5 12 f3 h6 (or if 12...c5!?, V.Eingorn-A.Zapata, Moscow 1989, 13 exf5!? gxf5 14 f4 +=) 13 ♗e3 f4 14 ♗f2 ♔h8 15 b4 axb4 16 axb4 ♖xa1 17 ♕xa1 ♘f6 18 c5 g5 19 ♕a5 ♗d7 20 ♘c4 +/- M.Hoerstmann-P.Visser, Soest 1996.

11 f3

The alternative 11 exf5 gxf5 12 f4 sets Black few problems, e.g. 12...♘f6 (or 12...h6 13 ♗h4 exf4 14 ♘f3 ♘f6 15 ♗xf6 ♖xf6 16 ♘d4 ♗d7 17 ♗h5 c6 18 ♕b3 ♕b6 19 ♕xb6 axb6 20 ♖xf4 = J.Pomes Marcet-K.Spraggett, Tarrassa 1990) 13 fxe5 (if 13 ♗h5?! e4 14 ♘b3 c5 15 dxc6 bxc6 16 ♔h1 d5 =+ B.Gelfand-E.Grivas, Haifa 1989) 13...dxe5 14 c5 h6 15 ♗xf6 ♖xf6 16 ♗c4 ♔h8 17 ♘f3 ♖g6 with the initiative D.Piza Cortizo-M.Campos Lopez, San Fernando 1991.

11...f4 12 ♗h4

Otherwise ...♗f6 forces the exchange of dark-squared bishops, e.g. 12 b4 ♗f6 13 ♗xf6 ♖xf6 14 c5 g5 15 ♘c4 ♖h6 planning to attack with ...♘f6, ...♕e8-h5 etc.

12...g5!? *(D)*

This pawn sacrifice aims to accelerate Black's kingside counterplay. Other moves give White the better game:

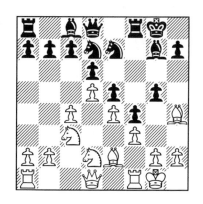

a) 12...♔h8 13 b4 h5 14 ♖c1 g5!? had a similar idea, but White's intermediary moves were more useful. After 15 ♗xg5 ♗f6 16 ♗xf6+ ♘xf6 17 c5 ♖g8 18 ♘c4 h4 19 ♔f2!? ♗d7 20 ♖g1 ♘g6 21 ♔e1 ♕e7 22 cxd6 cxd6 23 ♔d2 White was clearly better in N.Nikcevic-Z.Lanka, Cannes 1995.

b) 12...h5 13 b4 ♗h6 14 ♗f2 c5 (or 14...♘f6 g5 15 c5 ♘f6 16 ♘c4 g4 17 cxd6 cxd6 18 ♘b5 +/- E.Solozhenkin-M.Turner, French Team Ch. 1999) 15 dxc6 ♘xc6 16 ♘b3 ♘f6 17 b5 ♘e7 18 c5 +/- L.Gonda-P.Enders, Balatonlelle 2006.

c) 12...♗f6 13 ♗f2 g5 14 b4 ♘g6 15 c5 ♗e7 16 cxd6 (16 c6!? also deserves attention) 16...♗xd6 (Wl.Schmidt-S.Voitsekhovsky, Barlinek 2002) 17 ♘b5! ♘f6 (or if 17...♗xb4 18 ♖c1 ♗d6 19 ♕c2 targeting c7) 18 ♖c1 is good for White.

13 ♗xg5

Of course 13 ♗f2 is also possible, but then Black would be a valuable tempo up on the 10...f6 11 ♗e3 f5 12 f3 f4 13 ♗f2 line.

13...♗f6 14 ♗xf6 ♘xf6

14...♖xf6! seems more direct, e.g. 15 b4 ♖h6 16 c5 ♘g6 17 ♕e1 (or 17 ♘c4 ♕h4 18 h3 ♘f6 19 ♕e1 ♕g5) 17...♕g5 18 ♘b5 ♕h5 19 h3 ♘xc5! with a dangerous attack.

15 g4!? *(D)*

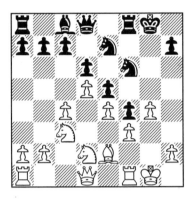

We are following the rapidplay game Y.Pelletier-F.Jenni, Basel 2004. White's move is an understandable reaction given the fast time limit, trying to lessen the opponent's initiative by neutralizing the open file. But as he doesn't succeed, he should probably just have pursued his own agenda with 15 b4 and c4-c5, ♘c4 etc.

15...fxg3 16 hxg3 ♘h5 17 ♖f2 ♔h8 18 ♘f1?

Correct was 18 ♖g2 and if 18...♖g8 19 ♔f2 ♘xg3 20 ♕g1! defends; but not 20 ♖xg3? ♖xg3 21 ♔xg3 ♘f5+! 22 exf5

♕g5+ 23 ♔f2 ♕h4+ with a winning attack (as 24 ♔e3? ♕d4 is mate).

18...♘xg3! 19 ♘xg3 ♖g8 20 ♖g2 ♗h3 21 ♕e1 ♗xg2 22 ♔xg2 ♘g6 23 ♕h1 ♘f4+ 24 ♔f2 c6!

The appearance of the black queen on the a7-g1 diagonal is decisive.

25 c5 ♕a5 26 ♖g1 ♕xc5+ 27 ♔f1 ♖g5 28 ♕h6 ♖ag8?

First 28...♖g6! and then 29...♖ag8 would have won.

29 ♕f6+ ♖8g7 ½-½.

Conclusion

White cannot expect a great deal from 8 ♗e3, as Black equalizes after both 8...♖e8 (line A1) and the standard manoeuvre 8...♘g4 9 ♗g5 f6 (line A2), irrespective of whether White retreats his bishop to h4 or c1.

The main line with 8 d5 ♘e7 gives White far greater possibilities, as we will see in the subsequent chapters. Here we examined only the 9th move sidelines. In particular, 9 ♗d2 (line B1) does not White offer much of an advantage; while after 9 ♗g5 (line B2) Black can hope for good chances after any of 9...h6, 9...♘h5 or 9...♘d7. However, the rarely played 9 ♗e3 (note 'e' to line B) certainly deserves more attention.

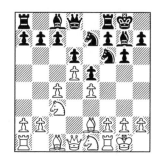

Chapter Nine

7...♘c6 8 d5 ♘e7 9 ♘e1

1 d4 ♘f6 2 c4 g6 3 ♘c3 ♗g7 4 e4 d6 5 ♘f3 0-0 6 ♗e2 e5 7 0-0 ♘c6 8 d5 ♘e7 9 ♘e1 *(D)*

Historically 9 ♘e1 is the most popular of White's continuations; indeed, in the early days of the Classical, it was used almost exclusively. The knight heads for d3 where it can support White's play both on the queenside (the c4-c5 advance) and the kingside (it controls the f4-square), while uncovering the e2-bishop prevents the black knight sally with ...♘h5-f4.

As in most variations of the King's Indian, White's chances are on the queenside, while Black can count on counterplay on the kingside. The simplistic 9...c5 (line A) doesn't offer so many chances for active play, so Black's primary idea is based on the standard ...f7-f5 thrust, for which the f6-knight has to withdraw. After 9...♘e8 (line B) White mostly chooses between 10 ♘d3 followed by f2-f4 (line

B1), and 10 ♗e3 with a subsequent c4-c5 (line B2).

Black's most popular response, played in 75% of games, is 9...♘d7 (line C) which renders the idea of f2-f4 less effective. Here we will discuss:

1) 10 ♗e3 f5 11 f3, when play usually continues 11...f4 12 ♗f2 g5.

2) 10 f3 f5 where White does not follow with ♗e3; in particular 11 g4 and 11 ♘d3 f4.

3) 10 ♘d3 f5 11 ♗d2 is the main line, and further 11...♘f6 12 f3 f4 13 c5 g5 (line C3222)

Both sides have numerous plans, ideas and tactical motifs which can be used in different positions and make the play extremely complicated.

Other seldom played moves do not give Black equality:

a) 9...b6?! 10 ♘d3 (or 10 f4) 10...♘e8?! 11 f4! +/- R.Vera-J.Polgar, Benidorm (rapid) 2002.

b) 9...c6 10 ♗e3 a6 (or 10...cxd5 11 cxd5 ♗d7 12 a4 ♘c8 13 a5 ♘e8 14 ♕b3 ♖b8 15 ♘d3 f5 16 f4 +/- M.Tal-J.Murey, Tel Aviv 1990) 11 ♖c1 cxd5 12 cxd5 b5 13 ♘d3 ♗d7 14 f3 ♘e8 15 ♕b3 +/= B.Lalic-J.Murey, Cappelle la Grande 1998.

c) 9...♗d7 10 ♘d3 c6 11 f4! cxd5 12 cxd5 ♖c8 13 fxe5 dxe5 14 ♕b3 += V.Neverov-I.Zaitsev, Orel 1994.

d) 9...a5 10 ♗e3 ♘d7 11 a3 f5 12 f3 ♔g8 (or 12...♘f6 13 c5) 13 b4 (in contrast to 9 ♘d2 a5 in the next chapter, White does not have to waste time with ♖a1-b1 here) 13...b6 14 ♘d3 ♘f6 15 ♖c1 f4 16 ♗f2 g5 17 c5 +/- F.Baragar-B.Bollenbach, Winnipeg 1996.

A: 9...c5 (D)

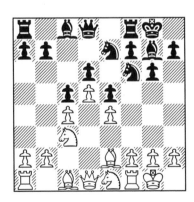

Black attempts to close the centre.

10 ♘d3

Black has no problems after 10 dxc6 bxc6 11 b4 d5 12 ♗g5 dxe4 13 ♘c2

♕xd1 14 ♖fxd1 ♘f5 15 ♗xf6 ♗xf6 16 ♘xe4 ♗e7 17 a3 h5 18 g3 ♗e6 19 ♔f1 ½-½ D.Anagnostopoulos-E.Grivas, Karditsa 1996; or 10 ♖b1 ♘d7!? 11 ♘b5 ♕b6 12 ♗e3 f5 13 f3 a6 14 ♘c3 ♕c7 15 b4 cxb4 ½-½ M.Horvath-K.Motuz, Slovakian Team Ch. 1998.

However, 10 f4! is very logical, striking in the centre before Black secures the dark squares: 10...exf4 (if 10...♘d7 11 f5! +/-) 11 ♗xf4 ♘e8 (not 11...♘d7? 12 ♗xd6) 12 ♘d3 f6 (if 12...f5 13 e5! dxe5 14 ♗xe5 ♗xe5 15 ♘xe5 +/- J.Lopez Martinez-M.Diez Fraile, Spanish Ch. 1999) 13 ♕d2 ♗d7 (or 13...♔h8 14 ♖ab1 ♘g8 15 b4 b6 16 bxc5 bxc5 17 ♘b5 ♖f7 18 ♗d1! ♖b7 19 ♗a4 +/- V.Korchnoi-V.Ciocaltea, Nice Olympiad 1974) 14 ♖ab1 g5 15 ♗g3 ♘g6 16 ♘d1 ♕e7 17 ♘1f2 ♗h8 18 h3 ♘g7 19 b4 b6 20 bxc5 bxc5 21 ♗g4 f5 22 exf5 ♘xf5 23 ♖be1 +/- G.Sosonko-R.Gunawan, Surakarta 1982.

10...♘e8

Alternatively:

a) 10...a6 11 f4 exf4 12 ♗xf4 b5 13 e5 dxe5 14 ♘xe5 b4 15 ♘a4 ♘e4 16 ♗f3 ♘d6 (N.Vasilev-V.Karasev, Severodonetsk 1982) 17 ♘xc5! ♕b6 18 ♔h1 ♕xc5 19 ♘d3 ♕c7 20 c5 ♘ef5 21 g4 +/-.

b) 10...♘d7 (probably best) 11 f4! (11 f3 f5 12 g4 is also possible, when 12...♔h8 – 12...c5 in C21, or 12...f4 13 ♗d2 ♘f6 – 13...c5 in C3221) 11...f5 12 fxe5 (or 12 ♔h1!? a6 13 a4 b6 14 ♗d2 ♖a7 15 ♖b1 ♖c7 16 g4 += S.Krivoshey-J.Becerra Rivero, Internet blitz 2003) 12...♘xe5 13 ♘f4 ♘g4?! (13...fxe4 ∞) 14 ♗xg4 ♗d4+ 15 ♔h1 fxg4 (L.Hrbolka-M.Vacek, Czech League 1995) 16 ♘b5

♗g7 17 ♘e6 ♗xe6 18 dxe6 a6 19 ♖xf8+ ♕xf8 20 ♘c7 ♖c8 21 ♘d5 +/=.

11 ♗d2

11 f4! is still very strong, e.g. 11...b6 (11...exf4 12 ♗xf4 – *10 f4 exf4 11 ♗xf4 ♘e8 12 ♘d3*) 12 ♕e1 (or 12 a3 f5, E.Serrano Salvador-A.Caravaca, Alcala de Henares 2006, and now 13 fxe5 dxe5 14 b4 with the initiative) 12...f5 13 ♗f3 fxe4 14 ♗xe4 exf4 15 ♗xf4 ♘f5 (M.Bucher-S.Kneifel, Zürich 2001) 16 ♕d2 +/=.

11 a3 is less clear, e.g. 11...f5 12 b4 b6 13 ♗d2 ♗d7 14 ♖b1 ♖c8 15 bxc5 dxc5 16 f3 ♘d6 ∞ P.Velikov-Kr.Georgiev, Plovdiv 1982.

11...f5 12 f3 f4 13 g4 (D)

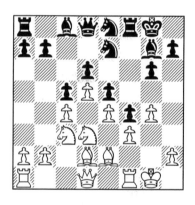

A typical motif against Black's kingside counterplay. Having waited for ...f5-f4 White avoids keeping tension on both sides of the board.

Nevertheless, we would rather recommend 13 ♖b1 or 13 a3, as in 9...♘d7 lines with ...c7-c5 later in the chapter. For instance, 13 ♖b1 g5 (13...♘f6 transposes to 12...c5 in line C32) 14 b4 b6 15 a4 h5 16 a5 += C.Pritchett-R.Britton, British Ch. 1983.

13...h5?!

13...♘f6!? would transpose to 13...c5 in line C3221, though Black has no need to play ...♘f6 just here. Instead, 13...♗d7 maintains his position with good counterplay.

14 h3

Better was 14 gxh5 gxh5 15 ♔h1 ♔h8 16 ♖g1 +/=.

14...♔f7 (D)

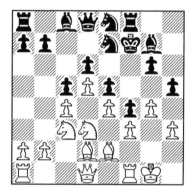

ECO gives this as unclear, quoting the game V.Lazarev-W.Uhlmann, Hartberg 1991, which continued **15 ♔g2 ♖h8 16 ♖h1 ♗f6 17 b4 b6 18 bxc5 bxc5 19 ♖b1 ♗h4 20 ♘b5 g5 21 ♕a4 ♘g6 22 ♗a5 ♕d7 23 ♕a3?!** [White should have preferred 23 ♘c3 ♕xa4 24 ♘xa4 ♗g3 with equality according to Uhlmann] **23...♗g3 24 ♘xd6+!?** [a desperate attempt to obtain some counterplay] **24...♕xd6 25 ♘xc5?** [and here 25 ♕xc5 ♕xc5 26 ♘xc5 with some compensation] **25...♘h4+ 26 ♔f1 ♘f6 27 ♗b4 a5! 28 ♗c3 hxg4** [stronger was 28...♘xf3! 29 ♗xf3 hxg4 30 hxg4 ♖xh1+ 31 ♗xh1 ♘xg4, threatening ...♘e3+ or ...♗f2 and wins] **29 hxg4 ♘d7 30 ♖b5 ♗a6 31 ♖xa5 ♘xf3! 32 ♖h5** [if 32 ♖xh8?

♖xh8 33 ♗xf3 ♗xc4+ 34 ♔g1 then 34...♖h1+! 35 ♗xh1 ♕h6 36 ♕b2 ♕h3 leads to mate] **32...♖xh5 33 gxh5 ♘xc5** [or 33...g4!, as 34 ♘xd7 ♕xd7 35 ♖xa6 fails to 35...♕b7!] **34 ♕xc5 ♕xc5 35 ♖xc5 g4! 36 ♖c7+ ♔f6 37 h6 ♔g5! 38 h7 ♖h8 39 d6 ♘h2+ 40 ♔g2 ♔h4! 41 ♖g7 f3+ 42 ♔g1 fxe2 43 d7 ♘f3+ 44 ♔h1** [if 44 ♔g2 e1♕ 45 ♗xe1 ♘xe1+ 46 ♔h1 ♔h3 47 ♖g8 ♗f2! 48 d8♕ ♗b7 and ...♗xe4 mate] **44...♗e1 45 ♗xe1+** [or 45 ♖g8 ♔g3! 46 d8♕ ♖xh7+ and mates] **45...♘xe1 46 d8♕+ ♖xd8 47 ♖g8 ♖xg8 48 hxg8♕ ♔g3 0-1** [there is no defence to ...♘f3, ...e1♕, etc].

B: 9...♘e8 (D)

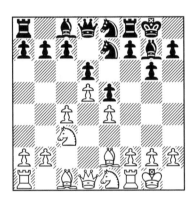

In many cases this leads to the 9...♘d7 main lines via a different move order, that is if the knight returns to f6. However, 9...♘e8 has a downside: it protects neither c5 nor e5; thus White can easily achieve c4-c5, or else play against the centre with f2-f4. On the other hand, on e8 the knight covers the c7- and d6-squares, and does not block the c8-h3 diagonal.

B1: 10 ♘d3 *218*
B2: 10 ♗e3 *221*

Other moves:

a) 10 b4 is not dangerous, e.g. 10...a5!? (10...f5 11 f3 f4 is also good) 11 bxa5 (or 11 ♕a4 ♗d7 12 b5 f5 13 f3, K.Davidsainen-J.Nykopp, Naan 1997, 13...c6 ∞) 11...♖xa5 12 ♘d3 f5 13 f3 f4 14 ♗d2 (U.Capo Vidal-J.Alvarez, Villa Giardino 2002) 14...c5 ∞.

b) 10 f3 f5 11 g4!? (otherwise 11 ♗e3 is line B2, while 11 ♘d3 is 11 f3 in line B1) 11...c6!? (increasing the tension still more; if 11...f4 12 h4! shuts down the kingside, A.Gipslis-B.Anetbaev, USSR 1972; instead 11...♘f6 transposes to 11...♘f6 in line C21, or 11...fxg4!? 12 fxg4 ♖xf1+ 13 ♔xf1 h6 14 h4 ♕d7 15 ♘d3 c5 16 ♗d2 a6 17 ♘f2 ♖b8 18 a4 b6 ½-½ P.Van Hoolandt-K.Bordi, Monte Carlo 2004) 12 ♗e3 cxd5 13 cxd5 ♘f6 14 ♘d3 f4 15 ♗f2 g5 16 a4 h5 17 h3 ♔f7 18 a5 ♖h8 19 a6 bxa6 20 ♕b3 hxg4 21 hxg4 ♘g6 ∞ A.Gipslis-E.Bukic, Olot 1973.

c) 10 f4!? (D)

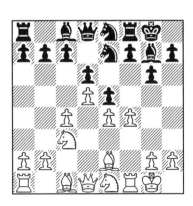

is very consistent, aiming to exploit the bad position of the e8-knight for any action in the centre, while pre-empting Black's standard counterplay on the kingside:

c1) 10...f5 11 fxe5 ♗xe5 (or 11...dxe5 12 exf5 gxf5 13 ♘f3 ♘g6 14 c5 ♘f6 15 ♗c4 +/= G.Loderbauer-G.Preusser, Passau 1999) 12 ♗h6 ♘g7 13 ♘f3 ♗f6 14 ♕d2 += J.Berrocal-M.Andrade, Bolivian Ch. 2003.

c2) 10...exf4 11 ♗xf4 f5 (if 11...c6 12 ♕d2 cxd5 13 exd5 ♘f6 14 ♔h1 ♗f5 15 ♘f3 a6 16 ♖ae1 ♖e8 17 ♘d4 ♘e4 18 ♘xe4 ♗xe4 19 ♗g4 with better play for White, P.Wells-V.Kupreichik, Regensburg 1997) 12 ♕d2 ♘f6 (if 12...♗xc3 13 ♕xc3 fxe4 14 ♘c2 ♘f5 15 g4 ♘fg7, A.Surender-W.Adamczyk, corr. 1999, then 16 ♗e3 ♖xf1+ 17 ♖xf1 with more than enough compensation for the pawn) 13 exf5 ♘xf5 14 ♘c2 h5 15 ♗g5 ♖f7 16 ♗d3 ♕f8 (T.Hillarp Persson-J.Hjartarson, Gausdal 1996) 17 ♗xf5!? ♗xf5 18 ♘d4 ♘g4 19 ♘e6 with better chances for White (Tisdall).

B1: 10 ♘d3 *(D)*

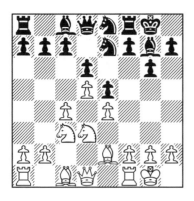

White increases his influence on the centre and is still ready to play f2-f4.

10...f5 11 f4

The most consistent. After other moves Black has sufficient counterplay:

a) 11 f3 f4 (or 11...c5!? 12 ♖b1 f4 13 b4 b6 14 bxc5 bxc5 15 ♗d2 g5 16 ♕a4 h5 17 ♘f2 ♖f7 ∞ A.Brkljaca-M.Vujic, Obrenovac 2005) 12 g4!? (if 12 ♗d2 g5, followed by ...h7-h5, ...♘g6, ...♖f7, ...♗f8 etc, and in comparison with the 9...♘d7 main lines of C322, Black gains from having the knight on e8) 12...♗f6! 13 ♗d2 h5 14 h3 ♔g7 15 ♗e1 ♖h8 16 ♔g2 ♘g8 17 ♗f2 ♗h4 18 ♕e1 ♗xf2 19 ♕xf2 g5 20 ♖h1 ♘e7 with good play for Black, B.Gelfand-J.Polgar, Linares 1994.

b) 11 exf5 gxf5 (11...♘xf5 12 f3 ♘f6 – *11 exf5* in line C3, or if 12 f4 ♕h4!? 13 fxe5 ♕d4+ ∞) 12 f4 e4 13 ♘f2 c5 14 dxc6 bxc6 15 ♗e3 ♘g6 16 ♕a4 ♗d7 17 ♖fd1 ♕b8 18 ♖d2 ♖f7 19 g3 a5 ∞ R.Cruz-P.Benko, Mar del Plata 1965.

c) 11 ♗d2 fxe4!? (11...♘f6 transposes to the main line C32) 12 ♘xe4 c6 13 dxc6 (or 13 ♕b3 ♔h8 14 f4 b5 15 c5 dxc5 16 ♘exc5 exf4 17 ♘xf4 ♘xd5 18 ♘xd5 ♖xf1+ 19 ♖xf1 ♕xd5 ∞ G.Sosonko-F.Nijboer, Dutch Ch. 1993) 13...bxc6 14 ♗c3 d5!? 15 ♘dc5 (or 15 ♘g3 e4 16 ♘c5 ♕b6 ∞) 15...♕b6 16 ♘a4 ♕b8 17 ♘ec5 (A.Hughes-D.Attig, corr. 1994) 17...♗f5 ∞.

11...exf4 *(D)*

Black has also tried:

a) 11...♘f6 12 fxe5 ♘xe4 (or 12...dxe5 13 ♘f2 += C.Goldwaser-C.Lallee, Argentine Team Ch. 2007) 13 exd6 cxd6 14 ♘xe4 fxe4 15 ♖xf8+ ♔xf8 16 ♘f2 += L.Zvolanek-J.Hujo, Bratislava 1990.

b) 11...c6 12 fxe5 dxe5 13 ♗g5 h6 14 ♗h4 cxd5 (or 14...g5 15 ♗g3 cxd5 16 cxd5 ♘g6 17 exf5 ♗xf5 18 ♗g4 += P.Petran-G.Kiss, Budapest 1995) 15 cxd5 ♘d6 16 ♘c5 ♕c7 17 ♗f2 b6 18 ♘e6 ♗xe6 19 dxe6 ♘xe4 20 ♘xe4 fxe4 21 ♖c1 ♕b7 22 ♕d7 ♕xd7 23 exd7 +/- R.Hübner-C.Herbrechtsmeier, German League 1983.

c) 11...fxe4 12 ♘xe4 c6 (or 12...exf4 – *11...exf4*) 13 dxc6 (or 13 fxe5 ♖xf1+ 14 ♕xf1 dxe5 15 ♗g5 cxd5 16 cxd5 ♕b6+ 17 ♘dc5 ♘f5 18 ♔h1 h6 19 ♗d2 ♘ed6 = P.Petran-M.Orso, Hungarian Ch. 1978) 13...♘xc6 14 ♗e3 ♘d4 15 ♗xd4 exd4 16 ♗f3 ♘f6 17 ♕e2 (17 ♕b3!?) 17...♔h8 18 ♖ae1 ♕c7 19 ♘xf6 ♗xf6 20 b3 = B.Enklaar-T.Ghitescu, Amsterdam 1971.

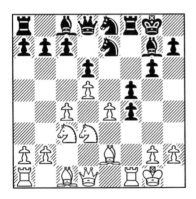

12 ♘xf4

Alternatively, 12 ♗xf4 and then:

a) 12...fxe4 13 ♘xe4 c6 (or 13...♘f5 14 ♗g5 ♘f6 15 g4 ♘d4 16 ♘df2 ♕e7 ½-½ T.V.Petrosian-M.Tal, Bled 1961) 14 dxc6 bxc6 15 ♕d2 ♘f5 16 ♖ae1 ♘f6 17 ♘c3 ♗e6 = L.Pliester-R.Caessens, Groningen 1988.

b) 12...♗xc3!? 13 bxc3 fxe4 14 ♘b4

(if 14 ♗g5 ♖xf1+ 15 ♕xf1 h6! 16 ♗xh6 ♘f5 17 ♕f4 exd3 18 ♗g5 ♕d7 19 ♗xd3 ♕g7 20 ♖c1 ♘f6! 21 ♗xf6 ♕xf6 22 g4 ♕e5 23 ♕xe5 dxe5 24 gxf5 ♗xf5 25 ♗e2 b6 -/+ M.Mädler-H.Berliner, corr. 1962) 14...♘f5 15 ♕d2 ♘f6 16 ♘c2 ♕e7 17 g4 (A.Gavrilov-A.Galkin, St Petersburg 1994) 17...♘g7 18 ♘e3 ♘ge8 19 ♖f2 ♕g7 ∞ Nunn.

12...fxe4

The simplest choice from a wide selection:

a) 12...♗xc3?! 13 bxc3 fxe4 14 ♘e6! ♗xe6 15 ♖xf8+ ♔xf8 16 dxe6 +/- T.Van Scheltinga-A.Van Oosten, Amsterdam 1969.

b) 12...♘f6?! 13 exf5 ♘xf5 14 g4! ♘e7 15 ♘e6 ♗xe6 16 dxe6 c6 17 ♗e3 d5 18 g5 +/- K.Murugan-R.Gupta, Indian Ch. 1988.

c) 12...c5 13 ♘d3 ♘f6 14 e5 dxe5 15 ♘xc5 f4 16 ♘5e4 ♘f5 17 ♘xf6+ ♕xf6 18 c5 ♘d4 (D.Vasiljevic-G.Tringov, Pancevo 1987) 19 ♘e4 +/=.

d) 12...c6 13 ♔h1!? ♘f6 (still if 13...♗xc3 14 bxc3 fxe4 15 ♘e6! +=) 14 exf5 ♘xf5 15 g4 ♘e7 16 ♗e3 +/= M.Donk-T.Seeman, Gent 1995.

e) 12...♗e5!? 13 ♘d3 ♗d4+ 14 ♘f2 ♗g7 15 g3?! (15 ♗e3 +=) 15...h6 16 ♗e3 ♘f6 17 c5?! fxe4 18 ♘fxe4 ♘xe4 19 ♘xe4 ♖xf1+ 20 ♕xf1 ♘f5 21 ♗f2 ♗xb2 =+ A.Yermolinsky-L.Van Wely, Wijk aan Zee 1997.

13 ♘xe4

Here 13 ♘e6 is ineffective after 13...♖xf1+ 14 ♕xf1 ♗xe6 15 dxe6 ♘f6 16 ♗g5 (or 16 g4 ♕f8 ∞) 16...♕f8 ∞ A.Finke-A.Van Leuken, corr. 1993.

13...♘f5 *(D)*

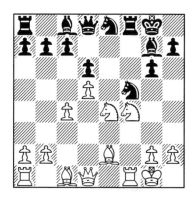

Black has a slightly cramped position, but if he can defend the e6-square successfully, he should be able to equalize.

14 ♔h1

14 ♗g4!? looks logical and gives White chances of a small advantage; e.g. 14...♗d4+ (14...♕e7 might be better) 15 ♔h1 ♘eg7 16 ♗xf5 (16 ♗h3!? +=) 16...♘xf5 17 g4 ♘e3 18 ♕xd4 ♘xf1 19 g5 ♕e7 (Y.Zats-S.Smith, Philadelphia 2000) 20 ♘e6! ♗xe6 21 ♘f6+ +/-.

14...♕e7

Also good is 14...♘f6 15 ♘g5 ♘g4 16 ♗xg4 ♕xg5 17 ♘e6 ♘g3+! 18 hxg3 ♖xf1+ 19 ♕xf1 ♕xg4 20 ♘xg7 ♔xg7 21 ♗d2 ♗f5 = L.Chiong-J.Howell, Calcutta 1996.

15 ♗d3 ♗e5 16 a4

So that the a1-rook can be activated via the third rank in some lines, though it gives White nothing special, as Black has developed well and solved his opening problems.

This was S.Atalik-F.Nijboer, Wijk aan Zee 1997, deviating from a game the month before: 16 g3 ♘eg7 17 ♘g2 ♕e8 18 ♖b1 ♗d7 19 b3 c5 20 ♖e1 ♕c8 (=

ECO) 21 ♗f4 ♗xf4 22 ♘xf4 ♕c7 23 b4 b6 24 bxc5 dxc5 25 ♘g5 ♘d4 ½-½ A.Yermolinsky-D.Rogozenko, Bad Zwesten 1997.

16...♘f6 17 ♘g5 ♘g4 *(D)*

17...♘d4 also guarantees Black good counterplay.

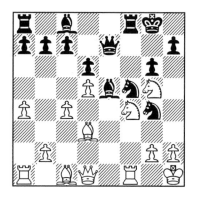

After the text the position is unclear according to *ECO*, and Atalik-Nijboer went on: **18 ♕xg4 ♘e3 19 ♘xg6** [winning a pawn temporarily, but Black has sufficient counterplay; instead, Huzman suggests 19 ♕g3 ♘xf1 20 ♗xf1 ♕f6 21 ♕h4 h5 22 g3, but the simple 22...♗xb2 23 ♗xb2 ♕xb2 24 ♖e1 ♕f2 25 ♖b1 ♗f5 26 ♖c1 ♕d2 27 ♖a1 ♕b2 leads to a forced draw] **19...♖xf1+ 20 ♗xf1 hxg6 21 ♕e4 ♕xg5** [not 21...♘xf1? 22 ♕xg6+ ♕g7 (or 22...♗g7 23 ♗f4) 23 ♕e8+ ♕f8 24 ♕xf8+ ♔xf8 25 ♗f4 ♗xb2 27 ♖xf1 +-] **22 ♗xe3 ♕h5 23 ♗f4 ♗f5 24 ♕e3 ♗xb2 25 ♖e1 ♗f6** [25...♖f8 looks simpler] **26 c5! ♗d7 27 ♕b3 ♖e8 28 ♖xe8+ ♗xe8 29 cxd6 cxd6 30 ♕xb7** [if 30 ♗xd6 ♕f5 31 ♗d3 ♗xa4! 32 ♕c4 b5! ∞] **30...♕f5 31 ♕b8 ♕xf4 32 ♕xe8+ ♔g7 33 ♕d7+ ♔h6 34 ♕h3+ ♔g7 35 ♕d7+ ♔h6 36 ♕h3+ ½-½.**

B2: 10 ♗e3 *(D)*

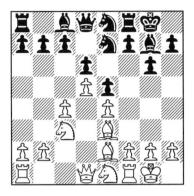

This development is very logical as it supports c4-c5. Moreover, the bishop may perform defensive tasks on the kingside, and sometimes it can even take the a7-pawn. On the other hand, it allows Black to gain a tempo with ...f5 followed by ...f4 and potentially another after ...g4-g3. As usual the arising positions are extremely sharp and difficult to assess.

10...f5 11 f3 f4

Black continues his main idea of an attack on the kingside. Other plans are usually connected with play in the centre or the activation of Black's dark-squared bishop:

a) 11...c5 12 ♘d3 (if 12 dxc6 bxc6 13 ♕d2 ♗e6 14 ♖d1 ♕c7 15 f4 exf4 16 ♗xf4 fxe4 17 ♘xe4 ♕b6+ 18 ♗e3 ♖xf1+ 19 ♔xf1 ♕xb2 = V.Korchnoi-F.Nijboer, Wijk aan Zee 1993) 12...f4 13 ♗f2 h5 14 b4 b6 15 a4 a5 16 bxc5 bxc5 17 ♖b1 g5 18 ♘xc5! (a typical sacrifice, which usually gives White excellent chances) 18...dxc5 19 ♗xc5 ♘g6 20 ♗b6 ♕f6 21 c5 with huge compensation for the piece, V.Korchnoi-F.Nijboer, Dutch Team Ch. 1993.

b) 11...♘f6?! is inaccurate here: while ...♘f6 may eventually be required to force through ...g5-g4, Black only restricts his options by playing it so early. For instance, 12 c5 f4 13 ♗f2 g5 transposes to the inferior 13...♘f6?! line below.

c) 11...♔h8 intends ...♘g8 and ...♗h6 to exchange dark-squared bishops or gain control of the c1-square. The downside of this plan is its slowness; e.g. 12 c5 ♘g8 13 a4 ♗h6 14 ♗f2 ♘gf6 15 a5 ♘h5 16 ♘d3 (better than 16 g3 fxe4 17 ♘xe4 ♘ef6 18 cxd6 cxd6 19 ♘c3 ♗h3 20 ♘g2 a6 21 ♗b6 ♕e7 22 ♖a4 ♘g7 ∞ V.Korchnoi-J.Polgar, Prague 1995) 16...♘ef6 17 ♖a4! (an original manoeuvre to take over the c-file; if 17 b4 a6! 18 ♘b2 ♘f4 19 ♘c4 ♕e7 ∞ B.Gelfand-J.Polgar, Dos Hermanas 1996) 17...♕e7 18 ♖c4 ♘e8 19 b4 (or 19 ♘b5!? +=) 19...a6 20 cxd6 ♘xd6 21 ♖c5 ♘f6?! 22 ♘xe5! fxe4 23 ♘c4 e3?! 24 ♗g3 ♗g7?! 25 ♖xc7! ♕xc7 26 ♗xd6 ♕d8 27 ♗e5 +/- V.Grabliauskas-L.Sandstrom, Copenhagen 1998.

12 ♗f2 g5 *(D)*

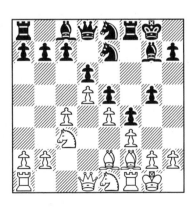

Black sometimes plays 12...h5 here, but this has no independent significance as ...g6-g5 inevitably follows, usually at once, with a transposition to whichever 13th move White prefers.

13 c5 (D)

The most consequential move: the knight on e8 does not prevent c4-c5, so preparatory moves such as 13 ♘d3 or 13 b4 are unnecessary.

White sometimes plays 13 a4, intending an early push to a5, but this will transpose to the relevant a2-a4 lines below after a later c4-c5. Note that 13...a5 (as in the 9...♘d7 main line C132) is not a good idea here, since Black is not in control of the c5-square; e.g. 14 c5 ♔h8 15 cxd6 ♘xd6 16 ♖c1 ♗d7 17 ♘d3 b6 18 b3 +/- E.Jiretorn-T.Stewart, Linköping 1995.

Worse is 13 g4?! fxg3 (13...c5!?) 14 hxg3 ♘g6 15 ♗e3 h5 16 ♘g2 ♗h3 17 ♖f2 h4 18 g4 ♗xg2 19 ♔xg2 ♘f4+ 20 ♔h2 b6 =+ T.Szentmihalyi-D.Boros, Budapest 1999.

B21: 13...♖f6 222
B22: 13...h5 224

Other moves are:

a) 13...♘f6?! (again too committal) 14 cxd6 cxd6 15 ♖c1 ♘g6 16 ♘b5 ♖f7 (not 16...g4?! 17 ♘c7 g3 18 ♘xa8 ♘h5 19 ♔h1! +- G.Burgess-F.Borkowski, Odense 1991) 17 ♘xa7 ♗d7 (or 17...g4 18 ♕b3 g3 19 ♗b6 gxh2+ 20 ♔xh2 ♕f8 21 ♘xc8 +/- D.Gurevich-L.Kaplan, US Open, Chicago 1989) 18 ♕b3 g4 19 ♗b6 ♕e7 20 ♗b5 gxf3 21 ♘xf3! ♘xe4 22 ♖c7

+/- M.Hrivnak-R.Flasik, Slovakian Team Ch. 1998.

b) 13...♘g6 14 a4 ♖f7 (14...h5 is B22) 15 a5 ♗f8 16 ♘d3 ♗g7 17 a6! bxa6 (or 17...b6 18 ♘b4 dxc5 19 ♘c6 ♕f6 20 ♘b5 ♘d6 21 ♘bxa7 += Korchnoi) 18 ♘b4 ♘f6 19 ♘c6 ♕d7 (19...♕e8 20 ♗xa6 +=) 20 ♘xa7 dxc5 21 ♘xc8 (or 21 ♗xa6 ♖xa7 22 ♗xc8 ♖xa1 23 ♗xd7 ♖xd1 24 ♗e6+ +/- Korchnoi) 21...♕xc8 22 ♖c1 += V.Korchnoi-L.Van Wely, Antwerp 1997.

c) 13...♔h8 14 a4 ♘g8 (or 14...a6 15 cxd6 ♘xd6 16 ♘d3 h5 17 ♘c5 ♖f6 18 ♖c1 ♖g6 19 b4 g4 20 ♗h4 += L.Johannessen-B.Socko, Bermuda 2002) 15 a5 h5 16 ♖c1 ♘h6 17 ♘b5 g4 18 ♔h1 a6 (if 18...♕g5 19 ♕d2!) 19 ♘a3 g3 (T.Rahman-C.Scholz, Dortmund 2004) 20 hxg3 fxg3 21 ♗xg3 +/-.

B21: 13...♖f6 (D)

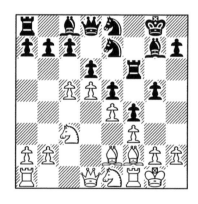

Heading for g6 to support ...g5-g4, or else to h6 to attack down the h-file.

14 cxd6

14 a4 may be more accurate, e.g. 14...♖g6 (if 14...h5 15 cxd6 cxd6 16 a5 ♘c7 17 ♘d3 ♖g6 18 ♔h1 g4 19 g3 h4 20

fxg4 hxg3 21 hxg3 ♖h6+ 22 ♔g2 ♘g6 23 ♖h1 +/- R.Vera-R.Perez Merlos, Spanish League 2004, or 14...♖h6 15 ♖c1! a6 16 a5 ♘f6 17 cxd6 cxd6 18 ♘a4 ♕e8 19 ♘b6 ♕h5 20 h4! +/-) 15 cxd6 cxd6 (or 15...♘xd6 16 ♘b5 ♗d7, R.Tuominen-J.Yrjola, Jyvaskyla 1996, 17 ♘d3! +/-Hazai) 16 a5! (better than 16 ♘b5 a6 17 ♘a3 g4 18 fxg4 ♘f6 19 h3 ♘xe4 20 ♗d3 ♘xf2 21 ♖xf2 ♖f6 ∞ R.Pogorelov-J.Guevara Pijoan, Mondariz 1996) 16...♗d7 (or 16...♘f6 17 ♘b5 +/- R.Pogorelov-J.Anton Veiga, Madrid 2002) 17 ♗b5 g4 18 ♗xd7 ♕xd7 19 fxg4 ♖xg4 20 ♕a4 +/- R.Pogorelov-R.Garcia Garcia, Navalmoral de la Mata 2004.

14...cxd6

14...♘xd6!?, planning ...♖h6 and ...♕e8-h5, looks a better plan here, e.g. 15 ♘d3 ♖h6 16 g4 (if 16 ♘c5 ♕e8 17 ♘e6!? ♗xe6 18 dxe6 ♖xe6 19 ♕b3 ♘c6 ∞) 16...fxg3 17 ♗xg3 ♘g6 18 ♔h1 ♘f4 19 ♖g1 ♕e8 20 ♘f2 ♖g6 21 ♗f1 ♗d7 22 ♖c1 ♖c8 23 ♖c2 ♕f7 24 a4 a6 ∞ R.Neininger-M.Füss, German League 1998.

15 ♖c1 *(D)*

White has less chance of advantage after 15 ♘d3 ♖g6 16 ♖c1 h5 17 ♔h1 g4 18 ♗g1 g3 19 ♘e1 gxh2 20 ♗f2 ♗f6 21 ♔xh2 ♔g7 22 ♖h1 ♘g8 23 ♔g1 h4 ∞ J.Pacheco-T.Coleman, Pan-American Junior Ch. 2001; or 15 ♘b5 a6 16 ♘a7 (16 ♘c3!?) 16...♗d7 17 ♕b3 ♕b8 18 ♕b6 h5 19 ♔h1 g4 with counterplay, S.Bromberger-B.Voekler, German League 2003.

After the text Black still has two attacking plans, but White should keep an edge with accurate play:

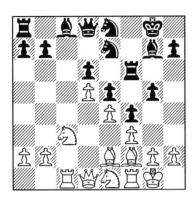

a) 15...♖h6 16 ♕c2 ♘f6 (if 16...a6 17 ♘d3 ♘f6 18 ♘a4 ♕e8 19 ♘b6 ♕h5 20 h4! or 18...♘d7 19 ♕c7 ♕e8 20 ♔h1 +/-) 17 ♘b5 g4 18 ♘c7? (correct was 18 ♕c7! +/-) 18...g3 19 hxg3 ♘h5 20 ♘xa8 ♘xg3 21 ♗xg3 fxg3 22 f4? (but if 22 ♕c7 ♕e8 23 f4 ♕g6! threatening ...♖h1+) 22...♘c6! 23 ♘f3 (P.Kalisvaart-T.Hendriks, Vlissingen 2000) 23...♘d4! -+.

b) 15...♖g6 16 ♘b5 ♗d7 (if 16...a6 17 ♘c7! ♘xc7 18 ♗b6 ♕e8 19 ♖xc7 ♖h6 20 ♔h1 += H.Waldmann-H.Knuth, German League 1996) 17 ♕b3 (or 17 ♘xa7!? +=) 17...a6 18 ♘c3 b5 19 ♘d3 g4 20 fxg4 ♗xg4 21 ♗xg4 ♖xg4 22 ♔h1 ♘g6 23 ♕d1 +/= G.Morrison-D.Kilgour, Scottish Ch. 1985, though White later went wrong: 23...♘f6 24 a4 ♕d7 25 ♖a1 b4 26 ♘xb4 ♘h4 27 ♖g1 ♘h5 28 h3? (better 28 ♘c6! and if 28...♘g3+ 29 hxg3 fxg3 30 ♘e7+! ♔h8 31 ♘f5 gxf2 32 ♕xg4 fxg1♕+ 33 ♖xg1 +/-) 28...♘g3+ 29 ♔h2 ♖g6 30 ♘d3 ♖f8 31 ♘e1 ♖h6 32 ♗xg3?? (32 ♘f3! and if 32...♘xg2 33 ♘g5! ∞) 32...fxg3+ 33 ♔xg3 ♘xg2! 34 ♕g4 ♖g6 35 ♘xg2 ♖xg4+ 36 hxg4 ♕b7 37 ♖ab1 ♕b6 38 ♖gf1 ♖xf1 39 ♖xf1 ♕xb2 40 ♖f3 ♗h6 0-1.

B22: 13...h5 *(D)*

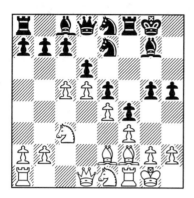

The start of a pawn storm on the opposing king.

14 a4

The most usual plan, intending to undermine the black queenside.

Alternatively:

a) 14 ♖c1 has the idea 14...♖f6 15 cxd6 cxd6 16 ♘b5 a6 17 ♘c7! ♘xc7 18 ♗b6 (the point) 18...♖g6 19 ♖xc7 ♕f8 20 ♕a4 g4 21 ♔h1 ♗f6 22 ♗b5 += J.Lopez Martinez-A.Garcia Luque, Seville 2007, or if 14...dxc5 15 ♗xc5 ♖f6 16 ♕b3 ♔h7 17 ♘d3 ♖g6 18 ♘b5 a6 19 ♘a7! ♖xa7 20 ♗xa7 b6 21 ♖c2 ♗d7 22 ♖fc1 ♘c8 23 ♗b8 ♘cd6 24 ♗xc7 ♘xc7 25 ♖xc7 ♘b5 26 ♖b7 +/- V.Korchnoi-G.Hernandez, Merida 1996.

Black does better with 14...♘g6 15 cxd6 (15 a4 is still an option) 15...cxd6 16 ♘b5 a6 17 ♘c3 (now if 17 ♘c7 ♘xc7 18 ♗b6 ♖f7! 19 ♕c2 g4 20 fxg4 hxg4 21 ♗xc7 ♕h4 22 ♗xd6 f3 ∞ D.Reizniece-E.Jiretorn, Stockholm 2002) 17...♘f6 18 ♘a4 g4 19 ♘b6 ♖b8 20 ♕b3 h4 21 fxg4 ♘xe4 ∞ K.Krüger-R.Ströher, corr. 2002.

b) 14 cxd6 is also possible, when 14...cxd6 15 ♖c1 ♘g6 is 14 ♖c1 above,

while 15 a4 is similar to the main line (albeit without the option of c5-c6) and will likely transpose. For instance, 15...♘f6?! – 14 a4 ♘f6; 15...♖f6 – 14 a4 ♖f6; 15...♘g6 16 a5 ♖f7 – 16...cxd6 in the main line.

If instead 14...♘xd6 15 ♘d3 ♘g6 16 ♘c5 (16 a4!? ♘g6 17 a5 is the main line again) 16...♖f7 17 ♘e6 ♕f6 18 ♘b5 ♘xb5 19 ♗xb5 c6 20 ♗c4 +/- G.Grigore-M.Cebalo, Arco 2003.

14...♘g6

Black has tried different ways of constructing his counterplay:

a) 14...♘f6?! (still premature) 15 a5 g4 16 cxd6 cxd6 17 ♘b5 g3 (if 17...a6? 18 ♗b6! ♕d7 19 ♘c7 ♖b8 20 ♖c1 and 21 ♗a7 +-; or 17...gxf3 18 ♗xf3 ♗g4 19 ♕e2 += G.Hildebrand-M.Schubert, corr. 1995) 18 ♗xa7 ♘g6 19 ♗b6 ♕e7 20 ♘c7 ♘d7! 21 h3! (not 21 ♘xa8? ♘xb6 22 ♘xb6 ♕h4 23 h3 ♗xh3 24 gxh3 ♕xh3 25 ♖f2 gxf2+ 26 ♔xf2 ♕g3+ 27 ♔f1 h4 -/+ Koutsin) 21...♘xb6 (or 21...♕h4 22 ♘e6 ♘xb6 23 axb6 ♗xe6 24 dxe6 ♖xa1 25 ♕xa1 +/- S.Koutsin-P.Zpevak, Slovakian Team Ch. 1999) 22 axb6 ♖xa1 23 ♕xa1 ♘h8 24 ♗c4 ♘f7 25 ♘e6 ♘g5 (or 25...♗xe6 26 dxe6 ♘d8 27 ♗d5 +- Gufeld) 26 ♘xg5 ♕xg5 27 ♘d3 ♕h4 28 ♖c1 ♗f6 (if 28...♗xh3 29 gxh3 ♕xh3 30 ♖c2 +/-) 29 ♖c2 ♗d8 30 ♕a5 ♕e7 31 ♘b4 ♔h8 32 ♘c6 +/- S.Krivoshey-O.Bindrich, Leutersdorf 2000.

b) 14...♔h8 15 a5 dxc5 16 ♗xc5 ♘d6 (or 16...♖f6 17 ♘b5 a6 18 ♘a3 ♘d6 19 ♘d3 ♖g6, V.Korchnoi-Xie Jun, San Francisco 1995, 20 ♕b3 g4 21 ♘c4 ♘xc4 22 ♕xc4 and 23 ♕c3 +/-) 17 a6 (or 17 ♘b5 ♘xb5 18 ♗xb5 ♖f6 19 ♖f2 ♘g8 20 a6 +/= K.Spraggett-F.Gonzalez Velez, Manresa 1993) 17...bxa6 18 ♗xa6 ♗d7 19 ♘d3 g4 20 ♔h1 ♘g6 21 ♗g1 ♘h4 22 ♘c5 += V.Ikonnikov-J.Gallagher, Geneva 1994.

c) 14...♖f6 (D), planning ...♖g6 and ...g5-g4, is a serious alternative:

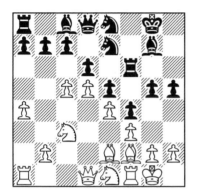

c1) 15 cxd6 ♘xd6 (if 15...cxd6 16 a5 ♘c7 17 ♘d3 ♖g6 18 ♔h1 g4 19 g3 h4 20 fxg4 hxg3 21 hxg3 += R.Vera-R.Perez Merlos, Spanish Team Ch. 2004) 16 ♘b5 (if 16 ♘d3 ♖g6 17 ♘c5 g4 18 ♗h4 ♕f8 19 ♘e6 ♗xe6 20 dxe6 ♗f6 21 ♗xf6 ♕xf6 22 fxg4 ♕g5 23 h3 ♘c6 ∞ N.Gongora Reyes-C.Diaz Ordonez, Havana 2008) 16...a6 17 ♘xd6 cxd6 18 ♘d3 ♖g6 19 ♕b3 g4 20 ♕b6 ♕f8 21 ♖fc1 g3! (better than 21...♕f6 22 ♗e1 ♔h7 23 ♖c7 gxf3 24 ♗xf3 ♗g4 25 ♔f1 ♖e8 26 ♕xb7 ♗xf3 27 gxf3 ♕g5 28 ♘f2 +/- T.Shaked-V.Babula, FIDE World Ch., Las Vegas 1999) 22 ♗e1 (or 22 hxg3 fxg3 23 ♗e3 ♗h6 24 ♗xh6 ♖xh6 25 ♕e3 ♕f6 26 f4 ♕h4 27 fxe5 ♗d7 28 ♗f3 ♖f8 ∞ A.Bormida-J.Copie, corr. 1999) 22...gxh2+ 23 ♔xh2 ♕f6 24 ♖c2 ♗h6 25 ♖ac1 ♗g5 26 ♗f1 ♗h4 ∞ A.Zawadka-J.Desmoitier, corr. 2000.

c2) 15 a5 ♖g6 16 cxd6 ♘xd6 17 ♘d3 (if 17 ♘b5 g4 18 ♘xd6 cxd6 19 ♗h4 ♕f8 20 ♕a4 ♗f6 21 ♗xf6 ♖xf6 22 ♖c1 ♘g6 23 a6 ♖f7 24 ♗b5 ♕d8! ∞ L.Ftacnik-A.Wojtkiewicz, Budapest 1993) 17...g4 18 ♗h4 ♕f8 19 g3 ♗f6 20 fxg4 hxg4 21 gxf4 (not 21 ♘xf4? exf4 22 ♖xf4 ♕h6 23 ♗xf6 ♖xf6 24 ♖xf6 ♕xf6 25 ♗xg4 ♘g6 -/+ A.Shirov-J.Nunn, Amsterdam 1995) 21...♗xh4 22 fxe5 ♕h6 23 ♘f4 with better chances for White, though Black still has some counterplay.

15 a5 ♖f7 (D)

Other moves:

a) 15...♘f6?! 16 cxd6 cxd6 17 ♘b5 g4 18 ♘xa7 (or 18 ♗xa7 g3 – 14...♘f6?!) 18...g3 (or 18...♗d7 19 ♗b6 ♕e7 20 ♗b5 g3 21 ♗xd7 ♘xd7 22 h3 +/- A.Nikitin-D.Frolov, St Petersburg 1997) 19 ♗b6 gxh2+ (or 19...♕e7 20 ♘xc8 ♖axc8 21 h3 +/- A.Pavlidis-A.Davletbakov, World Junior Ch. 2007) 20 ♔xh2 ♕e7 21 ♘xc8 ♖axc8 22 ♖h1 +/- P.Kiriakov-J.Ulko, Moscow 1999.

b) 15...dxc5?! 16 ♗xc5 ♘d6 17 ♘d3 ♖f7 18 a6 b6 19 ♗xd6 ♕xd6 20 ♘b5 ♕d7 21 ♘b4 ♘h4 22 ♖c1 +/- V.Korchnoi-I.Nemet, Swiss Team Ch. 1994.

c) 15...♗h6 16 ♘b5! (or 16 b4 ♔h7 17 cxd6 cxd6 18 ♘b5 g4!? 19 fxg4 hxg4 20 ♗xg4 ♗xg4 21 ♕xg4 ♘f6 22 ♕f3 ♕d7 23 ♘xa7 ♘g4, V.Korchnoi-G.Kasparov, European Team Ch., Debrecen 1992, 24 ♗b6! +/-) 16...a6 17 ♘a3 ♔h8 18 ♘c4 ♖g8 19 ♖a3 ♘f6 20 cxd6 cxd6 (V.Korchnoi-A.Shirov, Buenos Aires 1993) 21 ♕b3! ♕e7 22 ♕b4 ♖d8 23 ♘b6 ♖b8 24 h3 +/- is the suggestion of King's Indian expert Korchnoi.

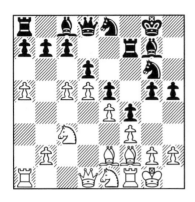

16 cxd6

White can develop his initiative in other ways too:

a) 16 ♖c1 ♗f8 17 ♘b5 a6 (17...dxc5!?) 18 ♘a3 ♖g7 19 cxd6 ♘xd6 20 ♘c4 ♗d7?! (20...♘xc4) 21 ♘d3 ♘xc4 22 ♖xc4 ♗d6 23 ♘c5 +/- T.Rahman-M.Abdul, Bangladeshi Ch. 2007.

b) 16 a6 b6 17 cxb6 cxb6 18 ♘d3 ♘f6 (18...♘c7!?) 19 ♘b4 g4 20 ♘c6 ♕f8 21 ♘b5 g3 22 ♗e1 +/- I.Arakelov-S.Voitsekhovsky, Vladimir 2004.

c) 16 c6!? bxc6 (or 16...♘f6 17 cxb7 ♗xb7 18 ♘d3 a6 19 ♘b4 ♗c8 20 ♘c6 ♕e8 21 b4 g4 22 ♔h1 ♗f8 23 b5 g3 24 ♗g1 ♗h3 25 gxh3 ♘h4 26 ♖f2 +/- K.Murugan-D.Neelotpal, Calcutta 1997) 17 dxc6 ♗e6 18 a6 ♘f6 19 ♕a4 g4 20 ♗c4 ♗xc4 21 ♕xc4 g3 22 hxg3 fxg3 23 ♗xg3 +/= E.Van Oosterom-M.Spaan, Houten 1993.

16...♘xd6

Alternatively, 16...cxd6 17 ♘b5 a6 18 ♘c3 ♘f6 (or 18...♗h6 19 ♘a4 ♖g7 20 ♘b6 ♖b8 21 ♖c1 ♗d7 22 ♖c3 ♘f6 23 ♘xd7 ♕xd7 24 ♕b3 g4 25 ♔h1 g3 26 ♗b6 +/- R.Rodriguez-R.Paramos Dominguez, Burela 1993) 19 ♘a4 ♗d7 (if

19...g4 20 ♘b6 ♖b8 21 ♘xc8 ♕xc8 22 ♖c1 ♕d7 23 ♗b6 +/= Hazai; 19...♘d7!? might be better) 20 ♘b6 ♔h8!? 21 ♘xd7! ♖xd7 22 ♗b6 ♕e8 23 ♘d3 +/- A.O'Kelly de Galway-T.Ghitescu, Sandefjord 1975.

17 ♘d3

If 17 ♘b5 ♘xb5 18 ♗xb5 g4 ∞ Kantsler, but 17 a6!? comes into consideration.

17...♗f6

Or 17...♗h6 18 ♘c5 (18 a6!? is still possible) 18...a6 19 b4 ♕f6 20 ♔h1 ♘f8 21 b5 ♖g7 22 bxa6 bxa6 23 ♕a4 g4 24 ♖fb1 (if 24 ♕c6 g3! or 24 fxg4 hxg4 25 g3 ♖h7 ∞) 24...g3 25 ♗g1 ♕g6 26 ♗f1 h4 27 ♖a2 h3 ∞ A.Belozerov-S.Gabrielsen, European Junior Ch. 1996.

18 ♘c5 ♘f8 19 ♘b5 *(D)*

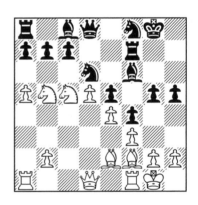

19 ♕b3 ♕e8 20 a6 b6 (if 20...bxa6 21 ♗xa6) 21 ♘b7 ♗e7 22 ♘b5 ♘xb5 23 ♗xb5 ♗d7 24 ♗xd7 ♕xd7 25 ♕a4 +/- V.Korchnoi-E.Relange, Cannes 1996, but 19...a6!? might improve.

The text was played in B.Gelfand-B.Kantsler, Israel 2001, which continued **19...♖g7 20 a6 bxa6 21 ♘xa6 g4 22**

♘xa7 g3 23 ♗c5 [if 23 hxg3!? fxg3 24 ♗c5 ♗g5! planning ...♗f4, ...♕h4] **23...♗h3?!** [the simple 23...gxh2+, intending ...♕e8-g6, guaranteed good counterplay] **24 gxh3?** [24 ♔h1! ♗xg2+ (if 24...♘g6 25 ♖e1 ♘h4 26 ♗f1 or 24...♗d7 25 ♘c6 ♕c8 26 ♘xc7! ♖xa1 27 ♕xa1 ♕xc7 28 ♕a3 +/-) 25 ♔xg2 ♘g6 (or 25...gxh2+ 26 ♔h1) 26 ♖g1 ♘h4+ 27 ♔f1 should parry the attack] **24...♕d7 25 ♗d3 ♕xh3 26 ♕e2 ♘g6?** [26...♘d7! followed by ...♔h7 and ...♖ag8 wins] **27 ♕g2 ♕d7 28 ♘xc7?** [28 hxg3 ♘h4 29 gxh4! ∞] **28...♘h4 29 ♕e2 ♕h3 30 ♘e6** [or 30 ♘xa8 ♘g2!] **30...♘g2! 31 ♖fc1 ♕xh2+ 32 ♔f1 ♕h1+ 33 ♗g1 ♘h4 34 ♘xg7 ♘xf3 0-1**.

C: 9...♘d7 (D)

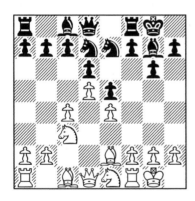

C1: 10 ♗e3 *228*
C2: 10 f3 *245*
C3: 10 ♘d3 *252*

Obviously these lines can transpose into each other in many places. White has also tried:

a) **10 f4?!** is ineffective with the knight on d7, e.g. 10...f5 11 fxe5 (or 11 exf5 ♘xf5 12 ♘d3 ♕e7 13 fxe5 ♘xe5 14 ♘xe5 ♗xe5 15 ♗f3? ♕h4 -+ B.Hönlinger-A.Dünmann, Vienna 1926; or 11 ♘f3 fxe4 12 ♘g5 ♘c5 13 fxe5 ♗xf3 =) 11...♘xe5 12 ♘f3 ♘xf3+ 13 ♗xf3 f4 14 ♗d2 g5 15 ♗g4 ♘g6 16 ♖c1 ♘e5 =+ Al Hamani-T.Hay, Skopje Olympiad 1972.

b) **10 b4** transposes elsewhere: 10...f5 11 f3 f4 12 ♘d3 – *12 b4* in line C22; or 10...a5!? 11 bxa5 ♖xa5 – *9 b4 a5 10 bxa5 ♖xa5 11 ♘e1 ♘d7* in Chapter 11 (note to line C1).

c) **10 ♗d2** f5 will transpose to line C3 if and when White plays ♘d3. Attempts to do without this move do not lead to much; e.g. 11 ♖c1 (11 ♘d3 – *10 ♘d3*) 11...♘f6 (or 11...♔h8 12 ♘d3 ♘f6 13 f3 – *10 ♘d3*) 12 f3 f4 (or 12...c5!? 13 dxc6 bxc6 14 ♘d3 ♗e6 ∞ A.Miles-E.Bukic, Bugojno 1978) 13 c5!? (13 ♘d3 g5 14 c5 – *10 ♘d3*) 13...dxc5 14 ♘a4 b6 15 b4 (A.Miles-J.Lind, Gausdal 1980) 15...c6 16 dxc6 ♘xc6 17 bxc5 ♘d4 ∞.

d) **10 ♗g5!?** hopes for 10...f5?! 11 exf5 gxf5 12 f4! ♘f6 (or 12...♗f6 13 ♗h6 ♖f7 14 ♘f3 ♗g7 15 ♗g5 e4 16 ♘d4 +/= H.Herraiz Lopez-D.Taboas Rodriguez, Torrelavega 2002) 13 fxe5 dxe5 14 ♘d3 h6 15 ♗e3 f4?! 16 ♗f2 ♘g6 17 ♘c5 +/- Sr.Cvetkovic-I.Nikolaidis, Corinth 1997.

Otherwise 10...f6 11 ♗e3 f5 or 11 ♗d2 f5 12 ♘d3 reaches the main lines a move behind (but not 11 ♗h4? g5 12 ♗g3 f5 13 f3 f4 14 ♗f2, when Black is a tempo up on the 10 ♗e3 main line). Similarly 10...h6 11 ♗e3 f5 or 11 ♗d2 f5, as the extra ...h7-h6 is not useful and Black will usually play ...h6-h5 anyway.

e) 10 ♔h1!? (a waiting move) 10...f5 11 exf5 ♘xf5! (better than 11...gxf5 12 f4! exf4 13 ♘d3 ♘g6 14 ♘xf4 ♘xf4 15 ♗xf4 += A.Miles-S.Nurkic, Toscolano 1996) 12 ♘c2 a5 13 ♘e4 ♘f6 14 ♗d3?! (14 ♗g5 = Hazai) 14...♘xe4 15 ♗xe4 ♕h4! 16 ♕d3 ♘g3+ 17 ♕xg3 ♕xe4 =+ A.Miles-A.Ziegler, Malmö 1996.

C1: 10 ♗e3 f5 11 f3 *(D)*

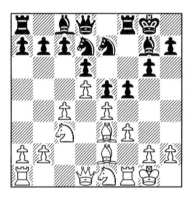

The plan with 10 ♗e3 (or 10 f3 f5 11 ♗e3) was known as early as the early 1950s, but after the game Szabo-Spassky, Bucharest 1953, it almost disappeared from tournament practice. It was not until the late 1980s that the variation became popular, due largely to Korchnoi, who played many fine games in this variation.

The position in the diagram is a starting point for one of the sharpest King's Indian variations. The e3-bishop takes up an ideal place, supporting the c4-c5 advance, and in some lines targeting the a7-pawn. From Black's perspective, the knight on d7 rules out any de-

fence with ...c7-c5, as the d6-pawn hangs after d5xc6. So he must rely on his kingside attack, which ...f5-f4 now accelerates, and ...g5-g4-g3 may later follow too. Black's queenside may be completely overrun, but if he succeeds on the other wing, he will win, since he is after the greater prize: the opposing king.

11...f4

The most logical move, played in nearly 90% of games. Others:

a) 11...♘f6?! makes little sense, as it allows c4-c5 at once: 12 c5! f4 13 ♗f2 g5, transposing to 13...♘f6?! in the 9...♘e8 line B2 above.

b) 11...b6?! (Black cannot prevent c4-c5 so shouldn't try) 12 ♘d3 ♘c5 13 b4 ♘xd3 14 ♕xd3 a5 15 a3 ♕d7 16 c5 +/- H.Harke-B.Bierwisch, Bad Wörishofen 2002.

c) 11...♖f7 12 ♖c1 b6?! (12...f4) 13 b4 a5 14 a3 ♘f6 15 c5 axb4 16 axb4 bxc5 17 bxc5 dxc5 18 ♘d3 +/- A.De los Santos Serrano-E.Benatar, corr. 2002.

d) 11...♔h8 12 ♘d3 (or 12 b4 ♘f6 13 c5 ♖f7 14 ♘d3 ♘eg8 15 a4 ♘e8 16 a5 ♗h6, T.Karolyi-T.Toshkov, Geneva 1989, 17 ♗xh6 ♘xh6 18 f4 +/-) 12...♘g8 (if 12...f4 13 ♗f2 g5 14 c5 ♖f6 15 cxd6 cxd6 16 ♘b5 a6 17 ♘a7 ♖g6 18 ♖c1 ♘f6 19 ♘xc8 ♖xc8 20 ♕b3 +/- G.Burgess-M.Hebden, British Ch. 1989) 13 c5 ♗h6 14 ♗xh6 ♘xh6 15 f4! exf4 16 cxd6 cxd6 17 ♘xf4 ♕b6+ 18 ♔h1 ♘e5 19 ♕d2 ♘hg4 20 ♗xg4 ♘xg4 21 ♖ae1 +/- M.Nikolov-J.Nikolov, Teteven 2004.

12 ♗f2 g5 *(D)*

This time it's a 91% choice. Of the rare alternatives:

a) 12...♘f6?! still allows 13 c5.

b) 12...a5?! is premature before a2-a4 has been played: 13 a3 b6 14 b4 axb4 15 axb4 ♖xa1 16 ♕xa1 ♘f6 17 ♕a7 ♗d7 18 ♘c2 g5 19 c5 +/- J.Ladstetter-L.Hanke, Eppingen 1988.

c) 12...h5 is quite playable, and generally transposes to ...h7-h5 lines below after a subsequent ...g6-g5, though it can hardly be more useful than 12...g5 at this precise moment.

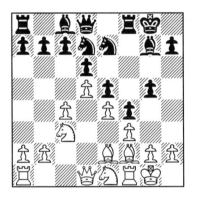

C11: 13 ♖c1 *231*
C12: 13 ♘b5 *233*
C13: 13 a4 *236*

White has also tried:

a) 13 c5?! ♘xc5 14 ♗xc5 (or 14 b4 ♘d7 15 ♖c1 a6 =+ J.Ager-K.Klundt, Austrian Team Ch. 2003) 14...dxc5 15 ♘d3 b6 16 b4 cxb4 17 ♘xb4 a5 18 ♘d3 ♔h8 =+ G.Khechumyan-V.Rajlich, Budapest 2000.

b) 13 g4 (trying to block the king-side before starting action on the other wing) 13...fxg3! (if 13...h5 14 h3 ♖f7 15 ♘d3 ♘f6 16 c5 ♗f8 17 ♔g2 ♘g6 18 b4

♖h7 19 ♖h1 ♕e7 20 ♖c1 ♘h4+ 21 ♔g1 ♗d7 22 c6 bxc6 23 dxc6 ♗e6 24 b5 += A.Zilberberg-Y.Zarubin, corr. 1967) 14 hxg3 ♘g6 15 ♘g2 (if 15 ♕d2 h5 16 ♗e3 ♗f6 intending ...h5-h4 = Nunn, or 16 ♘g2 h4 17 g4 ♘f4 18 ♔h2 ♘xg2 19 ♔xg2 ♖f7 20 b4 ♘f8 =/+ M.Socko-K.Kachiani Gersinska, Wuppertal 1998) 15...h5 16 ♘e3 h4 (or 16...a5!? 17 ♔h2 ♘c5 18 ♘a4 b6 19 ♘xc5 bxc5 20 ♕c2 h4 21 g4 ♗d7 22 ♘f5 ♗f6 ∞ V.Dydyshko-L.Van Wely, Yerevan Olympiad 1996) 17 g4 ♘f4 18 ♔h2 a5 19 ♘f5 ♗f6 20 ♕d2 b6 21 b3 ♘c5 22 ♖ab1 ♗d7 23 ♗d1 ♕c8 24 a3 ♕a6 ∞ D.Ruzele-R.Speckner, Regensburg 1998.

c) 13 ♘d3 ♘f6 (as White has now prepared c4-c5, the d7-knight moves away to support ...g5-g4; instead 13...♘g6 14 c5 ♘f5 – *13...♘f6*; or if 13...♘f6 14 c5 ♖h6 15 cxd6 cxd6 16 ♘b5 ♘f8 17 ♗e1 a6 18 ♘a3 b5 19 ♘c2 ♘d7 20 a4 bxa4 21 ♖xa4 ♘f6 22 ♘f2 += M.Taimanov-D.Bronstein, USSR Ch., Moscow 1952) 14 c5 *(D)* and now we have:

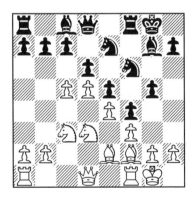

c1) 14...h5?! (premature, as it may be unnecessary) 15 ♖c1 g4 (if 15...a6 16 cxd6 cxd6 17 ♘a4 g4 18 ♗b6 ♕e8 19 ♗c7 +/- F.Döttling-V.Cziehso, Binz 1994; or 15...♘e8 16 ♘b5 a6 17 cxd6 axb5 18 dxe7 ♕xe7 19 ♕b3 ♔h8 20 ♘c5 +/- V.Korchnoi-C.Scholz, Münster 1996) 16 ♘b5 ♘e8 (now if 16...a6 17 cxd6 cxd6 18 ♘c7 g3 19 ♘xa8 gxf2+ 20 ♖xf2 ♘e8 21 ♕b3 b5 22 ♕c3 +- V.Neverov-S.Bjornsson, Pardubice 2003; or 16...g3 17 hxg3 fxg3 18 ♗xg3 ♗h6 19 ♖c3 +/- E.Gereben-B.Schwaegli, Switzerland 1982) 17 fxg4 a6 18 ♘c3 hxg4 19 ♗xg4 ♘f6 20 ♗xc8 ♖xc8 +/- A.Shirov-T.Radjabov, Morelia/Linares 2008.

c2) 14...♘g6 15 a4 (now if 15 ♖c1 ♖f7! 16 ♖c2 ♗f8 17 cxd6 cxd6 18 ♕d2 g4 19 ♖fc1 g3 20 hxg3 fxg3 21 ♗xg3 ♘h5 22 ♗h2 ♗e7 ∞ M.Taimanov-M.Najdorf, Zürich Candidates 1953, or 22 ♗f2 ♘gf4 ∞ S.Gligoric-A.Lukic, Yugoslav Ch. 1955) 15...h5 (if 15...♔h8 16 a5 ♖g8 – 13 a4 ♘g6 14 a5 ♔h8 15 ♘d3) 16 a5! (if 16 h3 ♖f7 17 c6 a5! 18 cxb7 ♗xb7 19 b4 ♗c8 20 bxa5 ♗h6 21 ♘b4?! g4 22 ♘c6 ♕f8 23 fxg4 hxg4 24 hxg4 ♗g5 25 ♗f3 ♕h6 -/+ V.Korchnoi-G.Kasparov, Amsterdam 1991) 16...g4 17 a6! (better than 17 c6 g3 18 hxg3 fxg3 19 ♗xg3 h4 20 ♗h2 ♘h5 21 cxb7 ♗xb7 22 f4 ♘hxf4 23 ♘xf4 ♘xf4 24 ♗xf4 exf4 25 ♗g4 ♕g5 ∞ V.Korchnoi-Xie Jun, Amsterdam 2001) 17...g3 (or 17...bxa6 18 ♘b4 g3 19 hxg3 fxg3 20 ♗xg3 h4 21 ♘c6 += N.Schouten-D.Webbink, Dutch Team Ch. 1995) 18 hxg3 fxg3 19 ♗xg3 h4 20 ♗h2 ♘h5 21 axb7 ♗xb7 22 f4 ♘hxf4 23 ♘xf4 ♘xf4 24 ♗xf4 exf4 25 ♗g4 += W.Harper-K.Waidyaratne, Foxwoods 2007.

d) 13 b4 *(D)* and now:

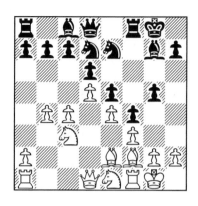

d1) 13...♘f6 14 c5 ♘g6 (or if 14...h5 15 cxd6 cxd6 16 ♖c1 g4 17 ♘b5 g3 18 hxg3 fxg3 19 ♗xg3 ♗h6 20 ♖c3 += D.Gurevich-K.Choobak, USA 1989) 15 ♖c1! (or 15 cxd6 cxd6 16 ♖c1 ♖f7 transposing; while 15 a4 – 13 a4 ♘g6 14 b4) 15...♖f7 16 cxd6 cxd6 17 a4 ♗f8 18 a5 ♗d7 19 ♘b5! (if 19 ♔h1 ♖g7 20 ♗b5 g4 21 ♗xd7 ♕xd7 22 fxg4 ♘xg4 23 ♘f3 ♗e7 24 ♗g1 ♘h4 ∞ D.Gurevich-H.Grünberg, New York Open 1991) 19...g4!? 20 ♘c7 (not 20 ♘xa7?! g3 21 ♗b6 ♕e7 22 h3? ♗xh3! 23 gxh3 ♕d7 -/+ Nikitin) 20...g3 21 hxg3 (not 21 ♘xa8? ♘h5! 22 ♔h1 gxf2 23 ♖xf2 ♘g3+! 24 ♔g1 ♕xa8 25 ♗c4 a6! 26 ♕d3 ♕a7 27 b5 axb5 28 ♗xb5 ♘h1 0-1 J.Piket-G.Kasparov, Tilburg 1989) 21...fxg3 22 ♗xg3 ♗h6 23 ♘xa8 ♘h5 24 ♗f2 ♘gf4? (but if 24...♗xc1 25 ♕xc1 ♕xa8 26 ♕e3 ♘gf4 27 ♔h2! ♕f8 28 ♖h1 +/-) 25 ♖c3! (not 25 ♖c7? ♗a4! 26 ♕xa4 ♘xe2+ -+ Nikitin) 25...♗a4 26 ♘c2 ♘xg2 27 f4! +- T.Teeriaho-J.Gwozdz, corr. 2000.

d2) 13...♖f6! 14 c5 (here 14 ♘d3?! ♖g6 15 c5 ♘f6 16 ♕b3 ♔h8 17 ♖fc1 g4 18 fxg4 ♗xg4 19 ♗f1 ♗f3 -/+ was L.Szabo-B.Spassky, Bucharest 1953)

14...♖h6 (now if 14...♖g6 15 cxd6 cxd6 16 ♖c1 ♘f6?! 17 ♘b5 g4 18 ♘c7 g3 19 ♘xa8 ♘h5 20 ♕c2 ♘c6 21 dxc6 ♕h4 22 ♗xg3! +- J.Tisdall-T.Scholseth, Norwegian Ch. 1989; but 14...a6!? is possible, when 15 ♖c1 – *13 ♖c1 a6 14 b4*, or if 15 c6 bxc6 16 dxc6 ♘f8 17 a4 ♔h8 18 b5 ♖h6 19 ♘d3 ♘e6 20 ♘b4 ♘d4 ∞ G.Kaganskiy-Ma.Tseitlin, Israeli Team Ch. 2000) 15 cxd6 cxd6 16 ♘b5 a6! (if 16...♕e8 17 g4 fxg3 18 ♗xg3 ♕d8 19 ♕c1 ♘f8 ∞ V.Korchnoi-W.Watson, Beersheba 1987, but 17 ♘xa7!? comes into consideration) 17 ♘a7 ♘f6 18 ♘xc8 ♖xc8 19 ♖c1?! ♖xc1 20 ♕xc1 g4 21 ♕c2 g3 22 hxg3 ♘h5 -/+ K.Engel-K.Richardson, corr. 1988.

C11: 13 ♖c1 (D)

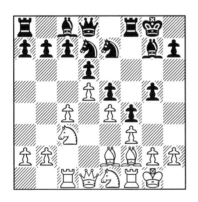

13...a6!? (D)

A relatively new idea: as ♘c3-b5 is integral to White's plan with 13 ♖c1, in particular to the sacrifice 14 c5!?, Black takes the time to prevent it. Previously Black just continued his play on the kingside with one of two moves:

a) 13...♘g6 (the most popular, though possibly not best) 14 c5!? (sacri-ficing a pawn to displace the black knight and open the c-file; instead 14 b4 ♘f6 15 c5 – *13 b4 ♘f6*, or 14 ♘d3 ♘f6 15 c5 – *13 ♘d3 ♘f6* but with 15 ♖c1 rather than 15 a4!) 14...♘xc5 (there is no point in declining: if 14...a6?! 15 ♘a4! h5 16 ♕b3 ♔h8 17 ♘d3 ♖g8 18 cxd6 cxd6 19 ♘b6 ♘xb6 20 ♗xb6 ♕f6 21 ♘f2 += A.Yermolinsky-R.Barcenilla, San Francisco 2000; while 14...♘f6?! 15 cxd6 cxd6 is 13...♘f6?! in line B2 again) 15 b4 ♘a6 (not 15...♘d7? 16 ♘b5 +/-) 16 ♘b5 (if 16 ♘d3 h5 17 ♘b5 ♗d7 18 a4 ♗h6 19 ♖c3 b6 20 ♗e1 ♖f7 21 ♘f2 ♘h4 22 ♘xd6 cxd6 23 ♗xa6 ♕e8 24 ♕e2 g4 ∞ J.Piket-G.Kasparov, Linares 1997; or even 21...♗c8!? 22 ♖a3 ♘xb4 23 ♗xb4 a6 24 ♘xd6 cxd6 25 ♖b3 ♗f8 ∞ I.Bern-W.Stern, corr. 2002) 16...♗d7 (not 16...b6?! 17 ♕a4 h5 18 ♘xd6 cxd6 19 ♗xa6 +/- P.Mascaro March-L.Tattersall Rodriguez, Palma 1999, or if 16...♖f7 17 ♘xa7 ♘xb4 18 ♕b3 ♘a6 19 ♘xc8 ♕xc8 20 a4 with good compensation, S.Atalik-R.Osterman, Bled 1999) 17 ♘xa7 h5 (or 17...♖f7 18 ♕c2 ♕f6 19 ♗xa6 bxa6 20 ♕xc7 ♗e8 21 ♕a5 ♖fxa7 22 ♗xa7 ♖xa7 23 ♖c8 ♔f7 ∞ D.Gurevich-R.Leitao, Groningen 1996) 18 a4 ♘xb4!? 19 ♕b3 g4! 20 fxg4 hxg4 21 ♕xb4 g3! 22 ♕xb7 gxf2+ 23 ♖xf2 f3! 24 ♘xf3 ♗h6 25 ♖c3 ♕b8! 26 ♕xb8 ♖fxb8 with compensation, V.Erdos-L.Kvaszinger, Hungarian Team Ch. 2005.

b) 13...♖f6 14 c5!? (the critical move; 14 ♘d3 and 14 b4 can now be met by 14...♖h6 15 c5 ♕e8! and ...♕h5 with strong play, while 15...a6!? transposes below) 14...♘xc5 (not 14...dxc5?! 15 ♘d3 b6 16 b4! cxb4 17 ♘b5 +/- H.Kallio-

J.Nordenbaek, Copenhagen 2003; or 14...a6?! 15 c6! bxc6 16 dxc6 ♘f8 17 ♘d3 ♘e6 18 ♘b4 ♖g6 19 ♘cd5 += L.Johannessen-M.Carlsen, Drammen 2004/05) 15 b4 ♘a6 16 ♘b5 (or 16 ♘d3 ♖h6 17 a4 ♕e8 18 ♔h1 ♗d7! 19 ♗g1 ♔h8 20 ♕b3 ♘g8 21 ♘f2 ♘f6 ∞ R.Vera-D.Lemos, Buenos Aires 2005) 16...♖h6! (better than 16...♗d7 17 ♘xa7 ♘xb4 18 ♕b3 b6 19 ♘b5 ♗xb5 20 ♗xb5 ♘a6 21 ♘d3 ♖g6 22 ♕c4 ♘c5 23 ♘xc5 bxc5 24 a4 with compensation, V.Iotov-D.Dochev, Bulgarian Ch. 2005) 16...♖h6 17 ♘xa7 ♗d7 18 ♗xa6 bxa6 19 ♕c2 g4 20 ♕xc7 ♕e8 21 fxg4 (if 21 g3 ♔h8 22 ♖c2 ♘g8 23 fxg4 ♗xg4 24 ♗b6 ♕g6 25 ♘c6 fxg3 -+ V.Korchnoi-I.Cheparinov, Amsterdam 2008) 21...♗xg4 22 ♘c6 ♘xc6 23 dxc6 ♕h5 24 h4 ♗f6 ∞ V.Iotov-V.Saravanan, Kalamaria 2008.

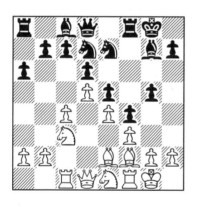

14 ♘d3

Not 14 c5? ♘xc5 15 b4 ♘d7 -/+ as there is no 16 ♘b5. But White also has:

a) 14 b4 ♖f6 15 c5 ♖h6 16 ♘a4 (if 16 cxd6 cxd6 17 ♘d3 b5! 18 a4 ♕e8 19 g4 fxg3 20 ♗xg3 ♘f6 21 ♘f2 ♗d7 ∞ H.Waldmann-H.Hoeckendorf, German League 2004) 16...♕e8 17 ♔h1 ♔h8 (or

17...♕h5 18 ♗g1 ♕h4 19 ♘d3 b5 20 cxb6 cxb6 21 ♕e1 += V.Korchnoi-I.Nataf, Cannes 1998; but 17...♖b8!? might be considered) 18 ♘d3 b5 19 cxb6 cxb6 20 ♗g1 b5 21 ♘b6 ♘xb6 22 ♗xb6 ♘g8 23 ♘f2 += B.Avrukh-B.Socko, European Team Ch., Leon 2001.

b) 14 ♘a4!? ♖f6 (if 14...b6 15 b4 +/=) 15 c5 ♖h6 16 ♕b3! (threatening 17 c6 or 17 cxd6 cxd6 18 ♘b6) 16...b5 17 cxb6 cxb6 18 ♘xb6!? (simpler 18 ♗xb6 ♘xb6 19 ♕xb6 ♕e8 20 ♕c7! ♕h5 21 ♗d3! +/-) 18...♖b8 19 ♘xc8 ♖xb3 20 ♘xe7+ ♕xe7 21 axb3 ♘c5 22 b4 ♘b3 23 ♖c8+ ♗f8 24 ♘c2 +/= V.Iotov-D.Dochev, Bulgarian Ch. 2004.

14...b6

If immediately 14...♖f6 15 c5 ♖h6 16 c6! (again if 16 ♘a4 ♕e8 17 ♔h1 ♖b8!? ∞) 16...bxc6 17 dxc6 ♘xc6 (or 17...♘f8 18 ♘b4 ♕e8 19 ♔h1 ♘e6 20 ♘cd5 ♘xd5 21 ♘xd5 ♔h8 22 b4 += V.Rogovski-T.Radjabov, Alushta 2001) 18 ♘xf4 ♘d4 19 ♘fd5 ♘f8 20 ♗c4 ♔h8 21 ♘e2 += M.Bluvshtein-E.Inarkiev, Moscow 2004.

15 b4 ♖f6 16 c5 ♖h6 *(D)*

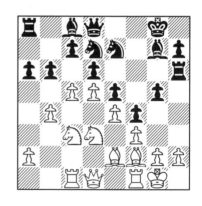

17 cxd6

Other moves:

a) 17 ♘a4 ♕e8 18 ♔h1 ♖b8!? 19 cxd6 cxd6 20 ♖c7 b5 21 ♘ac5!? dxc5 22 bxc5 ♗b7 23 ♖xb7 ♗xb7 24 a4 with sufficient compensation but no more than that, A.Khalifman-E.Inarkiev, 2nd match-game, FIDE World Cup, Khanty Mansyisk 2005.

b) 17 ♕b3 ♕e8 18 ♔h1 ♕h5 19 ♗g1 ♕h4 20 cxd6 cxd6 21 ♗d1 ♘f6 22 ♘e2 g4 23 ♘xe5 dxe5 24 d6+ ♘ed5 25 ♘c3 ♔f8 26 exd5 g3 27 ♘e4 ♗d7 28 a4 ♘e8 29 ♕c3 ♘xd6 30 ♘xd6 ♕g5 (threatening ...♖xh2+!) 0-1 O.Vodep-S.Giannetto, corr. 2000.

c) 17 ♔h1!? ♕e8 18 cxd6 cxd6 19 b5 ♘f6 20 bxa6 ♕h5 21 ♗g1 ♕g6 22 ♘f2 ♘h5 23 ♘h3 ♘g3+ 24 hxg3 ♗xh3 25 gxh3 fxg3? (but if 25...♖xh3+ 26 ♔g2 ♕h5 27 ♔f2 fxg3+ 28 ♔e1 or 25...♕h5 26 ♖f2! fxg3 27 ♖g2 ♕xh3+ 28 ♗h2 ♘g6 29 ♕e1! gxh2 30 ♖xg5 +=) 26 f4! exf4 27 ♗g4 +/- J.Berkvens-E.Inarkiev, Kemer 2007.

17...cxd6 18 g4

If instead 18 ♗e1 ♘f6 19 ♘f2 ♖g6! reverts to the breakthrough on the g-file; e.g. 20 ♗d2 (or 20 b5 a5 21 ♘a4 h5 22 h3 ♔h8 23 ♖c3 ♗d7 24 ♕c2 ♖c8 ∞ W.Pajeken-E.Chevelevitch, Hamburg 2006) 20...h5 21 g4 fxg3 22 hxg3 g4 23 f4 exf4 24 ♗xf4 h4 25 ♘d3 ♘h5 ∞ V.Iotov-L.Vajda, Dresden Olympiad 2008.

18...fxg3 19 hxg3 ♘g6 20 ♔g2 ♘f6 21 ♖h1 ♖xh1 22 ♕xh1 (D)

This was A.Khalifman-E.Inarkiev, 3rd matchgame, FIDE World Cup, Khanty Mansyisk 2005. White has negated the threats on the h-file but his

king remains vulnerable, while his queenside counterplay is rather ineffective:

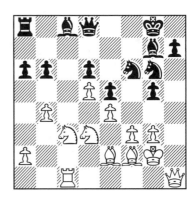

22...♗d7 23 b5 axb5 24 ♘b4 g4! 25 ♘c6 ♕f8 26 ♖c2 h5 27 ♕d1 [or 27 fxg4 ♘xg4 28 ♗xb6 h4! ∞] **27...♗h6 28 ♘xb5 h4! 29 ♘c7?** [but if 29 gxh4 ♘f4+ 30 ♔h1 ♔h7! with good play for the pawn] **29...hxg3! 30 ♗xg3 ♖a3 31 ♘e6 ♕f7** [or 31...♗xe6 32 dxe6 ♗f4, threatening ...♗xg3 or ...♕h6] **32 ♕h1? gxf3+ 33 ♗xf3 ♘xd5** with a winning position for Black, though time trouble later reduced it to a draw.

C12: 13 ♘b5 (D)

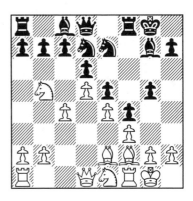

13...b6

The most frequent and solid response, blocking the attack on a7.

Not 13...a6? 14 ♘a7 ♖xa7 (otherwise Black loses his light-squared bishop, needed for his kingside attack) 15 ♗xa7 b6 16 b4 ♗b7 17 c5! dxc5 (if 17...bxc5 18 bxc5 ♕a8 19 ♗b6! cxb6 20 c6 +/-) 18 ♖c1 cxb4 (if 18...♘c8 19 bxc5 ♗a8 20 c6 ♘f6 21 ♗xb6 ♘xb6 22 ♗xa6 +/- V.Korchnoi-K.Hulak, Zagreb Interzonal 1987, or 19...♘xc5 20 ♖xc5 +/-) 19 d6 cxd6 (or 19...♘c6 20 ♗xa6! ♗xa6 21 ♖xc6 +/-) 20 ♕xd6 ♖f6 21 ♕c7 +/- T.Karolyi-V.Kupreichik, Lvov 1988.

However, 13...♘f6!? deserves attention: 14 ♘xa7 (if 14 c5 a6 15 ♘c3 ♘g6 ∞, or even 14...g4!?) 14...♗d7 15 ♘b5 (if 15 c5 ♖xa7 16 cxd6 ♘c8 17 dxc7 ♕xc7 18 ♗xa7 ♘xa7 19 ♕b3 ♕c5+ 20 ♔h1 ♘h5 21 ♘d3 ♕d6 ∞ B.Dimitrijewski-B.Buehler, Berlin 1992) 15...♘g6 (or 15...g4!? 16 fxg4 ♘xe4 ∞ A.Volk-G.Adocchio, German Junior Ch. 1989) 16 ♕c2 h5 17 c5 g4 18 c6 (if 18 cxd6 ♗xb5 19 ♗xb5 g3!? 20 hxg3 fxg3 21 ♗xg3 cxd6 ∞ Golubev) 18...bxc6 19 dxc6 ♗c8 with compensation, D.Gurevich-M.Golubev, Biel 1992.

14 b4

White sometimes plays 14 a4?!, but then 14...a6 15 ♘c3 a5 is just the 13 a4 a5 main line C132 with ...b7-b6 thrown in for free.

14...a6

Black can delay this move and transpose further down, but it makes no sense to omit it completely, as the white knight is clearly more effective on b5 than either c3 or a3; e.g. 14...♘f6

15 c5 ♘g6?! (15...a6) 16 cxd6 cxd6 17 ♖c1 ♖f7 18 ♖c6 ♘e8 19 ♘d3 h5 20 ♘b2 ♗f8 21 a4 ♖g7 22 ♘c4 +/- A.Czebe-G.Gnichtel, Budapest 1996.

15 ♘c3 *(D)*

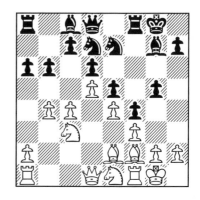

The alternative is 15 ♘a3!? h5 (if 15...a5 16 c5! axb4 17 cxd6 bxa3 18 dxc7 ♕e8 19 d6 ♔h8 20 dxe7 ♕xe7 21 ♕b3 +/- H.Keilhack-T.Kohler, Nuremberg 1990, or 17...cxd6 18 ♘b5 +=) 16 c5 b5 17 ♘ac2 (or 17 ♘b1 ♘f6 18 a4 bxa4 19 ♕xa4 ♘g6 20 ♕a5 ♕e7 21 b5 g4 22 ♘d2 g3 23 hxg3 fxg3 24 ♗xg3 h4 25 ♗f2 ♘f4 ∞ G.Bensberg-M.Schlögel, corr. 1998) 17...♘f6 (17...♕e8!?) 18 a4 bxa4 19 ♖xa4 ♘g6 20 b5 g4 21 ♘b4 (21 bxa6!?) 21...g3 22 hxg3 fxg3 23 ♗xg3 h4 24 ♘c6 ♕d7 25 ♗h2 ♗h6 26 f4 ♘xf4 ∞ A.Huzman-I.Smirin, Sverdlovsk 1987.

15...h5

Other moves:

a) 15...♘f6 16 a4 (planning to target b6; if 16 c5 ♖b8 17 cxb6 cxb6 18 b5 a5 19 ♖c1 ♗d7 20 ♘a4 g4 ∞ D.Gurevich-A.Shchekachev, Moscow 1992; or 16...h5 – *15...h5 16 c5*) 16...h5 (or 16...a5 17 c5 axb4 18 cxd6 cxd6 19 ♘b5 +=) 17 a5 ♘g6 18 axb6 cxb6 19 ♘a4 ♖b8 20 c5 bxc5 21 bxc5 g4 22 ♘b6 h4 23 ♘xc8 ♖xc8 24 fxg4 +/- A.Jovic-B.Pejovic, Yugoslav Team Ch. 1994.

b) 15...♘g6 16 ♘d3 (if 16 a4 a5 17 bxa5 ♖xa5 18 ♘d3 ♘f6 19 ♗e1 ♖a8 20 ♘f2 h5 21 h3 ♖f7 22 a5 += A.Smirnov-O.Gladyszev, St Petersburg 2000; instead 16...h5 – 15...h5 16 a4; but 16 c5! may be better here, and if 16...h5 17 cxb6 cxb6 18 ♘a4 +=) 16...♖f7 17 a4 ♗f8 18 a5 bxa5 19 ♖xa5 ♖b8 20 c5 ♘f6 21 b5 axb5 22 ♘b4 ♗d7 23 c6 ♗c8 24 ♖a7 h5 and although White looks better, it is not so easy to prove it; e.g. 25 ♘a6 (or 25 ♘xb5 g4 26 ♘a6 ♗xa6 27 ♖xa6 g3 ∞) 25...♗xa6 26 ♖xa6 b4 27 ♘b5 g4 28 ♕a4 g3 ∞ J.Piket-R.Douven, Dutch Ch. 1988.

c) 15...♖f6 16 ♘d3 ♖h6 17 c5 (or 17 ♗e1 ♘f6 18 ♘f2 ♖g6 19 a4 h5 20 h3 ♔h8 21 a5 ♘eg8 ∞ P.Van der Sterren-R.Douven, Dutch Team Ch. 1987) 17...♕e8 18 ♔h1 bxc5 19 bxc5 ♘f6 20 ♕d2 ♕h5 21 ♗g1 g4 22 fxg4 (not 22 ♘a4?? g3 23 cxd6 ♕g5! 24 dxe7 ♖xh2+! 0-1 J.Kiltti-V.Maki, Tampere 1998) 22...♗xg4 ∞.

16 ♔h1?! (D)

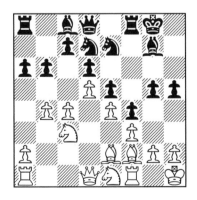

Rather unnecessary prophylaxis at this moment, especially as it encourages the sacrifice ...g5-g4-g3. Instead:

a) 16 a4 ♘g6!? (if 16...a5 17 c5 axb4 18 cxd6? bxc3 19 dxc7 ♕e8 20 d6 +/- I.Foldi-W.Winterstein, Budapest 1990; or 16...♘f6 – 15...♘f6) 17 a5 bxa5 18 ♖xa5 ♘f6 19 ♘d3 g4 20 ♕e1 ♗h6 21 ♔h1 ♖f7 22 c5 g3 23 ♗g1 (or 23 hxg3 fxg3 24 ♗xg3 h4 ∞) 23...gxh2 24 ♗f2 h4 ∞ J.Federau-C.Joecks, German League 1990.

b) 16 ♖c1 ♖f6 (or 16...♘f6 17 c5 – 16 c5) 17 ♕c2 ♖g6 18 c5 g4 19 cxd6 cxd6 20 ♔h1?! (but if 20 ♘d3 ♗h6 ∞) 20...g3 21 ♗g1 gxh2 22 ♗xh2 (G.Hertneck-J.Sieglen, German League 1987) 22...h4! intending ...♘f6-h5-g3 =+.

c) 16 c5 ♘f6 (if 16...bxc5?! 17 bxc5 ♘xc5 18 ♗xc5 dxc5 19 ♘a4 ♕d6 20 ♖c1+=, or 17...♘f6 18 cxd6 cxd6 19 ♖b1 ♘g6 20 ♘a4 += D.Gurevich-Cu.Jones, Las Vegas 1994) 17 ♖c1 g4 (not 17...♘g6?! 18 cxb6 cxb6 19 ♘a4! ♖b8 20 ♘xb6! +/- B.Lalic-A.Martin, Oberwart 1988; or 17...bxc5 18 bxc5 g4 19 ♕a4 g3 20 hxg3 fxg3 21 ♗xg3 ♗h6 22 ♖b1 ♘g6 23 ♗f2 ♘f4 24 ♘d3 += J.Hogenacker-A.Ljuboschitz, Germany 1996) 18 cxd6 cxd6 19 ♘a4 (obviously better than 19 ♔h1?! – 16 ♔h1) 19...♖b8 20 b5 a5 21 ♕d2 ♗d7 22 ♖c6!? ♗xc6 23 dxc6 with compensation, D.Gurevich-E.Yanayt, Las Vegas 2006, which continued 23...g3 24 hxg3 fxg3 25 ♗xg3 ♘g6 26 ♕c2 ♘e8 27 ♗c4+ ♔h8 28 ♘d3 ♗h6 ∞.

16...♘f6 17 c5 g4 18 cxb6 cxb6 19 ♖c1 g3! 20 ♗g1

Or 20 hxg3 fxg3 21 ♗xg3 ♘g6 22 ♗f2 ♗h6 with the usual counterplay.

20...gxh2 21 ♗f2 h4! 22 ♘a4 ♖b8 (D)

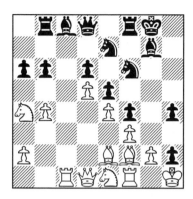

In comparison with other lines, such as 16 c5 above, White's queenside initiative is less advanced and the king being on h1 doesn't help him any. The game V.Korchnoi-Ye Jiangchuan, Novi Sad Olympiad 1990, continued:

23 b5

23 ♗xh4?! ♘h5 only helps Black, e.g. 24 ♖xc8 ♖xc8 25 ♗xa6 ♖b8 26 ♘d3 ♗f6 27 ♗f2 ♘g6 28 ♔xh2 ♗h4 29 ♖h1 ♗xf2 30 ♘xf2 b5 -+ V.Molnar-J.Helbich, Presov 1999.

23...axb5 24 ♗xb5 ♘h5 25 ♔xh2 ♘g3 26 ♖g1 ♘g6 27 ♘d3 ♔h7

Not yet 27...h3?! 28 gxh3 ♕h4 29 ♖xc8 ♖fxc8 30 ♗d7 and the bishop defends the kingside.

28 ♘b4?!

White might have tried 28 ♗xb6!? ♖xb6 29 ♖xc8 ♕xc8 30 ♘xb6 ♕b7 31 ♘d7 ♕xb5 32 ♘xf8+ ♗xf8!? 33 ♕c2 (Ye Jiangchuan), as it is hard for Black to continue his attack with no rooks.

28...h3! 29 ♖xc8

Or 29 gxh3 ♖h8 30 ♗xg3 fxg3+ 31 ♖xg3 ♗h6 with a strong attack; e.g. 32 f4 exf4 (not 32...♗xf4?? 33 ♕h5+) 33 ♖g1 f3! 34 ♕xf3 ♖f8 35 ♕h5 (35 ♕e2

♕h4 with an attack) 35...♘f4 36 ♖xc8 ♖xc8 37 ♕f3 ♖c7 =/+.

29...♖xc8 30 gxh3 ♖h8 *(D)*

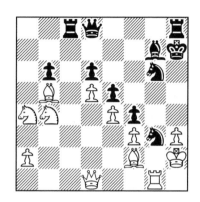

31 ♗xb6?!

Here 31 ♗a6!? b5 32 ♗xc8 ♕xc8 33 ♘b6 ♕xh3+!? 34 ♔xh3 ♔g8+ 35 ♔g2 ♘h4+ 36 ♔h2 ♘hf5+ is perpetual check.

31...♕e7 32 ♘d3 ♖b8 33 ♗c6 ♔g8 34 ♘f2 ♘h4 35 ♕d3 ♔f7?!

Stronger was 35...♕f7! and ...♕h5 (Ye Jiangchuan); e.g. 36 ♖b1 ♕h5 37 ♖b3 ♕g6! 38 ♘g4 ♘xf3+! 39 ♕xf3 ♖xh3+! 40 ♔g2 (or 40 ♔xh3 ♕h5+ 41 ♔g2 ♕h1+ 42 ♔f2 ♕h1 mate) 40...♖h4 41 ♗d7 ♘xe4 -+.

36 ♖c1?

A mistake in turn; necessary was 36 ♖b1 -/+ (Ye Jiangchuan). Now White loses material and the game:

36...♖xb6! 37 ♘xb6 ♕a7 38 ♕b3 ♖b8 39 ♖b1 ♗f6 40 ♕b4 ♘xf3+ 41 ♔g2 ♘h4+ 42 ♔g1 ♗d8 43 ♕xd6 ♖xb6 44 ♕e6+ ♔g7 45 ♖xb6 ♕xb6 46 ♕d7+ ♔h6 47 ♕e6+ ♘g6 48 ♔g2 ♔g7 49 ♕d7+ ♗e7 50 d6 ♘h4+ 51 ♔g1 ♕b1+ 52 ♔h2 ♘f1+ 0-1.

C13: 13 a4 *(D)*

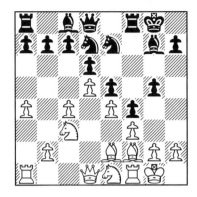

This move also has the idea of targeting a7 with ♘c3-b5. But as the immediate 13 ♘b5 (line C12 above) is met by 13...b6, White plans to pre-empt this defence by preparing (or playing) a4-a5 before sending the knight forward.

Black has two main replies:

C131: 13...♘g6 *238*
C132: 13...a5 *241*

Alternatives do not offer equality:

a) 13...♘f6?! just allows 14 c5 reaching 9...♘e8 positions, e.g. 14...h5 15 a5 g4 16 cxd6 cxd6 17 ♘b5 – *14...♘f6?!* in line B22, or similarly 14...♘g6 15 cxd6 cxd6 16 a5 h5 17 ♘b5 – *15...♘f6?!* in that line. Or if 14...a6 15 a5 ♕e8 16 cxd6 cxd6 17 ♘a4 g4 18 ♘b6 +/- P.Alexander-P.Groselj, Bled 1998.

b) 13...♖f7 14 ♘b5 (or 14 a5 ♗f8 15 c5!? ♘xc5 16 b4 ♘d7 17 ♘b5 a6 18 ♘a7 ♘f6 19 ♘xc8 ♖xc8 20 b5 += V.Ridky-M.Hala, corr. 2001; 14...♘g6 – *13...♘g6 14 a5 ♖f7*) 14...a6 (if 14...b6?! 15 a5 a6 16 axb6 +/-, or 14...♘f6 15 ♘xa7 ♗d7 16 ♘b5 ♗f8 17 c5 +/- G.Burgess-

F.Petersen, Aarhus 1991) 15 ♘a7 ♘f6 16 ♘xc8 ♕xc8 17 c5 g4 18 ♘d3 g3 19 ♗e1 gxh2+ 20 ♔xh2 ♘g6 21 ♖h1 +/- V.Ikonnikov-A.Kulagin, Katowice 1992.

c) 13...♖f6 14 ♘b5 (or 14 a5 a6 – *13...a6*) 14...a6 (if 14...b6?! 15 a5 a6 16 axb6 cxb6 17 b4 ♗b7 18 ♘c3 += P.Wells-R.Forster, Bad Wörishofen 1996) 15 ♘a7 ♖xa7 16 ♗xa7 ♖h6 17 ♘d3 ♘f6 18 ♘f2 ♗d7 19 c5 ♘c8 20 ♕b3! ♖xa7 21 ♕xb7 ♘c8 22 c6 ♗e8 23 ♗xa6 ♘e7 24 a5 +- A.Summerscale-R.Black, British League 2001.

d) 13...a6 14 a5 (or 14 ♘d3 ♖f6 15 c5 ♖h6 16 cxd6 cxd6 17 a5 ♕e8 18 ♗e1 ♔h8 19 ♘f2 ♘g8 20 ♘a4 += P.H.Nielsen-A.Volokitin, European Ch., Ohrid 2001) 14...♖f6 15 ♘d3 ♖h6 16 ♗e1 ♕e8 (or 16...♔h8 17 b4 ♘g8 18 ♖c1 ♗f8 19 ♘a4 ♘df6 20 ♘f2 += D.Reinderman-B.Socko, European Ch., Istanbul 2003) 17 ♘f2 ♖g6 18 ♘a4 h5 19 h3 ♔h7 20 b4 ♘g8 21 c5 +/= V.Ikonnikov-O.Simon, Bethune 2005.

e) 13...h5 *(D)* is sometimes played first, and then:

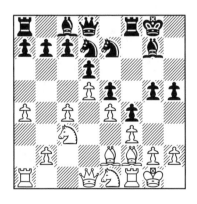

e1) 14 a5 a6 (here 14...♘g6 –

13...♘g6 below; again not 14...♘f6?! 15 c5 g4 16 cxd6 cxd6 17 ♘b5 – *14...♘f6?!* in line B22; or if 14...♖f7 15 c5!? ♘xc5 16 ♗xc5 dxc5 17 ♗c4 += P.Wells-R.Gallego Martinez, Escaldes 1998) 15 ♘d3 (if 15 ♘a4 g4 16 c5 g3! 17 hxg3 fxg3 18 ♗xg3 ♘g6 ∞ L.Friedman-L.Basin, Dearborn 1992) 15...♘f6 16 c5 g4 17 cxd6 cxd6 18 ♘a4 ♘g6 19 ♘b6 ♖b8 20 ♘xc8 ♖xc8 21 fxg4 ♘xe4 22 gxh5 ♘h4 23 ♗g4 += A.Maksimenko-A.Frolov, Nikolaev 1993.

e2) 14 ♘b5 ♘f6 (if 14...a5 15 ♘a7 ♖xa7 16 ♗xa7 b6 17 b4 += A.Bachmann-C.Sandipan, Berlin 1994; or 14...a6 15 ♘a7 ♘f6 16 ♘xc8 ♖xc8 17 c5 g4 18 ♗h4 g3 19 c6 += P.H.Nielsen-L.Degerman, Hinnerup 1995) 15 ♘xa7 ♗d7 16 c5 (or 16 ♘b5 g4 17 c5) 16...g4 17 cxd6 cxd6 18 ♘b5 g3 (if 18...♘g6?! 19 ♘xd6 g3 20 ♗c5! +/- A.Uberoi-D.Radovanovic, World Junior Ch. 1998) 19 hxg3 fxg3 20 ♗xg3 ♘g6 21 ♗f2 ♘e8 22 ♘d3 h4 23 f4! += L.Degerman-J.Eriksson, Lindesberg 1993.

C131: 13...♘g6 (D)

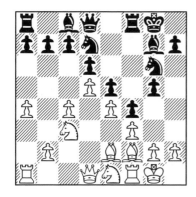

14 a5

Other moves:

a) 14 b4?! mixes plans, so that either a2-a4 or b2-b4 may be unnecessary, e.g. 14...♘f6! 15 c5 h5 16 a5?! g4 – *14 a5 h5 15 b4?!*, or if 16 c6!? ♗h6 17 b5 b6 18 a5 g4 19 axb6 cxb6 20 fxg4 hxg4 21 g3 ♖f7 22 ♗d3 ♘h7 23 ♔h1 ♘g5 ∞ V.Korchnoi-Xie Jun, Marbella 1999.

b) 14 ♘d3!? is better, as 14...♘f6 15 c5 returns to *13 ♘d3 ♘f6 14 c5 ♘g6 15 a4* which is reasonable for White. If instead 14...♖f7 (or 14...a5?! – *13...a5 14 ♘d3 ♘g6?!* in C132) 15 a5 ♗f8 (or 15...♘f6 16 c5 ♗f8 17 c6 bxc6 18 dxc6 += V.Ikonnikov-A.Belakovskaia, Katowice 1992) 16 a6 bxa6 17 ♘b4 g4 18 fxg4 ♖g7 19 ♘c6 ♕g5 20 ♕e1 ♘e7 21 ♘xa7 ♗b7 22 b4 +/- O.Borik-K.Volke, German League 1996.

c) 14 ♘b5!? ♘f6 (not 14...b6?! 15 a5 a6 16 axb6 ♘xb6 17 ♘c3 +/- R.Astrom-O.Lundberg, Stockholm 1990; or if 14...a5 15 ♘a7 ♖xa7 16 ♗xa7 b6 17 b4 +=) 15 ♘xa7 g4!? (if 15...♗d7 16 c5 g4 17 c6 g3 18 hxg3 fxg3 19 ♗xg3 ♘h5 20 ♗f2 += K.Cherenkova-M.Mozharov, Moscow 2006) 16 ♘xc8 g3 17 hxg3 ♘h5 18 gxf4 exf4 19 ♗d4?! (but if 19 ♘d3 ♖xc8 20 c5 ♘g3 21 ♘xf4 ♘xf4 22 ♗xg3 ♗d4+!, or 19 ♘xd6 cxd6 20 ♘d3 ♕g5 ∞) 19...♗xd4 20 ♕xd4 ♘g3 21 ♕d2 ♖xc8 22 ♘d3 ♘xf1 23 ♗xf1 = K.Mietus-W.Schmidt, Polanica Zdroj 1992.

14...h5 (D)

Black has tried various alternatives, but none of them is sufficient to equalize:

a) 14...♘f6?! 15 c5 h5 16 cxd6 cxd6 17 ♘b5 – *15...♘f6?!* in line B22 again.

b) 14...a6 15 ♘d3 (or 15 b4 ♖f7 16 c5

♗f8 17 c6 ♘f6 18 cxb7 ♗xb7 19 b5 h5 20 bxa6 ♗c8 21 a7 +/- K.Shantharam-P.Thipsay, India 1996) 15...♘f6 16 c5 h5 17 ♘a4 g4 18 cxd6 cxd6 19 ♘b6 ♖b8 20 ♘xc8 ♕xc8 21 ♕a4 gxf3 22 ♗xf3 ♘g4 23 ♗b6 ♘h4 24 ♖ac1 ♕e8 25 ♕xe8 ♖bxe8 26 ♖c7 +/- V.Korchnoi-B.Gelfand, Tilburg 1992.

c) 14...♔h8 15 ♘d3 (or 15 b4 ♘f6 16 c5 ♖g8 17 cxd6 cxd6 18 ♘b5 g4 19 ♘xa7 g3 20 ♗b6 gxh2+ 21 ♔xh2 ♕e7 22 ♖h1 +/- P.Pinho-L.Reis, Honra 1998; whereas if 15 ♘b5 ♘f6! 16 ♘xa7 ♗d7 17 c5 g4 18 c6 g3 19 hxg3 bxc6 20 ♘xc6 ♗xc6 21 dxc6 ♘h5 22 gxf4 exf4 ∞ A.Ziegler-Y.Shulman, Gothenburg 1999) 15...♖g8 16 c5 ♘f6 (or 16...♗f8 17 c6! bxc6 18 ♘b4! ♘e7 19 ♘xc6 ♘xc6 20 dxc6 ♘f6 21 ♘d5! ♗e6 22 b4 +/- V.Korchnoi-A.Shirov, Horgen 1994) 17 cxd6 cxd6 18 a6 b6 19 ♘b4 ♗f8 20 ♖c1 g4 21 fxg4 ♗h6 22 ♖c2 ♗g5 23 ♔h1 ♕d7 24 ♘b5 ♘xe4 25 ♖c7 ♕d8 26 ♘c6 ♕f6 27 ♘bxa7 f3 (A.Summerscale-M.Hebden, British Ch. 1998) 28 ♘xc8! +/-.

d) 14...♖f7 15 c5!? (thematic; but White has time to prepare it here with either 15 ♘d3 – *14 ♘d3 ♖f7* above, or 15 b4 ♘f6 16 c5 ♗f8 17 c6! ♖g7 18 cxb7 ♗xb7 19 a6 ♗c8 20 ♔h1 ♗d7 21 ♗b5 g4 22 ♗xd7 ♕xd7 23 fxg4 +/- P.H.Nielsen-Y.Kruppa, Minsk 1996; again if 15 ♘b5 ♘f6! 16 ♘xa7 g4 17 ♘xc8 g3 18 hxg3 ♘h5 19 gxf4 exf4 20 ♘d3 ♖xc8 21 ♕e1 ♕g5 ∞ A.Volodin-A.Purtov, Gyongyos 1995) 15...♘xc5 16 ♗xc5 dxc5 17 ♗c4 ♔h8 18 a6 bxa6 (if 18...♖f6 19 axb7 ♗xb7 20 ♘d3 ♗f8 21 ♖f2 c6 22 b3 ♗d6 23 ♖fa2 += A.Illner-J.Gonzalez Garcia,

Budapest 1995) 19 ♘d3 ♗f8 20 ♘a4 g4 21 ♘axc5 (or 21 fxg4 ♕g5 22 ♘f2 ♗d6 23 ♖a3 ♘h4 24 ♖h3 ♗d7 25 ♘c3 ♖g8 =+ A.Shirov-J.Nunn, Monte Carlo rapid 1995) 21...c6 22 ♘e6 ♗xe6 23 dxe6 ♖g7 24 ♔h1 gxf3 25 gxf3 ♕d4 ∞ J.Markauss-H.Uhle, corr. 1994.

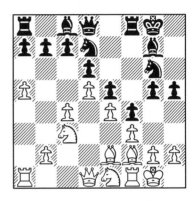

15 ♘b5

Continuing with the plan. The alternative is to aim for c4-c5 again:

a) 15 b4?! (essentially a wasted move) 15...♘f6 16 c5 g4 17 cxd6 cxd6 18 ♘b5 g3 19 hxg3 (or if 19 ♗xa7 ♘h7! followed by ...♕h4) 19...fxg3 20 ♗xg3 a6 21 ♘a3 h4 22 ♗f2 ♘h5 -/+ L.Ftacnik-I.Smirin, Biel Interzonal 1993.

b) 15 ♘d3 is again reasonable, when 15...♘f6 16 c5 g4 – *13 ♘d3*.

c) 15 ♔h1!? awaits ...♘f6, while making a useful defensive move: 15...♘f6 (falling in with White's plan; but if 15...♗h6 16 ♘b5 a6 17 ♘a7 ♘f6 18 ♘xc8 ♕xc8 19 c5 g4 20 cxd6 cxd6 21 ♗b6 += S.Krivoshey-C.Claverie, France 1995; or 15...♖f7 16 ♘b5 ♘f6 17 ♘xa7 ♗d7 18 c5 g4 19 cxd6 cxd6 20 ♗b6 ♕e7 21 ♘b5 += V.Zakharstov-A.Bragin, Krasnodar 1999) 16 c5 g4 (if 16...♖f7 17 cxd6 cxd6 18 ♘b5 a6 19 ♗b6 ♕e7 20 ♘c7 ♖b8, S.Krivoshey-F.Cordier, France 1995, 21 ♗a7! ♕xc7 22 ♖c1 +/- Krivoshey) 17 cxd6 cxd6 18 ♘b5 g3 19 ♗g1 gxh2 20 ♗xa7 h4 21 ♗b6 ♕e7 22 ♘c7 ♘h5!? 23 ♘xa8 ♘g3+ 24 ♔xh2 h3 25 ♘c7 ♕h4 26 ♘e6 ♔f7 27 gxh3 ♖h8 28 ♔g1 ♗f6 (S.Krivoshey-V.Stukalov, Pavlograd 1995) and now 29 ♗b5! ♕xh3 30 ♔f2 should parry the attack, e.g. 30...♘xe4+ (if 30...♕h2+ 31 ♘g2 ♘xf1 32 ♕xf1 ♘h4 33 ♖c1 ♖g8 34 ♔e1 ♘xg2+ 35 ♔d1 ♘e3+ 36 ♗xe3 fxe3 37 ♖c2, or 30...♗d7 31 ♕d3) 31 fxe4 ♕h2+ 32 ♘g2 ♕g3+ 33 ♔e2 ♕xg2+ 34 ♔e1 ♕xe4+ 35 ♕e2 ♗h4+ 36 ♔d1 ♕xd5+ 37 ♘d4 +/-.

15...♘f6

If 15...a6?! 16 ♘a7 ♘f6 17 ♘xc8 ♕xc8 (or 17...♖xc8 18 ♕b3) 18 c5 g4 19 ♖c1 +/-.

16 ♘xa7 ♗d7

The alternative is 16...g4 17 ♘xc8 g3 18 hxg3 fxg3 19 ♗xg3 h4 (if 19...♖xc8 20 ♘d3 h4 21 ♗h2 ♘h5 22 f4 ♘hxf4 23 ♗g4 +/- S.Solovjov-N.Nikolaev, St Petersburg 1998; or similarly 19...♕xc8 20 ♘d3 +/-) 20 ♗h2 ♘f4!? (if 20...♕xc8 21 ♘d3 ♗h6 22 f4 ♘xe4 23 ♗g4 +/- Z.Kozul-A.Sherzer, Biel Interzonal 1993) 21 ♗xf4 exf4 22 e5 ♘h5 (or if 22...dxe5 23 ♘d3 ♘h5 24 ♘f2 +/- T.Hillarp Persson-K.Trygstad, Gausdal 1996) 23 ♘d3 ♘g3 24 ♖e1 h3 25 gxh3 ♖xc8 26 ♗f1 +/- V.Sakalauskas-V.Tokmachev, Birstonas 2002.

17 c5 g4

If instead 17...♖xa7?! (or 17...dxc5? 18 ♗xc5 g4 19 ♕b3 ♔h8 20 ♕xb7 +- E.Kobylkin-A.Demchenko, Krasnodar 2004) 18 c6 ♕a8 (or 18...bxc6 19 ♗xa7 c5

20 ♘d3 ♕a8 21 ♗xc5 dxc5 22 ♘xc5 +/- P.Kiriakov-M.Manik, Pardubice 1995) 19 cxd7 ♖xa5 20 ♖c1 ♕d8 21 ♕c2 ♕xd7 22 ♕xc7 +/- V.Sakalauskas-A.Labuckas, Lithuanian Ch. 2001.

18 c6! *(D)*

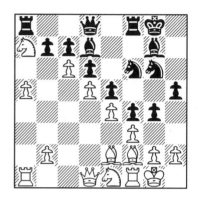

Other moves are less testing:

a) 18 ♔h1?! g3 19 ♗g1 (B.Finegold-B.Kreiman, US Ch. 1994) 19...gxh2 20 ♗f2 h4! 21 c6 bxc6 22 ♘xc6 ♕e8 ∞ Byrne/Mednis.

b) 18 cxd6?! g3 19 ♗c5 cxd6 20 ♗b6 gxh2+ 21 ♔h1 ♕e8! 22 ♕b3 h4 23 ♗b5 ♕b8 ∞ Te.Johansen-E.Gallardo, World Junior Ch. 1996.

c) 18 a6!? bxa6 (not 18...g3? 19 axb7! gxf2 20 ♖xf2 +- M.Tupy-R.Forster, Plzen 1995) 19 ♖xa6 g3 20 hxg3 fxg3 21 ♗xg3 h4 ∞ Golubev.

18...g3

18...bxc6 19 ♘xc6 ♗xc6 20 dxc6 g3 21 hxg3 fxg3 22 ♗xg3 h4 23 ♗f2 transposes below, while if 19...♕e8 20 ♘d3 ♗h6 21 ♕e1 ♖f7 22 a6 +/- P.Kiriakov-N.Kiseleva, Groningen 1997.

19 hxg3 fxg3 20 ♗xg3 h4

Black has also tried:

a) 20...bxc6 21 ♘xc6 ♕e8 22 ♘d3 h4

23 ♗f2 ♘h5 24 f4! ♘g3 (if 24...♘hxf4 25 ♗h5 +/-) 25 f5 +- V.Ikonnikov-M.Ahn, Le Touquet 1993.

b) 20...♖xa7 21 ♗f2! (better than 21 cxd7 ♘xd7 22 f4 ♘xf4 23 ♗xh5 ♘c5 24 ♗g4 ♕g5 ∞ B.Zlender-V.Conti, corr. 1999) 21...b6 (or 21...♕a8 22 cxd7 ♖xa5 23 ♘d3 +/- Hazai) 22 axb6 ♖xa1 23 ♕xa1 cxb6 24 cxd7 ♘xd7 25 ♗b5 ♘c5 26 ♕d1 +/- S.Koutsin-P.Durik, Slovakian Ch. 1998.

21 ♗f2 bxc6 22 ♘xc6 ♗xc6

If 22...♕e8 23 ♘c2 ♘f4 24 ♗xh4 ♕h5 25 g3 ♘xe4 26 ♘e7+ ♔h8 27 gxf4 ♖g8 28 fxe4 ♗h6+, then 29 ♗g5! (rather than 29 ♘xg8? ♕xh4 30 ♘xh6 ♕g3+ ½-½ P.Kiriakov-A.Cela, Halkida 1996) 29...♖xg5+ 30 fxg5 ♕xg5+ 31 ♗g4! ♗xg4 32 ♕c1 wins.

23 dxc6 ♘h5 24 f4! *(D)*

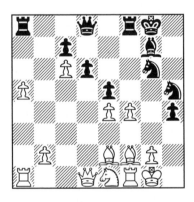

Forcing Black to capture with the h5-knight. Instead 24 ♗c4+ ♔h8 25 f4 ♘gxf4! 26 ♕g4 ♗f6 27 ♘f3 ♕e7 ∞ S.Siebrecht-V.Loginov, Budapest 1994.

24...♘hxf4 25 ♗c4+ ♔h8

Or 25...♔h7 26 ♕g4 d5 27 ♗xd5 +/- T.Likavsky-Z.Hagarova, Slovakian Team Ch. 1999.

26 ♕g4 ♕e7 27 a6 ♗h6 28 a7

White has complete control and won quickly in P.Kiriakov-D.Fernandez, Lake George 2005: **28...♕h7 29 ♖a3** [or 29 ♕d7!?] **29...h3 30 g3 ♘e7 31 ♖e3** [or 31 ♔h2!?] **31...♖f6 32 ♔h1 ♖g6 33 ♕d7 d5 34 exd5 ♘fxd5 35 ♖xe5 1-0.**

C132: 13...a5 *(D)*

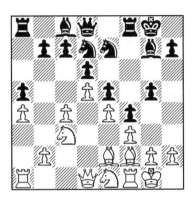

From being a relative sideline in the early years of this variation, 13...a5 is nowadays the most common response – no doubt due to its usage by Kasparov in 1996, Gallagher's subsequent recommendation in *Play the King's Indian*, and not least because Black's other options have not fared as well. Moreover, it is quite a logical response: the a4-pawn is prevented from advancing further, while White's inability to support b2-b4 with a2-a3, and thus achieve c4-c5, lessens his initiative on the queenside.

14 ♘d3

Threatening c4-c5, preparing b2-b4, and reorganizing the minor pieces. Other moves merely give Black more options while reducing White's own; e.g. 14 b4 axb4 15 ♘b5 ♖f6!? (or 15...♘c5!? 16 ♘d3 b6 transposing below) 16 ♕b3 ♘c5 (or 16...g4!?) 17 ♕xb4 ♘a6 ∞ M.Prusikhin-V.Georgiev, Regensburg 1997.

14...b6

The only consistent move, otherwise Black has weakened his queenside for nothing; e.g.

a) 14...♖f6 15 c5 ♖h6 16 ♕b3 ♔h8 17 ♖fc1 ♕e8 18 ♘b5?! (better 18 cxd6 cxd6 19 ♘b5 +/-) 18...♕h5 19 h3 ♘xc5 20 ♗xc5 ♗xh3 21 ♘f2 (P.Wells-N.Abbasi, London Lloyds Bank 1994) 21...♗xg2! 22 ♔xg2 ♕h2+ 23 ♔f1 dxc5 ∞.

b) 14...♘g6 15 c5 ♘f6 16 ♖c1 ♖f7 17 cxd6 cxd6 18 ♔h1 ♗f8 19 ♕b3 g4 20 ♗b6 ♕e7 21 ♘b5 g3 22 ♘c7 ♖b8 23 h3 ♗d7 24 ♘e6 ♘e8 25 ♗xa5 +/- A.Smirnov-S.Voitsekhovsky, St Petersburg 2003.

15 ♗e1 (D)

Switching the bishop to queenside action, while making room for the d3-knight to drop back in defence. The alternative is 15 b4 axb4 (D) and then:

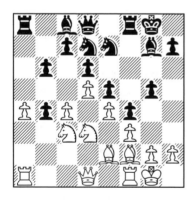

a) 16 ♘b5 ♘f6 (or 16...♘c5!? 17

♘xb4 g4 18 a5 g3 19 hxg3 fxg3 20 ♗xg3 ♖xa5 ∞ B.Züger-O.Cvitan, Geneva 1988; but not 16...h5?! 17 ♗e1 g4 18 ♗xb4 ♘f6 19 a5 bxa5 20 ♖xa5 ♖b8 21 ♖a7 g3 22 ♗a5 +/- B.Van der Velden-A.Bomans, Maastricht 2008) 17 ♗e1 (if 17 ♘xb4 g4 18 ♗h4 g3 19 h3 ♘g6 20 ♘c6 ♕d7 21 ♗xf6 ♖xf6 22 ♘ba7 ♘e7 23 a5 bxa5 24 ♖xa5 ♘xc6 25 dxc6, P.H.Nielsen-H.Harestad, Gausdal 1996, 25...♕d8! ∞) 17...g4 18 ♗xb4 g3 19 h3 ♘e8 (not 19...♗xh3? 20 gxh3 ♕d7 21 ♕c2 ♕xh3 22 ♗d1 ♘g6 23 ♕g2 ♕h6 24 ♘xc7 ♘h4 25 ♕d2! g2 26 ♖e1 +/- C.Persson-G.Calzolari, corr. 1998) 20 ♕d2 ♘g6 21 ♖fc1 ♘h4 22 ♘e1 ♖f6 23 ♗f1 ♖h6 ∞ N.Sulava-V.Nevednichy, Bad Wörishofen 2000.

b) 16 ♘xb4 ♘f6 (if 16...♘c5 17 ♘d3 ♘b7 18 ♘c1! ♖f6 19 ♘b3 ♗f8 20 ♘b5 ♗d7 21 ♕d2 c6 22 dxc6 ♘xc6 23 ♖fd1 ♖g6 24 c5 +/- Z.Franco Ocampos-G.Milos, Pamplona 1991) 17 ♘d3! (better than 17 ♖a3 ♗d7 18 ♘b5 ♔h8!? 19 ♗e1 ♖g8 20 g4 fxg3 21 hxg3 g4 22 ♔g2 gxf3+ 23 ♗xf3 ♗h6 =+ A.Yusupov-G.Kasparov, Yerevan Olympiad 1996; or 17 ♘c6?! ♘xc6 18 dxc6 ♕e8 19 ♘d5 ♖f7 20 a5 bxa5 21 ♕a4 g4 22 ♕b5 ♘xd5 23 cxd5 g3 24 hxg3 fxg3 25 ♗xg3 ♗h6 -/+ J.Van Oosterom-G.Timmerman, corr. 1996) 17...h5 18 ♘b5 ♗d7 (if 18...♘g6 19 a5 bxa5 20 ♗e1 g4 21 ♖xa5 ♖b8 22 ♘b4! ♖b7 23 ♘c6 ♕e8 24 ♖a8 +/- Z.Kozul-D.Rogic, Bled 1997) 19 ♗e1 ♕b8!? 20 ♔h1 g4 21 a5 bxa5 22 ♗xa5 ♕b7 23 ♗xc7 ♖xa1 24 ♕xa1 gxf3 25 gxf3 ♗b5 26 ♗xd6 ♗xc4 27 ♕xe5 ♖f7 ∞ S.Ghane Gardeh-V.Kotronias, Cappelle La Grande 2008.

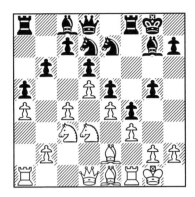

15...♘f6

The most precise. Instead:

a) 15...c5?! 16 dxc6 ♘b8 17 c7! ♕xc7 18 ♕b3 ♔h8 19 ♕a3 ♕d8 20 ♘b5 ♖f6 21 ♖d1 +/- Z.Kozul-P.Popovic, Pula 1991.

b) 15...♘c5 16 ♘b5 g4 17 ♘xc5 gxf3 18 ♗xf3 bxc5?! 19 ♗c3 ♘g6 20 ♕d2 ♖f7 21 ♗xa5 +/- V.Sakalauskas-G.Piesina, Lithuanian Ch. 2001.

c) 15...h5 16 ♘b5 (if 16 ♘f2 ♘f6 – *15...♘f6*) 16...♘c5!? (now if 16...♘f6 17 b4 axb4 18 ♗xb4 g4 – *15 b4 axb4 16 ♘b5 h5?!*, or 17...g4 18 bxa5 bxa5 19 c5 +=
S.Krivoshey-S.Demidenko, Ukrainian Ch. 2000) 17 b4 axb4 18 ♗xb4 ♘b7 (or 18...c6 19 dxc6 ♘xc6 20 ♗e1 ♘d4 21 ♘b4 ♗e6 22 ♗f2 += G.Vescovi-C.Braga, Sao Paulo 1996) 19 ♕d2 ♖f6 (if 19...♘a5 20 c5! ♘b3 21 cxd6 +/-) 20 a5!? c6 (if 20...bxa5 21 ♖xa5! ♘xa5 22 ♗xa5 +=) 21 a6 ♘c5 22 ♗xc5 cxb5 23 ♗f2 bxc4 24 ♘b4 b5 25 a7 g4 26 ♖fb1 += O.Sedlacek-C.Teichmann, corr. 1994.

16 ♘f2

Here 16 ♘b5 (or 16 b4 axb4 17 ♘b5 g4) 16...g4 17 b4 axb4 returns to *15 b4 axb4 16 ♘b5* above, or if 17 fxg4 ♘xe4 18 ♗f3 ♘g5 19 ♘f2 h5 ∞ Wl.Schmidt-

P.Dobrowolski, Polish Team Ch. 1997.
16...h5 17 h3 *(D)*

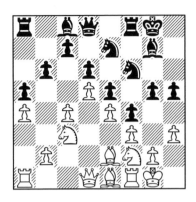

White has done what he can to hamper ...g5-g4, and now plans to develop his play on the other wing with b2-b4. Naturally Black's chances are still on the kingside, so he must find a way to invigorate his attack.

17...♔h8

Planning a reorganization ...♘eg8-h6 and ...♖f7-g7 to enforce the ...g5-g4 breakthrough. Other moves are:

a) 17...♘g6 18 ♘b5 ♘h4 19 b4 axb4 20 ♗xb4 g4 21 fxg4 hxg4 22 hxg4 +=, e.g. 22...f3 23 ♗xf3 ♘h5!? 24 gxh5 ♘xf3+ 25 gxf3 ♕g5+ 26 ♘g4 ♗xg4 27 fxg4 ♕e3+, and now rather than 28 ♔h2?? ♖xf1 29 ♕xf1 ♖f8 30 ♕g2 ♖f2 -+ S.Krivoshey-O.Strelnikov, Alushta 1999, White should have played 28 ♔g2! ♕xe4+ (or 28...♖xf1 29 ♕xf1 ♖f8 30 ♖e1) 29 ♔h2 +/-.

b) 17...♖f7 18 ♘b5 ♗f8 19 b4 axb4?! (19...♔h8 20 bxa5 bxa5 21 c5 ♘eg8 transposes below) 20 ♗xb4 merely accelerates White's initiative; e.g. 20...♔h8 21 a5 bxa5 22 ♖xa5 ♖xa5 23 ♗xa5 ♘eg8 24 ♕b3 +/- V.Ikonnikov-

G.Krachler, Werfen 1996.

18 ♘b5 ♘eg8 19 b4 ♖f7

Or 19...♘h6 20 bxa5 (or 20 c5 bxc5 21 bxc5 ♖f7) 20...bxa5 21 c5 ♖f7 – *21...♘h6* below.

Again 19...axb4?! 20 ♗xb4 only helps White; e.g. 20...♘d7 (not 20...♖f7 21 a5 ♗f8? 22 axb6 ♖xa1 23 bxc7) 21 a5 ♘c5 22 axb6 ♖xa1 23 ♕xa1 cxb6 24 ♕a7 ♘h6 25 ♕c7 ♕xc7 26 ♘xc7 ♗d7 27 ♖a1 += M.Narciso Dublan-X.Duran Albareda, Terrassa 1994.

20 bxa5

20 c5 bxc5 21 bxc5 comes to the same thing.

20...bxa5 21 c5 ♗f8 *(D)*

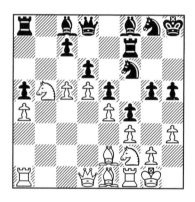

Or 21...♘h6 22 cxd6 cxd6 23 ♖c1 ♗f8 transposing, while 22 ♘a3!? ♗f8 is the next note.

22 cxd6

White has also tried:

a) 22 c6 ♘h6 23 ♖a3 ♖g7 24 ♗d2 g4 25 fxg4 hxg4 26 hxg4 ♘hxg4 27 ♘xg4 ♘xg4 28 ♕e1 ♔g8 ∞ S.Krivoshey-G.Schebler, German League 2004.

b) 22 ♗c3 ♘h6 23 ♕d2 g4 24 hxg4 hxg4 25 fxg4 ♗xg4 26 ♘xg4 ♘hxg4 27 ♗xg4 ♘xg4 28 ♖f3 dxc5 ∞ O.Loren-

tzen-E.Sterud, corr. 2004.

c) 22 ♘a3 ♘h6 23 ♘c4 g4 24 fxg4 (if 24 ♗xa5 gxh3 25 ♘xh3 ♗xh3 26 gxh3 ♘xd5!) 24...hxg4 25 hxg4 ♖g7 26 ♖a3 ♘hxg4 27 ♘xg4 ♘xg4 ∞ V.Zakhartsov-C.Voicu, Alushta 2005.

22...cxd6 23 ♖c1 ♘h6 24 ♖c4

We are following P.H.Nielsen-V.Kotronias, Hastings 2003/04. In a later game White went for 24 ♕c2 ♘e8 25 ♕b3 ♖g7 26 ♖c6!? ♗d7 27 ♗d2 ♗xc6 28 dxc6 with compensation, and was successful after 28...♕b6 29 ♖c1 g4?! 30 fxg4 ♗e7 31 ♕e6 ♘f6?? (31...♘g8 ∞) 32 c7 ♔h7 33 g5 +- P.H.Nielsen-M.Golubev, Internet blitz 2004.

24...♖g7?

More energetic was 24...g4! 25 fxg4 (if 25 ♕c2 ♗d7 26 ♘c7 ♗xa4!) 25...hxg4 26 hxg4 ♖g7, e.g. 27 g5!? ♖xg5 28 ♕c2 ♘h5 29 ♗f3? (better 29 ♗xh5! ♖xh5 30 ♖c7 ∞) 20...♘g3 30 ♘c7 (S.Krivoshey-N.Ortiz, Sort 2006) and now 30...♘xf1 31 ♔xf1 ♖g7 32 ♘xa8 ♗a6 -/+.

25 ♕c2 g4

If now 25...♗d7 26 ♘c7 ♖a7 27 ♘e6 ♗xe6 28 dxe6 g4 29 ♖c8 ♕e7 30 ♕b3 +=.

26 ♗xa5! *(D)*

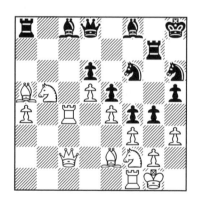

26...♕e8

No better is 26...♕xa5 27 ♖xc8 gxh3 28 ♘xh3 ♖xc8 (or 28...♘d7 29 ♘xd6 ♖xc8 30 ♘xc8 ♗c5+ 31 ♔h1 ♕a8 32 ♗b5 ♕xc8 33 ♕c3! +/- Kotronias) 29 ♕xc8 ♘h7 30 ♖c1 +/- J.Fang-B.Dean Kawamura, Parsippany 2008.

27 h4?

White obtains an edge after 27 fxg4! hxg4 28 ♘c7! ♖xc7 29 ♗xc7 ♗xc7 gxh3 30 ♘xh3 ♘hg4 31 ♗b6 +/- Avrukh.

27...gxf3 28 ♗xf3 ♗g4 29 ♗xg4 ♘fxg4! 30 ♗b6 ♕e7 31 ♘xg4 ♘xg4 32 ♗f2 f3! 33 g3?

Capitulation, but 33 ♖c7 fxg2 34 ♖e1 (if 34 ♖xe7 ♘h2!) 34...♕f6 35 ♖xg7 ♗xg7 36 ♔xg2 ♗h6 (Avrukh) or 33 ♖c3 fxg2 34 ♖a1 ♖g8 35 ♗g3 ♗h6 36 ♖aa3 ♗f4 (Kotronias) would still give Black a probably winning attack.

The game ended **33...♘e3! 34 ♗xe3 ♖xg3+ 35 ♔f2 ♖g2+ 36 ♔xf3 ♖xc2 37 ♖xc2 ♕xh4 38 ♖g1 ♖xa4 39 ♘c3 ♖c4 40 ♔e2 ♗h6 41 ♗b6** [if 41 ♗xh6 ♕h2+] **41...♖xe4+ 0-1** [since if 42 ♘xe4 ♕xe4+ 43 ♔d1 ♕d3+ etc].

C2: 10 f3 f5 (D)

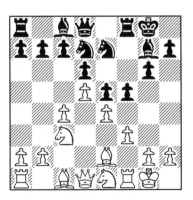

Often this variation has no independent significance, as a subsequent 11 ♗e3 returns to C1 above, while 11 ♘d3 ♘f6 12 ♗d2 heads for C32 (albeit via an inaccurate move order). In this section we will examine lines where White follows up f2-f3 with g2-g4.

C21: 11 g4 *245*
C22: 11 ♘d3 *249*

As noted above, 11 ♗e3 returns to line C1. 11 ♗d2 is also possible, but transposes after a subsequent ♘d3; e.g. 11...♘f6 12 ♘d3 is C32, while 11...f4 12 g4 g5 13 ♘d3 is *12...g5* in C22, or if 12 ♖c1 g5 13 ♘d3 – *12 ♗d2* again in C22.

C21: 11 g4 *(D)*

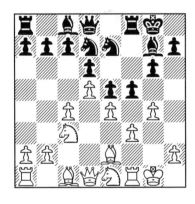

A Hungarian speciality, played first by B.Sandor, then taken up by Portisch and, later, GMs Lukacs and Pinter, IMs Dudas and Kiss, among others. White hopes to neutralize the black pawn storm by blocking the kingside and then develop his initiative on the other wing. Nevertheless, the position is usually full of tension and White must be careful as Black has some tactical motifs: in particular, a sacrifice on g4 (or sometimes on g5, depending on the pawn structure), followed by a march of the g- and h-pawns.

11...♔h8

Preparing to reorganize with ...♘g8. Black has various other plans:

a) 11...fxg4 12 fxg4 ♖xf1+ 13 ♗xf1 (or 13 ♔xf1 h6 14 h4 ♘f6 15 g5 ♘h7 16 ♗e3 ♕d7 17 ♔g1 ♕h3 18 ♘g2 hxg5 19 hxg5 += T.Ghitescu-J.Bolbochan, Varna Olympiad 1962) 13...♘f6 14 h3 c6 15 ♘c2 cxd5 16 cxd5 ♗d7 17 ♗e3 ♖c8 18 a4 += B.Sandor-E.Gereben, Hungarian Ch. 1952.

b) 11...h5 12 g5 h4 13 ♗e3 f4 14 ♗f2 ♔f7 (or 14...h3 15 ♔h1 ♔f7 16 ♘d3 ♖h8 17 c5 +/- T.Doering-J.Hogenacker, Dortmund 1987) 15 ♔h1 ♖h8 16 ♘d3 ♖h5 17 ♖g1 ♘f8 18 c5 ♘h7 19 cxd6 cxd6 20 ♖c1 ♘xg5 21 ♘b5 += S.Mirovshchikov-I.Brikov, Tula 2002.

c) 11...h6!? (intending ...f5xg4, ...g6-g5) 12 h4 (if 12 ♗e3 fxg4 13 fxg4 ♖xf1+ 14 ♔xf1 g5 15 ♘g2 ♘g6 16 ♗f2 ♘f4 17 ♘e3 ♘f6 ∞ J.Dudas-O.Cvitan, Basel 2001) 12...♘f6 13 ♘g2 (or 13 ♘d3 – *11...♘f6 12 ♘d3 h6*) 13...c6 14 ♗e3 cxd5 (or 14...♕d7!?) 15 cxd5 ♕d7 16 exf5 gxf5 17 g5 hxg5 18 ♗b5 ♕d8 19 hxg5 ♘h5 20 f4 ♘xf4 21 ♗xf4 exf4 22 ♘xf4 a6 23 ♕h5 axb5 24 ♖ae1 ∞ K.Nikolaidis-Kr.Georgiev, Athens 1993.

d) 11...f4!? 12 h4 (for 12 ♘d3 or 12 ♗d2 g5 13 ♘d3 see C22) 12...♔h8 (12...♘f6!? 13 ♘d3 – *11...♘f6 12 ♘d3 f4!?* below; or if 12...c5 13 a3 ♔h8 14 ♗d2 ♘g8 15 ♘g2 ♗f6 16 ♗e1 ♗e7 17 b4

+= P.Benko-L.Pachman, Portoroz Interzonal 1958) 13 ♖f2 (if 13 ♘g2 ♘g8 14 ♗d2 ♗f6 15 ♗e1 ♖f7! 16 ♔h2 ♕f8 17 b4 ♗d8 18 ♖c1 a5 19 a3 axb4 20 axb4 g5 21 h5, P.Lukacs-S.Zakic, Budapest 1991, 21...♘df6! 22 ♖h1 ♘h6 intending ♘fxg4! -/+ Lukacs; or 13 g5 h6 14 ♔g2 ♔g8!? 15 ♖h1 hxg5 16 hxg5 ♔f7 17 ♘d3 ♘g8 18 ♔f1 ♕xg5 19 ♘b5 ♕d8 =+ R.Hungaski-A.Melekhina, Pawtucket 2008) 13...♘g8 14 ♖h2 (or 14 g5 – *11...♔h8 12 h4 ♘g8*) 14...♗f6 15 ♘g2 ♗e7 16 ♖b1 a5 17 ♗d2 ♘gf6 18 ♗e1 c6 19 ♗f2 ♕c7 ∞ J.Sunye Neto-D.Di Berardino, Sao Paulo 2005.

e) 11...♘f6 (the main alternative) 12 ♘d3 (D) (if 12 ♘g2 c6 13 ♖b1 cxd5 14 cxd5 ♗d7 15 ♗e3 f4 16 ♗f2 g5 17 ♕d3 h5 18 h3 hxg4 19 hxg4 ♔f7 ∞ L.Portisch-L.Stein, Yerevan 1965; or 12 ♗e3 c5 13 ♘d3 h6 14 ♔h1 ♖f7 15 ♖g1 fxg4 16 fxg4 g5 ∞ E.Ovod-F.Amonatov, Moscow 2007) and then:

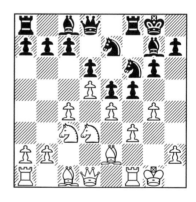

e1) 12...♔h8 13 ♗e3 c5 (or 13...c6 – *12...c6*) 14 ♖b1 f4 15 ♗d2 h5 16 g5 ♘h7 17 h4 ♘xg5 18 hxg5 ♘f5 19 ♖f2 ♕xg5+ 20 ♖g2 ♘g3 21 ♘f2 += A.Hauchard-Al.David, Brussels 1993.

e2) 12...c5 13 ♖b1 (or 13 ♗d2 – *12...c5 13 g4* in C32) 13...b6 14 b4 cxb4 15 ♖xb4 ♕c7 16 ♗e3 ♗d7 17 h3 ♖f7 ∞ L.Ftacnik-F.Borkowski, Groningen 1974.

e3) 12...h6!? 13 h4 c6 14 ♘f2 (or 14 ♗e3 b5! 15 dxc6 bxc4 16 ♘b4 ♗e6 17 ♘bd5 ♘xc6 18 ♗xc4 ♘d4 ∞ K.Petrosian-I.Nikolaidis, Budapest 1995) 14...a6 15 ♗e3 ♔h8 16 ♔g2 b5 ∞ G.Zaichik-M.Podgaets, Kutaisi 1978.

e4) 12...f4!? 13 h4 (13 ♗d2 is C3221; not 13 b4?! h5 14 g5 ♘h7 15 h4 ♘xg5! 16 hxg5 ♘xd5 17 ♘xd5 ♕xg5+ 18 ♔h1 ½-½ K.Grigorian-L.Yurtaev, Frunze 1979) 13...c6 (if 13...h5 14 g5 ♘h7 15 ♖f2 += A.Kochyev-U.Kaminski, Dresden 1984) 14 ♗d2 ♔h8 15 ♗e1 b5!? 16 b3 b4 17 ♘a4 (if 17 ♘xb4 ♕b6+ 18 ♔g2 ♕xb4 19 ♘b5 ♕c5 20 ♗f2 ♕b4 21 ♗e1 =) 17...cxd5 18 exd5 ♘exd5 19 cxd5 ♘xd5 20 ♘xb4 ♘e3 21 ♕d2 ♗b7 ∞ V.Chekhov-A.Kubicek, Berlin 1988.

e5) 12...c6 13 ♗e3 (if 13 ♘f2 a6! 14 ♕b3 ♔h8 15 ♗d2 ♘d7 16 ♕a3 c5 ∞ V.Maki-Y.Grünfeld, World Student Team Ch. 1981) 13...♔h8 (or 13...h6 14 h4 – *12...h6*; if instead 13...f4 14 ♗f2 g5 15 c5!? += J.Gralka-J.Konikowski, Polish Ch. 1977; or 13...cxd5 14 cxd5 f4 15 ♗f2 g5 16 a4 += A.Gipslis-E.Bukic, Olot 1973) 14 h3 b5 (14...h6!? is still possible) 15 ♘b4 bxc4 (if 15...cxd5 16 ♘bxd5 ♘exd5 17 ♘xd5 ♗b7?! 18 ♘xf6 ♖xf6 19 cxb5 += J.Pinter-A.Sznapik, Prague 1985; or 15...♗b7?! 16 dxc6 ♘xc6 17 ♘xc6 ♗xc6 18 cxb5 ♗b7 19 ♗c4 +/- P.Lukacs-V.Loginov, Budapest 1993) 16 ♘xc6 (or 16 ♗xc4 cxd5 17 ♘bxd5 ♘exd5 18 ♘xd5, M.Condie-J.Gallagher, London

1986, 18...♗e6 ∞) 16...♘xc6 17 dxc6 ♗e6 18 ♕a4 (J.Pinter-E.Mortensen, Copenhagen 1985) 18...d5! ∞.

12 ♘d3 *(D)*

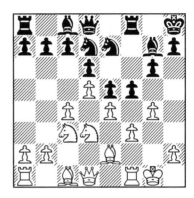

Here the knight is ready to support c4-c5, or drop back to f2 to defend the vulnerable e4- and g4-pawns. Other moves:

a) 12 ♘g2 ♘g8 (or 12...a5 13 h4 ♘c5 14 ♗e3 ♘g8 – *12...♘g8*) 13 h4 (13 ♗e3 – *12 ♗e3*) 13...a5 (13...f4!? – *11...f4*) 14 ♗e3 ♘c5 15 a3 (if 15 ♖b1 ♗d7 16 b3 b6 17 a3 a4 18 b4 ♘b3 =+ J.Pinter-J.Nunn, Thessaloniki Olympiad 1988; or 15 exf5 gxf5 16 g5 f4 17 ♗xc5 dxc5 18 ♘e4 ♘e7 19 ♘xc5 ♘f5 ∞ V.Zilberstein-A.Petrushin, USSR 1979) 15...fxg4 16 fxg4 ♖xf1+ 17 ♔xf1 ♘f6 18 ♗f3 h5 ∞ V.Shtyrenkov-E.Gleizerov, Kursk 1987.

b) 12 ♗e3 ♘g8 13 ♕d2 (instead 13 ♘d3 – *12 ♘d3*, or if 13 ♘g2 ♗h6 14 ♗f2 a5 15 a3 ♘c5 16 b4 axb4 17 axb4 ♖xa1 18 ♕xa1 ♘b3 19 ♕d1 ♘d2 ∞ G.Mouratidis-V.Kotronias, Thessaloniki 2005) 13...f4 (if 13...♘df6 14 h3 h5 15 ♔g2 ♘h7 16 ♘d3 hxg4 17 hxg4 ♘gf6 18 ♕d1 += J.Pinter-Kr.Georgiev, Warsaw 1987) 14 ♗f2 h5 15 h3 ♖f7 16 ♔g2

♗f6 17 ♘d3 ♖h7 18 ♖h1 ♗h4 with a good position, e.g. 19 ♗d1 ♘f8 20 c5 ♗xf2 21 ♕xf2 g5 22 cxd6 cxd6 23 ♖c1 ♗d7 24 ♗a4 ♗xa4 25 ♘xa4 ♘g6 26 b4 ♘f6 =+ D.Jacimovic-M.Vukic, Kastel Stari 1988.

c) 12 h4 *(D)* is more complicated, when Black has two main ideas:

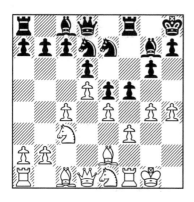

c1) 12...♘g8 (or 12...f4!? – *11...f4*) 13 g5 (or 13 ♘g2 – *12 ♘g2*) 13...f4 14 ♔g2 (or 14 ♖f2 h6 15 ♖g2 ♖f7 16 ♘d3 ♘f8 17 ♔f2 c6 18 ♕h1 b5!? ∞ M.Rodshtein-B.Avrukh, Maalot-Tarshiha 2008) 14...h6 15 ♖h1 ♖f7 16 ♘d3 ♗f8 17 ♕g1 ♖h7 18 ♔f1 ♗e7 (not 18...hxg5? 19 hxg5 ♖xh1 20 ♕xh1+ ♔g7 21 ♕h4! ♗e7 22 ♘xf4! exf4 23 ♗xf4 with a decisive attack, A.Gipslis-L.Muchnik, Moscow 1970) 19 ♘xf4 exf4 20 ♗xf4 ♖f7 21 ♗e3 h5 ∞ P.Van Hoolandt-J.Cabrera Trujillo, Cannes 2007.

c2) 12...♘f6 (or 12...c6!? 13 ♔g2 ♘f6 14 ♘d3 b5 15 b3 ♖b8 16 ♘f2 b4 17 ♘a4 ♗b7 =+ P.Eljanov-T.Radjabov, FIDE Grand Prix, Elista 2008) 13 ♘g2 (or 13 ♘d3 c6 14 ♗e3 b5 15 b3 a5 16 ♘f2 b4 17 ♘a4 c5 ∞ L.Barredo-M.Lee, US Chess League 2007) 13...c6 14 ♗e3 ♕d7 (or

14...a6!? 15 a4 a5 16 ♕d2 c5 ½-½ A.Sumets-Y.Zinchenko, Alushta 2006) 15 exf5 gxf5 16 g5 ♘h5 17 f4 ♘g3 18 ♖f3 ♘xe2+ 19 ♕xe2 b6 20 h5 ♔g8 21 ♖g3 ♗a6 with good play for Black, A.Defize-N.Faybish, Belgian Team Ch. 1998.

12...♘g8

The alternative is to try and block the queenside with 12...c5, when the most logical response is 13 a3 (not 13 dxc6?! bxc6 14 b4 d5 =+ I.Cervenka-Z.Lanka, Trnava 1986; while if 13 ♔g2 ♘g8 14 ♗e3 ♗h6 15 ♗f2 ♗g5 16 ♕e1 fxg4 17 fxg4 ♘df6 18 h3 h5 = G.Agzamov-Z.Lanka, USSR 1979; or 13 ♗d2 ♘g8 14 ♖b1 ♗h6 15 b4 cxb4 16 ♖xb4 fxg4 17 ♗xh6 ♘xh6 18 fxg4 ♖xf1+ 19 ♕xf1 ♘c5!? ∞ F.Baumbach-W.Uhlmann, Leipzig 1974) 13...♘g8 (or 13...a6 14 b4 b5!? 15 cxb5 axb5 16 bxc5 b4 17 cxd6 bxc3 18 dxe7 ♕xe7, W.Weisser-A.Müller, Hessen 1992, 19 a4 +=) 14 b4 b6 15 ♖b1 ♗h6 16 ♘b5 ♗xc1 17 ♕xc1 ♘df6 18 exf5 gxf5 19 g5 ♘e8 20 f4 += R.Almond-J.Kohout, Liberec 2005.

13 ♔h1

Vacating g1 for the rook. Otherwise 13 ♗e3 is mostly played, e.g. 13...♗h6 (other options are 13...f4 14 ♗f2 h5 15 h3 ♗f6 16 c5 ♗h4 17 cxd6 cxd6 18 ♔g2 ♗xf2 19 ♘xf2 ♖f7 20 ♖h1 ♖h7 ∞ B.Kovacevic-N.Fercec, Zadar 2002; or 13...♘gf6 14 c5 ♘xc5 15 ♘xc5 dxc5 16 ♗xc5 ♖f7 17 h3 ♘e8 ∞ P.Kazantzidis-D.Dochev, Nikea 2002; or even 13...♘h6!? 14 ♗f2 ♖f7 15 ♔g2 ½-½ G.Garcia Gonzales-W.Uhlmann, Potsdam 1985) 14 ♗f2 ♗g5 (or 14...a5 15

♔g2 b6 16 ♖h1 ♘c5 17 ♘xc5?! bxc5 18 h4 ♗f4 =+ P.Zarubin-E.Gleizerov, Voronezh 1987) 15 ♕e1 fxg4 16 fxg4 ♘h6 17 h3 a5 18 c5 dxc5 19 ♘xc5 ♘xc5 20 ♗xc5 ♖xf1+ 21 ♗xf1 ♘f7 22 a4 ♗d7 ½-½ E.Arlandi-M.Ghinda, Novi Sad Olympiad 1990.

13...f4 (D)

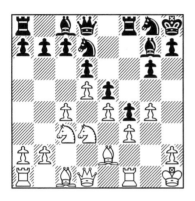

Planning to play on the h-file. If now 13...♗h6?! 14 gxf5 gxf5 15 f4! fxe4 16 ♘xe4 exf4 17 ♗xf4 += L.Sandstrom-M.Eklund, Stockholm 1993; but Black can also try 13...a6!? 14 ♗e3 ♗h6 15 ♕d2 ♕h4 16 ♖g1 fxg4 17 ♖xg4 ♗xe3 18 ♕xe3 ♕e7 = V.Khomyakov-A.Khait, Warsaw 1992; or 13...a5 14 ♖g1 ♖f7 15 g5?! f4! 16 ♗f1 ♗f8 17 b3 ♗e7 = R.Vaganian-W.Uhlmann, Niksic 1978.

14 ♖g1 g5

Alternatively, 14...♗f6 15 b4 (or 15 ♗d2 ♖f7 16 ♔g2 ♗h4 17 ♗e1 ♗xe1 18 ♕xe1 h5 19 h3 ♖h7 ∞ P.Kiss-L.Vajda, Balatonbereny 1996) 15...♗h4?! (15...a5 looks better here) 16 c5 ♘df6 17 ♗b2 ♗d7 18 a4 h5?! 19 ♘xf4! exf4 20 g5 +/- V.Belov-A.Grischuk, Russian Team Ch. 2009.

15 ♗d2 h5 16 h3 ♖f6 17 ♖c1 ♖h6 18

♔g2 ♗f8 19 b4 ♘e7 20 c5 ♘g6 21 cxd6 ♗xd6 22 ♘b5 ♘f6 23 ♘f2 ♗d7 24 a4 **½-½**

I.Cheparinov-A.Fedorov, FIDE World Cup, Khanty Mansyisk 2005. Neither side could really hope to achieve anything here.

C22: 11 ♘d3 (D)

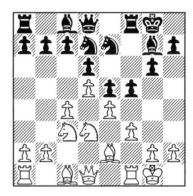

Playing f2-f3 and ♘d3 (or equivalently 10 ♘d3 f5 11 f3) without waiting for ...♘d7-f6 is slightly inaccurate, as Black can now defer the knight move or even omit it completely.

11...f4

The critical continuation. Alternatives mostly transpose elsewhere:

a) 11...♘f6 12 c5 (here 12 ♗d2 is the C32 main line; 12 ♗e3 f4 13 ♗f2 g5 is 13 ♘d3 in C1; and 12 g4 is 11...♘f6 in C21) 12...c6?! 13 ♕b3 ♔h8 14 ♗e3 fxe4 15 fxe4 cxd5 16 cxd6 += S.Skembris-E.Gufeld, Athens 1985.

b) 11...♔h8 12 ♗d2 heads for C321 after 12...♘f6 (or 12...♘g8 and ...♘df6 subsequently), but White does better with 12 ♗e3!, reaching 11...♔h8 in line C1.

c) 11...c5 12 dxc6 (or 12 g4, when 12...♔h8 is 12...c5 in C21, while 12...f4 13 ♗d2 is 12...c5 below) 12...bxc6 (or 12...♘xc6 13 ♗e3 +=) 13 c5 d5 14 exd5 cxd5 15 ♗g5 += R.Bauer-K.Dörr, Ladenburg 1992.

12 g4 *(D)*

This is the only real justification for White's move order, trying to close the kingside with the black f-pawn having already gone past. But as we saw in line C21 above, ...f5-f4 is not at all a bad plan in these positions. Instead:

a) 12 b4 (often unnecessary) 12...g5 (or 12...a5!? 13 bxa5 ♖xa5 14 ♗d2 ♖a8 15 g4?! ♗f6 16 ♗e1 h5 17 h3 ♔g7 18 ♔g2 ♖h8 =+ I.Miladinovic-V.Golod, Belgrade 1993) 13 c5 ♘f6 14 a4 ♖f7 (or 14...♔h8 15 ♗a3 ♖g8 16 a5 ♗f8 17 cxd6 cxd6 18 b5 g4 ∞ S.Lagrotteria-B.Socko, Saint Vincent 2001) 15 b5 ♗f8 16 ♗a3 ♘g6 17 a5 h5 18 ♕b3 g4 19 b6 cxb6 20 cxd6 g3 21 h3 ♘h7 22 ♖fc1 (B.Larsen-P.H.Nielsen, Valby 1991) 22...♗xh3! 23 gxh3 ♘g5 -/+.

b) 12 ♗d2 g5 (12...♘f6 is C322; or 12...c5!? 13 a3 g5 14 ♗e1 h5 15 b4 b6 16 ♖b1 ♘f6 17 bxc5 bxc5 18 ♕a4 a6 ∞ D.Obradovic-B.Cetkovic, Belgrade 2005) 13 g4!? (13 ♖c1 ♖f7 is 11...♖f7 in C3; while 13...♘f6 or 13...♘g6 14 c5 ♘f6 reaches C32222) 13...fxg3?! (otherwise we transpose to the line *12 g4 g5 13 ♗d2* below) 14 ♗xg5! (if 14 hxg3 ♘g6 followed by ...h7-h5-h4 ∞) 14...gxh2+ 15 ♔h1 h6 16 ♗h4 ♗f6 17 ♗xf6 ♖xf6 18 f4 exf4 19 ♘xf4 ♘e5 20 ♕d2 ♘7g6 21 ♘h5 ♖xf1+ 22 ♖xf1 ♕g5 23 ♕xg5 hxg5 24 ♔xh2 += D.Barlov-E.Mortensen, Budapest 1987.

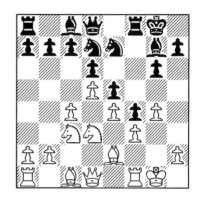

12...h5!?

A provocative reply, but perhaps not the best. Other ideas are:

a) 12...fxg3?! 13 hxg3 leaves Black with little counterplay, e.g. 13...h6 (or 13...♘f6 14 ♔g2 ♖f7 15 ♖h1 ♕f8 16 c5 a6 17 ♗e3 +/- D.Dupuy-P.Petermans, Naujac 2001) 14 ♗e3 g5 15 ♔g2 ♘g6 16 ♕d2 ♘f6 17 ♖ac1 += J.Vestergaard-J.Lind, Stockholm 1992.

b) 12...♘f6 – *11 g4 ♘f6 12 ♘d3 f4*, though it is unusual just here.

c) 12...c5 13 ♗d2 ♔h8!? (or 13...♘f6 – *13...c5* in C3221) 14 ♗e1 ♘g8 15 ♗f2 ♘h6 16 ♖b1 a5 17 a3 ♘f7 18 b4 += I.Miladinovic-J.Todorovic, Yugoslav Team Ch. 1990.

d) 12...♗f6!? 13 ♗d2 h5 14 h3 ♔f7 (or 14...♗h4!? 15 ♗e1 ♗xe1 16 ♕xe1 hxg4 17 hxg4 g5 18 b4 ♘g6 19 c5 ♘f6 ∞ D.Cherin-A.Srebrnic, Nova Gorica 2005) 15 ♗e1 ♖h8 16 ♔g2 ♘g8 17 ♖c1 ♗h4 = A.Dreev-B.Gelfand, Kramatorsk 1989.

e) 12...g5 (the most common response) 13 ♗d2 h5 (13...♘f6 – C3221; or 13...♘g6 14 ♗e1 ♖f7 15 ♗f2 ♗f8 16 b4 ♘f6 17 ♔g2 h5 18 h3 ♗e7 ∞

I.Miladinovic-P.Popovic, Yugoslav Ch. 1991) 14 h3 ♖f6 (or 14...♔f7 15 ♔g2 ♖h8 16 ♗e1 ♖h6 17 ♗f2 ♘g6 ∞ F.Schwarz-M.Hermann, German League 1994) 15 ♗e1 (or 15 ♔f2!? ♖h6 16 ♖h1 ♘g6 17 ♕g1 ♘f6 18 ♔e1 c5 19 a3 b6 20 b4 ♗d7 ∞ L.Portisch-S.Gligoric, Madrid 1960) 15...♖h6 16 ♗f2 ♘g6 17 ♔g2 ♘f6 18 ♖h1 ♗d7 19 c5 ♔f7 ∞ I.Miladinovic-R.Forster, World Junior Ch. 1990.

13 g5

Less consistent are 13 h3 ♔f7 14 ♔g2 ♖h8 15 ♖h1 ♘g8 16 ♗d2 ♗f6 ∞ H.Jung-M.Morgenstern, Saarland 1992; or 13 gxh5 ♗f6!? 14 ♔h1 ♔f7 15 ♗xf4!? exf4 16 ♘xf4 ♘c5 ∞ J.Banas-K.Mokry, Budapest 1981.

13...h4

Cutting off the g5-pawn, so as to attack it with ...♖h8-h5, but this plan is a little slow.

14 ♔h1

If 14 ♕e1 ♔f7 15 ♔h1 ♖h8 16 ♖g1 ♘f8 (not 16...♖h5? 17 ♗xf4! exf4 18 ♘xf4 +/-) 17 c5 ♗d7 18 b3 ♖h5 19 ♗a3 ♘c8 ∞ R.Wade-S.Reshevsky, Buenos Aires 1960.

14...♔f7 (D)

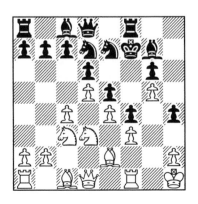

Otherwise the h-pawn falls for nothing; e.g. 14...b6?! 15 ♕e1! ♔f7 16 ♕xh4 ♖h8 17 ♕f2 ♘g8 18 ♖g1 ♘c5 (if 18...♖h5 19 ♗xf4! again) 19 ♗d2 ♖h5 20 b4 ♘xd3 21 ♗xd3 ♖xg5 22 ♖xg5 ♕xg5 23 ♖g1 +/-.

15 ♗d2 (D)

White can also consider:

a) 15 b4 ♖h8 (15...a5!? looks better) 16 c5 ♘f8 17 ♕b3 ♖h5 18 ♖g1 ♘h7 19 ♘xf4! exf4 20 ♗xf4 ♘g8 21 cxd6 cxd6 (R.Gabdrakhmanov-G.Kasparov, USSR Junior Ch. 1976) 22 ♖ac1!, and if 22...a6 23 ♗xd6! ♕xd6 24 f4 with a very strong attack.

b) 15 c5 (the most energetic) 15...♖h8 (if 15...dxc5?! 16 ♕b3 creates problems) 16 ♕b3 b6 (now if 16...♖h5 17 cxd6 cxd6 18 ♘b5 ♕b6 19 a4 a5 20 ♖g1 ♗f8 21 ♗d2 ♘g8 22 ♗e1 +/- J.Lucio-D.Markl, corr. 1994; or again 19 ♘xf4!? exf4 20 ♗xf4 +/-) 17 cxd6 cxd6 18 ♕a3 ♘c5 19 ♘xc5 bxc5 20 b4 += B.Larsen-M.Tal, 1st matchgame, Bled 1965.

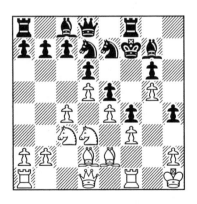

15...♖h8 16 b4 ♖h5 17 ♖g1 ♘g8

Or 17...♘f8 18 ♖c1 ♘h7 19 ♘xf4! exf4 20 ♗xf4 with compensation.

18 c5 a6

If instead 18...♘f8 (not 18...♖xg5? 19 ♖xg5 ♕xg5 20 ♘b5 +-) 19 ♖c1 (or 19 ♕b3 ♘h7 20 ♖ac1 ♘xg5 21 cxd6 cxd6 22 ♘b5 += S.Kupka-J.Siekaniec, Trinec 1998) 19...♗d7 20 ♘xf4! exf4 21 ♗xf4 ♕e7 22 ♕d2 with excellent compensation, R.Weinstein-R.Byrne, US Ch. 1964.

19 ♕b3 ♖xg5 20 c6 ♖xg1+ 21 ♖xg1 ♘f8 22 cxb7 ♗xb7 23 ♗e1 (D)

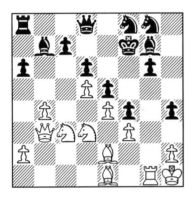

White has more than enough for the pawn, especially as Black has no counterplay. I.Miladinovic-O.Korneev, Vrsac 2006, continued **23...g5?!** [23...♗f6 might improve slightly] **24 b5 a5 25 ♘a4 ♗c8** [if 25...♘d7 26 ♘db2 and 27 ♘c4] **26 b6 cxb6 27 ♕xb6** [or 27 ♘xb6 a4 28 ♘xa4 +/-] **27...♗f6 28 ♘db2 ♗e7 29 ♕xd8 ♗xd8 30 ♘c4 ♖a6 31 ♗f2 ♘d7 32 ♖c1 ♘e7 33 ♘a3 ♖a8 34 ♘b5 ♖a6 35 h3 ♘f6** [or 35...♔f6 36 ♘c7 ♗xc7 37 ♗xa6 ♗xa6 38 ♖xc7 +-] **36 ♔g2 g4?! 37 hxg4 h3+ 38 ♔xh3 ♗xg4+ 39 fxg4 ♘xe4 40 ♗h4 ♘f6 41 ♗xf6 ♔xf6 42 ♘c7 ♖a7 43 ♘e8+ ♔g5 44 ♘c3 ♘xd5 45 ♘xd5 e4 46 ♘xd6 ♖h7+ 47 ♔g2 f3+ 48 ♗xf3 exf3+ 49 ♔g3 ♖d7 50 ♖c6 ♔g6 51 ♔xf3 1-0.**

C3: 10 ♘d3 f5 11 ♗d2 (D)

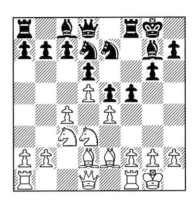

This is the most popular move, preparing ♖c1 and c4-c5. Instead, 11 f3 is C22 above, and White has occasionally tried:

a) 11 f4?! (no better than on the previous move) 11...exf4 (or 11...fxe4!? 12 ♘xe4 ♘f5 13 ♘g5 ♘d4 14 ♗g4 ♘c5 15 ♘xc5 dxc5 16 ♗xc8 ♕xc8 = G.Deloge-F.Robert, Checy 2002) 12 ♗xf4 (or 12 ♘xf4 ♘c5 13 exf5 ♘xf5 14 ♗d2 a5 15 ♘d3 ♕h4 =+ J.Cortes Parejo-M.Tissir, Seville 2002) 12...♗xc3 13 bxc3 fxe4 14 ♘b4 ♘f5 15 g4 ♘h4 16 ♕d2 ♕e8 =+ R.Wade-J.Penrose, Hastings 1961/62.

b) 11 exf5 ♘xf5 (or 11...gxf5 12 f4 e4 13 ♘f2 ♘c5 14 ♕c2 ♘g6 15 ♗e3 a5 = E.Kristiansen-O.Seuss, European Seniors Ch. 2006) 12 f3 ♘f6 13 ♘f2 ♘d4 (or 13...c6!? 14 ♘fe4 ♘xe4 15 ♘xe4 ♕b6+ 16 ♔h1 ♗d7 ∞ Hort) 14 ♘fe4 (if 14 ♗e3 ♘h5 15 ♖e1 a6 16 ♗f1 c5 17 ♘fe4 ♗f5 18 ♕d2 ♘f4 ∞ R.Dzindzichashvili-E.Geller, USSR Team Ch. 1975; or 14 ♗d3 c5 15 ♗e3 ♘h5 16 ♗e4, V.Hort-J.Van der Wiel, Reykjavik 1985, 16...♘f4!? ∞) 14...♘h5 15 ♗g5 ♕d7 16 g3 h6 17 ♗e3 c5!? (safer 17...♕e7 ∞) 18

♗xd4 exd4 19 ♘b5 a6 20 ♘bxd6 d3 21 ♕xd3 (here 21 ♗xd3 ♗d4+ 22 ♖f2! offered more chances) 21...♗d4+ 22 ♔g2 ♘xg3! 23 ♘xc8 ♘xf1 24 ♘b6 ♕c7 25 ♖xf1 ♕xb6 26 b4! ∞ S.Gligoric-R.Fischer, Bled 1961.

C31: 11...♔h8 *254*
C32: 11...♘f6 *256*

Black has several other moves:

a) 11...f4?! 12 ♗g4! (the reason ...♘f6 is played first) 12...h5 (or 12...c6 13 ♗e6+ ♔h8 14 ♖c1 f3!? 15 gxf3 ♘b6 16 c5! += F.Balabaev-R.Sakic, corr. 2003) 13 ♗e6+ ♔h7 14 f3 ♘f6 (or 14...g5 15 ♗e1 ♘f6 16 ♗xc8 ♖xc8 17 c5 += A.Gavrilov-L.Yurtaev, Pavlodar 1993) 15 ♗xc8 ♖xc8 16 ♕b3 b6 17 ♕d1 g5 18 a4 ♗h6 19 a5 g4 20 ♘b5 a6 (E.Ragozin-E.Ubilava, Linares 1996) 21 ♘a7!? ♖a8 22 axb6 cxb6 23 ♖xa6 ♕c7 24 ♕a4 +=.

b) 11...c5 12 f4!? (otherwise 12 ♖b1 ♘f6 13 f3 or 12 a3 ♘f6 13 f3 – *11...♘f6 12 f3 c5*) 12...a6 13 a4 (if 13 ♕b3 fxe4 14 ♘xe4 ♘f5 15 ♗g4 b5! ∞ M.Stean-P.Biyiasas, Buenos Aires Olympiad 1978) 13...exf4 14 ♘xf4 (if 14 ♗xf4 ♗xc3 15 bxc3 fxe4 16 ♘e1 ♘f5 ∞ L.Ftacnik-A.Sznapik, Dortmund 1981) 15...♗d4+ 15 ♔h1 ♘f6 16 exf5 ♘xf5 (R.Douven-F.Nijboer, Dutch Ch. 1989) 17 ♘e6! +/=.

c) 11...♖f7!? 12 f3 (if 12 ♕c2 fxe4!? 13 ♘xe4 ♘f5 ∞; while 12 ♖c1 ♕f8!? 13 f3 ♘f6 – *12...♖f7 in C32*, or if 13 b4 ♗h6 14 c5 ♘f6 15 f3 ♗xd2 16 ♕xd2 f4 17 cxd6 cxd6 18 ♘b5 ♕d8 19 ♘c7 ♖b8 20 ♘e6 ♗xe6 21 dxe6 ♖f8 22 b5 ½-½ M.Milicevic-Kr.Georgiev, Kragujevac

1984) 12...f4 (12...♘f6 is *12...♖f7 in C32* again) 13 ♖c1 g5 (not 13...h5?! 14 c5! ♘xc5 15 ♘xc5 dxc5 16 ♗c4 ♔f8 17 ♗e1 +/- A.Khalifman-W.Watson, London 1991) 14 c5!? (if 14 ♘b5 a6 15 ♘a3 ♗f8! 16 b4 ♘g6 17 c5 ♘f6 ∞ J.Lanz Calavia-E.Barrababe Menal, corr. 1985) 14...dxc5 (or 14...♘xc5 15 ♘xc5 dxc5 16 ♗c4 +=, while 14...♘f6?! transposes to 14...♖f7?! in C32222) 15 b4!? cxb4 16 ♘b5 with compensation.

d) 11...♘b6!? (D)

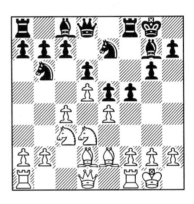

12 b3 (if 12 c5 fxe4! 13 cxb6 exd3 14 bxc7 ♕xc7 15 ♗xd3 ♕b6 ∞; but 12 ♕b3 might be better, and if 12...fxe4 13 ♘xe4 ♗f5 14 ♘g3 +=, or 13...♘f5 14 ♗c3 ♔h8 15 a4 += Z.Gyimesi-B.Szuk, Hungarian Junior Ch. 1994) 12...fxe4 13 ♘xe4 ♗f5 14 f3 c6! 15 dxc6 bxc6 (if 15...♘xc6 16 ♘df2! += N.Rashkovsky-M.Krasenkow, Cappelle la Grande 1990, or 15...♗xe4 16 fxe4 ♘xc6 17 ♖xf8+ ♕xf8 18 ♘e1 ♘d7 19 ♗e3 ♘c5 20 ♘c2 += O.Saether-M.Antonsen, Gausdal 1991) 16 ♖c1 d5 17 cxd5 cxd5 18 ♘g3 (M.Winz-P.Lukasevicius, corr. 2002) 18...e4! ∞ Krasenkow.

e) 11...fxe4!? 12 ♘xe4 ♘f5 (playing

11 exf5 lines two tempi down!) 13 ♗c3 (if now 13 f3 ♘f6 14 ♘df2 c6! = J.Sofrevski-L.Portisch, Skopje/Ohrid 1968; or 13 ♖c1!? ♘f6 14 ♘xf6+ ♕xf6 15 f3 ♘d4 16 ♘f2 ♘xe2+ 17 ♕xe2, S.Tomalak-T.Kirylo, corr. 1992, 17...e4!? ∞) 13...♘f6 (if 13...♘b6 14 ♕b3 – *11...♘b6*) 14 ♗f3 ♘xe4! (better than 14...♘h4 15 ♘xf6+ ♕xf6 16 ♗e4 ♗f5 17 ♕e2 ♗xe4 18 ♕xe4 ♕f5 19 ♖ae1 g5 20 f3 ♕xe4 21 ♖xe4 += Z.Gyimesi-D.Dumitrescu, European Junior Ch. 1993) 15 ♗xe4 ♕h4 16 ♖e1 (or 16 ♕e2, L.Ftacnik-F.Portisch, Bratislava 1983, 16...♘d4!? 17 ♗xd4 exd4 ∞) 16...b6 17 g3 ♕g5 18 ♘xe5!? (if 18 ♗g2 a5 ∞ V.Neverov-I.Belov, Podolsk 1989; or 18 ♕c1 ♕h5!) 18...♘xg3 (safer than 18...♗xe5!? 19 ♗xe5 dxe5 20 d6 ♗e6 21 ♗xa8 ♖xa8 22 f4 ♕f6, S.Kramer-D.Petrovic, corr. 2001, 23 dxc7! ♖c8 24 ♖xe5 ♔f7 ∞) 19 hxg3 ♗xe5 20 ♗xe5 ♕xe5 =, as 21 ♗xg6? fails to 21...♕f6! -/+ Sveshnikov.

C31: 11...♔h8 *(D)*

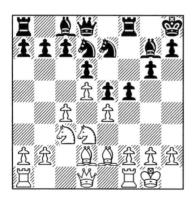

By far the most popular move here is 11...♘f6, increasing the pressure on

e4 and forcing White to support it with f2-f3 (see C32). However, the downside of ...♘f6 is that it gives up control of c5; so Black sometimes leaves the knight where it is and inserts this prophylactic king move. On seeing the reply, Black can then decide whether to play ...♘f6 after all (transposing to C321), or else seek independent ideas with ...♘g8 and/or ...c7-c5.

12 ♖c1

White continues as intended, ensuring that a later ...♘d7-f6 will not create any move order tricks.

Alternatively:

a) 12 b4 ♘g8 (12...♘f6 13 f3 is C3211) 13 ♖c1 (13 f3 – *12 f3 ♘g8 13 b4*) 13...♘gf6!? (13...♘df6 14 f3 f4 is C3211 again) 14 f3 f4 (if 14...♘h5 15 c5 ♘df6 16 a4 ♕e7 17 ♘f2 ♘f4 18 ♖e1 ♘6h5 19 ♗f1 += M.Notkin-D.Solak, Bucharest 1997) 15 g4 h5 16 g5 ♘h7 17 h4 ♘xg5 18 hxg5 ♕xg5+ = W.Liedl-S.Farago, Kecskemet 1991.

b) 12 f3 ♘g8 (12...♘f6 is just C321; and 12...f4 should also transpose as ...♘f6 will be necessary sooner or later, e.g. 13 ♖c1 h5 14 b4 g5 15 c5 ♘f6 etc) 13 a4!? (or 13 b4 ♗h6 14 ♗xh6 ♘xh6 15 ♕d2 f4 16 c5 ♘f6 – *13...♘eg8* in C3211; but if 13 ♖c1 c5! 14 ♖b1 ♗h6 15 b4 b6 16 bxc5 bxc5 17 ♖b3 ♗xd2 18 ♕xd2 f4 ∞ K.Spraggett-M.Marin, Spanish Team Ch. 1992) 13...♗h6 14 a5 a6 15 b4 ♗xd2 16 ♕xd2 f4 17 c5 ♕h4 18 cxd6 cxd6 19 ♘a4 += Z.Kozul-P.Pandavos, Corfu 1993.

12...c5!?

The most direct challenge to White's plan. Instead 12...♘f6 13 f3 is

C3212; while if 12...♘g8 13 exf5!? (13 b4 – *12 b4*, or 13 f3 – *12 f3*) 13...gxf5 14 f4 e4 15 ♘f2 (15 ♘b4!?) 15...♘df6 (if 15...c5 16 dxc6 bxc6 17 ♗e3 += V.Neverov-D.Bokan, Moscow 1989; or 15...♗d4!? 16 ♔h1!) 16 ♗e3 ♘h6 17 ♕d2 ♗d7 18 ♗d4 ♕e7 19 ♘cd1 c5 20 dxc6 bxc6 21 ♘e3 += V.Neverov-A.Frolov, Nikolaev 1995.

13 f4! *(D)*

Ineffective are:

a) 13 b4?! cxb4 14 ♘xb4 ♘c5 15 ♗f3 ♗d7 16 ♗e3 b6 =+ A.Khalifman-A.Shirov, Lvov 1990.

b) 13 dxc6 ♘xc6 (if 13...bxc6 14 c5! d5 15 exd5 cxd5 16 ♗g5 ♗b7 17 ♘b5 += A.Dreev-A.Shirov, World Junior Ch. 1989) 14 f3 (if 14 exf5 gxf5 15 f4 e4 16 ♘f2 ♗d4! 17 ♘b5 ♗xb2 18 ♗c3+ ♗xc3 19 ♖xc3 ♘c5 ∞ J.Hultin-V.Georgiev, Hallsberg 1991) 14...♘c5 15 ♗e3 ♘e6 16 ♕d2 b6 17 ♖fd1 ♗b7 18 ♘e1 ♘cd4 ∞ V.Akopian-A.Shirov, World Junior Ch. 1990.

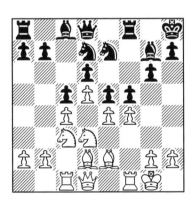

13...a6

White is also better after 13...exf4 14 ♘xf4 ♗d4+ 15 ♔h1 ♘f6 16 exf5 ♘xf5 17 ♕b3 += M.Drzazga-P.Torwong, corr.

2000; or 13...♘g8 14 exf5 gxf5 15 fxe5 ♘xe5 16 ♘f4 ♘f6 17 b3 ♕e7 18 ♕c2 += M.Kevorkyan-G.Karnovich, corr. 1993.

14 a4

Another option is 14 a3, since if 14...b5!? 15 cxb5 axb5 16 fxe5 ♘xe5 17 ♘xe5 ♗xe5 (T.Werbeck-T.Köhler, corr. 1993) 18 ♗xb5 and Black does not have enough for the pawn.

14...♘g8

If 14...exf4 15 ♗xf4! (stronger than 15 ♘xf4 ♘f6 16 exf5 ♘xf5 ∞) 15...♗d4+ (or 15...♘e5 16 ♘xe5 ♗xe5 17 ♗xe5+ dxe5 18 ♕d2 += E.Wiersma-T.Hansen, Kallithea 2008) 16 ♔h1 ♘e5 17 ♘xe5 dxe5 18 ♗g5 += R.Hafner-G.Beckhuis, Vienna 1998.

15 ♕c2 ♕e7 16 ♖ce1 exf4 17 exf5 g5 18 g4 fxg3 19 hxg3 ♘e5 20 ♘xe5 ♕xe5

Otherwise White supports the passed pawn with 20...♗xe5 21 g4 +=.

21 ♔g2 ♗xf5 22 ♗d3 ♗xd3 23 ♕xd3 ♕d4 24 ♕xd4 cxd4 25 ♘e4 *(D)*

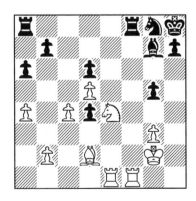

This was the game L.Ftacnik-P.Acs, German League 2005. White will regain the pawn and then stand clearly better due to his superior structure and better placed pieces, though he later went wrong: **25...h6** [or 26...♗e5 26 ♘xg6 +/-] **26 ♘xd6 ♖xf1 27 ♖xf1 ♘f6 28 b4** [simpler 28 a5! +/- Ftacnik] **28...b6 29 ♖f5 ♔h7 30 ♖e5 ♖f8 31 ♘e4 ♘xe4 32 ♖xe4 ♖d8 33 ♖e6 b5 34 axb5?** [a mistake in time trouble; instead 34 c5! ♖xd5 35 ♖xa6 bxa4 36 ♖xa4 +- Ftacnik] **34...axb5 35 c5 ♖xd5 36 c6 ♖d8 37 ♔f3 ♔g8 38 ♖e7 ♖c8 39 c7 ♔f8 40 ♖d7 ♗f6 41 ♔e4 ♔e8 42 ♖h7 ♗e7 43 ♖xh6 ♖xc7 44 ♖b6 ♖c2 45 ♔d3 ♖b2 ½-½.**

C32: 11...♘f6 12 f3 *(D)*

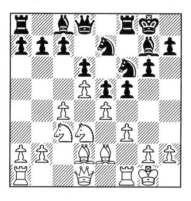

This is one of the most complicated variations in the Classical King's Indian, leading to mutual pawn-races on opposite sides of the board. White hopes to open the c-file and infiltrate the enemy camp with the manoeuvre ♘b5-c7-e6. Black, on the other hand, plans ...g6-g5-g4, followed by ...g4xf3, after which he can attack the opposing king.

C321: 12...♔h8 *257*
C322: 12...f4 *263*

Seldom played moves lead to a small advantage for White; e.g.:

a) 12...h5 (versus g2-g4) 13 exf5! (otherwise 13 c5 f4 or 13 ♖c1 f4 will transpose to C3222) 13...gxf5 (or 13...♘xf5 14 ♗g5 +=) 14 f4 e4 15 ♘f2 ♘g4 (or 15...c6 16 ♗e3 cxd5 17 cxd5 ♕a5, I.Stork-M.Van de Pol, Den Bosch 1992, 18 ♖b1 +=) 16 ♘xg4 fxg4?! (but if 16...hxg4 17 ♗e3 += Shirov) 17 ♘xe4 ♗xb2 18 ♖b1 ♗d4+ 19 ♔h1 +/- A.Shirov-J.Nunn, German League 1992.

b) 12...c5 13 ♖b1 (or 13 a3 f4 14 b4 b6 15 a4 g5 16 a5 cxb4 17 ♘xb4 bxa5 18 ♘d3 ♘g6 19 ♕a4 g4 20 ♕xa5 += H.Schaufelberger-A.Sznapik, Skopje Olympiad 1972; less good is 13 g4 ♗d7 14 ♘f2 ♖f7 15 a3 h6 16 h4 ♘h7 17 b4 f4 18 bxc5 dxc5 19 ♘d3 ♘c8 20 ♗e1 b6 ∞ B.Jansson-L.Portisch, Raach 1969; or 13 dxc6 bxc6 14 ♕a4 c5 15 b4, E.Arnlind-L.Monostori, corr. 1974, 15...cxb4!? ∞) 13...f4 (or 13...a5 14 b3 h5 15 a3 ♔h7 16 b4 axb4 17 axb4 b6 18 ♕c1 += G.Hertneck-W.Uhlmann, Austrian Team Ch. 2001) 14 b4 b6 15 bxc5 bxc5 16 ♕a4 (or 16 ♖b2) 16...g5 17 ♘f2 h5 18 h3 ♖f7 19 ♖b2 ♗f8 20 ♖fb1 ♖g7 (O.Panno-A.Zapata, Bogota 1978) 21 ♘b5! +=.

c) 12...♖f7 13 ♖c1 (or 13 c5 at once) 13...♕f8!? (13...f4?! 14 c5 g5 is 14...♖f7?! in C32222) 14 c5 ♗h6 15 cxd6 (if 15 ♘b5 fxe4 16 fxe4 ♘xe4 17 ♖xf7 ♔xf7 18 ♗xh6 ♕xh6 ∞ M.Roeder-Kr.Georgiev, Torcy 1991) 15 cxd6 cxd6 16 ♘f2 ♗d7 17 ♗b5 a6 18 ♗xd7 ♘xd7 19 ♖c2 ♖c8 (L.Weglarz-D.Pedzich, Police 1992) 20 ♕c1 ♗xd2 21 ♕xd2 intending ♖fc1 +=.

d) 12...c6!? 13 ♗e3 ♔h8 (if 13...f4 14

♗f2 c5 15 b4 b6 16 ♖b1 g5 17 a4 ♘g6 18 a5 += M.Richter-F.Voelzke, Hamburg 1999) 14 b4 (better 14 ♖c1! – *13...c6* in C3212) 14...b5!? 15 c5 cxd5 16 cxd6 d4 17 dxe7 ♕xe7 18 ♗f2 dxc3 19 ♗c5 ♕c7 20 ♗xf8 ♗xf8 with compensation, P.Harikrishna-K.Sasikiran, Asian Ch., Calcutta 2001.

C321: 12...♔h8 (D)

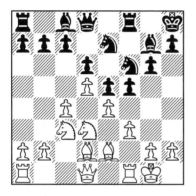

A flexible move, making room for the rook or knight, and useful in many variations. Also, by maintaining the central tension, Black renders the c4-c5 advance slightly problematic, due to the response ...c7-c6.

C3211: 13 b4 257
C3212: 13 ♖c1 260

Other moves are:

a) 13 a4 a5! (if 13...c6 14 a5 h6 15 ♘f2 g5 16 ♖e1 += G.Sosonko-J.Van der Wiel, Tilburg 1984) 14 g4 (not 14 c5?! dxc5! 15 ♘xc5 c6 =+) 14...c5 (or 14...c6!? 15 ♔h1 ♗d7 16 b4 axb4 17 ♘xb4 ♖f7 ∞ S.Feick-K.Berg, Berlin 1989) 15 ♔g2 f4 16 h4 h5

17 g5 ♘e8 18 ♖h1 ½-½ A.Khalifman-B.Gelfand, Reggio Emilia 1991/92.

b) 13 g4 c6 (if 13...c5 14 ♖b1 a5 15 b3 ♗d7 16 ♔h1 += J.Lautier-J.Fedorowicz, Wijk aan Zee 1991) 14 ♘f2 (instead 14 ♔h1 b5!?, L.Polugaevsky-E.Gufeld, Sochi 1981, 15 g5 ♘h5 16 cxb5 cxd5 17 exd5 ∞ Gufeld, or if 14 a4 a5! – *13 a4*) 14...♗d7 15 ♔g2 a6 16 a3 b5 17 b3 ♕b6 18 h3 ♖ac8 ∞ V.Gavrikov-A.Kochyev, Leningrad 1984.

c) 13 c5!? c6 (a typical response to an early c4-c5; if instead 13...dxc5!? 14 ♗e3 b6 15 b4 cxb4 16 ♘xb4 a5 17 ♘c2 with compensation, J.Hallam-J.Yoos, Vancouver 1999) 14 cxd6 (if 14 dxc6 ♘xc6 15 cxd6 ♕xd6 16 ♗e3 ♘d4!? ∞ R.Duijn-M.Van Delft, Apeldoorn rapid 2001) 14...♕xd6 15 ♗e3 b6 (or even 15...cxd5!? 16 ♗c5 ♕e6, E.Nasjleti-H.Alvarez Castillo, Buenos Aires 1992, 17 exd5 ♘fxd5 18 ♘xd5 ♘xd5 19 ♗xf8 ♗xf8 with compensation) 16 f4!? ♘xe4 17 fxe5 ♘xc3 18 exd6 ♘xd1 19 dxe7 ♘xe3 20 exf8♕+ ♗xf8 ∞ J.Hvenekilde-G.Schaefer, European Seniors Ch. 2007.

C3211: 13 b4 (D)

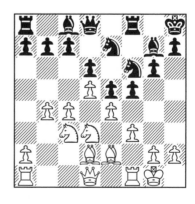

13...f4

Aiming to show that ...⌃h8 is more useful than b2-b4. Other moves may transpose after a later ...f5-f4, though there are some independent variations:

a) 13...h5 14 exf5!? (otherwise 14 c5 f4 15 ♖c1 heads for the main line, e.g. 15...g5 16 ♘f2 ♘eg8 or 16 ♘b5 ♘e8 17 cxd6 cxd6 18 a4) 14...gxf5 (or 14...♘xf5 15 ♘f2 c6! 16 ♗d3 cxd5 17 ♘xd5 ♘xd5 18 cxd5 ♗d7 ∞ C.Lutz-A.Shirov, World Junior Ch. 1990) 15 f4 e4 16 ♘f2 ♘g4 17 ♗xg4 (or 17 ♘xg4 hxg4 ∞, as 18 ♗e3 is not possible here) 17...hxg4 18 ♖c1 c6 19 ♗e3 a5 20 b5 c5 = J.Barkhagen-V.Bologan, Mamaia 1991.

b) 13...♘eg8 14 c5 (or 14 g4 f4 – *13...f4 14 g4*; if instead 14...♘e8 15 ♔h1 ♗d7 16 ♖g1 ♖f7 17 ♖c1 += Kir.Georgiev-H.Ree, Palma 1989) 14...♗h6 (again 14...f4 15 ♖c1 or 15 g4 returns to *13...f4* lines below) 15 ♗xh6 (or 15 a4!? ♗xd2 16 ♕xd2 f4 17 a5 g5 18 ♕b2 g4 19 b5 g3 20 h3 ♘h6 21 b6 ♘h5 22 ♖fc1 ♕h4 23 ♗f1 +/- Al.Gavrilov-A.Shchekachev, Russian Ch. 1992) 15...♘xh6 16 ♕d2 f4 17 a4 ♘f7 18 a5 g5 19 g4 fxg3 20 hxg3 h5 21 ♖f2 += Y.Rantanen-P.Houtsonen, Jyvaskyla 1994.

c) 13...c6!? 14 a4 (if 14 ♗e3 b5 – *12...c6*, or 14 ♖c1 b5 – *13 ♖c1 c6*) 14...cxd5 (if 14...f4 15 g4 h5 16 g5 ♘h7 17 h4 ♘xg5 18 hxg5 ♘xd5 19 ♖f2! ♘e3 20 ♗xe3 fxe3 21 ♖g2 ♗e6 22 ♕c1 += N.Rashkovsky-V.Tsarev, Kiev 1989; or 14...a5 15 bxa5 ♖xa5 16 ♖b1 c5 17 ♖b5 ♖a8 18 ♕b3 ♘eg8 19 exf5 gxf5 20 f4 e4 21 ♘f2 += J.Timman-J.Nunn, Cannes 1992) 15 cxd5 ♗d7 16 a5 ♖c8 17 ♕b3?! (better 17 ♘f2 +=) 17...fxe4 18 fxe4

♖xc3! 19 ♗xc3 ♘xe4 20 ♗e1 ♘f5 with excellent play for the exchange, M.Ziegler-M.M.Ivanov, Würzburg 1994.

14 ♖c1

The alternative is 14 g4 and then:

a) 14...h5 15 g5 ♘h7 16 h4 ♘xg5 17 hxg5 ♘f5 18 ♖f2 ♕xg5+ 19 ♖g2 ♘g3 20 ♘f2 += N.Rashkovsky-V.Loginov, Eger 1989.

b) 14...g5!? 15 ♔g2 h5 16 h3 ♘g6 17 ♗e1 ♖f7 18 c5 ♗f8 19 ♕b3 ♖h7 ∞ C.Lutz-V.Loginov, Budapest 1990.

c) 14...♘eg8 15 ♔g2 (if 15 c5 h5 16 h3 ♘e8 17 ♔g2 ♘h6 ∞ B.Maksimovic-G.Timoshenko, Cheliabinsk 1990; or 15 ♗e1 ♘e8!? intending ...h7-h5 ∞ Marin) 15...♘e8 16 c5 ♖f7 17 a4 h5 18 h3 ♗f6 19 a5 ♖h7 ∞ Z.Gyimesi-V.Loginov, Kecskemet 1992.

14...♘eg8

Or 14...g5 15 c5 (or 15 ♘f2 h5 16 c5 ♘eg8 – *14...♘eg8*) 15...h5 16 ♘b5 ♘e8 17 ♕c2!? ♗d7 18 ♘f2 a6 19 ♘a3 b5 20 cxb6 cxb6 (J.Hjartarson-A.Shirov, Reykjavik 1992) 21 b5! axb5 22 ♘xb5 ♘g8 ∞ Shirov.

15 c5 h5 *(D)*

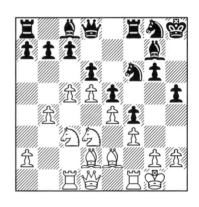

16 ♘f2

16 cxd6 cxd6 17 ♘b5 ♘e8 18 ♘f2 g5 transposes; while if 16 a4 g5 17 a5!? ♘h6 18 ♕a4 g4 19 c6!? bxc6 20 ♕xc6 ♗d7 21 ♕c4 h4 22 fxg4 ♘hxg4 23 b5 ♘e3 24 ♗xe3 fxe3 25 ♘b4 ♗h6 ∞ L.Stankevicius-M.Larsson, corr. 2002.

16...g5 17 cxd6

Other moves lead to the same positions, unless Black elects to deviate:

a) 17 a4 ♘h6 18 h3 (18 cxd6 cxd6 19 ♘b5 ♘e8 – *17 cxd6*) 18...a6!? (18...♖g8 19 cxd6 cxd6 20 ♘b5 ♘e8 – *20...♖g8*) 19 cxd6 cxd6 20 a5 b5 21 axb6 ♕xb6 22 ♘a4 ♕a7 23 ♖c6 g4 ∞ D.Sellos-Z.Lanka, Cannes 1993.

b) 17 h3 ♘h6 18 cxd6 cxd6 19 ♘b5 ♖f7!? 20 ♕c2 ♘e8 21 a4 ♗f8 22 ♘xa7 (if 22 ♕b3 ♖g7 23 ♖c2 g4 ∞ V.Sakalauskas-A.Kybartas, Radviliskis 1995; or 22 a5!? ♗d7 23 ♕b2 ♖g7 24 ♖c3 a6 25 ♘a3 b5 ∞ L.B.Hansen-V.Loginov, Stara Zagora 1989) 22...♖c7 23 ♘c6 bxc6 24 dxc6 ♖g7! 25 a5 g4 26 fxg4 hxg4 27 ♘xg4 ♘xg4 28 hxg4 ♗xg4 ∞ T.Rahman-A.Sznapik, Novi Sad Olympiad 1990.

17...cxd6 18 ♘b5 ♘e8 19 a4 ♘h6 20 h3 *(D)*

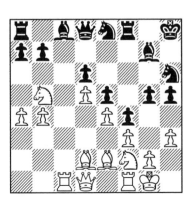

White may as well play this at once, rather than declare his hand. If instead 20 ♖c3 ♗d7 21 h3 ♖f6 22 ♕b3 a6 23 ♘a3 ♖g6 =+ A.Lesiege-S.Kindermann, Budapest 1992; or 20 a5 ♖f7 21 h3 ♗f6 22 ♖c3 ♖h7 23 ♕c2 g4 24 fxg4 hxg4 25 hxg4 ♗h4 26 ♖h3 ♗d7 27 ♕b2 ♔g8 ∞ G.Gislason-F.Nijboer, Reykjavik 1990.

20...♖f6

Another option is 20...♖g8 21 ♖c3 ♗f6, e.g. 22 ♕b3 (or 22 ♕c2 ♗d7 23 ♖c1 g4 24 fxg4 hxg4 25 hxg4 ♗h4 26 ♗e1 ♗g3 27 ♔f1 ♕h4 -/+ S.Silva-E.Favaro, World Junior Ch. 1992) 22...♖g7 23 ♖fc1 ♗d7 24 a5 g4 25 fxg4 hxg4 26 hxg4 ♗h4 27 ♖h3 ♔g8 ∞ I.V.Ivanov-P.H.Nielsen, Forli 1992.

21 ♖c3 a6 22 ♘a3 ♖g6 23 ♘c4 g4 24 fxg4 hxg4 25 hxg4 ♘f6 26 a5 ♘hxg4 27 ♘xg4 ♗xg4

Or 27...♘xg4!? 28 ♘b6 ♘e3! 29 ♗xe3 ♖xg2+! 30 ♔xg2 ♕g5+ 31 ♔h1 (not 31 ♗g4? ♗xg4 32 ♕d2 ♗h3+! -/+) 31...♕h4+ 32 ♔g1 ♕g3+ with a draw.

28 ♗xg4 ♘xg4 29 ♕e2 *(D)*

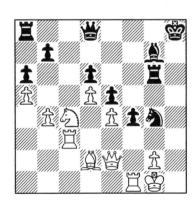

The position is roughly equal, as White is too concerned with defending to achieve anything on the other side.

Two games have finished:

a) 29...♕e7 30 ♖h3+ ♗h6 31 ♖ff3 ♖ag8 32 ♔f1 ♘f6 33 ♔e1 ♘h7 34 ♖h2 ½-½ J.Knudsen-A.Jorgensen, corr. 2002.

b) 29...♕g5 30 ♖h3+ ♔g8 31 ♗e1 ♕e7 32 ♖ff3 ♖c8 33 ♖c3 ♖f8 34 ♗f2 ♕d7 35 ♘b6 ♕e7 36 ♔h1 ♗f6 37 ♗g1 ♗h4 38 ♘c8 ♕g5 39 ♕f3 ♗g3? (time trouble; instead 39...♗e1 40 ♖c7 ♖f7 ∞) 40 ♖c7 ♖f7? (dropping a piece) 41 ♖xf7 ♔xf7 42 ♖xg3 ♕d8 43 ♘b6 ♕h4+ 44 ♖h3 ♕e1 45 ♘c4 ♕xb4 46 ♕b3 ♕e1 47 ♕xb7+ ♔f6 48 ♕b6 ♔g5 49 ♕b2?? (49 ♘d2! ♕xd2 50 ♕d8+ wins) 49...♖h6! 50 ♖xh6 ♔xh6 51 ♕a3 ♘f2+ 52 ♔h2 ♘g4+ 53 ♔h1 ½-½ G.Hertneck-J.Gallagher, European Team Ch., Leon 2001.

C3212: 13 ♖c1 *(D)*

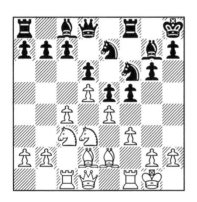

13...c5

A familiar idea from line C31 (11...♔h8 12 ♖c1 c5), and here White does not have f2-f4.

a) 13...f4 makes less sense now, as ...♔h8 is essentially a wasted tempo; e.g. 14 c5 g5 (14...dxc5!? 15 ♘xc5 c6 might be a better try) 15 cxd6 cxd6 16

♘f2 ♘g6 17 ♘b5 ♘e8 18 ♕c2 ♗d7 19 a4 += O.Berechet-D.Popescu, Bucharest 1996.

b) 13...♘eg8 14 c5 (if 14 b4 f4! – *13 b4*; or 14 exf5!? gxf5 15 f4 e4 16 ♘f2 c5 17 dxc6 bxc6 18 ♗e3 ♗e6 19 ♕a4 ♕c7 ∞ G.Barbero-J.Gallagher, Bern 1989) 14...♗h6 (14...f4 15 cxd6 cxd6 16 ♘b5 sees Black behind on C3211, e.g. 16...♖f7 17 ♕c2 ♘e8 18 a4 ♗f6 19 ♕c3 ♗d7 20 ♕b4 ♕b8 21 a5 g5 22 ♖c3 +/- V.Neverov-I.Manakov, St Petersburg 2000) 15 cxd6 (or 15 ♗xh6 ♘xh6 16 ♕d2 ♘f7 17 cxd6 cxd6 18 ♘f2 f4 19 ♘b5 ♘e8 20 a4 += P.Schwarz-S.Mohandesi, Giessen 1994) 15 cxd6 16 ♘f2 a6 17 a4 ♗xd2 18 ♕xd2 f4 19 ♘b1 g5 20 ♘a3 += D.Barlov-T.Lenz, Graz 1987.

c) 13...c6 *(D)* is the main alternative and then:

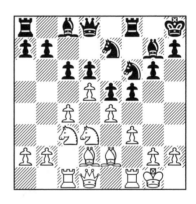

c1) 14 dxc6 – *13...c5 14 dxc6* below.

c2) 14 b4 b5! 15 dxc6 (if 15 ♘f2 bxc4 16 ♗xc4 cxd5 17 exd5 ♗b7 18 ♕b3 ♖c8 ∞ Z.Gyimesi-M.Mrva, Buekfuerdo 1995) 15...bxc4 16 ♘f2 (if 16 ♘b2 ♘b2 ♘xc6 17 ♘xc4 ♗e6 18 ♗e3 ♘d4 19 ♘a5 ♖c8 20 ♗a6 ♖c7 =+ A.Shirov-J.Nunn,

Wijk aan Zee 1993) 16...♘xc6 17 ♗xc4 ♘d4 (if 17...♘xb4?! 18 ♘b5 a5 19 ♗e3 ♖a6 20 ♕e2 with good compensation) 18 ♗e3 ♗b7 19 ♘d5 ♘xd5 20 ♗xd5 ♗xd5 21 exd5 ♕b6 ∞ V.Frias Pablaza-A.Sznapik, Thessaloniki Olympiad 1984.

c3) 14 ♘f2!? f4 (or 14...a5 15 a3 ♗d7 16 ♔h1 cxd5 17 cxd5 ♕b6 ∞ G.Sosonko-O.Renet, European Team Ch., Pula 1997) 15 dxc6 ♘xc6 (or 15...bxc6 16 b4 d5 17 cxd5 cxd5 18 exd5 ♘exd5 19 ♘xd5 ♕xd5! = Gelfand) 16 ♗d3 g5 17 ♘d5 h5 18 h3 ♗e6 19 ♗c3 ♖g8 ∞ K.Spraggett-A.Pablo Marin, Malgrat del Mar 1991.

c4) 14 ♗e3 a6 (if 14...f4?! 15 ♗f2 c5 16 b4 cxb4 17 ♘xb4 b6 18 a4 g5 19 a5 +/- J.Ehlvest-L.Van Wely, New York Open 1994) 15 c5!? (or 15 b4 cxd5 16 cxd5 ♗d7 17 ♘b2 b5 18 a4 bxa4 19 ♘bxa4 ♖b8 20 ♖b1 += B.Gelfand-V.Topalov, Amsterdam 1996) 15...cxd5 16 cxd6 ♕xd6 17 ♗c5 ♕d8 18 ♘xe5 ♘h5 (if 18...b6 19 ♗a3 ♗b7 20 exf5 += Gelfand) 19 f4 ♘xf4 20 ♖xf4 ♗xe5 21 ♗d4 ♘c6 22 ♗xe5+ ♘xe5 23 ♘xd5 += B.Gelfand-F.Nijboer, Wijk aan Zee 1998.

14 g4

White goes tit for tat, challenging Black's counterplay on the kingside. Instead:

a) 14 dxc6 ♘xc6 (not 14...bxc6?! 15 c5! d5 16 ♘xe5 ♘xe4 17 fxe4 ♗xe5 18 exd5 += J.Basta-W.Assmann, corr. 1998) 15 ♗e3 ♗e6 16 b3 ♘d4 17 ♘f2 ♘h5 18 ♖e1 ♘f4 19 ♗f1 ♗g8 = H.Schacht-C.Schubert, German League 1986.

b) 14 ♖b1 f4 (if 14...a5 15 a3 ♘eg8 16 b4 axb4 17 axb4 b6 18 ♕c1 +=

V.Neverov-I.Belov, Voskresensk 1990; but Black might try 14...♘eg8!? 15 b4 b6 16 bxc5 bxc5 17 ♕a4 a6! 18 ♕c6 ♖a7 19 ♖b8 ♖c7 ∞ Belov) 15 b4 b6 16 bxc5 bxc5 17 g4 g5 18 ♔f2 ♘g6 19 h3 h5 20 ♕a4 ♕e7 21 ♔e1 ♘h4 22 ♖f2 ∞ V.Ivanchuk-T.Radjabov, Dubai (rapid) 2002.

14...a6 (D)

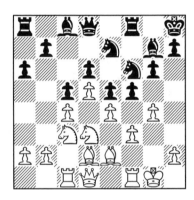

Securing the queenside further, without committing himself elsewhere. Other moves have been less successful:

a) 14...♘eg8 15 ♔g2 ♘e8 16 g5 f4 17 h4 ♖f7 18 ♖h1 ♗f8 19 ♕g1 ♘g7 20 ♗d1 ♘h5 21 ♘e2 +/= L.Ftacnik-J.Nunn, Vienna 1986.

b) 14...h6 15 h4 a6 16 ♖b1 (16 ♘f2 – 14...a6) 16...♘h7 17 ♔g2 ♘g8 18 ♖h1 ♗f6?! (18...b5!?) 19 ♕e1 ♗d7 20 ♕g3 ♗e7?! 21 f4 +/- Z.Kozul-A.Fedorov, European Team Ch., Pula 1997.

c) 14...♗d7 15 ♘f2 ♘eg8 (15...a6 – 14...a6) 16 ♔h1 f4 17 b4 (17 g5!? ♘h5 18 ♖g1 +=) 17...b6 18 ♘b5 a6 19 ♘a3 ♘e8 20 ♖b1 ♕h4 ∞ L.Ftacnik-E.Geller, Sochi 1977.

15 ♘f2 h6

If 15...♗d7 16 a3 (or 16 ♖b1 b5!? 17

cxb5 axb5 18 ♘xb5 ♗xb5 19 ♗xb5 ♖xa2 20 b4 +/= D.Rosenberg-N.McDonald, British Ch. 1991) 16...♘eg8 17 b4 b6 18 bxc5 bxc5 19 ♖b1 +/= L.Ftacnik-J.Ost Hansen, Esbjerg 1982.

16 h4

Not 16 ♔g2?! fxg4 17 fxg4 g5! 18 ♖b1 ♘g6 19 ♔g3 b6 20 b4 ♖a7 21 bxc5 bxc5 22 ♘a4 ♖af7 =+ T.Halasz-Wl.Schmidt, Dortmund 1991; or if 16 f4!? exf4 17 exf5 gxf5 18 gxf5 b5! 19 ♗xf4 b4 20 ♘ce4 ♘xf5 ∞ S.Daroczy-T.Schmidt, corr. 2001.

16...fxg4 17 fxg4 ♘eg8 18 ♔g2 ♘h7 19 ♖h1 ♗f6 20 g5!

White sacrifices a pawn for the initiative. This is forced in any case, since if 20 h5?! ♗h4 -/+, or 20 ♔g3 ♗xh4+ 21 ♖xh4 ♖xf2 22 ♕h1 ♕f8! (Kasparov) and if 23 ♗e3 g5! =/+.

20...hxg5 21 h5 ♕e8 *(D)*

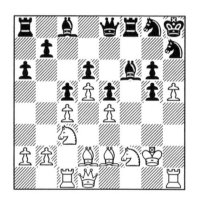

22 ♖h2

With the simple plan of doubling on the h-file. White has also tried:

a) 22 hxg6 ♕xg6 23 ♗h5 (if 23 ♖h2 ♗d8 – 22 ♖h2) 23...♕g7 24 ♗g4 ♘e7!? (24...♗d8 25 ♖h2 – 24 ♗h5 below) 25 ♘e2 ♘g6 26 ♘g3 ♘h4+ 27 ♔g1 ♗d8

(27...b5!? ∞) 28 ♗xc8 ♖xc8 29 ♘g4 ♕f7 30 ♗e3 ♕f3 31 ♕xf3 ♖xf3 32 ♗f2 ∞ B.Zlender-A.Praznik, corr. 1995.

b) 22 b4!? cxb4 (perhaps 22...b6!? ∞ Kasparov) 23 ♘a4 ♗d8 24 ♗xb4 ♗d7 (B.Gelfand-G.Kasparov, Linares 1990), and now either 25 ♘b2 ♖xf2+ 26 ♔xf2 ♘gf6 27 ♔g2! or 25 ♗xd6 ♗xa4 26 ♕e1! looks good for White.

c) 22 ♕a4 ♕f7 (or 22...b5!? 23 cxb5 ♗d7 ∞ Gelfand; but not 22...♗d7?? 23 hxg6 +-, or 22...♕xa4? 23 ♘xa4 +/- and Black has no counterplay) 23 ♖cf1 gxh5 24 ♗xh5 ♕g7 ∞ G.Blomstrand-D.King, corr. 1991.

22...♗d8 23 hxg6 ♕xg6 24 ♗g4

White may do better to insert 24 ♗h5 ♕g7 25 ♗g4, e.g. 25...♘gf6 (if 25...♗a5 26 ♕e2! +=, or 25...♘e7?! 26 ♗xc8 ♘xc8 27 ♕g4 +/- M.Diesner-M.Koch, corr. 1993) 26 ♗xc8?! (26 ♕e2! +=) 26...♖xc8 27 ♘e2 ♕f7 28 ♔g1 ♘h5 29 ♖c3 ♘f4 30 ♘g3 ♗a5 31 ♖b3 ♗xd2 32 ♕xd2 b5!? 33 cxb5 c4! ∞ A.Peluso-G.Poli, corr. 1992.

24...♗a5!

A novelty from the game J.Morgado-R.G.Alvarez, corr. 2001, which we now follow. Black aims to undermine the e4-pawn by eliminating both defending knights.

If instead 24...♘gf6 25 ♕f3!? +/= exploits the pin on the f-file, while White also seems to have the initiative after two other moves considered by Alvarez: 24...♕f7 25 ♗xc8 ♖xc8 26 ♕e2, and 24...b5 25 cxb5 axb5 26 ♗xc8 ♖xc8 27 ♕g4.

25 ♕e2 ♗xg4 26 ♘xg4

If 26 ♕xg4 ♖xf2!? (or 26...b5!? with

counterplay) 27 ♔xf2 ♘gf6 28 ♕e2 ♗xc3 29 ♗xc3 ♖f8 with compensation (Alvarez).

26...♔g7 27 ♖ch1 ♘hf6 28 ♘e3 ♘e7

Not 28...♘xe4?? 29 ♖h7+! and wins (Alvarez).

29 ♕d3

Perhaps 29 ♖h6 ♕xh6 30 ♖xh6 ♔xh6 31 ♘g4+ was the last hope of achieving anything, though 31...♔g6 seems to hold, e.g. 32 ♕e3 ♘h7 33 ♕h3 ♘g8.

29...♗xc3 30 ♘f5+ ♘xf5 31 exf5 e4! 32 fxg6

32 ♕f1 ♘xd5! also leads to a draw after 33 fxg6 ♖xf1 34 ♗xc3+ ♘xc3 35 ♖h7+ ♔xg6 36 ♖7h6+ ♔g7 37 ♖h7+ etc.

32...exd3 33 ♗xc3 ♖ae8 34 ♖h7+ ♔xg6 35 ♖7h6+ ♔g7 36 ♗xf6+ ♖xf6 37 ♖h7+ ♔g6 38 ♖7h6+ ♔g7 ½-½.

C322: 12...f4 *(D)*

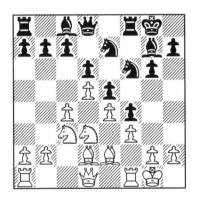

Having forced f2-f3, Black starts the race, planning to continue with ...g6-g5, ...h7-h5 and ...g5-g4. As usual, White's chances are on the queenside with the advance c4-c5, which can either be played at once, or after attempting to

neutralize the kingside attack with 13 g4.

C3221: 13 g4 263
C3222: 13 c5 267

---

13 ♖c1 g5 14 c5 is another route to C32222, unless Black wants to try 13...c5!? again, e.g. 14 ♖b1 g5 15 b4 b6 16 bxc5 bxc5 17 ♘f2 ♘g6 18 ♕a4 a6 19 ♕c6 ♖a7 20 ♖b8 ♘d7 21 ♖b2 ♖c7 22 ♕a4 h5 ∞ K.Embrey-O.Koskivirta, corr. 1991.

Note that 13 b4 would be a waste of time: White does not need to prepare c4-c5 further, and b2-b4 has little purpose otherwise in this variation.

C3221: 13 g4 *(D)*

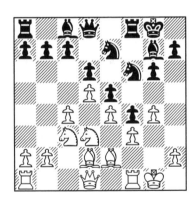

13...g5

Preventing g4-g5 in response to the intended ...h7-h5. Black has also tried:

a) 13...fxg3 (this exchange usually helps White) 14 hxg3 c6 (or 14...h5 15 ♗e3 ♘h7 16 c5 g5 17 ♖c1 ♘g6 18 cxd6 cxd6 19 ♘b5 ♖f7 20 ♘xa7 ♗h3 21 ♖f2 ♘f4 22 ♘b5 += E.Ragozin-Se.Ivanov,

Leningrad 1989) 15 a4!? (or 15 ♔g2 b5!? 16 dxc6 bxc4 17 ♘b4 ♗e6 18 ♕a4 ♔h8 19 ♗g5 ♕c8 20 ♖fd1 += A.Pablo Marin-J.Garriga Nualart, Malgrat del Mar 1991) 15...a5 16 ♗e3 h6 17 ♔g2 g5 18 ♖h1 ♕e8 19 c5 += P.Wells-P.Etchegaray, Benidorm 1991.

b) 13...h5 14 g5! ♘h7 15 h4 ♘xg5 (or 15...c5 16 ♖f2 ♗d7 17 b4 b6 18 bxc5 dxc5 19 ♕b3 ♘c8, Z.Hracek-L.Salai, Czechoslovakian Ch. 1990, 20 a4 +=) 16 hxg5 ♘f5 (if 16...♘xd5 17 ♖f2 ♘xc3 18 ♗xc3 ♕xg5+ 19 ♖g2 ♕f6 20 c5 += E.Nachev-D.Ilchev, Teteven 1991) 17 ♖f2 ♕xg5+ 18 ♖g2 ♘g3 19 ♘f2 ♕f6 20 ♗f1 (20 c5!?) 20...g5 21 ♖h2 ♕g6 (or 21...♘xf1 22 ♔xf1 ♕g6 23 ♔e2 g4 24 ♕h1 += K.Haydock-M.Rensen, corr. 1997) 22 ♗h3 += P.Lukacs-P.Spiriev, Budapest 1991.

c) 13...c6!? 14 ♔g2 (or 14 h4 – *11...♘f6 12 ♘d3 f4!? in C21*) 14...a5 (if 14...b5?! 15 ♘b4! c5 16 ♘c6 ♘xc6 17 dxc6 += F.Leveille-L.Poitras, corr. 1988) 15 a4 (or 15 ♗e1 b5! 16 dxc6 b4 17 ♘b5 ♘xc6 18 ♘f2 ♗e6 ∞ T.Halasz-K.Nickl, Dortmund 1991) 15...c5! 16 h4 h6 17 ♖h1 ♘e8 = A.Lein-A.Brustman, Palma 1989.

d) 13...c5!? 14 h4 (or 14 a3 ♘e8!? 15 b4 b6 16 bxc5 bxc5 17 ♖b1 ♗f6 18 ♕e1?! h5 19 h3 ♔g7 =+ L.Hjelmaas-I.Kourkounakis, Gausdal 1990) 14...♗d7 (if 14...h6 15 ♖f2 ♔h8 16 ♖h2 ♗d7 17 ♖b1 a5 18 b3 b6 19 a3 ♔h7 20 ♗e1 ♖f7 21 b4 += Z.Kozul-T.Radjabov, European Team Ch., Leon 2001) 15 ♔g2 a6 16 ♘f2 ♘e8 17 a3 ♘c8 18 ♖h1 ♗f6 19 h5 ∞ Z.Gyimesi-P.Enders, Budapest 1995.

14 ♗e1 *(D)*

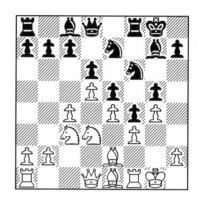

Black's plan is to play ...h7-h5, ...♘g6 and bring the rook to the h-file, either by ...♔f7 and ...♖h8 or, more usually, ...♖f7, ...♗f8, and ...♖h7. Although the latter manoeuvre takes a tempo more, it also brings the bishop to a more useful post.

For White, 14 ♗e1 covers the h4-square against a black knight invasion, while heading for the g1-a7 diagonal to support the queenside initiative based on c4-c5. Alternatives mostly transpose, as ♗e1 is usually played sooner or later:

a) 14 c5 h5 (or 14...c6!? ∞) 15 h3 ♘g6 16 ♗e1 is the main line, but Black can also try 15...c6!? ∞ ½-½ U.Dresen-G.Bluhm, German League 1991.

b) 14 ♖c1 h5 15 h3 ♘g6 16 c5 ♖f7 17 cxd6 cxd6 18 ♘b5 (or 18 ♗e1 ♗f8 – *17 cxd6* in the main line) 18...♗f8 19 a4 ♖h7 20 ♕c2 ♘e8 21 a5 hxg4 22 hxg4 a6 23 ♘a3 b5 24 axb6 ♕xb6+ 25 ♖f2 ♗d7 26 ♘c4 ♕a7 ∞ B.Skutta-V.Arbakov, Bad Zwesten 1998.

c) 14 b4!? (not strictly necessary) 14...h5 15 h3 *(D)* and now:

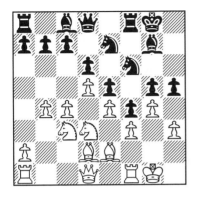

c1) 15...♔f7 16 ♔g2 (or 16 ♗e1 ♖h8 17 ♔g2 ♘g6 18 c5 hxg4 19 hxg4 ∞ B.Gelfand-G.Kasparov, Reggio Emilia 1991/92) 16...♖h8 17 ♖h1 ♘g6 18 c5!? ♗d7 (18...♘h4+) 19 a4 ♕e7 20 ♘b5 hxg4 21 hxg4 ♖xh1 22 ♔xh1 ♖h8+ 23 ♔g1 ♗xg4!? 24 cxd6 cxd6 25 fxg4 ♘xe4 26 ♖c1 (H.Veen-H.Lassen, corr. 1992) 26...♘g3! ∞.

c2) 15...♘g6 16 ♗e1 (if 16 c5 ♖f7 17 a4 ♗f8 18 a5, O.Gavriushin-S.Temirbaev, USSR 1990, 18...a6! ∞) 16...♖f7 17 c5 ♗f8 18 ♗f2 ♖h7 (if 18...♗e7 19 ♖c1 ♗d7 20 b5! ♖h7 21 c6 += Z.Gyimesi-B.Szuk, Budapest 1994) 19 ♔g2 ♗e7 20 ♖h1 ♔g7 (if 20...♘h4+ 21 ♗xh4 gxh4 22 b5! ♖g7 23 c6 ∞ Z.Gyimesi-S.Videki, Budapest 1996) 21 ♖c1 ♗d7 22 ♕b3 (if 22 a4 ♖h6 23 cxd6 cxd6 24 ♘b2 ♕h8 25 ♘b5 ♕h7! 26 ♖c7 ♖h8 -/+ P.Neuman-B.Szuk, European Junior Ch. 1995) 22...a6! (if 22...♕h8, J.Hjartarson-J.Fedorowicz, Philadelphia 1991, 23 c6! bxc6 24 bxc6 ♗xc6 25 ♕c4 += Grivas) 23 a4 hxg4 24 hxg4 ♘h4+ 25 ♗xh4 ♖xh4! 26 ♖xh4 gxh4 =+ P.Lukacs-E.Grivas, Budapest 1993.

14...h5

Black can play 14...♘g6 first, but ...h7-h5 inevitably follows at some point.

15 h3 ♘g6 *(D)*

The alternative is 15...♔f7 16 ♔g2 ♖h8 17 ♗f2 ♘g6 18 ♖h1 ♗d7 (or 18...hxg4 19 hxg4 ♖xh1 etc, though Black can consider 18...♘h4+!? 19 ♗xh4 gxh4 20 c5 hxg4 21 hxg4 ∞ M.Taggatz-D.Gross, German League 1997) 19 c5 hxg4 20 hxg4 ♖xh1 21 ♕xh1 ♕e7 (or 21...♕g8 22 ♖c1 ♗f8 23 c6 bxc6 24 dxc6 ♗e6 25 ♘b4 += S.Knott-I.Snape, British Ch. 2004) 22 ♕d1 ♖h8 23 ♕b3 b6 24 c6 ♗c8 25 ♖h1 ♖xh1 26 ♔xh1 ♕d8 27 ♕d1 += S.Knott-L.Wu, Southend 2004.

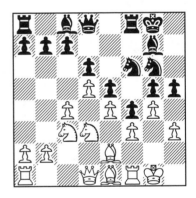

16 c5 *(D)*

White does not have to play this at once. Instead:

a) 16 b4 – *14 b4 h5 15 h3 ♘g6 16 ♗e1* above.

b) 16 ♗f2 ♖f7 (if 16...♔f7 17 ♔g2 ♖h8 – *15...♔f7*; or 16...c5!? 17 ♖b1 ♖f7 18 b4 b6 19 ♔g2 ♗f8 20 ♖h1 ♖h7 ∞ Kir.Georgiev-K.Spraggett, Tarrassa 1990) 17 c5 (if 17 a4!? ♗f8 18 ♔g2 ♗e7 19 a5 ♕f8! 20 ♘b5 ♗d8 21 ♘xa7 hxg4 22 hxg4 ♗xg4! 23 a6 bxa6 24 fxg4 ♘xe4 with a strong attack, H.Fiaramonti-O.Cvitan, Geneva 1995) 17...♗f8 18 cxd6 cxd6 (or 18...♗xd6 19 ♘c5 ♕e7 ∞) 19 ♔g2 (or 19 ♖c1 – *17 cxd6*) 19...♘h4+ 20 ♗xh4 gxh4 21 ♘f2 hxg4 22 hxg4 ♖g7 23 ♔h1 ∞ J.Vilela-D.Aldama, Cuban Ch. 1989.

c) 16 ♔g2 ♖f7 (or 16...♔f7 17 ♗f2 ♖h8 – *15...♔f7*) 17 ♖h1 (if 17 a4!? ♗f8 18 a5 ♗e7 19 ♗f2 – *16 ♗f2 ♖f7 17 a4*) 17...♗f8 18 ♗f2 ♖h7 (or 18...♗e7 19 c5 ♘h4+ 20 ♗xh4 gxh4 21 ♕b3 ♕f8 22 ♖ag1!? hxg4 23 hxg4 ♘h7 ∞ S.Knott-M.Hebden, British Ch. 2007) 19 c5 ♘h4+ 20 ♗xh4 gxh4 21 b4 ♕e8 22 ♔h2 hxg4 23 fxg4 ♖g7 24 ♗f3 ♘h7 ∞ S.Knott-M.Hebden, British Ch. 2004.

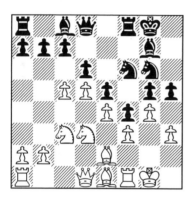

16...♖f7

16...♔f7 is still possible; e.g. 17 ♔g2 ♖h8 18 ♖h1!? (18 ♗f2 ♗d7 19 ♖h1 – *15...♔f7*; or 18 cxd6 cxd6 19 ♖c1 a6 ∞ G.Reis-H.Hepting, Lichtenfels 1994) 18...hxg4 19 hxg4 ♖xh1 20 ♔xh1 ♕h8+ 21 ♔g2 ♗d7 22 ♗f2 ♘h4+ 23 ♗xh4 ♕xh4 24 ♕e1 ♕h7 25 ♕h1 ♕g6 ∞ M.Hochgraefe-K.Gueldner, German Junior Ch. 1990.

17 cxd6

Otherwise Black might recapture with the bishop; e.g. 17 ♖c1 ♗f8 18 ♗f2 ♖h7 19 cxd6 ♗xd6!? (19...cxd6 returns to the main line) 20 ♔g2 ♗d7?! (better 20...hxg4!? 21 hxg4 ♘h4+ ∞ or 20...♘h4+!?) 21 ♕b3 a6?! 22 ♕xb7 ♕f8 23 ♖h1 ♖f7 (N.Rashkovsky-K.Spraggett, Paris 1990) 24 ♘c5! +/-.

17...cxd6 18 ♖c1

If 18 a4 ♗f8 19 a5 ♗e7 20 ♗f2 ♕f8! 21 ♔g2 ♗d8 22 ♖h1 a6 23 b4 ♗d7 =+ G.Vescovi-J.Rowson, World Junior Ch. 1993.

18...♗f8 19 ♗f2

Again if 19 a4 ♗e7 20 ♔g2 ♕f8! 21 a5 ♗d8 22 b4 ♗d7 =+ E.Bareev-B.Belotti, Aosta 1989; or 19 ♕b3 hxg4 20 hxg4 ♘h4 21 ♗xh4 gxh4 22 ♘f2 ♖g7 23 ♖c2 h3! 24 ♔h2 ♘h5 25 ♖fc1 ♕h4 26 ♘h1 ♘g3 ∞ D.Bredemeier-F.Micheel, German League 1995.

19...♖h7 20 ♕b3

If 20 ♔g2 hxg4 21 hxg4 ♘h4+ 22 ♗xh4 ♖xh4 23 ♖h1 ♖xh1 24 ♕xh1 ♕b6 25 ♕d1 ♗d7 26 ♕d2 ♖c8 = A.Mikhalev-O.Dobierzin, Krynica 1999.

20...hxg4 21 hxg4 ♘h4 22 ♗xh4 ♖xh4 23 ♘f2 a6 24 a4 ♖h7 25 ♔g2 ♗d7 (D)

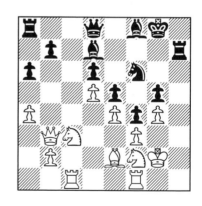

This was A.Khalifman-V.Spasov, Manila Interzonal 1990. White cannot take on b7 due to 26 ♕xb7? ♗xg4, while 26 ♖h1 ♖xh1 27 ♘xh1 ♖b8 is equal. So Khalifman tried **26 ♘b1 b5! 27 axb5 axb5 28 ♘a3 ♕b6 29 ♘xb5!?** ♗xb5 [if 29...♖b8 30 ♖c6! ♗xc6 31 dxc6+ ♔g7! 32 c7 ♕xc7 33 ♘xc7 ♖xb3 34 ♘e6+ ♔g8 35 ♗c4 ∞] **30 ♕xb5 ♕xb5 31 ♗xb5 ♖b8 32 ♗c6 ♖xb2 33 ♖a1 ♗e7?** [correct was 33...♘d7! 34 ♖fb1 ♖xb1 35 ♖xb1 ♘c5 36 ♖a1 ♘b3 and ...♘d4 = Khalifman] **34 ♖fb1 ♖xb1 35 ♖xb1** [now Black is very passive and Khalifman ground out a win] **35...♔f7 36 ♖b8 ♖g7 37 ♘d1 ♖g8 38 ♖b7 ♖d8 39 ♘c3 ♘h7 40 ♘b5 ♘f8 41 ♘a7 ♔f6 42 ♔f2 ♘g6 43 ♗d7 ♘h4 44 ♔e2 ♖a8 45 ♗e6 ♖d8 46 ♘c6 ♖e8 47 ♖d7 ♗f8 48 ♖f7+ ♔g6 49 ♖a7 ♔f6 50 ♗d7 ♖e7 51 ♘xe7 ♗xe7 52 ♔f2 ♗d8 53 ♖a6 ♔e7 54 ♗f5 ♗c7 55 ♔e2 ♘g2 56 ♖a7 ♔d8 57 ♖a8+ ♔e7 58 ♖g8 1-0.**

C3222: 13 c5 *(D)*

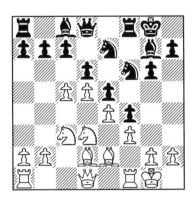

13...g5

Black wants to defend c7 (after c5xd6, ♖c1, ♘b5) with ...♖f7, so must not delay reorganizing accordingly. 13...♖f7!? first is acceptable, but not 13...h5?! as Black would have to play ...♘e8 prematurely; i.e. 14 cxd6 cxd6 15 ♖c1 g5 16 ♘b5 ♘e8 (see 14...h5?! in C32222). Other ideas are also inferior:

a) 13...c6 14 cxd6 ♕xd6 15 dxc6 ♘xc6 16 ♘b5 ♕e7 17 ♘b4 ♗e6 18 ♘xc6 bxc6 19 ♘a3 ♕c5+ (or 19...♘d7 20 ♕c2 +/= G.Sosonko-R.Hübner, Wijk aan Zee 1982) 20 ♔h1 ♘h5?! 21 ♗c4! ♗xc4 22 ♕c2 ♕e7 23 ♕xc4+ ♖f7 24 ♖fd1 ♗f8 25 ♗e1 +/- L.Ftacnik-E.Gufeld, Tallinn 1981.

b) 13...dxc5 14 ♕b3 ♔h8 15 ♘xc5 c6 (or 15...♕d6 16 ♘d3 c6 17 dxc6 ♘xc6 18 ♘b5 +=) 16 ♘xb7 ♗xb7 17 ♕xb7 cxd5 18 exd5 ♘exd5 19 ♖fd1 +/= S.Yuferov-E.Mochalov, Belarus Ch. 1980.

After the text we have a final split:

C32221: 14 cxd6 *268*
C32222: 14 ♖c1 *271*

Obviously these two lines will converge if 14 cxd6 is followed by ♖a1-c1, so in C32221 we will concentrate on independent variations where White leaves c1 free for the f1-rook.

Of the rare alternatives, 14 g4 returns to 14 c5 in C3221 above (note that 14...fxg3?! would still be weak); while 14 ♘b5 can be met by 14...a6 (or 14...♘g6) 15 ♘a3 g4 16 cxd6 cxd6 17 ♘c4 g3! 18 ♗a5 ♕e8 19 ♕e1 (not 19 ♘xd6? ♕h5 20 h3 ♗xh3! etc) 19...♘h5 20 ♘xd6 (if 20 h3 ♗xh3 21 gxh3 ♕c8! 22 ♘f2 gxf2+ 23 ♖xf2 ♖f6 ∞, or 21 ♘xd6 ♕g6! 22 ♕b4 ♗d7 followed by ...♘f6 and ...♕h5 with a strong attack) 20...♕g6 21 ♘xc8 gxh2+ 22 ♔xh2 ♖axc8 ∞ B.Gurgenidze-M.Tal, USSR Team Ch. 1955.

C32221: 14 cxd6 cxd6 *(D)*

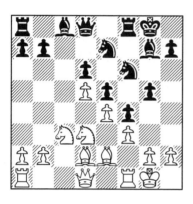

15 ♘f2

Having clarified the position on the queenside, White drops the d3-knight back to strengthen the kingside. Otherwise 15 ♖c1 ♘g6 transposes to C32222; or if 15...♗d7 (or 15...a6 16 ♗e1! h5 17 ♗f2 ♘g6 18 ♘a4 += A.Lambert-M.Soellig, corr. 1998) 16 ♕b3 b5? (but 16...♘g6 17 ♘b5 is *16...♗d7?!* in C32222) 17 ♘xe5 dxe5 18 d6+ ♔h8 19 dxe7 ♕xe7 20 ♘xb5 ♖fb8 21 ♗b4! ♕d8 22 ♘d6 +/- W.Nitsche-J.Dille, corr. 1987.

15...h5

This will be required sooner or later, though Black sometimes plays other moves first; e.g. 15...♘g6 (or 15...♖f7 16 ♕c2 ♘g6) 16 ♕c2 ♖f7 17 ♖fc1, when 17...a6 18 a4 h5 19 h3 transposes to the text, albeit without the option of an early ...g5-g4 (see below). If instead 17...h5, White can throw in 18

♘b5! ♘e8 19 a4 *(D)* (not yet 19 ♘xa7? ♗d7 20 ♘b5 g4! 21 a4 g3 -/+ B.Maksimovic-J.Todorovic, Arandjelovac 1991) and then:

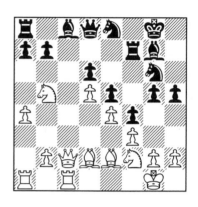

a) 19...♘h4 20 ♘xa7! ♗d7 (if 20...♖c7 21 ♗a5! ♖xc2 22 ♗xd8 ♖xc1+ 23 ♖xc1 ♗d7 24 ♗xg5 +/-) 21 ♘b5 ♗f8 22 ♕d1 ♖g7 23 h3 g4 24 fxg4 hxg4 25 hxg4 ♘f6 (or 25...♗e7 26 ♖a3 ♘g6, Z.Kozul-A.Sznapik, Tbilisi 1988, 27 ♗b4 +/-) 26 ♗e1 ♘h5 27 ♘c7 ♘g3 28 ♘xa8 ♘xg2 29 ♔xg2 ♕h4 (M.Stean-E.Agdestein, Gausdal 1982) 30 ♖c7! ♖xe2 31 ♖a3! +/-.

b) 19...♗f8 20 a5! (if now 20 ♘xa7 ♖c7! 21 ♗a5 ♖xc2 22 ♗xd8 ♖xc1+ 23 ♖xc1 ♗d7 24 ♗b6 ♗xa4 =, or 20 ♖a3 a6 21 ♖c3 ♗d7 22 ♘a3 ♖g7 23 h3 ♘h4 24 ♕d1 ♘f6 25 a5 g4 26 fxg4 hxg4 27 hxg4 ♘h5! 28 ♖h3 ♘g3 ∞ N.Grotnes-E.Gullaksen, Norwegian Ch. 1992) 20...♖g7 21 ♖a3 ♘h4 (or 21...g4 22 fxg4 hxg4 23 ♖c3 ♗d7 24 ♘xg4 ♘h4 25 h3 ♕xa5 26 ♗e1 +=) 22 h3 ♕f6 23 ♕xc8! ♖xc8 24 ♖xc8 ♕g6 25 ♘xa7 +/- Z.Kozul-E.Miroshnichenko, Bled 1999.

16 h3

Again 16 ♖c1 ♘g6 transposes to C32222 (see the note with *16 ♘f2 h5*).

16...♘g6

If 16...♖f7 17 ♕c2 a6!? (17...♘g6 – *16...♘g6*) 18 a4 ♗f8 19 a5 ♖g7 20 ♘a4 g4 21 hxg4 (not 21 ♘b6? gxh3! 22 ♘xa8 ♖xg2+ 23 ♔h1 ♕e8 24 ♖g1 ♕g6 -+ G.Sosonko-R.Gadjily, European Team Ch., Pula 1997) 21...hxg4 22 fxg4 ♗xg4 (or 22...♘xg4, V.Zakharstov-S.Mihajlovskij, Krasnodar 1996, 23 ♘b6 ♖b8 24 ♖ac1 +=) 23 ♘xg4 ♘xg4 24 ♘b6 ♖b8 (Gadjily) 25 ♕c3 +=.

17 ♕c2

The alternative is 17 a4 ♖f7 18 ♘b5 ♗f8 19 ♕c2 *(D)* and then:

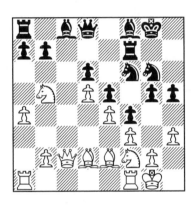

a) 19...a6 20 ♘a3 ♖g7 21 ♘c4! (if 21 ♖fc1 ♘h4 22 ♕d1 ♗d7! 23 ♘c4 g4 24 hxg4 hxg4 25 fxg4 ♘xg2 26 ♔xg2 ♘xg4 27 ♗xg4 ♗xg4 28 ♕xg4! ♖xg4+ 29 ♘xg4 ∞ S.Yuferov-G.Kasparov, Minsk 1978) 21...g4 (or 21...♘h4 22 ♗a5 ♕e8 23 ♕d1 +=) 22 ♗a5 ♕e8 23 fxg4 hxg4 24 hxg4 ♘h4 25 ♕d1! ♕g6 26 ♘b6 ♗xg4 27 ♘xg4 ♘xg4 28 ♗xg4 ♖e8 29 ♗f3! ♘xg2 30 ♔f2 ♘e3 31 ♕b3 ♖h7 32 ♗e2! +/- M.Chovanec-W.Lührig, corr. 2000.

b) 19...g4 20 fxg4 hxg4 21 hxg4 a6 22 ♘a3 ♖g7 (22...♗d7! ∞) 23 ♖fc1 (or 23 ♘c4 ♘h4 24 ♗a5 Ligterink) 23...♘h4 24

♕d1 ♗xg4 25 ♘xg4 ♘xg2 (R.Cabrera-W.Browne, Las Palmas 1977) 26 ♔f1! and if 26...♘xg4? 27 ♗xg4 ♕h4 28 ♗e6+ ♔h8 29 ♖c3! +- Crouch.

17...♖f7

Black can also play 17...g4!? immediately: 18 fxg4 hxg4 19 hxg4 ♘e8! 20 a4 (if 20 ♖fc1 ♗f6 21 ♗e1 ♗h4 22 ♘b5 ♗d7 23 ♕b3 ♗g3 =+ A.Resende-H.Van Riemsdijk, Brazilian Team Ch. 1995) 20...♗f6 21 ♘h3 ♗h4 22 ♘d1 ♖f7 23 ♘df2 ♖h7 24 ♖a3 ∞ G.Möhring-W.Uhlmann, Halle 1981.

18 ♖fc1 *(D)*

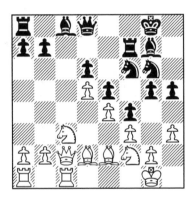

18...a6

18...♗f8 allows 19 ♘b5! ♘e8 20 a4 += (as in the note with 15...♘g6 above), but 18...g4! may be stronger, e.g. 19 fxg4 hxg4 20 hxg4 ♘e8! 21 a4 ♗f6 22 ♖a3 ♗h4 23 ♘cd1 ♗g3 24 ♘h3 ♕h4 25 ♘df2 ♘f6 (not 26...♗d7 26 ♕d1 ♖h7?, G.Sosonko-V.Liberzon, Amsterdam 1978, 27 ♘h1! +/-) 26 ♕d1 ♗d7 27 ♘h1!? ♘xe4 28 ♕c2 ♘xd2 29 ♘xg3 f3! 30 ♕xg6+ ♖g7 31 ♘f5 ♗xf5 32 ♕xf5 fxe2 = E.Bang-H.Ziewitz, corr. 1989.

19 a4 ♗f8 *(D)*

19...g4 20 fxg4 hxg4 21 hxg4 ♗f8 22

a5 transposes to the text. If instead 19...♘h4 20 a5 g4 21 fxg4 hxg4 22 hxg4 b5 23 axb6 ♕xb6 24 ♘a4 ♕a7 25 ♗a5 +/- Z.Kozul-V.Arapovic, Croatian Team Ch. 1998; or 19...b6 20 ♘a2 ♗f8 21 ♘b4 ♖g7 22 ♖a3 ♘h4 23 ♗e1 g4 24 fxg4 hxg4 25 ♘c6 ♕e8 26 ♘xg4 ♘xg4 27 hxg4 +/- A.Gavrilov-A.Korotylev, Moscow 1996.

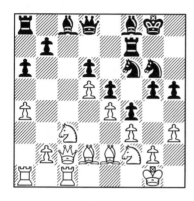

20 a5 g4

Black has also tried 20...b5 (or 20...♗d7 21 ♘a4 ♖c8 22 ♕b3 ♖xc1+ 23 ♖xc1 g4 24 fxg4 hxg4 25 hxg4 ♗xa4 26 ♕xa4 +/- Z.Kozul-G.Gislason, Kallithea 2008) 21 axb6 ♕xb6 22 ♘a4 (or even 22 ♘b5!? g4 23 ♗a5 ♕e3 24 ♖a3 +/-) 22...♕a7 23 ♗a5 ♖b7 (if 23...g4 24 ♘b6! g3 25 ♘xa8 ♕xf2+ 26 ♔h1 ♗xh3 27 ♗f1 +-) 24 ♔f1 ♗d7 25 ♖a3 ♗e7 26 ♖c3 ♗d8 27 b4 ♕b8 28 ♖c6 ♗xa5 29 bxa5 ♗xc6 30 dxc6 ♖c7 31 ♘b6 ♖aa7 (G.Sosonko-J.Fedorowicz, Cannes 1992) 32 ♘d3 intending ♘b4 +/-.

21 fxg4 hxg4 22 hxg4 b5!?

If 22...♖g7 23 ♘a4 ♘h4 24 ♕d1! ♗xg4 (or 24...♘xg2!? 25 ♖xc8! ♖xc8 26 ♔xg2 ♘h5 27 ♘b6 ♖cc7 28 ♗f3 ♘g3 29 ♖c1 +/-) 25 ♘xg4 ♘xg2 26 ♖a3! ♘e3 27

♗xe3 fxe3 28 ♖xe3 ♘xg4 29 ♗xg4 ♕h4 30 ♔g2 ♖xg4+ 31 ♕xg4+ ♕xg4+ 32 ♖g3 ♕xg3+ 33 ♔xg3 +/- J.Hybl-J.Vaindl, corr. 2001.

23 axb6 ♕xb6 24 ♘a4 ♕a7 25 ♗a5 (D)

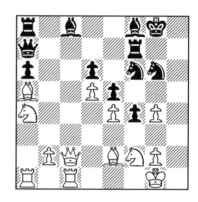

25...♖b8?

25...♖b7 is the last try, and if 26 g5 ♘h7! with some counterplay.

26 ♗c7!

Not 26 ♗b6? ♖xb6 27 ♘xb6 ♕xb6 28 ♕xc8 ♘xe4 29 ♖f1 ♘g3 -+ E.Ermenkov-Z.Lanka, Jurmala 1978; or 26 g5 ♘g4! 27 ♗xg4 ♗xg4 28 ♖a3 (or if 28 ♕c6 ♗e2! 29 ♗b6 ♕e7 -/+) 28...f3! with excellent counterplay for Black, Z.Azmaiparashvili-O.Cvitan, Tilburg 1993.

26...♖b4

If 26...♖b7 27 ♗xd6 ♗xd6 28 ♕xc8+ ♘f8 29 ♔f1 +- G.Sosonko-D.Rogic, Bled 1997.

27 ♗xd6 ♘xe4 28 ♘c5

Or 28 ♗c5 ♗xc5 29 ♘xc5 ♕xc5 30 ♕xc5 ♘xc5 31 ♖xc5 ♗b7 32 ♗c4 ♔g7 33 b3 +/-.

29...♘xd6 29 ♗xa6 ♗f5

If 29...♗g4 30 ♗c8 or 30 ♗d3 +/-.

30 gxf5 ♘xf5 31 d6! ♗xd6 32 ♗c4 ♖xc4

33 ♕xc4 ♕xc5 34 ♕xc5 ♗xc5 35 ♖xc5

The exchange up with an outside passed pawn, White won easily in W.Vertongen-P.Boreux, corr. 2005: **35...♖g7 36 ♘g4 ♘gh4 37 ♖a8+ ♔h7 38 ♘f6+ ♔g6 39 ♖a6 ♔h6 40 ♘e8+ ♖g6 41 ♖xg6+ ♔xg6 42 ♖xe5 ♘e3 43 ♖e6+ ♔f7 44 ♖e4 ♘g6 45 b4 ♘d5 46 ♘d6+ ♔f6 47 b5 ♘e5 48 ♘c4 ♘d7 49 ♖e1 1-0.**

C32222: 14 ♖c1 (D)

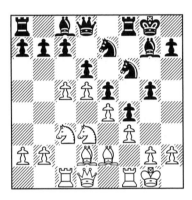

This time White intends to press on at once on the queenside with ♘b5 and c5xd6.

14...♘g6

Hurrying to meet White's plan in the optimum way, which is by ...♘g6 and ...♖f7. Other moves are weaker:

a) 14...h5?! 15 ♘b5 ♘e8 gives Black an inferior version of the main line: usually the knight only drops back in answer to ♘b5 and ♕c2, whereas here the white queen can go straight to b3, saving a tempo; e.g. 16 cxd6 cxd6 17 a4! ♘g6 (or 17...♖f6 18 ♘f2 ♖g6 19 h3 ♔h8 20 ♕b3 ♘g8 21 ♖c3 ♘h6 22 ♖fc1 += V.Neverov-A.Khalifman, Lvov 1985) 18 ♘f2 ♖f7 19 ♕b3 ♗f8 20 ♖c2 ♖g7 21 h3

(or just 21 ♖fc1 ♗d7 22 a5 +=) 21...♘h4 22 ♖fc1 a6?! (but if 22...♗d7 23 ♗b4 a6 24 ♘a3 ♖c8 25 ♘c4 +/= R.Wahrenberg-J.Teixeira, Bad Zwischenahn 2002) 23 ♘c7! ♖xc7 24 ♖xc7 ♘xc7 25 ♗a5 ♘e7 26 ♖xc7 +/- P.Wells-C.Thomson, British Ch. 1985.

b) 14...♘e8?! is similar to line 'a', and in fact 15 ♘b5 ♖f7 16 a4! ♘g6 17 cxd6 cxd6 18 ♘f2 h5 or 18...♗f8 19 ♕b3 h5 just transposes.

c) 14...♖f7?! runs into 15 ♘b5! a6? (but if 15...♘g6 16 ♗a5! – see *14...♘g6 15 ♘b5 ♖f7*) 16 cxd6 axb5 17 dxe7 (17 dxc7! looks even stronger) 17...♕xe7 18 ♘f2 +/- D.Curnow-G.Wagner, Cheltenham 2003.

d) 14...a6?! (preventing ♘b5 but weakening b6) 15 ♕b3 (not yet 15 ♘a4 b5! 16 cxb6 cxb6 17 ♕b3 b5 18 ♘c3 ♘g6 19 a4 g4! ∞ F.Nordstrom-D.Hansson, Swedish Ch. 1972) 15...♖b8 16 ♘a4 g4 (now if 16...b5 17 cxb6 cxb6 18 ♘b4! +/- Huzman) 17 ♗a5 b6 18 cxb6 cxb6 19 ♘xb6 gxf3 20 ♘xc8 fxe2 21 ♗xd8 exf1♕+ 22 ♔xf1 ♖xb3 23 ♘xe7+ ♔f7 24 axb3 ♖xd8 25 ♘c6 ♖a8 26 ♘f2 +- D.Svetushkin-D.Salinnikov, Alushta 1999.

15 cxd6

An important alternative is 15 ♘b5!? a6 (if 15...♖f7 16 ♗a5! b6 17 cxb6 axb6 18 ♗e1 ♗f8 19 ♘b4 ♘e8 20 ♖c3 +/- M.Najdorf-W.Uhlmann, Moscow 1956, or 17...cxb6 18 ♗b4 ♗f8 19 ♖c6 ♘e8 20 a4! += I.Sudakova-T.Dmitrieva, St Petersburg 2001) 16 cxd6! (otherwise 16 ♘a3 g4! 17 cxd6 cxd6 18 ♘c4 g3! 19 ♗a5 gxh2+ 20 ♔xh2 ♕e7 21 ♖h1 ♘h5 22 ♘b6 ♘g3 23 ♔g1 ♖b8 24 ♖h2 ∞

M.Yudovich-E.Arnlind, corr. 1970) 16...axb5 17 dxc7 *(D)*

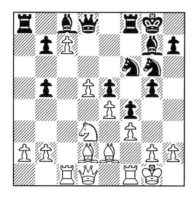

17...♛d7 (if 17...♛e8?! 18 ♛b3 g4 19 ♘c5 ♘h4 20 fxg4 ♛g6 21 ♗e1 +/- G.Fissore-M.Petrillo, corr. 1984, or 18...b6 19 ♖c6 ♖f7 20 ♘f2 ♗f8 21 ♗xb5 ♗d7 22 ♖fc1 ♗c5 23 ♗b4 +/- O.Biriukov-S.Solovjov, St Petersburg 2001) 18 ♛b3 ♘e8! (if 18...g4?! 19 ♗b4 ♖f7 20 d6 g3 21 ♖fd1 gxh2+ 22 ♔xh2 b6 23 ♗a3 ♛e8 24 ♘b4 ♗e6 25 ♗xb5! +- A.Shariyazdanov-S.Klimov, St Petersburg 1997) 19 ♘c5 (if 19 ♗b4 ♖f6! 20 ♘c5 ♛f7 21 ♘e6 ♖xe6! 22 dxe6 ♗xe6 23 ♛c2 ♖c8 ∞) 19...♛d6 (not 19...♛xc7? 20 d6+ ♛f7 21 d7 +/-) 20 ♘e6! (if 20 ♗b4?! ♛b6 21 ♔h1 ♖f7 22 ♖fd1 ♗f8 =+ Soloviov) 20...♖xe6! (not 20...♛b6+? 21 ♔h1 ♗xe6 22 dxe6 ♘xc7 23 e7+ ♖f7 24 ♗c4 ♘h8 25 ♖fd1 +/- O.Biriukov-S.Soloviov, St Petersburg 1999) 21 ♗b4 ♛b6+ 22 ♗c5 ♛a5 23 dxe6 ♘xc7 24 ♗xf8 ♔xf8 25 ♖fd1 ♛b6+ 26 ♔f1 (or 26 ♔h1 ♘xe6 27 ♛b4+ ♔g8 ∞ Soloviov) 26...♗f6! 27 ♖d7 ♘xe6 28 ♖cd1 ♖d8 ∞.

Although the defence appears to be holding at the moment, White's sacrifice is still very dangerous and may be critical for the whole 9 ♘e1 variation.

15...cxd6 16 ♘b5

16 ♘f2 *(D)* is sometimes played here, or may arise via C32221:

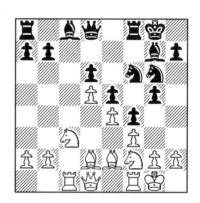

a) 16...h5 17 ♘b5 (if 17 h3 ♖f7 18 a4 ♗f8 19 ♘b5 ♘h4 20 ♛c2, Black can omit ...♘e8 and play 20...g4! 21 fxg4 hxg4 22 hxg4 ♖g7, e.g. 23 ♘c7?! ♗xg4! 24 ♗xg4 ♘xg4 with a strong attack, or if 23 ♛d1, A.Pavlov-M.Lushenkov, Voronezh 2001, 23...a6 24 ♘a3 ♛b6! 25 a5 ♛a7 ∞) 17...♖f7 (not 17...♘e8?! 18 a4 +=; or 17...g4?! 18 ♘c7 ♖b8 19 ♛b3 +=) 18 ♛c2 ♘e8 (not 18...a6?! 19 ♘c7 ♖b8 20 ♘e6 +/- B.Pohlig-H.Jung, Dudweiler 1995) 19 a4 transposes to the main line.

b) 16...♖f7 17 ♘b5 ♗f8 (17...h5 – 16...h5; but Black can also try 17...a6!? 18 ♘a3 b5, e.g. 19 ♘c2 ♛b6 20 ♘b4 g4 21 ♖c6 ♛c7 22 ♛c2 ♗b7 23 fxg4 a5 24 g5, V.Neverov-B.Siwiec, Katowice 1993, 24...♘e8 ∞) 18 ♛c2 (or 18 a4 h5) 18...♘e8 19 ♘xa7?! (19 a4 h5 is the main line again) 19...♘c7! 20 ♗a5 ♖xc2 21 ♗xd8 ♖xe2 22 ♘xc8 ♖xb2 = P.Hanko-L.Dobrovolsky, Prievidza 1978.

c) 16...a6!? 17 a4 (if 17 ♛b3 h5 18 h3 ♘h4 19 ♖c2 ♖f7 20 ♖fc1 ♗f8 21 ♘a4 b5

22 ♞b6 ♛xb6 23 ♜xc8 ♜xc8 24 ♜xc8 g4 =+ S.Furman-W.Browne, Wijk aan Zee 1975) 17...h5 (or 17...♜f7 18 b4 b6 19 ♞b1 h5 20 h3 ♝f8 21 ♞a3 ♜g7 ∞ A.Korotylev-F.Amonatov, Russian Team Ch. 2007) 18 b4 ♝d7!? h5 19 a5 b5 20 axb6 ♛xb6 21 h3 g4 22 hxg4 hxg4 23 fxg4 ♝h6 ∞ G.Levtchouk-K.Spraggett, Quebec 1981.

16...♜f7 (D)

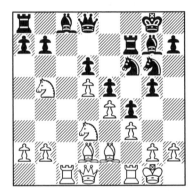

The only consistent continuation, covering c7 and planning to join the kingside attack from g7 or h7. Instead:

a) 16...g4?! 17 ♞c7 gxf3 18 ♝xf3 ♜b8 19 ♛b3 ♜f7 20 ♞e6 ♝xe6 21 dxe6 ♜e7 (R.Stone-J.Zendrowski, London, Canada 1993) 22 ♝e1 +=.

b) 16...♛b6+?! 17 ♞f2 g4 18 ♞c7 ♜b8 19 ♛b3 ♛xb3 20 axb3 g3 (P.Selick-R.Zuk, Canadian Ch. 1972) 21 hxg3 fxg3 22 ♞d3 +=.

c) 16...♝d7?! 17 ♛b3! (not 17 ♞xd6? ♛b6+) 17...♛b6+ 18 ♞f2 g4 19 ♞c7 ♛xb3 20 axb3 g3 21 hxg3 fxg3 22 ♞h1 +/- J.Kocandrle-J.Jensen, corr. 2003.

d) 16...♞e8?! 17 a4 is good for White for the same reasons as 14...h5?! 15 ♞b5 ♞e8 etc.

17 ♛c2

Encouraging the f6-knight to drop back to cover c7, so that it no longer supports ...g5-g4. Otherwise 17 ♞f2 returns to 16 ♞f2 ♜f7 17 ♞b5 above.

17...♞e8

Although this falls in with White's intentions, it also holds up his queenside initiative considerably, so Black has no reason to demur. Nevertheless, proceeding on the kingside is possible too: 17...g4!? (not 17...♛b6+?! 18 ♞f2 g4 19 ♞c7 ♜b8 20 ♛b3! += M.Litinskaya-D.Savereide, Alicante 1979; the extra ...♜f7 on 16...♛b6+ makes no real difference) 18 ♞c7 gxf3 19 gxf3 ♝h3 20 ♞e6 (D) (taking the rook leads to a draw: 20 ♞xa8 ♞xe4! 21 fxe4 ♛g5+ 22 ♔f2 ♛h4+ ½-½ O.Averkin-M.Tal, USSR Ch., Moscow 1969) and now:

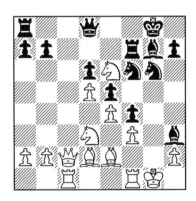

a) 20...♝xe6 21 dxe6 ♜e7 22 ♞b4 += H.Bouwmeester-E.Cobo Arteaga, Siegen Olympiad 1970.

b) 20...♛b6+ 21 ♜f2 ♝h6 (or 21...♝xe6 22 dxe6 ♜e7 23 ♛a4 ♞f8 24 ♝a5 ♛e3, M.Podgaets-M.Gurevich, Sverdlovsk 1984, 25 ♜c3 +=) 22 ♛b3! (if 22 ♛a4 ♞f8! 23 ♞xf8 ♜axf8 ∞

G.Sosonko-R.Keene, Barcelona 1975) ♕xb3 23 axb3 ♘f8 24 ♘c7 ♖d8 25 ♘b5 a6 26 ♘a3 ♘e8 27 ♗f1 += Y.Lobanov-V.Doroshkievich, Sochi 1974.

c) 20...♕d7 21 ♖f2 ♗xe6?! (21...♗h6) 22 dxe6 ♕xe6 23 ♘b4 ♘e7 24 ♗c4 d5 25 ♘xd5 ♘fxd5 26 ♕b3 ♕g6+ 27 ♖g2 ♕b6+ 28 ♔h1 ♕xb3 29 ♗xb3 +/- M.Pac-F.Van de Bos, corr. 2000.

d) 20...♕e7! 21 ♖f2 (if 21 ♖fd1 ♗xe6 22 dxe6 ♕xe6 23 ♘b4 ♕h3! ∞) 21...♗h6 (not now 21...♗xe6?! 22 dxe6 ♕xe6 – 20...♕d7) 22 ♔h1 ♔h8 23 ♕b3 ♗xe6 24 dxe6 ♖g7 ∞ L.Ftacnik-I.Ivanov, Hastings 1983/84.

18 a4 h5 19 ♘f2 ♗f8 *(D)*

The alternative is 19...♗d7 20 ♕b3 and then:

a) 20...♗f6!? 21 ♖c2 ♕b8 22 a5 ♗d8 23 ♘a3 (if 23 ♖fc1 a6 24 ♘a3 b5! 25 axb6 ♗xb6 ½-½ A.Davidovic-D.Sahovic, Nis 1985) 23...a6 (otherwise 24 ♗b5) 24 ♘c4 ♗b5 25 ♗b4 ♗c7 26 ♖fc1 ♕d8 27 ♕a3 += L.Ftacnik-I.Hausner, Czechoslovakia 1984, though it is not easy for White to make progress.

b) 20...♗f8 *(D)* and further:

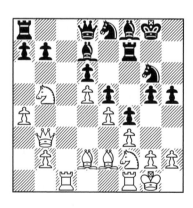

b1) 21 h3 usually transposes below

after 21...♖g7 22 ♖c2 (or somewhere) 22...a6 23 ♘a3, but Black can also try 21...♗e7!? (or even 21...♕b8!?) 22 ♖c2 ♕b8 23 ♖fc1 ♗d8 24 a5 a6 25 ♘a3 b5 26 ♗b4 ♖g7 ∞ M.Vukic-D.Sahovic, Tuzla 1983.

b2) 21 ♖c2 a6 (not here 21...♕b8?! 22 ♖fc1 a6 23 ♘a3 ♗e7 24 a5 ♗d8 25 ♘c4 ♗b5 26 ♗b4 +/- G.Kacheishvili-D.Sharavdorj, Lubbock 2009) 22 ♘a3 ♖g7 23 h3 ♘h4 (or 23...♘f6 24 ♖fc1 ♘h4, but not 24...g4?! 25 fxg4 hxg4 26 hxg4 ♘h4 27 ♖c7! ♗e7 28 ♗e1 +/- L.Ftacnik-G.Ligterink, Amsterdam 1977) 24 ♖fc1 ♘f6 (not 24...g4?! 25 fxg4 hxg4 26 hxg4 ♖c8 27 ♖xc8 ♗xc8 28 ♘c4 ♘f6 29 ♗a5 ♕e8 30 ♕h3 ♗h7 31 ♘b6 ♗d7 32 ♘xd7 ♘xd7 33 g5 +/- N.Rashkovsky-A.Vitolinsh, Daugavpils 1978; or 24...♖b8?! 25 ♘c4 b6 26 a5! g4 27 fxg4 ♘f6 28 ♘xb6 hxg4 29 hxg4 +/- and if 29...♘xg2?, as in V.Ivanchuk-J.Timman, 4th matchgame, Hilversum 1991, 30 ♔xg2! ♘xg4 31 ♗xg4 ♗xg4 32 ♔f1 ♗d7 33 ♔e2 +-J.Knap-M.Petrov, corr. 2004) 25 ♗e1 (or 25 ♖c7 ♖b8 26 a5 ♘e8 27 ♖7c2 ♘f6 = H.Grünberg-P.Hesse, East German Ch. 1984) 25...g4 26 fxg4 hxg4 27 hxg4 ♘xg4 28 ♗xg4 ♗xg4 29 ♘xg4 ♖xg4 30 ♕h3 ♕g5 ½-½ F.Quiroga-E.Maggiolo, Buenos Aires 2000.

b3) 21 ♖c3 a6 22 ♘a3 ♖g7 23 h3 ♘f6 (or 23...♘h4) 24 a5 (if 24 ♖fc1 ♘h4! intending ...g5-g4 again; or 24 ♕d1, G.Taylor-R.Pelts, Montreal 1981, simply 24...g4! with counterplay) 24...♘h4 25 ♗e1 ♖c8 26 ♘c4 g4 27 fxg4 hxg4 28 hxg4 ♘xg4 29 ♘xg4 ♗xg4 30 ♗xg4 ♖xg4 31 ♗xh4 ♕xh4 32 ♖h3 (if 32 ♕xb7 ♖xc4! 33 ♖xc4 ♖xg2+ draws) 32...♕e7 ∞

S.Conquest-P.Thipsay, British Ch. 1986.
b4) 21 ♖c4!? (this has only been tried once) 21...a6 22 ♘a3 ♖g7 23 a5 ♘f6 24 ♕b6!? (24 ♖b4!?) 24...♕e8?! (24...♕xb6 25 axb6 ♖b8 =) 25 h3 (25 ♗b4!? looks critical) 25...g4 26 fxg4 hxg4 27 hxg4 ♘h4 28 ♖c7 ♕g6?! (28...♖g6! unpins the d7-bishop) 29 ♗e1? (this was the moment for 29 ♕xb7! +/-) 29...♖h7! 30 ♕b3 (if now 30 ♕xb7?? ♕h6! 31 ♘h3 ♘xg2 wins) 30...♘xe4 31 ♕d3 ♘g3 32 ♖xb7 (Z.Kozul-T.Radjabov, Sarajevo 2003) 32...♗f5! 33 ♖xh7 ♗xd3 34 ♗xd3 ♔xh7 35 ♗xg6+ ♘xg6 -/+ Gallagher.

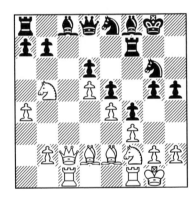

20 h3

Other moves:

a) 20 ♘xa7 ♖c7! (otherwise Black must sacrifice a pawn, but 20...♗d7?! 21 ♘b5 ♖g7 22 b3!? g4 23 fxg4 ♘h4 24 h3 hxg4 25 ♘xg4 ♘f6, B.Kliesch-L.Beroun, corr. 1997, and now 26 ♕c7! ♘xe4 27 ♕xd8 ♖xd8 28 ♗e1 ♘f5 29 ♗d3 leaves White with the better chances, or if 22...♘h4 23 ♕d1! +=) 21 ♗a5 (if 21 ♘c6 bxc6 22 dxc6 ♘e7! 23 ♗b5 ♗e6 ∞ Z.Jurik-J.Dolezel, corr. 1993) 21...♖xc2 22 ♗xd8 ♖xe2 23 ♘xc8

♖xa4 (not 23...♖xb2?! 24 a5 +=) 24 ♘d3 (or 24 ♘d1 ♘h4!) 24...g4 25 ♖f2 ♖e3 26 ♘e1 ♖a8 27 ♖fc2 ♖b3 28 ♔f2 ♖a2 29 ♖b1 ♔f7 30 ♔e2 ♗e7 31 ♘xe7 ♘xe7 32 ♘d3 ♖a8 33 ♗xe7 ♔xe7 = I.Novikov-I.Glek, Lvov 1985.

b) 20 b4!? has the idea 20...♖g7? 21 ♘xa7 ♖c7 22 ♘c6! bxc6 23 dxc6 +/- N.Rashkovsky-E.Gufeld, Daugavpils 1978; but Black should be fine after 20...a6 21 ♘a3 ♖g7 22 ♘c4 ♘h4 23 a5 g4 ∞ P.Malbon-C.Kidd, corr. 1999.

c) 20 ♕b3!? ♖g7?! (this allows White to omit h2-h3; 20...♘f6!? may be more accurate, or else 20...♗d7, transposing to 19...♗d7 above) 21 ♖c3! (21 h3 returns to the main line) 21...a6 (or 21...♘h4 22 g3! g4 23 fxg4 hxg4, V.Neverov-A.Istratescu, Bucharest 1993, 24 gxf4! +/-) 22 ♘a3 ♘f6 23 ♘c4 b5!? 24 axb5 g4 25 fxg4 axb5 26 ♕xb5 ♗xg4 (26...♖b7!?) 27 ♗xg4 hxg4 28 ♕b6 ♕e7 29 ♘xd6 +/- H.Cording-A.Sundin, corr. 1972.

20...♖g7 21 ♕b3

The usual continuation, though White has also tried:

a) 21 ♘xa7 ♖c7! (the extra h2-h3 makes little difference; if instead 21...♗d7!? 22 ♘b5 ♘h4 23 ♕b3 ♔h8! 24 ♖c3 g4 25 fxg4 ♘f6 26 ♕d1 hxg4 27 hxg4 ♘h5! ∞ V.Frias Pablaza-M.Wilder, New York 1984, but 23 b3!? is again possible) 22 ♗a5 (or 22 ♘c6 bxc6 23 dxc6 ♘e7 24 ♗b5 ♗e6 ∞ A.Allen-G.Canfell, Australian Ch. 1991) 22...♖xc2 23 ♗xd8 ♖xe2 24 ♘xc8 ♖xa4 25 ♘d3 g4 26 ♖f2 ♖e3 27 ♘e1 g3 28 ♖fc2 ♖b3 29 ♔f1 ♖a2 30 ♖b1 ♔f7 31 ♔e2 ♖a8 = O.Averkin-G.Kasparov, USSR Spartakiad 1979.

b) 21 a5!? ♘h4 22 ♗e1 (if 22 ♗b4 a6 23 ♘a3 g4 24 fxg4 ♘f6 25 ♕d1 hxg4 26 hxg4, G.Piesina-M.Chiburdanidze, Vilnius 1978, 26...♘h5! ∞) 22...♗d7 23 ♕b3 a6!? (or just 23...♔h8-g8-h8 etc, since White cannot do anything from his current configuration) 24 ♘a3 ♘f6 25 ♖c2 ♖c8! 26 ♖xc8 ♗xc8 27 ♘c4 g4 28 hxg4 hxg4 29 fxg4 ♘xg4 30 ♘xg4 ♗xg4 31 ♗xg4 ♖xg4 (H.Schaufelberger-D.Marovic, Birseck 1971) 32 ♗xh4 ♕xh4 33 ♕h3 ♕g5 =.

21...♘h4 22 ♖c2 (D)

The alternative is 22 ♖c3 a6 23 ♘a3 ♘f6 24 ♕d1!? (if 24 ♗e1 g4 25 fxg4 hxg4 26 hxg4 ♘xg4 27 ♘xg4 ♗xg4 28 ♗xg4 ♖xg4 29 ♗xh4 ♖xh4 30 ♖h3 ♖b8 = F.Visser-F.Hoorweg, corr. 1986) 24...g4?! (24...♗d7! is fine) 25 fxg4 hxg4 26 hxg4 ♘h5? 27 gxh5! ♘xg2 (B.Christensen-M.Nielsen, Ringsted 1995) 28 ♗g4! ♗xg4 (or 28...♘e3 29 ♗xe3 fxe3 30 ♖xe3 ♕h4 31 ♔g2!) 29 ♘xg4 ♕h4 30 ♖f2 ♘e3 31 ♗xe3 ♖xg4+ 32 ♕xg4 ♕xg4+ 33 ♖g2 +/-.

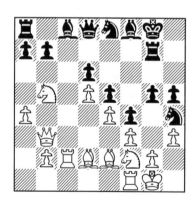

22...a6

It makes sense to insert this, though Black can also play 22...♘f6 (not yet

22...g4?! 23 fxg4 ♘f6 24 ♗e1! hxg4 25 hxg4 ♘h5, V.Ivanchuk-I.Cheparinov, Sofia 2008, 26 ♘d1! +=; or if 24...♔h8 25 g3!?) 23 ♖fc1 g4 24 ♖c7 (or 24 fxg4 hxg4 25 hxg4 ♗xg4 26 ♗xg4 ♘xg4 27 ♘xg4 ♖xg4 28 ♗e1 f3! 29 ♗xh4 ♕xh4 30 ♕xf3 ♖xe4 = K.Langeweg-J.H.Donner, Amsterdam 1971) 24...♖g6!? 25 fxg4 hxg4 26 hxg4 ♗xg4 27 ♘xg4 ♘xg4 28 ♕h3 ♘e3 29 ♗xe3 fxe3 30 ♖xb7 (or 30 ♗g4 ♕g5 31 ♗e6+ ♔h8 32 ♖1c2 a6 33 ♘c3 ♗h6 ∞ E.Martinovsky-D.Fleetwood, corr. 1990) 30...♖xg2+ 31 ♔h1 ♕g5 32 ♘xa7 (if 32 ♘c7 ♕f4! 33 ♖f1 ♕xe4 34 ♗f3 e2 35 ♕e6+ ♔h8 36 ♕f6+ ♗g7 37 ♗xe4 ♗xf6 38 ♗xg2 ♖g8! 39 ♖e1 ♖xg2 =) 32...♔h8 33 ♖cc7 ♖g1+ ½-½ A.Haarer-H.Grimm, corr. 1988.

23 ♘a3 ♘f6

23...♗d7!? transposes to *19...♗d7 20 ♕b3 ♗f8 21 ♖c2* etc.

24 ♗e1

If 24 ♖fc1 g4 25 fxg4 hxg4 26 hxg4 ♗xg4 27 ♗xg4 ♘xg4 28 ♘xg4 ♖xg4 29 ♗e1 f3 30 ♗xh4 ♕xh4 = P.Bergen-F.Brandstätter, Finkenstein 1993.

24...g4 25 hxg4 hxg4 26 ♘xg4

If 26 fxg4 ♘h5!? (or 26...♘xg4 – 26 ♘xg4 ♘xg4) 27 ♘h1 ♗xg4 28 ♗xg4 ♖xg4 29 ♕h3 ♕g5 30 ♗xh4 ♖xh4 31 ♕e6+ ♔h8 32 ♖f3 ♖g4 ∞ H.Anaya Oger-T.Crespo, corr. 1985.

26...♘h5!?

Or simply 26...♘xg4 27 fxg4 ♗xg4 28 ♗xg4 ♖xg4 29 ♕h3 (if 29 ♕xb7 ♘xg2! 30 ♖xg2 ♖xg2+ 31 ♔xg2 ♖b8, T.Einarsson-M.Westeras, corr. 1992, 32 ♗h4! =) 29...♕g5 30 ♗xh4 ♖xh4 31 ♕e6+ ♔h8 32 ♖f3 ♗e7 ∞ K.Nickl-M.Raubal, Finkenstein 1990.

27 ♘c4 ♘g3 28 ♗xg3 fxg3 29 ♕b6

Not 29 ♖fc1?! ♘xf3+ 30 gxf3 ♕h4 (Van Dyck), or 29 ♘b6? ♘f5! and wins.

29...♕e7 30 ♘ce3 ♖h7 31 ♖fc1 ♗xg4!

If 31...♘g6?! 32 ♖c7 ♕g5 (or 32...♕h4? 33 ♖xh7 ♔xh7 34 ♘f5! +/- C.Van Dyck-R.Chapman, corr. 1985) 33 ♖xh7 ♔xh7 34 ♖c7+! ♔g8 25 ♘f1 (Van Dyck) is good for White.

32 ♘xg4 ♘g6 33 ♖c7 ♕g5 34 ♖xh7 ♕xc1+ 35 ♗f1 ♔xh7 36 ♕xb7+ ♘e7! 37 ♕xa8 ♗h6 38 ♕a7 ♔g6 (D)

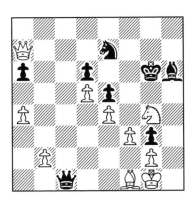

Despite the two pawns deficit, Black draws thanks to his complete control of the dark squares:

a) 39 ♕xa6 ♗e3+ 40 ♔h1 ♗c5 41 b4 ♗xb4 42 ♕c4 ♕d2 =.

b) 39 ♕d7 ♗e3 ½-½ E.Bang-P.Hertel, corr. 1988, since if 40 ♘xe3 ♕xe3+ 41 ♔h1 ♔f7! 42 ♕xd6 ♕c1 =.

c) 39 ♕b6 ♘c8 40 ♕b3 a5! 41 ♕c3

♘e7!? (or just 41...♕xc3 42 bxc3 ½-½ S.Kramer-M.Lecroq, corr. 2000) 42 ♕xc1 ♗xc1 43 b4 axb4 44 a5 ♘g8 45 a6 ♘f6 46 a7 ♘xg4 47 a8♕ ♗e3+ 48 ♔h1 ♘f2+ etc.

Conclusion

Black cannot hope for much after 9...c5 (line A) as White can attack on the other side with f2-f4. The retreat 9...♘e8 (line B) grants White more freedom, who can play for f2-f4 again, or else ♗e3 and c4-c5, with good chances for the advantage in either case. Therefore the knight usually goes back to d7, when there are now two lines which need to be considered:

After 10 ♗e3 f5 11 f3 f4 12 ♗f2 g5 (line C1), White has tried numerous ideas without proving an edge. Korchnoi's 13 a4 is the most testing, but Black has sufficient resources if he looks first to his defence with 13...a5 (line C132) before proceeding on the kingside.

The most principled variation is 10 ♘d3 f5 11 ♗d2 ♘f6 12 f3 f4 (line C322), leading to extremely complicated positions with mutual chances. As theory runs to great depth in this line, some players prefer to circumvent it, such as by the pre-emptive g2-g4 for White (lines C2 and C3221), or for Black the flexible ...♔h8 (lines C31 and C321).

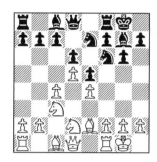

Chapter Ten

7...♘c6 8 d5 ♘e7 9 ♘d2

1 d4 ♘f6 2 c4 g6 3 ♘c3 ♗g7 4 e4 d6 5 ♘f3 0-0 6 ♗e2 e5 7 0-0 ♘c6 8 d5 ♘e7 9 ♘d2 *(D)*

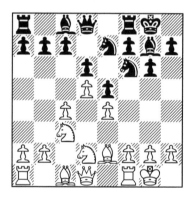

The move 9 ♘d2 first appeared in tournament practice in the early 1960s and became popular a few years later. As with 9 ♘e1 in the previous chapter, 9 ♘d2 enables White to support the centre with f2-f3, and prevents the black knight from going to h5. On the queenside White intends to advance with b2-b4 and c4-c5, and then to place

the knight on c4, where it will be more active than on d3. On the downside, the knight is temporarily badly placed on d2 and obstructs the c1-bishop, while ideas with f2-f4 will be less effective.

For Black, the standard replies to 9 ♘e1, 9...♘e8 and 9...♘d7, both allow White to make substantial strides before Black achieves anything on the kingside. These lines may still be playable, but counteraction on the queenside first is usually preferred. To this end 9...c5 is logical as it leaves the d2-knight misplaced, but the natural advance b2-b4, prepared by ♖b1 or a2-a3, gives White the slightly freer game, even if Black's position is very solid.

The main line begins with 9...a5, a standard idea in many King's Indian variations. Again, White will aim for b2-b4, after 10 ♖b1 or 10 a3 (the two moves often just transpose), and then Black's most principled response is

10...♘d7, followed by 11...f5 12 b4 ♔h8, leading to sharp positions with mutual chances.

A: 9...♘e8 *279*
B: 9...♘d7 *284*
C: 9...c5 *287*
D: 9...a5 *290*

Rarely played alternatives are:

a) 9...♗d7 10 b4 c6 11 ♗a3 a6 12 dxc6 ♗xc6 (if 12...bxc6, Sherbakov-I.Zaitsev, USSR Ch., Moscow 1991, 13 ♘b3 +/=) 13 ♖e1 b5 14 ♗f1 ♕b6 15 ♘b3 += V.Korchnoi-I.Zaitsev, USSR Ch., Riga 1970.

b) 9...♗h6 10 b4 (or 10 c5!? dxc5 11 ♘c4 ♗g7 12 ♗e3 b6 13 f4 with very strong compensation for the pawn) 10...a5 11 bxa5 ♘d7 12 ♘b3 ♗xc1 13 ♖xc1 f5 (J.Kaplan-H.Camara, Sao Paulo 1977) 14 c5!? ♘xc5 15 ♘xc5 dxc5 16 ♗c4 ♔h8 17 f4 with the initiative.

c) 9...c6 10 a3!? (instead 10 dxc6 bxc6 – 9...c5; or if 10 b4 a5 11 bxa5 ♕xa5 12 ♕c2 c5 13 a4 ♘d7 14 ♘b5 ♖a6 15 ♘b3 ♕d8 16 ♗e3 f5 17 f3 f4 18 ♗f2 g5 19 a5 h5 20 ♖fb1 += P.Pelts-R.Byrne, Chicago 1994) 10...♘e8 (or 10...cxd5 11 exd5 ♗d7 12 b4 ♖c8 13 a4 a6 14 a5 += S.Sabaev-G.Pukropski, corr. 1999) 11 b4 f5 12 ♕b3 ♔h8 13 ♗b2 ♘f6 14 ♖ad1 fxe4 15 dxc6! ♘xc6 16 ♘cxe4 ♘xe4 17 ♘xe4 ♘d4 18 ♗xd4 exd4 19 ♕g3 +/= M.Gurevich-V.Bologan, 1st match-game, Saint Pierre 2000.

A: 9...♘e8 *(D)*
The knight on e8 has the same dis-

advantages as in the 9 ♘e1 variation: it is neither hinders c4-c5, nor controls the e5-square. On the plus side, it leaves the c8-h1 diagonal open for the bishop, and covers d6, which White is planning to target by c4-c5, ♘c4 and ♗a3.

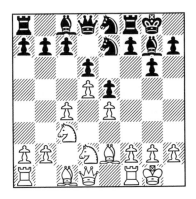

10 b4

Preparing this further just wastes a tempo; e.g. 10 ♖b1 f5 11 b4 ♘f6 12 f3 f4 13 c5 g5 14 ♘c4 ♘g6 15 a4 ♖f7 16 ♗a3 ♗f8 17 a5 ♖g7 18 b5 b6! 19 cxd6 cxd6 20 ♘a2 g4! 21 fxg4 ♘h4! -/+ G.Kamsky-G.Kasparov, Paris (rapid) 1992.

10...f5

Other moves allow White an easy advantage:

a) 10...♗h6 (this loses time and control of e5) 11 ♘b3 ♗xc1 12 ♕xc1 f5 (or 12...c6 13 dxc6 bxc6 14 a4 ♗e6 15 b5 f5 16 f4! +/- H.Mecking-R.Naranja, Palma Interzonal 1970) 13 f4! ♘f6 14 fxe5 dxe5 15 ♕g5 +/- M.Taimanov-V.Zhelian-dinov, USSR Ch., Kharkov 1967.

b) 10...a5 11 bxa5 ♖xa5 12 ♘b3 ♖a8 13 ♗e3 (also good is 13 a4 f5 14 c5 ♘f6 15 f3 f4 16 ♗a3 ♖f7 17 a5 g5 18 cxd6 cxd6 19 ♘a4 +/- S.Skembris-L.Radice,

---

Cannes 1991; or even 13 c5!? dxc5 14 ♘xc5 ♘d6 15 ♗e3 b6 16 ♘b3 += C.Crouch-R.McFarland, British League 2003) 13...f5 14 f3 f4 15 ♗f2 g5 16 c5 ♘g6 17 a4 h5 18 a5 +/- T.Civin-J.Maskova, Czech League 1997.

11 c5

The most natural continuation. Instead:

a) 11 f3 (an inaccurate move order) 11...f4 (if 11...♗h6 12 ♘b3 ♗xc1 13 ♖xc1 f4 14 c5 g5 15 a4 h5 16 a5 += Wl.Schmidt-B.Andersen, Nice Olympiad 1974; or 11...a5 12 bxa5 ♖xa5 13 ♘b3 ♖a8 14 c5 += A.Zabihi-U.Adianto, World Junior Ch. 1980; but Black can consider 11...c6!? 12 ♕b3 ♔h8 13 a4 a5 ∞ T.Fordan-S.Farago, Budapest 1999) 12 c5 g5 (or 12...h5 first, avoiding g2-g4 ideas) 13 ♘c4 (if 13 g4!? ♔f7 14 ♘c4 ♖h8 15 ♔g2 ♘g6 16 h3 h5 17 ♖h1 ♗d7 ∞ T.Teske-E.Zizer, Württemberg 1996) 13...♘g6 (13...♘f6 – *11 c5*, or else 13...h5 14 a4 ♖f6!? 15 ♗a3 ♖g6 16 a5 g4 17 b5 g3 18 h3 ♔h7 19 b6 ♘c6 20 ♖e1 ♕h4 ∞ G.Lock-M.Singleton, Portsmouth 2002) 14 a4 (or 14 ♗a3 ♖f7 15 b5 ♗f8 16 b6 dxc5 17 bxc7 ♘xc7 18 d6 ♘e6 ∞ H.Van Kooten-H.Bonte, Haarlem 2001) 14...♖f7 15 ♗a3 ♗f8 16 a5 h5 17 h3 ♖g7 18 b5 g4 19 fxg4 hxg4 20 ♗xg4 ♘h4 ∞ J.Hjartarson-L.Yurtaev, Moscow Olympiad 1994.

b) 11 a4 ♘f6 12 a5!? (12 f3 f4 13 c5 or 12 c5 – *11 c5*) 12...♗h6 (if 12...fxe4 13 ♘dxe4 ♘f5 14 ♗g5 h6 15 ♗xf6 ♗xf6 16 a6! +=, or 12...f4 13 c5 g5 14 h3!? ♗d7 15 ♘c4 ♘c8, D.Kolbus-L.McShane, Hastings 1994/95, 16 a6 +=) 13 c5 ♗xd2 14 ♗xd2 ♘xe4 15 ♘xe4 fxe4 16 ♗g5 ♕e8

17 ♖c1 ♘f5 18 ♖c3 ♗d7 ∞ V.Epishin-V.Akopian, Tbilisi 1989.

11...♘f6 *(D)*

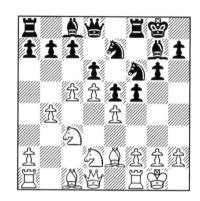

This position arises via 9...♘e8 and 9...♘d7 with equal frequency; some 9 b4 variations can also end up here (e.g. 9...♘e8 10 c5 f5 11 ♘d2). Other moves:

a) 11...f4?! (as usual, this is premature before f2-f3) 12 ♗g4! g5 (or 12...♗xg4 13 ♕xg4 h5 14 ♕e2 ♘f6 15 a4 g5 16 f3 ♘g6 17 ♗a3 +/- R.Jedynak-G.Mittermayr, Balatonlelle 2004) 13 ♗xc8 ♕xc8 14 f3 ♘g6 15 ♘c4 ♖f7 16 a4 ♗f8 17 c6 +/- S.Iskusnyh-L.Yurtaev, Seversk 1997.

b) 11...fxe4 12 ♘dxe4 ♘f5 (or 12...♘f6 13 ♘xf6+ ♗xf6 14 ♘e4 ♗g7 15 ♗c4 += Duong The-Phung Nguyen Tuong, Phu Quoc 2007) 13 ♗g5 ♘f6 14 ♖c1 h6 15 ♗xf6 ♗xf6 16 cxd6 cxd6 17 ♘b5 a6 18 ♘c7 ♖b8 19 ♗g4 ♕e7 20 b5 += J.Dorfman-S.Iuldachev, Elista Olympiad 1998.

c) 11...♔h8 12 a4! (if 12 f3 f4 13 ♘c4 h5 14 a4 g5 15 ♗a3 ♖f6 16 b5 dxc5 17 ♗xc5 ♖g6 18 h3?! ♘g8 19 ♕d3 ♘h6 20 ♘d1 g4 21 fxg4 hxg4 22 hxg4 ♘xg4 -/+ G.Flear-M.Hebden, London 1990, or 18 a5 ♘g8 19 ♕b3 g4 20 fxg4 hxg4 21 g3 ♕g5 ∞ D.Anagnostopoulos-J.Rowson, Richmond 1994) 12...a5!? (12...♘g8 – 9 b4 ♔h8 in the next chapter; or 12...c6?! 13 ♘c4! fxe4 14 ♗g5 +/- E.Arlandi-A.Profumo, Bratto 1998) 13 ♗a3 axb4 14 ♗xb4 fxe4 15 cxd6 (better 15 ♘dxe4 +=) 15...♘xd6 16 ♘dxe4 ♘xe4 17 ♘xe4 ♖f4 18 ♗xe7 ♕xe7 ∞ I.Bern-A.Sousa, Cappelle la Grande 1995.

d) 11...a5!? deserves more attention; e.g. 12 ♗a3 axb4 13 ♗xb4 fxe4 (if 13...dxc5 14 ♗xc5 b6 15 ♗b4 ♘d6 16 ♘c4 fxe4 17 ♘xd6 cxd6 18 ♘xe4 += M.Taimanov-F.Portisch, Zalaegerszeg 1969) 14 ♘dxe4 ♘f5 15 ♗b5 (or 15 a4 ♘d4 16 ♗c4 ♗f5 17 ♖e1 ♖f7 ∞ K.Weber-H.P.Köhler, corr. 1997) 15...♘d4 16 ♗xe8 dxc5 17 ♗xc5 ♖xe8 18 d6 ♗f5 ∞ A.Lombard-D.Yanofsky, Siegen Olympiad 1970.

12 f3

White sometimes holds this move back:

a) 12 cxd6 cxd6 13 ♗a3 (or 13 b5 ♗h6 14 ♗d3 fxe4 15 ♘dxe4 ♗xc1 16 ♖xc1 ♗f5 ∞ G.Flear-A.J.Mestel, Bath 1987) 13...♗h6 14 exf5 (not 14 f3? ♕b6+ 15 ♔h1 ♕d4 -/+) 14...gxf5 (or 14...♗xf5!?) 15 ♘c4 ♘g6 16 b5 ♘e8 17 b6 (or 17 ♖e1 ♖f7 ∞) 17...a6 18 ♗h5 ♖f6 19 ♗c1 ♗xc1 20 ♖xc1 (E.Postny-I.Nataf, Portuguese Team Ch. 2006) 20...♗d7!? ∞.

b) 12 a4 f4!? (safer is 12...♗h6 13 cxd6 cxd6 14 f3 ♗e3+ 15 ♔h1, A.Beliavsky-V.Zheliandinov, Bled 1999, 15...♗d4 16 ♖a3 a6 ∞; or 12...fxe4 13 ♘dxe4 ♘f5 14 ♗g5 h6 15 ♗xf6 ♗xf6 16 ♗g4 ♗g7 ∞ D.Antic-Z.Grujic, Serbian Team Ch. 2007) 13 ♘c4 g5 14

♘b5!? (14 f3 – 11 c5; or if 14 cxd6 cxd6 15 b5 g4 16 ♗a3 f3 17 gxf3, M.Taimanov-R.Klovsky, USSR Team Ch. 1968, 17...gxf3 18 ♗xf3 ♘e8 intending ♘g6 ∞; 14 ♗a3 g4 is similar) 14...♘e8 (perhaps 14...♘xe4!? 15 ♗d3 ♗f5 ∞) 15 ♗a3 ♘g6 16 ♗g4 ♘h4 17 ♗xc8 ♖xc8 (J.Werle-F.Vallejo Pons, Wijk aan Zee 2009) 18 ♕g4 +/-.

c) 12 ♗a3!? ♗h6?! (this turns out badly here, but if 12...fxe4 13 ♘dxe4 ♘xe4 14 ♘xe4 ♘f5 15 b5 += C.Conrad-D.Thomaschke, Hamburg 1999; or 12...♖f7 13 b5 ♘e8 14 ♘c4 g5, H.Schussler-E.Ermenkov, Thessaloniki Olympiad 1984, 15 ♗h5 ♘g6 16 exf5 ♗xf5 17 ♘e3 +=) 13 f3! ♗e3+ 14 ♔h1 f4 (or similarly 14...♘h5 15 ♘c4 ♗d4, B.Hala-M.Holoubkova, Czech League 1999, 16 ♘b5! +/-) 15 ♘c4 ♗d4 16 cxd6 (or 16 ♘b5! ♗xa1 17 ♕xa1 ♘e8 18 ♘xc7! +/- O.Panno-O.Yepez, Quito 1976) 16...cxd6 17 ♘b5! ♗xa1 18 ♕xa1 ♘e8 19 ♘bxd6! ♘xd6 20 ♕xe5 +/- W.Browne-M.Maloney, USA 1997.

12...f4 (D)

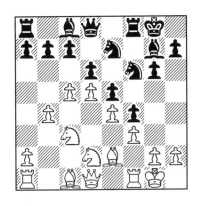

If now 12...a5?! 13 bxa5! dxc5 14 ♘c4 ♗d7 15 ♖b1 ♘c8 16 ♗e3 +/- E.Geller-

I.Zaitsev, USSR Ch., Moscow 1969; or 12...♗h6 13 ♘c4 ♗xc1 14 ♖xc1 f4 15 a4 g5 16 ♘b5 ♘e8 17 cxd6 cxd6 18 a5 += E.Bukic-F.Portisch, Virovitica 1978.

13 ♘c4

Another option is 13 a4 (if 13 ♗a3 g5 14 ♘c4 or 14 b5 ♘e8 15 ♘c4 – *13 ♘c4*) 13...g5 14 ♗a3 (or if 14 a5 h5! ∞, but not 14...♘g6?! 15 a6! b6 16 ♗b5 +/- B.Malich-B.Schmitz, East German Ch. 1968) 14...♘g6 15 b5!? (delaying ♘c4) 15...dxc5 (if 15...♖f7 16 b6! +=) 16 ♗xc5 ♖f7 17 a5!? (17 ♘c4 returns to the main line) 17...♗f8 18 ♗f2 h5 19 b6 cxb6 20 axb6 a6 21 ♘b5 dxc5 (if 21...♘e8 22 ♘a7! ♗d7 23 ♖c1 +=) 22 ♘c7 g3! 23 hxg3 fxg3 24 ♗xg3 h4 25 ♗f2 ♘f4 ∞ A.Pomaro-G.Caprio, Italian Junior Ch. 2007.

13...g5 14 a4

White has two further possibilities:

a) 14 g4!? ♘g6 (or 14...♖f7 15 cxd6 cxd6 16 ♘b5 ♘e8 17 a4 ♗f8 18 ♗d2 h5 19 h3 ♖h7 20 ♔g2 ♘g6 ∞ L.Ftacnik-J.Maiwald, Austrian Team Ch. 2005, but not 14...fxg3?! 15 hxg3 ♘h5 16 ♔g2 ♘g6 17 ♖h1 ♘h4+ 18 gxh4 gxh4 19 ♔f2 h3 20 ♔e3 +/- R.Sherbakov-A.Motylev, Ekaterinburg 1997) 15 ♗d2 ♖f7 16 ♗e1 h5 17 h3 ♗f8 18 c6 bxc6 19 dxc6 ♗e6 20 ♘a5 ♕e8 21 b5 hxg4 22 hxg4 ♖h7 23 ♗c4 ♔g7 ∞ M.Ulibin-M.Pavlovic, Biel 2005.

b) 14 ♗a3 (omitting a2-a4) 14...♘g6 (or 14...♘e8 15 b5 b6!? 16 cxd6 cxd6 17 ♗b4 ♖f6 18 a4 ♗d7 19 a5 ♖b8 20 axb6 axb6 21 ♘b2, M.Sorokin-J.Seminara, Buenos Aires 1994, 21...h5 intending ...♖g6, ...g5-g4 ∞) 15 b5 ♘e8 (15...dxc5 16 ♗xc5 ♖f7 17 a4 is the main line

again, but White can avoid this with 17 ♔h1! h5 18 d6 ♗e6 19 ♕a4 g4 20 ♖ad1 c6 21 bxc6 bxc6 22 ♕a5 +/- R.Buhmann-J.Maiwald, Austrian Team Ch. 2008) 16 b6 cxb6 17 cxb6 (or 17 ♘xd6 bxc5 18 ♘xe8 ♖xe8 19 ♗b5 ♗d7 20 d6 b6 ∞ R.Vaganian-A.Shirov, Manila Interzonal 1990) 17...axb6 18 ♕b3 h5 19 ♖ab1 g4 20 ♘xb6 ♕g5! 21 ♔h1 (if 21 ♘xa8 g3! 22 h3 ♕h4 with a very strong attack) 21...♘h4 22 ♘xc8 ♖xc8 23 ♖g1 ♖f7 24 ♖bc1 ♗f8 25 ♘a4 ♖xc1 26 ♗xc1 ♖g7 ∞ V.Bogdanovski-M.Golubev, Skopje 1991.

14...♘g6 15 ♗a3

If instead 15 cxd6 cxd6 16 ♘b5 ♘e8 17 ♗d2!? ♖f7 18 ♗e1 ♗d7! 19 ♗f2 (or 19 ♘a5 ♕b8 20 ♗f2 ♗f6 21 ♕b3 ♗d8 22 ♖fc1 ♗xa5 23 bxa5 h5 24 ♕d1 ♕d8 25 a6 bxa6 26 ♘xa7 g4 ∞ Y.Pelletier-J.Maiwald, German League 2000) 19...♗xb5 20 axb5 b6 21 ♕d3 ♖c8 22 ♖fc1 ♖fc7 23 ♕d1 ♘f6 24 ♘d2 ♖xc1 25 ♖xc1 ♖xc1 26 ♕xc1 ♘e7 27 ♕c2 h5 ∞ M.Gurevich-A.Shirov, Wijk aan Zee 1993.

15...♖f7 16 b5 (D)

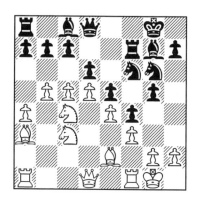

This kind of position appears many

times. White intends to break up the queenside with b5-b6, while Black's chances, as always, lie on the kingside with ...g5-g4. Although White's play is well advanced here, Black's attack remains dangerous as it aims for the greater prize.

16...dxc5!

16...♗f8 allows White to carry out his plan straightaway: 17 b6! cxb6 (if 17...dxc5 18 bxc7 ♖xc7 19 ♘b5 ♖g7 20 ♗b2 a6 21 ♘ba3 ♘d7 22 d6 += I.Nemet-J.Fricker, Mendrisio 1987; or 17...axb6 18 cxb6 cxb6 19 ♕b3 ♖a6 20 ♘b5 ♘e8 21 ♖fc1 += M.Tratar-A.Grilc, Slovenian Junior Ch. 1994, continuing 21...h5? 22 ♘cxd6! ♘xd6 23 ♗xd6 g4 24 ♗xf8 ♘xf8 25 ♕c3 +-) 18 cxd6! (if 18 cxb6 a6! ∞, or 18 ♘xd6 ♖g7! 19 ♘xc8 ♖xc8 20 d6 bxc5 21 ♘b5 ♖c6 ∞ V.Epishin-V.Akopian, Minsk 1990) 18...♘e8 19 ♘b5 ♗d7 20 ♗b2 (or 20 ♘c7!? ♘xc7 21 dxc7 ♕xc7 22 ♖c1 ♕d8 23 ♕b3 with compensation, M.Reischl-E.Lipok, German League 1997) 20...a6 (if 20...♕f6, L.Ftacnik-V.Akopian, Groningen 1991, then 21 ♕b3! ♘xd6 22 ♘cxd6 ♗xd6 23 ♘xd6 ♕xd6 24 ♗a3 ♕f6 25 ♖ac1 +=) 21 ♘ba3?! (Ftacnik suggests 21 ♘c7 ♘xc7 22 dxc7 ♕xc7 23 d6 with the initiative) 21...♗xd6 22 ♘xd6 (or if 22 ♔h1, K.Sakaev-V.Stotika, Leningrad 1990, 22...b5!? 23 axb5 axb5 24 ♘xd6 ♘xd6 25 ♕b3 g4 ∞) 22...♘xd6 23 ♘c4 ♘xc4 24 ♗xc4 ∞ R.Brglez-P.Riegler, Bled 1992.

17 ♗xc5 h5

Still not 17...♗f8?! 18 ♗xf8 ♕xf8 19 a5 h5 20 b6 g4 21 bxc7 ♖xc7 22 d6 += I.Farago-Kr.Georgiev, Baile Herculane 1982.

18 a5

18 ♔h1 g4 19 a5 g3 19 b6 transposes; or if 18 h3 ♗f8 19 ♗f2 g4 20 hxg4 hxg4 21 fxg4 ♗d6 22 a5?! ♖h7 23 ♗f3 ♔g7 intending ...♕h8 -/+ D.Tishin-M.Golubev, Alushta 2006.

18...g4 19 b6

If 19 ♗f2 g3! 20 hxg3 fxg3 21 ♗xg6 h4 22 ♗h2 (or 22 ♗xe5 ♘h5 23 ♗xg7 ♖xg7 24 f4 ♘hxf4 25 ♔h1 ♕g5 26 ♗f3 ♗d7 ∞ R.Ribeiro-M.Lorenzi, corr. 2002) 22...♘h5 23 ♖a2 ♘gf4 24 ♘e3 ♕g5 ∞ L.Riska-J.Havlik, Tabor 2005.

19...g3 20 ♔h1 *(D)*

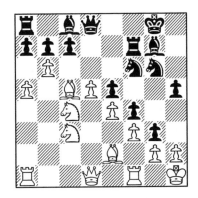

20...♘h7!?

The start of a lovely trap, but other moves may be better:

a) 20...♗f8!? 21 ♗g1 (not 21 ♗xf8? ♘e4! -+) 21...♘h4 22 ♖e1? (but if 22 hxg3 fxg3 23 ♕e1 ♘f5! ∞, or 22 ♖a2 ♘xg2! 23 ♘xe5 ♘h4 24 ♗c4 ♗h3 25 hxg3 fxg3 26 ♘xf7 ♕d7 ∞) 22...♘xg2! 23 ♔xg2 ♖g7 24 ♘xe5 gxh2+ 25 ♔h1 ♘xe4 0-1 T.Roussel Roozmon-P.Charbonneau, Montreal 2008.

b) 20...♘e8 21 bxc7 (or 21 ♘b5 ♗f8 22 ♗g1 ♕g5 23 ♖e1 h4 24 ♗f1 h3 =+ G.Siegel-J.Maiwald, German League

1998) 21...♖xc7 22 ♗g1 ♗f8 (or 22...♘h4!?) 23 d6 (if 23 ♘b5 ♖g7 24 ♘xa7 ♗h3! 25 gxh3 ♕h4 -/+) 23...♖g7 24 ♕d5+ ♔h7 25 ♘xe5 ♘f6 26 ♕d4 ♘xe5 27 ♕xe5 ♗xd6 ∞ V.Babula-R.Polzin, Austrian Team Ch. 2004.

21 d6

Or 21 ♘b5 ♕h4 22 ♗g1 ♗h3 23 gxh3! (not 23 ♖e1?? ♗xg2+! 24. ♔xg2 ♕h3+! 25 ♔xh3 ♘g5+ 26 ♔g2 ♘h4+ 27 ♔f1 g2+ 28 ♔f2 ♘h3 mate, V.Epishin-O.Cvitan, Switzerland 1997) 23...♕xh3 24 ♖f2 gxf2 25 ♗xf2 axb6 (M.Genutis-J.Cabrera Trujillo, Budapest 2008) 26 d6! +=.

21...♕h4 22 ♗g1 ♗h3 23 bxc7??

Missing the threat. White should have played 23 gxh3 ♕xh3 24 ♖f2! gxf2 25 ♗xf2 axb6 (or 25...cxb6 26 axb6 a6 27 ♗f1) 26 ♘d5! b5 27 ♘xc7 ♖d8 28 ♘xb5 += Ftacnik.

23...♗xg2+! 24 ♔xg2 ♕h3+! 25 ♔xh3 ♘g5+ 26 ♔g2 ♘h4+ 0-1

White resigned in L.Ftacnik-O.Cvitan, German League 1997, since 27 ♔h1 g2 is mate.

B: 9...♘d7 (D)

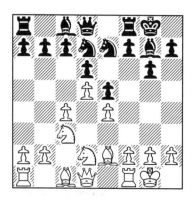

10 b4

Again, there is little point in delaying this. For instance, after 10 a3 (or 10 ♖b1 f5 11 b4 ♘f6 – *9...♘e8*) 10...f5 (10...a5 – *9...a5*) 11 b4 ♘f6 12 f3 f4 13 c5 g5 14 ♘c4 ♘g6 15 a4 (M.Koen-A.Botsari, European Team Ch., Debrecen 1992), Black is a tempo ahead on line A and should have no problems.

10...a5!?

A natural response, breaking up the white pawn structure and taking control of the c5-square. Play is similar to that after 9 b4 a5 in Chapter Eleven and can in fact transpose. Instead:

a) 10...♗h6 11 ♘b3 (or 11 c5!? f5 12 ♘b5 ♘f6? 13 ♘xc7! ♗xd2 14 cxd6 ♕xd6 15 ♘b5 ♕d8 16 ♗xd2 +/- V.Epishin-W.Uhlmann, Frankfurt 1990) 11...♗xc1 12 ♕xc1 f5 13 f4! +/= D.Yanofsky-S.Krstic, Siegen Olympiad 1970.

b) 10...f5 (D) is the most popular move, which generally transposes to line A (9...♘e8) after a subsequent ...♘d7-f6.

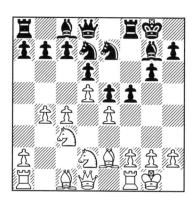

b1) 11 ♘b3 ♘f6 (or 11...fxe4! 12 ♘xe4 ♘f6 13 ♘g3 ♘f5 14 ♘xf5 ♗xf5 = V.Korchnoi-S.Gligoric, Havana 1969)

12 f3 f4 13 c5 g5 14 a4 ♘g6?! (14...h5! 15 a5 g4 ∞) 15 a5 h5 16 a6! +/- F.Andersson-A.Somerfield, British League 2005.

b2) 11 a4 a5!? (11...♘f6 – 9...♘e8) 12 bxa5 ♖xa5 13 ♘b3 ♖a8 – 10...a5 (note with 13 a4).

b2) 11 f3 f4 12 a4 (or if 12 c5 g5 13 ♘c4 ♘f6! – 9...♘e8) 12...g5 13 ♗a3 ♘g6 14 c5 ♖f7? (14...♘f6! – 9...♘e8) 15 c6! ♘f6 16 cxb7 ♗xb7 17 ♘c4 ♗c8 18 ♘a5 h5 19 ♘b5 a6 20 ♘a7 ♗d7 21 ♘7c6 +/- V.Korchnoi-M.Udovcic, Rovinj/Zagreb 1970.

b4) 11 c5!? dxc5 (11...♘f6 – 9...♘e8) 12 bxc5 ♘xc5 13 ♗a3 b6 (if 13...♘xe4 14 ♘dxe4 fxe4 15 ♘xe4 ♖f4 16 d6! += M.Gurevich-C.Mann, German League 2005) 14 ♗xc5 bxc5 15 ♘b3 (or 15 ♕b3 ♔h8 16 ♕c4 c6! 17 ♕xc5 cxd5 = P.Eljanov-A.Beliavsky, European Ch., Warsaw 2005) 15...♔h8 16 ♕d2 (or 16 ♗c4 ♖b8 17 ♘xc5 ♕d6 18 ♘b3 c6 =+ M.Taimanov-J.Sofrevski, Skopje 1970) 16...♖b8 17 ♖ad1 ♖b4 18 f3 ♕d6 19 ♕e3 ♕b6 20 ♖b1 ♘g8 21 ♘xc5 ♗h6 22 ♕f2 ♘f6 ∞ D.Mohrlok-I.Kopylov, corr. 1999.

11 bxa5!

11 ♗a3 axb4 12 ♗xb4 transposes to Chapter Eleven (see 12 ♘d2 in line C23).

11...♖xa5

Otherwise Black has problems regaining the pawn, e.g. 11...f5 12 ♘b3 ♘f6 (or 12...♔h8 13 f3 ♘g8 14 ♕c2 ♘gf6 15 exf5 gxf5 16 ♗g5 += L.Ftacnik-M.Mrva, Presov 1999) 13 f3 c5 14 dxc6 bxc6 15 ♕c2 ♗e6 16 ♗a3 ♘c8 17 ♖ad1 +/= B.Brinck Claussen-N.Borge, Copenhagen 1990.

12 ♘b3

If 12 a4 f5 13 ♗a3 (13 ♘b3! ♖a8 is the next note) 13...♖a8 14 ♗b4 is Chapter Eleven again (12 ♘d2 in line C23).

12...♖a8 13 ♗e3

White can also play 13 a4 f5 (D) and then:

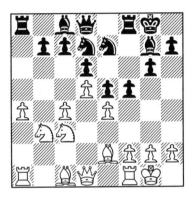

a) 14 a5 fxe4 (or 14...♘f6 15 f3 c5!? ∞ G.Grigore-L.Vajda, Rumanian Ch. 1998) 15 fxe4 ♘f6 16 ♘xf6+ ♗xf6 ∞ N.Krug-H.Schaack, German League 2004.

b) 14 ♗a3 b6! (or 14...♘f6!? 15 f3 ♗h6 16 c5 ♗e3+ 17 ♔h1 ♘h5 18 ♕e1 f4 19 ♘d1 ♘f5 20 exf5 ♘g3+ 21 hxg3 ♕g5 ∞ V.Vojvodic-Z.Popovic, Banja Luka 2008) 15 a5!? (15 ♗b4 is Chapter Eleven once more) 15...♘c5!? 16 ♘xc5 bxc5 17 ♗b2 fxe4 18 ♘xe4 ♘f5 ∞ M.Nacu-D.Dumitrescu, Rumanian Team Ch. 2005.

c) 14 f3! ♔h8 (if 14...b6 15 a5! ♘c5 16 axb6 ♖xa1 17 dxc7 +/-, or 15...bxa5 16 ♗e3 ♘f6 17 c5 a4 18 ♘d2 += N.Skalkotas-C.Escondrillas, Skopje Olympiad 1972; or 14...♘f6 15 c5) 15 a5 ♘g8 16 ♗e3 ♗h6 17 ♗f2 fxe4 18 fxe4 ♖xf2 19 ♔xf2 ♕h4+ 20 ♔g1 ♗e3+ 21

♔h1 (½-½ R.Schlaap-K.Bachmann, German League 1995) 21...♗f4 22 ♖xf4! ♕xf4 23 ♘b5 +=.

13...f5

13...b6 14 a4 ♘c5 (or 14...f5 15 f3) 15 a5 f5 16 f3 transposes below, or if 15...♕xb3 bxa5 17 c5 c6 (R.Tozer-P.Girinath, Oakham 1988) 18 cxd6 ♕xd6 19 ♕b6! +=.

14 f3 b6

It would be inconsistent for Black to give up on the queenside now; e.g. 14...f4 (or 14...♘f6 15 c5) 15 ♗f2 g5 16 c5 ♘f6 17 a4 h5 18 a5 ♘g6 19 cxd6 cxd6 20 ♘a4 (or 20 ♘b5 ♘e8 21 ♗b6 +/- K.Robatsch-J.Macles, Nice Olympiad 1974) 21...g4 21 ♘b6 +/- A.Tikovsky-B.Moldawskij, German League 1996.

15 a4 ♘c5 (D)

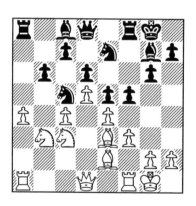

Again if 15...f4 (or 15...♘f6 16 a5 bxa5 17 c5 +=; or 15...♔h8 16 a5 ♖b8 17 axb6 cxb6 18 ♘b5 += M.Manolache-L.Vajda, Bucharest 2001) 16 ♗f2 g5 17 a5 bxa5?! (17...♘c5) 18 c5 ♘f6 19 ♘xa5 h5 20 ♕b3 +/- M.Shadarevian-C.Reyes Najera, Novi Sad Olympiad 1990.

16 a5

It is too soon for 16 ♘xc5?! bxc5,

when Black has few problems; e.g. 17 ♕d2 (or 17 ♘b5 f4 18 ♗f2 g5 19 ♕b3 h5 20 ♖fd1 ♖a6 ∞ I.Farago-G.Kluger, Hungarian Ch. 1965) 17...f4 18 ♗f2 g5 19 ♖fb1 ♔h8 20 ♖b3 h5 21 h3 ♘g8 22 a5 ♘h6 =+ S.Brittner-R.Jones, Istanbul Olympiad 2000.

16...♗d7

Black has also tried:

a) 16...f4 17 ♗f2 g5 18 ♕c2 h5 19 axb6 ♖xa1 20 ♖xa1 cxb6 (O.Panno-J.Granda Zuniga, Buenos Aires 1993) 21 ♘b5 +=.

b) 16...fxe4 17 fxe4 ♖xf1+ 18 ♗xf1 ♘xb3 19 ♕xb3 ♔h8 20 ♘b5! ♘g8 21 ♕c3 ♘f6 22 axb6 ♖xa1 23 ♕xa1 cxb6 24 ♕a8 +/- A.Beliavsky-Xie Jun, Belgrade 2000.

c) 16...♘xb3 17 ♕xb3 ♖xa5 (or 17...bxa5 18 c5 += R.Van Wessel-G.Regniers, Ghent 2008) 18 ♖xa5 bxa5 19 c5 += J.Johansson-A.Saastamoinen, Jyvaskyla 1996.

17 ♕c2! (D)

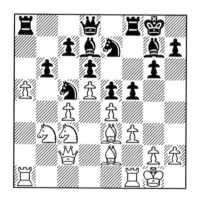

Not yet 17 ♘xc5 bxc5 18 a6 ♕c8! =, or 17 axb6 ♖xa1 18 ♘xa1 cxb6 19 ♕c2 ♘c8 ∞ J.Emberger-H.Kotz, Austrian Team Ch. 1996. But now 18 ♘xc5 bxc5

19 a6 is a real threat and White has a strong initiative.

B.Gelfand-A.Morozevich, Monte Carlo (rapid) 2007, continued **17...fxe4** [committal, but if 17...♖a6 18 ♖fb1! or 17...♘xb3 18 ♕xb3 ♖xa5 19 ♖xa5 bxa5 20 c5!] **18 fxe4 ♖xf1+ 19 ♗xf1 ♔h8 20 ♘xc5! dxc5** [if 20...bxc5 21 a6! ♕c8 22 ♕a2] **21 ♕b2 ♕b8 22 axb6 ♖xa1 23 ♕xa1 cxb6 24 ♕b2 ♕c7 25 ♘b5 ♕b8 26 ♗g5 ♘c8?!** [26...♘g8!? was possible] **27 ♗d8!** [threatening ♗c7] **27...♗xb5 28 ♕xb5 ♕d6 29 ♗c7 ♕e7** [not 29...♕xc7?? 30 ♕e8+] **30 ♕c6 ♗f8 31 g3 ♕g5 32 ♕e6?** [32 ♔g2!] **32...♕e3+ 33 ♔g2 ♕xe4+ 34 ♔f2 ♕f5+ 35 ♕xf5 gxf5 36 ♗xe5+ ♔g8** and Black managed to hold the draw.

C: 9...c5 *(D)*

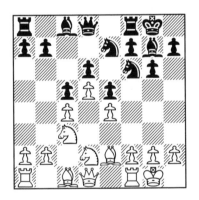

Quite an apposite move: since White's strategy is based on playing c4-c5 and ♘d2-c4, Black aims to puts a stop to it straightaway. Furthermore, compared with 9 ♘e1 c5, the position of White's knight on d2 makes a reaction with f2-f4 less effective.

10 ♖b1

Black has no problems after 10 dxc6 bxc6 11 b4 (or 11 ♘b3 d5!? 12 cxd5 cxd5 13 exd5 ♘exd5 14 ♘xd5 ♘xd5 15 ♗f3 ♗b7 16 ♕d2 ♖b8 17 ♖d1 ♘f4 = E.Gleizerov-P.Steiner, Oberwart 1996) 11...d5 12 b5 (or 12 ♗a3 ♖e8 13 ♖e1 ♗e6 14 ♗f1 dxe4 15 ♘dxe4 ♘xe4 16 ♘xe4 ♘f5 = M.Ulibin-V.Bologan, Chalkidiki 1992) 12...d4 13 ♘a4 ♘h5 14 ♘c5 ♘f4 15 ♘db3 (S.Lputian-A.Fedorov, Elista Olympiad 1998) 15...♘xe2+!? 16 ♕xe2 a6 ∞.

10 a3!? seems a wasted tempo as White will have to play ♖b1 sooner or later, but at least he does not have to reckon with ...c5xb4 (as in the note with 10...b6 below). Then 10...♘d7!? (10...♘e8 11 b4 b6 12 ♕b3!? f5 13 a4 fxe4 14 ♘dxe4 ♘f5 15 ♗g5 ♘f6 16 ♗d3 ♘d4, U.Goy-C.Gustavsson, Porz 1991, 17 ♕b2 +/=) 11 b4 b6 12 ♘b5 ♘f6 13 ♖b1 ♘e8 14 ♘b3 a6 15 ♘c3 f5 16 f3 ♗d7 17 ♗d2 (P.Hesse-Zsu.Polgar, Leipzig 1984) 17...cxb4!? 18 axb4 a5 ∞.

10...♘e8

The most logical continuation. Other moves give White an advantage:

a) 10...a5 11 a3 – *9...a5 10 a3 c5 11 ♖b1* in line D2.

b) 10...♗h6 11 a3!? ♘e8 12 b4 b6 (or 12...f5 13 ♘b3 ♗xc1 14 ♕xc1 b6 15 f4! +/- M.Frolik-T.Zeleny, Czech League 2005) 13 ♘b3 ♗xc1 14 ♕xc1 ♔g7 15 f4 +/- S.Giemsa-L.Thiede, German League 1994.

c) 10...♘d7 11 ♘b5! ♘b8 (or 11...♕b6 12 b4 cxb4 13 a3! bxa3 14 c5! ♘xc5 15 ♗xa3 ♕d8 16 ♘xd6! +/- S.Lputian-A.Khalifman, USSR Ch., Minsk 1987) 12 a3 f5 13 b4 ♘a6 14 ♘b3 b6 15 bxc5!

♘xc5 16 ♘xc5 bxc5 17 f3 ♔h8 18 ♗d2 ♘g8 19 ♕a4 (Li Wenliang-E.Gufeld, Beijing 1996) 19...a6 20 ♘c3 ♗d7 +=.

d) 10...b6 11 b4 cxb4!? (otherwise 11...♘e8 – *10...♘e8*) 12 ♖xb4 ♘d7 13 ♖b1 ♘c5 14 ♘b3 f5 15 ♘xc5 bxc5 (a main line position with a pair of knights exchanged) 16 ♗d2 (simpler 16 f3 +=) 16...fxe4 17 ♘xe4 ♘f5 18 ♗d3 ♘d3 19 f3 ♕c7 20 ♕a4 ♗f5 21 ♕a5 ♕d7 22 ♖b2 ♖ab8 23 ♖fb1 ♖xb2 24 ♖xb2 ♗xe4 25 ♗xe4 (E.Bukic-S.Gligoric, Yugoslavia 1971) 25...♕g4! ∞.

11 b4 b6

11...cxb4 makes little sense with the knight on e8, while if 11...f5 12 bxc5 dxc5 13 a4 ♘d6 14 ♗a3 b6 15 a5 ♗h6 16 ♗c1 ♗d7 17 ♗d3 += L.Ogaard-C.Micheli, Skopje Olympiad 1972.

12 bxc5

The alternative plan is 12 a4 f5 13 a5, but then Black can try 13...♗h6!? 14 ♗d3 ♘f6 15 axb6 axb6 16 bxc5 bxc5 17 ♘b3 ♗xc1 18 ♕xc1 ∞ P.Sinkovics-Zsu.Polgar, Hungarian Ch. 1986.

12...bxc5

Worse is 12...dxc5?! 13 a4 a5 14 ♕b3 ♖b8 (or 14...♖a6 15 f4 exf4 16 ♘f3 g5 17 ♘xg5 ♘g6 18 ♘f3 ♗g4 19 h3 +/= G.Orlov-Kr.Georgiev, Belgrade 1988) 15 f4 exf4 16 ♘f3 ♗h6! 17 ♘b5 g5 (V.Bogdanovski-Kr.Georgiev, Belgrade 1988) 18 e5!? +=.

13 ♘b3 (D)

13 ♕a4!? is another option; e.g. 13...f5 (or 13...♗h6 14 ♘b3 ♗xc1 15 ♖fxc1 a5 16 ♘d2 f5 17 ♕b3 ♖a6 18 ♕d1 ♘f6 19 ♖b8 += K.Sakaev-M.Erdogdu, Saint Vincent 2005) 14 ♘b3!? (if 14 f3 ♗h6 15 ♘b3 ♗xc1 16 ♖fxc1 ♘f6 ∞

S.Otterstätter-D.Hausrath, German Junior Ch. 1992) 14...fxe4 15 ♘xe4 ♘f6 16 f3 += S.Gligoric-V.Ciocaltea, Hastings 1971/72.

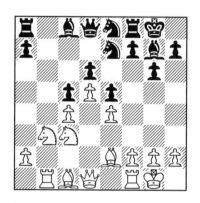

13...f5

Black has also tried:

a) 13...a5 14 a4 ♘c7 15 ♘xc5 dxc5 16 d6 ♘e6 17 dxe7 ♕xe7 18 ♘d5 += K.Lerner-O.Renet, Geneva 1988.

b) 13...♔h8 14 ♕c2!? f5 15 f4 ♘g8 16 exf5 ♗xf5 17 ♗d3 ♖b8 18 ♗d2 += V.Baikov-M.Krasenkow, Moscow 1989.

c) 13...h6!? 14 ♗d2 f5 15 f3 ♘f6 16 ♗d3 f4 17 ♘b5 ♘e8 18 ♗a5 ♕d7 19 ♗c2 += V.Bogdanovski-M.Sarwinski, Bytom 1988.

14 ♗g5

If 14 ♗d2 ♘f6!? 15 f3 ♘h5 with counterplay, K.Helmers-P.Popovic, World Junior Ch. 1977.

14...h6

Other moves give White better play:

a) 14...♔h8 15 exf5 gxf5 16 f4 h6 17 ♗h4 exf4 18 ♕d2 ♘f6 19 ♗xf6 ♗xf6 20 ♗h5 ♗a6 21 ♘e2 ♗xc4 22 ♕xf4 ♗xd5 23 ♕xh6+ ♔g8 24 ♘f4 with the initiative, L.Polugaevsky-G.Timoshenko, Moscow 1990.

b) 14...♘f6 15 ♘xc5 dxc5 16 d6 ♗e6 17 dxe7 ♕xe7 18 ♘d5 ♕d7 19 ♗xf6 ♗xf6 20 ♖b5 +/= C.Shephard-A.O'Duill, corr. 1982.

c) 14...♗f6 15 ♗d2 ♔h8 16 ♔h1 (if 16 f3 f4 17 ♕c1 g5 18 ♘d1 h5 19 ♘f2 ♘g8 20 ♘a5 ♘h6 21 ♘c6 ♕d7 ∞ P.Lukacs-P.Thipsay, Kolhapur 1987) 16...♘g8 17 ♘c1 ♗g7?! (but if 17...♗g5 18 exf5 ♗xf5 19 ♗d3 += Lobron) 18 exf5 gxf5 19 f4 +/- E.Lobron-A.Kovalev, Debrecen 1992.

15 ♗xe7

Also good is 15 ♗d2 g5 (or 15...♔h8 16 ♘b5 ♘g8 17 f3 ♘gf6 18 ♗d3 f4 19 ♘a5 g5 20 ♘c6 ♕d7, K.Sakaev-A.Fedorov, Moscow 2005, 21 ♗c3 +=) 16 ♘b5 a6?! (if 16...fxe4 17 ♗a5 ♕d7 18 ♘d2 +/=; or 16...♘g6 17 ♗h5 ♕f6 18 ♘a5 with the initiative; but 16...♗d7!? is possible) 17 ♗a5 ♕d7 18 ♘c3 ♘g6 19 exf5 ♕xf5 20 ♘a4 ♖b8 21 ♘b6 += M.Gurevich-A.Fedorov, Belfort 1999.

15...♕xe7 16 ♘a5 (D)

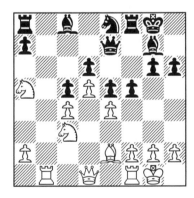

16...♘f6

The usual continuation, though Black has tried numerous others:

a) 16...♕h4 17 ♕a4 (threatening ♕c6; S.Bell-L.Keely, Sheffield 1999)

17...♕d8 18 ♘b7 ♕d7 19 ♕xd7 ♗xd7 20 ♖b3 +=.

b) 16...♗f6 17 ♕a4 ♘g7 18 ♘c6 ♕d7 (G.Schebler-F.Portisch, Budapest 1993) 19 exf5 +=.

c) 16...♕g5 17 exf5 (if 17 ♕a4 ♘f6! 18 ♕c6 ♘xe4 ∞) 17...gxf5 18 ♖b3 ♗d7 19 ♘c6 ♔h8 20 ♔h1 ♖g8 21 f4 exf4 22 ♗f3 += S.Bell-D.Walker, Newcastle 1995.

d) 16...♖f7 17 exf5 gxf5 18 ♗h5 ♖f8 19 ♘c6 += G.Andruet-J.M.Degraeve, French Ch. 1987.

e) 16...h5 17 ♘c6 ♕g5 18 exf5 ♗xf5 19 ♖b7 e4 20 ♕c1 += G .Flear-D.Sellos, Paris 1988.

17 ♘c6 ♕e8

The alternative is 17...♕d7 18 exf5 (or 18 ♕c2 f4 19 f3 ♘h7 20 ♖b2 ♗f6 21 ♖fb1 ♗d8 22 a4 ♘f6 23 a5 with the initiative, W.Beilfuss-R.Schoene, German League 1992) 18...gxf5 19 ♕c2!? ♖e8 20 ♖b3 e4 21 ♕d2 ♗b7 22 ♘a5 (22 ♕f4!? +/=) 22...♗a6 23 ♖fb1 ♘g4 (V.Kozlov-B.Taborov, Belgorod 1989) and now 24 ♘c6 with a slight edge for White.

18 ♗d3

18 f3 ♖f7 19 ♕a4 (R.Dautov-M.Krasenkow, Moscow 1990) 19...♘h5!? with counterplay. Or 18 exf5 gxf5 19 ♕a4 (19 ♘b5) 19...♖f7 20 ♘b5 ♕d7 21 ♖b3 f4 22 ♖fb1 ♗f8 23 ♕a5 ♖g7 ∞ M.Krasenkow-V.Neverov, Odessa 1989.

More promising is 18 ♘b5 ♕d7 19 exf5 gxf5 20 ♖b3 ♖f7 (if 20...♔h8, M.Gurevich-A.Shirov, Prague rapid 2002, 21 f4!? +/= Tsesarsky) 21 ♖a3 (or 21 f4!? +/=) 21...a6 22 ♘c3 e4 23 ♕d2 f4 24 ♘a4 f3 (I.Cosma-A.Fedorov, Rumania 1995) 25 gxf3 +/= Cosma, and if 25...♕h3? 26 ♘b6 gives Black serious problems; e.g. 26...♘h5 27 fxe4 ♕xa3 28 ♗xh5 +-, or 26...♘d7 27 ♘xa8 exf3 28 ♖xf3 ♖xf3 29 ♗xf3 ♕xf3 30 ♕e3 ♕g4+ 31 ♔h1 +-.

18...♖f7!

If 18...f4 19 ♘b5 ♕d7 20 f3 g5 21 ♕e1! ♘e8 (21...a6 22 ♕a5 +/=) 22 ♕a5 ♗f6 23 ♘bxa7 +/- Y.Dokhoian-M.Wahls, German League 1991.

19 ♖b3 (D)

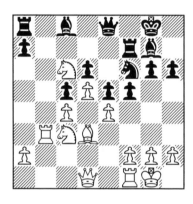

19 f4!? comes into consideration. The text was tested by Mikhail Gurevich in a couple of games:

a) 19...♗f8 20 ♕c2 f4 21 f3 (21 ♗e2 – *19...f4*) 21...g5 22 ♗e2 ♗g7 23 ♖fb1 ♗d7 24 ♖b8 ♖xb8 25 ♖xb8 ♕h5! 26 ♘d8 g4 27 fxg4 ♕h4 (or 27...♘xg4 28 h3 ♕h4! 29 hxg4 ♕e1+ 30 ♗f1 ♕e3+ 31 ♕f2 ♕xc3 = Bologan) 28 ♕d2 (not 28 h3? ♗xg4! -+) 28...♗xg4 29 ♘e6 ♗xe6 30 dxe6 ♕h3 31 ♗f3 ♕xe6 = M.Gurevich-V.Bologan, Belfort 1999.

b) 19...f4 20 ♗e2 ♗f8 21 ♕c2 ♗d7!? (21...g5 is still possible) 22 ♖fb1 (if 22 ♘a5 g5 23 ♖fb1 g4 with counterplay, Tsesarsky) 22...♗xc6 23 dxc6 ♕xc6 24 ♘d5 (White has sufficient compensation for the pawn, but Black is fine as

well) 24...♔g7 25 ♖b5 ♗e7 26 ♕d3 ♗d8 27 ♗d1 a6! 28 ♖5b2 ♖aa7 29 h3 ♗a5 30 a3 h5 31 ♗c2 ♘h7 ½-½ M.Gurevich-M.Hebden, Clichy 2001.

D: 9...a5 (D)

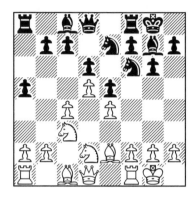

The main line, hampering b2-b4 and c4-c5. White now has to expend two moves (a2-a3, ♖b1) to achieve his plan, whereas Black has only spent one (...a7-a5).

D1: 10 ♖b1 *291*
D2: 10 a3 *293*

Naturally these transpose if White follows each move up with the other one. Alternative ideas offer little chance of an advantage:

a) 10 f4 exf4 11 ♖xf4 ♘d7 12 ♘f3 (or 12 ♖f1 f5 with counterplay) 12...♘c5 13 ♗e3!? ♗h6 14 ♕d2 ♗xf4 15 ♗xf4 f6 16 ♗h6 ♖f7 17 ♖f1 ♗d7 18 ♕d4 ♕e8 ∞ P.Ricardi-G.Milos, Buenos Aires 1990.

b) 10 c5!? dxc5 11 ♘c4 ♘e8 12 f4 (I.Nemet-F.Maurer, Swiss Ch. 1999) 12...exf4 13 ♗xf4 ♘d6 ∞.

c) 10 ♘b3 ♘d7 11 ♗e3 b6 12 ♘d2 f5 13 f3 f4 14 ♗f2 g5 15 a3 ♘f6 16 b4 g4 17 fxg4 axb4 18 ♘b5 bxa3 19 ♖xa3 ♖xa3 20 ♘xa3 ♘g6 ∞ J.Corral Blanco-L.Bass, Alcobendas 1994.

d) 10 b3 ♘d7 (or 10...c5 11 a3 ♘e8 12 ♖b1 f5 13 b4 axb4 14 axb4 b6 15 ♕b3 ♘f6 16 ♗d3 ♗h6! 17 ♖b2 ♖a1 18 ♕c2 ♗f4 ∞ A.Karpov-G.Kasparov, 17th matchgame, Seville 1987) 11 ♗a3 f5 12 b4 (playing 9 b4 a5 10 ♗a3 a tempo down) 12...axb4 13 ♗xb4 ♗h6 14 ♘b3 b6 15 a4 fxe4 (or 15...♘c5!?) 16 ♘xe4 ♘f5 17 ♗d2 ♕h4 18 ♘g3 ♘c5 19 ♘xc5 bxc5 ∞ J.Ehlvest-Y.Shulman, New York Open 1998.

D1: 10 ♖b1 (D)

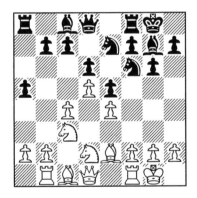

10...♗d7

The main move here is 10...♘d7, when 11 a3 transposes to D22. If immediately 11 b4 axb4 12 ♖xb4 f5 13 f3 f4 14 ♖a4 ♖xa4 15 ♕xa4 (or 15 ♘xa4 h5 16 ♘c3 g5 with counterplay, V.Dambrauskas-M.Esses, corr. 2001) 15...♘c5 16 ♕a3 ♗d7 ∞ B.Naves Miranda-S.Castelao Rodriguez, Gijon 1999.

Against other continuations White

plays 11 a3, so these are covered via 10 a3, 11 ♖b1 in the notes to D2.

11 b3 (D)

Forestalling ...a5-a4. Instead 11 a3 transposes to D21, while 11 b4 again leads to an unclear position after 11...axb4 12 ♖xb4 b6 (12...♘c8!?) 13 a4 ♘e8 14 ♕c2 f5 15 ♘b5 ♘f6 16 f3 f4 17 ♗b2 h5 ∞ M.Dominguez-F.Prates, Roque Saenz Pena 1997.

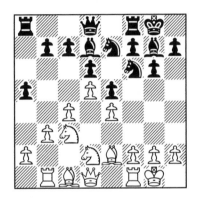

11...c5

White obtains an advantage after:

a) 11...♗h6 12 c5! dxc5 13 ♘c4 ♗g7 14 ♗g5 ♘e8 15 d6 cxd6 16 ♘xd6 ♗c6 (L.Ftacnik-I.Smirin, Polanica Zdroj 1995) 17 ♘xb7! ♕xd1 18 ♖bxd1 f6 19 ♗e3 ♗xb7 20 ♖d7 +/- Ftacnik.

b) 11...♔h8 12 a3 ♘eg8 13 b4 axb4 14 axb4 ♘e8 15 c5 f5 16 f3 ♘gf6 17 ♘c4 ♘h5 18 g3 ♘ef6 19 ♖f2 ♕e7 20 b5 dxc5 21 b6 c6 22 d6 ♕e8 23 ♘a4! fxe4 24 ♘xc5 exf3 (L.Ftacnik-Z.Lanka, Hamburg 2001) 25 ♖xf3!? += Ftacnik.

c) 11...♘c8 12 a3 ♘b6 13 ♕c2 ♕e7 (or 13...♗h6 14 ♘b5 ♕e7 15 b4 axb4 16 axb4 ♖fc8 17 c5 ♘a4 18 ♖a1 ♕e8 19 ♘a3 ♗f8 20 ♘b3 +/- L.Psakhis-V.Spasov, Debrecen 1992) 14 b4 axb4 15 axb4 ♘a4 16 ♘xa4 ♗xa4 17 ♕c3 ♗h6 18 ♕d3! c6 19 ♘f3 ♗g7! 20 ♗g5 += M.Gurevich-I.Smirin, Elenite 1994.

However, two other moves deserve attention:

d) 11...c6!? 12 a3 ♕c7 (or 12...♕b8 13 b4 axb4 14 axb4 cxd5 15 cxd5 ♖c8 16 ♗b2 b5 17 ♗d3 ♕b6 18 ♘b3 ♗h6 19 ♘a5 ♖c7 ∞ I.Nemet-J.Gallagher, Swiss Team Ch. 1994) 13 ♗b2 ♘e8 14 b4 axb4 15 axb4 f5 16 ♕b3 cxd5 17 cxd5 (N.Nikcevic-M.Tosic, Yugoslav Ch. 1991) 17...♘f6 with counterplay.

e) 11...♘e8!? 12 a3 f5 13 b4 axb4 14 axb4 ♘f6 15 c5 (or 15 f3 c6 16 dxc6 ♘xc6 17 ♘b5 ♗e6 18 ♕c2 ♖c8 19 ♕d3 ♘h5 20 g3 ♕g5 21 ♘b3 f4 22 g4 ♖fd8 23 ♗d2 ♘f6 ∞ R.Sherbakov-J.Nunn, Hastings 1993/94) 15...fxe4 (if 15...♔h8 16 f3 ♘h5 17 ♘c4 ♘f4 18 ♗e3 ♘c8 19 ♔h1! +/= M.Gurevich-B.Gelfand, Munich 1993) 16 ♘dxe4 ♘f5 17 ♗g5 h6 18 ♗xf6 (or if 18 ♘xf6+ ♗xf6 19 ♗d2 ♗g7 20 ♗d3 ♕e7 21 ♕c1, L.Ftacnik-J.Polgar, Bled Olympiad 2002, 21...♔h7 22 ♕c2 ♕f6 23 ♖be1 ♘d4 24 ♕b2 = Ftacnik) 18...♗xf6 19 b5 b6 20 c6 ♗c8 21 ♗d3 ♗g5 22 ♖a1 ♖xa1 23 ♕xa1 (E.Gleizerov-J.Nunn, Leeuwarden 1995) 23...♘d4 ∞.

12 a3 ♘e8 13 b4 axb4

Worse is 13...b6?! 14 bxc5 dxc5 (or 14...bxc5 15 ♕b4 +=) 15 ♕b3!? ♘c8 16 ♗b2! ♘ed6 17 ♖be1 ♖e8 18 ♕c2 +/- Y.Dokhoian-W.Uhlmann, German League 1993.

14 axb4 b6 15 ♕b3

If instead 15 bxc5 bxc5 16 ♘b3 (16 ♕b3 ♘c8 transposes below) 16...f5 17 ♗g5 h6 18 ♗d2 fxe4 19 ♘xe4 ♘f5 20 ♖a1 ♘f6 21 ♗d3 ♘xe4 22 ♗xe4 ♕f6 =

H.Harestad-E.Gullaksen, Norwegian Team Ch. 1997; or 15 ♘b3 cxb4!? (15...f5) 16 ♘b5 f5 17 f3 ♘f6 (17...♘c8!?) 18 ♗d3 ♗xb5 19 cxb5 ♘d7 20 ♗d2 ♘c5 21 ♗xb4 ♗h6 ∞ Z.Azmaiparashvili-J.Nunn, Amsterdam 1990.

15...♘c8 *(D)*

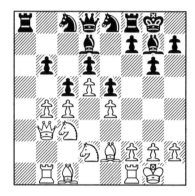

The most solid continuation, covering b6 and d6. Other moves give White more chances:

a) 15...♗h6 16 bxc5 bxc5 17 ♕b6 ♕c8 18 ♘f3 ♗xc1 19 ♖fxc1 +/= G.Van Laatum-W.Uhlmann, Dieren 1990.

b) 15...f5 16 bxc5 bxc5 17 ♕b6 ♗h6 18 ♕xd8 ♖xd8 19 ♖b6 ♘c8 20 ♖b7 ♘f6 21 exf5 gxf5 22 ♘f3 ♗xc1 23 ♖xc1 += L.Portisch-M.Paragua, Linares 2000.

c) 15...♘c7 16 ♘b5 ♘xb5 17 cxb5 ♗h6 18 bxc5 dxc5 19 ♘c4 ♗xc1 20 ♖fxc1 += M.Frolik-R.Szczepanek, Karvina 2001.

16 ♘f3

White can also insert 16 bxc5 bxc5 and then 17 ♘f3 (or 17 ♗b2 ♗h6 18 ♘f3 ♖a6 19 ♖a1 ♖b6 20 ♕c2 f5 21 ♖fb1 ♘f6 22 exf5 e4 ∞ T.Tuomala-W.Watson, Jyvaskyla 1991) 17...f5 (or 17...h6 18 ♘e1 f5 19 f3 f4 20 ♘d3 g5 21 ♘f2 h5 22

♗d2 ♘f6 23 h3 g4 24 fxg4 hxg4 25 hxg4 ♗h6 ∞ L.Müller-J.Gallagher, Lenk 1992) 18 ♗g5 ♘f6 19 ♗d2 g5 20 exf5 ♗xf5 21 ♖a1 ♖xa1 22 ♖xa1 e4 23 ♘e1 ♗d4 24 ♖a2 ♗xf2+ 25 ♔xf2 e3+ 26 ♔g1 exd2 27 ♖xd2 ∞ T.Henrichs-A.Bachmann, Bad Wiessee 2008.

16...f5

Or 16...h6 17 ♘e1 f5 18 f3 f4 19 ♘d3 h5 20 ♗d2 g5 21 ♘f2 ♖f6 (or 21...♘f6) 22 h3 ♖g6 23 bxc5 bxc5 ∞, but not 22...dxc5? 24 ♘b5 +/- G.Beckhuis-O.Dannevig, Gausdal 1992, as Black has just created a lot of weaknesses.

17 ♗g5 ♗f6 18 ♗d2 g5 (D)

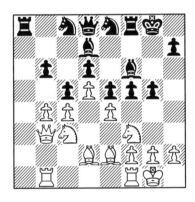

Black has typical kingside counterplay. L.Ftacnik-B.Socko, Czech League 2004, concluded **19 h3** [if 19 exf5 ♗xf5 20 ♖a1 ♖xa1 21 ♖xa1 e4 22 ♘e1 ♗d4 ∞] **19...g4 20 hxg4 fxg4 21 ♘h2 ♗g5 22 ♕d1 h5** [or 22...♗xd2 23 ♕xd2 cxb4 24 ♖xb4 ♕h4 =] **23 g3 ♕f6 24 bxc5 bxc5 25 ♖b7 ♖a7 26 ♖xa7 ♘xa7 27 f3 ♗xd2 28 ♕xd2 gxf3 29 ♘xf3 ♕g7 30 ♕g5 ½-½**.

D2: 10 a3 (D)

The main line, and now Black has two main responses:

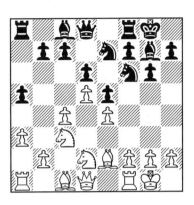

D21: 10...♗d7 *294*
D22: 10...♘d7 *296*

Also occasionally played are:

a) 10...c6 11 ♖b1 (if 11 ♖a2!? ♗d7 12 b4 axb4 13 axb4 ♖xa2 14 ♘xa2 b5 15 dxc6 ♘xc6 16 cxb5 ♘d4 with compensation, L.Ftacnik-S.Bercys, Philadelphia 2006) 11...b5!? (or 11...♕c7 12 dxc6 bxc6 13 b4 axb4 14 axb4 d5 15 b5 += A.Blees-V.Moskalenko, Budapest 1990) 12 dxc6 b4 13 axb4 axb4 14 ♘b5 ♘xc6 15 ♘b3 ♗e6 16 ♕d3 ♘e8 17 ♗e3 +/- V.Epishin-J.Nunn, Vienna 1991.

b) 10...c5 11 ♖b1 ♘e8 12 b4 axb4 13 axb4 b6 14 bxc5 bxc5 15 ♘b3 (if 15 ♕b3 f5 16 ♕b6 ♕b6 ♕d7 17 ♘f3 h6 18 ♗d2 ♘f6 19 ♗d3 ♖a6 20 ♕b2 ♘h5 ∞ L.Ftacnik-A.Sznapik, Prague 1985) 15...f5 16 f3 (if 16 ♗g5 h6 17 ♗d2 ♘f6 18 f3 g5 19 ♖a1, A.Shirov-M.Antonsen, World Junior Ch. 1988, 19...♖xa1 20 ♕xa1 ♘g6 ∞ Shirov) 16...♔h8 17 ♗d2 ♘g8 18 ♖a1 ♖xa1 19 ♕xa1 ♗h6 20. exf5 gxf5 21 ♗xh6 ♘xh6 22 f4 += L.Psakhis-J.Pigott, Oostende 1993.

c) 10...♘e8 11 ♖b1 f5 12 b4 axb4 (or 12...♘f6 13 c5! axb4 14 axb4 transposing) 13 axb4 ♘f6 (this more often arises via 10...♘d7, though it makes little sense via that move order; here if 13...g5 14 exf5 ♗xf5 15 ♘de4 h6 16 ♗d3 ♘f6 17 ♘xf6+ ♖xf6 18 ♘e4 ♗xe4 19 ♗xe4 ♘f5 20 ♗b2 ♕d7 21 ♖a1 with the initiative, L.Ftacnik-Z.Lanka, Koszalin 1999) 14 c5! ♔h8 (if 14...fxe4 15 ♘dxe4 ♘f5 16 ♘xf6+ ♗xf6 17 ♗g4 h5 18 ♗f3 ♗e7 19 c6 b6 20 ♗e4 += M.Ulibin-S.Kositsin, Pavlodar 1991; or 14...♗h6 15 cxd6 cxd6 16 f3 ♗e3+ 17 ♔h1 f4 18 ♘c4 ♗xc1 19 ♕xc1 g5 20 ♘b5 += A.Shneider-B.Asanov, Pavlodar 1982) 15 f3 ♘h5 (or 15...f4 16 ♘c4 ♘e8 17 ♘a4 ♖b8 18 b5 +/- K.Sakaev-Ma.Tseitlin, St Petersburg 1997) 16 ♘c4 ♘g8 (or 16...♘f4 17 ♗e3 g5 18 b5 dxc5, A.Khalifman-S.Dolmatov, Moscow rapid 1992, 19 ♗xc5 +/- Khalifman) 17 b5 b6 18 cxd6 cxd6 19 ♗e3 ♖b8 20 ♘a4 +/- A.Khalifman-F.Nijboer, Ter Apel 1993.

D21: 10...♗d7 *(D)*

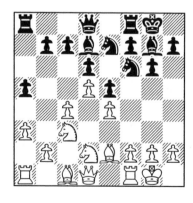

11 ♖b1

Alternatively:

a) 11 b3 usually returns to D1 after a subsequent ♖b1 (11...c5 12 ♖b1, 11...c6 12 ♖b1, 11...♘e8 12 ♖b1, etc), but ♗b2 is sometimes tried instead; e.g. 11...c6!? (other lines are 11...c5 12 dxc6?! bxc6 13 c5 d5 14 ♗b2 ♖b8 15 ♖e1 ♗e6 ∞ I.Nemet-B.Heim, Bern 1988; or 11...♘e8 12 ♗b2 f5 13 b4 ♘f6 14 c5, R.Douven-F.Nijboer, Dutch Ch. 1990, 14...fxe4 15 ♘dxe4 ♘f5 with counterplay) 12 ♗b2 (or 12 ♖a2!? c5 13 ♖b2 ♘e8 14 b4 axb4 15 axb4 b6 16 bxc5 bxc5 17 ♕b3 ♘c8 18 ♘f3 h6 ∞ M.Gurevich-L.Kritz, Metz 2004) 12...♗h6 (if 12...c5 13 ♘b5 ♘e8 14 b4 axb4 15 axb4 ♖xa1 16 ♕xa1 ♗h6 17 ♘xd6! ♘xd6 18 bxc5 ♗xd2 19 cxd6 ♘c8 20 c5 with a strong initiative, M.Ulibin-A.Galkin, Russian Ch. 1996) 13 c5 (or 13 dxc6 ♘xc6 14 ♘b5 ♗e6 15 ♗d3 ♘d7 16 ♘b1 ♘c5 17 ♘1c3 ♘a7 18 ♘xa7 ♖xa7 19 ♗c2 ♖a6 ∞ Shen Yang-L.Van Wely, Moscow 2009) 13...dxc5 14 ♘c4 cxd5 15 exd5 e4 16 ♘a4 ♘exd5 17 ♘xc5 ♗c6 18 ♕d4 ♘f4 19 ♕xd8 ♘xe2+ 20 ♔h1 ♖fxd8 21 ♗xf6 ♖e8 22 ♘d6 ♗f8 23 ♘xe8 ♗xc5 with compensation, R.Jannsen-F.Nijboer, Dutch Ch. 1999.

b) 11 ♖a2!? causes Black few problems after 11...c5 (if 11...a4 12 b4 axb3 13 ♘xb3 b6 14 a4 ♔h8 15 ♗e3 ♘fg8 16 ♕d2 f5 17 f3 ♘f6 18 ♖fa1 f4 19 ♗f2 g5 20 a5 bxa5 21 c5 += W.Beisswanger-M.Krämer, German League 2004) 12 dxc6 (if 12 b3 ♘e8 13 ♖b2 f5 14 b4 axb4 15 axb4 b6 ∞ G.Kamsky-A.Shirov, Dos Hermanas 1995; or 12 ♕c2 ♘e8 13 b4 axb4 14 axb4, A.Isoev-A.Kudriashov, USSR Team Ch. 1991, 14...cxb4!? 15 ♘b5 f5 with counterplay) 12...bxc6 13 b4 axb4 14 axb4 ♖xa2 15 ♞xa2 ♕a8 16 ♞c3 d5 ∞ G.Flear-M.Gurevich, Tel Aviv 1989.

11...a4 *(D)*

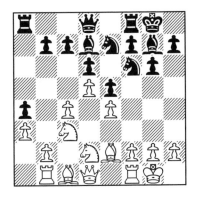

The only consistent continuation; otherwise White gains a tempo on 10 ♖b1 ♗d7 11 b3 lines from D1, having played b2-b4 in one go.

12 b4

The usual move; although White spoils his pawn structure, he can still develop an initiative on the queenside by means of c4-c5 or a4-a5.

If 12 f4 exf4 13 ♞f3 ♞h5!? 14 ♞g5 ♗h6 15 ♞h3 ♗xh3 16 gxh3 ♞g7 ∞ T.Southam-J.Nunn, London Lloyds Bank 1990.

12...axb3 13 ♞xb3

Black has fewer difficulties after:

a) 13 ♕xb3 b6 14 a4 ♞h5 15 ♗xh5 gxh5 16 ♕b4 f5 17 f3 h4 with the initiative, E.Solana Suarez-L.Van Wely, Las Palmas 1993.

b) 13 ♖xb3 ♗c8!? (if 13...b6 14 a4 ♞e8 15 ♖a3 f5 16 f3 ♞f6 17 ♞b3 f4 18 a5 bxa5 19 ♞xa5 += M.Agopov-M.Al Modiahki, Benasque 1999) 14 a4 ♞d7 15 ♖a3 c5 16 ♞b5 ♖a6 17 ♗b2 f5 18 ♕a1

♗h6 19 ♗c3 ♖f7 ∞ V.Malykin-E.Inarkiev, Pardubice 2002.

13...b6

Preventing c4-c5. Other moves allow White an advantage:

a) 13...♗a4 14 c5! dxc5 15 ♞xa4 ♖xa4 16 f3 b6 17 ♞xc5 +/- M.Ulibin-F.Nijboer, Leeuwarden 1997.

b) 13...c5 14 dxc6! ♗xc6 15 ♕d3 ♞e8 (or 15...♞h5 16 ♗xh5 gxh5 17 ♖d1 f5 18 ♗g5 fxe4 19 ♞xe4 ♖xa3 20 ♞xd6 +/- K.Sakaev-R.Har Zvi, Groningen 1992) 16 ♖d1 f5 17 f3 ♔h8 18 a4 b6 19 ♗e3 ♞c8 20 c5 bxc5 21 ♞xc5 ♕e7 22 ♞a6 ♞f6 23 ♖a1 ♗b7 24 ♞b4 +/= K.Sakaev-V.Baklan, Panormo 2001.

14 ♖a1 ♕e8!? *(D)*

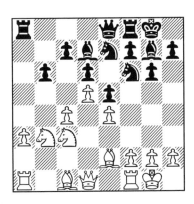

Trying to prevent a3-a4 as well. Black has also tried:

a) 14...♗a4 15 ♞xa4 ♖xa4 16 ♗d3 ♕a8 17 ♕e2 (if 17 ♞d2 ♞d7 18 ♞b1 ♞c5 19 ♞c3 ♖a6 20 ♗c2 ♔h8 21 ♞b5 ♕d8 with counterplay, L.Ftacnik-V.Kupreichik, Cuxhaven 1992) 17...♔h8 18 ♗c2 ♞d7 19 ♗b2 ♞g8 20 g3 ♞gf6 21 ♖a2 (21 f4!?) 21...♔g8 22 ♖fa1 h5 23 ♗c3 ♗h6 24 ♞c1 ♖a7 25 ♞d3 h4 26 a4 +/- K.Sakaev-J.M.Degraeve, Paris 1996.

b) 14...♘e8 15 a4 f5 (if 15...c5 16 dxc6
♗xc6 17 ♗e3 f5 18 f3 ♘f6 19 ♕d3 ♘h5,
B.Ostenstad-R.Djurhuus, Gausdal 1993,
20 ♖fd1 ♘c8 21 c5! +/- Knaak) 16 f3 ♘f6
(or 16...♔h8 17 ♗e3 ♘g8 18 a5 bxa5 19
♘xa5 ♗h6 20 ♗xh6 ♘xh6 21 ♕d2 ♘f7
22 c5 += S.Lputian-V.Kupreichik, USSR
Ch., Minsk 1987) 17 ♗e3 ♔h8 18 a5
bxa5 19 c5 a4 20 ♘d2 dxc5
(M.Gurevich-E.Inarkiev, Spanish Team
Ch. 2007) 21 ♗xc5! +=.

15 ♗e3

This natural developing move is the
latest try. If instead:

a) 15 ♗b2 ♔h8 16 g3 ♘fg8 17 f4 f5
18 ♕d2 exf4 19 gxf4 fxe4 20 ♘xe4 ♘f5
∞ L.Ftacnik-S.Kindermann, Vienna
1996.

b) 15 ♕d3 ♘h5!? 16 ♗xh5 gxh5 17
♘b5 (N.Ioseliani-V.Hort, Prague 1995)
17...♗c8 18 a4 (or 18 ♘a7 ♖a8 19 ♘b5
♖c8 =) 18...f5 with counterplay.

c) 15 ♕c2 ♘h5!? 16 ♘b5 ♖c8 17 a4 f5
18 f3 (if 18 a5 bxa5 19 ♖xa5 fxe4 ∞)
18...♘f4 19 a5 bxa5 20 ♖xa5 g5 21 c5
♕h5 ∞ D.Komarov-M.Pavlovic, Yugoslav Team Ch. 1998.

15...♔h8 16 ♘d2

Or 16 f3 ♘h5 17 ♘b5 ♕d8 18 a4 ♘f4
19 a5 bxa5 20 ♖xa5 ♖xa5 21 ♘xa5 ♕a8
∞ E.Arlandi-M.Erdogdu, European
Ch., Kusadasi 2006.

16...♘fg8 17 a4 ♗h6

If 17...f5 18 f3 ♗h6 19 ♗xh6 ♘xh6 20
a5!? ♖xa5 21 ♖xa5 bxa5 22 c5 with the
initiative, or 20...♕b8 (L.Kaufman-
J.Fedorowicz, Mashantucket 1999) 21
a6!? ♕c8 22 c5 bxc5 23 ♗c4 with compensation.

18 ♗xh6 ♘xh6 19 a5 (D)

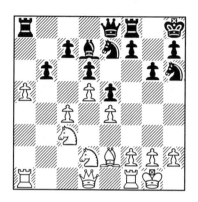

A thematic pawn break, so that if
19...♖xa5 (or 19...bxa5 20 c5) 20 ♖xa5
bxa5 21 c5 and White has a useful initiative.

Instead, M.Gurevich-V.Baklan, Deizisau 2005, went on: **19...♘c8?! 20** axb6
[20 a6!? again comes into considera-
tion] **20...♘xb6 21 ♖xa8 ♕xa8 22 c5
dxc5 23 ♕c1** [White is slightly better
here, though it proves difficult to win]
23...♔g7 24 ♘b3 c4 25 ♘d2 [if 25 ♘c5
♕a5 26 ♘xd7 ♘xd7 27 ♗xc4 ♖b8 with
counterplay (Gurevich)] **25...♕a5 26
♘xc4 ♘xc4 27 ♗xc4 c6! 28 ♕b2 ♕c5 29
♗e2 f6 30 ♖c1 cxd5 31 ♘xd5 ♕d6 32
♖c7 ♖f7 33 ♕c3** [or if 33 ♕c1!? f5! 34 f3
fxe4 35 fxe4 ♘f5 =] **33...♘f5!** [not
33...f5? 34 f4 +-] **34 exf5 ½-½**.

D22: 10...♘d7

The most frequent choice, increasing Black's control over c5 and immediately preparing ...f7-f5.

11 ♖b1 f5 12 b4 ♔h8 (D)

This flexible continuation was discovered in the late 1980s and soon became the main defence to 9 ♘d2. Black
does not want to commit himself with

either ...f5-f4 or ...♘d7-f6, and so plays a useful waiting move, clearing the g8-square for the e7-knight and f8-rook.

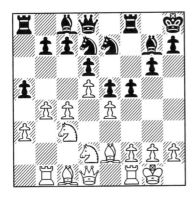

White has better chances after:

a) 12...♘f6?! allows simply 13 c5! (see 10...♘e8 above).

b) 12...f4?! is met by 13 ♗g4!, e.g. 13...h5 14 ♗e6+ ♔h7 15 ♗b2 b6 16 f3 ♗f6 17 ♕c2 g5 18 ♘b3 +/- M.Marin-R.Aloma Vidal, La Massana 2008.

c) 12...b6 13 f3 (if 13 ♘b3 axb4 14 axb4 fxe4 15 ♘xe4 ♘f6 16 ♘xf6+ ♗xf6 17 ♗h6 ♗g7 18 ♗xg7 ♔xg7 19 f4 exf4 20 ♕d4+ ♔g8 21 ♖xf4 ♘f5 22 ♕d2 ♕e7 = I.Farago-L.Riemersma, Amsterdam 1987) 13...♗h6 (or 13...f4 14 ♘a4 axb4 15 axb4 g5 16 c5 ♘f6 17 cxd6 cxd6 18 b5 += G.Kasparov-I.Smirin, USSR Ch., Moscow 1988) 14 ♘b3 ♗xc1 15 ♖xc1 axb4 16 axb4 ♘f6 17 c5 ♔g7 18 cxb6 cxb6 19 ♖a1 ♗d7 20 ♕d2 +/= A.Blees-K.Berg, Dieren 1987.

d) 12...axb4 (this is fine, but delaying the exchange reduces White's options) 13 axb4 ♗h6 (if 13...♘f6?! 14 c5! again; while after 13...♔h8, apart from 14 ♕c2 and 14 f3, White can consider 14 ♖b3!? ♘g8 15 ♖a3 ♖b8 16 ♕c2 ♘gf6

17 ♘b5 += S.Citak-P.Mohajerin, Istanbul 2004) 14 f3 (or 14 c5!? dxc5 15 ♕b3 ♔g7 16 ♘f3 ♗xc1 17 ♖bxc1 with compensation, M.Gurevich-K.Mohsen, Tanta 1997) 14...♘f6 (if 14...c5 15 bxc5 ♘xc5 16 ♘b3 ♗xc1 17 ♕xc1 b6 18 ♘xc5 bxc5 19 f4! += I.Smirin-V.Golod, Vienna 1998) 15 ♘b3 ♗xc1 16 ♖xc1 f4 17 c5 g5 18 ♘d2 ♗d7 19 ♘c4+= A.Schneider-A.Whiteley, Cappelle la Grande 1994.

D221: 13 f3 *298*
D222: 13 ♕c2 *303*

White has also tried:

a) 13 ♗b2 ♘f6 14 exf5 gxf5 15 f4 exf4 16 ♖xf4 ♘g6 17 ♖f1 axb4 18 axb4 ♗d7 19 ♕c2 ♘e5 ∞ M.Novikov-S.Klimov, St Petersburg 2003.

b) 13 ♘b3 axb4 14 axb4 ♘f6 15 f3 f4 (instead 15...♘df6 – *13 f3 ♘g8 14 ♘b3*; or 15...b6 16 c5 bxc5 17 bxc5 ♘h5 18 g3 ♘g8 19 ♗d2 ♘hf6 20 ♘c1 fxe4 21 fxe4 ♗h3 22 ♖f2 h5 23 ♗f1 ♘g4 24 ♖xf8 ♕xf8 25 ♘d3 ∞ J.Kristiansen-E.Mortensen, Esbjerg 1984) 16 c5 h5 17 ♗d2 g5 18 ♖a1 ♖xa1 19 ♕xa1 g4 20 ♕a5 b6 ♘e8 21 ♘b5? (21 ♗e1) 21...♘xd5! 22 exd5 g3 -/+ I.Pastukhov-S.Popovich, Lvov 1996.

c) 13 bxa5!? ♘c5 (or 13...♖xa5 14 ♘b3 ♖a8 15 f3 f4 ∞ M.Ulibin-R.Barcenilla, World Junior Ch. 1991) 14 a4 ♖xa5 15 ♗a3 b6 16 ♗xc5 bxc5 (if 16...dxc5?! 17 ♘b3 ♖a8 18 a5 += Z.Azmaiparashvili-F.Hellers, Reykjavik 1990) 17 ♖b8 c6 18 ♕b3 ♗h6 19 ♖d1 ∞ E.Gleizerov-P.Thipsay, New Delhi 2009.

D221: 13 f3 *(D)*

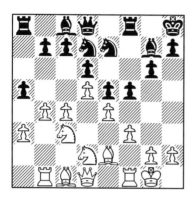

The most straightforward move, supporting the centre.

13...♘g8

The most frequent and consistent response, though Black has tried several others:

a) 13...♘f6?! 14 c5! axb4 15 axb4 is *10...♘e8* again.

b) 13...b6 14 ♕c2 f4 (or 14...c5 15 bxc5 ♘xc5 16 ♘b3 += A.Chernin-A.Groszpeter, Munich 1993) 15 ♘a4 axb4 16 axb4 c6 17 ♘c3 g5 18 dxc6 ♘xc6 19 ♘b5 += A.Shneider-A.Frolov, Groningen 1993.

c) 13...axb4 (again this might be delayed) 14 axb4 c6!? (14...♘g8 will probably transpose to the text; if instead 14...f4?! 15 ♕b3!? g5 16 ♗a3 ♘f6 17 c5 ♖g8 18 b5 dxc5 19 ♘c4 b6 20 ♘xe5 +/- M.Krasenkow-I.Glek, Pinsk 1986) 15 ♔h1 ♘f6 16 ♘b3 cxd5 17 cxd5 f4 (or 17...♘eg8 18 ♘a5 ♘h5 19 ♗e3 ♗h6 20 ♗f2 += D.Dumitrache-D.Vasiesiu, Rumanian Ch. 1994) 18 ♘b5 g5 19 ♕c2 ♘e8 20 ♗d2 ♗d7 21 ♖a1 += A.Beliavsky-T.Radjabov, European Team Ch., Plovdiv 2003.

d) 13...f4!? (this leads to very sharp play) 14 ♘a4 (if 14 ♘b5 b6 15 c5 bxc5 16 bxc5 ♘xc5 17 a4 c6 18 dxc6 ♘xc6 19 ♘c4, A.Gofman-S.Safin, Kramatorsk 1989, 19...♘d4 ∞; or 14 ♘b3 axb4 15 axb4 g5 16 ♗d2 ♘g6 17 ♖a1 ♖xa1 18 ♕xa1 ♘f6 19 ♕a7 g4 20 fxg4 ♘xg4 21 h3 ♘h6 22 ♗e1 ♖g8 23 ♘d2 ♗f6 with a very strong attack, L.Ljubojevic-G.Kasparov, Linares 1993) 14...axb4 15 axb4 c6 16 ♗b2 (if 16 c5 cxd5 17 cxd6 ♘c6 18 exd5 ♘d4 19 ♘c3 ♘b6 20 ♘de4 ♗f5 ∞ V.Salov-J.Nunn, Rotterdam 1989) 16...♘f6 17 dxc6 ♘xc6 18 c5 dxc5 19 ♘xc5 ♘d4 (or 19...♘xb4 20 ♘c4 ♕e7 21 ♕d6 ♕xd6 22 ♘xd6 b6 23 ♘d3 ♘xd3 24 ♗xd3 with good compensation, M.Sheehan-T.Jobe, corr. 1998) 20 ♘c4 ♘h5 21 ♖f2 b6 22 ♘d3 ♘g3 23 ♗f1 ♘xf1 24 ♖xf1 +/= L.Polugaevsky-F.Hellers, Biel 1989.

e) 13...c6!? also deserves attention, e.g. 14 ♔h1 (if 14 ♕c2 ♘f6 15 ♘b3 axb4 16 axb4 b5!? 17 dxc6 bxc4 18 ♗xc4 ♘xc6 19 b5 ♘b4 20 ♕e2 fxe4 21 fxe4 ♗g4 intending ...d6-d5 with counterplay, Ju Wenjun-Ding Liren, Shandong 2007) 14...f4 (14...axb4 15 axb4 ♘f6 – *13...axb4*) 15 dxc6 ♘xc6 16 ♘b5 axb4 17 axb4 ♘f6 18 ♕c2 (if 18 ♘b3!? ♘h5 19 ♔g1 ♘g3! 20 ♖f2, R.Sherbakov-V.Syrtlanov, Koszalin 1997, 20...♘xe2+! 21 ♕xe2 ♗e6 22 ♗d2 ♖a4 with counterplay) 18...♕e7 19 ♖d1 ♖d8 20 ♘b3 (or 20 ♖b3 g5 21 ♗b2 g4 22 fxg4 ♘xg4 23 ♗xg4 ♗xg4 ½-½ E.Vassia-H.Tiemann, corr. 2002) 20...♘xb4 21 ♕d2 ♘c6 22 ♘xd6 ½-½ E.Gleizerov-Y.Shulman, Calcutta 1999.

14 ♕c2 *(D)*

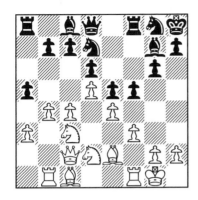

White reinforces the e4-pawn and adds support to his play on the c-file. Alternatives are less testing:

a) 14 exf5 gxf5 15 ♕c2 ♘e7 16 f4 (White is a tempo down on D222) 16...axb4 17 axb4 ♘g6 18 fxe5 ♘dxe5 19 ♘f3 ♗d7 (or 19...♕e7!? ∞ Lputian) 20 ♘g5 ♕e7 21 ♘b5 (S.Lputian-I.Smirin, USSR Team Ch. 1990) 21...f4! ∞.

b) 14 c5!? axb4 15 axb4 dxc5 16 bxc5 ♘xc5 17 ♘c4 (or 17 ♘b3 ♘d7 18 ♗e3 c6 19 ♕d2 fxe4 20 dxc6 bxc6 21 ♘xe4 ∞ L.Ftacnik-H.Grünberg, Stara Zagora 1990) 17...fxe4! 18 fxe4 ♖xf1+ 19 ♕xf1 ♘a4 20 ♘xa4 ♖xa4 21 ♗b2 ♕e7 22 d6 ♕e6 ∞ R.Hernandez-R.Henao, Bogota 1991.

c) 14 ♘b3 axb4 15 axb4 ♘df6 (if 15...b6 16 c5!? bxc5 17 bxc5 ♘df6 18 ♕c2 ♘h5, H.Schussler-E.Mortensen, Espoo 1989, 19 ♗b5 with the initiative) 16 c5 (or 16 ♗d2 ♘h5 17 g3 ♘hf6 18 ♖f2 ♘h6 19 ♖a1 ♖xa1 20 ♕xa1 ♘f7 21 ♕c1 f4! ∞ A.Karpov-G.Kasparov, Skelleftea 1989) 16...♘h5 17 g3 (17 ♗c4!?) 17...♘hf6 18 ♗d2 fxe4 19 fxe4 ♗h3 20 ♖f2 ♘h6 ∞ E.Peralta-R.Watanabe, World Student Team Ch. 1991.

14...♘gf6

A logical move: the f6-knight joins in kingside operations, while the other maintains control of the c5-square. 14...axb4 15 axb4 ♘gf6 or 15...♘df6 transposes below. Other moves do not promise equality:

a) 14...♖f7 15 ♘b5! ♗f8 16 exf5 gxf5 17 f4 c6 18 ♘c3 axb4 19 axb4 e4 (V.Chuchelov-M.Roeder, Berlin 1994) 20 ♗b2 +/=.

b) 14...b6 15 ♘b5 (or 15 exf5!? gxf5 16 f4 +/- E.Gleizerov-U.Kaminski, Dresden 1994, as the extra ...b7-b6 has only weakened Black's position) 15...♗h6 16 ♘b3 a4 17 ♗xh6 ♘xh6 18 ♘d2 f4 19 ♖bc1 g5 20 g4 fxg3 21 hxg3 ♗a6 22 ♔g2 ♖f6 23 ♖h1 +/- R.Dautov-G.Timoscenko, USSR Team Ch. 1990).

c) 14...♗h6 15 ♘b3 (or 15 c5!? axb4 16 axb4 dxc5 17 bxc5 ♘xc5 18 ♘b5 b6 19 ♘b3 with compensation, E.Lobron-S.Kindermann, Baden Baden 1992) 15...axb4 16 axb4 ♘df6 17 c5 ♘h5 18 ♘b5 ♘f4 19 ♔h1 fxe4 20 fxe4 ♗d7 21 ♗xf4 ♗xf4 22 g3 ♗xb5 23 ♗xb5 ♗h6 24 ♘a5 +/- W.Browne-A.Zapata, Linares 1994.

d) 14...♘h6!? 15 ♘b5 axb4 16 axb4 ♘f6 17 c5 ♘h5 18 ♘c4 ♖a6 (or 18...♗d7 19 ♘c3 ♘f4 20 ♗e3 fxe4 21 fxe4 ♕g5 22 ♗f3 ♘g4 23 ♗xg4 ♗xg4 24 ♔h1 += O.Peker-E.Van den Doel, Antwerp 1997) 19 ♘c3 fxe4 (if 19...♘f4 20 b5 ♖a8 21 b6! +/- G.Schnepp-J.Dietzel, German League 1999) 20 fxe4 ♖xf1+ 21 ♗xf1 ♘g4 22 ♘e3 ♖a8 23 ♘xg4 ♗xg4 24 ♘b5 +/- A.Beliavsky-V.Kotronias, Turin Olympiad 2006.

e) 14...♘df6 may transpose to the

text if the knights go to h5 and f6 anyway, but it also allows White to play ♘c4 (instead of ♘b5) after 15 c5 axb4 16 axb4 ♘h5 *(D)* and then:

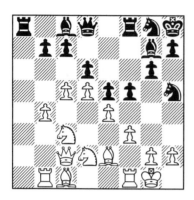

e1) 17 g3 ♘gf6 (if 17...♘hf6 18 ♘c4 fxe4 19 fxe4 ♗h3 20 ♖f3 ♗h6 21 b5 +/= A.Peter-E.Kahn, Hungarian Team Ch. 1998) 18 ♘c4!? (18 ♘b5 – *14...♘gf6*) 18...fxe4 19 fxe4 ♗h3 20 ♖f3 ♘g4 21 ♕d1!? ♖xf3 22 ♗xf3 ♘hf6 23 ♕e2 h5 24 ♗g2 ♗xg2 25 ♔xg2 ♕e7 26 h3 ♘h6 27 ♗e3 += A.Korotylev-M.Hochstrasser, Swiss Ch. 2003.

e2) 17 ♘c4!? ♘f4 (or if 17...fxe4 18 fxe4 ♖xf1+ 19 ♗xf1 ♘gf6, A.Watanabe-Ong Chong Ghee, World Junior Ch. 1991, then 20 b5! intending b5-b6) 18 ♗e3 ♘f6 19 b5 fxe4 (or 19...♘6h5 20 b6 ♕g5 21 ♗d3 +/- E.Gleizerov-J.Tihonov, Minsk 1996) 20 fxe4 ♗g4 21 ♗xf4 exf4 22 ♖xf4 ♗xe2 23 ♘xe2 dxc5 24 b6 +/- W.Browne-A.Sherzer, US Ch. 1992.

15 ♘b5

The direct continuation, preparing c4-c5 and an immediate queenside initiative.

However, 15 ♗d3 *(D)* is a significant alternative. By putting pressure on

the f5-pawn, White induces the advance 15...f4, after which the f6-knight is misplaced (and having just taken two moves to get there). White then has a choice of how to proceed:

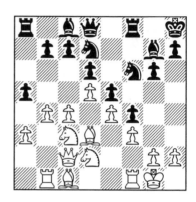

a) 16 ♘b5 b6 (16...♘e8!? may be stronger, and if 17 c5 axb4 18 axb4 dxc5! 19 bxc5 c6!? ∞ L.Gustafsson-T.Mercier, corr. 1998; or 17 ♗e2 axb4 18 axb4 c6!? ∞ U.Leth-S.Kramer, corr. 1993) 17 c5!? (if 17 ♗b2 ♘e8 18 ♘b3 a4 19 ♘d2 g5 20 ♘c3 ♖g8 21 ♘xa4 g4!? 22 fxg4 h5 23 gxh5 ♘df6 ∞ E.Arlandi-Al.David, Mondariz 2000; or 17 ♗e2 h5 18 ♗b2 ♘e8 19 c5 bxc5 20 bxc5 ♘xc5 21 a4 g5 22 ♗a3 ♘a6 23 ♖fc1 g4 24 ♘b3 ♖g8 ∞ P.Lukacs-B.Szuk, Hungarian Team Ch. 1995) 17...dxc5 (if 17...bxc5 18 ♘b3 a4 19 ♘a5 ♘e8 20 ♕xa4 ♕h4 21 ♕c2 += A.Khalifman-G.Kamsky, Biel Interzonal 1993) 18 bxa5 ♖xa5 19 ♘c4 ♖a8 20 a4 ♘e8 21 a5 ♗a6 22 ♗d2 ♗xb5 23 ♖xb5 ♘d6 ∞ V.Ivanchuk-G.Kasparov, Linares 1992.

b) 16 ♘a4!? axb4 17 axb4 g5 18 c5 g4 19 fxg4 (if 19 c6 g3! 20 h3 ♘h5! Ye Jiangchuan) 19...♘xg4 20 ♘f3 ♗h6 21 c6 ♘df6 22 b5 b6 23 ♘b2 ♘e3 24 ♗xe3 fxe3 25 ♖be1 ♖g8 =+ S.Lputian-Ye Ji-angchuan, Shenzhen 1992.

c) 16 ♗e2 ♖g8! 17 ♘a4 (if 17 ♗b2 ♗f8 18 ♘d1 g5 19 ♘f2 h5 20 h3 ♗e7 21 ♖fc1 ♘f8 ∞ A.Korotylev-N.Kabanov, Novokuznetsk 2008) 17...axb4 18 axb4 ♗f8?! (better 18...g5!? 19 c5 g4 20 fxg4 ♗f8 21 c6 bxc6 22 dxc6 ♘b6 23 ♘xb6 cxb6 24 b5 ♖a7 ∞ B.Lalic-N.Stanec, Moscow Olympiad 1994; or 18...c6!? 19 dxc6 bxc6 ∞ R.Casafus-Y.Dennis, corr. 1995) 19 c5 dxc5 (or 19...♗e7 20 ♘c4 g5 21 b5 ♖xa4 22 ♕xa4 ♘xc5 23 ♕c2 g4 24 ♗a3 g3 25 ♗xc5 gxh2+ 26 ♔xh2 +/- P.Van der Sterren-B.Gelfand, Munich 1994) 20 ♘xc5 ♘xc5 21 bxc5 b6 22 cxb6 cxb6 23 ♗b2 ♗c5+ 24 ♔h1 +/- P.Lukacs-C.Lingnau, Budapest 1994.

d) 16 ♗b2!? h5 (16...b6 17 ♘b5 – *16 ♘b5*; if now 16...♖g8 17 ♘b5 ♗f8 18 c5 ♘e8 19 ♘c4 +/- K.Sakaev-M.Harti-kainen, Kuopio 1995; or 16...♘e8 17 ♗e2 h5 18 c5 ½-½ P.Lukacs-Ye Jiang-chuan, Budapest 1992, 18...dxc5 19 bxc5 ♘xc5 20 ♘b5 with excellent compensa-tion) 17 ♘b5 (or 17 c5!? dxc5 18 bxc5 ♘xc5 19 ♗e2 with compensation, K.Sakaev-P.Smirnov, Panormo rapid 2002) 17...♘e8 18 c5 dxc5 19 bxc5 c6 20 dxc6?! (instead 20 ♘d6! ♘xd6 21 cxd6 cxd5 22 exd5 looks good for White) 20...bxc6 21 ♘d6 ♘xc5 22 ♕xc5 ♕xd6 ∞ D.Sharavdorj-J.De Boni, Dos Hermanas (blitz) 2004.

15...axb4

15...♘h5 generally comes to the same thing after a subsequent ex-change on b4; e.g. 16 g3 axb4 17 axb4. Or if 15...b6 16 exf5!? gxf5 17 f4 axb4 18 axb4 exf4 19 ♘f3 ♘e5 20 ♗xf4 ♘e4 21

♘d2 += K.Lerner-I.Smirin, USSR Ch., Odessa 1989.

16 axb4 ♘h5 17 g3

Not yet 17 c5?! ♘f4! 18 ♘c4 dxc5 19 ♗xf4 exf4 20 d6!? cxd6 21 ♘cxd6 fxe4 =+ V.Epishin-S.Dolmatov, Novosibirsk 1993.

17...♘df6 18 c5 (D)

If 18 ♖b3 fxe4 19 ♘xe4 ♗h3 (or 19...♘xe4 20 fxe4 ♖xf1+ 21 ♗xf1 c6 22 ♘c3 ♘f6 23 dxc6 bxc6 24 b5 cxb5 25 cxb5 ½-½ A.Beliavsky-E.Ubilava, Ma-nila Olympiad 1992) 20 ♖d1 ♘xe4 21 fxe4 ♕d7 22 ♖f3 (if 22 c5!? ♘f6 23 c6 bxc6 24 dxc6 ♕c8 25 ♘c3 ♕b8! ∞) 22...♘f6 23 ♘c3 ♖f7 = E.Lobron-B.Gelfand, Dortmund 1990.

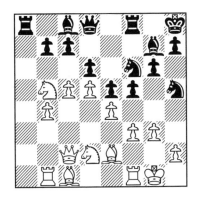

18...♗d7

The sacrifice 18...♘xg3?! 19 hxg3 ♘h5 is premature, as after 20 ♖f2 ♘xg3 21 ♘f1 ♘xe2+ 22 ♕xe2 ♗f6 (or 22...h5 23 ♖g2 fxe4 24 fxe4 ♗h3 25 ♗g5 ♕d7, A.Butnorius-R.Djurhuus, Norway 1992, 26 ♖g3 +/-) 23 ♖h2 fxe4 24 fxe4 ♗g5 25 ♗xg5 ♕xg5+ 26 ♖g2 ♕e7 27 ♕e3 ♖f4 28 ♘d2 ♗g4 29 ♖f1 g5 30 ♕c3 h5 31 cxd6 cxd6 32 ♕c7, Black has in-sufficient compensation for the piece,

M.Tratar-M.Borriss, Kecskemet 1991.

Instead, 18...fxe4 19 fxe4 ♗h3 is simpler, e.g. 20 ♖f2 (or 20 ♖e1 ♘e8 21 ♘f3 h6 22 ♘h4 ♔h7 23 ♖b3 ♘hf6 ∞ P.Van der Sterren-F.Nijboer, Dutch Ch. 1992) 20...♕e7! 21 ♖b3 (if 21 cxd6 cxd6 22 ♕c7 ♕xc7 23 ♘xc7 ♖a2! ∞ T.Hedlund-J.Becker, corr. 1995) 21...♗h6 22 ♖c3 (or 22 ♘a3 ♗d7 23 ♖c3 ♘g4 24 ♖xf8+ ♖xf8 25 ♘f3 ♗xc1 26 ♕xc1, Kir.Georgiev-J.Ehlvest, Brussels rapid 1992, 26...♘hf6 ∞) 22...♘g7 23 ♕b1 ♘ge8 ∞ V.Palciauskas-I.Kopylov, corr. 1989, which concluded 24 ♘b3 ♗xc1 25 ♖xc1 ♘g4 26 ♖xf8+ ♕xf8 27 ♗xg4 ♗xg4 28 ♖f1 ♕e7 29 ♕b2 ♗h3 30 ♖a1 ♖xa1+ 31 ♕xa1 ♕g5 32 ♕e1 ½-½.

19 ♖b3

Reinforcing the third rank, while preparing to double on the c-file. 19 cxd6 cxd6 20 ♕c7 (not 20 ♘xd6? ♗a4 21 ♕c5 b6 -/+) 20...♕xc7 21 ♘xc7 ♖a2 is fine for Black.

19...♘xg3!?

If now 19...fxe4?! 20 fxe4 ♗h3 21 ♖e1 ♗h6 22 ♘f3 ♗xc1 23 ♖xc1 ♘g4 (B.Gelfand-G.Kasparov, Paris rapid 1991) 24 ♖c3 +=.

But 19...♗h6 is possible, e.g. 20 ♖c3 ♗f4 (or 20...♘g7!? 21 ♖d1 ♘ge8 22 ♗b2, V.Epishin-S.Dolmatov, Russian Team Ch. 1992, 22...♖f7! ∞ Epishin) 21 cxd6 cxd6 (not 21...♘xg3? 22 hxg3 ♘h5 23 gxf4 ♘xf4 24 ♗c4 ♘h3+ 25 ♔h1 ♕h4 26 ♘b3 +- G.Kamsky-G.Kasparov, Dortmund 1992) 22 ♘c7 ♗xg3!? 23 hxg3 (not 23 ♘xa8? ♘xd5! -/+) 23...♘xg3 24 ♖f2 ♖c8 25 ♘f1 (or if 25 ♗d3 ♘fh5 ∞ Ftacnik) 25...♘fxe4 26 fxe4 ♘xe4 27 ♖ff3 ♘xc3 28 ♖xc3 f4 ∞ R.Druon-

E.Ruch, corr. 1996.

20 hxg3 ♘h5 21 f4! *(D)*

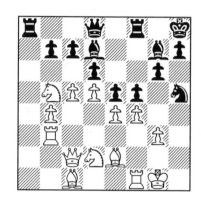

The critical defence. Not 21 ♔g2? ♘xg3 22 ♔xg3 f4+ 23 ♔f2 ♕h4+ 24 ♔g1 ♗h3 -+ Kasparov; or 21 ♖e1? ♘xg3 22 ♘f1 ♕h4 23 ♗c4 ♕h1+ 24 ♔f2 ♘xf1 -+ C.Bouton-C.Lingnau, Dortmund 1992; while 21 ♖f2 ♘xg3 22 ♗c4 (or 22 ♘f1 ♘xe2+ 23 ♕xe2 fxe4 ∞ Kasparov) 22...♕h4 23 ♖h2 ♕g5 24 ♖g2 (if 24 ♔f2 fxe4 or 24...♖a1!? ∞) 24...♕h4 25 ♖h2 ♕g5 is a draw.

21...♗xb5

Improving on 21...exf4 22 c6! bxc6 23 dxc6 ♘xg3 24 ♖xg3 fxg3 25 cxd7 g2 (A.Karpov-G.Kasparov, Tilburg 1991) when 26 ♖f2! ♕xd7 (or 26...♕h4 27 ♖xg2 fxe4 28 ♘f1) 27 exf5 (Kasparov) would have been good for White.

22 ♗xb5 exf4 23 exf5

White has also tried:

a) 23 gxf4 ♘xf4 24 ♘f3 fxe4 25 ♕xe4 ♕c8! 26 ♘h2 (or 26 ♗xf4!? ♕g4+ 27 ♔h1 ♖xf4 28 ♕e2, E.Kobylkin-P.Smirnov, European Junior Ch. 1993, 28...♕f5! 29 ♖d1 ♖a2 30 ♕xa2 ♖xf3 31 ♖e1 ♕h5+ 32 ♕h2 ♕xd5 =) 26...♘h3+ 27 ♔g2 ♖a2+ 28 ♗b2! ♖xf1 29 ♗xf1 ♖xb2+

30 ♖xb2 ♗xb2 31 ♕e3 dxc5 32 bxc5 ♕f5 33 ♕e8+ ½-½ A.Khalifman-S.Kindermann, Munich rapid 1991.

b) 23 ♗b2 ♘xg3 (or 23...♕g5!? 24 exf5 ♘xg3 25 ♘f3 ♕h5 ∞ Khalifman) 24 ♗xg7+ ♔xg7 25 ♕c3+ ♔g8 26 ♖xf4 ♘h5 27 ♖f2 fxe4 28 ♖xf8+ ♕xf8 29 ♘xe4 ♕f5 ∞ A.Beliavsky-A.Khalifman, Reggio Emilia 1991/92.

23...♘xg3 24 ♖xf4 ♘xf5 25 ♘f3 dxc5 26 bxc5 ♕xd5

Black should not delay taking on d5, as 26...♖a1 27 ♖d3! is good for White, e.g. 27...♕e7 28 ♔h2 ♖fa8 29 ♗b2 ♖1a2 30 ♖b3 +/- V.Epishin-J.Piket, Wijk aan Zee 1992.

27 ♖d3

Or 27 ♗b2 ♗xb2 28 ♕xb2+ ♘g7 29 ♖xf8+ ♖xf8 30 ♕c3 ♖f5 31 c6 b6 ∞ J.Kobryn-J.Knap, Poland 2003.

27...♖a2! *(D)*

Not 27...♕e6 28 ♗d7 +/- Epishin. But after the text Black seems to be okay:

a) 28 ♕c4 ♕xc4 29 ♗xc4? (29 ♖xc4 ♘g3 =) 29...♖a1 30 ♖d1 ♖xc1 31 ♖xc1 ♗h6 -/+ S.Kitte-T.Oral, World Junior Ch. 1992.

b) 28 ♖xd5 ♖xc2 29 ♗d2 c6 30 ♗a4 cxd5 31 ♗xc2 ♖c8 32 ♗xf5 gxf5 33 ♗b4 ♗f8 ½-½ S.Rublevsky-A.Pugachov, Russia 1992.

D222: 13 ♕c2 *(D)*

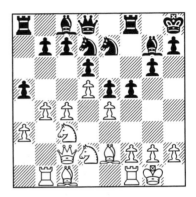

A refinement in move order: White may yet play f2-f3 after all, but maintains the option of f2-f4.

13...♘g8

Again the consistent continuation, though Black has tried numerous other moves:

a) 13...b6 14 ♘b5 (or 14 f3 – *13 f3*) 14...axb4 15 axb4 ♗a6 16 ♘c3 fxe4 17 ♘dxe4 ♘f5 18 ♕d1 ♘d4 19 ♗d3 += V.Chuchelov-E.Ragozin, USSR Army Ch. 1990.

b) 13...♗h6 14 bxa5 ♗xd2 (or 14...♘c5 15. ♘b3 ♗xc1 16. ♘xc5 ♗xa3 17. ♘xb7 ♗xb7 18. ♖xb7 +/- W.Koch-J.Kraschl, Finkenstein 1994) 15 ♗xd2 ♖xa5 16 ♘b5 ♖a8 17 f4 with the initiative, L.Brunner-S.Neurohr, German League 1991.

c) 13...fxe4 14 ♘dxe4 (if 14 ♘cxe4 ♘f5 15 ♘f3 ♘f6 16 ♗g5, M.Gurevich-M.Van Delft, Hoogeveen 1999, 16...h6!

=) 14...♘f5 15 ♗g5 (or 15 ♗d3 ♘f6 16 ♗g5 h6, S.Anapolsky-A.Shchekachev, Jurmala 1991, 17 ♗xf6 ♗xf6 18 ♘xf6 ♕xf6 10 ♕d2 +=) 15...♘f6 16 ♕c1 axb4 17 axb4 ♘d4 18 ♗d3 ♗f5 (S.Kishnev-L.Hazai, Budapest 1991) 19 f3 +=.

d) 13...axb4 is of course possible, with a likely transposition below after 14 axb4 ♘g8 or 14...♘f6, though there is nothing to be gained by exchanging pawns so soon.

e) 13...♘f6!? *(D)* is Gallagher's recommendation, and then:

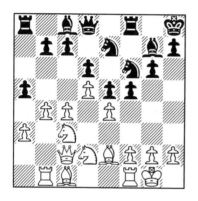

e1) 14 ♖d1 axb4 15 axb4 ♗d7 (if 15...c6?! 16 c5 fxe4 17 ♘dxe4 ♘xe4 18 ♘xe4 ♗f5 19 ♗d3 cxd5 20 ♘xd6 += E.Arlandi-J.Gallagher, Pula 2003) 16 f3 c6 17 c5 cxd5 18 exd5 ♘fxd5 19 ♘c4 ♘xc3 20 ♕xc3 e4 21 ♕e1 d5 22 ♘b6 ♖a2 ∞ E.Arlandi-T.Radjabov, Saint Vincent 2005.

e2) 14 ♗b2 fxe4 (or 14...axb4 15 axb4 c6 16 ♖bd1 fxe4 17 ♘dxe4 ♗f5! 18 ♗d3 cxd5 19 ♘xf6 ♗xd3 20 ♕xd3 dxc4 21 ♕xd6 = E.Cornblum-H.Sjøl, corr. 2001) 15 ♘cxe4 (or 15 ♘dxe4 ♘f5 16 ♘xf6 ♘d4 17 ♕d2 ♕xf6 = Gallagher) 15...♘f5 16 ♘f3 ♗d7 17 ♗d3 ♘h5 18 g3 ♕e7 19

c5 axb4 20 axb4 (E.Gleizerov-T.Gareev, Kaluga 2003) 20...♘f6! ∞.

e3) 14 f3 axb4 (if 14...♘h5 15 c5 axb4 16 axb4 ♘f4 17 ♘c4 g5 18 ♗e3 ♘eg6 19 cxd6 cxd6 20 ♘b5 ♖a6 21 ♖a1 += Wl.Schmidt-A.Sznapik, Polish Ch. 1992) 15 axb4 c6 16 ♔h1!? (if 16 dxc6 ♘xc6 17 ♘b5 fxe4 18 ♘xe4 ♘xe4 19 fxe4 ♖xf1+ 20 ♗xf1 ♘d4 21 ♘xd4 exd4 22 ♕d3 ♗e6 = M.Gurevich-Ye Jiangchuan, Belfort 1999) 16...f4 17 dxc6 ♘xc6 18 ♘b5 ♕e7 19 ♖d1 ♗e6 20 ♘b3 ♖fd8 ∞ V.Ruban-S.Dolmatov, Novosibirsk 1993.

14 exf5!?

Otherwise 14 f3 returns to D221 above. White has also tried:

a) 14 ♘b5 axb4 15 axb4 ♘df6 16 ♗d3 (if 16 f3 c6! 17 ♘c3 ♗h6 18 ♔h1 ♘h5 19 ♘b3 ♕h4 ∞ M.Agopov-M.Hartikainen, Finnish Team Ch. 2005) 16...♘h5 17 ♘f3 ♘gf6 18 ♗g5 ♘f4 19 ♘d2 ♘xd3 20 ♕xd3 ♗d7 21 ♖a1 ♗xb5 22 cxb5 ♕d7 ∞ R.Vaganian-M.Marin, Manila Interzonal 1990.

b) 14 ♗b2!? deserves attention, e.g. 14...♘df6 (if 14...♘gf6 15 ♖bd1 f4?! 16 c5 h5 17 ♘c4 +/- O.Danielian-Y.Yarovik, Moscow 1995; or 15...♘e8 16 exf5 gxf5, J.Pinter-A.Sznapik, European Team Ch., Haifa 1989, 17 f4!? +/=) 15 ♖bd1 ♘h5!? (if 15...♗d7 16 exf5 gxf5, M.Illescas Cordoba-A.Khalifman, Manila Interzonal 1990, 17 c5! ♕e7 18 cxd6 cxd6 19 ♘c4 +/= Khalifman) 16 ♗xh5 gxh5 17 f4! axb4 18 axb4 ♘h6 19 h3 ♗d7 20 fxe5 dxe5 21 c5 += O.Danielian-A.Istratescu, World Junior Ch. 1992.

14...gxf5 15 f4 *(D)*

The characteristic idea of the 13 ♕c2 variation.

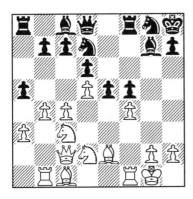

15...♘e7

The knight returns whence it came, after which it can go on to g6 or, more usually, support play against the white centre with ...c7-c6.

Here, too, Black has a number of other options, but most of them do not offer equality:

a) 15...♘gf6 16 ♘f3 ♘b6 17 fxe5 dxe5 18 ♘xe5 axb4 19 axb4 ♘fxd5 20 ♘xd5 ♘xd5 21 ♖d1 c6 22 cxd5 ♗xe5 23 ♗b2 +/- V.Ruban-M.Roeder, Balassagyarmat 1990.

b) 15...♘df6 16 fxe5 (if 16 ♘f3 axb4 17 axb4 e4 18 ♘g5 ♘e7 – 15...♘e7) 16...dxe5 17 ♘f3 e4 18 ♘g5 ♘e7 19 ♗e3 axb4 20 axb4 ♗d7 21 ♖bd1 +/- E.Gleizerov-P.Karnik, Pardubice 1992.

c) 15...e4 16 ♘b3 axb4 17 axb4 ♘df6 18 ♗e3 ♕e7 19 ♘d4 ♘h6 20 h3 ♗d7 21 c5 += S.Lputian-V.Loginov, USSR Team Ch. 1991.

d) 15...♘h6!? 16 ♘f3 e4 17 ♘g5 (if 17 ♘e1 axb4 18 axb4 ♘f6 19 h3 c6 20 ♗e3 cxd5 21 cxd5 ♗d7 ∞ O.Danielian-S.Anapolsky, Jurmala 1991) 17...♘f6 18 ♘d1 axb4 19 axb4 c6 20 ♘e3 += J.Sosa Macho-D.Langier, Rancagua 1993.

e) 15...exf4 (the main alternative) 16 ♘f3 ♘e5 (if 16...axb4 17 axb4 ♘df6 18 ♗d3! ♘e7 19 ♘e2 ♘h5 20 ♘xf4 ♘xf4 21 ♗xf4 ♘g6 22 ♗c1! intending ♗b2 += M.Gurevich-A.Shchekachev, French Team Ch. 2002) 17 ♗xf4 axb4 (if 17...♘xf3+ 18 ♗xf3 axb4 19 axb4 ♘h6 20 ♔h1 ♘g4 21 c5 ♘e5 22 ♘b5 += S.Lputian-E.Torre, Manila Interzonal 1990; or 19...♗d7 20 ♔h1 ♖a3 21 ♖b3 ♖xb3 22 ♕xb3 ♕f6 23 ♘e2 intending ♗e3-d4 += S.Lputian-Ye Jiangchuan, Beijing 1991) 18 axb4 ♗d7 19 ♔h1 ♘e7 20 ♕d2 ♘7g6 21 ♗g5 ♘xf3 22 ♗xf3 ♕e8 23 ♘e2! +/= E.Gleizerov-A.Petrushin, Balakovo 1994.

16 ♘f3 (D)

White gets little from either 16 fxe5 ♘xe5 17 ♘f3 ♘xf3+ 18 ♗xf3 ♘g6 19 ♘e2 axb4 20 axb4 ♕e7 21 ♘f4 ♗d7 = K.Berg-A.Fishbein, Kerteminde 1991; or 16 ♗b2 exf4 17 ♗d3 axb4 (17...♘e5!?) 18 axb4 ♘e5 19 ♘e2 ♘7g6 20 ♘xf4 ♕g5! 21 g3 (S.Atalik-J.Ehlvest, Reykjavik 2004) 21...♘xf4!? 22 ♖xf4 ♖a2 with counterplay, or if 21 ♘xg6+ hxg6 22 ♗d4 ♕h4 ∞.

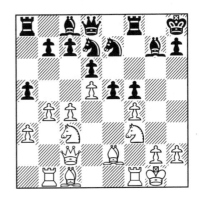

16...axb4

Black can still hold this back, but there's no real reason to do so now. Instead, 16...e4 will just transpose below after 17 ♘g5 (or 17 ♘e1 axb4 18 axb4) 17...♘f6 followed by 18...axb4 19 axb4.

Other ideas are worse, e.g. 16...♘g6 17 ♘g5 ♘f6 18 fxe5 dxe5 19 ♗e3 b6 20 ♖bd1 axb4 21 axb4 f4 22 ♗f2 ♘xd5 23 ♘xh7 ♗f5 24 ♗d3 ♘xb4 25 ♗xf5 ♘xc2 26 ♖xd8 ♖fxd8 27 ♗xg6 += M.Kosiorek-K.Jedryczka, Czestochowa 1998; or 16...exf4 17 ♗xf4 ♘g6 18 ♗g5 ♘f6 19 ♖be1 axb4 20 axb4 h6 21 ♘h4 ♘e5 22 ♗f4 ♘h5 23 ♗xe5 ♕xh4 24 ♗xg7+ ♘xg7 25 ♕d2 += E.Arlandi-J.Polgar, Portoroz 1991.

17 axb4 e4

If immediately 17...c6 18 dxc6 (or 18 fxe5 ♘xe5 19 ♗g5 ♕e8 20 ♘xe5 ♗xe5 21 ♗f3 += L.Ftacnik-S.Robovic, Munich 1992) 18...bxc6 19 ♖d1 ♕c7 20 b5 cxb5 21 ♘xb5 ♕c5+ 22 ♔h1 ♘f6 23 ♘e1 +/= as in A.Schneider-J.M.Degraeve, Cap d'Agde 1994.

18 ♘g5

The alternative is 18 ♘e1 c6! 19 ♗e3 (if 19 dxc6 ♘xc6 20 ♘b5 d5 21 cxd5 ♘d4 22 ♘xd4 ♗xd4+ 23 ♔h1 ♘b6 24 ♗b2 ♗xb2 25 ♕xb2+ ♕f6 26 ♘c2 ♘xd5 = V.Chuchelov-V.Kotronias, Greek Team Ch. 2004) 19...♘g6!? (or 19...cxd5 20 ♘xd5 ♘xd5 21 cxd5 ♘b6 22 ♕d2 ♗d7 23 ♗d4 ∞ Lputian; but if 19...♘f6 20 dxc6 bxc6 21 ♕d2 ♗e6 22 ♘c2 ♕c7 23 ♖fd1 += S.Lputian-L.Van Wely, Helsinki 1992) 20 dxc6 (if 20 ♕d2 ♖a3 21 ♖c1 ♕f6 22 ♘b1 ♖xe3! 23 ♕xe3 ♕d4! 24 ♕xd4 ♗xd4+ 25 ♔h1 ♘xf4 with compensation, M.Bellegotti-G.Calzolari,

corr. 1999) 20...bxc6 21 ♕d2 ♖a3 22 ♘d1 ♕f6 23 ♘c2 ♖a2 24 ♖b3 d5 25 ♘c3 ♖xc2 26 ♕xc2 d4 -/+ M.Boguslawsky-H.Theissen, Dortmund 1993.

18...♘f6 *(D)*

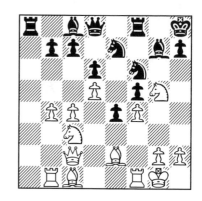

19 ♕b3

A recent try. Other moves are:

a) 19 ♔h1 axb4 19 axb4 h6 20 ♘h3 c6 21 dxc6 bxc6 22 ♖d1 d5 ∞ P.Van der Sterren-A.Fishbein, Kerteminde 1991.

b) 19 ♗b2 c6 20 dxc6 bxc6 21 ♖fd1 ♕c7 22 ♕d2 h6 23 ♘h3 ♖d8 (or 23...♕b6+ 24 ♔h1 ♕xb4 25 ♕xd6 =) 24 b5 ♗e6 ∞ A.Shirov-A.Fishbein, Kerteminde 1991.

c) 19 ♖d1!? c6! 20 dxc6 (if 20 ♗e3 h6 21 ♘e6 ♗xe6 22 dxe6 ♘c8! 23 g4 ♕e8! 24 gxf5 ♘e7 25 ♘xe4 ♘xf5 26 ♗f2 ♘xe4 27 ♕xe4 ♕g6+ 28 ♕g2 ♕xe6 -/+ M.Gurevich-M.Wahls, Tastrup 1992) 20...bxc6 21 ♗e3 (21 ♗b2 – 19 ♗b2) 21...h6 22 ♘h3 ♘g4 (L.Ftacnik-L.D.Nisipeanu, German League 1999) 23 ♗xg4 fxg4 24 ♘f2 ♘f5 25 ♕d2 ♘xe3 26 ♕xe3 ♖a3 27 ♘fxe4 ♗f5 with good compensation.

d) 19 ♗e3 h6 (still 19...c6! ∞) 20 ♘e6! (not 20 ♘h3?! ♘g4 21 ♗c1 c6 22 ♖d1

♕b6+ 23 ♔h1 ♘e3 =+ P.Genov-A.Kolev, Bulgarian Ch. 1992) 20...♗xe6 21 dxe6 ♖e8 (21...♕c8!?) 22 g4! ♖a3 23 g5 ♘g4? 24 ♗d2 ♘c6? 25 ♗xg4 ♘d4 26 ♕c1 +- A.Beliavsky-M.Illescas Cordoba, Barcelona 2007.

19...c6 20 ♗e3 h6 21 ♘h3 cxd5

An improvement on 21...♘g4?! 22 ♗xg4 fxg4 23 ♘f2 ♘f5 24 ♘cxe4 cxd5 (24...b5!?) 25 cxd5 ♖e8 26 ♗d2 ♘d4 27 ♕d3 +/- S.Ionov-A.Smirnov, St Petersburg 2005.

22 ♘xd5?

The exchange of knights only helps Black. 22 cxd5 ♗d7 23 ♘f2 is equal.

22...♘fxd5 23 cxd5 ♗d7 (D)

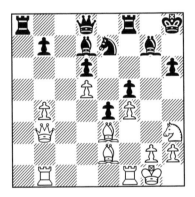

Black is now clearly better: his pieces are far better coordinated (the white knight on h3 is a very poor piece) and this enables him quickly to take over the initiative.

E.Gleizerov-V.Kotronias, Stockholm 2007, concluded **24 ♕d1** [if 24 b5 ♕a5! followed by 25...♖fc8 -/+] **24...♖a3! 25 ♗d4 ♖g8 26 ♔h1 ♕f8! 27 ♗c4 ♗a4! 28**
♕d2 ♗xd4 29 ♕xd4+ ♕g7 30 ♕xg7+ ♔xg7 [White's position is a mass of weaknesses] **31 b5 ♖c3 32 ♖b4 ♖xc4 33 ♖xc4 ♗xb5 34 ♖fc1 ♗xc4 35 ♖xc4 ♖c8 0-1.**

Conclusion

The straightforward 9...♘e8 (line A) leaves Black lagging behind in the attacking race, and therefore involves a degree of brinkmanship. If Black's breaks through on the kingside, he has good winning chances, but only if he hasn't been wiped out on the other side. The alternative retreat 9...♘d7 (line B) comes to the same thing if Black follows up with ...f7-f5 and ...♘d7-f6, but he can also counter with 10 b4 a5!?. In this case, however, he should be prepared for 9 b4 a5 positions from Chapter 11, to which it can transpose.

More often Black takes pre-emptive action on the queenside. 9...c5 (line C) deserves attention as a logical response to the plan of c4-c5 and ♘d2-c4, though White can probably count on a slightly better game.

The main defence is based on 9...a5 (line D). After 10 a3 ♘d7 11 ♖b1 f5 12 b4 ♔h8, White has sought to pose problems with 13 f3 ♘g8 14 ♕c2 ♘gf6 15 ♗d3 or 15 ♘b5 (line D221) and 13 ♕c2 ♘gf6 14 exf5 gxf5 15 f4 (line D222). Black seems to have sufficient counterplay, but if desired he can bypass these variations and try 13 f3 c6!? or 13 ♕c2 ♘f6!?.

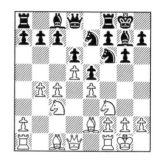

Chapter Eleven

Bayonet Attack:
9 b4 without 9...♘h5

1 d4 ♘f6 2 c4 g6 3 ♘c3 ♗g7 4 e4 d6 5 ♘f3 0-0 6 ♗e2 e5 7 0-0 ♘c6 8 d5 ♘e7 9 b4 *(D)*

This energetic pawn thrust initiates the so-called "Bayonet Attack". White refrains from any preparatory moves and begins active play on the queenside straightaway. Furthermore, by leaving the knight on f3, White can consider answering ...f7-f5 with the disruptive ♘f3-g5-e6, seeking to remove the dangerous light-squared bishop, even at the cost of a whole pawn.

Black has two consequent replies. Firstly, with the e2-bishop still obstructed Black can pursue the standard plan of ...f7-f5 while placing his f6-knight on the more aggressive square h5. 9...♘h5 is the main line and is the subject of the next chapter. Secondly, as the b-pawn has been advanced without preparation, Black can seek to undermine queenside operations by swiping

at it with 9...a5. This is examined in line C below.

The possibility of 9...♘h5, in particular, saw the Bayonet Attack languishing in relative obscurity for many years. However, that all changed in the mid 1990s as new ideas were discovered for White, so that 9 b4 is now the most popular move and regarded as a dangerous weapon against the King's Indian. All this attention has naturally led to Black's resources being refined, so that he too can count on his share of the chances available.

Apart from the two main moves 9...♘h5 and 9...a5 outlined above, Black tried numerous other ideas, such 9...♔h8, 9...♘e8, 9...♘d7, 9...c6, etc. However, there is a reason these are seen less frequently, as in all cases White has comparative freedom of action and good prospects for acquiring an opening advantage with straightforward play.

A: 9...♔h8 *310*
B: 9...♘e8 *312*
C: 9...a5 *314*

Black occasionally plays:

a) 9...c5?! is positionally unjustified, weakening the queenside pawn structure: 10 bxc5 dxc5 11 a4 (not 11 ♘xe5?! ♘d7! =) 11...a5 (or 11...♘e8 12 ♗e3 b6 13 a5 ♖b8 14 ♘b5 +/- D.Galkiewicz-A.Kruszynski, Suwalki 2000) 12 ♖b1 ♘e8 13 ♘e1 f5 14 ♘d3 b6 15 ♕b3 ♖a6 16 f4 +/- B.Ahlander-M.Mudelsee, Berlin 1994.

b) 9...♘d7 does not equalize after 10 ♗e3! (other moves transpose elsewhere: 10 ♘d2 – *9 ♘d2 ♘d7 10 b4*, line B in the previous chapter; similarly 10 a4 f5 11 ♘d2 or 10 c5!? dxc5 11 bxc5 ♘xc5 12 ♗a3 b6 13 ♘d2 f5 etc; while 10 c5!? f5 11 ♘g5 ♘f6 – *9...♘e8*) 10...f5 (or 10...h6 11 ♘d2 +=, as after 8 ♗e3 h6 9 d5 in Chapter Eight) 11 ♘g5 ♘f6 12 f3 f4 (if 12...h6 13 ♘e6 ♗xe6 14 dxe6 c6, V.Meskanen-R.Tuominen, Espoo 2001, 15 ♕d2 +=; or 12...♗h6 13 ♗d2! f4 14 ♘e6 ♗xe6 15 dxe6 c6 16 ♗e1 += M.Manolache-D.Hristodorescu, Rumanian Team Ch. 1994) 13 ♗f2 h6 14 ♘e6 ♗xe6 15 dxe6 ♕c8 16 ♘d5 ♖e8 17 ♖c1 c6 (R.Petetta-G.Della Torre, Villaguardia 2000) 18 ♘xe7+ ♖xe7 19 ♕xd6 ♖xe6 20 ♕d3 +/=.

c) The move 9...c6!? *(D)* is interesting, increasing the tension in the centre, while keeping the option of playing on either side, or even both sides, of the board.

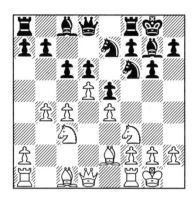

c1) 10 ♘d2 – *9 ♘d2 c6 10 b4* in Chapter Ten.

c2) 10 ♗a3 (intending 11 dxc6, 12 b5 to target the d6-pawn) 10...cxd5 (if 10...a6!? 11 dxc6! bxc6, V.Golod-L.Gofshtein, Hoogeveen 1998, 12 ♕d2 d5 13 exd5 e4 14 ♘d4 cxd5 15 c5 += or 11...♘xc6 12 ♕d3 ♘h5 13 ♘d5 +/=) 11 cxd5 ♗g4 (if 11...♗d7 12 b5 ♘e8 13 ♘d2 ♘c8 14 ♗b4 f5 15 a4 += G.Gajewski-M.Vokac, Litomysl 2005) 12 h3 ♖c8 13 ♕b3 ♗xf3 14 ♗xf3 ♘d7 15 ♖ac1 ♗h6 16 ♖c2 f5 ∞ L.Van Wely-V.Bologan, Dresden Olympiad 2008.

c3) 10 dxc6!? bxc6 (or 10...♘xc6 11 a3 +=) 11 ♗g5!? ♗e6 (if 11...h6 12 ♗xf6 ♗xf6 13 ♕d2 ♖b8 14 ♖ab1 g5 15 ♖fd1 +/- V.Babula-M.Vokac, Czech League 2000) 12 ♕d2 ♕c7 13 ♖ac1 ♖fd8 14 ♗xf6 (or just 14 b5 +/-) 14...♗xf6 15 ♘d5! ♗xd5 16 cxd5 ♕b7? 17 dxc6 ♘xc6 18 ♕d5 ♖ac8 19 ♗b5 1-0 A.Truskavetsky-O.Loskutov, Alushta 2005.

c4) 10 a3!? ♔h8 11 ♕b3 (or 11 dxc6!? +=) 11...cxd5 12 cxd5 ♘eg8 (12...♘e8!? immediately looks better) 13 a4 ♘e8 14 a5 +/= R.Kalod-M.Vokac, Czech Ch. 2000.

---

c5) 10 a4 a5 11 bxa5 ♕xa5 (11...c5 leaves Black a tempo down on line C1) 12 ♗d2 ♘e8 (or if 12...c5 13 ♕b3 ♘h5 14 ♖fb1 ♘f4 15 ♗f1 += W.De Winter-A.Campos Campos, Mexico City 2006) 13 ♖b1 f5 14 ♘g5 h6 (M.Orso-S.Vajda, Budapest 2000) 15 ♘e6! ♗xe6 16 dxe6 ♕c7 17 ♕b3 with better chances for White.

A: 9...♔h8 (D)

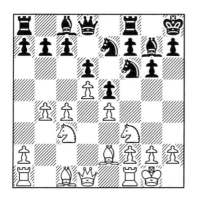

The main idea behind this move is to avoid any knight sallies to e6 by delaying ...f7-f5. The obvious drawback is that it is rather slow.

10 c5

White can also play 10 a4 first, when 10...♘eg8 transposes below after 11 c5 or 11 ♘d2 ♘e8 12 c5. Alternatively, 10...♘e8 is *9...♔h8 10 a4 ♘e8* in line B; while 10...a5!? 11 ♗a3 is similar to 9...a5 10 ♗a3 (line C2) and may even transpose, though ...♔h8 seems a little early here.

10...♘fg8?! makes less sense, e.g. 11 c5 dxc5 12 bxc5 f5 13 ♘d2 fxe4 14 ♘dxe4 ♘f6 15 ♗c4 +/- V.Epishin-H.Sikorsky, Bad Wildbad 2000.

10...♘eg8

The consistent move. Instead, 10...♘e8 is *9...♘e8 10 c5 ♔h8* in line B; or if 10...♘h5 11 cxd6 (11 a4 is the next note; while 11 ♖e1 – *9...♘h5 10 ♖e1 ♔h8 11 c5*) 11...cxd6 12 ♘g5 ♘f4 13 ♗xf4 exf4 14 ♖c1 h6 15 ♘f3 g5 16 ♘b5 ♘g6 17 a4 g4 18 ♘e1 f3! 19 gxf3 gxf3 20 ♘xf3 ♗h3 21 ♖e1 ∞ Comp Fritz 5.32-J.Polgar, Budapest (rapid) 1999.

11 ♘d2

If 11 a4 ♘h5! 12 ♖e1 (or 12 ♘d2 ♘f4 13 ♘c4 f5 14 cxd6 cxd6 15 ♘b5 fxe4 16 ♘bxd6 ♘f6 ∞ S.Savchenko-M.Hebden, Elista Olympiad 1998) 12...f5 13 ♗g5 (if 13 ♘g5?! ♘f4! 14 ♗xf4? exf4 is the tactical point; or 13 ♘d2 ♘f4 14 ♗f1 ♘f6 15 g3 ♘4h5 16 f3 ♕e7 ∞ B.Lalic-M.Hebden, Cambridge 1996) 13...♘hf6 14 exf5! gxf5 15 ♖c1 +/= D.Komljenovic-M.Hebden, Cappelle la Grande 2003.

11...♘e8 12 a4

Another option is 12 ♘c4 f5 13 exf5!? (or 13 f3 f4 14 a4 ♘h6 15 c6 g5 16 cxb7 ♗xb7 17 g4 ♘g8 18 ♘a5 += V.Popov-V.Dimitrov, Pardubice 1999) 13...gxf5 14 f4! (along the lines of D222 in Chapter Ten) 14...exf4 (or 14...e4 15 ♗b2 ♘gf6 16 ♖c1 += A.Ramirez-R.Sousa, World Junior Ch. 2008) 15 ♘c4 ♘e7 16 ♖xf4 ♘g6 17 ♖f2 += H.Pinheiro-C.Santos, Portuguese Team Ch. 2001.

12...f5 13 ♗a3 (D)

Or 13 a5!? ♘h6 (or 13...♘gf6 14 a6 b6 15 f3 ♗h6 16 ♘b3 ♗xc1 17 ♖xc1 += Wl.Schmidt-T.Markowski, Polish Ch. 1993) 14 a6 b6 15 ♗b5 bxc5 16 bxc5 dxc5 17 ♗a3 ♘d6 18 ♗xc5 ♘xb5 19 ♘xb5 ♖f6 20 ♘xa7 ♖xa6 21 ♖xa6 ♗xa6

22 ♖e1 fxe4 23 ♘xe4 += D.Collas-M.Hebden, Montpellier 2003.

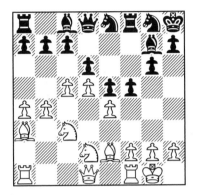

13...♘gf6

Black has also tried:

a) 13...f4?! 14 ♗g4! ♗xg4 15 ♕xg4 ♘gf6 16 ♕e2 g5 17 f3 ♖g8 18 a5 ♗f8 19 g4 fxg3 20 hxg3 ♘h5 21 ♕h2 +/-S.Estremera Panos-J.Rivadulla Horrillo, Seville 2002.

b) 13...♘h6 14 b5 f4?! (but if 14...dxc5 15 ♗xc5 ♘d6 16 a5 += V.Golod-M.Hebden, Albufeira 1999; or 14...fxe4 15 ♘cxe4 ♘f5 16 ♖c1 += P.Eljanov-N.Mariano, Dubai 2004) 15 ♘c4 g5 16 a5 (or 16 g4!? ♖f6 17 c6 bxc6 18 bxc6 +/- D.Komarov-M.Hebden, Albufeira 1999) 16...g4 17 g3 f3 18 ♗d3 ♖f6 19 b6 axb6 20 axb6 cxb6 21 cxd6 ♘f7 22 ♕b3 +/- V.Chuchelov-R.Meessen, Antwerp 1999.

c) 13...fxe4 14 ♘dxe4 ♘gf6 15 b5 dxc5 (or 15...♗f5 16 ♘g3 e4?! 17 c6 bxc6 18 bxc6 +/- V.Babula-M.Vokac, Czech Ch. 2005) 16 ♗xc5 ♘d6 17 ♗f3 += V.Tukmakov-M.Hebden, Lausanne 2000.

14 b5

The immediate 14 a5 might be met

by 14...a6!? ∞; while if 14 f3 ♘h5! 15 ♖e1 ♗h6 16 ♘c4 ♗f4 17 ♗f1 ♕h4 18 g3 ♘xg3 19 hxg3 ♕xg3+ 20 ♗g2 ♕h2+ 21 ♔f1 ♗g3 -/+ M.Maleki-M.Hebden, Neuchatel 2003.

14...dxc5

Instead 14...fxe4 15 ♘dxe4 – *13...fxe4* above; or if 14...♗h6 15 a5 ♗xd2 16 ♕xd2 ♘xe4 17 ♘xe4 fxe4 18 b6 +/- S.Lputian-F.Donguines, Moscow Olympiad 1994.

15 ♗xc5 ♘d6 16 ♕c2 b6 17 ♗a3 fxe4 18 ♘dxe4 *(D)*

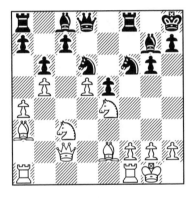

White has a nice advantage with more active pieces and potential targets at e5, d6 and c7.

J.Hjartarson-T.Shaked, Bermuda 1997, continued **18...♗f5** [18...♘fxe4 19 ♘xe4 ♖f4 might be a better try, and if 20 ♘xd6 cxd6 21 ♕c6 ♗f5 22 ♕xd6 (Hjartarson) 22...♖d4!? +=] **19 ♗d3 ♘h5** [now if 19...♘fxe4 20 ♗xe4 ♗xe4 21 ♘xe4 ♖f4 22 ♗xd6 cxd6 23 ♖ac1 ♗h6 24 ♕d3 +/- Hjartarson] **20 g3 ♗h6 21 ♖fe1 ♕d7 22 ♗c1 ♗xc1 23 ♖axc1 ♖ae8 24 ♘g5 ♘g7** [or 24...♗xd3 25 ♕xd3 ♕g4 26 ♘ce4! ♘xe4 27 ♘xe4 ♘f4 28 ♕d1 +/-] **25 ♘ce4 ♖c8 26 ♘d2 ♘f7 27**

♗xf5 ♘xf5 28 ♘e6? [28 ♘xf7+! ♕xf7 29 ♖xe5 ♘d4 30 ♕c3 ♕xf2+ 31 ♔h1 (Hjartarson) should win] **28...♕xd5?** [28...♖fe8! += Hjartarson] **29 ♘xf8 ♖xf8 30 ♕c3 ♘d4 31 ♕c4 ♕d7 32 ♕xc7** and White went on to win.

B: 9...♘e8 (D)

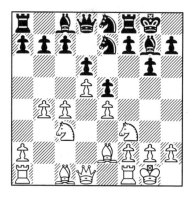

Preparing the usual ...f7-f5. Although Black's move looks passive (compared with 9...♘h5 for instance), after the possible invasion ♘f3-g5-e6 the e8-knight may go to g7 or c7 to win the e6-pawn.

10 c5

There is no reason to delay this advance. Nevertheless White sometimes plays:

a) 10 ♘d2 returns to *9 ♘d2 ♘e8 10 b4*, line A in the previous chapter.

b) 10 ♕b3 f5 (if 10...h6 11 c5 f5 12 ♘d2 ♔h7 13 ♗a3 ♘g8 14 b5 += J.Tisdall-O.Dannevig, Norwegian Ch. 1990) 11 ♘g5 (or 11 c5 – *10 c5 f5 11 ♕b3*) 11...♘f6 12 f3 h6 13 ♘e6 ♗xe6 14 dxe6 (J.Meyer-N.Fenske, Passau 1997) 14...c6 ∞.

c) 10 a4!? f5 (if 10...♔h8 11 c5 f5 12

♘d2! ♘g8 – *9...♔h8*, rather than 12 ♘g5 h6 13 ♘e6 ♗xe6 14 dxe6 fxe4! 15 cxd6 ♘xd6 ∞ S.Gligoric-L.Evans, Amsterdam 1971; but Black might prefer 10...a5!? 11 ♗a3 axb4 12 ♗xb4 f5, e.g. 13 ♘d2 c5!? 14 dxc6 ♘xc6 15 ♗a3 ♘d4 16 c5 ♗e6 ∞ H.Pascua-A.Stukopin, World Junior Ch. 2007) 11 ♘g5 (otherwise 11 ♘d2 or 11 a5!? ♘f6 12 ♘d2 – *9 ♘d2 ♘e8* again, or if 12 ♗g5!? ♘h5 13 exf5 gxf5 14 ♕d2 ♘f6 15 c5, V.Ivanchuk-T.Radjabov, Wijk aan Zee 2009, 15...a6 ∞ Radjabov) 11...h6 12 ♘e6 ♗xe6 13 dxe6 ♕c8 (13...c6!?) 14 ♘d5 ♕xe6 15 ♘xe7+ ♕xe7 16 exf5 gxf5 17 ♕d5+ ♔h8 18 ♕xb7 ♘f6 19 ♖a3 += F.Leveille-A.Ibrahim, Quebec 1997.

10...f5

Instead:

a) 10...h6?! 11 ♘d2! f5 is the 10 ♘d2 line with ...h7-h6 virtually a wasted move; e.g. 12 f3 f4 13 a4 g5 14 ♗a3 ♘g6 15 a5 ♖f7 16 b5 +/- C.Van den Berg-L.Te Velde, Dutch Ch. 1963.

b) 10...♔h8 11 ♗a3!? (otherwise 11 a4 – *10 a4 ♔h8*; or 11 ♘d2 f5 – *9 ♘d2 ♘e8* as above) 11...f5 12 b5 dxc5 13 ♗xc5 ♘d6 14 ♘g5 h6 15 ♘e6 ♗xe6 16 dxe6 fxe4 17 ♘d5 += A.Gokhale-S.Soumya, Indian Women's Ch. 2006.

c) 10...a5 is still possible, but then 11 ♗a3 axb4 12 ♗xb4 transposes to the inferior 9...a5 10 ♗a3 axb4 11 ♗xb4 ♘e8 variation in the notes to line C23.

11 ♘g5 (D)

The thematic continuation, though the most popular move is 11 ♘d2, returning to 9 ♘d2 ♘e8 in Chapter Ten. If instead 11 ♕b3 ♘f6 12 cxd6 cxd6 13 ♗d3 fxe4 14 ♘xe4 ♗f5 15 ♘xf6+ ♗xf6

16 ♗xf5 ♘xf5 = A.De Groot-J.Vetter, corr. 1997; or 11 ♗a3 ♘f6 12 ♘d2 ♗h6 13 ♗f3 ♗xd2 14 ♕xd2 f4 15 ♖ac1 g5 16 ♗e2 g4 ∞ P.Ricardi-B.Roselli Mailhe, Pinamar 2001.

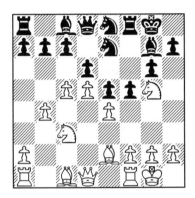

11...♘f6

This also arises via 9...♘h5 and 9...♘d7 so we will treat it as the main line, although in this precise position, in the absence of other threats (♗xh5, ♘e6), 11...h6 is often preferred.

a) 11...fxe4 12 ♗c4 (or 12 ♗g4 ♘f5 13 ♘gxe4 ♘d4 14 ♗xc8 ♕xc8 15 ♗e3 += T.Florian-A.Arulaid, Tallinn 1957; while 12 ♘gxe4 – *9 ♘d2 ♘e8 10 b4 f5 11 c5 fxe4*) 12...♘f6 13 ♘gxe4 ♘xe4 14 ♘xe4 h6 15 a4 ♘f5 16 a5 += N.Nesic-D.Misedakis, Chania 2000.

b) 11...h6 (obviously critical) 12 ♘e6 ♗xe6 13 dxe6 fxe4! 14 cxd6 (if 14 ♘xe4 d5 15 ♘g3 c6 =+ E.Ausmins-M.Scalcione, Viareggio 2001; or 14 ♗c4 ♘f6 15 cxd6 cxd6 16 ♘d5 ♖c8 17 ♗b3 ♘exd5 18 ♗xd5 ♕e7 -/+ R.Jedynak-T.Zeleny, Pardubice 2005) 14...♘xd6 (or 14...cxd6 15 ♘xe4 b6 16 b5 d5 17 ♗a3 ♘c7 ∞ J.Eslon-F.Del Hoyo Estades, Alicante 1992) 15 b5 (or 15 ♗e3 ♘ef5 16

♗c5 ♕g5 ∞ S.Ernst-R.Duchene, Dieren 1998) 15...♔h7 (or 15...♘ef5 16 ♕d5 c6!? 17 bxc6 bxc6 ∞ V.Epishin-J.Maiwald, Vienna 1998) 16 ♗a3 ♘ef5 17 ♖c1 ♖c8 18 ♗g4 ♖e8 ∞ E.Bareev-C.Gabriel, German League 2002.

12 f3

Other moves hardly test Black:

a) 12 cxd6?! cxd6 13 f3 (or 13 ♗f3? h6 14 ♘e6 ♗xe6 15 dxe6 fxe4 16 ♗xe4, A.Lauber-L.Vajda, Gyula 2000, 16...♖c8 17 ♗b2 ♖xc3 -+ Huzman) 13...♕b6+ 14 ♔h1 h6 15 ♘e6 ♗xe6 16 dxe6 fxe4 17 fxe4 ♕xb4 18 ♕d3 ♖ac8 19 ♗d2 ♕d4 =+ A.Kryschilovskij-M.Rogovoi, St Petersburg 1996.

b) 12 exf5 gxf5 (12...♘xf5!?) 13 f4 (if 13 ♕b3?! h6 14 cxd6 cxd6 15 ♘e6 ♗xe6 16 dxe6 d5 =+ S.Djuric-R.Byrne, New York Open 1990) 13...h6 14 ♘e6 ♗xe6 15 dxe6 e4 = M.Zeihser-J.Böhm, corr. 1995.

12...♔h8

Moving away from any tricks on the a2-g8 diagonal. If instead 12...f4?! 13 ♗c4 h6 14 ♘e6 ♗xe6 15 dxe6 ♔h7 16 ♗a3 +/- M.Pribyl-P.Scheffknecht, Triesen 2000; or 12...dxc5 13 bxc5 (13 ♗c4!?) 13...h6 14 ♘h3! (not 14 ♘e6? ♗xe6 15 dxe6 ♕d4+! 16 ♕xd4 exd4 -/+ A.Kornev-Y.Shabanov, Moscow 2000) 14...fxe4 15 fxe4 ♗xh3 16 gxh3 +=.

But 12...h6! at once is possible, as long as Black follows 13 ♘e6 ♗xe6 14 dxe6 with 14...d5! (if 14...dxc5 15 ♕xd8! ♖fxd8 16 bxc5 += S.Panzalovic-W.Reyher, Griesheim 2002) 15 exd5 ♘fxd5 16 ♘xd5 ♕xd5! (if 16...♘xd5 17 ♗c4 c6 18 ♗b2 ♕e7 19 ♗xd5 ♖fd8 20 ♗b3! ♖xd1 21 ♖axd1 +/- I.Farago-

M.Scalcione, Nereto 2000) 17 ♕xd5 ♘xd5 18 ♗c4 c6 19 ♖d1 ♖fd8 (or 19...♖fe8!? 20 ♗xd5 cxd5 21 ♖xd5 e4 with counterplay) 20 b5 ♗f8! ∞, rather than 20...♔f8 21 bxc6 bxc6 22 ♖b1 ♘c3 23 e7+! ♔xe7 24 ♖b7+ ♔e8 25 ♖d6! +- V.Anand-A.Ramaswamy, Madras (simul) 1998.

13 ♗e3!

Facing the prospect of 13...h6 etc, this is the most useful move for White. 13 ♖b1 h6 14 ♘e6 ♗xe6 15 dxe6 d5 16 exd5 ♘fxd5 17 ♘xd5 ♕xd5 18 ♕b3 ♕xb3 19 ♖xb3 ♘c6 20 ♗b2 ♖fe8 21 ♗c4 ♖ad8 was fine for Black in E.Ubilava-K.Kranthi, New Delhi 2008.

13...♗h6!?

Now if 13...h6 14 cxd6! cxd6 15 ♘e6 ♗xe6 16 dxe6 d5 17 exd5 ♘fxd5 18 ♘xd5 ♕xd5 19 ♕xd5 ♘xd5 20 ♗c5 is slightly better for White with the two bishops; or 13...f4 14 ♗f2 h6 15 ♘e6 ♗xe6 16 dxe6 d5 17 ♕b3 d4 18 ♖fd1 +/= M.Barbaric-M.Schönfelder, Bad Wiessee 1998.

14 ♘f7+ ♖xf7 15 ♗xh6 f4 16 ♖c1 ♘eg8 17 ♗g5 *(D)*

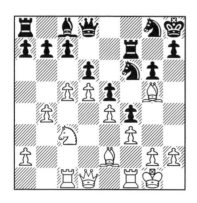

The position is good for White: his queenside initiative is well underway, while the bishop on g5 is a disruptive influence on the other side. Two games have seen:

a) 17...h6 18 ♗h4 g5 19 ♗f2 ♖g7 20 ♕c2 (20 ♘b5 g4 21 ♗h4 looks better) 20...g4 21 ♗h4 ♕e8! 22 fxg4 ♘xg4 23 ♗xg4 ♗xg4 24 ♔h1 ♕h5 25 ♕f2 ♖f8 with good play for Black, M.Najdorf-C.Cuartas, Buenos Aires 1973.

b) 17...♖g7 18 g4!? (or 18 ♘b5 again) 18...h5 19 h3 ♖h7 20 ♔g2 ♗d7 21 ♖h1 ♖c8?! (21...♕f8) 22 ♕g1 ♖a8 23 a4 ♕f8 24 a5 ♘h6 25 ♗h4 g5 26 ♗f2?! (26 ♗xg5! +/-) 26...a6 27 ♔f1 ½-½ E.Bacrot-T.Radjabov, FIDE World Ch., Tripoli 2004.

C: 9...a5 *(D)*

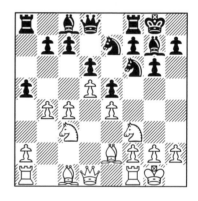

A natural reaction, breaking up the white pawn phalanx (since a2-a3 is not possible) and consequently gaining more control over the c5-square. Nevertheless, White still has an initiative on the queenside, can support c4-c5 with ♗a3, and counter ...b7-b6 with a2-a4-a5. Meanwhile Black's kingside counterplay with ...f7-f5 is not as violent as in other variations, and his a8-rook is often passive.

First of all White must decide how to meet the challenge to his b-pawn.

C1: 10 bxa5 315
C2: 10 ♗a3 319

Nothing else is worth considering; for instance 10 ♕b3 axb4 11 ♕xb4 ♘d7 12 ♘e1 f5 13 f3 f4 14 ♘d3 b6 15 ♗d2 h5 (M.Barasiant-K.Smokina, Bucharest 1999) sees Black well ahead on normal lines, especially as 16 a4 g5 17 a5? bxa5 18 ♖xa5? loses to 18...c5!.

C1: 10 bxa5 (D)

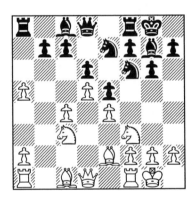

By exchanging rather than defending the b-pawn, White keeps his options open with his dark-squared bishop. The drawback is that it allows Black an additional possibility too.

10...c5 (D)

The critical response, suppressing White's queenside initiative somewhat. Alternatively, Black can recapture with 10...♖xa5 at once, though ...c7-c5 is of-

ten only deferred. For example:

a) 11 a4 ♘h5 (if 11...♘d7 12 ♘d2 – *9 ♘d2 ♘d7 10 b4 a5*; while 11...c5 – *10...c5*, except for 12 dxc6 bxc6, e.g. 13 ♗d2 ♖a8 14 c5 d5 15 exd5 ♘fxd5 16 ♗c4 ♗e6 ∞ H.Herndl-S.Cigan, Austrian Team Ch. 1996) 12 ♖e1 f5 13 ♘d2 ♘f6 14 ♗a3 b6 15 ♗d3 ♗h6 16 ♗b4 ♖a8 17 ♘b5 ♗d7 ∞ V.Dydyshko-S.Mihajlovskij, Belarus Ch. 2006.

b) 11 ♘e1 ♘d7 12 ♘d3 f5 13 ♗d2 ♖a8 (or 13...c5 – *10...c5 11 ♘e1*) 14 f3 b6 (14...f4 15 ♘b5 g5 16 ♗b4 b6 17 a4 ♘c5 18 a5 += I.Veltmander-V.Skotorenko, Rostov on Don 1954) 15 a4 ♘f6 16 ♕b3 ♔h8 17 ♕b4 ♖g8 18 ♘f2 ♘h5 19 ♘b5 ♘f4 ∞ M.Amanov-I.Kovalenko, Alushta 2007.

c) 11 ♘d2 c5 (again 11...♘d7 12 ♘b3 ♖a8 – *9 ♘d2 ♘d7 10 b4 a5*; while 11...♘e8 12 ♘b3 ♖a8 – *9 ♘d2 ♘e8 10 b4 a5*) 12 dxc6 (otherwise 12 a4 – *11 a4*; or 12 ♘b3 ♖a6 – *10...c5 11 ♘d2*) 12...bxc6 13 ♘b3 ♖a8 14 ♕c2 ♕c7 15 a4 ♗e6 16 ♗a3 ♖fd8 17 ♖fd1 ♘e8 18 a5 f5 with counterplay, N.Ristic-F.Pancevski, Obrenovac 2005.

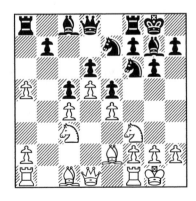

11 a4

White has several alternatives:

a) 11 dxc6 bxc6 (if 11...♘xc6 12 ♗e3 ♕xa5 13 ♕b3 ♗g4 14 ♗b6 ♕b4 15 ♖fb1 ♕xb3 16 axb3 ♘d4, B.Raedeker-F.Ott, German League 1996, 17 ♘xd4 exd4 18 ♗xd4 ♗xe2 19 ♘xe2 ♘xe4 20 f3 with a better ending for White) 12 ♗e3 (if 12 ♘d2 ♕xa5 13 ♗b2 ♖d8 14 ♘b3 ♕b4 15 ♕c2 ♗e6 16 ♘d1 ♘d7 =+ M.Najdorf-J.Penrose, Leipzig Olympiad 1960; or 12 ♗g5 h6 13 ♗xf6 ♗xf6 14 ♕d2 ♔g7 15 c5 dxc5 16 ♕c2 ♕xa5 17 ♘d1? ♘d5! 18 exd5 e4 -/+ C.Wichmann-R.Kasim-dzhanov, German League 1998) 12...♕xa5 13 ♕xd6 ♕xc3 14 ♕xe7 ♘xe4 ∞ A.Fayard-M.Roeder, Cannes 1989.

b) 11 ♗d2 ♖xa5 12 ♕c2 ♖a6 (if 12...♔h8 13 ♖fb1 ♘h5 14 g3 ♖a6 15 ♖b2 ♘g8 16 ♕c1 ♕e7 17 ♖ab1 f5 18 ♘g5 += G.Beckhuis-V.Bologan, German League 1994) 13 ♖fb1 h6 (if 13...♘d7?! 14 ♕c1! ♔h8 15 ♖b3 ♘g8 16 g3 ♗f6 17 ♖ab1 ♗e7 18 ♗f1 +/= C.Lutz-S.Dolmatov, Dortmund 1993) 14 ♘e1 ♘h7 15 ♘d3 f5 16 f3 g5 ∞ G.Beckhuis-A.Shirov, German League 1994.

c) 11 ♘e1 ♖xa5 (if 11...♕xa5 12 ♗d2 ♘e8 13 a4 ♕d8 14 ♖a3 f5 15 exf5 gxf5 16 f4 e4 17 g3 ♘g6 18 ♘g2 ♗d4+ 19 ♔h1 ♖f7 20 ♘b5 += A.Yermolinsky-J.Fedorowicz, US Ch. 2000) 12 ♘d3 (12 a4 – *11 a4*) 12...♘d7 13 ♗d2 f5 14 exf5 (14 f3 ♖a6 15 a4 h6 16 ♖a3 ♘f6 17 ♖b3 g5 18 ♕c2 f4 ∞ L.Van Wely-J.Gonzalez Garcia, New York Open 1993) 14...gxf5 15 f4 ♘g6 (15...e4!? 16 ♘c1 b5! ∞) 16 ♕c2 ♖a6 17 ♔h1 exf4 18 ♘xf4 ♘xf4 19 ♗xf4 ♘e5 20 ♖ab1 += C.Lutz-I.Smirin, Groningen 1993.

d) 11 ♘d2 ♖xa5 12 ♘b3 (or 12 a4 –

11 a4) 12...♖a6 13 a4 ♘d7 (if 13...♘e8 14 a5 b6, H.Alber-T.Michalczak, German League 1996, 15 axb6 ♖xa1 16 ♘xa1 ♕xb6 17 ♕b3 +=) 14 ♗d2 (or 14 ♗e3 f5 15 f3 f4 16 ♗f2 g5 17 a5 ♖f7 18 ♘b5 ♗f8 19 ♘xd6! ♖xd6 20 ♘xc5 ♘xc5 21 ♗xc5 with compensation, V.Epishin-T.Shaked, New York Open 1997) 14...f5 15 f3 ♔h8 16 ♕c2 ♘g8 17 exf5 gxf5 18 ♗d3 ♘e7 19 ♖a2 ♘f6 20 ♘b5 ♘h5!? ∞ S.Skembris-K.Moutousis, Athens 1995.

11...♖xa5 12 ♖a3 (D)

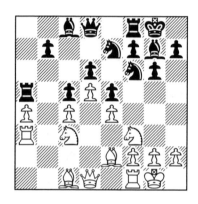

White's last two moves are typical for this system: a2-a4 gains space and aims to advance further, while the a3-rook can play on either side of the board. White has various set-ups for his other pieces. For instance:

a) 12 ♘e1 ♘d7 13 g4!? f5 14 f3 ♘f6 (14...h6!? intending ...f5xg4, ...g6-g5, ...♘g6) 15 ♘g2 ♗d7 16 ♗d2 ♕c8 17 h3 ♖a6 18 ♕c2 ♘e8 19 a5 fxe4 20 ♘xe4 +/= L.Gofshtein-E.Sutovsky, Israeli Ch. 2002.

b) 12 ♘d2 ♖a6 (if 12...♘d7 13 ♘b5 ♖a6 14 ♖a3 – *12 ♖a3*) 13 ♗b2 (otherwise 13 ♖a3 – *12 ♖a3* again, while 13 ♘b3 – *11 ♘d2* above) 13...♘d7 14 ♘b5 f5 15

exf5 gxf5 16 f4 ♘g6 17 fxe5 ♘dxe5 18
♕b3 (or 18 ♖a3 ♗d7 ½-½ W.Browne-
J.Fedorowicz, US Ch. 1998) 18...f4 19
♘f3 ♗f5 20 ♗c3 ♕d7 ∞ I.Umanskaya-
S.Dolmatov, Moscow 1998.

c) 12 ♗d2!? ♖a6 13 ♖b1 h6 14 ♕c1
♔h7 15 g3!? ♘fg8 (or 15...♘e8 16 ♘h4
f5 17 exf5 ♘xf5 18 ♘xf5 gxf5 19 f3 h5?!
20 ♔h1 ♔g8 21 ♗g5 ♗f6 22 f4 +/-
V.Topalov-A.Morozevich, Nice rapid
2008) 16 ♘h4 f5 17 exf5 ♘xf5 18 ♘xf5
gxf5 19 ♔h1 ♕f6 20 ♖b3 ♕g6 21 ♕b1
♘f6 22 ♖b6 ♖xb6 23 ♕xb6 f4 ∞
V.Mikhalevski-J.Zawadzka, Queenstown 2009.

12...♖a6

The rook will have to retreat at
some stage, so Black maintains flexibility by moving it at once, while covering the squares weakened by ...c7-c5.
Instead:

a) 12...h6 13 ♘d2 ♖a6 14 ♘b5 ♘h7
15 ♗b2 f5 16 exf5 (16 f4!?) 16...♘xf5 17
♗d3 h5 18 ♗c2 ♗h6 19 ♘e4 +/=
V.Malakhatko-M.Stryjecki, Krakow
1999.

b) 12...♔h8 13 ♘d2 ♘eg8 14 ♗b2
♕e7 15 ♘b5 ♗d7 16 ♕a1 (this set-up is
worth remembering) 16...♖aa8?! 17 f4
exf4 ½-½ A.Kharlov-V.Ivanchuk,
European Ch., Istanbul 2003; although
18 ♖xf4 would have very good for
White, e.g. 18...♘e8 19 ♘c7! ♖xa4 20
♖xa4 ♗xa4 21 ♘xe8 ♗xb2 22 ♕xb2+
♕e5 23 ♕xe5+ dxe5 24 ♖f3 ♗xe8 25 ♖b3
etc.

c) 12...♘e8 13 ♘b5 (if 13 ♘e1 f5 14
exf5 ♘xf5 15 ♘e4 ♘f6 16 ♗d3 ♘xe4 17
♗xe4 ♗d7 18 ♗d2 ♖a7 19 ♘f3 ♕a8 20
a5 b5! =+ E.Postny-I.Smirin, Maalot-

Tarshiha 2008) 13...♖a6 14 g3!? f5 15
exf5 gxf5 (better 15...♘xf5 ∞) 16 ♘h4
♘g6 17 ♘g2 ♘f6 18 f4 ♘e4 19 ♗d3 exf4
20 ♘xf4 += D.Antic-D.Radovanovic,
Serbian Ch. 2002.

13 ♘d2

White has also tried:

a) 13 ♘e1 ♘d7 14 ♘d3 ♘b6!? (if
14...f5 15 f4! exf4 16 ♘xf4 ♗d4+ 17 ♔h1
♘f6 18 ♘b5 ♗e5 19 ♘d3 fxe4 20 ♘xe5
dxe5 21 ♗e3 +/- A.Rychagov-
H.Banikas, Greek Team Ch. 2000) 15
♕b3 f5 16 exf5 ♘xf5 17 ♘b5 ♘d7 18 f4
e4!? 19 ♘f2 ♖e8 20 ♕c2 ♘f6 21 ♗b2
♗d7 22 ♗xf6 ♗xf6 23 ♘xe4 ♘d4 24
♘xd4 ♗xd4+ 25 ♔h1 ♖xa4 26 ♖xa4
♖xa4 27 ♕xa4 ♖xe4 = S.Lputian-
I.Smirin, Kemer 2007.

b) 13 ♖e1!? ♔h8 (if 13...♘e8 14 ♘b5
♔h8 15 ♗f1 f5 16 exf5 ♘xf5 17 ♗d3 ♘f6
18 ♘g5 18...♘d4 19 ♘xd4 cxd4 20 h3 h6
21 ♘e6! ♗xe6 22 dxe6 ♕e8 23 c5! with
the initiative, B.Gulko-I.Smirin, World
Team Ch., Beersheba 2005) 14 ♕c2 ♘e8
15 ♘b5 ♘g8 16 ♗f1 f6 17 g3 ♘h6 18
♗g2 ♘f7 19 ♗d2 ♗d7 = R.Stern-
Z.Lanka, Rostock 2002.

13...♘d7 *(D)*

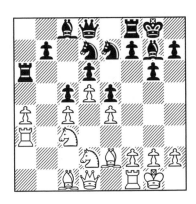

Keeping an eye on the e5-square in readiness for f2-f4. If instead 13...♘e8 14 ♘b5 f5 15 exf5 gxf5?! (15...♘xf5) 16 f4! exf4 17 ♖xf4 ♘g6 18 ♖f1 ♘f6 19 ♕c2 ♕e7 20 ♘f3 +/= A.Yermolinsky-J.Fedorowicz, New York Open 2000. But Black can also consider 13...♗d7!? 14 ♘b5 ♗h6 15 ♗b2 ♘c8 16 g3 ♖e8 17 ♗d3 ♘h5 = A.Barsov-Ye Jiangchuan, FIDE World Ch., Moscow 2001.

14 ♘b5 f5

There is no point in delaying this move; e.g. 14...♔h8 15 ♕c2 f5 16 exf5 gxf5 (if 16...♘xf5 17 ♘e4 ♘f6 18 ♗g5 +=) 17 ♘f3 h6 18 ♘h4 e4? (but if 18...♘f6 19 f4, or 18...f4!? 19 g3 +=) 19 f3! exf3 20 ♖axf3 ♘e5 21 ♖g3 +/- B.Gulko-D.Reinderman, FIDE World Ch., Las Vegas 1999.

15 exf5

If 15 ♗b2 ♗h6 16 exf5 ♘xf5 (or 16...gxf5!? 17 ♖h3 ♗g7 18 f4 ♘g6 19 fxe5 ♘dxe5 ∞ M.Rodshtein-D.Vocaturo, World Junior Ch. 2006) 17 ♘e4 ♘f6 18 ♘xf6+ ♖xf6 19 ♗g4 ♘d4 20 ♗xc8 ♕xc8 21 g3 ♖f7 22 ♔g2 ♕f5 23 ♗xd4 cxd4 = S.Gligoric-F.Jenni, Zürich 1998.

15...gxf5!?

Safer is 15...♘xf5 16 ♘e4 ♘f6 17 ♗g5 h6 18 ♗xf6 ♗xf6 19 ♗g4 ♖f7 20 ♗h3 ♗g7 21 ♕d2 ♔h7 22 ♖e1 ♗d7 = A.Korobov-P.Kostenko, Moscow 2004. Black is slightly passive, but it is hard for White to do anything either.

16 ♘f3

Following Gulko's idea from his game with Reinderman. White has also tried:

a) 16 f4 exf4 17 ♖xf4 ♘g6 18 ♖f1 ♘de5 ∞ and ½-½ F.Doettling-I.Nataf, French Team Ch. 2007.

b) 16 ♗b2 ♘g6 17 g3 ♘f6 18 f4 exf4 19 gxf4 ♗h6 20 ♖g3 ♘g4 21 ♗xg4? (better 21 h3 ♗xf4 22 ♖xf4 ♘xf4 23 hxg4 ♕h4 24 ♘f1 ♘h3+ 25 ♖xh3 ♕xh3 26 g5 ∞ Tsesarsky) 21...fxg4 22 ♖xg4 ♗xf4 23 ♘e4 ♗xg4 24 ♕xg4 (E.Bareev-I.Smirin, Moscow rapid 2002) and now 24...♗xh2+! (Tsesarsky) was the simplest win.

16...♘g6!?

If 16...h6 17 ♘h4! ♘f6 18 f4 or 17...f4 18 g3 +=.

17 ♘g5 ♘f6 (D)

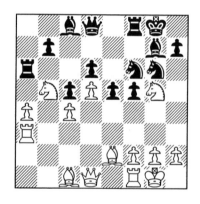

This double-edged position was reached in R.Vera-F.Fiorito, Santa Clara 2000. Compared with other games in the notes, White can throw in a disruptive ♘e6, but was unable to find a good moment to do so. Instead, he tried a different idea and went wrong in the complications: **18 ♕c2** [if 18 ♘e6!? ♗xe6 19 dxe6 ♕e7! 20 ♕c2 ♘e8 ∞ Vera] **18...♖e8 19 f3** [if 19 ♖d1!? h6 20 ♘e6 ♗xe6 21 dxe6 e4 22 ♗e3 ♕b8! 23 ♕d2 ♖xe6!, as 24 ♗xh6 is met by 24...e3! 25 ♗xe3 f4 26 ♕d3 fxe3 27

♕xg6 exf2+ 28 ♔f1 d5 ∞ Vera] **19...♘f8 20 ♗d3 h6 21 ♘h3** [or 21 ♘e6!? ♘xe6 22 dxe6 f4 23 ♗g6 ♖xe6 24 ♖d1 with compensation (Vera)] **21...♕d7 22 ♔h1 ♘g6 23 g4!?** [this is White's idea] **23...e4 24 fxe4?** [24 ♗e2 was correct, intending to follow with g4-g5; now Black takes over the initiative] **24...fxg4 25 ♘f4 ♘xf4 26 ♖xf4 ♕e7 27 ♗b2 ♘h5 28 ♖f1 ♖f8 29 e5?** [White was already worse and this doesn't help] **29...dxe5 30 d6 ♖xf1+ 31 ♗xf1 ♕f6 32 ♗g2 ♘f4 33 ♗e4 ♔h8 34 ♕d2 ♘e6 35 ♖a1 ♖xa4 36 ♖e1 ♘g5 37 d7 ♗xd7 38 ♕xd7 ♘xe4 39 ♕c8+ ♔h7 0-1**.

C2: 10 ♗a3 (D)

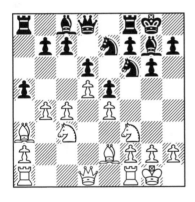

This move may be more accurate than 10 bxa5. Firstly, White immediately threatens c4-c5; secondly, Black cannot play ...c7-c5 himself as the d6-pawn hangs.

C21: 10...♘h5 *320*
C22: 10...b6 *322*
C23: 10...axb4 *326*

10...b6 11 bxa5 and 10...axb4 11 ♗xb4 often lead to the same position. For instance, 10...axb4 11 ♗xb4 b6 12 a4 is equivalent (with one fewer move) to 10...b6 11 bxa5 ♖xa5 12 ♗b4 ♖a8 13 a4, which is the main line of C22.

10...♘d7 is another move order, controlling the c5-square and preparing ...f7-f5. Then 11 bxa5 ♖xa5 12 ♗b4 ♖a8 transposes to 10...axb4 11 ♗xb4 ♘d7 (line C23), though 12...♖a6!? is also possible. While there is the danger of a discovered attack from the e2-bishop after c4-c5, the rook may be better placed should White play ♘g5-e6. For example, 13 a4 (D), and then:

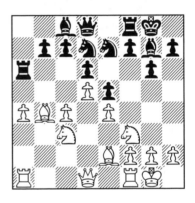

c1) 13...♘c5 14 a5 ♔h8 15 ♘d2 ♘g8 16 ♗xc5 dxc5 17 ♘b3 ♕e7 18 ♘a4 b6 (F.Baumbach-H.Berliner, corr. 2001) 19 d6!? cxd6 20 ♘xb6 +/=.

c2) 13...f5 14 a5 ♘c5 (14...♗h6 – *13...♗h6*) 15 ♗xc5 dxc5 16 ♘d2 ♗h6?! 17 ♘b3 b6 18 axb6 cxb6? 19 d6 ♖xa1 20 ♘xa1 1-0 V.Kramnik-'ICClover', Internet blitz 1999.

c3) 13...♗h6 14 a5 f5 15 ♘d2 ♔h8 16 ♘b3!? (if 16 ♘a4 ♘f6 17 c5 fxe4 18 ♗xa6 ♘exd5 19 ♘xe4 ♘exd5 20 ♘xf6,

L.Van Wely-E.Inarkiev, Moscow 2003, 20...bxa6! ∞) 16...♘f6 17 c5?! (17 f3!?) 17...fxe4 18 ♗xa6 bxa6 19 cxd6 cxd6 20 ♕e2 ♗b7 =+ S.Irwanto-Wan Yunguo, Kuala Lumpur 2007.

C21: 10...♘h5 *(D)*

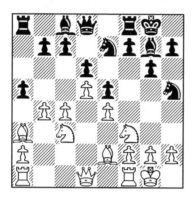

A cunning move; Black hopes to transpose to 9...♘h5 10 ♖e1 ♘f4 11 ♗f1 a5, but with White having played 12 ♗a3 already (whereas 12 bxa5! is regarded as the strongest continuation).

11 c5

The best response, taking immediate action on the queenside. Instead:

a) 11 ♖e1?! ♘f4! 12 ♗f1 gives Black his desired transposition (see line E1 in the next chapter, note with 12 ♗a3).

b) 11 bxa5 ♘f4 (11...♖xa5 12 ♗b4 ♖a8 13 c5 returns to the main line) 12 c5 (or 12 ♗b4 f5 13 ♖b1 fxe4 14 ♘d2 ♘f5 15 ♘cxe4 ♘d4 with compensation, P.Skalik-P.Bobras, Polish Team Ch. 1997) 12...f5 13 cxd6 cxd6 14 ♘d2 ♖xa5 15 ♘c4 (R.Hangweyrer-C.Lovrinovic, Austrian Team Ch 2006) 15...♖a6 16 ♘b5 ♗d7! ∞.

c) 11 g3 f5 12 ♘g5 ♘f6 (or 12...h6!)

13 c5 h6 14 cxd6 cxd6 15 ♘e6 ♗xe6 16 dxe6 fxe4 17 bxa5 ♘f5 18 ♘b5 d5 19 ♗xf8 ♗xf8 20 ♖c1 ♖xa5 with compensation, M.Taimanov-V.Ciocaltea, Moscow 1956.

11...axb4

Not yet 11...♘f4?! 12 b5! (threatening b5-b6) 12...b6 (or 12...♗g4 13 ♘d2 ♘xe2+ 14 ♘xe2 dxc5 15 ♗xc5 b6 16 ♗a3 ♖e8 17 ♘c4 +/- J.Piket-J.Nunn, Amsterdam 1995) 13 cxd6 cxd6 14 ♖c1 ♗h6 15 ♘d2 f5 16 ♖e1 ♗b7 17 ♗f1 ♖c8 18 ♘c4 ♖f6 19 ♖c2 +/- V.Topalov-J.Polgar, Frankfurt (rapid) 1999.

12 ♗xb4 dxc5

Now if 12...♘f4 13 cxd6! cxd6 14 ♘b5 ♖a6 (or 14...♘xe2+ 15 ♕xe2 ♖a6 16 ♘d2 f5 17 ♘c4 +/- D.Erhembayar-N.Sakr, Beirut 2000) 15 ♗c4 g5 16 ♘d2 g4 17 ♖e1 f5 18 ♗f1 ♖f6 19 a4 ♖h6 20 ♖c1 ♗d7 21 g3 += R.Pogorelov-T.Hillarp Persson, Reykjavik 2004.

13 ♗xc5 ♘f4 14 ♗c4 ♗g4 *(D)*

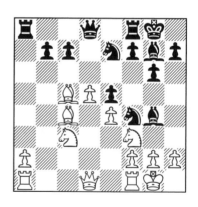

15 h3!

A useful insertion. White stands better in the diagram position, but Black is not without counterplay. For example:

a) 15 ♖e1?! b6 16 ♗b4 c5 17 dxc6 ♘xc6 18 ♗xf8 ♘d4 with excellent play for the exchange, C.Babos-N.Alfred, Budapest 2003.

b) 15 ♘b5 b6 16 ♗b4 ♔h8 17 ♕b3 f5 18 d6 cxd6 19 ♗xd6 fxe4! (not 19...♘c6? 20 ♗xf8 ♕xf8 21 ♘g5 +/- Ch.Pedersen-M.Paragua, Alushta 2004) 20 ♘g5 (or 20 ♘xe5 ♘f5! 21 ♘xg4 ♘xd6 22 ♖ad1 ♕g5 ∞) 20...h6 21 f3 (if 21 ♘xe4 ♘xg2! with very strong counterplay) 21...exf3 22 ♘xf3 ♗xf3 23 ♕xf3 ♖a4 ∞.

15...♗h5!?

15...♗xf3 16 ♕xf3 gives White a clear positional advantage, J.Nill-J.Gilbert, European Women's Ch., Kusadasi 2006.

16 ♘b5

The critical line was 16 ♔h2! g5! 17 g3!, when Mikhalevski gives a fantastic variation: 17...♘xh3! 18 ♔xh3! g4+ 19 ♔h4! *(D)*

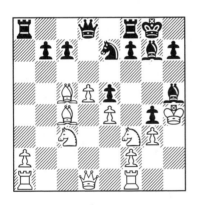

19...f5!? (if 19...♘xd5+ 20 ♔xh5 ♘f6+ 21 ♔h4, or 19...gxf3 20 ♔xh5! f5 21 ♗xe7 ♕e8+ 22 ♔h4 ♕xe7+ 23 ♔h3, or 19...♗g6 20 ♘g5 ♗f6 21 ♕xg4 h6 22 ♔h3 +/-) 20 d6+ ♘d5+ 21 ♘g5 h6 22 ♕d2! ♗f6 23 f4! gxf3 24 ♗xd5+ ♔g7 25 ♔h3! hxg5 26 exf5 ♖h8 27 ♔h2 cxd6 28 ♗e3 and White should win.

16...g5

If 16...b6 17 ♗b4 ♔h8 18 ♕b3 f5 (as in the note with 15 ♘b5) White can try 19 ♖fe1!; e.g. 19...fxe4 (or 19...♗xf3 20 ♕xf3 fxe4 21 ♕xe4 ♖a4 22 a3 ♘fxd5 23 ♕c2) 20 ♘g5 ♘exd5 21 ♗xf8 ♕xg5 22 ♗xg7+ ♔xg7 23 ♕g3 +=.

17 ♕b3 ♖a6

Heading over to the kingside. However, it might have been better to play 17...c6!? 18 dxc6 ♘xc6! 19 ♗xf8 ♗xf8 with compensation for the exchange.

18 ♖fd1! ♖f6

Threatening ...♘xh3.

19 ♘xe5! *(D)*

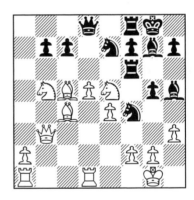

White responds with an exchange sacrifice of his own, completely seizing the initiative and gaining a clear advantage.

V.Babula-T.Hillarp Persson, European Team Ch., Gothenburg 2005, continued **19...♗xd1 20 ♖xd1 ♖d6 21 ♘xd6 cxd6 22 ♗b6 ♕c8 23 ♘g4 f5 24 exf5 ♘xf5 25 ♗f1 h5 26 ♘e3 ♘h4 27 ♘c4 ♕d7 28 ♔h1 g4**, and now 29 g3! ♘xh3 30 ♗xh3 gxh3 31 gxh4 (Mikhalevski) would have won for White. Instead, the game ended in a messy draw, presumably in mutual time trouble.

C22: 10...b6 *(D)*

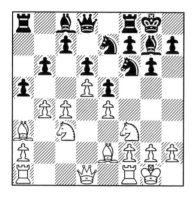

Black strengthens his control over the c5-square, so White must now aim for a4-a5 to undermine the queenside.

11 bxa5 ♖xa5

11...♘h5!? *(D)* is an interesting alternative, actively preparing ...f7-f5 and ...♘f4. On the downside, the knight does not control c5; hangs after ...f7-f5, e4xf5; while ...♘f4 prevents the f5-pawn from advancing further. In response White has tried several moves:

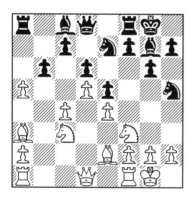

a) 12 ♗b4 bxa5 13 ♗a3 ♘f4 14 c5 ♘xe2+ 15 ♘xe2 ♗a6 16 ♖e1 h6 17 ♖c1 f5 18 exf5 gxf5 19 ♘g3 ♖f7 ∞ A.Wirig-N.Mamedov, Neustadt an der Weinstrasse 2009.

b) 12 ♘d2 ♘f4 13 ♘b3 bxa5 14 c5 (if 14 ♖e1, S.Gligoric-M.Pavlovic, Yugoslav Team Ch. 1998, 14...a4 15 ♘d2 c5!? ∞ Nataf) 14...♘xe2+ 15 ♘xe2 f5 16 ♘c3 fxe4 17 ♘xe4 ♘f5 (or 17...a4!?) 18 ♖b1 ♖f7 19 ♖e1 dxc5 20 ♘bxc5 ♘d4 ∞ C.Hernaez Fernandez-V.Strautins, corr. 2002.

c) 12 ♘b5 ♖xa5 13 ♗b4 ♖a6 14 ♘d2 (if 14 a4 f5 15 a5 ♘f4 16 ♘d2 ♖f6 17 ♗f3 c5!? ∞ I.Ivanisevic-D.Antic, Yugoslav Team Ch. 2000) 14...♘f4 15 ♖e1 ♘xe2+ 16 ♕xe2 f5 17 a4 fxe4 18 ♘xe4 ♘f5 19 ♕d1 ♖f7 20 a5 bxa5 21 ♖xa5 h6 22 ♕a1 ♖xa5 23 ♕xa5 += L.Van Wely-V.Topalov, Monte Carlo (rapid) 2000.

d) 12 g3 f5 13 ♘g5 (if 13 ♗b4 bxa5 14 ♗a3 ♘f6 15 c5 ♘xe4 16 ♘xe4 fxe4 17 ♘d2, C.Lutz-J.Nunn, German League 2000, 17...♗h3! 18 ♖e1 e3 19 fxe3 ♘f5 20 ♗d3 ♗h6 with excellent play for Black; or 13 exf5 gxf5 14 ♘g5 ♘f6 15 ♕b3 ♖xa5 16 ♗b4 ♖a8 17 a4 ♔h8 ∞ J.Cox-P.Doggers, Amsterdam 2006) 13...♘f6 14 ♗b4 (perhaps White should try 14 axb6!? ♖xa3 15 ♘b5 ♖a5 16 bxc7 ♕d7 17 ♘e6 ∞) 14...bxa5 15 ♗a3 fxe4 (better 15...h6! 16 ♘e6 ♗xe6 17 dxe6 ♘xe4 18 ♘xe4 fxe4 19 ♕c2 ♕c8 =+) 16 ♘gxe4 ♘f5 17 c5 ♘xe4 18 ♘xe4 ♖f7 = D.Rogozenko-Z.Lanka, Hamburg 2006.

e) 12 ♖e1 (vacating f1 for the bishop) and then:

e1) 12...♖xa5 13 ♗b4 ♖a8 14 a4 – *11...♖xa5 12 ♗b4 ♖a8 13 a4 ♘h5 14 ♖e1.*

e2) 12...♘f4 13 ♗f1 f5 14 ♘d2 (if 14 g3!? fxe4 15 ♘xe4 ♘h3+ is fine for Black) 14...♖xa5 (or 14...fxe4 15 ♘dxe4 ♘f5 16 g3 ♘h5 17 ♘b5 ♖xa5 18 ♗b4 ♖a8 19 a4 += V.Golod-I.Bitansky, Israeli Team Ch. 1999) 15 ♗b4 ♖a8 16 ♘b5! ♗d7 17 a4 ♗xb5 18 cxb5 fxe4 19 ♘xe4 ♔h8 20 ♗c4 += S.Savchenko-D.Reyhan, European Ch., Istanbul 2003.

e3) 12...f5 13 ♗b4 bxa5 14 ♗a3 ♘f4 (if 14...♘f6 15 ♗d3 fxe4 16 ♘xe4 ♗g4 17 ♘xf6+ ♖xf6 18 ♗e4 +/= V.Kramnik-I.Smirin, Belgrade 1999) 15 ♗f1 (the energetic 15 c5! may be better, e.g. 15...fxe4 16 ♘xe4 ♘xe2+ 17 ♕xe2 ♘f5 18 ♕c2 h6 19 ♖ac1 ♖f7 20 ♕a4 ♗f8 21 ♖c3 +/= E.Bacrot-N.Djukic, Dresden Olympiad 2008) 15...fxe4 16 ♘d2 ♘d3 (if 16...♘f5 17 ♘dxe4 ♘d4 18 ♔h1 ♕h4 19 f3 ♖f5 20 ♘g3 ♖f7 21 ♘b5 ♘xb5 22 cxb5 ♗b7 23 ♘e4 ♕h5 24 b6 +/- B.Gelfand-N.Djukic, Dresden Olympiad 2008) 17 ♗xd3 exd3 18 ♘de4 ♘f5 19 ♕xd3 h6!? (if 19...♗h6 20 ♗c1! ♗xc1 21 ♖axc1 a4 22 ♕d2 ♘d4 23 ♘b5 ♘xb5 24 cxb5 += F.Elsness-T.Hirneise, Gausdal 2008) 20 ♖ab1 ♕d7 21 ♘b5 ♗a6 22 ♗c1 a4 23 ♖b4 c6!? 24 ♘bxd6? (White had to play 24 dxc6 ♕xc6 ∞) 24...♘xd6 25 dxc6 ♕f5 26 ♕xd6 ♖ad8 27 c5 ♗d3 -/+ E.Iturrizaga-N.Mamedov, Cappelle la Grande 2009.

12 ♗b4 ♖a8 13 a4 *(D)*

Although 11...♖xa5 allows play to start on the queenside immediately, Black can prepare for it quite well. As noted above, 10...axb4 11 ♗xb4 b6 12 a4 also reaches this position and is, in fact, the more usual move order, but it aids organization to consider it via 10...b6.

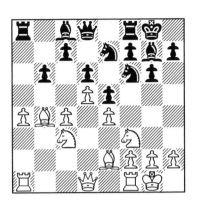

13...♖e8!?

Developed by the Latvian grandmaster, Zigurds Lanka, in the late 1990s; the idea is to protect the d6-pawn with ...♗f8 and play ...c7-c5. Other plans involve moving the f6-knight:

a) 13...♘d7 (combining ...b7-b6 and ...♘d7 is rather passive) 14 a5 ♘c5 (if 14...bxa5 15 ♗xa5 ♗a6 16 ♘b5 ♗xb5 17 cxb5 ♘c5 18 ♕c2 f5 19 ♘g5 +/- S.Estremera Panos-Lin Yi, Barcelona 2000) 15 axb6 ♖xa1 16 ♕xa1 cxb6 17 ♖b1 f5 (or 17...♗h6 17 ♕a7 f5 18 ♗xc5 bxc5, J.Ulko-V.Dobrov, Moscow 2000, 19 ♖b6 +/-) 17 ♗xc5 bxc5 18 ♖b8 ♕c7 19 ♕a8 ♗d7 20 ♖b7 ♖xa8 21 ♖xc7 ♖d8 22 ♘g5 ♗f6 23 ♘e6 ♗xe6 24 dxe6 +/- A.Veingold-J.Vakeva, Karhula 1994.

b) 13...♘h5 (the c7-pawn is often vulnerable here) 14 ♖e1 (this can arise via various move orders, including 9...♘h5 10 ♖e1 a5 or 10...♘f4 in the next chapter; if instead 14 a5 bxa5 15 ♗xa5 ♘f4 16 ♘d2 ♕d7 17 ♖e1, V.Anand-J.Polgar, Dos Hermanas 1997, 17...c6! with counterplay) 14...♘f4 15 ♗f1 f5 (if 15...♗g4 16 h3 ♗xf3 17 ♕xf3 f5 18 ♘b5 fxe4 19 ♕xe4 += I.Tsesarsky-I.Bitansky, Petah Tiqwa 1996) 16 h3 (if 16 a5 fxe4 17 ♘d2 bxa5 18 ♖xa5?! ♖b8! 19 ♖b5 ♗d7 20 ♖xb8 ♕xb8 =+ Ax.Smith-M.Mader, Cappelle La Grande 2008; or 16 ♘d2 c5!? 17 dxc6 ♘xc6 18 ♗a3 ♘d4 ∞ A.Bellaiche-P.Mai, Paris 1998) 16...h6 17 a5 bxa5 18 ♗xa5 fxe4 19 ♘xe4 ♗f5 20 ♘fd2 ♕d7 21 ♗b4 g5 22 ♖e3 ♗g6 23 ♖ea3 ♖ab8 24 ♗c3 += A.Karpov-V.Maki, Helsinki (clock simul) 1996, although Karpov eventually lost.

c) 13...♘e8 *(D)* is the main alternative, freeing the f-pawn and defending the d6-pawn, so that White has to reckon with both ...f7-f5 and ...c7-c5.

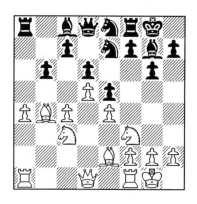

c1) 14 a5?! c5! 15 dxc6 ♘xc6 16 ♗a3 (or 16 ♕d5 ♗b7 17 a6 ♘xb4 18 ♕xb7 ♖b8 =+ D.Akdag-O.Kanmazalp, World Junior Ch. 2007) 16...♘xa5 17 ♘b5 ♗b7 18 ♕d3 f5 19 ♘d2 ♗h6 =+ G.Heinatz-K.Isgandarova, Turin Olympiad 2006.

c2) 14 ♘b5 f5! 15 ♘d2 ♗h6 (if 15...c6 16 dxc6 ♘xc6 17 ♗a3 ♗e6 18 ♗f3 ♕d7 19 ♕c2 += L.Van Wely-M.Solleveld, Dieren 1999; or 15...♗d7 16 ♗f3 ♔h8 17 ♗c3 ♖b8 18 ♖b1 ♘g8 19 a5 bxa5 20 ♗xa5 ♘gf6 21 ♘c3 += A.Shneider-

V.Iordachescu, Enakievo 1997) 16 a5 (if 16 ♗f3 ♘f6 17 a5 bxa5 18 ♖xa5 ♗a6 19 ♕c2 c5 20 ♖fa1 cxb4 21 ♖xa6 ♖xa6 22 ♖xa6 ♗xd2 23 ♕xd2 fxe4 24 ♗e2 ♘f5 25 ♕xb4 e3 -/+ A.Evdokimov-D.Khismatullin, Russian Junior Ch. 2002) 16...c6 17 dxc6 ♘xc6 18 ♗c3 ♘xa5 18 ♘b3 ♗b7 19 ♘xa5 bxa5 20 ♕b3 a4 21 ♖xa4 ♖xa4 22 c5+ ♔h8 23 ♕xa4 dxc5 24 ♗xe5+ ♗g7 = P.Lopepe-P.Spitz, corr. 1999.

c3) 14 ♘d2 f5 15 ♕b3 (or 15 ♘b5 – *14 ♘b5*) 15...♔h8 (or 15...♖b8 16 ♘b5 – *14 ♕b3*) 16 a5 c5 17 axb6! ♖xa1 18 ♖xa1 cxb4 19 ♕xb4 ♗b7 20 ♘b3 ♘c8 21 c5! (if 21 ♘a5, B.Gelfand-A.Istratescu, Yerevan Olympiad 1996, 21...♕e7! Gelfand; e.g. 22 ♗d1 ♗h6 23 ♗a4 ♗d2 24 ♗c6 ♘f6 25 ♗xb7 ♘xe4 26 ♗xc8 ♗xc3 ∞) 21 c5 dxc5 22 ♘xc5 ♖f7 23 ♘xb7 ♖xb7 24 ♖a8 += S.Shmat-V.Guivan, Alushta 2006.

c4) 14 ♕b3 ♖b8!? (if 14...f5 15 a5! bxa5 16 ♗xa5 fxe4 17 ♘xe4 ♗f5 18 ♘fd2 +/= D.Matulik-P.Kovacocy, Slovakian Team Ch. 2005; and not 15...c5?! 16 dxc6 ♘xc6?? 17 c5+ ♔h8 18 cxb6 +- E.Stauch-G.Brunner, Bad Wiessee 2001) 15 ♘b5 (not 15 a5?? bxa5 16 ♖xa5 c5 -+) 15...f5 16 ♘d2 (or 16 a5 fxe4 17 ♘d2 bxa5 18 ♗xa5 ♘f5 19 ♘xe4 ♘d4 20 ♕d1 += Z.Dub-M.Müller, Budapest 2002) 16...♘f6 17 a5 bxa5 18 ♗xa5 ♘xe4 19 ♘xe4 fxe4 20 ♕c2 ♖b7 21 c5 with compensation, O.Vodep-J.Nielsen, corr. 1998.

14 ♕d3

Overprotecting the e4-pawn to prepare 15 ♘b5 followed by 16 a5. White has also tried:

a) 14 a5 c5! 15 dxc6 ♘xc6 16 ♗xd6 ♖xa5 (or 16...♘d4!? 17 ♘xd4 exd4 18 ♘b5 ∞ S.Joksic-A.Colovic, Padova 1999) 17 ♖xa5 (T.Radjabov-J.Tihonov, Minsk 2000) 17...♘xa5! 18 ♗xe5 ♕xd1 19 ♗xd1 ♘xc4 20 ♗xf6 ♗xf6 =.

b) 14 ♘d2 c5! 15 ♗a3 (or 15 dxc6 ♘xc6 16 ♗a3 ♘d4 17 ♘b5 ♘xb5 18 axb5 ♗h6 with counterplay, J.Gustafsson-S.Joachim, German League 2001) 15...♖f8 16 ♗b2 ♘e8 17 ♘b5 ♗h6 18 ♕c2 f5 ∞ D.Rogozenko-B.Miljanic, Bucharest 2002.

c) 14 ♕c2!? c5 15 ♗a3 ♘h5 (or 15...♖f8 16 ♖fb1 ♘e8 17 ♗c1 h6 18 ♖a3 += E.Ovod-A.Toth, Budapest 2002) 16 ♖fb1 ♘f4 17 ♗f1 ♗g4 (E.Ovod-I.Sudakova, European Women's Ch., Warsaw 2001) 18 ♘e1 ♘c8 19 ♗c1 +/=.

d) 14 ♖e1 (the main alternative) 14...♗f8 15 h3 (if 15 ♗f1 c5 16 dxc6 ♘xc6 17 ♗a3 ♗g4! 18 h3 ♗xf3 19 ♕xf3 ♘d4 20 ♕d1 ♘d7 21 ♖b1 ♘c5 22 ♗c1 ♗g7 ∞ L.Van Wely-M.Golubev, Dieren 1999; or 16 ♗a3 ♗h6 17 ♗b2 ♖f8 18 g3 ♘e8 19 ♘b5 f5 with counterplay, P.Eljanov-R.Ponomariov, Kharkov 2001) 15...♗b7 16 ♗f1 c5 (D) and then:

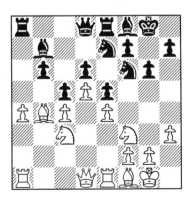

d1) 17 dxc6 ♘xc6 18 ♗a3 ♘d4! gives Black good counterplay; e.g. 19 ♘d5 (if 19 ♘xd4 exd4 20 ♕xd4 ♗g7 = Ye Jiang-chuan; or 19 ♖a2!? V.Epishin-A.Cherniaev, Geneva 2002, 19...♘e6! 20 ♘d5 ♘d7 21 ♕b3 ♗c6 ∞) 19...♗g7 20 ♘xd4 exd4 21 ♗d3 ♗c6 22 ♗b4 ♖e6! 23 ♖a3 ♘d7 24 ♕c2 (if 24 ♘f4 ♖e8 25 ♗xd6?? ♕f6 wins a piece) 24...♘c5 25 ♖ea1 ♖e8 = I.Farago-S.Joachim, Böblingen 2001.

d2) 17 ♗a3 ♗c8 (or 17...♗g7 18 ♗c1 ♗c8 19 ♖b1 ♗d7 20 ♘b5 ♘c8 21 g3 += L.Van Wely-Ye Jiangchuan, FIDE World Ch., Moscow 2001) 18 ♘b5 ♗g7 19 ♗b2 ♖f8 (although Black has spent *six* tempi moving his rook and bishops back and forth, he has achieved his aim of closing the position and does not stand too badly) 20 ♖a3 ♘e8 21 ♕a1 ♗d7 (21...f5!? is quite possible) 22 a5 bxa5 23 ♗c3 ♘c8 24 ♗xa5 ♕e7 25 ♕c1 +/= R.Kasimdzhanov-Ye Jiangchuan, Istanbul Olympiad 2000.

14...♘d7

This is considered the best response. Instead:

a) 14...♗f8 15 ♘b5 ♗b7 16 a5 c5 17 ♗c3 is good for White, e.g. 17...♘h5 18 g3 bxa5 19 ♖a4 f5 20 ♘d2 ♘f6 21 f3 h5?! 22 f4! +/- A.Shabalov-D.Sharavdorj, Qingdao 2002.

b) 14...♘f5!? 15 a5! (not 15 exf5? e4 ∞) 15...bxa5 16 ♖xa5 ♖b8 16 ♘b5 ♘d4 17 ♘fxd4 exd4 18 f3 +/- T.Kotanjian-D.Petrosian, Iranian Team Ch. 2005.

c) 14...♘h5 15 g3 f5 16 a5 bxa5 17 ♗xa5 fxe4 18 ♘xe4 ♗f5 19 ♘fd2 ♕d7 20 ♗c3 ♘f6 21 ♘xf6+ += D.Rogozenko-N.Djukic, Bucharest 2002.

15 ♕b1! *(D)*

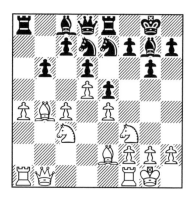

The immediate 15 a5 allows 15...c5!? (if 15...bxa5 16 ♗xa5 ♘c5 17 ♕c2 += Golubev; while 15...♘c5 16 ♕b1! f5 is the next note) 16 dxc6 ♘xc6 17 ♗xd6 ♖xa5 18 ♖xa5 ♘xa5 19 ♘b5 ♘b7 20 ♖d1 ♕f6 21 ♕a3 ♘dc5 ∞ S.Bromberger-M.Golubev, Bad Wiessee 1999. Or if 15 ♘b5 ♘c5 16 ♗xc5 bxc5 17 a5 ♗a6 18 ♖fb1 ♖f8 intending ...f7-f5 with counterplay (Tsesarsky).

The text was a subtle novelty from V.Ivanchuk-Ye Jiangchuan, FIDE World Ch., Moscow 2001, which we now follow:

15...♗h6

The salient point is that 15...♘c5 16 a5 f5 (or 16...bxa5 17 ♗xc5 dxc5 18 ♘a4 ♕d6 19 ♕b5 +/- Ivanchuk) 17 axb6 ♖xa1 18 ♕xa1 cxb6 19 ♗xc5 bxc5 20 ♖b1 ♖f8 transposes to the inferior 13...♘d7 variation, where 21 ♖b8 (18 ♖b8 in the above note) is good for White.

15...♗f8!? (Ivanchuk) 16 ♖d1!? f5 17 a5 ♘c5 18 axb6 ♖xa1 19 ♕xa1 cxb6 (V.Babula-M.Tratar, Graz 2001) leads to similar positions after 20 ♗xc5 bxc5

21 ♖b1.

16 a5 ♘c5

If 16...c5 17 dxc6 ♘xc6 18 ♗xd6 ♖xa5 19 ♘d5! ♖xa1 20 ♕xa1 +/- Ivanchuk.

17 axb6 ♖xa1 18 ♕xa1 cxb6 19 ♖b1 *(D)*

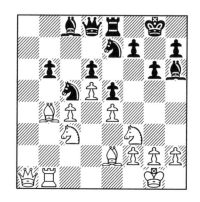

19...♕c7?

Merely wasting a couple of moves. Instead 19...f5 (Ivanchuk) leads again to 13...♘d7 type positions; e.g. 20 ♗xc5 bxc5 21 ♕a7 ♗d7 22 ♖b7 ♘c8 23 ♕b8 with the initiative.

20 ♘b5 ♕d8

There is nothing better: if 20...♕d7 21 ♗xc5 bxc5 22 ♕a5 +/- Tsesarsky; or 20...♕b8 21 ♘xe5!? dxe5 22 d6 ♘a6 23 d7 ♗xd7 24 ♕xa6 +/-.

21 ♗xc5 bxc5 22 ♕a7 ♗g4?!

22...f5 should still have been tried, when Ivanchuk gives 23 ♗d3 fxe4 24 ♗xe4 ♘f5 25 ♕c7 +/-. Whereas now Black has no counterplay and White wins smoothly.

23 h3 ♘c8 24 ♕b8 ♗xf3 25 ♗xf3 ♗g5 26 ♖a1 h5 27 ♖a6 ♗e7 28 ♖c6 ♖f8 29 ♖c7 ♗g5 30 ♕b7 ♗d2 31 h4 ♗a5 32 ♖c6 ♗e1 33 g3 ♗a5 34 ♔f1! ♕d2 35 ♗e2 ♘e7 36 ♕xe7 ♗xf2 37 ♔xf2 1-0.

C23: 10...axb4 11 ♗xb4 *(D)*

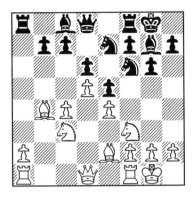

11...♘d7

With the text Black achieves two goals: he controls the c5-square and prepares ...f7-f5. The advantage is that White has no direct way to develop his initiative as a4-a5 does not aim at a target on b6. On the downside, the light-squared bishop is obstructed; sooner or later Black will have to move the d7-knight again, and this will allow White to play c4-c5.

Instead, 11...b6 12 a4 transposes to line C22 above. 11...♘e8 makes less sense due to 12 c5! and then:

a) 12...f5 13 ♘g5! (13 ♘d2 – *9 ♘d2 ♘e8 10 b4 f5 11 c5 a5!?* in Chapter Ten) 13...fxe4 (or 13...dxc5 14 ♗xc5 ♘d6 15 ♕b3 ♔h8 16 ♖ad1 += E.Relange-E.Juglard, Corsica rapid 1997) 14 ♗g4 ♘f5 15 ♘cxe4 ♗f6 16 ♘e6 += J.Paasikangas Tella-T.Lematschko, Yerevan Olympiad 1996.

b) 12...h6 13 a4 f5 14 ♘d2 f4?! (but if 14...dxc5 15 ♗xc5 ♘d6 16 f3 += A.Al Ghasra-A.Kassis, Arabian Ch. 2000) 15 ♘c4 ♖f6 16 cxd6 cxd6 17 ♘b5 ♗f8 18 ♕b3 ♔h7 19 ♕a3 ♗d7 (G.Di Benedetto-

M.Ibar, Argentine Ch. 2004) and now 20 ♘bxd6! ♖xa4 21 ♘xe8 ♖xa3 22 ♘xf6+ ♔g7 23 ♗xa3 ♔xf6 24 ♗b2 +-.

c) 12...♗h6 13 cxd6 cxd6 14 ♘d2 f5 15 ♘c4 fxe4 16 ♘xe4 ♘f5 17 a4 += L.Ostrowski-S.Farago, Budapest 1998.

d) 12...dxc5 13 ♗xc5 ♘d6 14 ♕b3 ♔h8 15 ♖ac1 f5 16 ♘d2 (or 16 exf5!? ♗xf5 17 ♘g5 +=) 16...♗h6 17 f4! with the initiative, I.Weltmander-G.Borisenko, corr. 1956.

12 a4 *(D)*

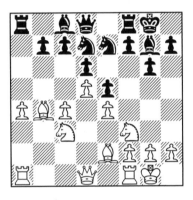

The advance a2-a4-a5 is essential for White, lest a more timely ...b7-b6 stop all his queenside play.

12 ♘d2 is slightly less accurate as it loses the option of ♘g5. Thus 12...f5! 13 a4 (or 13 ♘b3 b6 14 a4 ♘c5! 15 f3 ♗d7 16 a5 ♘a6 17 ♗a3 bxa5 18 ♘xa5 ♗h6 = J.Pietila-O.Alivirta, Finnish Team Ch. 1993) 13...fxe4!? (13...♗h6 returns to the main line; but not 13...♘f6?! 14 c5!, e.g. 14...dxc5 15 ♗xc5 fxe4 16 ♗c4 ♔h8 17 ♘dxe4 +/- V.Mikhalevski-N.Gelbmann, Vienna 1998) 14 ♘dxe4 ♘f5 15 c5 (or 15 a5 ♘d4 16 ♗d3 ♖f4 ∞ V.Rührig-W.Zbikowski, German League 1985) 15...dxc5 16 ♘xc5 ♘xc5 17 ♗xc5

(B.Lalic-M.Van Schaardenburg, Haarlem 1994) 17...♖f7 ∞.

12...♗h6

The standard move here, preventing ♘g5 in response to ...f7-f5, while anticipating the removal of a knight on d2 to increase the pressure on e4. Other lines are good for White:

a) 12...b6 returns to a lesser variation in C22 above (see the note with 13...♘d7).

b) 12...f5 13 ♘g5! (13 ♘d2 – *12 ♘d2 f5 13 a4*) 13...♘c5 (if 13...♘f6 14 c5 fxe4 15 ♘gxe4 ♘f5 16 ♗c4 += I.Gulkov-S.Timofeev, Tula 2000) 14 ♗xc5 dxc5 15 ♗f3 ♖a6 16 a5 ♔h8 17 ♘e6 ♗xe6 18 dxe6 f4 19 ♕xd8 ♖xd8 20 ♖fb1 ♖b8 21 ♘d5 ♘xd5 22 cxd5 +/- V.Kramnik-G.Kasparov, Moscow blitz 1998.

c) 12...h6 13 a5 f5 14 ♘d2 h5!? (if 14...♘f6 15 c5 fxe4 16 cxd6 cxd6 17 ♘dxe4 ♘e8 18 ♘b5 +/- M.Dehne-T.Kuhnen, Dortmund 2001) 15 exf5?! (15 ♘b3 += *ECO*) 15...gxf5 16 ♗xh5 e4! ∞ D.Antic-P.Panchev, Negorski Bani 1997.

d) 12...♘c5 (intending ...♘a6) 13 ♗xc5! dxc5 14 a5 ♗d7 (if 14...b6?! 15 axb6 ♖xa1 16 ♕xa1 cxb6 17 ♖b1 +/- E.Gausel-D.Rogozenko, Yerevan Olympiad 1996; or 14...f5 15 ♘d2 c6 16 ♘b3 +/- J.Tisdall-M.Carlson, Stockholm 1996) 15 ♕b3 ♖b8 (or 15...♖a7 16 a6! b6 17 ♘b5 ♗xb5 18 cxb5 ♘c8 19 ♘d2 ♘d6 20 ♗d3 +/- J.Lautier-M.Novik, Dubai rapid 2002) 16 ♖fd1 ♘c8 17 a6 b6 18 ♘b5 ♗xb5 19 cxb5 ♘d6 20 ♘d2 f5 21 ♘c4 += Se.Ivanov-P.Laveryd, Swedish Team Ch. 1999.

e) 12...♔h8 13 a5 ♘g8 14 ♘d2 f5 15 ♘b3 ♘gf6 (or 15...♘df6 16 c5 ♘xe4 17 ♘xe4 fxe4 18 cxd6 cxd6 19 ♘d2 ♘f6 20 ♘c4 += I.Farago-N.Stewart, Senden 2000) 16 c5 ♘e8 17 cxd6 ♘xd6 (or 17...cxd6 18 ♘d2 ♘df6 19 f3 ♗h6 20 ♘c4 +/- A.Adamov-D.Shtanko, Ukrainian Junior Ch. 1999) 18 ♘d2 ♘f6 19 f3 ♘h5 20 ♘c4 ♘f4 21 ♖f2 ♖f7 22 ♘xd6 cxd6 23 ♗f1 += F.Baumbach-I.Kopylov, corr. 1989.

13 a5

The most flexible response, though White has also tried:

a) 13 ♘e1?! f5 14 ♘d3 (the knight is misplaced here) 14...♘f6 15 ♗f3 (or 15 f3 c5 16 ♗a3 ♗e3+ 17 ♘f2 ♗d4 =+ D.Muhvic-S.Zelenika, Rijeka 2001) 15...fxe4 16 ♘xe4 ♘f5 17 c5 ♖a6 18 cxd6 cxd6 19 ♘b2 ♘d4 =+ J.Hernando Rodrigo-M.Roeder, Barbera 1998.

b) 13 ♕b3 ♔h8 14 a5 f5 15 ♕a3!? (15 ♗d3 – *14 ♗d3 ♔h8 15 ♕b3*) 15...♘f6?! (15...g5!? looks better, and if 16 c5 dxc5 17 ♗xc5 ♘xc5 18 ♕xc5 g4 19 ♘xe5 ♗g7 ∞) 16 c5 ♘xe4 17 ♘xe4 fxe4 18 cxd6 ♘xd5 (or 18...cxd6 19 ♘xe5!) 19 dxc7 ♕f6 20 ♘d2 +/- E.Najer-L.Valdes, Linares 2003.

c) 13 ♘d2 f5 14 ♘b3?! (instead 14 a5 transposes below; as does 14 ♗f3 ♔h8 15 a5, or if 14...b6 15 a5 ♘c5 16 axb6 ♖xa1 17 ♕xa1 cxb6 18 ♕a2 += B.Gelfand-G.Schebler, German League 1996) 14...♘f6 (14...b6 15 a5 ♘c5 is also fine, e.g. 16 exf5 gxf5 17 ♘b5 ♘g6 18 ♖e1 e4 ∞ I.Sokolov-B.Gelfand, Groningen 1996; or 16 ♖a3, R.Kasimdzhanov-G.Schebler, Groningen 1997, 16...♘xe4!? 17 ♘xe4 fxe4 18 axb6 ♖xa3 19 bxc7 ♕xc7 20 ♗xa3 ♘f5 ∞ Krnic) 15

♗f3 (or 15 exf5 gxf5 16 c5 ♘g6 17 cxd6 cxd6 ½-½ T.Halasz-Z.Ballai, Hungarian Team Ch. 2001) 15...fxe4 (or 15...g5!? again) 16 ♘xe4 ♘xe4 17 ♗xe4 ♗f5 = A.Von Gleich-H.Degenhardt, German League 1992.

13...f5

Now White has two moves:

C231: 14 ♘d2 329
C232: 14 ♗d3 330

C231: 14 ♘d2 *(D)*

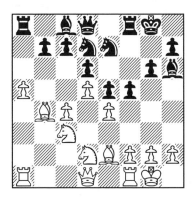

14...♘f6

Otherwise 14...♔h8 15 ♗d3 transposes to C322, unless White wants to try:

a) 15 ♘b3 ♘f6! 16 ♗f3 (not 16 f3? ♗e3+ 17 ♔h1 ♘h5 18 ♕d3? ♘g3+! 19 hxg3 f4 -+ I.Jelen-B.Socko, Groningen 1998) 16...fxe4 17 ♘xe4 ♘xe4 18 ♗xe4 ♘g8 = V.Sakalauskas-P.H.Nielsen, Koszalin 1997.

b) 15 ♗f3 ♘g8 16 ♘b3 ♖f7 (if 16...♘gf6 17 c5 fxe4 18 ♗xe4 ♘xe4 19 ♘xe4 ♕h4 20 ♕e1 += F.Baumbach-K.Richardson, European Seniors Ch.

2006) 17 c5 ♗f8 18 cxd6 ♗xd6 19 ♗xd6 cxd6 20 ♘b5 ♘df6 ∞ V.Popov-Y.Yarovik, Novgorod 1999.

15 c5 ♗xd2 16 ♕xd2 fxe4!

This seems better than exchanging knights with 16...♘xe4!? 17 ♘xe4 fxe4 *(D)* and then:

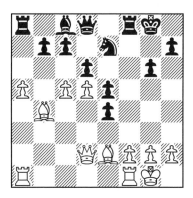

a) 18 cxd6 cxd6 19 ♗c3 (or 19 ♖fe1 ♘f5 20 ♗d1!? e3 21 fxe3 b6 22 ♗a4 bxa5 23 ♗c6 ♖b8 24 ♗xa5 += I.Tsesarsky-U.Weissbuch, Petah Tikva 1998) 19...♘f5 20 ♖a4 b6! (not 20...♘d4? 21 ♖xd4! exd4 22 ♕xd4 +- V.Mikhalevski-F.Jenni, Zürich 1999) 21 a6 (or if 21 ♖xe4 bxa5 22 f4 ♕b6+ 23 ♔h1 ♗a6 with counterplay) 21...♕d7 22 ♖fa1 b5 23 ♖4a3 ♕a7 24 ♗b4 ♕b6 = D.Kuhne-T.Irzhanov, corr. 2003.

b) 18 ♗c3! ♘f5 (not 18...dxc5?! 19 ♗c4 ♕d6 20 ♖ae1 +/- J.Mertanen-J.Filipek, Halkidiki 2002) 19 ♖a4! ♕h4 (or 19...♘h4 20 ♖xe4 g5 21 ♖b4 ♘g6 22 cxd6 cxd6 23 ♖b6 ♘f4 24 ♗b4 +/- V.Kramnik-L.Van Wely, Monte Carlo blindfold rapid 1997) 20 cxd6 (or 20 ♖c4!? +=; but not 20 g3? e3! =+) 20...cxd6 21 f4 e3 22 ♕d1 ♗d7 23 ♖b4 exf4 24 ♖fxf4 ♕g5?! (but if 24...♕h6 25 ♖f3!? +=)

25 ♖g4 ♕e7 26 ♖xb7 +/- V.Babula-A.Istratescu, Krynica 1998.

17 cxd6

Delaying only gives Black more options; e.g. 17 ♘b5 ♘f5 18 cxd6 (or 18 ♖ac1 ♖f7 19 ♖fe1? dxc5 20 ♗xc5 c6 21 ♘d6 e3 -/+ I.Ivanisevic-S.Safin, Elista Olympiad 1998) 18...♘xd6!? (18...cxd6 is the main line) 19 ♖ac1 ♖f7 20 ♖fd1 ♗g4 21 ♘c3 ♕d7 22 h3 ♗xe2 23 ♕xe2 ♕f5 ∞ V.Babula-E.Inarkiev, Elista Olympiad 1998.

17...cxd6 18 ♘b5

18 ♘a4!? might be a better try; e.g. 18...♘f5 19 ♘b6 ♖b8 20 ♖ac1 ♗d7 21 ♖fe1 ♗e8 22 ♗c4 h6 23 ♗b1 += A.Evdokimov-I.Kurnosov, Russian Junior Ch. 2002.

18...♘f5 19 ♖a3

Or 19 ♖ac1 ♘e8 20 ♖c4 b6 21 ♖a1 ♗a6 22 ♖c6?! (but if 22 ♖cc1 ♗xb5 23 ♗xb5 ♘d4 =+) 22...♗xb5 23 ♗xb5 bxa5 24 ♗c3 ♘f6 25 ♖c4? e3! 26 fxe3 ♕b6 -+ A.Shalamberidze-T.Mgeladze, Batumi 2003.

19...♘e8 20 ♕c2 b6! *(D)*

The simplest solution; Black eradicates his weakness.

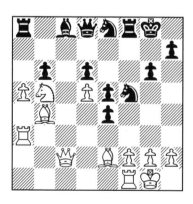

21 ♕c6

Or if 21 axb6 ♖xa3 22 ♗xa3 ♗a6 23 b7 ♗xb7 24 ♕xe4 ♗a6 25 ♖b1 ½-½ C.Sergel-H.Van de Wynkele, corr. 2000.

21...♖a6 22 ♖c1 ♘e7 23 ♕c3 bxa5!

Eschewing any complications such as 23...♘xd5 24 ♗c4 ♗e6 25 ♕b3 ♕f6 26 ♖f1 ♘xb4 27 ♗xe6+ ♔h8 28 ♗c8!? ∞.

24 ♗xa5 ♕d7 25 ♘c7 ♘xc7 26 ♕xc7 ♖a7

And not 26...♕f5? 27 ♗xa6 ♕xf2+ 28 ♔h1 ♗xa6 because of 29 ♗b6! ♘xd5 30 ♗xf2 ♘xc7 31 ♗b6 and wins (Beckhuis).

27 ♕xd7 ♗xd7 ½-½ G.Beckhuis-T.Pähtz, Gelsenkirchen 1997.

Beckhuis gives the final variation 28 ♗b4 ♖xa3 29 ♗xa3 ♖c8 30 ♖xc8+ ♘xc8 31 ♗a6 ♔f7 32 ♗xc8 ♗xc8 33 ♗xd6 ♗b7 34 ♗xe5 ♗xd5 when the game has reduced to a dead draw.

C232: 14 ♗d3 ♔h8

Black wants to play ...♘d7-f6 to increase pressure on the e4-pawn, but doing so immediately would allow 15 c5, so he makes a useful waiting move. Instead:

a) 14...♖f7 15 ♖e1! (or 15 ♕b3 g5 16 ♖fd1 g4 17 ♘d2 b6 18 ♘b5 bxa5 19 ♕c2 += L.Van Wely-J.Piket, 4th matchgame, Monte Carlo 1997; but 15...fxe4! improves, and if 16 ♗xe4 ♘f5, or 16 ♘xe4 ♖xf3! 17 gxf3 ♘f5 18 ♕d1 ♕h4 with compensation) 15...f4? (releasing the tension is a mistake as White quickly breaks through on the queenside; no better is 15...♘f6? 16 c5 fxe4 17 ♘xe4 ♘exd5 18 ♗c4 ♘xb4 19 cxd6 +/- L.Van Wely-A.Morozevich, Monte Carlo blindfold rapid 2007; while if 15...♔h8 16 ♘b5! += as Black would have preferred ...♘g8 to ...♖f7 here) 16 ♘b5 g5 17 c5 dxc5 18 ♗c4 cxb4 19 d6 +/- L.Van Wely-G.Schebler, Dutch Team Ch. 2000.

b) 14...♘f6 15 c5! fxe4 16 ♘xe4! (better than inserting 16 cxd6 cxd6 17 ♘xe4 ♘xe4 18 ♗xe4 ♗f5 19 ♖e1 ♗xe4 20 ♖xe4 ♘f5 21 ♖b1 ♖c8 ∞ D.Bunzmann-S.Kindermann, German League 2000) 16...♘xe4 17 ♗xe4 ♗f5 18 ♖e1 ♗xe4 (or 18...♕d7 19 ♖b1 ♔h8 20 ♗c3 ♖a7 21 ♕d3 += J.Lautier-M.Roeder, German League 2001) 19 ♖xe4 ♘f5 (or 19...♖f4 20 ♖xf4 ♗xf4 21 ♕b3 ♘f5 22 ♗c3 +/= R.Sakic-F.Balabaev, corr. 2003) 20 ♕b3! b6 21 cxb6 cxb6 22 a6 b5 23 ♕c2 ♕b6 24 ♕c6 ♕xc6 25 dxc6 ♗g7 26 ♖a5 += K.Müller-J.Monacell, corr. 2001.

15 ♘d2

If he hasn't played ♘d2 already (e.g. 14 ♘d2 ♔h8 15 ♗d3), White can also try:

a) 15 ♕b3 fxe4 (15...♘f6?! 16 c5 += is similar to 14...♘f6 above; but 15...g5!? comes into consideration) 16 ♗xe4 (or 16 ♘xe4 ♖xf3!? 17 gxf3 ♘f5) 16...♘f5 17 ♕c2 ♕e7 18 ♖fe1 ♘b8 19 ♘b5 ♘a6 20 ♗a3 ♗g7 ∞ P.Taboada-A.Acevedo Millan, corr. 1997.

b) 15 ♖e1! ♘g8 (if 15...♘f6?! 16 c5 += again) 16 h3 (16 ♘d2! – *15 ♘d2 ♘g8 16 ♖e1* while avoiding the next note) 16...♘df6?! (better 16...fxe4 17 ♘xe4 ♘df6 or 17 ♗xe4 ♘gf6! ∞) 17 c5 fxe4 18 ♗xe4! ♖f7 (if 18...♘xe4 19 ♘xe4 ♘f6? 20 cxd6 wins) 19 ♗c2 ♗f5 20 ♗b3 ♘e8 21 c6 +/- P.Smirnov-F.Jenni, Istanbul 2004.

15...♘g8 (D)

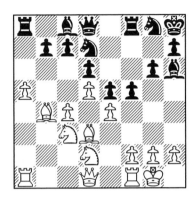

The usual continuation, although in this precise position 15...♘f6! is critical, when 16 c5 can be met by 16...dxc5 17 ♗xc5 b6!; e.g. 18 axb6 ♖xa1 19 ♕xa1 cxb6 20 ♗xe7 ♕xe7 = L.Lamarche Rodriguez-I.Hristov, corr. 2001, or 18 ♗b4 c5! 19 dxc6 bxa5 20 ♗xe7 ♕xe7 = S.Soucha-J.Pletanek, corr. 1999.

16 ♕c2

Other moves:

a) 16 ♘b3?! ♘df6 17 c5 (or 17 exf5 gxf5 18 c5 ♘e7 19 cxd6 cxd6 20 ♘b5 ♖a6 21 ♘c3 ♖a8 = M.Sorokin-D.Valerga, Buenos Aires 1996) 17...fxe4 18 ♘xe4 ♘xe4 19 ♗xe4 ♘f6 20 ♗f3 ♗f5 = N.Sretenskij-M.Erdogdu, Dos Hermanas 2004.

b) 16 ♘b5 fxe4 17 ♘xe4 ♘gf6 18 ♖a3 (if 18 ♘xc7!? ♕xc7 19 ♗xd6 ♕d8 20 ♗xf8 ♕xf8 ∞) 18...♘xe4 19 ♗xe4 ♘f6 20 ♗f3 ♗d7 = T.Kotanjian-N.Mamedov, Iranian Team Ch. 2005.

c) 16 ♖e1 is also good; e.g. 16...♖f7 17 ♕c2 (or 17 ♘b5 ♖a6 18 ♕c2 ♘df6 19 c5 fxe4 20 ♗xe4 ♗d7 21 ♘c3 +/= L.Van Wely-V.Ivanchuk, Wijk aan Zee 1999) 17...♘df6 18 c5 fxe4 19 ♘dxe4 ♘xe4 20 ♘xe4 ♘f6 21 cxd6 ♘xe4 22 ♗xe4 (22

Ξxe4! cxd6 23 Ξc4 looks stronger) 22...cxd6 23 ♕b3 b6! ∞ A.Polatel-M.Erdogdu, Turkish Ch. 2004.

16...Ξf7

If 16...♘df6?! 17 c5 ♗xd2 18 ♕xd2 fxe4 19 ♗xe4 ♘xe4 20 ♘xe4 ♗f5 21 ♘c3 ♘f6 22 f4 +/- V.Babula-T.Balabaev, Olomouc 2004.

17 Ξad1!?

Alternatively, 17 ♘a4!? (or 17 Ξe1 – 16 Ξe1) 17...fxe4 18 ♘xe4 ♘df6 19 ♘ac3 ♗f5 20 ♘g3 ♗xd3 21 ♕xd3 ♕f8 22 Ξab1 += Y.Pelletier-O.Renet, European Team Ch., Pula 1997.

17...♘df6 18 c5! dxc5?!

Black should prefer 18...fxe4 19 ♘dxe4 ♘xe4 20 ♘xe4 ♘f6 when he is only slightly worse.

19 ♗xc5 fxe4 20 ♘cxe4 *(D)*

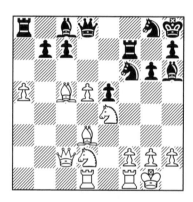

This position was reached in L.Van Wely-A.Morozevich, Monte Carlo (blindfold rapid) 2006. White stands better: the e5-pawn is a target, and the d1-rook is now well placed opposite the black queen.

Unfortunately, without sight of the board neither player was able to show complete accuracy and in the end Black came out on top. The game concluded **20...♗f5?!** [but if 20...Ξxa5?! 21 ♘c4 +/- or 20...b6 21 axb6 cxb6 22 ♗b4 ♘xd5 23 ♗d6! +/=] **21 ♘f3! Ξxa5?!** [21...♘xe4 22 ♗xe4 ♗g7] **22 ♘xe5 Ξg7 23 ♘c4?!** [23 ♘xf6 ♘xf6 24 ♕c3 is very strong] **23...♗xe4?!** [23...Ξb5] **24 ♘xa5 ♗xg2 25 ♔xg2 b6 26 Ξfe1? ♕xd5+ 27 ♗e4 ♕g5+ 28 ♔h1 bxc5 29 ♘c6 ♕h4 30 f3 ♗f4 31 Ξe2 ♘h5 32 ♔g1 g5 33 ♕xc5??** [33 ♗f5] **33...g4! 34 ♕f2 gxf3+ 0-1**.

Conclusion

If Black wishes to avoid the 9...♘h5 main lines, he has several possibilities. Of these, 9...♔h8 (line A) is perhaps a bit too subtle, allowing White good chances for an advantage. 9...♘e8 (line B) is more acceptable, but only if Black is prepared for 9 ♘d2 ♘e8 lines in the previous chapter.

Instead, 9...a5 (line C) offers the best equalizing chances. White should probably prefer 10 ♗a3 (to 10 bxa5) as it eliminates any ideas of an early ...c7-c5. For Black the main problem is that, by delaying his kingside counterplay to respond on the queenside, he can often end up in a slightly passive position, as in the main lines C22 and C232. It may be for this reason that Black has recently been investigating 11...♘h5!? leading to interesting play (see the notes to C22).

Chapter Twelve

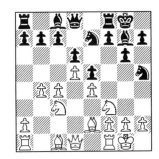

Bayonet Attack: 9 b4 with 9...♘h5

1 d4 ♘f6 2 c4 g6 3 ♘c3 ♗g7 4 e4 d6 5 ♘f3 0-0 6 ♗e2 e5 7 0-0 ♘c6 8 d5 ♘e7 9 b4 ♘h5 *(D)*

The most frequent and principled continuation; Black takes the chance to prepare ...f7-f5 while posting his knight actively on h5, with the additional option of ...♘f4. If the knight is allowed to come forward, Black can either remove the e2-bishop, increasing his control over the key g4-square in anticipation of ...g6-g5-g4; or in the event of ♗c1xf4, strongly activate his own dark-squared bishop after ...e5xf4.

For White the standard retreats, 10 ♘d2 and 10 ♘e1, fail to challenge this plan, so that Black obtains his traditional counterplay with the knight already participating. More subtle are 10 ♕c2 and 10 ♕b3, which have the idea of exchanging on f4 and then attacking in the centre, but Black has sufficient resources whether he falls in with White's intentions or not. The straight-

forward 10 c5 hopes to exploit the absence of the king's knight for defensive purposes by breaking through quickly on the queenside; but the consequent elimination of one of White's bishops is more significant, so that he has little hope of an advantage here either.

In the early days of the variation White mostly opted for 10 g3, crudely keeping the knight out of f4, while answering ...f7-f5 with ♘g5. The obvious drawback is that g2-g3 weakens the white king's position, which may be punished by, for example, 10...f5 11 ♘g5 ♘f6 12 f3 f4!?.

However, it was the emergence of 10 ♖e1 in the mid 1990s which led to the rejuvenation of the Bayonet Attack for White, and this move is now played in 70% of games. The simple idea is to answer 10...♘f4 with 11 ♗f1, leaving the knight at somewhat of a loss. If instead 10...f5 11 ♘g5 ♘f4, then 12 ♗xf4! exf4 13 ♖c1 also gives good prospects.

Naturally Black has other possibilities, such as 10...a5!?, leading to positions reminiscent of 9...a5 in the previous chapter, or 10...f5 11 ♘g5 ♘f6!, which is regarded as the main line. In the latter case White can support the centre with either 12 f3 or 12 ♗f3, both of which lead to interesting and unique play.

A: 10 ♘d2 *334*
B: 10 ♕c2 *337*
C: 10 c5 *340*
D: 10 g3 *345*
E: 10 ♖e1 *353*

A: 10 ♘d2 *(D)*

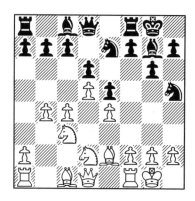

Moving the knight over to the queenside while attacking its counterpart on h5; but this plan is too simplistic to offer White any real hope of an edge.

10 ♘e1 ♘f4 11 ♘d3, with the same idea, fails to exert much pressure either; e.g. 11...f5 12 f3 g5 (or 12...a5 13 bxa5 ♖xa5 14 ♖b1 g5 15 ♘f2 ♘xe2+ 16 ♕xe2 f4 17 ♖b5 ♖a8 18 ♘d3 b6 =+

B.Korsus-M.Pena Gomez, Bad Wiessee 2008) 13 ♗e3 ♘eg6 14 ♖c1 h5 15 c5 ♘xe2+ 16 ♕xe2 f4 17 ♗f2 g4 with a good game for Black, D.Surma-B.Socko, European Junior Ch. 1996.
10...♘f4 11 ♗f3
Instead:

a) 11 a4 f5 12 ♗f3 transposes below, but Black might just play 11...♘xe2+!? 12 ♕xe2 f5 13 f3 f4 with a standard sort of game, e.g. 14 ♗a3 g5 15 c5 ♘g6 (or 15...♖f6, ...♖g6, etc) 16 a5 ♖f7 17 b5 ♗f8 ∞ K.Kaunas-G.Piesina, Lithuanian Ch. 1994.

b) 11 c5 c6! (a logical reaction to White's temporarily clumsy configuration; on 11...f5 12 ♗c4!? looks best, e.g. 12...g5 13 f3 ♘eg6 14 exf5 ♗xf5 15 ♘de4 += J.Malmström-D.Camper, corr. 1997) 12 cxd6 (if 12 dxc6 ♘xc6 or 12 ♘c4 dxc5) 12...♕xd6 13 ♘c4 ♕xb4 14 d6? (Tsakhaev-E.Szapunov, Briansk 1995; but if 14 ♗d2 b5! 15 ♘e3 a6 =+) 14...♘xe2+ 15 ♕xe2 ♗e6 -+.
11...f5
The usual move, though Black can also try:

a) 11...a5!? 12 bxa5 ♖xa5 13 a4 f5 14 ♗a3 (14 ♘b3 and 15 a5 looks better) 14...b6! 15 ♘b5 ♖a8 16 ♗b4 ♗d7 17 ♖a3 fxe4 18 ♘xe4 ♘f5 19 g3 ♘h3+ 20 ♔h1 ♘d4 ∞ F.Baumbach-M.Lecroq, corr. 1994.

b) 11...♘d3!? 12 ♗a3 a5 13 bxa5 ♖xa5 14 ♘b5 (if 14 ♘cb1!? ♖a6 15 ♕b3 ♘f4 16 c5 ♘exd5! or 16 g3 ♘h3+ 17 ♔h1 f5 ∞) 14...♗d7 15 ♘b3 ♖a4 16 ♗xd6 (if 16 ♕xd3 ♗xb5 17 cxb5 ♖xa3 or 17 ♘d2 ♗d7 18 ♗d1 ♖a6 = Gelfand) 16...cxd6 17 ♕xd3 ♗xb5 18 cxb5 ♗h6 19 ♗d1

♗g7 with compensation, V.Anand-B.Gelfand, Dortmund 1997.

12 a4

Or 12 c5 g5!? (12...a5 looks safer here) 13 exf5 ♞xf5 14 g3 ♞h3+ (or 14...♞d3 15 ♞de4 ♞xc1 16 ♖xc1 ♞d4 17 ♗g4 h6 18 ♗xc8 += T.Cuno-C.Pilalis, corr. 2001; but 14...♞d4!? is interesting, e.g. 15 gxf4 ♞xf3+ 16 ♕xf3 g4 17 ♕d3 exf4 18 ♗b2 ♕h4 19 ♖fe1 f3 with a strong attack for the piece, F.Baumbach-K.Widmann, corr. 1992) 15 ♔g2 g4?! 16 ♗xg4 ♞xf2 17 ♔xf2 ♞h6+ 18 ♗f3 ♗h3 (18...♞g4+ 19 ♔g1 ♞e3 20 ♕e2 ♞xf1 21 ♞de4! +/-) 19 ♔g1 ♗xf1 20 ♞xf1 a5 21 ♞e4 +/- J.Manion-A.Sherzer, New York Open 1994.

12...g5!? *(D)*

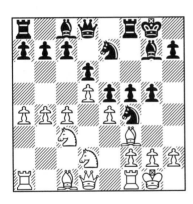

This leads to breakneck complications. Otherwise Black can consider:

a) 12...a5!? 13 bxa5 ♖xa5 – *11...a5!?* above.

b) 12...♔h8!? 13 ♞b3 (or 13 a5 ♞g8 14 c5 ♞f6 15 ♗a3 g5 16 exf5 ♗xf5 17 ♗e4 ♗xe4 18 ♞dxe4 ♞4xd5 19 ♞xd5 ♞xe4 ∞ J.Manion-F.Nijboer, Newark 1995) 13...g5 14 exf5 ♞xf5 15 g3 ♞h3+ 16 ♔g2 ♞h6!? 17 ♗e4 ♞g4 18 ♖a2 ♕e8

19 f3 ♞f6 20 ♗b1 ♕h5 ∞ G.Sosonko-F.Nijboer, Dutch Ch. 1996.

c) 12...♗d7!? 13 c5 g5 14 exf5 ♞xf5 15 g3 ♞h3+ 16 ♔g2 ♕c8! 17 ♗e4 g4 18 ♞b3 ♖f6 (18...♞d4!?) 19 c6 bxc6 20 dxc6 ♗e6 21 ♞d5 ♖f7 22 b5? (better 22 f3, although 22...gxf3 23 ♖xf3 ♔h8! and ...♕g8, ...♖af8 still gives Black good play) 22...♔h8! 23 f3 gxf3+ 24 ♖xf3 (D.Zagorskis-G.Beckhuis, Münster 1994) and now 24...♞h4+! 25 gxh4 ♗xd5 26 ♖xf7 (or 26 ♗xd5 ♕g4+ 27 ♔f1 e4) 26...♗xe4+ 27 ♔g3 ♕g8! would have won.

13 exf5 ♞xf5 14 g3

A key position; Black has to decide where to move his f4-knight.

14...♞h3+

The knight has also gone to other squares:

a) 14...♞g6?! 15 ♞de4 ♞d4 16 ♗h5 ♗h3 17 ♗xg5 ♕d7 18 ♖e1 +/- D.Zagorskis-A.Pushkarjow, Minsk 1994.

b) 14...♞d3 15 ♞de4 (or 15 ♗a3!? a5 16 bxa5 e4 17 ♞cxe4 ♗xa1 18 ♕xa1 with strong compensation for the exchange) 15...♞xc1 16 ♖xc1 ♞d4 17 ♗g4 ♗xg4 (17...a5!? straight away may be better, e.g. 18 bxa5 ♖xa5 19 ♞b5 ♗xg4 20 ♕xg4 ♞f3+ 21 ♔g2 ♖xa4 =) 18 ♕xg4 a5 19 bxa5 ♖xa5 20 ♔g2 h6 ∞ J.Manion-S.Tennant, USA 1996.

c) 14...♞d4!? 15 gxf4 ♞xf3+ (15...exf4! is more accurate, and if 16 ♞de4 ♞xf3+ 17 ♕xf3 g4 etc) 16 ♞xf3 (if 16 ♕xf3 g4 17 ♕h1?! exf4 18 ♗b2 ♗f5 19 ♖fe1 f3! 20 ♞de4 ♕h4 21 h3? ♗e5! -+ T.V.Petrosian-S.Gligoric, Rovinj/Zagreb 1970; or 17 ♕d3 ♗f5 18 ♞de4 exf4 19 f3 gxf3 20 ♖xf3 ♗xc3 21 ♕xc3 ♗xe4 22 ♖xf4 ♕g5+ 23 ♕g3 ♕xg3+ 24 hxg3 = Gligoric) 16...g4 (not 16...e4? 17 ♘xg5 ♗xc3 18 ♖a3 ♗g7 19 ♖g3 1-0 A.Martin-R.Britton, British Ch. 1991) 17 ♔h1 gxf3 18 ♕xf3 ♗f5 19 ♖g1 ♗g6 20 ♗d2 ♕d7 21 ♘e4 ♖ae8 ∞ I.Kourkounakis-I.Smirin, Gausdal 1990.

15 ♔g2 ♕d7!

Reinforcing Black's x-ray control of the c8-h3 diagonal. Not yet 15...g4?! 16 ♗xg4 ♘xf2 17 ♔xf2 ♘h6+ 18 ♗f3 ♘g4+ 19 ♔g1 ♘e3 20 ♕e2 ♘xf1 21 ♘de4! ♗h3 22 ♗g5 ♕d7 23 ♗g2 +/- J.Parker-J.Gallagher, Hastings 1991/92.

16 ♗e4 (D)

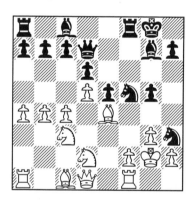

The most solid-looking move. Not 16 ♗g4? ♘xf2! -/+ or 16 ♘de4?! ♘d4 17 ♗h5? ♘f4+! 18 gxf4 ♕h3+ 19 ♔h1 g4 -+ (Cvetkovic); while if 16 ♘b3?! ♘d4 17 ♘xd4 exd4 18 ♘b5 c6 19 ♘a3 ♖xf3! 20 ♕xf3 g4 with a strong attack, R.Keene-L.Kavalek, Teesside 1975.

16...g4

Giving the h3-knight a retreat square. 16...♕f7!? and 16...a5!? also deserve attention; whereas 16...♘xf2!? 17 ♔xf2 ♘xg3+ 18 ♔g1 ♘xf1 19 ♘xf1 sees

Black with a rook and two pawns for two knights, but White stands better as his minor pieces control all the key squares; e.g. 19...♕h3 20 ♘g3 ♗g4 21 ♕d3 ♖f4 22 ♖a2! ♖af8 23 ♖c2 (or 23 ♗g2 ♕h4 24 ♘ce4 +/=) 23...♗f3?! 24 ♗xf4 exf4 25 ♘f1 ♕g4+ 26 ♔f2 ♕g2+ 27 ♔e1 ♗xe4 28 ♘xe4 ♕g1 29 h3 +/- D.Ruzele-D.Lapienis, Lithuanian Ch. 1993.

17 ♘b3 ♕e7 18 ♕d3 h5

Here 18...♘g5 19 ♗xg5 ♕xg5 is roughly equal, though not then 20 c5 ♖f6 21 ♘b5 ♕h5? 22 ♔g1 ♖h6 23 h4! +/- D.Zagorskis-D.Gross, Pardubice 1995.

19 c5 (D)

Or 19 f3!? ♘g5 20 fxg4 ♘xe4 21 ♘xe4 hxg4 =.

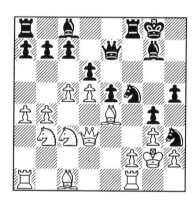

Now either 19...♘g5 or 19...a5!? would have given Black good play.

Instead, in J.Manion-I.Smirin, Kissimmee 1997, he went for broke with **19...♘f4+?! 20 gxf4 exf4 21 f3** [or 21 ♔h1!? ♗xc3 22 ♗xf5 ♗xa1 23 ♗xc8 ♖axc8 24 ♘xa1 ♖ce8 25 ♗xf4 ♕e4+ 26 ♕xe4 ♖xe4 27 ♗g3 with the better ending] **21...♗e5 22 ♖a2 ♕g7 23 ♘d1 g3 24 ♖g1 gxh2+ 25 ♔xh2 ♘g3 26 ♖gg2 ♕g5 27 ♘f2 ♔h8 28 ♘d4 ♕h4+ 29 ♔g1**

♖f7 30 ♘e6? [30 ♘e2! +/-] **30...♗xe6 31 dxe6 ♖g7 32 ♗b2?** [32 ♗f5 dxc5! (or 32...♖ag8 33 ♗h3) 33 ♗g4! ∞] **32...♖ag8 33 ♗xe5 dxe5 34 ♘g4 ♕h1+ 35 ♔f2 hxg4 36 fxg4 ♖xg4 37 ♗f3 e4 38 ♕d4+ ♖4g7 0-1**.

B: 10 ♕c2 (D)

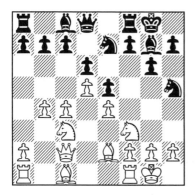

This is the pet line of Russian grandmaster Vladimir Epishin. White defends the c3-knight in advance, so that after 10...♘f4 11 ♗xf4 exf4 he can continue 12 ♖ad1 and ♘d4 or c4-c5 with the initiative, though Black does not have to fall in with this plan. 10 ♕b3 (D) has similar intentions, and:

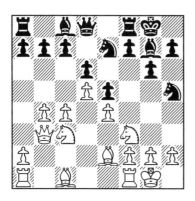

a) 10...h6 11 a4 (instead 11 c5 – *10 c5 h6 11 ♕b3*; or if 11 g3!? f5 12 ♘d2 ♘f6 13 f3 h5 14 ♖f2 ♗h6 15 ♘f1 ♗xc1 16 ♖xc1 ∞ C.Buhr-P.Mai, Schoeneck 1996; 11...♗h3!? 12 ♖e1 f5 also looks good) 11...f5 (if 11...♘f4 12 ♗xf4 exf4 13 a5 +=) 12 exf5 ♘xf5 (not 12...gxf5?! 13 ♘xe5, or if 12...e4!? 13 ♘h4! +=) 13 ♖a2 ♘h4 (13...a5!?) 14 ♘e4 ♗f5 15 ♘g3 ♘xf3+ 16 ♗xf3 ♘f6?! (16...♘xg3 ∞) 17 ♖e1 ♕d7 18 a5 += S.Skembris-A.Vragoteris, Athens 1991.

b) 10...f5!? 11 ♘g5 (again 11 c5 – *10 c5 f5 11 ♕b3*; or if 11 exf5, L.Hajsman-R.Wadura, Rakovnik 2001, 11...♘xf5 12 ♘e4 h6 ∞) 11...♘f4 (or 11...♘f6!? – *9...♘e8 10 ♕b3*) 12 ♗xf4 exf4 13 ♖ae1 ♗f6 (or 13...♘c6 14 dxc6 ♕xg5 15 c5+ ♔h8 16 cxd6 cxd6 17 b5 +=) 14 ♘e6 ♗xe6 15 dxe6 ♗xc3 16 ♕xc3 fxe4 17 ♗d1 +=.

c) 10...♘f4 11 ♗xf4 exf4 12 ♖ad1 h6 (if 12...♗g4 13 ♘d4 ♗d7 14 c5 += B.Guyard-R.Forster, Metz 1994) 13 c5 g5 14 e5!? (sacrificing a pawn to activate his pieces, but the outcome remains unclear and simply 14 h3!? might be better) 14...dxe5 (if 14...g4 15 exd6 cxd6 16 ♘d4 += S.Ernst-E.Sziva, Groningen 1998; or 14...♘f5 15 exd6 cxd6 16 h3 h5 17 ♘h2 ♘d4 18 ♕c4 ♘xe2+ 19 ♘xe2 += A.Stickler-W.Uhlmann, German League 1991; but 14...dxc5!? might be considered, e.g. 15 bxc5 g4 16 ♘d4 ♗xe5, or 15 d6 ♘c6 16 dxc7 ♕xc7 17 ♘d5 ♕b8!, or 15 h3 cxb4 16 ♕xb4 ♘g6 17 e6 ♕d6 ∞) 15 d6 ♘f5 (or if 15...cxd6 16 ♖xd6 ♕e8, E.Najer-P.Kotsur, Elista 2000, 17 ♗b5 ♘c6 18 ♘d5 ♗e6 19 ♖e1 with compensation –

Huzman) 16 dxc7 (or 16 h3!? cxd6 17 ♘e4 d5 18 ♖xd5 ♕e7 19 ♗c4 with compensation, S.Skembris-Al.David, Cannes 1991) 16...♕xc7 17. ♘d5 ♕b8 18. ♗d3 ♖e8 19. ♗b5 ♖f8 20. ♗d3 ♔h8 21. ♕c4 g4 22. ♕e4 gxf3 23. ♘e7 ∞ F.Lambrecht-D.Edelman, Biel 1994.

10...a5

A logical reaction to 10 ♕c2; note that after 10 ♕b3 a5?! White could just play 11 c5, but here he does not have that option. Otherwise Black has the same set of replies as above:

a) 10...h6 11 ♖e1 (or 11 c5 f5 12 ♖d1 fxe4 13 ♘xe4 ♘f4 14 ♗xf4 exf4? 15 ♖ac1 ♘f5 16 cxd6 cxd6 17 ♕c7 +/- V.Epishin-T.Kabisch, Deizisau 2004; but the standard 14...♖xf4 is fine for Black) 11...f5 (if 11...♘f4 12 ♗f1 a5 13 bxa5 ♖xa5 14 a4 f5 15 ♗xf4 exf4 16 e5 g5 17 ♖ad1 g4 18 exd6 cxd6 19 ♘d4 +/= V.Epishin-M.Paragua, Turin 2000; or just 12 ♗xf4 exf4 13 ♖ac1 +=) 12 ♘d2 (12 ♗d3!?) 12...♘f4 13 ♗f1 fxe4 14 ♘cxe4 ♘f5 (14...b5!?) 15 ♗b2 ♘e7 16 ♕b3 ♔h7 17 ♖ad1 ♗f5 18 ♔h1 ♕d7 19 ♘g3 ♖ad8 20 a4 ♗f6 21 ♘de4 += M.Kozakov-L.Rouillon, Mans 2001.

b) 10...f5!? 11 ♘g5 (or 11 c5 fxe4 12 ♘xe4 ♘f4 13 ♗xf4 ♖xf4 14 g3 ♖f8 15 ♖fd1 ♗f5 16 a4 a5 ∞ V.Epishin-I.Nataf, Reykjavik 2004) 11...♘f4 (or 11...♘f6!? 12 ♗f3 h6 13 ♘e6 ♗xe6 14 dxe6, A.Yermolinsky-D.Sharavdorj, Berkley 2005, 14...♕c8! 15 ♘d5 ♘fxd5 16 cxd5 c6 =+) 12 ♗xf4 exf4 13 ♖ae1 ♘c6! 14 dxc6 (or 14 ♘e6 ♘d4 15 ♘xd4 ♗xd4 16 ♗f3 ♗e5 ∞ V.Epishin-V.Menoni, Bratto 1999) 14...♕xg5 15 ♗f3 bxc6 16 b5 ♗d7 17 exf5 ♕xf5 ∞ V.Epishin-F.Nijboer,

Apeldoorn (rapid) 2001.

c) 10...♘f4 11 ♗xf4 exf4 12 ♖ad1! h6 *(D)* reaches a key position.

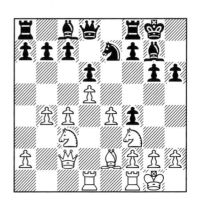

c1) 13 c5 g5 14 e5 (compared with 10 ♕b3 ♘f4, here the queen is better placed on c2) 14...dxe5 (if 14...♗f5 15 ♗d3 ♗xd3 16 ♕xd3 dxe5, S.Brittner-L.Rama, European Team Ch., Leon 2001, 17 d6! cxd6 18 ♕e4! with a strong initiative; but Black might try 14...g4!? 15 exd6 cxd6 16 ♘d4 dxc5 17 bxc5 f3! 18 gxf3 ♘xd5 19 fxg4 ♘xc3 20 ♕xc3 ♖e8 with compensation) 15 d6 ♘f5 (or 15...♘c6 16 dxc7 ♕xc7 17 ♘d5 ♕b8 18 b5 ♘d4 19 ♘xd4 exd4 20 ♗c4 += M.Karttunen-M.Hartikainen, Finnish Team Ch. 2000) 16 dxc7 ♕xc7 17 ♘d5 ♕d8 (or 17...♕b8 18 ♗d3 ♘d4 19 ♘xd4 exd4 20 ♘e7+ ♔h8 21 ♗f5 +=) 18 ♘b6 ♘d4 19 ♘xd4 axb6 20 ♘e6 ♗xe6 21 ♖xd8 ♖fxd8 22 ♗c4 += M.Karttunen-T.Franssila, Kuopio 2001.

c2) 13 ♘d4 g5 14 ♗h5 (forestalling ...♘g6-e5, after which Black would stand well) 14...a5 15 b5! (White can play this here as the knight on d4 makes ...b7-b6 unpalatable) 15...♔h8 (if 15...♗e5 16 ♘f3 f6?! 17 c5 ♗d7 18 c6

♗e8 19 ♗xe8 ♕xe8 20 b6 +/- S.Atalik-B.Brkic, Bosnian Team Ch. 2001; or 15...♗d7 16 ♘ce2 c5 17 dxc6 bxc6 18 a4 ♕b6 19 ♕d2 cxb5 20 cxb5 ♖ac8 21 ♕a2! += S.Atalik-R.Speckner, Pula 2005) 16 h3!? (intending ♗g4; if 16 ♖fe1 ♘g8 17 h3 ♘f6 ∞ Atalik) 16...♘g6!? 17 ♗xg6 fxg6 18 ♘e6!? ♗xe6 19 dxe6 ♖e8 20 e5?! (better 20 ♘d5 ♖xe6 21 c5 ♖c8 22 c6 b6 23 ♕d3 with compensation, Atalik) 20...♖xe6 21 exd6 ♖xd6 22 c5 ♖xd1 23 ♖xd1 ♕e7 24 ♘d5 ♕f7 25 c6 bxc6 26 ♕xc6 ♖d8 -/+ S.Atalik-W.Uhlmann, Dresden 2005.

11 bxa5 ♖xa5

Not 11...c5?! 12 dxc6 bxc6 13 ♖d1 ♕c7 (or 13...♖xa5 14 a4) 14 ♗e3 +/- V.Epishin-J.Henrichsen, Bad Wiessee 2000; but 11...♘f4!? is possible, e.g. 12 ♘d2 ♘xe2+ 13 ♘xe2 ♖xa5 14 ♗b2 c6 15 ♘b3 ♖a6 ∞ M.Karttunen-O.Sepp, Helsinki 2000, or if 12 ♗xf4 exf4 13 ♖ac1 ♖xa5 14 ♕d2 (Atalik) 14...f5! 15 ♕xf4 fxe4 16 ♕xe4 ♖a3 17 ♘b5 (or 17 ♘d4 ♘f5!) 17...♗f5 18 ♕h4 ♖xa2 ∞.

12 ♖e1 *(D)*

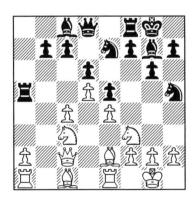

This useful move has the same ideas as 10 ♖e1 in the main line, and

with Black already committed to 10...a5!? 11 bxa5 ♖xa5. On the other hand, 12 ♕c2 would not be White's move of choice in line E2 below.

Instead, 12 ♖d1 would prevent 12...c5?! due to 13 dxc6! etc, but 12...♘f4! 13 ♗xf4 exf4 14 ♘d4 g5 gives Black a good version of 10...♘f4 above; e.g. 15 ♖ac1 ♘g6 16 ♘cb5 ♗d7 17 h3 ♘e5 18 c5?! f3! 19 gxf3 dxc5 20 ♕xc5 c6 =+ Z.Gyimesi-V.Sikula, Hungarian Team Ch. 2008.

12...c5

A standard idea, aiming to prevent c4-c5 forever.

The alternative is 12...f5 13 a4 (or 13 exf5 ♘xf5 14 ♗g5 ♕d7 15 ♖ad1 h6?! 16 ♗d2 ♘f6 17 ♗d3 b6 18 a4 += S.Atalik-A.Fedorov, Moscow 2005; but Atalik's 15...♗h6! improves for Black) 13...fxe4 (now if 13...c5 14 exf5! ♗xf5 15 ♘e4 ♕d7 16 ♘fd2 ♘f4 17 ♗d1 h6 18 ♕b3 ♘c8 19 ♘f1 += A.Yermolinsky-M.Paragua, Philadelphia 2000) 14 ♘xe4 ♘f4 15 ♗d1 ♘f5?! (15...h6 intending ...g6-g5 looks better) 16 ♗d2 ♖a7 17 ♖a3 ♗f6 18 ♗xf4 exf4 19 ♕d2 g5 20 ♗c2 g4 21 ♘xf6+ ♕xf6 22 ♗xf5 ♗xf5 23 ♘d4 += L.Forslof-P.Schumacher, corr. 2001.

13 a4!?

Epishin's latest try, though he has also played:

a) 13 dxc6 (as after 11...c5?!, but the extra rook moves make this okay for Black) 13...bxc6 14 ♗e3 ♘f4 15 ♖ad1 ♗g4 16 ♕d2!? (if 16 ♗xf4 exf4 17 ♘d4 h5 18 ♕d2 ♕b6 19 h3 ♗c8 20 ♘b3 ♖a7 =+ V.Epishin-A.Fedorov, European Ch., Saint Vincent 2000) 16...♘xe2+ 17 ♕xe2 d5 (or 17...♕c7! 18 h3 ♗xf3 19 ♕xf3 f5 with excellent play for Black) 18 cxd5 cxd5 19 exd5 ♘xd5 20 ♕d2 ♗e6 21 ♘g5 ♕a8 22 ♘xe6 fxe6 23 a4 ♖c8 = V.Epishin-V.Baklan, Northeim 2005.

b) 13 ♖b1 h6 (or 13...♔h8 14 a4 – *13 a4*) 14 ♖b3 f5 15 exf5 ♘xf5 16 ♘e4 ♘f6 17 ♗d3 ♘xe4 18 ♗xe4 g5 19 h3 ♖a6 ∞ V.Epishin-R.Palliser, Port Erin 2002.

13...♔h8

Instead, 13...f5 returns to 12...f5 above, or if 13...♘f6 14 ♗d2 ♖a6 15 ♖a3 ♔h8 16 ♖b3 ♘eg8 17 ♖eb1 ♗h6 18 ♗e1 += V.Epishin-N.Ambrosini, Geneva 2005.

14 ♖b1 ♘g8 15 ♖b5 ♖a6 16 ♘d2 *(D)*

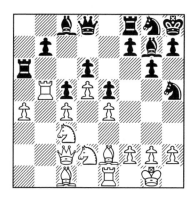

An interesting position; although White has little advantage objectively, he is well set to meet any kingside threats and can hope for an eventual breakthrough with a4-a5 and ♘a4-b6. For example:

a) 16...♘hf6 17 ♘f1 ♘e8 18 ♗d1 ♕h4 19 ♘g3 ♗h6 20 ♖f1 ♘g7 21 ♗xh6 ♘xh6 22 ♕d2 g5 23 ♖e1 f6 24 a5 ♘f7 25 ♘a4 ♖a7 26 ♘b6 ♕h6 27 ♕b2 ♕g6 28 ♘xc8 ♖xc8 29 ♖xb7 +- V Epishin-K Le Quang, Bethune 2005.

b) 16...♘f4 17 ♗f1 ♕g5 18 ♘f3 ♕g4 19 ♔h1 g5 20 ♘g1 ♕h5 21 g3 ♘g6 22 ♕d1 g4 23 ♗g2 ♗h6 (23...f5 24 exf5 ♘6e7! and ...♘xf5 would give Black good play) 24 ♘ge2 ♗xc1 25 ♕xc1 ♘h6 26 a5 f6?! (still 26...f5) 27 ♖f1 ♘e7 28 ♘a4 ♗d7 29 ♖xb7 ♗xa4 30 ♖xe7 ♖xa5 31 ♘g1 ♖aa8 32 f4 +/- V.Epishin-C.Jimenez Hernandez, Seville 2007.

C: 10 c5 *(D)*

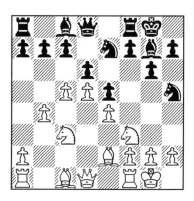

The most straightforward move; White makes the thematic advance before Black changes his mind and plays ...a7-a5. The drawback is that it may cost White one of his bishops.

10...♘f4

This immediate leap is the most frequent continuation, though Black quite often plays:

a) 10...h6?! (not strictly necessary) 11 ♘d2! (the usual move; instead 11 ♕b3!? f5 – *10...f5 11 ♕b3 h6* below, and 11 ♖e1! – *10 ♖e1 h6* in line E; worse is 11 g3?! ♗h3! 12 ♖e1 f5. e.g. 13 ♘h4 ♘f6 14 ♗f3 fxe4 15 ♘xe4 g5 =/+ S.Mahmud-A.Iswana, Singapore 2004) 11...♘f4 12 ♘c4 f5 13 f3 and then:

a1) 13...g5 14 ♗e3! ♘eg6 15 cxd6 cxd6 16 ♘b5 is good for White, e.g. 16...♘h4?! 17 g3 ♘h3+ 18 ♔h1 f4 19 ♗xa7 fxg3 20 hxg3 g4 (L.Karlsson-A.Sznapik, Pohja 1985) 21 fxg4! ♖xa7 22 ♘xa7 ♘f2+ 23 ♖xf2 ♖xf2 24 ♕e1 +-.

a2) 13...♗d7!? 14 a4 ♘c8 15 ♔h1 ♔h7 (U.Kottke-K.Juhnke, German League 1990) 16 ♗e3 +/=.

a3) 13...♘xe2+ 14 ♕xe2 f4 is similar 9 ♘d2 ♘e8 lines in Chapter Ten, except that Black is even further behind here; e.g. 15 a4 (or 15 ♗a3!? g5 16 ♘b5! dxc5 17 bxc5 c6 18 ♘bd6! cxd5 19 exd5 ♘xd5 20 ♕d3 ♗e6 21 ♖ae1 ♕c7 22 ♖e4 +/- J.Tisdall-N.De Firmian, US Junior Ch. 1976) 15...g5 16 ♗a3 (or 16 a5!? h5 17 cxd6 cxd6 18 ♘b5 ♖f6 19 ♕f2 g4 20 fxg4 hxg4, Y.Kuzubov-A.Motylev, European Ch., Warsaw 2005, 21 ♘xa7! +/- Avrukh) 16...♖f6 17 b5 ♘g6 18 b6 (Korchnoi's 18 a5!? ♗f8 19 b6 dxc5 20 bxc7 ♕xc7 21 d6 also looks good) 18...axb6 (or 18...cxb6 19 cxd6 +/-) 19 cxd6 cxd6 20 ♕b2 ♖a6 21 ♘b5 g4 (M.Gurevich-B.Gelfand, Belgrade 1991) 22 ♗xd6! +/-.

b) 10...f5 *(D)* (rightly unafraid of ♘f3-g5) and then:

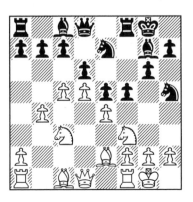

b1) 11 ♖e1!? – *10 ♖e1 f5 11 c5* in the notes to line E3.

b2) 11 ♘d2!? also transposes elsewhere: 11...♘f4 12 ♗f3 – *10 ♘d2 ♘f4 11 ♗f3 f5 12 c5* (see line A); while 11...♘f6!? – *9 ♘d2 ♘e8* in Chapter Ten.

b3) 11 exf5?! e4! 12 ♘d4 ♘xf5 13 ♘xf5 ♗xf5 14 ♗d2 ♕h4 15 ♗xh5 gxh5 16 ♕e1 ♗e5 17 f4 ♗d4+ 18 ♔h1 ♕xe1 19 ♖axe1 e3 -/+ C.Remling-M.Grabics, Budapest 1994.

b4) 11 ♕b3!? h6 (or 11...fxe4!? 12 ♘xe4 ♘f4 13 ♗c4 ♗g4 14 ♗xf4 ♖xf4 15 ♘fd2 ♘f5 16 ♖fe1 ♘d4 17 ♕d3 ♕f8 18 ♖ac1 ♗h6 ∞ A.Veingold-J.Fedorowicz, Candas 1992) 12 a4 (if 12 exf5 ♘xf5 13 ♘e4, Peng Zhaoqin-Wang Pin, Subotica Interzonal 1991, 13...♘f6! ∞) 12...fxe4 (or 12...♔h8 13 exf5 ♘xf5 14 ♗d3 g5 15 ♗e4 ♘d4 ∞ J.Tisdall-R.Djurhuus, Oslo 1992) 13 ♘xe4 ♘f4 14 ♗xf4 ♖xf4 15 cxd6 cxd6 16 ♗d3 b6 (or 16...♗g4!? 17 ♘fd2 ♘f5) 17 ♖fe1 ♗b7 18 ♘c3 ♖c8 ∞ E.Grivas-J.Nunn, 4th matchgame, Athens 1991.

b5) 11 ♘g5 ♘f4! (or 11...♘f6!? – *9 b4 ♘e8* in Chapter Eleven) 12 ♗c4 (if 12 ♗xf4 exf4 13 ♖c1 ♗f6 14 ♘e6 ♗xe6 15 dxe6 ♗xc3! 16 ♖xc3 fxe4 17 ♕d4 d5 -/+ I.Penillas Mendez-P.Llaneza Vega, Candas 1997) 12...h6 (not 12...fxe4?! 13 ♘gxe4 ♘f5 14 f3 ♘h4 15 g3 ♘h3+ 16 ♔h1 ♘f5 17 ♔g2 += D.Goodman-A.Arnason, Reykjavik 1982) 13 ♘e6 ♗xe6 14 dxe6 fxe4 15 g3!? (or 15 ♘d5 ♘fxd5 16 ♗xd5 c6 17 cxd6 ♘xd5 18 e7 ♘xe7 19 dxe7 ♕xe7 -/+ L.Karlsson-A.Olsson, Swedish Ch. 2001) 15...d5 (if 15...♘h5!? 16 ♕b3 ♘f6 17 ♖d1 ∞) 16 ♗b3 ♘xe6 (16...a5!?) 17 ♘xd5 ♔h7 18

♘xe7 ♕xe7 19 ♕d5 ♘d4 20 ♕xe4 c6 =+ N.Gamboa-L.Perez, Santa Clara 1998.

11 ♗xf4

The most consistent reply. Instead, 11 ♘d2 – *10 ♘d2 ♘f4 11 c5* in line A; or if 11 ♗c4 ♗g4 (not 11...f5?! 12 ♗xf4 exf4? 13 e5 or 12...fxe4 13 ♗xe5 exf3 14 ♗xg7 +/- Granda Zuniga) 12 h3 ♗h5 13 ♖e1 g5!? (if 13...a5?! 14 ♖b1 ♘c8?! 15 a3 axb4 16 axb4 ♔h8 17 ♗f1 f5 18 exf5 gxf5 19 ♗xf4 exf4 20 ♘b5 +/- J.Granda Zuniga-J.Nunn, Amsterdam 1995) 14 ♗f1 f5 15 ♗xf4 exf4 16 ♖c1 a5 17 a3 axb4 18 axb4 ♗xf3 19 ♕xf3 ♖a3! 20 cxd6 cxd6 21 ♕d3 fxe4 22 ♖xe4 ♘g6 ½-½ Z.Gyimesi-A.Pankratov, corrrespondence 1999.

11...exf4 12 ♖c1 (D)

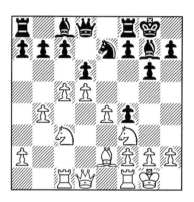

Again the key position; White defends and unpins the c3-knight and can put the other one on d4 in support of his queenside initiative. From the other side, Black has activated his dark-squared bishop and has control of the e5-square.

Alternatively, White sometimes puts the rook on d1:

a) 12 ♕b3 ♗g4 (or 12...h6 13 ♖ad1 –

10 ♕b3 ♘f4 in the notes to line B) 13 ♖ad1 ♗xf3 14 ♗xf3 g5 15 ♗h5 (or 15 ♗g4 ♘g6 16 ♘e2 ♘e5 17 ♕h3 ♘xg4 18 ♕xg4, W.Vögel-K.Neumeier, Austrian Team Ch. 1997, 18...a5 ∞) ♘g6 16 ♗xg6 hxg6 17 ♘b5 ♖e8 18 ♖fe1 a6 19 ♘a3 g4 20 ♘c4 ♗e5 = A.Schneider-E.Gufeld, Helsinki 1992.

b) 12 ♕d2 h6 (or 12...♗g4 13 ♖ac1 ♗xf3 14 ♗xf3 g5 15 ♗g4 ♘g6 16 ♖fd1 ♕e7 ∞ B.Larsen-S.Gligoric, Lugano 1970) 13 ♖ad1 g5 14 e5!? g4! (not 14...dxe5? 15 d6; or 14...♘f5 15 exd6 cxd6 16 h3 +/- T.Welin-T.Scholseth, Gausdal 1987; while if 14...dxc5!? 15 d6 cxd6 16 exd6 ♘c6 17 bxc5 g4 18 ♘e1 b6 19 ♘e4 ♘d4 20 c6! +=) 15 exd6 cxd6 16 ♘e1 ♘g6 ∞ (P.Littlewood), e.g. 17 ♘e4 dxc5 18 bxc5 ♗e5 19 d6 ♗f5 20 ♘d3 f3! 21 gxf3 ♗xh2+ 22 ♔xh2 ♕h4+ 23 ♔g1 ♗xe4 24 fxe4 g3 with a draw.

12...h6

Black has also tried:

a) 12...♗g4?! 13 ♘d4 ♗xe2 14 ♘cxe2 g5 15 ♕c2 ♘g6 16 f3 ♗e5 17 cxd6 cxd6 18 ♕c7 ♕f6 19 ♘f5 +/- Z.Azmaiparashvili-J.Rodriguez Talavera, San Roque 1996.

b) 12...f5!? is now risky, due to 13 e5! dxe5 14 d6 cxd6 (or 14...♘c6 15 ♕d5+ ♔h8 16 b5 etc) 15 cxd6 ♘c6 16 ♕d5+ ♔h8 17 b5 ♘d4 (if 17...♘b4 18 ♕c5 ♕a5 19 a3! +/- Suba, but 18...a5!? deserves attention, e.g. 19 a3 ♗e6! 20 axb4 ♖c8 21 ♕a7 axb4 22 ♘b1 ♖xc1 23 ♖xc1 e4 24 ♘d4 ♗g8 25 ♕c5 f3! 26 ♘xf3 exf3 27 ♗xf3 ♖f7 28 ♕xb4 ♖d7 =) 18 ♘xe5 ♕e8! (if 18...♘xe2+?! 19 ♘xe2 ♕e8, C.Hertan-P.Simon, Toronto 1985, then 20 ♖c5! threatening ♘xf4 is strong, e.g. 20...b6 21 ♖c7 ♗e6 22 ♕b7! ♖b8 23 ♕xa7 ♖a8 24 ♕xb6 ♗xe5 25 ♖e7 or 22...♗d5 23 ♘c6 ♕e4 24 ♘xf4! +/-) 19 ♕xd4 ♕xe5! (if 19...♗xe5 20 ♕b4 ♗e6 21 ♗f3 += M.Suba-W.Uhlmann, Zinnowitz 1983) 20 ♕xe5 ♗xe5 21 ♖fd1 ♖d8 22 ♖d5 ♗g7 23 ♗f3 ♗e6 24 ♖d3 ∞ J.Vilela-L.Perez, Villa Clara 1998.

c) 12...a5!? (a logical move, activating the a8-rook, though it allows a rook incursion at c7) 13 ♘b5 (or 13 a3 axb4 14 axb4 f5!? 15 exf5 ♘xf5 16 ♘b5 g5 ∞ I.Samarin-D.Salinnikov, Nizhnij Novgorod 1999) 13...axb4 (if 13...♗g4 14 a3 +=) 14 cxd6 cxd6 15 ♕b3 (if 15 ♕d2 f5! 16 ♗d3 fxe4 17 ♗xe4 ♖a4 18 ♖c4, R.Henley-K.Spraggett, New York 1983, 18...♗d7! 19 ♘xd6 ♗c3 ∞) 15...♗g4 16 ♖c7 (or 16 ♖c2 ♕b6 17 ♕xb4 ♗xf3 18 ♗xf3 ♗e5 ∞ T.Halasz-I.Borocz, Hungarian Team Ch. 1996) 16...♘c8! 17 ♘fd4 ♗xe2 18 ♘xe2 f3 19 gxf3 ♘a7 20 ♖xb7 ♘xb5 21 ♖xb5 ♕g5+ 22 ♔h1 ♖a3 23 ♕xb4 ♖xa2 with compensation, F.Schirm-G.Schmid, German League 1991.

13 ♘d4 *(D)*

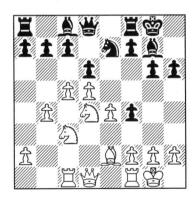

The knight takes up its central post.

White has two significant alternatives:

a) 13 h3 g5 (13...f5!? may be better, e.g. 14 cxd6 cxd6 15 exf5, J.Fedorowicz-J.Boudy, Mexico 1978, 15...♗xf5! 16 ♘d4 ♖c8 17 ♕d2 ♕b6 with good play for Black) 14 a4 ♘g6 15 a5! ♗e8 (or) 16 ♘d2 ♘e5 (if 16...♗xc3?! 17 ♖xc3 ♕f6 18 ♕c2 ♘e5 19 ♖c1 ♔g7 20 ♕d1 ♖h8 21 ♗h5 +/- B.Malich-E.Bukic, Vrnjacka Banja 1972; or 16...f5!?, G.Sosonko-L.Van Wely, Dutch Ch. 1995, 17 ♗h5! +/-) 17 cxd6 cxd6 18 ♘b5 ♖e7 19 ♕c2 a6 20 ♘d4 += M.Diesen-L.Day, Lone Pine 1977.

b) 13 ♘d2 g5 (if 13...a6 14 ♘c4 f5 15 cxd6 cxd6 16 ♗d3 fxe4 17 ♗xe4 ♗f5 18 ♗f3 ♖c8 19 ♘e4 ♗xe4 20 ♗xe4 += C.Danschczyk-F.Sawatzki, German League 1994; but 13...f5!? is again possible, e.g. 14 cxd6 cxd6 15 ♘b5 fxe4 16 ♘xe4 ♘f5 17 ♗g4 ♗e5 ∞ P.Littlewood-L.McShane, British League 1996) 14 ♘c4!? a6 (if 14...♘g6 15 ♗g4 ♘e5 16 ♘xe5 ♗xe5 17 ♗xc8 ♖xc8 18 ♘b5 ♕f6 19 c6 +/- A.Lein-M.Rohde, New York 1977) 15 a4 (15 ♘a4!? also looks good) 15...♘g6 16 cxd6 cxd6 17 a5 ♖e8 18 ♘b6 ♖b8 19 ♗h5 ♘e5 20 h3 ♕f6 21 f3 += S.Skembris-G.Milos, Novi Sad Olympiad 1990, and if 21...♘d7 22 ♘ca4 ♕d4+ 23 ♔h1 ♕xd1 24 ♖fxd1 ♘f6 (Milos) then 25 ♗xf7+! ♔xf7 26 ♖c7+ ♔g6 27 ♖dc1 gives Black serious problems.

13...g5 *(D)*

Intending ...♘g6-e5 which White now prevents. Other moves:

a) 13...♔h8 14 a4 ♘g8 15 a5 ♘f6 16 ♖e1 h5 17 ♕d2 ♔h7 18 a6! ♗h6 19 axb7 ♗xb7 20 ♗f3 ♘g4 21 cxd6 cxd6 22 ♘c6

+/- A.Beliavsky-B.Gelfand, Paris (rapid) 1991.

b) 13...a6 14 ♖e1!? ♗d7 15 a3 ♔h7 16 ♘b3 f5 17 ♗f3 fxe4 18 ♘xe4 ♘f5 19 ♘a5 b6 20 cxb6 cxb6 21 ♘c6 +/- L.Psakhis-B.Kantsler, Israeli Team Ch. 2002.

c) 13...c6!? 14 ♗f3 a5 15 a3 axb4 16 axb4 g5 17 ♘b3 ♘g6 18 dxc6 bxc6 19 ♘a5 ♘e5 20 ♘xc6 ♘xc6 21 e5 ♘xb4 22 ♗xa8 ♗a6 ∞ S.Tschann-H.Reichmann, Dresden 1998.

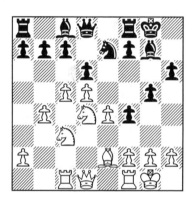

14 ♗h5 a5!?

This was suggested by Beliavsky as a favourable transposition. Other moves allow White an advantage:

a) 14...a6 15 a3 ♔h8 16 h3 ♖b8 17 ♖e1 ♘g8 18 ♗g4 += V.Karpman-A.Frolov, Kherson 1990.

b) 14...♔h8 15 ♖e1 ♘g8 16 h3 ♘f6 17 ♗f3 ♖e8 18 cxd6 cxd6 19 ♘cb5 ♖e7 20 ♖xc8! ♖xc8 21 ♘f5 ♖d7 22 ♘bxd6? (better simply 22 a3! and if 22...a6 23 ♘bxd6, or 22...♘e8 23 ♗g4) 22...♖xd6 23 ♘xd6 ♕xd6 24 e5 ♕xb4 25 exf6 ♗xf6 = Se.Ivanov-I.Smirin, Moscow 2003.

c) 14...c6!? 15 ♘b3 cxd5 (if 15...dxc5 16 bxc5 cxd5, then 17 ♘xd5! ♗e6 18 ♕c2 ♘xd5 19 exd5 ♕xd5 20 ♗f3 with

strong compensation) 16 exd5 a5 17 ♘b5 a4 18 ♘a5 dxc5 19 d6 ♘f5 20 ♖xc5 b6 21 ♘c6 +/- A.Beliavsky-A.Romero Holmes, Leon 1994.

15 a3 axb4 16 axb4 c6! *(D)*

A.Beliavsky-V.Spasov, Manila Olympiad 1992, arrived at this position via 12...a5!? 13 a3 axb4 14 axb4 h6 15 ♘d4 g5 16 ♗h5?! c6! (though 16 ♘cb5! is good in that case) and we take up that game here.

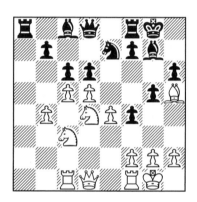

17 ♘de2

Or 17 ♘b3 dxc5 18 bxc5 ♖a3 19 d6 ♘g6 20 ♗xg6 fxg6 21 ♕d3?! f3! 22 g3 ♕d7 23 ♘d2 (A.Guseinov-M.Zulfugarli, Azeri Ch. 1996) and now 23...b6! would have been strong.

17...b6!?

If 17...cxd5 18 exd5 ♗d7 19 ♕b3 ♘f5 20 ♖fe1 ♗e5 21 h3 ♕e7 22 ♘e4 +/- U.Loseries-W.Haufe, corr. 1995; but 17...♗e5!? is possible and given as equal by Beliavsky.

18 dxc6 dxc5 19 b5 ♗e6 20 ♕c2 ♕c7 21 h3 ♕e5?!

Beliavsky suggested 21...♖a5!? as a better idea, when Black might follow with ...♗c4 or ...♘c8.

22 ♗g4 ♗c4 23 ♘a4! ♗xb5 24 ♘xb6 ♗xc6 25 ♘xa8 ♗xe4 26 ♕xc5 ♕xc5 27 ♖xc5 ♖xa8 28 ♖d1 *(D)*

Black still has reasonable chances with a pawn for the exchange and everything on one side, but he was unable to hold on over the board.

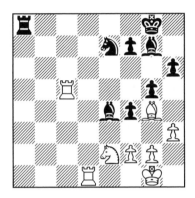

The game concluded **28...♖a3?** [28...♘g6 += Beliavsky] **29 ♖d8+ ♔h7 30 ♖d7 ♗f6 31 ♖cc7 ♖a1+ 32 ♔h2 ♘d5 33 ♖c4 ♗d3 34 ♖c5 ♖e1 35 ♖xf7+ ♔g6 36 ♗h5+! ♔xh5 37 ♖xf6 1-0** [since if 37...♘xf6 38 ♘xf4+ ♔h4 39 g3 mate].

D: 10 g3 *(D)*

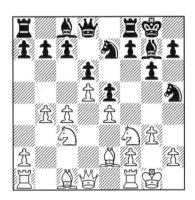

For many years 10 g3 was consid-

ered an almost obligatory move, in order to prevent 10...♘f4. The obvious drawback is that White weakens his kingside light squares, and it was largely for this reason that 9 b4 remained unpopular. Nevertheless, Black needs to play with purpose if he is to achieve a good game.

10...f5

Alternatives are rare, but seem quite playable:

a) 10...a5 should be met by 11 bxa5, when 11...f5 12 ♘g5 ♘f6 13 f3 transposes to *10...f5 11 ♘g5 ♘f6 12 f3 a5 13 bxa5* below; rather than 11 ♗a3 – *9...a5 10 ♗a3 ♘h5 11 g3* (notes to line C21 in Chapter Eleven).

b) 10...c6!? 11 dxc6 (or 11 ♘h4 ♘f6 12 ♗e3 ♘e8 13 ♕d2 f5 14 exf5 gxf5, L.Van Wely-A.Shirov, Monte Carlo rapid 1998, 15 f4 +=) 11...♘xc6 (or 11...bxc6 12 b5) 12 ♖b1 ♘f6 13 ♕d3 += L.Van Wely-A.Shchekachev, French Team Ch. 2000.

c) 10...h6!? 11 ♘d2 (or 11 ♘h4 ♘f6 12 ♗e3 ♘h7 13 ♕d2 g5 14 ♘g2 f5 15 f4 ∞ C.Garcia Palermo-V.Topalov, Elgoibar 1991) 11...♗h3 12 ♖e1 ♘f4! 13 ♗f1 (if 13 gxf4 exf4! threatens ...♗xc3 or ...♘xd5) 13...♗xf1 14 ♘xf1 ♘h5 15 ♘e3 ♕c8 ∞ A.Brito Garcia-C.Valiente, Asuncion 1992.

d) 10...♗h3!? 11 ♖e1 h6 12 ♘h4 (or 12 ♘d2 – *10...h6*) 12...♘f6 13 ♗e3 (or 13 ♗d2 ♘h7 14 ♗f1 ♗c8 15 ♖c1 g5 16 ♘g2 f5 ∞ A.Sznapik-G.Sax, European Team Ch., Bath 1973) 13...g5 14 ♘g2 a5 15 bxa5 ♖xa5 16 ♗d2 ♖a3 17 ♕b1 ♕c8 ∞ G.Timoscenko-H.Mynn, Istanbul Olympiad 2000.

11 ♘g5

The only worthwhile continuation. Retreating the knight makes no sense; for instance 11 ♘d2?! ♘f6 is the same as 9 ♘d2 ♘d7 10 b4 f5 11 g3?! ♘f6, which is clearly ridiculous for White.

11...♘f6 12 f3 *(D)*

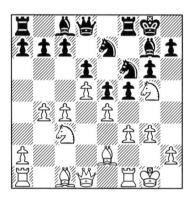

White reinforces his centre to reach the standard starting position for this variation. As the knight has no retreat (h3 is not a safe square) it will have to jump into e6 at some point. The resulting exchange of the c8-bishop helps secure White's kingside light squares, but creates a forward e6-pawn which is both strong and vulnerable at the same time. Sometimes White is able to support it by ♘d5 or ♕b3. Other times it can be attacked by ...♕c8 or ...c7-c6 and ...♘e8-c7; in this case White must look for compensation by opening the b-file or attacking the d6-pawn.

Again, alternatives are hardly worth considering; e.g. 12 exf5 ♘xf5! 13 ♘ge4 a5 14 b5 ♘xe4 15 ♘xe4 ♘d4 16 f3 ♗f5 17 ♗d3 ♕d7 18 ♗e3 ♖ae8 = G.Kuzmin-M.Taimanov, USSR Ch., Kharkov 1967; or 12 ♗f3 h6 13 ♘e6 ♗xe6 14 dxe6 fxe4 15 ♘xe4 ♘xe4 16 ♗xe4 c6 17 ♗e3 d5 18 cxd5 cxd5 19 ♗g2 (A.Shneider-I.Zakurdjaeva, Aghios Kirykos 2008) 19...b6! =+.

Black also has three other moves at his disposal:

a) 12...a5 13 bxa5 (if 13 b5!? b6 14 ♗e3 ♘h5 15 ♗f2 ♗f6 16 ♕d2 f4 17 ♘e6 ♗xe6 18 dxe6 ♘g7 19 c5 dxc5 20 ♖ad1 with compensation, G.Sosonko-C.Baljon, Dutch Ch. 1979; or else 13...f4!? ∞) 13...♖xa5 14 ♕b3 (or 14 a4 f4!? 15 ♗d2 ♘h5 16 g4 ♗f6 17 ♘h3 ♗h4!? 18 ♗e1 ♗xe1 19 ♕xe1 ♘f6 20 ♘f2, B.Ivkov-W.Uhlmann, Beverwijk 1961, 20...g5 21 ♘d3 b6 intending ...h7-h5 with counterplay, Shipov) 14...♔h8 15 ♗d2 (if 15 ♗e3 f4 16 ♗f2 fxg3 17 hxg3 ♘h5 18 ♘e6 ♗xe6 19 dxe6 ♘c6 =+ W.Lowy-Z.Gofshtein, Netanya 1993) 15...♖a8 16 ♗d3 b6 17 ♔g2 f4 18 a4 ♗h6 ∞ A.Veingold-S.Atalik, Oviedo (rapid) 1993.

b) 12...♔h8 13 ♗e3 (if 13 ♔g2 c6!? 14 ♗d2 h6 15 ♘h3 g5 16 ♘f2 cxd5 17 cxd5 f4 ∞ K.Murugan-M.Kaabi, Moscow Olympiad 1994) 13...f4!? (or 13...♘eg8 14 ♕d2 f4!? 15 gxf4 ♘h5 16 f5 gxf5 17 exf5 ♗xf5 ∞ E.Gleizerov-V.Kupreichik, Warsaw 1991) 14 ♗f2 ♗h6 15 ♘e6 ♗xe6 16 dxe6 fxg3 17 hxg3 ♕c8 18 ♘d5 ♕xe6 19 ♘xc7 ♕h3 20 ♕b3? (a misplaced winning attempt; instead 20 ♕xd6 ♗e3! 21 ♗xe3 ♕g3+ is a draw, S.Grimm-W.Winterstein, German

League 1991) 20...♘c6! 21 ♖fd1 (or 21 ♘xa8 ♘d4 22 ♕d3 ♗f4! 23 gxf4 ♘h5 -+) 21...♘g4! 22 fxg4 ♖xf2 -+ M.Zeihser-H.Schanzenbach, corr. 1995.

c) 12...h6 (this is more often delayed, but there's nothing wrong with playing it straight away) 13 ♘e6 ♗xe6 14 dxe6 c6 *(D)* (the usual move; though 14...f4!? is also possible, when 15 ♔g2, 15 b5 and 15 c5 transpose to their respective 12...f4, 13...h6 lines in D2)

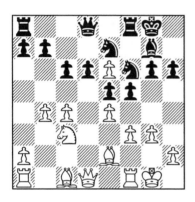

c1) 15 ♗e3 ♕c7 (or 15...♘e8 16 ♕b3 ♘c7 17 ♖ad1 ♔h7 18 c5 d5 19 exd5 ♘exd5! 20 ♗c4 ♘xe3 21 ♖xd8 ♖fxd8 ∞ J.Donaldson-K.Arakhamia Grant, Liechtenstein 1994; while 15...f4!? 16 ♗f2 – *14...h6* in line D1) 16 b5 ♖fd8 17 ♕d2 ♕c8! (or 17...♔h7 18 ♖fc1 fxe4! 19 fxe4 ♕c8 20 bxc6 bxc6 21 ♘d5, C.Garcia Palermo-J.Gallagher, Aosta 1990, 21...cxd5! 22 cxd5 ♘xe4 ∞) 18 ♗xh6 ♕xe6 19 ♗xg7 ♔xg7 20 bxc6 bxc6 21 ♖b1 ♖d7 =+ M.Raeber-J.Gallagher, Bad Ragaz 1994.

c2) 15 b5 ♕c7 (if now 15...♘e8 16 bxc6 bxc6 17 ♗a3! c5 18 ♕a4 ♘c7 19 ♕d7 ♕xd7 20 exd7 ♘c6 21 ♗d1 += L.Van Wely-D.Reinderman, Dieren

1990, or 17...♖f6 18 ♖b1 ♖xe6 19 ♕a4 with compensation, L.Van Wely-V.Kupreichik, German League 1994) 16 ♖b1 ♖fd8 17 ♕a4 ♕c8 18 bxc6 bxc6 19 ♗e3 ♕xe6 20 ♖b7 a5 (if 20...♖d7 21 ♖fb1 ♔h7 22 ♕a6! h5 23 ♖xd7 ♘xd7 24 ♕b7 ♖b8 25 ♕xa7 ♖xb1+ 26 ♘xb1 += Wl.Schmidt-R.Hübner, Skopje Olympiad 1972) 21 ♖fb1 ♔h8 22 ♖a7 ♖xa7 23 ♗xa7 ♕d7 24 ♕xa5 d5 ∞ K.Panczyk-M.Hawelko, Polish Ch. 1981.

D1: 12...c6 *(D)*

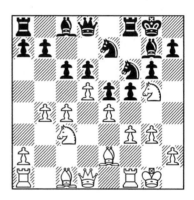

More flexible than 12...h6 13 ♘e6 ♗xe6 14 dxe6 c6 above. Black may indeed opt for ...h7-h6 after all, but by playing 12...c6 first he gives himself more options.

13 ♗e3

White has to be wary of ...h7-h6 appearing at an unfavourable moment. For instance:

a) 13 ♕b3?! h6 14 ♘e6 ♗xe6 15 dxe6 ♕c8 16 ♖d1 ♖d8 17 b5 ♕xe6 18 bxc6 bxc6 19 ♗a3 c5 =+ M.Kekelidze-H.Grünberg, German League 2000.

b) 13 ♔g2 h6 14 ♘h3!? (if 14 ♘e6 ♗xe6 15 dxe6 ♘e8 16 ♕b3 ♘c7 17 c5,

J.Speelman-V.Akopian, European Team Ch., Debrecen 1992, 17...fxe4! 18 fxe4 ♖xf1 19 ♗xf1 d5 -/+) 14...cxd5 15 exd5 g5 16 ♗d2 ♔h8 17 ♘f2 ∞ J.Tisdall-A.Kolev, Andorra 1993.

c) 13 b5 is the main alternative, and is usually met by 13...h6 14 ♘e6 ♗xe6 15 dxe6 returning to 12...h6; though Black can also try 13...c5!? (or 13...cxd5!? 14 cxd5 h6 15 ♘e6 ♗xe6 16 dxe6 ♖c8, I.Zlatilov-Kir.Georgiev, Bulgarian Team Ch. 1988, 17 ♗b2! ∞; but not 13...♘e8?, J.Donaldson-J.Schroer, Philadelphia 1986, 14 dxc6 bxc6 15 c5! h6 16 ♗c4+ +/-) 14 ♕d3 (or if 14 ♘e6!? ♗xe6 15 dxe6 h6!) 14...h6 15 ♘e6 ♗xe6 16 dxe6 ♘e8 17 ♘d5 ♘c7 18 ♖d1? (better 18 ♘xc7 ♕xc7 19 a4 and sit tight) 18...♘xe6 19 ♘xe7+ ♕xe7 20 ♕xd6 ♕f7 -/+ G.Beckhuis-J.Howell, Münster 1994.

13...f4!?

Alternatively, 13...h6 14 ♘e6 ♗xe6 15 dxe6 is 12...h6 again, unless Black follows with 15...f4!? 16 ♗f2, for which see the next note. Other moves are worse:

a) 13...♗h6 14 ♔h1 (threatening 15 ♘e6) 14...♘fxd5 (or 14...f4 15 gxf4 exf4 16 ♗xf4 ♘fxd5 17 ♘xd5 ♘xd5 18 ♘e6 ♗xe6 19 ♗xh6 +/- J.Donaldson-J.Benjamin, Seattle 1986) 15 cxd5! f4 16 gxf4 exf4 17 dxc6 ♗xg5 (A.Miles-Kr.Georgiev, Komotini 1992) 18 ♗c4+! ♔h8 19 cxb7 ♗xb7 20 ♗xa7 +/-.

b) 13...♘e8 14 c5! cxd5 15 ♘xd5 ♘c6 (or 15...h6 16 cxd6! ♘xd6 17 ♗c5) 16 ♗c4 ♔h8 17 h4!? h6 18 ♔g2 +/- L.Van Wely-W.Von Alvensleben, Dortmund 1992.

14 ♗f2 ♘e8 *(D)*

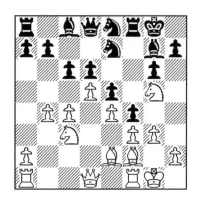

This used to be considered the main line, but Black should perhaps prefer:

a) 14...h6! (at last!) 15 ♘e6 ♗xe6 16 dxe6, when T.Ghitescu-B.Kantsler, Cappelle la Grande 2000, continued 16...♘h7! 17 ♔g2 ♘g5 18 ♕b3 ♔h7 19 c5 d5 20 exd5 cxd5 21 ♖ad1 d4 22 ♘e4 and ½-½ in this unclear position; or if 22 h4!? fxg3 23 ♗xg3 (not 23 ♗g1? ♘h3! 24 ♔xh3 ♘f5 -/+) 23...♘f5 24 ♗f2 ♔h8 ∞ Kantsler.

Alternatives are again worse:

b) 14...fxg3 15 hxg3 ♘h5 16 c5! (if 16 ♘e6 ♗xe6 17 dxe6 ♘f4! 18 gxf4 exf4 19 ♖c1 ♘f5 20 exf5 ½-½ H.Wegner-A.Kurz, German League 1992) 16...♔h8 17 cxd6 ♕xd6 18 dxc6 ♕xc6 19 ♘d5 ♘xd5 20 exd5 ♕e8 21 ♕d2 +/- M.Mraz-I.Schütt, corr. 1999.

c) 14...♗h6 15 ♘e6 ♗xe6 16 dxe6 fxg3 17 hxg3 ♘e8 18 ♕b3 ♘c7 19 ♖ad1 ♔h8 20 c5 d5 (P.H.Nielsen-B.Socko, Helsingør 2008) 21 ♘xd5! +/-.

15 ♕b3

15 c5!? is also possible, e.g. 15...cxd5 16 exd5 (if 16 ♘xd5?! h6 17 cxd6 ♘xd6 18 ♗c5 ♘c6 19 ♘c7 ♕xg5 ∞) 16...♘f5 17 ♘e6 ♗xe6 18 dxe6 fxg3 19 hxg3 ♘d4 20

♗c4 ♔h8 21 ♗xd4 exd4 22 ♘d5 +=
L.Van Wely-M.Valvo, New York Open
1995.

15...fxg3

Instead:

a) 15...♘f5 16 exf5 ♕xg5 17 fxg6?!
(better 17 ♘e4! ♕xf5 18 c5 += as in the
main line) 17...♕xg6 18 ♖ad1 ♗f5 19
dxc6 bxc6 20 b5!? ♗c2 21 ♕a3 fxg3 22
hxg3 ♗xd1 23 ♖xd1 with compensation, Z.Rahman-A.Al Khateeb, Doha
1992.

b) 15...♔h8 16 ♖ad1 (16 c5! is more
accurate, and if 16...♘xd5 17 exd5
♕xg5 18 ♘e4 ♕d8 19 ♖ad1, or 16...cxd5
17 exd5 ♘xd5 18 ♘ce4!, or 16...dxc5 17
♘e6! ♗xe6 18 dxe6 cxb4 19 ♕xb4 with
great compensation) 16...♘xd5?!
(16...cxd5! 17 cxd5 ♘xd5 improves this
for Black) 17 exd5 ♕xg5 18 ♘e4 ♕e7 19
c5! fxg3 20 hxg3 cxd5 21 ♕xd5 ♗e6 22
cxd6 ♕f7 23 ♕a5 +/- A.Veingold-
M.Hartikainen, Helsinki 1995.

16 hxg3 ♘f5

No better is 16...cxd5 17 cxd5 ♘c7
18 ♔g2 ♖f6 19 ♗e3 h6 20 ♘h3 +=
M.Bertok-D.Minic, Zagreb 1965; or
16...h6 17 ♘e6 ♗xe6 18 dxe6 ♘c7 19
♖ad1 ♔h7 20 c5 d5 21 ♘xd5! cxd5 22
exd5 ♘exd5 23 ♗c4 ♘xe6 24 ♗xd5 ♘d4
25 ♗xd4 exd4 26 ♔g2 ♕c7 27 ♗e4 +=
A.Miles-A.Shirov, Biel 1992.

**17 exf5 ♕xg5 18 ♘e4 ♕xf5 19 c5 ♔h8
20 cxd6 ♗d7 21 ♖ad1!**

Improving on 21 g4 ♕f7 22 ♘g5
½-½ A.Shariyazdanov-S.Dyachkov,
Russian Junior Ch. 1995.

**21...cxd5 22 g4 ♕f4 23 ♘c5 ♘f6 24
♘xd7 ♘xd7 25 ♕xd5** (D)

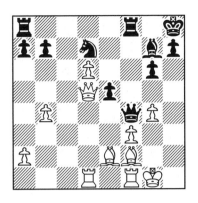

White has a big advantage due to
his domination in the centre, the strong
d-pawn and the bishop pair. S.Webb-
G.J.Timmerman, corr. 1996, continued
25...b6 26 ♕c4 ♕f6 27 ♗e3 ♖ac8 [if
27...♗h6 28 ♗xh6 ♕h4 29 ♔g2 ♕xh6 30
♕e6 +/-] **28 g5 ♕f5 29 ♕e4 ♕e6 30 ♗b5
♖fd8 31 ♖f2 ♘f8 32 d7! ♖c3** [not
32...♘xd7? 33 ♖fd2 ♖c7 34 ♗xd7 ♖cxd7
35 ♖xd7 ♖xd7 36 ♖xd7 ♕xd7 37 ♕a8+
mates] **33 ♖c2 ♖xc2 34 ♕xc2 ♕e7 35
♕e4 ♘e6 36 f4 ♖f8 37 fxe5 ♘xg5 38
♕g4 ♘e6** [not 38...♘f3+? 39 ♕xf3! etc]
**39 ♗c4 ♘d8 40 e6 ♖f5 41 ♔g2 ♗f6 42
♗b3 ♔g7 43 ♖f1 ♖xf1 44 ♔xf1 h6 45
♔e2 ♕d6 46 ♕e4 ♕h2+ 47 ♔d3 ♕d6+
48 ♗d5 g5** [if 48...♘c6 49 ♗f4! ♘xb4+
50 ♔d2 +-] **49 ♗d4 ♕e7 50 a3 h5 51
♕f5 ♗xd4 52 ♔xd4 a5** [or 52...♕f6+ 53
♕e5! +-] **53 ♔e5 1-0** [White wins after
♗e4 etc].

D2: 12...f4 (D)

The most popular continuation;
Black begins direct action against the
white king (see the line 13 b5 h6, for
example).

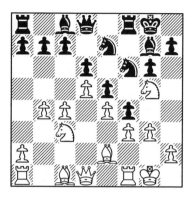

13 ♔g2 *(D)*

The king sees to his own defence, reinforcing the g3-pawn and covering h3 against a possible bishop or queen invasion. There are two significant alternatives:

a) 13 c5 and then:

a1) 13...fxg3 14 hxg3 ♘h5!? (or 14...h6 15 ♘e6 ♗xe6 16 dxe6 – *13...h6*) 15 ♔g2 (if 15 ♕e1, L.Stein-E.Gufeld, USSR Team Ch. 1969, 15...h6! 16 ♘e6 ♗xe6 17 dxe6 dxc5! ∞) 15...♘f4+ 16 gxf4 exf4 17 ♕e1! ♘f5 (or if 17...♗xc3 18 ♕h4! h5 19 ♗xf4 with compensation, Van Wely) 18 ♗xf4 ♗xc3 19 ♕xc3 ♘h4+ (L.Van Wely-O.Cvitan, Moscow Olympiad 1994) 20 ♔h1!? ♖xf4 21 ♖g1 +=.

a2) 13...dxc5!? 14 bxc5 (or 14 ♗c4!? cxb4 15 d6+ ♔h8 16 ♘b5 h6 17 ♘f7+ ♖xf7 18 ♗xf7 cxd6 19 ♘xd6 ♗h3 20 ♖f2 ♘c8 21 ♗e6! ♘xd6 22 ♗xh3 ∞ J.Novotny-M.Zavrel, corr. 1993) 14...h6 15 ♘e6 ♗xe6 16 dxe6 ♕d4+ (or 16...fxg3 17 ♖b1!?) 16...♕d4+ 17 ♕xd4 exd4 18 ♘b5 fxg3 19 ♖b1!? gxh2+ 20 ♔xh2 ∞ J.Sieglen-T.Düster, German League 1989.

a3) 13...h6 14 ♘e6 ♗xe6 15 dxe6 fxg3 (or just 15...d5! 16 exd5 ♘fxd5 17 ♘xd5 ♘xd5 18 ♗c4 ½-½ J.Donaldson-G.Markzon, New York Open 1991) 16 hxg3 d5! 17 exd5 ♘fxd5 18 ♘xd5 ♘xd5 19 ♗c4 c6 20 e7! ♕xe7 21 ♗xd5+ cxd5 22 ♕xd5+ ♔h7 23 ♕e4 a5 24 ♗e3 axb4 25 ♖ab1 has occurred several times. White has a slight initiative after 25...♖a4 (or 25...♖xa2 26 ♖xb4 K.Panczyk-D.Klimaszewski, Augustow 1983) 26 ♖xb4 ♖xb4 27 ♕xb4 ♕d7 (K.Panczyk-Z.Beil, Decin 1982) 28 ♔g2, though the odds are on a draw.

b) 13 b5!? *(D)* seems to be Van Wely's current preference.

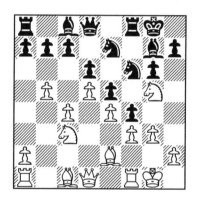

It looks anti-positional, but it is not. The idea is to discourage ...c7-c6, so that after the forcing exchange on e6 White can follow with ♘d5.

b1) 13...fxg3 14 hxg3 ♘h5!? (again 14...h6 15 ♘e6 ♗xe6 16 dxe6 – *13...h6*) 15 ♕e1! (if 15 ♔g2 ♘f4+! 16 gxf4 exf4 17 e5 ♗xe5 18 ♘ge4 ♘f5, M.Taimanov-E.Gufeld, USSR Ch., Moscow 1961, 19 ♕d3 ∞) 15...h6 (or 15...c6 16 dxc6 bxc6 17 c5!, since if 17...d5 18 bxc6 h6 19 exd5 hxg5 20 ♗xg5 is very strong) 16

♘e6 ♗xe6 17 dxe6 ♕c8 18 ♘d5 ♕xe6 19 g4! ♘f4 20 ♘xc7 ♕c8 21 ♘xa8 ♕c5+ 22 ♔h2 ♖xa8 23 ♕f2 +/- G.Prakash-K.Sashirikan, Indian Ch. 2001.

b2) 13...c6!? (anyway) 14 bxc6 (if 14 dxc6?! bxc6 15 c5 d5 16 bxc6 h6! or 15 ♗a3 c5! ∞) 14...bxc6 15 ♖b1 h6 16 ♘e6 ♗xe6 17 dxe6 d5? (17...♕c7) 18 cxd5 cxd5 19 ♘xd5 ♘fxd5 20 exd5 ♕xd5 21 ♕xd5 ♘xd5 22 ♗c4 ♘e7 23 ♖b7 ♗f6 24 ♗a3 +- L.Szabo-A.Anastasopoulos, Leipzig Olympiad 1960.

b3) 13...h6 14 ♘e6 ♗xe6 15 dxe6 fxg3 16 hxg3 ♕c8 (now White has to play energetically) 17 ♘d5 ♕xe6 18 ♘xc7 ♕h3! 19 ♖f2 (D) (not 19 ♘xa8?? ♕xg3+ 20 ♔h1 ½-½ L.Pachman-M.Taimanov, Havana 1967, due to Huzman's 20...♘h5! with a strong attack, e.g. 21 ♕e1 ♕h3+ 22 ♔g1 ♘g3 23 ♘c7 ♘ef5! 24 exf5 e4 25 ♘e6 e3! -+) and now:

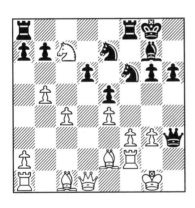

b31) 19...♖ac8! 20 ♖h2 ♕xg3+ 21 ♖g2 ♕h3 22 ♕xd6 ♖f7 23 c5! ♘f5! (not 23...♗f8? 24 ♘e6 ♘xe4 25 ♕xe5 ♘c3 26 ♗c4 ♕h4 27 ♕xc3 1-0 L.Van Wely-M.Golubev, Rumanian Team Ch. 2000) 24 exf5 ♖fxc7 25 ♖xg6 ♔h7! (Golubev)

seems to hold for Black; e.g. 26 ♗b2 ♕xf5 27 ♗d3 e4! 28 ♖xf6 ♕g5+ 29 ♔f1 exd3 30 ♕xd3+ ♔h8 31 ♖g6 (or 31 ♕d6 ♔h7) 31...♕h5 32 ♗xg7+ ♖xg7 33 ♖xg7 ♔xg7 34 ♕d7+ ♔f6 =.

b32) 19...♘xe4!? (a risky winning attempt) 20 fxe4! (if 20 ♖h2?! ♕d7 21 ♘xa8 ♘xg3 gives Black excellent compensation, e.g. 22 ♗xh6 ♗xh6 23 ♖xh6 ♔g7 24 ♖h2 ♘ef5 25 ♔f2 ♖xa8 26 ♗d3 ♕c7 =+ L.Van Wely-J.M.Degraeve, Mondariz 2000) 20...♗xf2 21 ♔xf2 ♖f8+ 22 ♔e3! ♕xg3+ 23 ♔d2 ♖f2 24 ♘e8 h5 25 ♘xg7 ♔xg7 26 ♕b3 ♕g2 27 ♕e3 ♘g8 28 c5! dxc5 29 ♗b2 ♕h2 30 ♖e1 ♘f6 31 ♔d1 +/- L.Van Wely-T.Radjabov, Dresden Olympiad 2008.

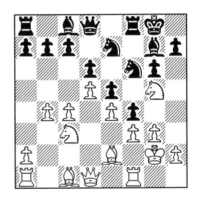

13...h6

Black has several other interesting possibilities:

a) 13...fxg3?! 14 hxg3 ♘h5 (White is ready for this) 15 ♖h1! h6 16 ♘e6 ♗xe6 17 dxe6 c6 (or 17...♘c6 18 ♘d5 ♖e8 19 c5 ♘d4 20 e7 +/- V.Bogdanovski-Z.Gicov, Macedonian Ch. 1993) 18 ♗e3 ♕c7 19 ♕d2 ♔h7 20 ♖af1 ♘g8 21 f4 +/- T.Ghitescu-R.Milu, Bucharest 1991.

b) 13...a5!? 14 bxa5 ♖xa5 15 ♕b3 (if

15 a4 ♘e8 16 ♕b3 ♘f5! 17 exf5 ♕xg5 18 fxg6 ♕xg6 ∞ G.Tunik-A.Pugachev, Chelyabinsk 1991) 15...♘e8 16 ♗d2 ♖a8 (better 16...h6 17 ♘e6 ♗xe6 18 dxe6 ♖a7!? ∞) 17 c5 ♔h8 18 cxd6 ♘xd6 19 ♘e6 ♗xe6 20 dxe6 ♘c6 21 ♘d5 ♖e8 22 ♗c3 += E.Lobron-E.Gelfand, Munich 1992.

c) 13...♘h5!? 14 g4 (or 14 c5!? fxg3 15 hxg3 – *13 c5,* though Black might try 14...♘f5!?) 14...♗f6! (clearing g7 for the knight) 15 ♘e6 ♗xe6 16 dxe6 ♘g7 17 c5 ♔h8 18 cxd6 cxd6 19 ♘b5 ♘c8 20 ♗c4 ♖e8 21 ♗d5 ∞ L.Van Wely-A.Zapata, Matanzas 1995.

d) 13...♔h8 14 c5! h6 15 cxd6 ♕xd6 16 ♘b5 ♕b6 17 a4 ♘fxd5! 18 exd5 hxg5 19 a5 ♕f6 20 ♘xc7 ♖b8 21 g4 ♖d8 (or 21...e4 = Nunn; but not 21...♗d7? 22 b5 ♖fc8 23 d6 +/- L.Van Wely-J.Nunn, Wijk aan Zee 1992) 22 b5 (A.Vlaskov-E.Mamedov, Kirov 1993) 22...♘xd5! 23 ♘xd5 ♕f7 ∞.

e) 13...c6! is also critical; e.g. 14 ♕b3 (if 14 b5 c5! 15 ♕d3 ♘e8 16 ♘e6 ♗xe6 17 dxe6 ♘c7 18 ♖d1 ♘c8 19 e7 ♕xe7 20 ♘d5 ♘xd5 21 ♕xd5+ ♔h8 =+ B.Finegold-G.Michelakis, Groningen 1993; or 14 c5 cxd5 15 exd5 ♘f5 16 ♘ge4 a5 17 cxd6 axb4 18 ♘b5 ♕d7! -/+ J.Malmström-F.Toumani, corr. 1997) 14...h6 15 ♘e6 ♗xe6 16 dxe6 ♕c8 17 ♖d1 ♖d8 18 ♘d5!? (if 18 c5 d5 19 exd5 ♘fxd5! 20 ♘e4 ♕xe6 -/+ L.Van Wely-R.Pruijssers, Dutch Team Ch. 2006) 18...cxd5 19 cxd5 g5 20 ♗d2 ♖f8 21 g4 h5 22 h3 ♘g6 23 ♖dc1 ♕b8 24 ♗e1 hxg4 25 hxg4 ♘e8 26 a4 ∞ L.Van Wely-A.Fedorov, European Team Ch., Batumi 1999, as it is hard for Black to do

anything with his extra piece.

14 ♘e6

14 ♘h3!? is also possible, though White can hardly hope for any advantage; e.g. 14...g5 15 ♘f2 h5 16 ♗d2 ♘g6 17 c5 ♖f7 18 a4 ♗f8 19 cxd6 cxd6 20 ♔h1 ♖g7 21 ♖g1 ∞ D.Chaplicky-P.Golovenchenko, corr. 1993.

14...♗xe6 15 dxe6 c6

If instead 15...♘c6!? 16 ♘d5 ♖e8 17 gxf4 exf4 (or 17...♖xe6 18 ♗e3) 18 ♗xf4 ♘h5 19 ♗e3 ♗xa1 20 ♕xa1 ♖xe6 21 ♔h1 with compensation.

16 b5

Not 16 gxf4?! ♘h5 17 fxe5 ♗xe5 with an attack (Ye Jiangchuan), but 16 ♖b1 is an alternative.

16...♕c7

16...c5!? sees Black essentially a tempo down on 13...c6 14 b5 c5 lines, having played ...h7-h6 to induce ♘g5-e6; e.g. 17 ♘d5 ♘e8 18 ♖f2!? ♘c7 19 ♘xc7 ♕xc7 20 ♗f1 with the initiative (Michelakis).

17 bxc6 bxc6 18 ♗a3 ♖fd8 19 ♕a4 ♕c8 20 ♖ab1 (D)

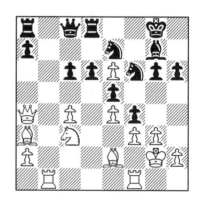

The typical method of seeking compensation for the pending loss of the e6-pawn: White prepares to infiltrate on the squares which ...♕xe6 surrenders (b7 and a6).

20...♔h8

The immediate 20...♕xe6 21 ♖b7 (21 ♕a6!?) 21...h5 22 ♖d1 g5 23 ♕b4 c5 24 ♕b5 g4 25 ♘d5 ♘exd5 26 cxd5 ♕c8 27 ♕c6 turned out well for White in C.Lutz-G.Beckhuis, German League 1993; but Black might consider 20...a5!?.

21 ♖fd1 ♕xe6

Here, too, 21...a5!? (Van Wely) looks like an improvement.

22 ♕a6!

If 22 ♖b7 a5!? gives Black a good game; e.g. 23 c5?! (23 ♖xe7!? ♘xe7 24 ♕xc6 is perhaps the best try) 23...d5 24 ♗c1 g5 25 ♖b6 d4 26 ♘b5 ♘e8 27 ♗c4 ♕g6 -/+ I.Badenas-L.Cabanas, corr. 1995.

22...h5 23 ♖b7 g5 24 ♖xa7 *(D)*

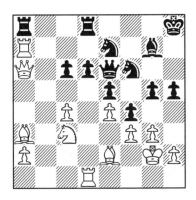

White has recovered his pawn with a good position. L.Van Wely-Ye Jiangchuan, Biel Interzonal 1993, continued **24...♖ab8 25 ♕a5** [if 25 ♖b7!? ♕c8! ∞, but not 25...♖a8? 26 ♖xd6! ♖xa6 27 ♖xd8+ ♘fg8 28 ♖e7! +/-] **25...♘e8 26 ♖b1 ♖bc8 27 gxf4?!** [here 27 c5! was

correct, and if 27...d5? 28 ♖bb7 ♗f8 29 ♕a6! d4 30 ♘d5 +-] **27...gxf4 28 ♔h1 ♗f6 29 ♖g1 ♗h4 30 c5 d5!** [now Black is better] **31 exd5** [or 31 ♕a6 ♘c7! =+] **31...cxd5 32 ♖a6 ♘c6 33 ♕a4 ♘f6 34 ♗b2?** [34 ♗f1 was necessary, when 34...♖g8 35 ♖xg8+ ♖xg8?? loses to 36 ♕xc6] **34 ♗b2 ♖g8 35 ♖xg8+ ♖xg8! 36 ♗f1** [too late; but if 36 ♕xc6? ♕h3! mates] **36...♘g4! 37 ♘d1 ♕g6 38 fxg4 ♕xg4 39 ♗xe5+ ♘xe5 40 ♖h6+ ♔g7 41 h3 ♕f3+ 42 ♗g2 ♕g3 43 ♕a6 ♕e1+ 44 ♗f1 ♕e4+ 45 ♗g2 f3 0-1.**

E: 10 ♖e1 *(D)*

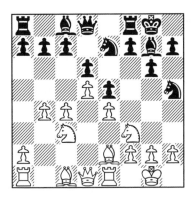

Although 10 ♖e1 had been played as early as the 1970s, it was two wins by Ivan Sokolov en route to the 1995 Dutch Championship title that signalled its true arrival on the chess scene. Since then 10 ♖e1 has been White's move of choice, and has featured in literally thousands of games.

The main idea is to neutralize 10...♘f4 by giving the bishop a retreat square. On f1 the white bishop fulfils useful defensive functions, whereas the knight now stands awkwardly on f4, hindering ...f5-f4, and vulnerable to a timely ♗c1xf4 or g2-g3.

The statistics make pleasant reading for White: a 61% overall score, with a 44%-22% win ratio – not at all what Black is looking for from his counter-attacking opening. Consequently, the King's Indian declined in popularity somewhat; while Garry Kasparov, after losing to Kramnik at Novgorod 1997, gave up the King's Indian altogether.

Inevitably, Black's game has since been strengthened, in particular by the decision to dispense with ...♘f4, after ...f7-f5, and instead return the knight to f6, as in the traditional ...♘e8 and ...♘d7 variations. The difference here is that the battle mostly takes place in the centre, rather than on opposite wings, and Black aims simply for equality. The reduction of White's percentage (in line E32) to 57% shows the relative success of Black's strategy.

E1: 10...♘f4 *354*

E2: 10...a5 *358*

E3: 10...f5 *362*

Alternatives are inferior:

a) 10...h6 11 c5! (or 11 ♘d2 ♘f4 12 ♗f1 f5 13 c5 etc) 11...f5 12 ♘d2 ♘f4 13 ♗f1 and then:

a1) 13...g5?! 14 g3 (or 14 cxd6 cxd6 15 ♘c4 g4 16 b5 ♖f6 17 ♕b3 ♔h7 18 b6 a6 19 ♗a3 +/- I.Sokolov-L.Van Wely, Dutch Ch. 1995) 14...♘fg6 15 ♘c4 f4 (or 15...♔h8 16 cxd6 cxd6 17 ♘b5 fxe4 18 ♘bxd6 b5 19 ♘xb5 ♘xd5 20 ♘bd6 ♗e6 21 ♕h5 +/- R.Hess-C.Neidhardt, Ger-

man League 1992!) 16 ♗a3 ♖f6 17 b5 b6 18 cxd6 cxd6 19 ♗b4 g4 20 a4 h5 21 a5 +/- S.Iskusnyh-A.Fedorov, Omsk 1996.

a2) 13...fxe4 14 ♘dxe4 ♘f5 15 g3 ♘h5 16 ♗g2 ♘f6 17 a4 ♘xe4 18 ♘xe4 ♘d4 19 ♗e3 ♘f5 20 ♖c1 ♖f7 21 ♕d3 += D.Jakovenko-T.Radjabov, Sochi 2008.

b) 10...♔h8 11 ♘d2! (if 11 c5 f5!? – *10...f5 11 c5 ♔h8 below*) 11...♘f4 12 ♗f1 f5 13 a4 fxe4 (or 13...a5 14 bxa5 ♖xa5 15 ♘b3 ♖a8 16 a5 fxe4 17 ♘xe4 += I.Sokolov-K.Arakhamia, Gibraltar 2009) 14 ♘dxe4 ♘f5 15 ♔h1 ♘h6 16 f3 ♘g8 17 c5 ♘f6 18 ♘xf6 ♗xf6 19 ♘e4 += E.Bacrot-I.Nataf, French Ch. 2008.

c) 10...c6!? is a standard move in this variation (see line E322) but seems a bit premature here; e.g. 11 dxc6!? (or 11 ♘d2 ♘f4 12 ♗f1 h5 13 a4 ♗g4 14 ♕b3 g5 15 ♘d1!? ♗h6 16 ♘e3 ♗d7 17 ♗b2 += Y.Pelletier-J.Balcerak, Biel 2000) 11...bxc6 (or 11...♘xc6 12 b5 += Huzman) 12 b5 ♘f4 13 ♗xf4 exf4 14 ♖c1 ♗g4 15 e5 dxe5 16 ♘xe5 ♗xe5 17 ♗xg4 ♕xd1 18 ♗xd1 f6 19 ♗f3 +/- A.Evdokimov-F.Amonatov, Sochi 2005.

E1: 10...♘f4 *(D)*

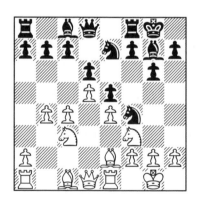

This is usually connected with ...a7-a5, but in that case the immediate 10...a5 (line E2) is probably more accurate. Black also has to watch out for ♗c1xf4 occurring at an unfortunate moment.

11 ♗f1

Taking the knight would be entirely inconsistent, even if it's not objectively too bad; e.g. 11 ♗xf4 exf4 12 ♖c1 h6 13 c5 g5 14 ♘d4 ♘g6 15 cxd6 cxd6 16 ♘cb5 a6 17 ♘c7 ♖b8 18 b5 ♕f6 19 ♘b3 axb5 20 ♘xb5 ♖a8 = Huang Qian-I.Krush, Beijing (blitz) 2008.

11...a5 *(D)*

A logical continuation, breaking up the queenside pawns before White can play c4-c5. Other moves are weaker:

a) 11...h6 12 c5! g5 13 ♘d2 f5 – *10...h6 above.*

b) 11...f5?! 12 ♗xf4 exf4 13 e5! dxe5 (if 13...a5 14 bxa5 ♖xa5 15 ♕d2 dxe5 16 ♘xe5 transposes; or 13...g5 14 ♘xg5 dxe5 15 c5 h6 16 ♗c4 hxg5 17 d6+ ♔h7 18 dxe7 ♕xe7 19 ♘d5 +/- B.Lalic-B.Gicev, Skopje 1995) 14 ♘xe5 a5 15 bxa5 (or 15 c5 axb4 16 ♕b3 ♔h8 17 ♕xb4 ♘xd5 18 ♘xd5 ♕xd5, L.Psakhis-S.Weeramantry, Honolulu 1997, 19 ♗c4! +/- Psakhis) 15...♖xa5 16 ♕d2! g5 17 ♖ad1 ♘g6 (or 17...♕d6 18 ♘d3 b6 19 ♘b5 +/- S.Pedersen-A.Esenov, Beijing rapid 2008) 18 ♘xg6 hxg6 19 ♘b5 c6 20 ♘d6 +/- V.Baikov-D.Markosian, Moscow 1996.

c) 11...c6 12 a4 (or 12 ♘d2 – *10...c6 11 ♘d2)* 12...a5 (if 12...h6 13 a5 g5 14 dxc6 bxc6 15 b5 ♗e6 16 a6 += N.Rashkovsky-C.Navrotescu, Cappelle la Grande 2000) 13 bxa5 (or 13 dxc6

♘xc6 14 b5 += Rashkovsky) 13...♕xa5 (13...♖xa5?! – *11...a5* with the inferior 13...c6?!) 14 ♖a3 h6 15 dxc6 ♘xc6 16 ♘b5 +/= V.Rajlich-S.Farago, Budapest 2000.

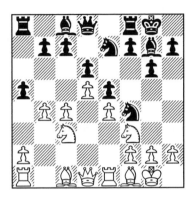

12 bxa5

Khalifman considers this response the strongest. Instead:

a) 12 ♗a3 is inferior due to 12...axb4 (12...♗g4!? 13 h3 ♗xf3 14 ♕xf3 axb4 15 ♗xb4 transposes; or if 13 ♖e3 f5! 14 h3 ♗h5 15 ♕b3!? a4 16 ♕c2 fxe4 17 ♘h2 ♘f5 18 ♘xe4!, J.Granda Zuniga-Al.David, Yerevan Olympiad 1996, 18...g5 19 ♖ee1 ♘d4 20 ♕d2 ♕d7 with excellent play for Black) 13 ♗xb4 ♗g4! (13...b6 14 a4 transposes to the previous chapter; see 13...♘h5 14 ♖e1! in the notes to line C22) 14 h3 ♗xf3 15 ♕xf3 c5!, when White is forced to capture en passant, but cannot follow with ♗xd6 as his queen has left the d-file. V.Kramnik-B.Gelfand, Dortmund 1996, continued 16 dxc6 ♘xc6 17 a3 ♘e6! 18 ♘b5 ♘ed4 19 ♕d3 ♘xb4 20 axb4 ♕b6 21 ♘xd4 exd4 (opposite-coloured bishops make the position very drawish) 22 ♕d2 ♖a7 23 ♖ec1 ♖fa8 24 ♖xa7 and

½-½, since 24...♕xa7 25 c5 dxc5 26 ♖xc5 ♖d8 is equal (Gelfand).

b) 12 b5!? deserves attention. It is unusual for White to block the queenside in the King's Indian, but here he hopes to exploit his space advantage on the rest of the board; e.g. 12...b6 13 a4 ♘h5 14 ♖a3 ♔h8 (if 14...f5 15 exf5 ♘xf5 16 ♘e4 +/= Mikhalevski) 15 g3 ♘g8 16 ♗g2 ♗h6?! (16...♘gf6!? Mikhalevski) 17 ♗b2 ♘g7 18 ♘e2! f5 19 exf5 ♗xf5 (if 19...gxf5 20 ♘xe5! dxe5 21 ♗xe5 with strong compensation, Mikhalevski) 20 ♘d2 ♘f6 21 f4! exf4 22 ♘xf4 ♗xf4 23 gxf4 ♕d7 24 ♖ae3! ♖ae8 25 ♗xf6 (or 25 ♖xe8!? ♘gxe8 26 ♘f3 ♘g7 27 ♘d4 +/-) 25...♖xf6 26 ♖xe8+ ♘xe8 27 ♕a1 += V.Mikhalevski-A.Chow, Chicago 2005.

12...♖xa5

The immediate 12...c5 generally transposes after a subsequent ...♖xa5, unless Black wants to investigate 13 a4 (or 13 ♘d2 ♖xa5 – line E2) 13...h6 (13...♖xa5 – 12...♖xa5) 14 ♘b5 g5 15 ♘d2 ♔h8!? (still 15...♖xa5 16 ♖a3 ♖a6 – 15...h6 16 ♘d2 g5 in the main line) 16 ♖a3 ♘g8 17 g3 ♘g6 (not 17...♘h3+?? 18 ♗xh3 ♗xh3 19 g4 +- Lautier) 18 ♗e2! (Se.Ivanov) 18...♘6e7 19 ♗g4 f5 20 exf5 ♗xf5 (or 20...♘f6 21 ♘e4 ♘xe4 22 ♖xe4 ♖xa5 23 ♗d2 ♖a6 24 f6! ♖xf6 25 ♗xc8 ♕xc8 26 a5 +/= Lautier) 21 ♘e4 ♗xe4 22 ♖xe4 ♘f6 23 ♖ee3 ♘xg4 24 ♕xg4 ♘f5 25 ♖f3 ♘d4 (if 25...♕xa5 26 ♗xg5! +/-) 26 ♖xf8+ ♕xf8 27 ♗b2 +/- J.Lautier-V.Spasov, European Team Ch., Leon 2001.

13 a4

13 ♘d2 again transposes to line E2, but there is no need to hurry with this move. The knight can sometimes be useful on f3, and White keeps the option of ♗xf4.

13...c5

13...f5!? is better than on the 11th move, as 14 ♗xf4 exf4 15 e5 dxe5 16 ♘xe5 reaches the same position but with 16 a4 (rather than 16 ♕d2!) inserted; e.g. 16...♕d6 17 ♕e2 f3 18 gxf3 f4 19 ♘b5 ♕d8 20 ♖ad1 ♘f5 ∞ M.Palacios Perez-D.Pribeanu, Mondariz 2003.

Instead, White should probably prefer 14 ♖a3! (14 ♘d2 – 13...f5 14 a4 in line E2) 14...h6 (not 14...c5?! 15 ♘g5! ♗f6 16 ♗xf4 exf4 17 ♘e6 ♗xe6 18 dxe6 ♗e5 19 ♘d5 +/- Cu.Hansen-M.Krakops, Istanbul Olympiad 2000; or if 14...fxe4 15 ♘xe4 ♗g4 16 h3 ♗xf3 17 ♖xf3 ♕d7 18 ♖a3 += S.Prudnikova-M.Petrovic, Yugoslav Women's Ch. 1999) 15 exf5 ♘xf5 16 g3 (if 16 ♘e4?! g5! 17 g3 ♘g6 ∞ E.Bareev-V.Spasov, Elista Olympiad 1998) 16...♘h5 17 g4 ♘d4 18 ♘xd4 exd4 19 ♘b5 ♘f4 20 ♘xd4 ♗e5 21 h3 += S.Romanov-D.Konca, corr. 2001.

14 ♖a3

Or 14 ♘b5 ♖a6 15 ♖a3 transposing; but 14 ♖b1!? is another option, e.g. 14...h6 15 ♘d2 ♖a6 16 ♘b3 g5 (if 16...f5 17 ♗xf4! exf4 18 e5 ♗xe5 19 ♖xe5! dxe5 20 ♘xc5 with compensation, Glek) 17 a5 f5 18 g3 ♘fg6 19 exf5 ♘xf5?! (better 19...♗xf5 20 ♘e4 g4 ∞) 20 ♗d3 e4!? 21 ♘xe4 ♘e5 22 f4 gxf4 23 ♗xf4 ♘h4 24 ♗e2 ♘hg6 25 ♗e3 ♖f7 26 ♖f1 ♗f5 27 ♘bd2 ♖xa5 28 ♖xf5 ♖xf5 29 ♗g4 += I.Sokolov-I.Glek, Wijk aan Zee 1997.

14...♖a6 15 ♘b5 (D)

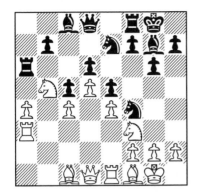

15...h6

Black has also tried:

a) 15...♗d7 16 ♗xf4!? (if 16 ♘d2 ♕c8!? 17 ♔h1, Xu Jun-K.Sasikiran, Asian Ch., Udaipur 2000, 17...f5! 18 g3 ♘h5 = A.Martin) 16...exf4 17 ♕c1 ♗e5 (17...♔h6 18 e5 +/- Khalifman) 18 ♘xe5 dxe5 19 ♕c3 f6 20 a5 +/= A.Polatel-B.Marmont, corr. 2003.

b) 15...♔h8 16 ♘d2 (again 16 ♗xf4!? exf4 17 ♕c1 comes into consideration) 16...♘g8 17 g3 ♘h5 18 ♗e2 ♘hf6 19 f4 exf4 20 gxf4 ♘d7 21 ♘f3 += S.Iskusnyh-V.Zaitsev, Novosibirsk 1998.

c) 15...♘h5 16 g3 ♔h8 17 ♘h4 (or 17 ♘d2 ♘g8 – *15...♔h8*) 17...♘g8 18 ♘g2 ♘hf6 19 ♗b2 ♘d7 20 ♕a1 f5?! (better 20...♘h6 += Tsesarsky) 21 exf5 gxf5 22 f4 +/- M.Kobalia-P.Smirnov, Russian Ch. 2001.

16 ♘d2

Now Black has taken control of g5, the white knight moves away. If here 16 ♗xf4 exf4 17 e5 ♘f5 18 ♗d3 dxe5 19 ♘xe5 ♕a5 (19...♘h4!?) 20 ♘f3 ♗d7 21 ♗xf5?! ♗xf5 22 ♕d2 ♕xd2 23 ♘xd2 ♖fa8 -/+ G.Dimopoulos-Kr.Georgiev, Athens 1997.

16...g5

Giving the f4-knight a retreat square.

If instead 16...♗d7 17 g3 ♘h5 (not 17...♘h3+?? 18 ♗xh3 ♗xh3 19 g4! +-) 18 ♗b2 (planning ♕a1 and f2-f4 to attack the e5-fortress) 18...♗e8!? (an imaginative defence) 19 ♗e2 ♘f6 20 f4 ♘d7 21 ♕a1 += V.Topalov-F.Nijboer, Wijk aan Zee 1998; although Black developed interesting counterplay after 21...f5 22 ♔h1 g5!? 23 ♖f1 ♗g6 24 ♗d3 g4 25 exf5 (25 a5!? +=) 25...♘xf5 26 ♕b1 exf4 27 ♗xg7 ♔xg7 28 ♖xf4 ♘e5! 29 ♗xf5 (if 29 ♖xf5 ♗xf5 30 ♗xf5 ♕g5! 31 ♘c7 ♗xf5 -/+) 29...♖xf5 30 ♖xf5 (or 30 ♘d4 cxd4! 31 ♕xb7+ ♘f7 32 ♕xa6 ♕e8 ∞) 30...♕d7 31 ♖e3 ♕xf5 32 ♕xf5 ♗xf5 33 ♘xd6 ♖xd6 34 ♖xe5 ♔f6 35 ♖e8 ♖a6 =.

17 g3 ♘fg6 18 ♗e2

Planning ♗g4 to exchange the light-squared bishops. Another option is 18 ♕h5!? (intending ♗h3) 18...♕d7!? (not 18...♗d7?! 19 ♗h3 ♕c8 20 ♗xd7 ♕xd7 21 ♘c3 ♘h8 22 h4 f6 23 hxg5 fxg5 24 ♘f1 ♘c8 25 ♘e3 +/- E.Miroshnichenko-R.Mamedov, Dubai 2004) 19 ♗e2 ♘h8! 20 ♘f1 f5 21 ♘e3 (or 21 exf5 ♘xf5 22 ♗g4 ♕f7! = Spasov) 21...f4 22 ♘g4 ♔h7 23 ♔g2 ♘g8 24 h4 ∞ and ½-½ V.Babula-V.Spasov, Krynica 1998.

18...f5

18...♕d7!? is possible here too: 19 ♗h5 (intending f2-f3, ♗g4) 19...f5 20 exf5 ♕xf5 21 ♖f3 (if 21 f3 ♕d7 22 ♘e4 ♕d8 23 ♕d3 ♘h8!? planning ♘f5, ♘f7, ♘d4 ∞ Marin) 21...♗f4!? was agreed drawn in S.Kiselev-R.Milu, Bucharest 1998. White is better after 22 gxf4 g4 23 ♗xg4 ♕xg4+ 24 ♔h1 ♖xf4 25 ♖xf4

♕xd1 26 ♖xd1 exf4 27 ♖e1 ♗e5 28 ♘e4!, but Black has good drawing chances as material leaves the board, e.g. 28...♗d7 29 ♘exd6 ♗xd6 30 ♘xd6 ♘xd5 31 ♘xb7 ♘c3 32 ♘xc5 ♗c6+ 33 ♔g1 ♖a5.

19 exf5 ♘xf5 20 ♗h5 ♘ge7 21 ♗g4 (D)

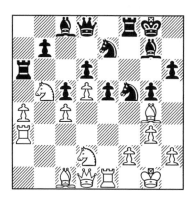

White is better here with options on both sides of the board, whereas Black has often struggled to find counterplay. For instance:

a) 21...e4? 22 ♖xe4 ♘g6 23 ♘f3! ♘e5 24 ♘xe5 ♗xe5 25 f4 ♗g7 26 fxg5 hxg5 27 ♖f3 ♘d4 28 ♖xf8+ ♕xf8 29 ♗xc8 ♕xc8 30 ♕h5 +- M.Krasenkow-A.Fedorov, Vilnius 1997.

b) 21...♔h8 22 ♘e4 ♘g8 23 ♖f3 ♗d7 24 ♗b2 ♘ge7?! 25 ♘exd6 ♘xd6 26 ♖xf8+ ♕xf8 27 ♗xd7 ♘xc4 28 ♗a1 ♘b6 29 ♗e6 +/- A.Rychagov-A.Cela, Greek Team Ch. 1998.

c) 21...♗d7 22 ♘e4 ♔h8 23 ♗b2 ♗e8 24 ♗h5 ♘g6 25 ♕b1 ♘fe7 26 ♖b3 ♗f7 27 a5 ♘c8 28 ♘bc3 +/- S.Savchenko-K.Arakhamia Grant, World Team Ch., Lucerne 1997.

d) 21...♘d4! (probably best) 22 ♗xc8 (or 22 ♘e4!? += Krasenkow) 22...♕xc8

23 ♘e4 ♕d7 24 ♗b2 (24 f3!? +=) 24...♘ef5 25 ♗xd4 ♘xd4 26 ♘xd4 cxd4 27 c5 dxc5 28 ♘xc5 ♕d6 29 ♘xa6 ♕xa3 30 ♘c7 ♖f7 31 ♘e6 ♕a2 32 ♕e2 = P.Lopepe-C.Blanco Gramajo, corr. 1999.

E2: 10...a5 (D)

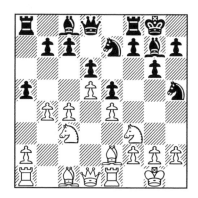

As we mentioned above, this is more accurate than 10...♘f4 11 ♗f1 a5. Black leaves ...♘f4 for a more suitable moment, and may not play it at all.

11 bxa5

11 ♗a3 ♘f4 12 ♗f1 or 11...axb4 12 ♗xb4 ♘f4 13 ♗f1 transposes to the inferior (for White) variation 10...♘f4 11 ♗f1 a5 12 ♗a3 in the notes to E1 above.

11...♖xa5

This is not obligatory, but if Black does not take on a5 soon, he must reckon with additional possibilities for White, such as ♘d2-b3 defending the a5-pawn, or a5-a6. For example:

a) 11...c5 12 ♘d2 ♘f4 13 ♘b3!? (otherwise 13 ♗f1 ♖xa5 transposes below) 13...♘xe2+ 14 ♕xe2 f5 15 ♘a4 +/= Va.Popov.

b) 11...f5 12 ♘d2 ♘f6 (if 12...♘f4 13

♘b3! ♘xe2+ 14 ♖xe2 f4 15 ♖c2 f3!? 16 gxf3 h6 17 c5 g5 18 cxd6 cxd6 19 ♘a4 ♘g6 20 ♘b6 ♘h4 21 ♘d2 ♖b8 22 ♕f1! +/- A.Shirov-V.Babula, Czech Team Ch. 2000) 13 c5! ♖xa5 14 cxd6 cxd6 15 ♘c4 ♖a6 16 ♗g5 fxe4 17 ♘d2 ♖a8 18 ♘dxe4 ♘f5 19 ♘b5 h6 20 ♗xf6 ♗xf6 21 a4 += A.Shariyazdanov-I.Smirin, Bosnian Team Ch. 2001.

12 ♘d2

On 12 a4, Black can refrain from 12...♘f4 13 ♗f1 (as in line E1) and play 12...c5 (others are 12...f5!? 13 ♘d2 ♘f6 14 ♗a3 b6 15 exf5 gxf5 16 ♗b4 ♖a8 17 ♘f3 ♘g6 18 a5 ∞ P.Harikrishna-A.Fedorov, Dubai 2004; or 12...♖a8!? 13 ♖a3 ♘f6 14 a5 c5 15 ♕a4 b6 16 ♕c2 bxa5 17 ♘b5 ♘e8 18 ♗d2 f5 ∞ E.Bacrot-V.Bologan, Odessa rapid 2007) 13 ♖a3 ♖a6 14 ♘b5 ♘f6 15 ♗f1 ♘e8 16 g3 h6 17 ♘h4 g5 18 ♘g2 f5 19 exf5 ♘xf5 ∞ A.Spielmann-O.Gladyszev, Nancy 2009.

It is also worth noting that 12 ♕c2!? would transpose to line B, though it has never been played via this move order.

12...♘f4 13 ♗f1 c5 (D)

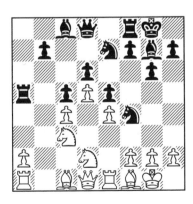

The familiar continuation, closing

the centre (unless White captures en passant) and ruling out c4-c5. Black has also tried:

a) 13...b6 (rather passive) 14 a4 ♗d7 15 ♗a3 ♖e8 16 ♗b4 ♖a8 17 ♘b5 ♘c8 18 a5 bxa5 19 ♗xa5 ♗xb5 20 cxb5 ♘b6 21 ♕c2 ♗h6 22 g3 ♘h5 23 ♗h3 +/- K.Landa-J.Maiwald, German League 2009.

b) 13...f5 14 a4 fxe4 (not 14...g5?! 15 g3! ♘fg6 16 ♘b3 ♖a8 17 ♗xg5 f4 18 ♕h5 +/- P.Petran-D.Goldenberg, Budapest 2000; otherwise 14...♖a8 – *13...♖a8*; and 14...♔h8 – *10...♔h8*) 15 ♘dxe4 ♘f5 16 ♘b5 ♘d4? (but if 16...♘e7 17 c5 dxc5 18 d6 cxd6 19 ♘bxd6 +/- Khalifman) 17 ♘xd4 exd4 18 ♗xf4 ♖xf4 19 ♕d2 +- Xu Jun-E.Sutovsky, Bad Homburg 1997.

c) 13...♖a8 14 a4 f5 (if 14...♘h5 15 c5 dxc5 16 ♘c4 b6 17 a5 += S.Iskusnyh-V.Bologan, Russian Team Ch. 2007) 15 ♖a3 fxe4 16 ♘dxe4 b6 (or 16...♘f5 17 ♘b5 ♘d4 18 ♘xd4 exd4 19 ♗b2 +/- A.Shchekachev-O.Loskutov, St Petersburg 1999) 17 ♘b5 ♔h8 18 g3 ♘h5 19 a5 bxa5 20 ♗d2 ♗f5 21 ♖xa5 += L.Van Wely-E.Bacrot, Dortmund 2005.

14 a4

Planning to develop the rook on a3 where it fulfils both offensive and defensive functions.

Alternatives cause Black fewer problems, e.g. 14 ♖b1 (if 14 dxc6 bxc6 15 ♘b3 ♖a8 16 a4 ♘e6 17 ♗a3 ♘d4 18 c5 d5 = N.Nogin-V.Moliboga, Kyiv 2006; or 14 ♘b3 ♖a6 15 a4 f5 16 g3 ♘h5 17 exf5 ♘xf5 18 ♘e4 ♘f6 = A.Ruzhkovich-D.Salinnikov, Russian Team Ch. 1999) 14...♖a6 15 ♖b3 (or 15 g3 ♘h5 16 ♗g2 ♘f6 17 ♖b3 ♘d7 18 ♖a3

♖xa3 19 ♗xa3 f5 ∞ G.Prakash-K.Sasikiran, Guntur 2000) 15...h6 16 g3 ♘h5 17 ♗e2 ♘f6 18 ♘f3 ♘h7 19 ♗d2 f5 ∞ V.Tukmakov-T.Christensen, Copenhagen 1996.

14...♖a6

The most flexible continuation, defending the d6-pawn and pre-empting any tricks on the exposed rook. Black has several alternatives at his disposal, though the course of the game will depend more on the chosen plans than on a particular move:

a) 14...g5 15 g3!? ♘h3+ (if 15...♘eg6?! 16 gxf4 exf4 17 ♗b2 g4 18 f3 and Black's attack looks insufficient) 16 ♗xh3 ♗xh3 17 ♘b3 ♖a6 18 ♗xg5 += S.Kuemin-A.Pitkaaho, Oulainen 2003.

b) 14...h6 15 ♖a3 (better than 15 ♘b3 ♖a6 16 a5 f5 17 g3 ♘h5 18 ♗g2 ♘f6 ∞ T.Bae-A.Vouldis, Bled Olympiad 2002) 15...♖a6 (or 15...g5 16 ♘b5 ♖a6) 16 ♘b5 returns to line E1.

c) 14...♘h5!? 15 ♖a3 ♘f6 16 ♘b5 ♘e8 17 ♗b2 f5? (too soon; instead 17...♖a6! – 14...♖a6 15 ♖a3 ♘h5) 18 f4! exf4 19 e5 dxe5 20 ♗xe5 ♗xe5 21 ♖xe5 g5 22 ♘b3 ♖a6 23 ♘xc5 ♖h6 24 d6 ♘xd6 25 ♖d3 ♖ff6 26 a5! +/- L.Van Wely-A.Fedorov, European Team Ch., Leon 2001.

d) 14...♔h8!? (to activate the e7-knight) 15 ♖a3 ♘g8 16 ♘b5 ♘h6!? (covering g4 so that g2-g3 can still be met by ...♘h3; otherwise 16...♖a6 – *14...♖a6 15 ♖a3 ♔h8*) 17 ♘f3!? (threatening ♗xf4; if 17 ♗b2 ♖a6 18 g3?! ♘h3+ 19 ♗xh3 ♗xh3 20 f4, A.Bykhovsky-B.Avrukh, Israeli Ch. 2004, 20...f6! gives Black a very solid position with the

bishop pair) 17...♖a6 (not 17...f5? 18 ♗xf4! exf4 19 e5 dxe5 20 ♘xe5 ♘g4 21 ♘d3 +/- Mikhalevski; or 17...f6? 18 ♗xf4 exf4 19 ♕d2 ♘f7 20 ♕xf4 +/- J.Dorfman-V.Bologan, French Team Ch. 2004; note that 19...g5 runs into 20 ♘xd6!) 18 ♗xf4 exf4 19 e5 ♘f5! 20 exd6 ♘xd6 21 ♘d2 ♕a5 (Eljanov suggests 21...g5! as a better try, e.g. 22 ♘b3 ♘xb5 23 cxb5 ♖h6 24 ♘xc5 g4 or 22 ♘xd6 ♖xd6 23 ♘e4 ♖h6 with the initiative) 22 ♘e4 ♖e8 23 ♘ec3 ♖e5 24 ♖xe5 ♗xe5 25 ♕e2 f6 26 ♘xd6 ♖xd6 27 ♘e4 ♖d8 28 ♖b3 += P.Eljanov-A.Fedorov, Dubai 2004.

15 ♖a3 (D)

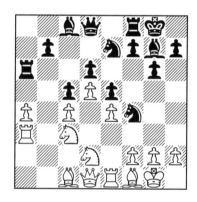

White's set-up with a2-a4, ♖a3 (strengthening the third rank), ♘b5 (attacking the d6-pawn and keeping the a6-rook passive), ♘d2, g2-g3, ♗b2, followed by ♗e2 (or ♗g2) and f2-f4 seems the most dangerous in this structure. Plans with ♖b1 or ♘b3 (blocking the third rank) are less logical and leave White with fewer possibilities to create real threats.

15...♘h5!?

A relatively new idea; Black intends

to consolidate his defences before seeking counterplay. The loss of time involved in playing ...♘f6-h5-f4 and back again is not so important if White cannot force anything. Other moves:

a) 15...h6 16 ♘b5 transposes to line E1 above.

b) 15...♔h8 16 ♘b5 ♘g8 17 g3 ♘h5 (not 17...♘h3+?? 18 ♗xh3 ♗xh3 19 g4 ♕h4 20 ♖g3 +-) 18 ♗g2 (or 18 ♗e2 ♘hf6 19 f4 += S.Iskusnyh-V.Zaitsev, Novosibirsk 1998) 18...♗h6 19 ♗b2 f6 (or 19...♘g7 20 ♖f1 f5 21 exf5 gxf5 22 f4 e4 23 ♕h5 +/-) 20 ♖f1! ♗d7 21 ♘f3 ♕c8 22 ♘e1 ♖f7 23 ♘d3 +/- I.Stohl-M.Muse, German League 1998.

c) 15...g5 is probably too committal:

c1) 16 g3 ♘h3+! 17 ♗xh3 ♗xh3 18 ♕h5 ♕d7 19 ♕xg5 f5! (not 19...h6?! 20 ♕e3! f5 21 ♕e2 f4 22 ♘b5 ♔h7 23 gxf4 exf4 24 ♔h1 ♗g4 25 ♘f3! ♘g6 26 ♖g1 +/- V.Kramnik-G.Kasparov, Novgorod 1997) 20 ♘b5 f4! 21 ♘f3? (but if 21 f3 ♖f6 22 g4 ♖g6 with at least a draw) 21...h6! 22 ♕h4 ♘g6 23 ♕h5 ♖f6 -/+ B.Thompson-D.Petrovic, corr. 2003.

c2) 16 ♘b5! continues as planned, when Black seems to have nothing better than 16...h6 and line E1 again. If 16...♗d7 17 g3 ♘fg6 18 ♕h5! intending ♗h3 +=; or 16...g4 17 g3 ♘fg6 (if 17...♘h3+?! 18 ♗xh3 gxh3 19 f4 +/- V.Malakhatko-A.Motylev, Swidnica 1998) 18 h3! h5 19 hxg4 hxg4 20 ♗e2 ♕d7 21 ♘f1 f5 (V.Golod-D.Zaltz, Modiin rapid 2002) 22 ♘h2! intending exf5 += Golod.

d) 15...♗d7!? is worth considering, hurrying to take control of the c8-h3 diagonal; e.g. 16 ♘b5 ♕c8! 17 ♗b2 (or if

17 ♘f3 f6!? 18 ♔h1 g5 19 ♘g1 h6 20 g3 ♘fg6 21 ♗d3 f5 22 exf5 ♘xf5 23 ♗e4 ♖f6 ∞ S.Gligoric-M.Pavlovic, Ulcinj 1998) 17...g5 18 ♕a1 ♘eg6 19 ♔h1 h5 20 ♕d1 ♗g4 (20...h4!?) 21 f3 ♗d7 22 g3 ♘h3 23 ♕e2 f6 24 ♗g2 ∞ F.Handke-V.Saravanan, Biel 2000.

16 ♘b5 ♘f6 17 ♗b2 ♘e8!

Improving on 17...♘d7 18 g3 f5 19 f4! g5?! (but if 19...exf4 20 ♗xg7 ♔xg7 21 gxf4 fxe4 22 ♘xe4 with the initiative, Xu Jun) 20 fxg5 f4 21 ♗h3 ♘b6 22 ♗xc8 ♘exc8 23 a5 ♘d7 24 ♕g4 ♖xa5 25 ♖xa5 ♕xa5 26 ♗c3 ♕d8 27 ♖a1 ♘db6 28 ♗a5 +/- Xu Jun-V.Magai, Istanbul Olympiad 2000.

18 ♕e2!

This seems like the best response, aiming for a breakthrough in the centre. Black had no problems after 18 ♘f3 h6 19 g3 f5 20 exf5 ♘xf5 21 ♘d2 ♘f6 = L.Aronian-T.Radjabov, Sofia 2008; or 18 g3 f5 19 exf5 (if 19 f4 exf4 20 ♗xg7 ♘xg7 ∞) 19...♘xf5 20 ♘e4 h6 21 ♗g2 ♘f6 = Tan Zhongyi-Ju Wenjun, Chinese Team Ch. 2008.

18...h6 *(D)*

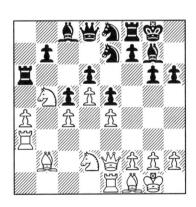

Now if 19 f4 exf4 20 ♗xg7 ♘xg7 21

e5 ♘ef5! 22 exd6 ♘e3 ∞ T.Kotanjian-R.Aloma Vidal, Athens 2008; while against other 19th moves Black should probably play 19...g5 and 20...♘g6 with a solid position.

Instead, A.Klimov-A.Pavlidis, World Junior Ch., Vung Tau City 2008, continued **19 g3 f5!?** [very risky, since White is just waiting for this move] **20 f4! exf4 21 ♗xg7 ♔xg7 22 e5 fxg3 23 hxg3 ♘g8 24 e6** [24 ♘b3! looks better and if 24...♕g5 25 exd6! or 24...b6 25 a5 +=] **24...♕g5! 25 ♗g2 ♘gf6 26 ♘f1 ½-½**.

E3: 10...f5 (D)

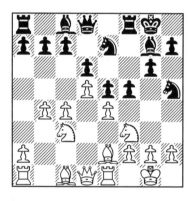

Despite falling in with White's intentions, this standard King's Indian move is nevertheless the most popular response to 10 ♖e1, featuring in over 50% of games. Undeterred, Black faces his opponent down, challenging White to do his worst.

11 ♘g5

The usual way to fight for the initiative, uncovering an attack on the h5-knight and preparing to jump into e6. White occasionally tries other moves:

a) 11 ♘d2 ♘f6 12 c5 (if 12 f3 c6! 13 dxc6 ♘xc6 14 b5 ♘d4 =+ A.Simutowe-I.Smirin, FIDE World Ch., Moscow 2001; or 12 a4 f4!? 13 c5 g5 14 a5 ♘g6 15 ♗a3 g4 with very dangerous counterplay, P.Gelazonia-M.Mchedlishvili, Georgian Ch. 2007) 12...♗h6 (or 12...♔h8!? 13 f3 f4 14 ♘c4 g5 15 ♗a3 ♘e8! 16 b5 b6 17 cxd6 cxd6 18 ♗b4 ♖f6 19 a4 ♗d7 20 a5 ♖b8 21 axb6 axb6 22 ♘b2 h5 23 ♘d3 ♖g6 ∞ G.Sosonko-F.Nijboer, Dutch Ch. 1992) 13 ♗d3 fxe4 14 ♘dxe4 ♘xe4 15 ♗xe4 ♗xc1 16 ♖xc1 ♘f5 17 ♕d2 ♘d4 18 ♘e2 ♘xe2+ 19 ♖xe2 ♗f5 = B.Gelfand-A.Shirov, Wijk aan Zee 1998.

b) 11 c5 fxe4 (also possible are 11...♘f6 12 ♘d2 – *11 ♘d2*, or if 12 ♗g5 ♘xe4 13 ♘xe4 fxe4 14 ♘d2 h6 15 ♗xe7 ♕xe7 16 ♘xe4 ♗f5 = A.Zontakh-E.Relange, Sabac 1998; and 11...♔h8!? 12 ♘d2 ♘f6 – *11 ♘d2* again, while 12 ♘g5 ♘f6 13 f3 is the main line E3212) 12 ♘xe4 ♘f4 13 ♗xf4 ♖xf4 14 ♘fd2!? (or 14 cxd6 cxd6 15 ♘fd2 ♔h8 16 g3 ♖f8 17 ♘c4 ♘f5 ∞ P.Nielsen-A.Brustman, Koszalin 1997) 14...dxc5! 15 ♗c4 ♔h8 16 ♘xc5 ♘xd5 17 ♘de4 c6 18 b5 ∞ V.Kramnik-B.Gelfand, Novgorod 1996.

c) 11 a4 ♘f6 (if 11...♘f4 12 ♗xf4 exf4 13 ♖a3 ♗xc3 14 ♖xc3 fxe4, H.Thallinger-R.Hangweyrer, Vienna 2003, 15 ♘d2 +=; but 11...a5!? comes into consideration) 12 a5!? (12 ♘d2 – *11 ♘d2*) 12...♘xe4 (or 12...h6 13 ♘d2 g5 14 exf5 ♗xf5 15 ♗f1 ♘g6 16 ♘de4 += H.Knoll-R.Polzin, Austrian Team Ch. 2009) 13 ♘xe4 fxe4 14 ♘g5 ♘f5 (14...e3!?) 15 ♘xe4 ♘d4 16 ♗g5 ♕e8 17 ♗d3 += M.Suba-K.Berbatov, Albacete 2008.

E31: 11...♘f4 *363*

E32: 11...♘f6 *365*

E31: 11...♘f4 *(D)*

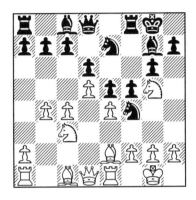

Although this knight move looks very active, practice indicates that it is not the best.

12 ♗xf4 exf4 13 ♖c1 ♗f6

The most popular continuation, and leading to forcing play, though Black has tried numerous alternatives:

a) 13...♘c6?? (as in the line 10 ♕c2 f5!?) loses to 14 dxc6 ♕xg5 15 ♕d5+ ♔h8 16 cxb7 +-.

b) 13...c6? 14 dxc6! bxc6 15 c5! ♗xc3 16 ♖xc3 d5 17 exd5 ♘xd5 18 ♗c4 +- M.Chernov-P.Maleev, Siberian Ch. 2008.

c) 13...h6 14 ♘e6 ♗xe6 15 dxe6 c6!? (if 15...♗xc3 16 ♖xc3 fxe4 17 ♗f1 e3 18 fxe3 f3 19 gxf3 ♘f5 20 f4 +/- C.Crouch-S.Buckley, British Ch. 2000; or 15...fxe4 16 ♘xe4 ♘c6 17 ♗f3 ♕e7 18 ♘c3! +/- C.Duncan-C.Baker, British League 2001) 16 ♗f3 ♕c7 17 c5 ♖ad8 18 cxd6 ♕xd6 19 ♕b3 ♔h7 20 b5 += M.Cebalo-

S.Cucancic, Croatian Ch. 1996.

d) 13...♗h6 14 ♘f3! (not 14 ♘e6?! ♗xe6 15 dxe5 f3!) 14...g5!? 15 ♖c2 a5 16 b5! (controlling c6 in advance of ♘d4-e6) 16...♔h8 17 ♘d4 ♗g7 18 ♘e6 ♗xe6 19 dxe6 c6 20 ♗d3 +/- H.Rau-T.Hänsel, German Junior Ch. 2002.

e) 13...♔h8 14 ♗f3 ♗e5 15 ♘e6 ♗xe6 16 dxe6 c6 17 b5 ♕c8 (or 17...♖f6 18 exf5 gxf5 19 bxc6 bxc6 20 ♘e2 += I.Stohl-V.Kupreichik, German League 1998) 18 bxc6 bxc6 19 exf5 gxf5 20 ♖xe5! dxe5 21 ♕d6 with excellent compensation, A.Truskavetsky-A.Nechaev, Alushta 2005.

f) 13...♗e5 14 ♗f3! fxe4 15 ♗xe4 (if 15 ♘cxe4 ♘f5 16 ♘e6 ♗xe6 17 dxe6 c6 18 b5, S.Savchenko-V.Kupreichik, European Ch., Istanbul 2003, 18...♘d4!? ∞) 15...♘f5 16 ♘f3! ♗g7 17 ♘e2 ♘h4 18 ♘ed4 ♘xf3+ 19 ♗xf3 += S.Soucha-F.Hlavac, corr. 2003.

g) 13...fxe4 14 ♘cxe4 ♘f5!? (otherwise 14...h6 15 ♘e6 ♗xe6 16 dxe6 – *13...h6*) 15 ♗g4 (if 15 c5?! ♘d4! 16 cxd6 cxd6 17 ♗g4 ♗xg4 18 ♕xg4 ♖f5 ∞ D.Dumitrache-V.Kupreichik, Yerevan Olympiad 1996) 15...♘d4 (if 15...♗h6!? 16 h4! +=; or 15...h6 16 ♘e6 ♗xe6 17 dxe6 ♕e7 18 c5 ♘d4, V.Malakhatko-E.Miroshnichenko, Polanica Zdroj 1998, 19 ♖c4! d5 20 ♖xd4 ♗xd4 21 ♕xd4 dxe4 22 ♕xe4 +=) 16 ♗xc8 ♕xc8 17 ♘f3 (to prevent ...f4-f3!) 17...♘xf3+ 18 ♕xf3 ♕f5 19 c5 ♗e5 (or 19...♖ad8 20 cxd6 cxd6 21 ♖c7 += N.Arkhipov-P.Smirnov, Prokojevsk 1997) 20 h3 (or just 20 b5! += Timoshenko) 20...♔g7 21 b5 h6 22 a4 += G.Timoshenko-I.Kutsyk, Kharkov 1997.

h) 13...a5!? should be met by 14 b5!, when play transposes to other variations; e.g. 14...♗f6 (or 14...♗h6 15 ♘f3 g5 16 ♖c2 – *13...♗h6*) 15 ♘e6 ♗xe6 16 dxe6 ♗xc3 17 ♖xc3 fxe4 is the main line (with 17...a5) after 18 ♗g4 or 18 ♗f1.

14 ♘e6 ♗xe6 15 dxe6 ♗xc3 16 ♖xc3 fxe4 (D)

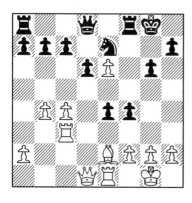

A key position in this variation. Given the chance Black will advance ...f4-f3, e.g. 17 ♕b1 f3! 18 gxf3 ♘c6 19 ♖e3 ♕g5+ with a good game, A.Veingold-R.Cheutshenko, Estonian Ch. 1999; so the bishop must move.

17 ♗f1

The alternative, and possibly stronger, is 17 ♗g4 and then:

a) 17...d5? 18 cxd5 ♘xd5 (Browne) 19 e7! ♘xe7 20 ♕b3+ ♔g7 21 ♖d1 ♕e8 22 ♖xc7 +- Khalifman.

b) 17...e3 18 fxe3 ♘c6? (but if 18...fxe3 19 ♖exe3 intending ♖f3 +/-) 19 exf4 ♖xf4 20 e7! ♘xe7 21 ♗e6+ ♔g7 22 ♕a1 +- F.Doettling-H.Rudolf, German League 2007.

c) 17...♘c6 18 ♖xe4 ♘e5 (or 18...♕f6 19 ♖c1 ♖ae8 20 c5 +/= H.Hentze-W.Ritter, corr. 2004) 19 c5! ♕e7 20 ♗h3

g5 21 ♖c2 ♖ad8 22 ♖d2 f3! 23 cxd6 cxd6 24 ♖ed4 ♖f6 25 g3 g4? 26 ♗xg4 ♘xg4 27 ♖xg4+ ♔h8 28 ♕a1 +- A.Lauber-J.Loxine, Dresden 2005.

d) 17...a5 18 b5 e3 19 fxe3 c6 20 ♖d3 d5 21 bxc6 bxc6 22 cxd5 cxd5 (Zhu Chen-Xie Jun, Beijing 1998) 23 e4! ♕b6+ 24 ♔h1 dxe4 25 ♖xe4 +/- Huzman.

17...e3

Apart from 17...a5 18 b5 e3 19 fxe3 transposing to 18...a5 in the next note, there is little else worth considering as White just takes on e4 with a clear advantage; e.g. 17...♖f5 18 ♖xe4 ♕f8 19 b5 +/- P.Szilagyi-G.Horvath, Hungarian Team Ch. 1998; or if 17...d5?! 18 exd5 ♘xd5 19 ♗c4! +/- Kramnik.

18 fxe3 fxe3

Other moves:

a) 18...♘c6 19 exf4 ♖xf4 20 b5 ♘e5 21 g3! ♖f6 22 ♗g2 c6 23 c5 +/- R.Fyllingen-R.Djurhuus, Norwegian Ch. 1999.

b) 18...f3 19 gxf3 ♘f5 20 f4 ♕f6 (P.Lafuente-D.Lemos, Chapadmalal 2003) 21 ♖a3 ♕xe6 22 ♕d5 +/=.

c) 18...a5 19 b5 fxe3 (if 19...c6 20 exf4 ♖xf4 21 ♕d2 += P.Taboada-C.O'Hare, corr. 1999) 20 ♖cxe3 c6 21 c5! dxc5 (or 21...d5 22 b6!? ♖f4 23 ♗d3 ♕f8 24 ♖f1 ♕f6 25 ♖f3 += Alvarez, e.g. 25...♖xf3 26 ♕xf3 ♕xe6 27 ♗a6!! bxa6 28 b7 ♖e8 29 ♕f4 +/-) 22 ♕d7! with a strong initiative, R.G.Alvarez-R.Berdichesky, corr. 1999.

d) 18...c6!? should be met by either 19 ♔h1 or 19 a3!? (Browne) and a slight edge for White. If 19 exf4 ♖xf4 20 ♕d2 then 20...♕b6+! 21 c5 ♕xb4 22 cxd6 ♖d4! 23 ♕f2 ♘f5 24 ♖b3 ♕xd6 25 ♖xb7

♖f4 gives Black good counterplay; while 19 ♕d4 ♘f5 20 ♕xf4 ♕f6 21 ♖d3 ♕xe6 was just equal in A.Szeberenyi-N.Resika, Budapest 1998.

19 ♖cxe3 c6 (D)

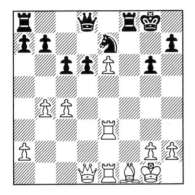

White has an accumulation of small pluses: strong e6-pawn, extra space, more active pieces, weak black d-pawn, and safer king. Nevertheless Black has good chances to hold once he activates his position.

20 ♔h1

Prophylaxis against ...♕b6. 20 a3!? also comes into consideration. Instead, 20 ♕d2!? d5 21 cxd5 cxd5 22 ♕d4 ♕d6 23 ♕c5 ♕f4?! 24 ♖f3 ♕g5 25 ♖f7! was good for White in V.Kramnik-A.Shirov, Tilburg 1997; but Black can improve with 20...♕b6!; e.g. 21 ♔h1 ♖ad8 22 a3 d5 23 c5 ♕c7 = A.Pankratov-R.Berdichesky, corr. 1998.

20...d5 21 ♖f3!

If 21 cxd5 cxd5 22 ♗e2 ♖f4 23 ♗f3 ♖xb4 24 ♖d3 (P.Peelen-D.Stellwagen, Amsterdam 2006) 24...♖b5! =.

The text was played in E.L'Ami-D.Stellwagen, Wijk aan Zee 2006, which continued **21...♖xf3** [if 21...♕b6

22 ♖f7! ♕xb4 23 ♕e2 with a strong initiative] **22 ♕xf3 ♕f8 23 ♕g3 ♕f6 24 cxd5 cxd5 25 ♗d3 ♖f8 26 ♕c7?!** [26 ♕d6 looks better] **26...♕h4?!** [missing the chance for 26...♖c8! and if 27 ♕xb7 ♕xe6! 28 ♖f1 ♕e3 =] **27 ♖b1 ♖f2?! 28 ♕xb7?** [the wrong pawn; correct was 28 ♕b8+! ♔g7 29 ♕xa7 +/-] **28...♕g4!** [forcing a draw] **29 ♕b8+** [if 29 ♖g1 ♖xg2! 30 ♖xg2 ♕d1+ or 29 ♗f1 ♕xe6 30 ♕xa7 ♕f5 =] **29...♔g7 30 ♕e5+ ♔g8 31 ♕b8+ ½-½.**

E32: 11...♘f6 (D)

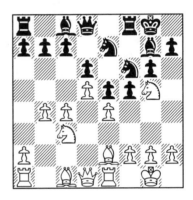

As we have seen many times already, the black knight's return to f6, exerting pressure on the e4-pawn, is a standard manoeuvre in the King's Indian. The difference here is that Black often follows up playing against the centre with ...c7-c6, rather than the usual kingside attack.

White can now choose between:

E321: 12 f3 *366*
E322: 12 ♗f3 *372*

E321: 12 f3 *(D)*

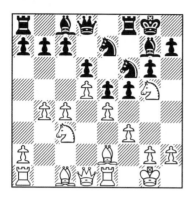

The most natural continuation, simply maintaining the pawn centre. The subsequent variations equate to those after 10 g3 f5 11 ♘g5 ♘f6 12 f3, though the fact that White has not weakened his kingside here should be in his favour. On the other hand, Black had good counterplay in line D, and a lot of the play is quite similar.

E3211: 12...♘h5 *367*
E3212: 12...♔h8 *369*

Other moves:

a) 12...f4?! makes little sense here; e.g. 13 c5! h6 14 ♘e6 ♗xe6 15 dxe6 d5 (or 15...dxc5 16 ♕xd8 ♖axd8?! 17 bxc5 c6 18 ♖b1 +/- A.Veingold-D.Ayza Leon, Lorca 2004) 16 exd5 ♘fxd5 17 ♘xd5 ♕xd5 18 ♕xd5 ♘xd5 19 ♗c4 +/- D.Bunzmann-S.Maitesian, Bethune 2000.

b) 12...♘e8?! is also too slow; e.g. 13 c5! a5 14 cxd6 ♕xd6 15 ♘b5 ♕b6+ 16 ♔h1 ♘d6 17 bxa5 ♖xa5 18 ♘xd6 cxd6 19 ♗d2 ♖a8 20 ♖b1 ♕a7 21 ♗c4! ♗d7

22 ♗e3! ♕b8 23 ♘e6 +/- A.Khalifman-Peng Xiaomin, Shanghai 2001.

c) 12...h6!? (a standard move, though it's not usually played so soon) 13 ♘e6 ♗xe6 14 dxe6 c6 (if 14...♖e8!? 15 b5 fxe4 16 fxe4 ♔h7, M.Notkin-V.Nevednichy, Bucharest 1997, 17 ♕d3! += Nevednichy) 15 ♗e3! (15 ♔h1 ♘e8 is fine for Black; e.g. 16 ♕b3 ♘c7 17 c5 d5 18 exd5 cxd5 19 ♗b2 b6!? 20 cxb6 axb6 21 ♖ad1 ♕b8 = E.L'Ami-F.Nijboer, Dutch Ch. 2008) 15...♕c7 (now if 15...♘e8?! 16 ♕b3 ♘c7 17 ♖ad1! ♔h7 18 c5 d5 19 exd5 cxd5 20 ♘xd5 ♘exd5 21 ♗c4 +/- A.Veingold-J.Candela Perez, Burgas 2001) 16 ♖b1 ♖fd8 17 b5 ♕c8 18 bxc6 bxc6 19 ♕a4 ♔h7 20 ♖ed1 ♕xe6 21 ♖b7 ♖d7 22 ♕a6 with compensation, D.Komljenovic-A.Kuzmin, Benasque 1999.

d) 12...c6 (more flexible than the immediate ...h7-h6) 13 ♗e3 (if 13 ♔h1 h6! 14 ♘e6 ♗xe6 15 dxe6 – *12...h6*; or 13 b5 c5!? 14 exf5 ♘xf5 15 ♗d3 ♘d4 16 ♗e3 ♘h5 17 ♘ge4 ♘f4 = Ye Jiangchuan-Wang Pin, Beijing 1996) 13...♗h6!? (otherwise 13...h6 14 ♘e6 ♗xe6 15 dxe6 is *12...h6* again) 14 h4! (14 ♔h1?? f4 just wins a piece here) 14...cxd5 15 cxd5 ♗d7 (if 15...f4 16 ♗f2 ♗xg5 17 hxg5 ♘h5 18 ♖c1 ♗d7 19 ♗b5! += J.Berkvens-P.Smirnov, Patras 2001) 16 ♖c1 a6 17 b5 ♗xb5 (again if 17...f4 18 ♗f2 ♗xg5 19 hxg5 ♘h5 20 ♕b3 a5 21 b6 ♘c8 22 ♗b5! += Se.Ivanov-H.Rudolf, Panormo 2001) 18 ♗xb5 axb5 19 ♘xb5 fxe4 20 fxe4 ♘xe4!? 21 ♘xe4 (not 21 ♕g4? ♗xg5 22 hxg5 ♖a4! -/+ S.Brynell-V.Kotronias, Stockholm 2006) 21...♗xe3+ 22 ♖xe3 ♕b6 23 ♕b3 ♘f5 24

♖ce1 ♘xe3 25 ♖xe3 ♖xa2 26 ♘bxd6 ♖a1+ 27 ♔h2 ♕d8 28 ♖h3! +/-.

E3211: 12...♘h5 *(D)*

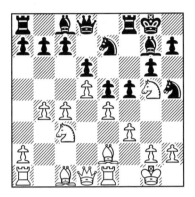

An almost contemptuous move: having encouraged White to close the e2-h5 diagonal, the knight nonchalantly returns to its active position, heading for the weakened f4-square.

13 c5

The critical reply; White begins his queenside action, preparing to open the c-file, while freeing c4 for the e2-bishop. Instead:

a) 13 ♕b3 ♘f4 14 c5 – *13 c5 ♘f4 14 ♕b3!?*.

b) 13 ♗e3 ♘f4 14 g3 ♘xe2+ 15 ♖xe2 f4 16 gxf4 exf4 17 ♗d4 ♘f5 18 exf5 ♕xg5+ 19 ♖g2 ♕xf5 =+ Z.Gyimesi-W.Uhlmann, Austrian Team Ch. 2002.

c) 13 g3? prevents ...♘f4 but weakens the kingside, which Black can immediately exploit by 13...f4! 14 g4 (or 14 ♔g2 ♘f5! 15 exf5 ♕xg5 16 ♘e4 ♕h6 17 fxg6 ♘xg3! -/+ A.Voyna-N.Stull, corr. 2001) 14...♗f6! 15 ♘e6 ♗xe6 16 dxe6 ♘g7 17 c5 dxc5 18 ♕xd8 (or 18 bxc5 ♕d4+ 19 ♕xd4 exd4 20 ♘d5 ♘xd5 21

exd5 d3 -+ D.Tishin-A.Sumets, Alushta 2006) 18...♖fxd8 19 bxc5 ♗h4 20 ♖f1 ♘c6 -/+ P.Eljanov-Z.Efimenko, Ukrainian Team Ch. 2002.

13...♘f4 14 ♗c4

Black has few problems after:

a) 14 ♗xf4 exf4 15 ♖c1 h6 (or 15...♗f6) 16 ♘e6 ♗xe6 17 dxe6 dxc5 18 bxc5 ♗d4+ (exploiting the weakened dark squares) 19 ♔h1 ♗e3 20 ♖c2 c6 ∞ S.Collins-G.Jones, Hastings 2007/08.

b) 14 ♕b3!? ♔h8 (14...fxe4 15 fxe4 ♔h8 leads to the same position) 15 ♗xf4 exf4 16 ♖ad1 fxe4 17 fxe4 ♘c6 (or 17...♘f5!? 18 exf5 ♕xg5 19 ♘b5 ♕e7 20 fxg6 hxg6 21 ♗f3 ♗e5 ∞ Z.Gyimesi-G.Timoshenko, Nagykanizsa 2003) 18 ♘f7+ ♖xf7 19 dxc6 ♖f8 20 e5 bxc6 21 exd6 cxd6 22 cxd6 (Y.Pelletier-I.Smirin, Biel 2002) 22...♖b8! ∞ Pelletier.

14...♔h8

Weaker is 14...a5?! 15 bxa5 (or 15 b5 h6 16 ♘e6 ♗xe6 17 dxe6 fxe4 18 fxe4 dxc5 19 ♗e3 += Goloshchapov) 15...♖xa5 16 cxd6 ♕xd6 17 ♕b3 += A.Goloshchapov-M.Golubev, Ukrainian Ch. 2001.

15 ♖b1! *(D)*

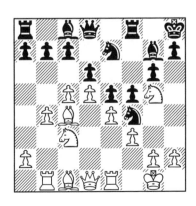

Bareev's idea; White makes a useful prophylactic move, while waiting for Black to play ...h7-h6. Instead:

a) 15 ♗xf4 exf4 16 ♖c1 fxe4 (or 16...dxc5!? 17 bxc5 h6 18 ♘e6 ♗xe6 19 dxe6 ♕d4+ 20 ♔h1 ♕xc5! ∞) 17 ♖xe4 ♗f5 18 ♘e6 ♗xe6 19 ♖xe6?! (19 dxe6 ∞) 19...♘f5 20 ♕d3 a5 =+ D.De Ruiter-D.Klein, Dieren 2008.

b) 15 g3 h6 16 gxf4 (or 16 ♘e6 ♘xe6 17 dxe6 fxe4 18 fxe4 ♘c6 ½-½ A.Shneider-Z.Efimenko, European Ch., Istanbul 2003) 16...exf4 17 e5!? hxg5 18 exd6 cxd6 19 ♗b2 ♗d7 ∞ A.Korobov-S.Bogner, Aarhus 2005.

c) 15 ♘e6 ♗xe6 16 dxe6 fxe4 17 fxe4 ♘c6! 18 cxd6 (if 18 ♗e3 ♘d4 =+ V.Tukmakov-Z.Efimenko, Lausanne 2001) 18...cxd6 19 ♘b5 ♕e7 20 ♕xd6 ♕g5 with compensation, J.Berkvens-Z.Efimenko, Hengelo 2001.

15...dxc5!?

Black has also tried:

a) 15...♘exd5? 16 ♘xd5 ♕xg5 17 ♗xf4 exf4 18 ♘xc7 +/- L.Van Wely-I.Mutschnik, Kuppenheim 2005.

b) 15...fxe4?! 16 ♘gxe4 (not 16 fxe4? ♘exd5! 17 ♘xd5 ♕xg5 =+ Zhu Chen-Ye Jiangchuan, Jinan 2003, as 18 ♗xf4 exf4 19 ♘xc7 now fails to 19...f3! -+) 16...♘f5 17 g3 ♘h3+ 18 ♔g2 ♘d4 19 ♖f1 a5 20 ♘e2 ♗f5 21 ♘xd4 exd4 22 ♕d3 += K.Landa-E.Chevelevitch, Hamburg 2007.

c) 15...h6 16 ♘e6 ♗xe6 17 dxe6 fxe4 18 fxe4 ♘c6 19 ♗xf4?! (better 19 ♘b5 +=) 19...exf4 20 ♘d5 dxc5 21 bxc5 ♖b8 ∞ W.Brandhorst-H.Dullemond, corr. 2004.

d) 15...a6!? 16 ♔h1 h6 (having run

out of things to do) 17 ♘e6 ♘xe6!? (if 17...♗xe6 18 dxe6 fxe4 19 fxe4 ♘c6 20 cxd6 cxd6 21 b5 += Liang Chong-Ye Jiangchuan, Xiapu 2005) 18 dxe6 ♘c6 19 b5! ♘d4 20 bxa6 bxa6 21 ♗a3 ♖e8 22 ♗d5 c6 (or 22...♖a7 23 ♘b8 ♘xe6 24 ♗xe6! ♖xe6 25 ♕b3 +/-) 23 cxd6 ♗xe6 24 ♗xe6 ♖xe6 25 ♗c5 ♘b5 26 ♕b3 ♕e8 27 ♖ed1 +/- E.Bareev-T.Radjabov, Wijk aan Zee 2003.

16 bxc5

If 16 d6 ♕xd6 (or 16...♘c6!?) 17 ♕xd6 cxd6 18 bxc5 dxc5 19 ♘f7+ ♖xf7 20 ♗xf7 ♘c6! (Mikhalevski) and Black has two good pawns for the exchange.

16...♘exd5 (D)

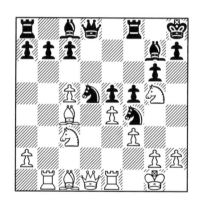

17 ♘xd5?!

At this critical juncture Mikhalevski suggests two possible improvements:

a) 17 ♗xf4 exf4 18 ♘b5 ♕xg5 19 exd5 ♕d8 20 d6 cxd6 21 ♘xd6 with more than enough compensation for the pawn.

b) 17 h4!? h6 (not 17...♘xc3? 18 ♘f7+! +-) 18 ♘xd5 hxg5 19 exf5 ♘xd5 (if 19...gxf5 20 hxg5 or 19...gxh4 20 ♘xf4 exf4 21 ♕xd8 ♖xd8 22 hxg6 +/-) 20 ♕xd5 ♕xd5 21 ♗xd5 c6 22 ♗c4 ♗xf5 23

♖xb7 gxh4 24 ♗g5 and White has the better chances.

After the text Black has survived the opening at least. L.Van Wely-D.Stellwagen, 1st matchgame, Maastricht 2005, went on **17...♕xg5 18 ♘xf4** [if 18 ♗xf4 exf4 19 e5!? ♗e6! 20 ♖xb7 ♗xd5 21 ♗xd5 (or 21 ♕xd5 ♖ad8 22 ♕c6 ♗xe5!) 21...♕e7 ∞] **18...exf4 19 e5 ♕e7 20 ♕b3 ♖e8?!** [better 20...♕xc5+ 21 ♔h1 ♕e7! 22 ♗xf4 c6 ∞] **21 ♗xf4** [or 21 c6!? bxc6 22 e6! += Mikhalevski] **21...b6 22 ♕e3 ♗e6 23 ♗b5 ♖ec8 24 ♗c6 ♖ab8 25 ♖bc1 ♗f8 26 ♗g5?** [missing the threat; either 26 ♕f2 or 26 ♔h1 maintains White's edge] **26...♕xc5! 27 ♖xc5??** [one mistake follows another; 27 ♕f2 keeps White in the game] **27...♗xc5 28 ♔f2 ♗xe3+ 29 ♔xe3 b5 30 ♔d4 b4 31 ♔c5 b3 32 axb3 ♖xb3 33 ♗d5 ♗xd5 34 ♔xd5 ♔g7 35 ♔e6 c5 36 ♗f6+ ♔f8 37 ♔d7 ♖e8 38 ♗g7+ ♔f7 39 e6+ ♖xe6 40 ♖xe6 ♔xg7 41 h4 ♔h6 0-1**.

E3212: 12...♔h8 (D)

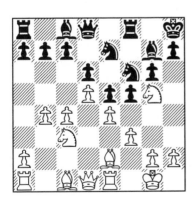

This line has become very topical lately, due in large part to the successes of GM Radjabov. Generally the point of

...♔h8 in the King's Indian is to free g8 for the other pieces; here its main purpose is to vacate the a2-g8 diagonal and avoid any problems arising from ♘e6 and/or c4-c5. As after 12...c6 above, Black will probably follow up with ...h7-h6, but waits to see how White responds before committing himself.

13 ♗e3

The most frequent reply, though White has tried numerous others:

a) 13 ♕b3!? h6 (13...c6 14 ♖d1) 14 ♘e6 ♗xe6 15 dxe6 ♘c6 (or 15...c6 16 ♖d1) 16 ♗e3 fxe4 17 fxe4 ♘d4 18 ♗xd4 exd4 19 ♘d5 += C.Duncan-I.Snape, British League 2004.

b) 13 b5 ♘h5 (or 13...♘e8!? 14 ♗e3 ♗f6 15 ♘e6 ♗xe6 16 dxe6 ♘g7 17 ♗h6 ♘xe6 18 ♗xf8 ♕xf8 with compensation, M.Carlsen-V.Ivanchuk, Foros 2008) 14 ♗f1 ♗f6 15 ♘e6 ♗xe6 16 dxe6 ♘g7 17 ♗h6 ♖e8 18 ♘d5 ♘g8 19 ♗xg7+ ♗xg7 =+ F.Abbasov-N.Mamedov, Azeri Ch , Baku 2009.

c) 13 c5 h6 (or 13...dxc5 14 bxc5 h6 15 ♘e6 ♗xe6 16 dxe6 ♕d4+! 17 ♕xd4 exd4 18 ♘b5 fxe4 19 fxe4 d3, Z.Gyimesi-T.Radjabov, Moscow 2005, 20 ♗xd3! a6 21 ♘d4 = Avrukh) 14 ♘e6 ♗xe6 15 dxe6 d5! 16 exd5 ♘fxd5 17 ♘xd5 ♕xd5 18 ♕b3 (or 18 ♕xd5 ♘xd5 19 ♗c4 ♘xb4 20 ♖b1 ♘c6 = G.Rechlis-B.Avrukh, Israeli Team Ch. 2003) 18...♕xb3 19 axb3 ♘c6 20 ♖a4 ♖fe8 21 ♗c4 a6 22 b5!? axb5 23 ♖xa8 ♖xa8 24 ♗xb5 ♖e8 25 ♖d1 ♖xe6 26 ♖d7 ♗f8 27 ♖xc7 ♗xc5+ 28 ♔f1 ♖e7 29 ♖xe7 ♗xe7 = A.Grischuk-T.Radjabov, Linares 2009.

d) 13 ♖b1!? h6!? (13...c6 looks safer; e.g. 14 ♗e3 h6 15 ♘e6 ♗xe6 16 dxe6

♘e8! 17 b5 ♘c7 18 bxc6 bxc6 19 ♖b7 ♘xe6 20 ♕a4 ♘d4 =+ R.Markus-Y.Dembo, Budapest 2002; though White might try 14 b5!?) 14 ♘e6 ♗xe6 15 dxe6 fxe4 16 fxe4 ♘c6 17 ♘d5 ♘g8! 18 ♗d3 ♘d4 19 ♕g4 g5! 20 h4!? (improving on 20 ♕h3 c6 21 ♘e3 ♕f6 22 ♘g4?! ♕e7 23 ♗e3 ♘xe6 =+ R.Ponomariov-T.Radjabov, Wijk aan Zee 2003) 20...♘f6 21 ♕g3 gxh4? (21...♘xe6 22 hxg5 ♘xd5! was correct, and if 23 exd5 ♘xg5 ∞ Ftacnik, or 23 gxh6 ♗f6 24 exd5 ♗h4) 22 ♕xh4 ♘xe6 23 ♗xh6 ♔g8 (this was previously thought defensible, but...) 24 ♕h3! ♗xh6 25 ♕xh6 c6 26 ♖e3 ♔f7 27 ♖f1 cxd5 28 exd5 ♔e7 29 dxe6 ♔xe6 30 ♖ef3 a5 31 ♗e4 1-0 L.Van Wely-T.Radjabov, Wijk aan Zee 2009.

e) 13 ♘e6!? (not waiting for ...h7-h6) 13...♗xe6 14 dxe6 ♘h5 *(D)* (not 14...fxe4 15 fxe4 ♘c6 16 ♘d5 ♘xe4 17 ♗f3 ♘f6 18 b5 +/- L.Van Wely-T.Radjabov, FIDE World Cup, Khanty-Mansiysk 2005; but 14...♖e8 is possible, e.g. 15 ♘d5 fxe4 16 ♘xf6 ♗xf6 17 fxe4 ♘c6 18 ♗g4 ♘d4 19 ♗e3 c6 20 ♗xd4 exd4 21 ♖f1 ♖f8 = A.Grischuk-T.Radjabov, FIDE Grand Prix, Elista 2008) and then:

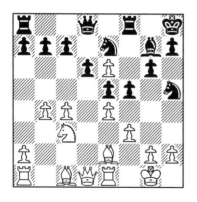

e1) 15 g3 ♗f6 16 c5 (or 16 exf5 ♘xf5 17 g4 e4 18 ♘xe4 ♗xa1 19 ♗g5 ♗d4+ 20 ♔h1 ♕e8 21 e7 ♘xe7 22 ♕xd4+ ♘g7 ∞ I.Cheparinov-T.Radjabov, Sofia 2008) 16...f4! 17 ♔g2 (if 17 g4 ♘g7 18 ♗c4 ♘c6 19 cxd6 cxd6 20 ♘e2 ♖c8 -/+ L.Van der Wely-T.Radjabov, Wijk aan Zee 2007) 17...♘c6 18 cxd6 cxd6 19 ♘d5 ♘d4 20 ♗b2 ♘xe6 21 g4 ♘hg7 ∞ A.Shirov-T.Radjabov, Wijk aan Zee 2007.

e2) 15 c5 ♘f4 16 ♗c4 fxe4 17 ♖xe4 ♘f5! (not 17...d5?! 18 ♗xf4 dxe4 19 ♗g5 += Radjabov) 18 g3 (or 18 ♗xf4 exf4 19 ♘d5 ♖e8 20 ♘xf4 c6 21 e7 ♖xe7 22 ♘e6 ♕b8 23 ♘xg7 ♖xg7 24 cxd6 ♘xd6 = L.Van Wely-T.Radjabov, Monte Carlo blindfold rapid 2007) 18...♘h3+ 19 ♔g2 ♘g5 20 ♖g4 ♘xf3! 21 ♔xf3 e4+ 22 ♘xe4 ♗xa1 23 ♗g5 ♘e7+ 24 ♔g2 ♗e5 ∞ L.Van Wely-T.Radjabov, Biel 2007. Although Black is not objectively better in these positions, it is worth noting that Radjabov won almost every time.

13...♗h6!?

Radjabov's favoured continuation. As after 12...c6, this is an interesting way of avoiding ...h7-h6 lines with ♗e3. The difference is that the position of the black king allows White a small tactic. Instead:

a) 13...h6?! 14 ♘e6 ♗xe6 15 dxe6 c6 16 ♕d2 f4 17 ♗f2 ♕c7 18 b5 += A.Veingold-I.Skrjabin, Helsinki 2003.

b) 13...♘e8 14 exf5 (or 14 c5 f4 15 ♗f2 ♘xd5!? 16 ♘xd5 ♕xg5 17 cxd6 cxd6 18 ♖c1 with compensation, A.Korobov-A.Volokitin, Ukrainian Junior Ch. 2001) 14...gxf5 (or 14...♘xf5 15 ♗d2) 15 f4 ♘g6 16 ♘h3 exf4 17 ♗d4

♗e5 18 ♗h5 ♕f6 19 ♗xe5 dxe5 20 ♗xg6 hxg6 21 ♕e2 e4 22 ♖ac1 += I.Jelen-M.Makaj, Ptuj 2007.

c) 13...♘h5!? also seems fine; e.g. 14 c5 (or 14 ♖c1 ♘f4 15 ♗f1 h6 16 ♗xf4 exf4 17 ♘e6 ♗xe6 18 dxe6, I.Farago-L.Hazai, Hungarian Team Ch. 2003, 18...c6!? ∞ Farago) 14...♘f4 15 ♗c4 fxe4 16 ♘gxe4 ♘f5 17 ♗f2 ♘d4 18 ♖c1 ♗f5 ∞ A.Rychagov-N.Pokazanjev, Novokuznetsk 2008.

14 ♘f7+

Trading the knight for the other bishop. If here 14 h4 f4 15 ♗f2 ♗xg5 16 hxg5 ♘h5 17 c5 ♘g8 18 ♕d2 h6! 19 ♖ec1 ♖f7 20 ♖c2 hxg5 21 ♖ac1 g4 -/+ M.Thejkumar-K.Ramu, Hyderabad 2006.

14...♖xf7 15 ♗xh6 f4 (D)

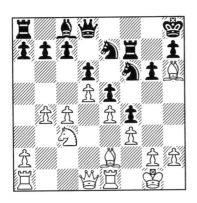

Black intends to make use of g8 after all, chasing the white bishop down to accelerate his kingside counterplay.

16 g4

Or 16 c5 ♘eg8 17 ♗g5 h6 18 ♗h4 g5 19 ♗f2 ♖g7 20 g4 (or 20 ♔f1 g4 21 ♗c4 a5 22 bxa5 gxf3 23 gxf3? ♗h3+ 24 ♔e2 ♘g4! -+ P.Eljanov-A.Grischuk, Moscow blitz 2008) 20...fxg3!? (20...h5) 21 hxg3

♘h5 22 ♔h2 g4 23 ♖h1 ♕g5 24 fxg4 ♘hf6 25 ♕c1 ♘xg4+ 26 ♔g2 ♕g6 ∞ R.Pogorelov-I.Nataf, Reykjavik 2004.

16...♘eg8 17 ♗g5 h6

Improving on 17...h5?! 18 gxh5 ♖h7?! (but if 18...♖g7 19 ♔h1! gxh5 20 ♖g1 +=) 19 h4? (missing 19 hxg6! ♖h5 20 h4 +/- Gyimesi, when 20...♖xg5+ 21 hxg5 ♘xd5 fails to 22 ♔f2! ♘xc3 23 ♖h1+ ♔g7 24 ♖h7+! ♔xg6 25 ♕h1 +/-) 19...♖xh5 20 ♔f2 a5 21 b5 ∞ Z.Gyimesi-P.Acs, Hungarian Ch , Budapest 2004.

18 ♗h4 g5 19 ♗f2 h5 20 h3 ♖h7 (D)

The position is reminiscent of 9 ♘e1 ♘d7 lines with g2-g4 (see C2 and C3221 in Chapter Nine) and, as there, Black's chances seem sufficient.

B.Gelfand-T.Radjabov, FIDE Grand Prix, Sochi 2008, continued **21 c5 ♘e7 22 ♔g2 ♘g6 23 ♖h1 ♗d7 24 b5 dxc5 25 ♗xc5 ♔g7 26 d6 hxg4?!** [26...♖c8! looks preferable, e.g. 27 ♖c1 (or 27 ♗b4 c5) 27...cxd6 28 ♕xd6 ♘e8 29 ♕d5 ♘f6 =] **27 hxg4 ♖xh1 28 ♔xh1 ♕h8+ 29 ♔g2 ♘h4+ 30 ♔g1 c6 31 bxc6 bxc6 32 ♔f2** [32 ♖b1 +=] **32...♘e6?!** [32...♖xf3!? 33 ♗xf3 ♘xg4+ with complications] **33 ♖b1 ♔g6 34 ♔e1 ♖d8 35 ♔d2** [now

White is clearly better] **35...♖d7 36 ♕a4 ♕c8 37 ♔c2 ♘e8 38 ♖d1 ♘g2 39 ♗a6 ♕a8 40 ♗c4 ♘g7 41 ♘d5! cxd5 42 exd5 ♕e8 43 dxe6 ♘xe6 44 ♗xa7 ♔f6 45 ♗b5?** [time trouble; 45 ♗b3 consolidates] **45...♕c8+ 46 ♔b2 ♖b7 47 d7??** [47 ♖d5 ♕a8 48 ♕e4 ♖xa7 49 ♕xe5+ still draws] **47...♕c6 48 ♔a1 ♖xb5 49 ♕a3 ♖d5 0-1**.

E322: 12 ♗f3 *(D)*

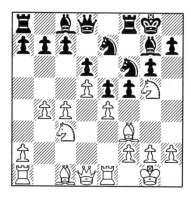

The second main line in the 10 ♖e1 f5 variation. The advantage over 12 f3 is that White maintains control of h5, while the bishop can also become active on the long diagonal. The disadvantage is that White's pawn centre is less secure.

12...c6 *(D)*

So Black increases the central tension. The direct 12...h6 13 ♗e6 ♗xe6 14 dxe6 c6 is also quite playable, when White's choice of 15th move transposes to its respective 13th below (see lines with 13...h6), but 12...c6 is slightly more flexible. Black has also tried the following:

a) 12...a5 13 bxa5 fxe4 14 ♘cxe4 ♖xa5 15 ♗d2 ♖a8 16 ♘e6 ♗xe6 17 dxe6 += P.Lafuente-O.Di Diego, Buenos Aires 2003.

b) 12...fxe4 13 ♘cxe4 (if 13 ♘gxe4 ♘f5 14 ♗g5 ♘d4 15 ♘b5 ♘xf3+ 16 ♕xf3, V.Kramnik-B.Gelfand, Vienna 1996, then 16...a6! 17 ♘bc3 ♘xe4 18 ♗xd8 ♖xf3 19 ♘xe4 ♖f7 20 ♘g5 ♖f5 = H.Zimmer-W.Franz, corr. 1998) 13...♘f5 14 ♗b2! (keeping the knight out of d4) 14...a5 (or 14...♘xe4 15 ♘xe4 a5 16 b5) 15 b5 ♘xe4 16 ♘xe4 b6 17 g3 (17 ♗g4!?) 17...♗d7 18 ♗g2 g5 19 a4 h6 20 ♖f1 ♕e8 21 ♗f3 ♘d4 22 ♗h5 ♕c8 23 ♖a3 +/= R.Sherbakov-F.Balabaev, Karaganda 1999.

c) 12...♖b8!? (defending b7 in advance of ♘e6 and exf5) 13 ♗b2! (better than 13 b5 h6 14 ♘e6 ♗xe6 15 dxe6 ♕c8 16 ♘d5 ♕xe6 17 exf5, V.Mikhalevski-I.Nataf, Montreal 2005, 17...gxf5!? 18 ♘xc7 ♕d7 19 ♘d5 ♘exd5 20 ♗xd5+ ♘xd5 21 ♕xd5+ ♕f7 22 ♕xd6 ♖fd8 with compensation, Mikhalevski; or if 17 ♘xc7? H.Hernandez-E.Espinosa, Cuban Ch. 2007, 17...♕f7! 18 exf5 e4 -/+) 13...h6 14 ♘e6 ♗xe6 15 dxe6 ♕c8 16 ♘d5 ♕xe6 17 ♘xc7 ♕d7 (or 17...♕f7 18 exf5 +/- J.Sadorra-M.Illingworth, Kuala Lumpur 2007) 18 c5 fxe4 19 cxd6! ♘f5 (or 19...exf3 20 dxe7 ♕xe7 21 ♗xe5 +/-) 20 ♗e2 += T.Polak-R.Chytilek, Brno 2008.

d) 12...♔h8!? deserves attention; e.g. 13 ♗b2 h6!? (13...♘eg8 14 c5 ♕e7 15 ♕b3 ♖b8 16 ♖ad1 += V.Golod-G.Timoshenko, Vienna 1998) 14 ♘e6 ♗xe6 15 dxe6 (V.Malakhatko-D.Blot, Rhone 2008) and now 15...fxe4!? 16 ♘xe4 ♕c8 ∞.

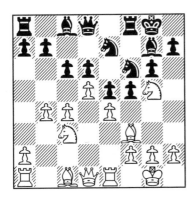

E3221: **13 b5** *373*
E3222: **13 ♗e3** *375*
E3223: **13 ♗b2** *380*

Other lines are:

a) 13 ♖b1 h6 14 ♘e6 ♗xe6 15 dxe6 fxe4 (or 15...♕c7 16 b5 ♖ad8 17 bxc6 bxc6 18 ♗a3 ♕c8 19 ♗xd6 ♕xe6 20 c5 ♘e8 ∞ I.Tsesarsky-Y.Dembo, Petah Tiqwa 1997) 16 ♘xe4 ♘xe4 17 ♗xe4 d5! 18 ♗c2 ♕d6 19 ♕g4 h5!? (19...♖f6!? and 19...e4 are also possible) 20 ♕h3 (if 20 c5!? ♕b8! 21 ♕h3 ♘f5 ∞) 20...e4 21 ♗e3 b6 22 b5 ∞ E.Bareev-T.Radjabov, Sarajevo 2003.

b) 13 ♗a3 cxd5 (or just 13...h6 14 ♘e6 ♗xe6 15 dxe6 fxe4 16 ♗xe4 d5! 17 b5 ♘xe4 18 ♘xe4 dxe4 19 ♕xd8 ♖fxd8 20 ♗xe7 ♖e8 21 ♗c5 ♖xe6 = R.Astrom-Y.Shulman, Gothenburg 1999) 14 exd5!? (if 14 cxd5 h6 15 ♘e6 ♗xe6 16 dxe6 fxe4 17 ♗xe4 d5 18 b5! ♘xe4 19 ♘xe4 dxe4 – *13 b5 cxd5 14 cxd5 h6 15 ♘e6 ♗xe6 16 dxe6 fxe4* in line E3221, but Black can improve with 16...♖c8! 17 ♕b3 d5 18 exd5 e4 19 ♗e2 ♘fxd5 20

♘xd5 ♕xd5 21 ♕xd5 ♘xd5 =+ R.Jedynak-A.Motylev, Panormo 2001) 14...e4! 15 ♗e2 ♘fxd5!? 16 ♘xd5 ♗xa1 17 ♘xe7+! ♕xe7 18 ♕d5+ ♔g7 19 ♖xa1 ♕xg5 20 ♗b2+ ♔h6 21 ♕xd6 ♖f7 22 ♖d1 f4! 23 ♖d5 ♗f5 ∞ L.Portisch-P.Acs, Rethymnon 2003.

c) 13 ♕b3 (preventing the ...d6-d5 idea, but rather slow) 13...h6 14 ♘e6 ♗xe6 15 dxe6 ♕c8! 16 ♖d1 (if 16 c5?! fxe4 17 cxd6 exf3 18 dxe7 ♖e8 19 ♗b2 ♖xe7 20 ♖xe5 ♕c7 21 ♖ee1 fxg2 -/+ Y.Pelletier-E.Inarkiev, European Ch., Istanbul 2003; or 16 b5 ♕xe6 17 ♗a3 c5! 18 exf5 gxf5 19 ♗xb7 ♖ab8 20 ♗d5 ♘fxd5 21 cxd5 ♕f7 22 ♗b2 e4 =+ A.Korobov-D.Yevseev, Russian Team Ch. 2008) 16...♖d8 17 b5 ♕xe6 18 bxc6 bxc6! (better than 18...♘xc6 19 exf5 ♕xf5 20 ♕xb7 ♘d4 21 ♗d5+ ♔h7 22 ♗e3! += E.Bacrot-T.Radjabov, FIDE World Ch., Tripoli 2004) 19 ♗a3 ♔h7 20 ♕a4 ♖ab8 21 ♕a6 fxe4 22 ♘xe4 ♘f5 23 ♘xf6+ ♕xf6 24 ♗xc6 ♖b6 25 ♕a4 ♘d4 ∞ Y.Pelletier-Al.David, La Roche sur Yon 2007.

E3221: **13 b5** *(D)*

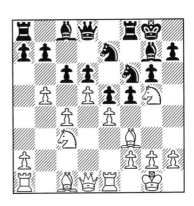

Forcing Black to clarify the situation in the centre.

13...cxd5

Black can also play 13...h6 14 ♘e6 ♗xe6 15 dxe6 fxe4! 16 ♘xe4 ♘xe4 17 ♗xe4 d5 18 cxd5 cxd5 transposing to 16...fxe4 below. If instead 15...♕a5?! 16 ♗b2 fxe4 17 ♘xe4 ♘xe4 18 ♖xe4 d5 19 cxd5 cxd5 20 ♖xe5! ♗xe5 21 ♗xe5 +/- Y.Pelletier-H.Nakamura, Biel 2005; or 15...♕c7 16 ♗a3 ♖ad8 17 ♕a4 ♕c8 (U.Volber-R.Janicke, corr. 1997) 18 ♖ad1 +=.

14 cxd5 h6

Or 14...fxe4 15 ♘gxe4 ♘xe4 16 ♘xe4 ♗f5 (or 16...♘f5 17 a4 +=) 17 a4 ♗xe4 18 ♗xe4 ♘f5 19 ♕d3 ½-½ Wl.Schmidt-W.Uhlmann, Dresden 2008, though White is slightly better here with the two bishops.

15 ♘e6 ♗xe6 16 dxe6 *(D)*

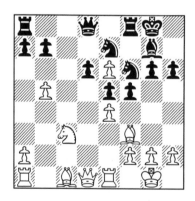

16...♖c8!?

Opting for complications. Otherwise 16...fxe4! leads to a level endgame after 17 ♘xe4 ♘xe4 18 ♗xe4 d5 19 ♗a3! dxe4 20 ♕xd8 ♖fxd8 21 ♗xe7 ♖e8, e.g. 22 ♗c5 (½-½ O.Danielian-M.Golubev, Moscow 1996) 22...♖xe6 23 ♗e3 a6 24

b6 ♗f6 25. g3 ♖d8 26. ♖ac1 ♔f7 27. h4 h5 28. ♖c7+ ♖e7 29. ♖c4 ½-½ V.Malakhatko-E.Moradiabadi, Manama 2009.

17 ♕b3

The alternative 17 ♗b2!? fxe4 18 ♘xe4 ♘xe4 19 ♖xe4! d5 (or 19...♕b6!? 20 ♕e2 ♗c5 ∞ J.Rindlisbacher-Y.Zhou, Mersin 2008) 20 ♖xe5! ♗xe5 21 ♗xe5 ♕b6 22 ♗b2 is equivalent to the 13 ♗b2 main line E3223, but with the extra moves b4-b5 and ...♖ac8. If anything this should ease Black's defence as his rook is more active; e.g. 22...♖c4 (not 22...♕h7?! 23 ♕e2 d4 24 h4 ♖f6 25 ♖e1 d3? 26 ♕e5 +- T.Nyback-D.Stellwagen, German League 2005) 23 ♕e2 ♕c7 24 ♕e3 ♕f4 25 ♕xa7 ♖c2 26 ♗a3 ♕e5 27 ♖f1 ♖xa2 28 ♕c5 ♖xf3 29 gxf3 ♕g5+ 30 ♔h1 ♕f5 31 ♔g2 ♕g5+ = Peng Zhaoqin-Li Shilong, Wijk aan Zee 2008.

17...d5 18 ♘xd5

If 18 exd5 e4 19 d6 ♕xd6 20 ♗a3 ♕c7 (Ponomariov) or 18 ♖d1 d4 with an excellent game for Black.

18...♘fxd5 19 exd5 e4 20 d6 *(D)*

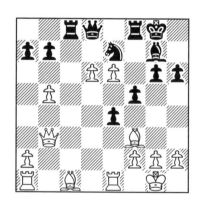

20...♕xd6

20...♖c3?! 21 dxe7! (if 21 ♗a3? ♖xb3 22 dxe7 ♖xa3 23 exd8♕ ♖xd8 24 ♖ad1,

Kir.Georgiev-R.Ponomariov, Istanbul Olympiad 2000, 24...♖e8! -/+ Ponomariov) 21...♕xe7 22 ♕a4 exf3 23 ♗b2 is good for White, e.g. 23...♕g5 (or 23...♖d3 24 ♗xg7 ♔xg7 25 ♕xa7 fxg2 26 ♖ad1 +/-) 24 g3 ♕g4 25 ♕xg4 fxg4 26 ♖ad1 ♖c7 27 e7 ♖e8? 28 ♖d8 1-0 S.Savchenko-F.Guilleux, Le Touquet 2007.

Or if 20...♗xa1 21 dxe7 ♕xe7 22 ♗a3 ♕f6 23 e7+ ♖f7 (S.Savchenko-M.Mozharov, Russian Team Ch. 2008) 24 ♗e2 ♔h7 25 b6! +=.

21 ♗a3 ♕d5

Worse is 21...♕b6?! 22 ♗xe7 ♖fe8 23 ♗b4! exf3 (or 23...♗xa1 24 ♖xa1 ♕xe6 25 ♗e2 +/-) 24 e7+ ♔h7 25 ♖ad1 and Black has unsolvable problems.

22 ♖ad1!

If 22 ♗xe7 ♕xb3 23 axb3 ♗xa1 24 ♗xf8 ♗c3! or 22 ♕xd5 ♘xd5 23 ♖ad1 ♗c3! with an excellent ending; e.g. 24 ♗xf8 ♔xf8 25 ♗xe4 (or 25 ♖f1? ♖c5! 26 ♗e2 ♘f4 -+) 25...fxe4 26 ♖xe4 ♖c5.

22...♕xb3 23 axb3 exf3

Now if 23...♗c3?! 24 ♖f1 ♖fe8 25 ♗e2! ♗f6 26 ♗c4! intending ♖d7 +/- (Mikhalevski).

24 ♗xe7 ♖fe8 25 ♖d7 (D)

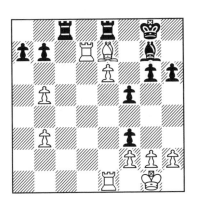

Black is still in a little difficulty here, despite the two draws after:

a) 25...♖c2 26 gxf3 (correct was 26 ♖xb7! ♗d4 27 ♖f1 ♖e2 28 b4! intending ♗c5) 26...♗d4! 27 ♔h1 (if 27 ♖xd4 ♖xe7 28 ♖d7 ♔f8 =) 27...♗xf2 28 ♖e5 ♗b6 29 ♗f6 ½-½ (due to 29...♖c7 =) K.Kameneckas-P.Ilyes, corr. 2002.
b) 25...♗f6 26 ♗xf6? (26 ♗b4! is much better) 26...♖xe6! 27 ♖a1 ♖xf6 28 ♖xb7 ♖f7 29 ♖xf7 ♔xf7 30 ♖xa7+ ♔f6 and Black easily held the rook endgame, Xu Jun-Ye Jiangchuan, Taiyuan 2004.

E3222: 13 ♗e3 (D)

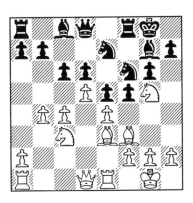

The most frequent move in tournament practice, after being popularized by Kramnik. Obviously Black can drive the bishop away again, but White doesn't mind the time wasted as ...f5-f4 takes the pressure off his centre.

13...h6!

This seems the most accurate response. Other moves:

a) 13...♘e8?! (V.Dobrov-V.Shinkevich, Pardubice 2000) loses a pawn after 14 dxc6 bxc6 15 exf5 ♗xf5 16 ♗xc6 ♘xc6 17 ♕d5+ ♔h8 18 ♕xc6 +/-.

b) 13...a5 14 bxa5 ♕xa5 15 ♕b3 cxd5 16 cxd5 h6 17 a4!? (or just 17 ♘e6 +/=) 17...b5 (not 17...hxg5? 18 ♗b6 +-) 18 ♘e6 ♗xe6 19 dxe6 += V.Kramnik-J.Piket, Monte Carlo (blindfold rapid) 1998.

c) 13...♔h8 14 a4! h6 (if 14...♘e8 15 c5 f4 16 ♗c1 h6 17 ♘e6 ♗xe6 18 dxe6 d5 19 exd5 e4 20 ♘xe4 cxd5 21 ♘d6! ♘xd6 22 cxd6 ♗xa1 23 ♗a3 ♗c3 24 b5 +/- M.Raidaru-G.Henrich, corr. 2002) 15 ♘e6 ♗xe6 16 dxe6 fxe4 17 ♘xe4 d5 (or 17...♘xe4 18 ♗xe4 d5 19 ♗c5 dxe4 20 ♕xd8 ♖fxd8 21 ♗xe7 ♖e8 22 ♗d6 ♖xe6 23 c5 += Huzman) 18 cxd5 cxd5 19 ♘xf6 ♖xf6 20 ♕b3 ♖xe6 21 ♖ad1 ♖d6 (21...e4 22 ♗c5 ♕c7 23 ♗g4 ♖e5 24 a5!? +/= Huzman) 22 ♗c5 ♖d7 23 ♗xe7 ♕xe7 24 ♖xd5 ♖xd5 25 ♗xd5 += E.Bacrot-I.Nataf, Bermuda 1999.

d) 13...f4!? (going along with White's idea) 14 ♗c1 h6 15 ♘e6 ♗xe6 16 dxe6 ♘c8! 17 b5!? *(D)* (or 17 ♕b3 ♕e7 18 c5 ♖e8 19 ♗e2 ♔h7 20 ♗a3 ♕xe6 21 ♗c4 ♕e7 22 ♖ad1 b5 23 cxb6 ♘xb6 24 b5 ♘xc4 25 ♕xc4 c5 ∞ M.Krasenkow-Y.Shulman, Vilnius 1997) and then:

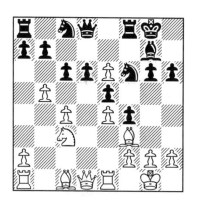

d1) 17...♕e8 18 bxc6 bxc6 19 c5 ♕xe6 20 ♗a3 ♖d8! (better than 20...dxc5?! 21 ♘a4 ♘b6 22 ♘xc5 ♕f7 23 ♕c1! += V.Kramnik-B.Gelfand, Belgrade 1997) 21 ♕d3 d5! (not 21...♖d7?! 22 ♕a6! dxc5 23 ♘a4 +/- Stohl) 22 exd5 cxd5 23 ♖ad1 ♘e7 24 c6 e4! (if 24...♘xc6 25 ♘xd5 += Stohl) 25 c7 ♖d7 26 ♗xe7 ♖xe7 27 ♗xe4! dxe4 28 ♕d8+ ♕e8 29 ♕xa8 ♖xa8 30 ♖d8+ ♕e8 31 ♖ed1 (D.Ortmann-R.Döhn, Kassel 2003) 31...♔h7! 32 ♖xa8 ♕xa8 33 ♖d8 ♕b7 34 c8♕ ♕b2 ∞.

d2) 17...♕e7 18 bxc6 bxc6 19 c5 dxc5!? (otherwise 19...♕xe6 – *17...♕e8*) 20 ♗a3 ♘b6 21 ♘a4 ♘xa4 (or 21...♖fd8 22 ♕c2 ♘xa4) 22 ♕xa4 ♕xe6 23 ♗xc5 ♖fd8 24 ♗d1 ♔h7 25 ♗b3 ♕c8 26 f3 with compensation, E.Akhmilovskaya-Wang Pin, Shanghai 2002.

e) 13...cxd5?! has been played more often, usually transposing to the main line after 14 cxd5 h6 15 ♘e6 ♗xe6 16 dxe6 fxe4 17 ♘xe4 ♘xe4 18 ♗xe4 d5, but it gives White a strong alternative in 14 exd5! *(D)* and then:

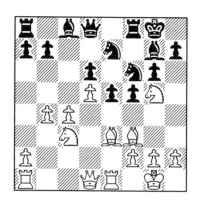

e1) 14...h6 15 ♘e6 ♗xe6 16 dxe6 e4 17 ♗e2 ♘g4 18 ♗d4 ♘e5 19 ♖c1 ♘7c6

20 ♘d5 +/- C.Gouw-S.Moncher, corr. 2003.

e2) 14...e4 15 ♗e2 ♘g4 (not 15...♘fxd5? 16 ♘xd5 ♗xa1 17 ♘xe7+ ♕xe7 18 ♕d5+ ♔g7 19 ♖xa1 +- D.Collas-H.Saldano Dayer, Campillos 2004) 16 ♗d4 e3 17 ♗xg4 exf2+ 18 ♔xf2 fxg4+ 19 ♔g1 ♗xd4+ 20 ♕xd4 +/- M.Jedrzejowski-A.Jorgensen, corr. 2000.

e3) 14...♘e8 15 ♖c1 h6 (or 15...♘c7 16 c5 f4 17 cxd6 fxe3 18 dxe7 exf2+ 19 ♔xf2 ♕xe7 20 ♘ce4 +/- B.Jacobs-U.Starace, corr. 2002) 16 ♘e6 ♗xe6 17 dxe6 e4 18 ♗e2 ♔h7 19 ♕d2 ♕c8 20 ♘b5 ♕xe6 21 ♗xa7 ♘c6 22 ♗e3 +/= W.Siewert-K.Piersig, corr. 2003.

As there is no simple route to equality in this line, Black should probably avoid this move order altogether.

14 ♘e6 ♗xe6 15 dxe6 fxe4!

Black has a few alternatives himself here:

a) 15...f4!? 16 ♗c1 – *13...f4* above.

b) 15...♔h7!? 16 b5 fxe4 17 ♘xe4 d5 18 ♘xf6+ ♗xf6 19 cxd5 cxd5 20 ♖c1 b6 21 ♕b3 e4 22 ♗g4 h5 23 ♗h3 ♕d6 ∞ T.Thamtavatvorn-V.Kotronias, Turin Olympiad 2006.

c) 15...g5!? 16 exf5 ♘xf5 17 ♕d3 ♘e3 (or 17...♘h4!? 18 ♗e2 ♕e7 19 g3 e4! 20 ♘xe4 ♘xe4 21 ♕xe4 ♗xa1 22 ♖xa1 ♘f5 ∞) 18 ♖xe3 ♕e7 19 ♖d1 ♖ad8 20 ♘e4 ♘xe4 (not 20...g4?! 21 ♘xf6+ ♕xf6 22 ♗xg4 ♕xf2+ 23 ♔h1 +/- V.Kramnik-F.Nijboer, Wijk aan Zee 1998) 21 ♗xe4 ♕xe6 22 b5 ♕d7 23 ♖e2 ♔h8 24 ♖ed2 ♕c7 ∞ V.Andriulaitis-J.Marcinkiewicz, corr. 1999.

16 ♘xe4 ♘xe4 17 ♗xe4 d5 18 cxd5

Not 18 ♗c5? dxe4 19 ♕xd8 ♖fxd8 20 ♗xe7 ♖d4 -/+ H.Tabatt-B.Traub, German League 1998.

18...cxd5 *(D)*

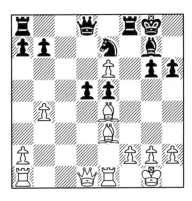

The key position of the 13 ♗e3 variation. Black has managed to demolish the white centre and advance his d-pawn, and threatens to round up the stray pawn on e6. However, his own centre may now come under attack.

19 ♗c2!?

This leads to extremely complicated play. The light-squared bishop is heading for b3 to increase the pressure on the d5-pawn, while the other one threatens to go to c5.

The immediate 19 ♗c5 reaches a level endgame after 19...dxe4 20 ♕xd8 ♖fxd8 21 ♗xe7 ♖e8, almost identical to the one arising from 16...fxe4! in line E3221 (White's b-pawn is one square further back here) and the result should be the same; e.g. 22 ♗c5 (or 22 ♗h4 ♖xe6 23 ♖xe4 ♖c8 24 ♗g3 b5 25 ♔f1 ♖c2 = M.Klauser-F.Jenni, Swiss Ch. 2002) 23 ♖xe4 ♖d8 24 h4 (or 24 ♗xa7 ♖a6 25 ♗e3 ♖xa2 = A.Spielmann-I.Nataf, French Team Ch. 2004) 24...a6

25 a4 ♖d5 26 ♗e3 ♖c6 = Z.Gyimesi-V.Baklan, Rumanian Team Ch. 2005.

19...b6!

Preventing ♗c5. Other moves are weaker:

a) 19...♕d6 20 ♗c5 ♕xe6 21 ♗xe7 ♕xe7 22 ♕xd5+ ♔h7 23 ♕e4 += G.Mikanovic-A.Luksza, Montreal 2003.

b) 19...d4 20 ♗d2 ♕d6 (or 20...d3 21 ♗b3 ♕b6 22 ♗e3 ♕xb4 23 ♖c1 ♖fd8 24 ♗c5 ♕h4 25 ♖e3 e4 26 ♖c4 +/- Psakhis) 21 ♗b3 (or 21 ♕g4) 21...♔h7 22 ♖c1 ♖ac8 23 ♕g4 b5 24 ♕e4 ♖c6 25 h4 +/- V.Evelev-J.Belanger, Montreal 2000.

c) 19...e4 20 ♖c1 d4? (but if 20...b6 21 ♗d4 ♖c8 22 ♗xg7 ♔xg7 23 ♗a4 ♖xc1 24 ♕xc1 ♕d6 25 ♕b2+ ♔h7 26 ♗d7 += Khalifman) 21 ♗d2 e3 22 fxe3 d3 23 ♗b3 ♕d6 24 ♕g4 ♗e5 25 ♖f1! ♗xh2+ 26 ♔h1 ♕g3 27 ♕d4 ♕e5 28 ♖f7! +- V.Kramnik-J.Polgar, Linares 1997.

20 ♕g4 (D)

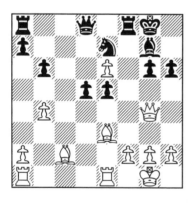

And here other moves are good for Black:

a) 20 b5 ♕d6 21 ♗c1 ♖ad8 22 ♗b3 ♔h7 23 a4 ♕xe6 24 ♗a3 ♖d7 -/+ V.Malakhatko-S.Sivokho, Polanica Zdroj 1999.

b) 20 ♗b3 ♕d6 21 ♕g4 h5 22 ♕h3 ♖f5 23 ♖ed1 e4 24 ♖ac1 ♖af8 25 b5 ♗e5 =+ E.Ovod-V.Rajlich, Budapest 2002.

c) 20 ♗a4 ♕d6 21 ♗d7 (defending the e6-pawn, but not doing much else) 21...♕xb4! 22 ♖b1 ♕h4 23 f3 ♖f5!? 24 ♗f2 ♕f6 25 ♗g3 h5 26 h3? (better 26 ♕a4!? and if 26...♖f8 27 ♗b5! brings the bishop back into play) 26...♖f8 27 ♔h1 ♕g5 28 ♗h2 e4! 29 fxe4 ♖f2 30 ♖g1 dxe4 -/+ V.Malakhatko-F.Jenni, Istanbul Olympiad 2000.

20...e4

The alternative is to play for the e6-pawn with 20...♖f6 (or 20...♕d6 21 ♖ad1 ♖ad8 22 b5 ♖f6 23 ♗b3 transposing) 21 ♗b3 ♕d6 22 ♖ad1 ♖d8 23 b5 (if 23 ♖xd5 ♘xd5 24 ♖d1 ♕xe6 25 ♗xd5 ♕xd5! 26 ♖xd5 ♖xd5 27 ♕c4 ♖fd6 = Huzman) 23...♕xe6 24 ♕xe6+ (if 24 ♕a4 ♖d7 25 f4, S.Gligoric-I.Nataf, Cannes 1998, 25...exf4! 26 ♗d4 ♕d6 =) 24...♖xe6 25 ♗c1 ♔f7 26 ♗a3, when White has a slight initiative in the endgame; e.g. 26...e4 27 g3 (if 27 ♗xe7 ♔xe7 28 ♖xd5 ♖xd5 29 ♗xd5 ♖e5 30 ♖xe4 ♔d6 31 ♖xe5 ♔xe5 = V.Mikhalevski-M.Klinova, Gibraltar 2008) 27...♖d7 28 ♗xe7 ♔xe7 29 ♖xd5 ♖xd5 30 ♗xd5 ♗c3 31 ♖e2 ♖e5 32 ♗xe4 g5 33 a4 += V.Kramnik-A.Shirov, Linares 1998, though the opposite-coloured bishops mean that a draw is the most likely result.

21 ♖ad1 ♕c7 22 ♗b3 ♖f5 (D)

A strong move, defending the d5-pawn and blocking the white queen off from e6. Now both sides must play carefully: Black in case he falls prey to a tactic, White in case the e6-pawn drops off for nothing.

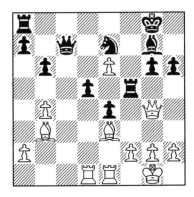

23 ♖d2

In order to double major pieces on the d-file. Instead:

a) 23 ♗d4?! ♖af8 24 ♕g3 ♕c6 25 h4 ♔h7 26 ♗xg7 ♔xg7 27 ♖c1 ♕xe6 -/+ F.Christenson-P.Bank, Aarhus 2003.

b) 23 ♖e2 h5! (if 23...♕c3 24 b5 ♖af8 25 ♖c2 ♕e5, V.Mikhalevski-Al.David, Vlissingen 2000, 26 ♕g3! sees White becoming very active) 24 ♕h4 (if 24 ♕h3!? ♕c6 =+) 24...♗f6 25 ♕g3 ♗e5 26 ♕h4 ♗f6 with a draw by repetition in Xu Jun-R.Ponomariov, FIDE World Cup, Shenyang 2000.

c) 23 ♖c1 ♕d6 24 ♖ed1 ♖af8 25 b5?! (25 ♕xe4! ♗b2! 26 ♖b1 ♗e5 ∞) 25...♔h7 26 h3 ♗e5 27 ♔h1 ♗f4 28 ♗xf4 ♖xf4 29 ♕g3 (L.Gerzhoy-V.Rajlich, Budapest 2002) 29...d4! -/+.

d) 23 b5!? (this non-committal move may be White's best here) 23...♖af8 (or 23...♕e5 24 ♗c1! ♖af8? 25 ♗a3 h5 26 ♕g3! ♕xe6, L.Lenic-A.Jankovic, Croatian Team Ch. 2006, 27 ♕d6! +/-) 24 ♖e2 ♕c8 25 ♗c1 (25 ♖c2!?) 25...h5 26 ♕h4 ♗f6 27 ♕h3 ♔h7 28 ♗a3 ♕xe6 29 g3 ♖d8 30 f3 ♕c8 31 ♖c2 ♕b8 =+ M.Bosiocic-I.Saric, Split 2005.

23...♕c3!?

The most active-looking continuation, though others deserve attention too:

a) 23...♗c3? 24 ♖c1 ♕e5 25 ♖xd5! ♘xd5 26 ♕xg6+ ♔h8 27 ♕xh6+ ♔g8 28 e7! +- R.Sherbakov-S.Iskusnyh, Tula 1999.

b) 23...♔h7 24 ♖ed1 ♕c6 25 ♖c2 ♕xe6?! (25...♕d6 ∞) 26 ♖c7 a5 27 bxa5 bxa5?! 28 ♗c5 h5 29 ♕h3 ♘c6 30 ♖xd5 ♕f6 (B.Lalith-A.Lahiri, New Delhi 2009) 31 ♖dd7 +/-.

c) 23...♕c6 24 b5!? ♕xe6 (or 24...♕xb5 25 ♖c1 ∞) 25 f3! exf3 26 ♗f2 ♕f6 27 ♖xe7 ♕xe7 28 ♗xd5+ ♖xd5 29 ♖xd5 = Z.Straka-D.Fridman, corr. 2004.

d) 23...♖af8!? 24 ♖ed1 ♕c6 25 ♖c2! ♕d6 (if 25...♕xe6?! 26 ♖c7 += Ponomariov) 26 ♕xe4!? ♗e5! 27 ♖xd5 ♗xh2+ 28 ♔h1 ♖xd5 29 ♗xd5 ♗f4! 30 ♖d2 ♗xe3 31 ♕xe3 ♘xd5 32 ♕xh6 ♕xe6 33 ♖xd5 ♕xd5 34 ♕xg6+ ½-½ A.Kozlowicz-F.Schwarz, corr. 2003.

24 ♕d1

Or 24 ♖ed1 ♕xb4 25 ♗d4? (better 25 ♕e2! intending g2-g4 or ♕a6) 26...♖c8 26 ♕e2 ♗xd4 27 ♖xd4 ♕c5 28 g4 ♖e5 -/+ J.Werle-Al.David, Amsterdam 2000.

24...♖d8 (D)

Black has also tried:

a) 24...♕xb4 25 g4!? ♖f6?! (25...♖f3!? ∞) 26 ♖d4 ♕d6 27 ♖xd5! ♘xd5 28 ♕xd5 ♕xd5 29 ♗xd5 ♖e8 30 ♗c1 += S.Soucha-J.Hostinsky, corr. 2003.

b) 24...♖af8 25 b5 ♔h7 (25...♕b4!?) 26 ♖c2 ♕e5 27 ♗c1! ♖h5 28 h3 ♕xe6 29 ♗a3 ♕e5 30 ♖d2 ♖hf5 31 ♖ee2 d4 32 ♗c2 ♖f4 33 ♗xe7 ♕xe7 34 g3 = W.Stummer-Z.Straka, corr. 2003.

The text was played in another Xu Jun-Ye Jiangchuan clash, this time at Shanghai 2001, which concluded **25 b5 ♕c8 26 ♗d4?!** [better 26 g4!? ♖ff8 27 ♗xd5 ♗c3 28 ♗xe4 ♗xd2 29 ♗xd2 ♕xe6 30 ♕e2 with compensation (Tsesarsky), e.g. 30...♘d5 31 ♗xh6 ♘f4 32 ♗xf4 ♖xf4 33 f3 =] **26...♗xd4 27 ♖xd4 ♕c5!** [not 27...♕xe6?? 28 ♖dxe4! +-] **28 ♖e2** [nor 28 ♖exe4?? ♖xf2! -/+] **28...♖df8 29 a4 ♖e5 30 h3 ½-½**

E3223: 13 ♗b2 *(D)*

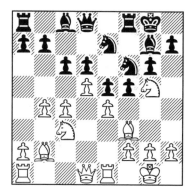

This has been the most popular move of late, due to the dangerous attack White achieves in the main line, even if Black has little to fear objectively speaking.

13...h6

13...cxd5 is less common here, though it allows both sides some additional possibilities:

a) 14 cxd5 h6 (14...♕b6!? is also possible) 15 ♘e6 ♗xe6 16 dxe6 fxe4 17 ♘xe4 ♘xe4 18 ♖xe4 ♕b6!? (18...d5 is the main line) 19 ♕b3 d5! 20 ♖xe5 ♗xe5 21♗xe5 ♕xe6 =+ I.Naumkin-F.Galassi, Porto Mannu Palau 2008.

b) 14 exd5!? h6 (better than 14...♘e8 15 ♕b3 += P.Van der Sterren-J.Piket, Dutch Ch. 1997) 15 ♘e6 ♗xe6 16 dxe6 e4 17 ♗e2 d5! (if 17...♕b6 18 ♕b3 += M.Kazhgaleyev-M.Dziuba, Moscow 2009) 18 ♘xd5 (or 18 cxd5 ♘fxd5 19 ♕b3 ♖c8! ∞) 18...♘fxd5 19 ♗xg7 ♔xg7 20 cxd5 ♕xd5 ∞ Piket.

14 ♘e6 ♗xe6 15 dxe6 fxe4!

Other moves are inferior:

a) 15...♕c7 16 ♕b3 ♖ad8 17 ♖ad1 fxe4 18 ♘xe4 ♘xe4 19 ♗xe4 ♕c8 20 ♕h3 ♖f6 21 ♗c2 ♖xe6 22 f4 += W.Paschall-D.Karatorossian, Budapest 2004.

b) 15...♔h7!? 16 b5! fxe4 17 ♗xe4 (17 ♘xe4 ♘xe4 18 ♖xe4 d5 19 ♖e3! looks better, and if 19...♕d6 20 cxd5 ♘xd5 21 e7 ♕xe7 22 ♗xd5 cxd5 23 ♕xd5 +=) 17...d5 18 ♗a3 ♘xe4 19 ♘xe4 dxe4 20 ♕xd8 ♖fxd8 21 ♗xe7 ♖e8 = V.Babula-Y.Shulman, Czech League 1997.

16 ♘xe4 ♘xe4 17 ♖xe4!

Planning to sacrifice the exchange. If 17 ♗xe4 d5! again gives Black a good game, e.g. 18 cxd5 cxd5 19 ♗f3 (or 19 ♗c2 ♕b6 20 ♕d2 e4 21 ♗xg7 ♔xg7 22 ♗b3 ♖f5 =+ M.Peek-Al.David, Amsterdam 2000) 19...♕d6 20 ♕b3 e4 21 ♗xg7 ♔xg7 22 ♗g4 ♖f6 =+ P.Dziadyk-V.Sikula, Kiev 2003.

17...d5

The most principled, but Black is not obliged to play it, e.g. 17...♖f6!? (it is hard to see anything wrong with this) 18 c5 (if 18 ♗g4 ♘f5) 18...♖xe6 19 cxd6 ♕xd6 20 ♕xd6 ♖xd6 21 ♗xe5 ♖e6 22 ♗xg7 ½-½ N.Shavtvaladze-A.Pavlidis, Halkidiki 2008.

18 cxd5 cxd5 19 ♖xe5! ♗xe5 20 ♗xe5 *(D)*

For the exchange White has two

strong bishops and a promising attack on the insecure black king.

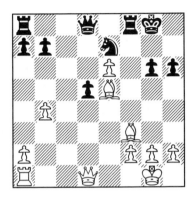

20...♕b6 21 ♗b2!

Shirov's novelty from the game A.Shirov-T.Radjabov, Linares 2004, which we now follow.

Earlier practice showed that Black is fine if he can safely take the white e-pawn; e.g. 21 ♕d2 ♕xe6 22 ♖e1 ♖xf3! 23 gxf3 ♘f5 24 ♗g3 ♕f7 25 ♖c1 d4! 26 ♖c7 ♕d5 with an excellent position for Black, S.Kingso-W.Stern, corr. 1997.

With the text White plans to line up on the a1-h8 diagonal straight away, thus safeguarding the e6-pawn due to 21...♕xe6? 22 ♕d4 (and if 22...♘f5 23 ♕h8+ ♔f7 24 ♕h7+ ♔e8 25 ♕xb7 +/-). Note 21 ♗c3?! is worse as 21...♖ac8 gains time, and the b4-pawn is relatively insignificant anyway.

21...♔h7!?

Improving the king's position is perhaps not the best here. Instead:

a) 21...♖ac8 22 ♕e2 ♖f5 23 g4?! (better 23 ♕d2! ♕xe6? 24 ♕xh6 +/- or 23...♔h7 24 ♖e1 with good play) 23...♖xf3! 24 ♕xf3 ♕xe6 25 h3 ♖c2 ∞ M.Mrva-S.Sarno, Zemplinska Sirava 2004.

b) 21...♖ad8! seems the best defence; e.g. 22 ♕d2 (now if 22 ♕e2 ♕xb4! 23 ♕e5? d4 -/+) 22...♕xe6! 23 ♖e1 (if 23 ♕xh6 d4!, or 23 ♕d4 ♘f5 24 ♕h8+ ♔f7 25 ♕h7+ ♔e8 26 ♕xb7 ♖f7! 27 ♕b5+ ♔f8 ∞) 23...♕f7 24 ♕xh6 d4 ∞ E.Vassia-M.Boccia, corr. 2004.

22 ♕e2 d4!

Closing the long diagonal. White's attack is very strong if he is allowed to co-ordinate his forces; e.g. 22...♕xb4? 23 ♕e5 ♖g8 24 ♖c1 ♖ac8 25 ♖xc8 ♘xc8 26 ♗xd5 ♘e7 27 ♗f3 ♘f5 28 g4 ♘g7 29 e7 ♘e8 30 h4! +- Shirov, or 22...♖ae8? 23 ♕e5 ♖g8? 24 ♕f6 1-0 T.Franzen-H.Da Silva Araujo, corr. 2005; or if 22...♕d6 23 h4! ♘f5 24 h5 ♘h4 25 hxg6+ ♘xg6 26 ♖d1 ♖f5 27 ♕d3 ♕f8 28 e7! ♕f7 29 ♗xd5 +- L.Rubio Mejia-J.Trepat Herranz, Balaguer 2008.

23 h4! ♖f6 24 ♖e1 ♕xb4 25 a3!

Not yet 25 h5?! because of 25...♖xf3! 26 gxf3 ♖g8 ∞ Shirov.

25...♕d6

25...♕a5? drops the d4-pawn, while 25...♕b6 leads to a better ending for White after 26 ♕e5 ♖f5 27 ♕xd4 ♕xd4 28 ♗xd4 ♘c6 29 ♗c3! (Shirov), though Black might hope to draw this.

26 h5 ♖af8

Against other rook moves Shirov gives 26...♖e8 27 ♕b5! ♖d8 28 hxg6+ ♘xg6 29 ♕xb7+ ♕e7 30 a4! ♕xb7 31 ♗xb7 ♘e7 32 ♗a3 +/=, or 26...♖d8 27 ♗xb7 gxh5 28 ♕d3+ ♔g8 29 ♖e4 ♘f5 30 ♗a6! still with compensation.

27 ♕e4 ♘c6 28 hxg6+ ♔g7 29 ♗c1! *(D)*

Threatening 30 ♗xh6+!, to which Black has no real answer. If 29...h5 30 ♗xh5 ♕c5 31 ♗f3 ♖xg6 32 ♗b2 continues the attack (Shirov), while 30...♖h8?! fails to 31 e7! ♖e8 32 ♗h6+! ♔xh6 33 g7 ♕xe7 34 ♗xe8 ♕xe4 35 ♖xe4 (or 35 g8♘+! first) 35...♔xg7 36 ♗xc6 and 37 ♖xd4 with a winning rook endgame.

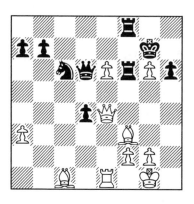

29...♕e7 30 ♗xh6+! ♔xh6 31 ♕h4+ ♔xg6 32 ♗xc6 bxc6 33 ♖e5 ♕xe6?

The last chance was 33...♖xe6!? 34 ♕h5+ ♔g7 35 ♖g5+ ♕xg5 36 ♕xg5+ ♖g6 37 ♕e5+ ♔g8 38 ♕xd4 ♖f7 when White has more difficulty making progress, but after 39 ♕d8+ (not 39 g3 ♖fg7! = Shirov) 39...♖f8 (if 39...♔h7 40 ♕d3! ♔h6 41 ♕h3+ ♔g7 42 g3) 40 ♕d7 ♖f7 41 ♕e8+ ♔g7 42 g3 ♖gf6 43 f4 White still went on to win in M.Casella-I.Zenyuk, US Ch. 2004.

34 ♖xe6 ♖xe6 35 ♕g4+ ♔f7 36 ♕xd4

Now White is winning more easily. The game concluded **36...a6 37 g4 ♖g8 38 f3 ♖f6 39 ♔f2 ♖e8 40 ♕c4+ ♔g7 41 ♕xa6 ♖ef8 42 ♕d3 c5 43 a4 ♖a8 44 ♕c3 ♔g6 45 ♕xc5 ♖fa6 46 ♔g3 ♖xa4 47 ♕d6+ ♔f7 48 g5 ♖8a6 49 ♕d7+ ♔g6 50 f4 ♖a1 51 ♕d3+ ♔g7 52 ♕d4+ ♔g8 53 ♔g4 ♖1a2 54 ♕d8+ ♔g7 55 ♕c7+ ♔g8 56 f5 ♖a7 57 ♕d8+ ♔g7 58 f6+ ♔h7 59 ♕d3+ ♔h8 60 ♔f5 ♖a8 61 ♕h3+ ♔g8 62**

♔g6 ♖2a7 63 ♕e6+ ♔f8 64 ♕d6+ ♔g8 65 ♕d5+ ♔h8 66 ♕h1+ 1-0.

Conclusion

White cannot count on any advantage after 10 ♘d2 ♘f4 (line A), as Black gains an active position without problems. The queen moves 10 ♕b3 or 10 ♕c2 (see line B) are more interesting ways of circumventing the main lines, but objectively Black has little to fear here either. Against the direct 10 c5 (line C) Black should equalize with either 10...♘f4 or 10...f5!?. While 10 g3 (line D), preventing ...♘h5-f4, is too committal to bring White any benefits; Black has good play after 10...f5 11 ♘g5 ♘f6 12 f3 and then 12...c6 or 12...f4, or indeed other 12th moves.

This leaves the main line with 10 ♖e1. Now 10...♘f4 (line E1) is probably premature, as the prepared 11 ♗f1 gives White the better of things. If Black wants to play this way he should begin with 10...a5 (line E2) and only venture ...♘f4 if it seems appropriate. In the same way, 10...f5 11 ♘g5 ♘f4 12 ♗xf4! exf4 13 ♖c1 (line E31) also gives White more freedom.

The critical variations follow 10...f5 11 ♘g5 ♘f6!. If White then supports his centre with 12 f3 (line E321), Black can count on reasonable chances after several moves: 12...h6, 12...c6, 12...♘h5 or 12...♔h8, the latter currently being the most popular. White's other plan, 12 ♗f3 (line E322), allows Black to assault the centre with ...c7-c6, ...h7-h6, ...cxd5 and ...fxe4, when he again seems to have sufficient counterplay.

Index of Variations